MW01114755

Northwest Iowa Plains
Iowan Surface
Des Moines Lobe
Southern Iowa Drift Plain
Loess Hills
Missouri Alluvial Plain
Southern Iowa Drift Plain
Mississippi Aluvial Plain

Natural Regions of Iowa

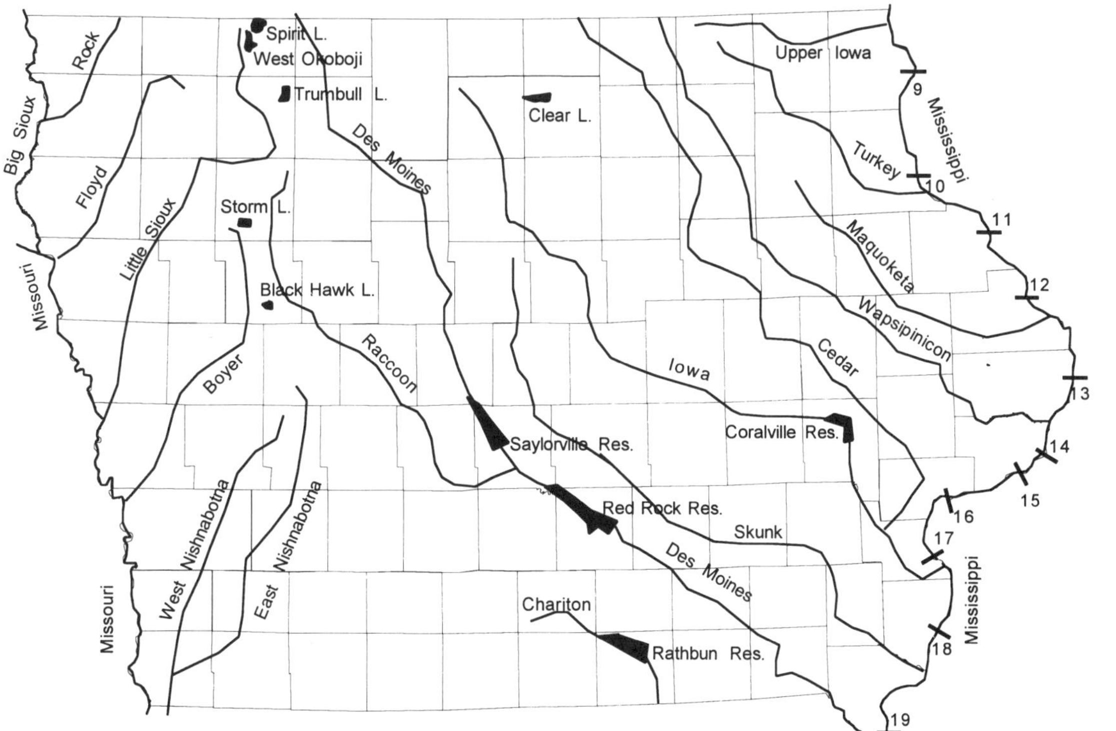

Rock
Big Sioux
Floyd
Little Sioux
Missouri
Spirit L.
West Okoboji
Trumbull L.
Storm L.
Black Hawk L.
Des Moines
Clear L.
Upper Iowa
Turkey
Mississippi
Maquoketa
Wapsipinicon
Cedar
Iowa
Raccoon
Boyer
Coralville Res.
Saylorville Res.
Red Rock Res.
Skunk
Des Moines
West Nishnabotna
East Nishnabotna
Missouri
Chariton
Rathbun Res.
Mississippi
9
10
11
12
13
14
15
16
17
18
19

Rivers, reservoirs, lakes, and Mississippi River dams

Birds in Iowa

Thomas H. Kent

and

James J. Dinsmore

Published by the authors

Iowa City and Ames

1996

Copyright 1996 Thomas H. Kent and James J. Dinsmore

International Standard Book Number: 0-87414-106-0

Library of Congress Catalog Card Number: 96-94857

Authors and publishers:
Thomas H. Kent, 211 Richards Street, Iowa City, Iowa 52246
James J. Dinsmore, 4024 Arkansas Drive, Ames, Iowa 50014

Cover: American Goldfinch by Paul Hertzel

Printed by: Thomson-Shore, Inc., Dexter, Michigan

CONTENTS

Preface, v
Acknowledgments, vi
List of Abbreviations, vii

Chapter 1. The State List, 1

Chapter 2. Geography and Birding Areas, 11

Chapter 3. History of Iowa Ornithology, 17

Chapter 4. Species Accounts, 25
GAVIIFORMES
Loons (Family Gaviidae), 28
PODICIPEDIFORMES
Grebes (Family Podicipedidae), 32
PELECANIFORMES
Pelicans (Family Pelecanidae), 38
Cormorants (Family Phalacrocoracidae), 41
Darters (Family Anhingidae), 43
Frigatebirds (Family Fregatidae), 44
CICONIIFORMES
Bitterns and Herons (Family Ardeidae), 45
Ibises and Spoonbills (Family Threskiornithidae), 57
Storks (Family Ciconiidae), 61
ANSERIFORMES
Swans, Geese, and Ducks (Family Anatidae), 62
FALCONIFORMES
American Vultures (Family Cathartidae), 101
Kites, Eagles, Hawks, and Allies (Family Accipitridae), 103
Caracaras and Falcons (Family Falconidae), 118
GALLIFORMES
Partridges, Grouse, Turkeys, and Quail (Family Phasianidae), 123
GRUIFORMES
Rails, Gallinules, and Coots (Family Rallidae), 129
Cranes (Family Gruidae), 138
CHARADRIIFORMES
Plovers and Lapwings (Family Charadriidae), 141
Stilts and Avocets (Family Recurvirostridae), 146
Sandpipers, Phalaropes, and Allies (Family Scolopacidae), 148
Skuas, Gulls, Terns, and Skimmers (Family Laridae), 172
Auks, Murres, and Puffins (Family Alcidae), 196
COLUMBIFORMES
Pigeons and Doves (Family Columbidae), 198
PSITTACIFORMES
Lories, Parakeets, Macaws, and Parrots (Family Psittacidae), 201

CUCULIFORMES
Cuckoos, Roadrunners, and Anis (Family Cuculidae), 202
STRIGIFORMES
Barn Owls (Family Tytonidae), 205
Typical Owls (Family Strigidae), 207
CAPRIMULGIFORMES
Goatsuckers (Family Caprimulgidae), 215
APODIFORMES
Swifts (Family Apodidae), 218
Hummingbirds (Family Trochilidae), 219
CORACIIFORMES
Kingfishers (Family Alcedinidae), 221
PICIFORMES
Woodpeckers and Allies (Family Picidae), 222
PASSERIFORMES
Tyrant Flycatchers (Family Tyrannidae), 228
Larks (Family Alaudidae), 239
Swallows (Family Hirundinidae), 240
Jays, Magpies, and Crows (Family Corvidae), 244
Titmice (Family Paridae), 251
Nuthatches (Family Sittidae), 253
Creepers (Family Certhiidae), 255
Wrens (Family Troglodytidae), 256
Muscicapids (Family Muscicapidae),
Old World Warblers, Kinglets, and Gnatcatchers (Subfamily Sylviinae), 263
Solitaires, Thrushes, and Allies (Subfamily Turdinae), 266
Mockingbirds, Thrashers, and Allies (Family Mimidae), 274
Wagtails and Pipits (Family Motacillidae), 278
Waxwings (Family Bombycillidae), 279
Shrikes (Family Laniidae), 281
Starlings and Allies (Family Sturnidae), 283
Vireos (Family Vireonidae), 284
Emberizids (Family Emberizidae)
Wood-Warblers (Subfamily Parulinae), 289
Tanagers (Subfamily Thraupinae), 318
Cardinals, Grosbeaks, and Allies (Subfamily Cardinalinae), 321
Emberizines (Subfamily Emberizinae), 326
Blackbirds and Allies (Subfamily Icterinae), 349
Fringilline and Cardueline Finches and Allies (Family Fringillidae), 358
Old World Sparrows (Family Passeridae), 368

Appendixes
Appendix A. Selected Other Species Reported in Iowa, 370
Appendix B. Species Not Represented by a Specimen, 375
Appendix C. Year of First Record for Species, 376

Literature Cited, 378

Index to Species Accounts, 385

PREFACE

The purpose of this book is to describe the distribution and frequency of wild birds that have been accepted as occurring in Iowa. The list of species is based on those accepted by the Records Committee of the Iowa Ornithologists' Union through 1995 (Kent 1996). Records of birds include those reported through 1995 and a few important sightings from winter and spring of 1996.

The major previous publications that have described the distribution and frequency of birds in Iowa include those of Anderson (1907), DuMont (1933), Brown (1971), and Dinsmore, Kent, Koenig, Petersen, and Roosa (1984). The later of these publications covered data through 1982. More data on Iowa birds have accumulated since 1982 than in all previous history. The reasons for this include more active and serious "birders," more emphasis on search for vagrants (birds out of their "normal" range), and more systematic reporting of bird sightings. Most of the information is recorded in the quarterly Field Reports published in *Iowa Bird Life*, the journal of the Iowa Ornithologists' Union. The publication by Dinsmore et al. (1984) also served to identify the need for new information and to stimulate more reporting of early and late birds and vagrants. We believe that the information in *Birds in Iowa* will also serve as a framework for new information. We know that some of the information will be out of date before the book can be printed.

Compared to previous works on Iowa's birds, we have expanded the information on distribution to provide more detail on occurrence in Iowa and to include where each species fits in terms of world-wide distribution. In some cases, we indicate whether Iowa is on the edge or center of the wintering or breeding range. We have included maps for those species not found in all areas of the state. In order to better illustrate the frequency of each species, we either list all records or show the frequency on a "timeline" or both. We believe that anyone evaluating the possibility of a rare or unusual bird needs to know how likely it is to occur at a specific location at the given time of year—it is a major goal of this work to provide that information for Iowa birds.

We follow the format of many other books on birds of states in not trying to cover identification, habitat, or behavior except in circumstances where that information bears on the accuracy of data or distribution of the species in Iowa. Readers should consult standard field guides for that information. We also do not attempt to provide a guide to birding areas of Iowa, but we do provide a general introduction to birding areas of Iowa in Chapter 2. We recommend the *Iowa Sportsman's Atlas* for county maps and for names, locations, and descriptions of all of Iowa's public recreation areas (Sportsman's Atlas Co., P.O. Box 132, Lyton, Iowa 50561, 1-800-568-8334). For all records cited in *Birds in Iowa*, we include the county location.

Other information included in this book includes a brief history of Iowa ornithology (Chapter 3) and more information about the state list in the appendices. Anderson (1907), DuMont (1933), and Dinsmore et al. (1984) made reasonably complete citations of all rare birds reported in the literature. We have decided for purposes of brevity and clarity not to cite reports that do not meet the standards for acceptance by the Records Committee. In many instances we allude to the existence of such records in the previous literature. The Records Committee has reviewed all known reports of accidental species except for old records of a few species that were once common (e.g., Greater Prairie-Chicken).

ACKNOWLEDGMENTS

We thank all who provided the information in the historical record that is the foundation of this work. Giants among contributors to Iowa ornithology include Rudolph M. Anderson and Philip A. DuMont, whose thorough early books on Iowa birds are invaluable; Woodward H. Brown, who started the Field Reports in *Iowa Bird Life* and provided an annotated update of the Iowa list; and Fred J. Pierce and Peter C. Petersen, who each edited *Iowa Bird Life* for many years.

Probably the most important and yet least recognized contributors to Iowa ornithology are the hundreds of individuals who have sent in their observations to the Field Reports section of *Iowa Bird Life*. These range from individuals who regularly send in detailed records for each season to others who have sent in a single observation. Collectively these reports provide much of the data that we have reviewed in preparing this book. Although it is impractical to cite these individuals here or in the Species Accounts, we and they know who they are, and we thank them.

We are indebted to the Records Committee of the Iowa Ornithologists' Union for the careful evaluation of rare birds that have occurred in Iowa since 1980 and for the retrospective evaluation of all old records of accidental species. The following individuals have served on the Records Committee: Eugene Armstrong, Carl J. Bendorf, Tanya E. Bray, Robert Cecil, Raymond L. Cummins, James J. Dinsmore, Stephen J. Dinsmore, Ann M. Johnson, Thomas H. Kent, Darwin Koenig, Francis L. Moore, Robert K. Myers, Michael C. Newlon, Peter C. Petersen, Mark Proescholdt, Joseph P. Schaufenbuel, Thomas K. Shires, W. Ross Silcock, and Barbara L. Wilson.

We thank Bruce Peterjohn and Ken Brock as Regional Editors of *American Birds/Field Notes* for publication of Iowa data and feedback on individual records.

We thank the authors of *The Iowa Breeding Bird Atlas* for access to their data prior to publication, and especially Carol Thompson for facilitating review of their maps. Bob Cecil reviewed drafts of our vireo and warbler accounts.

Ross Silcock provided information on Nebraska records, and he and Jim Fuller made comments on birds that might occur in Iowa in the future.

We are indebted to the following people for advice and patience in teaching us the techniques of book production: Jim Scheib (maps), Carol Thompson (maps), Les Finken (maps), Holly Carver (layout and production), and Roxanne Vincent (word processing). We thank Linda Fisher for proof reading.

We are indebted to Paul Hertzel for the superb drawing of American Goldfinch that is on the cover of this book.

We thank our wives, Ann and Pat, for ultimate patience during the four years we have worked on this book.

List of Abbreviations

In general, abbreviations are only used in charts and references, and only abbreviations that are self explanatory are used.

Months: Jan, Feb, Mar, Apr, May, Jun, Jul, Aug, Sep, Oct, Nov, Dec

Locations:

A.	Area
Co.	County
F.	Forest
Is.	Island
L.	Lake
M.	Marsh
N. W. R.	National Wildlife Refuge
P.	Park
R.	River
R. A.	Recreation Area
Res.	Reservoir
S. F.	State Forest
Sl.	Slough
S. P.	State Park
W. A.	Wildlife Area

Birds:

ad.	adult
alt.	alternate
imm.	immature
juv.	juvenile
yg.	young

Other:

ca.	circa
Univ.	University

Journals:

Acad.	*Academy*
Amer.	*American*
Bull.	*Bulletin*
IBL	*Iowa Bird Life*
J.	*Journal*
Nebr.	*Nebraska*
Proc.	*Proceedings*
Sci.	*Science*

Chapter 1. THE STATE LIST

Iowa species and their status: The number of species accepted as having occurred in Iowa by the end of 1995 was 397 (Kent 1996), which is an increase of 36 species since 1982 (Kent et al. 1982, Dinsmore et al. 1984). We also include 1 species Accepted in 1996 (Neotropic Cormorant), making the total 398. Of these, 300 are classified as Regular, 15 as Casual, 79 as Accidental, 2 as Extirpated, and 2 as Extinct. There is also 1 species of Uncertain Origin (Fulvous Whistling-Duck; see Appendix A). Additional species that may have occurred in the state, but lack sufficient evidence to be Accepted, are presented in Appendix A.

The status of Iowa species, as currently defined by the Records Committee of the Iowa Ornithologists' Union, is shown below. The status of species seen 3, 4, or 8 of the last 10 years is determined by majority vote of the committee.

Regular: seen every year or nearly every year, at least 8 of last 10 years.

Casual: seen many years but not all, at least 3 and fewer than 9 of last 10 years.

Accidental: seen once to several times, but fewer than 5 of last 10 years.

Extirpated: once regular or casual, but not seen in 50 years.

Extinct: no populations exist anywhere.

Origin Uncertain: acceptable identification of species, but it is uncertain whether the bird(s) occurred naturally or escaped from captivity. Species in this category are not counted in the state list total.

Species whose normal range, whether it be in winter, summer, or migration, overlaps with a geographic area are said to be *regular* in that area. The term *casual* is often used to describe a species whose range is nearby or sometimes overlaps with the area under consideration. The terms *vagrant* and *accidental* are often applied to species that are out of their normal range. The term *vagrant* puts more emphasis on the bird being away from its usual location, while the term *accidental* emphasizes that the bird is unlikely in the area to which it wandered. In this sense, most accidentals are vagrants, but there are exceptions. We follow the Iowa Ornithologists' Union Records Committee in adopting a frequency-based definition of regular, casual, and accidental rather than a range-based definition. This follows the practice of the majority of books on birds of states, although many use the terms in both senses. Basing the definitions on frequency has the advantage of being more operational; that is, the records can be counted. A range-based definition of occurrence is more descriptive, but its application is seriously limited by the difficulty of defining normal and casual ranges.

The term *accidental* has been used by some to mean only 1 or 2 records, that is, the species is not likely to occur again. The Records Committee of the Iowa Ornithologists' Union adopted the terminology used here because it is operationally defined and also does a reasonable job of categorizing species that have occurred in Iowa. Species that are vagrants in Iowa are usually not accidental in the sense that they are totally unexpected. They are part of a continental pattern of occurrence that can be discerned when the records of the species outside its normal range are viewed over a larger area than Iowa and over a long time period. For this reason we have included in the species accounts a discussion of the vagrancy patterns of accidental species. The Iowa records for a vagrant species do not always correspond exactly to the regional or continental pattern of vagrancy, but for most species the findings fit reasonably well.

Species that once occurred in Iowa on a regular or casual basis but no longer do so are categorized as *extinct* if no populations occur anywhere or as *extirpated* if there are no acceptable records for Iowa in the last 50 years. The extinct species are the Passenger Pigeon, which was once abundant, and the Carolina Parakeet, which was probably much less common and localized to riparian habitat in the southern parts of the state. The extirpated species are Sharp-tailed Grouse, which disappeared early after settlement began, and Eskimo Curlew, a migrant that became nearly extinct. Several other species disappeared when the marsh and prairie habitat was turned into farmland, but have been seen occasionally in the last 50 years.

The one species of Uncertain Origin, Fulvous Whistling-Duck, is held in captivity by several waterfowl game breeders and collectors in Iowa. The year-around pattern of reports in other states makes it difficult to tell whether there is a pattern of vagrancy for this species or whether birds escaped from game farms.

Breeding birds in Iowa: There are 198 species for which nesting has been confirmed in Iowa and 4 for which the evidence is considered probable. The data for nesting are based on the work of Dinsmore (1981) and a review of questionable nesting accounts by the Records Committee. The criteria are those used in *The Iowa Breeding Bird Atlas* (Jackson et al. 1996) and are shown in abbreviated form below.

Confirmed nesting:
- nest with eggs
- adult incubating on nest
- young seen or heard in nest
- downy young
- young seen away from nest but unable to fly

Probable nesting:
- bird building nest or excavating nest hole
- distraction display by adults
- recently used nest
- recently fledged young
- adult carrying fecal sac
- adult with food
- adults entering or leaving nest site

Possible nesting:
- singing male in territory on multiple days
- copulation

Of the 198 confirmed nesting species, 151 are currently regular nesting species, 34 are irregular or occasional nesting species with at least 1 nesting record in the last 50 years, and 13 formerly nested in Iowa. In the Species Accounts, we provide maps for species that do not nest throughout the state. These data are derived from the maps in *Iowa Birds* (Dinsmore et al. 1984), maps from *The Iowa Breeding Bird Atlas* (Jackson et al. 1996), data in the summer Field Reports in *Iowa Bird Life*, and, occasionally, other sources.

History of the state list: The first known list of birds for Iowa is that of Thomas Say at Engineer Cantonment near Council Bluffs in 1819-1820 (James 1823). This was a local list with Nebraska and Iowa sightings not separated. Allen (1868) published a list of 108 summer birds seen in west-central Iowa, and Parker (1871) added 54 species to this list. In the meantime, Allen (1870) published a "Catalogue of the Birds of Iowa" as an appendix to C. A. White's *Report on the Geological Survey of the State of Iowa.* Allen's 1870 list contained 283 species, including the 108 he personally saw. He does not indicate the basis for including the other species, but they probably represent species expected to occur rather than actual sightings. There was very little literature available at the time on which to base a list.

In 1889, Keyes and Williams published a list of 254 species, mostly from Charles City, Des Moines, and Iowa City and mostly based on specimens. Only 2 species listed by Keyes and Williams (Western Bluebird and Bachman's Sparrow) are not on the current state list. Otherwise, the Keyes and Williams list can be considered the first valid and reasonably representative state list. Currently accepted species not on the Keyes and Williams list are given in Appendix C, in the order of the year of the first acceptable record. Carolina Parakeet and Rock Wren, although on the Keyes and Williams list, are included in Appendix C because the citations by Keyes and Williams were not judged acceptable. Rock Dove is not listed because no first record was found.

Osborn (1891) published a list based on the Keyes and Williams list with the addition of Scaled Quail. Later it was judged that this bird was probably introduced or an escapee. Two reports of the Committee on State Fauna of the Iowa Academy of Sciences (Nutting 1893, 1895) added several species to the state list. In 1897 a committee of the Iowa Ornithologists' Association was formed to compile the state list (Savage 1897), but there is no evidence that this was ever completed.

Anderson (1907), in the first exhaustive treatise on Iowa birds, listed 354 species plus 24 hypothetical species for the state. Bailey (1906, 1910) published a book for use in schools, *200 Wild Birds of Iowa*, and in the second edition listed 352 species that are nearly the same as those given by Anderson.

DuMont (1933), in the second major treatise on Iowa birds, listed 364 species and 18 hypothetical species. DuMont (1935a, 1935b, 1944) updated his list and investigated available specimens. Musgrove (1949, 1952) published a list of 373 species and subspecies of Iowa birds to update DuMont's list.

In 1954, a committee of the Iowa Ornithologists' Union published a list of 297 species with seasonal and geographic distribution, based on a 15-year period with input from many observers (Ennis et al. 1954). They also listed 69 extinct, accidental, and hypothetical species, based on the works of Anderson, DuMont, and Musgrove.

Grant (1963) published a list of 361 species, with complicated codes for frequency, seasons, geographic location, and occurrence in Iowa. Brown (1971), in the third major treatise on Iowa birds, provided an annotated list of 369 species of which 7 were considered hypothetical. Brown gathered information on early and late migration dates from the literature and from many observers that he knew.

In 1977, the Checklist Committee of the Iowa Ornithologists' Union listed 378 species reliably identified in Iowa up to May 1977 (Brown et al. 1977). In 1980, the Checklist Committee was replaced by the Records Committee. This seven-member committee set up criteria for evaluation of records and used these criteria to critically review many old and current records, and a new "Official Checklist of Iowa Birds: 1982 Edition" with 361 species was published (Kent et al. 1982). Changes in nomenclature and taxonomic order had also occurred since the 1977 list, which was based on the 1975 edition of the *A.B.A. Checklist: Birds of Continental United States and Canada* (Checklist Committee of the American Birding Association 1975). The 1982 Iowa Checklist followed the "Thirty-fourth Supplement to the American Ornithologists' Union Check-list of North American Birds" (American Ornithologists' Union 1982).

Since 1980, year-by-year changes in the state list are noted in the annual reports of the Records Committee, which are published in *Iowa Bird Life*. The new birds by year are shown in Appendix C. New editions of the official checklist were published in 1986 (I.O.U. Records Committee 1986), 1991 (Kent and Bendorf 1991), and 1996 (Kent 1996). The number of species on the list increased from 361 in 1982 to 371 in 1986, to 384 in 1991, and to 397 in 1996. More species were added to the state list from 1970 to 1995 than from all previous decades in the Twentieth Century (chart). Of the 29 species predicted to occur in Iowa by Dinsmore et al. (1984), 21 were found over a 14-year period.

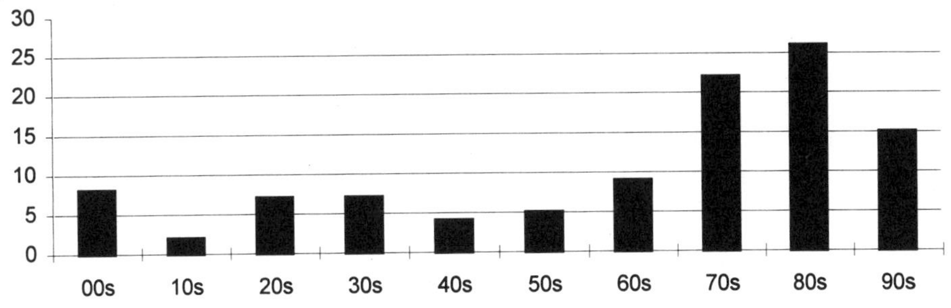

Number of new species for Iowa by decade, 1900 to 1995.

Potential species for Iowa: Although many species have been added to the Iowa list in the 1970s, 1980s, and 1990s, there are still many more that are possible. Listed below are species that could occur in Iowa in the future. Species considered here are those that have occurred in states that border Iowa (except for a few such as Crested Caracara, Spruce Grouse, Willow Ptarmigan, Rock Ptarmigan, Greater Roadrunner) and selected species that show a vagrancy pattern that potentially could involve Iowa. This does not guarantee that all species that will occur in Iowa have been included. Some Eurasian and Neotropical species have been found far from expected locations. Splitting of species by the American Ornithologists' Union Checklist Committee could also add species to the state list.

It is difficult to be sure that all pertinent records in the literature have been located and to judge the accuracy of some records. References that were most frequently used to obtain information on the normal ranges and vagrancy patterns as described in this chapter and in the Species Accounts include the following (journals in italics, complete book citations in Literature Cited): World—American Ornithologists' Union 1983; North America—The Regional Reports in *American Birds/Field Notes*, DeSante and Pyle 1986, National Geographic Society 1987, Peterson 1980, 1990; Mexico—Howell and Webb 1995; Canada—Godfrey 1986; Arkansas—James and Neal 1986, White 1995; California—Garrett and Dunn 1981, Small 1994; Colorado—Andrews and Righter 1992; Connecticut—Zeranski and Baptist 1990; Florida—Stevenson and Anderson 1994; Georgia—Haney et al. 1986; Illinois—*Meadowlark*, Bohlen 1978, 1989; Indiana—Keller et al. 1986; Kansas—Thompson and Ely 1989, 1992; Kentucky—Monroe 1994; Massachusetts—Veit and Petersen 1993; Michigan—Payne 1983, McPeek and Adams 1994; Minnesota—*Loon*, Janssen 1987; Mississippi—Toups and Jackson 1987; Missouri—*Bluebird*, Robbins and Easterla 1992; Montana—Skaar et al. 1985; Nebraska—*Nebraska Bird Review*, Bray et al. 1985; Ohio—Peterjohn 1989; Oklahoma—Wood and Schnell 1984, Baumgartner and Baumgartner 1992; Oregon—Gilligan et al. 1994; South Carolina—Post and Gauthreaux 1989, McNair and Post 1993; South Dakota—South Dakota Ornithologists' Union 1991; Tennessee—Robinson 1990; Texas—Oberholser 1974, Texas Bird Records Committee 1995; Utah—Behle et al. 1985; Wisconsin—*Passenger Pigeon*, Robbins 1991; Wyoming—Dorn and Dorn 1990, Scott 1993; Ontario—James 1991; Nova Scotia—Tufts 1986.

Most likely species: The following 17 species, in estimated order of probability, are judged most likely to be recorded in Iowa based on their occurrence in states that border Iowa and on their pattern of vagrancy.

White-tailed Kite: This nonmigratory species of the southern and western United States tends to wander, and the number of extralimital records appears to be increasing. There are 12 records from states bordering Iowa involving all of those states except Minnesota. Records are from April to August, with the most in May.

Sprague's Pipit: This species, which winters in the south-central United States and breeds in the northern Great Plains, should occur in Iowa during migration in April–May and in October. There are records from all states bordering Iowa and many other eastern states. This species inhabits grassy areas (short-grass prairie), where it is difficult to find and to view. Its behavior after flushing and its song are characteristic, but a good view and careful description are needed to confirm its occurrence.

Painted Bunting: This species breeds in the southeastern and south-central United States. There are multiple records from all states bordering Iowa except for South Dakota. Over-migrants occur in the upper Midwest from late April to early June and involve males, which are easy to identify. In the Midwest, there are only a few fall records.

Yellow-billed Loon: This species breeds in the Arctic from central Canada to Alaska and winters on the Pacific Coast. In the 1980s and 1990s, there are 15 fall–winter records from Minnesota, Illinois, Missouri, Tennessee, and Texas, with most from November and December. Identification is difficult, but with a close view and photographs the key field marks can be ascertained.

Anna's Hummingbird: Midwest records are from Oklahoma (1), Kansas (3), Arkansas (1), Missouri (3), Tennessee (1), Minnesota (2), and Wisconsin (2), with almost all from the 1990s and from October–November. Other vagrants are from the South, with none from the Northeast. Birds are found at feeders where they can be studied, photographed, and mist-netted. Males are easily identified; females and immatures may be more difficult.

Band-tailed Pigeon: This species of the mountains and forest of the western United States has shown a steady, low-frequency vagrancy pattern that includes more than half of the states and provinces in eastern North America. It can be seen in any month, but is most likely from September to December. Some appear at feeders and may remain for more than one day.

White-winged Dove: This easily identified large dove has been found in about half of the states and provinces north of its range, which is on the southern edge of the United States. It has shown a steady pattern of vagrancy that is uniformly spread from April to December.

Glaucous-winged Gull: This species breeds on the northern Pacific Coast and winters to the south on coastal waters. Increasing numbers have been found in the interior of western North America, and, in the 1990s, 6 have been found in North Dakota, Nebraska, Minnesota, and Illinois from September to April. Most of the vagrants are in first-alternate plumage, and very few are adults.

Hermit Warbler: This species of the mountainous West Coast states shows a steady but very low-grade spring over-migration pattern from Texas to Ontario in late April to May. There are December records from Missouri and Nova Scotia and a November record from Massachusetts. A good view and careful description are needed to substantiate this species.

Purple Sandpiper: This shorebird of rocky coasts breeds in Greenland and Baffinland and winters on the East Coast and occasionally on the Gulf Coast west to Texas. Although there are many records from states adjacent to Iowa, almost all are from the Great Lakes. A few have reached Kentucky, Tennessee, Arkansas, and Oklahoma. One might occur on rocky shores of large rivers or reservoirs in eastern Iowa, most likely from October to January and less likely from March to June.

Arctic Tern: This Arctic breeder migrates at sea to the southern hemisphere. The many records from adjacent states are almost all from the Great Lakes from May to July. Identification is difficult.

Swainson's Warbler: This species of the southeastern United States has bred in southern Missouri and southern Illinois. There are about 10 records of spring over-migrants in May from eastern Nebraska, northern Illinois, and southern Wisconsin, but not from northern Missouri. A good view and careful description are needed to substantiate this species.

Brambling: This Eurasian species is a regular winter vagrant to Canada and the northern United States, with Iowa lying on the southern edge of the recorded vagrants. It is found from October to May and often remains at feeders for extended periods.

Northern Wheatear: This Eurasian species breeds in the Arctic of North America, so it is not surprising that some of them attempt to winter on this continent. Most are found in the Northeast, but there are scattered records as far south as Florida, Louisiana, Texas, New Mexico, and California. Although there are relatively few records from the Midwest, an Iowa record would not be unexpected. Most are found in fall from August to November, but some occur in May and June. Identification is not difficult.

Fork-tailed Flycatcher: Most records of this easily identified South American visitor are from September to November with a secondary peak in May–June. Most are found in eastern North America with a few west to Wisconsin, Minnesota, Arkansas, and Texas. There are also single records from California and Idaho.

Ash-throated Flycatcher: This common bird of the southwestern United States is a regular vagrant to states along the Gulf Coast and the East Coast, with very few records in the Upper Midwest. Most Midwest records are from October to December, with 2 in May–June. Identification requires careful attention to details.

McCown's Longspur: This species winters from Oklahoma and southeastern Arizona south to northern Mexico and breeds in the high western plains from Wyoming to southern Alberta and Saskatchewan. A few have been found in Missouri, Minnesota, and western Ontario, and there are records from Michigan and Massachusetts. These records are prior to 1990 and have occurred from October to May. Although this species should be blown off course in spring and found in Iowa with other longspurs, the data do not support this hypothesis.

Species with a weak vagrancy pattern that have been recorded in states bordering Iowa: Some of these species may be as likely to occur in Iowa as those listed above.

Wilson's Plover: There are records of this coastal species from Oklahoma, Tennessee, Indiana, Ohio, Minnesota (3), Michigan (2), and Ontario (2) from April to September, with most in May.

Magnificent Hummingbird: The range of this species barely reaches the southwestern United States, but it often strays to Colorado, and there are records from Wyoming (3), eastern Kansas, Minnesota (3), Michigan–Ontario, Arkansas, and the Gulf Coast from June to October.

Violet-green Swallow: There are records of this western species from Illinois (3), Minnesota (1), western Ontario, Tennessee, New Jersey, New Hampshire, and Nova Scotia from March to November. This species is regular in western Nebraska and South Dakota.

Phainopepla: There are several records of this southwestern species from Colorado and Kansas and records from Oregon, Wyoming, Nebraska, Wisconsin, Ontario, Rhode Island, and Massachusetts (2) from May to February with most from September–October.

Virginia's Warbler: This western species is a very rare vagrant to the East. The closest records to Iowa are from eastern Kansas, western Nebraska, Michigan, and Ontario (3), all in May. There are also records from Labrador, New Brunswick, and Nova Scotia.

Painted Redstart: This southwestern species strays to California, Utah, Colorado, and the Gulf Coast. There are also records from Minnesota, Wisconsin, Michigan, Ohio, Ontario, Pennsylvania, and Massachusetts with most in fall.

Cassin's Sparrow: This species of the southern Great Plains and Southwest has been reported in Missouri, Illinois, Indiana (2), Michigan, Ontario (6), New Jersey, and Nova Scotia with most records from May–June.

Brewer's Sparrow: This western species has been reported from southwestern Minnesota (2), northeastern Illinois (2), New Jersey, and Massachusetts in both spring and fall.

Scott's Oriole: There are records of this southwestern species from southwestern Kansas, northeastern Minnesota, western Ontario, and Wisconsin, with 2 from spring, 1 from fall, and 1 from winter.

Species whose ranges and/or vagrancy patterns stop short of Iowa: These species could occur in Iowa, but the data do not indicate much tendency to do so.

Northern Gannet: Almost all inland records of the Atlantic Ocean species are from the Great Lakes from October to December.

Tufted Duck: This Eurasian species is a regular vagrant to the West Coast and less common on the East Coast. Inland records along the Great Lakes are from Illinois (4), Michigan (2), Ohio (1), and Ontario (5) from October to March.

Royal Tern: The few inland records of this coastal species are from the Great Lakes in Wisconsin (3), Illinois (2), Ohio, and Ontario from June to September.

Broad-tailed Hummingbird: This western species reaches South Dakota, Nebraska, and Kansas without any records from farther east in the Midwest.

Williamson's Sapsucker: The eastward extent of this western species includes records from Nebraska (3), South Dakota (1), and Minnesota (2) in April and May.

Kirtland's Warbler: This rare species that breeds locally in Michigan has been found in Minnesota, Wisconsin, Illinois, and Missouri. Finding one in Iowa would be lucky and require careful documentation.

Baird's Sparrow: This species winters mainly in north-central Mexico and breeds in the northern Great Plains including extreme northwestern Minnesota. There is a well-substantiated record from Wisconsin. Finding and substantiating this grassland species in Iowa is unlikely based on past data.

Species that are undergoing a range expansion that could reach Iowa in a few years: New records of some of these species have sometimes jumped states.

Harris's Hawk: This nonmigratory species of the southwestern United States and Mexico has recently been noted north of its usual range from October to May with a few in Oklahoma, Kansas, and Colorado and single records from Nebraska, Missouri, and Wisconsin. This relatively tame hawk is often kept by falconers; therefore, the origin of some records has been questioned.

Eurasian Collared-Dove: This Eurasian species spread through Europe beginning in the 1930s and in Florida in the 1980s. Some have reached Georgia, Alabama, Louisiana, Arkansas, Oklahoma, Colorado, New Mexico, Virginia, and Pennsylvania. The expansion is likely to continue and could reach Iowa.

Monk Parakeet: This introduced species from South America has become established in Florida, Texas, and the northeastern United States. It also nests in the Chicago area. If the present trend continues, it is likely to become established in other areas.

Cave Swallow: This species is expanding in the Southwest, and the West Indies form is being found along the East Coast. There are recent records north to Nebraska and Ontario. This species might be easily overlooked and requires careful substantiation.

Shiny Cowbird: This South American species spread through the West Indies beginning in the early 1900s and reached Florida in 1985. Although still only regular in south Florida, some have been found north to Georgia, Alabama, Louisiana, Texas, Oklahoma, Tennessee, South Carolina, North Carolina, Virginia, Maine, and New Brunswick.

Species found only a few times in states bordering Iowa with minimal evidence of vagrancy pattern: These species are not expected in Iowa, but occasionally new state birds are unexpected.

Band-rumped Storm-Petrel: There are specimens of this pelagic species found inland after storms in Missouri, Tennessee, Indiana, and Ontario.

Mottled Duck: There is a record of this Gulf Coast species from central Nebraska and others north to central Kansas.

Clapper Rail: This coastal species was collected in central Nebraska.

Common Crane: Of 10 North American records of this Eurasian species, 5 have been from Nebraska.

Mountain Plover: This species of the northwestern Great Plains is casual in western Nebraska and western South Dakota and is not a vagrant to the East.

Black Turnstone: There are records of this West Coast species from east-central Wisconsin and Montana.

Western Gull: This Pacific Coast species does not often stray from salt water. There is an Illinois specimen and records from southwestern and southern Texas. Separation of this species from other black-backed gulls is difficult.

Sandwich Tern: Records from Illinois, Minnesota, Michigan, and Ontario may have been of the same bird.

Sooty Tern: This bird of tropical oceans has been found after storms in Arkansas, Tennessee, Wisconsin, and Ontario.

Large-billed Tern: There are records of this South American species from Illinois and Ohio.

White-winged Tern: This Eurasian species is a regular vagrant to the East Coast and has been recorded in Wisconsin and Indiana.

Dovekie: There are old records (1881 to 1962) of this North Atlantic alcid from Minnesota (2), Wisconsin (2), and Michigan (2) and a recent record from north-central Illinois.

Inca Dove: This small dove of the Southwest is casual to Arkansas and Kansas, and there are records from central and northwestern Missouri, Nebraska (3), North Dakota, and western Ontario.

Boreal Owl: There are old records from Illinois and Nebraska and a few records from southern Minnesota and Wisconsin. This species might reach Iowa in an invasion year.

Common Poorwill: There are specimen records of this western species from west-central Minnesota and James Bay in Ontario and a possible record from southwestern Missouri.

White-throated Swift: This western species is a vagrant to Kansas, Oklahoma, and Arkansas, and there are specimen records from southeastern Missouri and south-central Michigan.

Calliope Hummingbird: There are records from western Nebraska and western South Dakota and a fall–winter record from Minnesota.

Red-naped Sapsucker: This western species reaches the Black Hills of South Dakota. Any record east of there would require very detailed substantiation.

Three-toed Woodpecker: The nearest records to Iowa for this northern and western species are from the Twin Cities in Minnesota and from northwestern Nebraska.

Hammond's Flycatcher: There are specimens of this western empid from Nebraska and Michigan and records from Massachusetts, Rhode Island, and Alabama, all from fall–winter.

Black Phoebe: This southwestern species has reached Kansas, and there is a record from southwestern Minnesota.

Cassin's Kingbird: This species occurs in southwestern South Dakota (nest records) and northwestern Nebraska, where it tends to remain later in the fall than other kingbirds. There are a few records from Ontario, Massachusetts, and Virginia, but not from intermediate locations.

Steller's Jay: This species of the western mountains is accidental to the western parts of the Great Plains states. There are records from northeastern Kansas (2) and Quebec.

Chihuahuan Raven: This southwestern species migrates north to Colorado and Kansas. There are several records from south-central Nebraska.

Carolina Chickadee: This common resident of southern Missouri and southern Illinois is not a known vagrant to the north.

Brown-headed Nuthatch: This species of the southeastern United States was found in Wisconsin in the winter of 1971-1972.

Canyon Wren: This resident wren of western mountains is found in the Black Hills of South Dakota, but is not a vagrant to the east except for 1 record in northeastern Nebraska.

American Dipper: This species of western mountain streams occurs in the Black Hills of South Dakota, and there are extralimital records from central Nebraska and northeastern Minnesota.

Fieldfare: This northern thrush breeds from Greenland to central Asia and is a rare vagrant to northeastern North America. There are records from Ontario (3) and northeastern Minnesota.

Gray Vireo: This southwestern species was collected in southeastern Wisconsin.

Hepatic Tanager: This southwestern species was found in west-central Illinois just south of Iowa. Other extralimital records are from Wyoming and Louisiana.

Canyon Towhee: This southwestern species is resident north to Colorado and southwestern Kansas, but there is only 1 report from western Nebraska.

Bachman's Sparrow: This species of the southeastern United States is rare in southern Missouri and southern Illinois, and there are old records from farther north in these states and from Kansas, Michigan, and Ontario.

Bronzed Cowbird: This southwestern species was collected in northwestern Missouri.

Cassin's Finch: This western species occurs in the western parts of South Dakota, Nebraska, and Kansas, mainly in winter, but there are nest records for South Dakota and Nebraska. There are 2 reports from Ontario.

Lesser Goldfinch: This western species has been recorded in western Nebraska and western South Dakota. There are single records from Wisconsin, Ontario, Missouri, Arkansas, and Kentucky from all seasons of the year.

Species recorded in the Midwest but not in states bordering Iowa: These species may have "skipped over" Iowa.

Spotted Redshank: This Eurasian shorebird is a regular vagrant to Alaska and northeastern North America with additional records from Ontario, Ohio, Saskatchewan, and Kansas.

Heermann's Gull: One was observed in Michigan and Ohio over a 3-year period. Otherwise, the most easterly records of this unlikely vagrant are from Texas (2), Oklahoma (1), and Wyoming (2).

Gull-billed Tern: One on the Indiana–Kentucky border may be the only acceptable record for the Midwest.

Black Skimmer: This coastal species has been recorded inland in Quebec, Ontario, Indiana, Tennessee, Arkansas, Kansas, and Oklahoma.

Green Violet-ear: This hummingbird from Middle America and South America now occurs annually in Texas and has occurred north to Oklahoma, Arkansas, Michigan, and Ontario.

Broad-billed Hummingbird: This southwestern species was way out of range in Ontario.

Allen's Hummingbird: This West Coast species is a vagrant to the Gulf Coast. A specimen from Massachusetts was very unusual and precludes considering all vagrant *Selasphorus* hummingbirds as Rufous.

Black-chinned Hummingbird: This widespread western species has strayed to Nova Scotia and Massachusetts and from Kansas and North Carolina south to the Gulf Coast.

Dusky Flycatcher: There is a December specimen of this western empid from Pennsylvania.

Gray Flycatcher: There is a specimen of this western empid from Massachusetts and a photographed bird from Ontario, both from fall.

Lucy's Warbler: There is a record of this southwestern species from Massachusetts. Other extralimital records are from California, Utah, Colorado, Texas, and Louisiana.

Sage Sparrow: The only eastern record for this western species is from Nova Scotia.

Chapter 2. GEOGRAPHY AND BIRDING AREAS

Physical setting: Iowa lies between 42 degrees 20 minutes and 43 degrees 30 minutes north latitude and between 90 degrees and 96 degrees 30 minutes west longitude near the center of the continental United States. Two of the world's principal rivers bound the state—the Mississippi on the east and the Missouri on the west. The maximum east-west distance is approximately 340 miles, and the greatest north-south distance is slightly over 200 miles. The total area is 55,986 square miles. Elevation varies from 480 feet above sea level in the southeast to 1,670 feet in the northwest.

Climate: Iowa's climate is characterized as extreme mid-continental or humid continental, warm summer, with a small portion of northern and northeastern Iowa in the cool-summer subtype. These climatic types are characterized by warm or occasionally hot summers with rainfall in the form of showers and thunderstorms. Iowa is subjected to seasonal extremes and frequent local, rapid weather changes due to the convergence of cold, dry Arctic air, moist maritime air from the Gulf of Mexico, and Pacific air masses that have lost their moisture while crossing the Rocky Mountains. The relatively flat character of Iowa, allowing air masses to move without impediment, results in these frequent changes in weather patterns. Average annual temperatures range from 46° F along the northern border to 52° F in the southeastern corner. Average July maximum temperatures range from 86° to 90° F, with average minimums of 60° to 66° F. The lowest temperatures occur in the northern portion, where minimums of –20° to –25° F are not uncommon. In southern Iowa, comparable lows of –10° to –15° F occur. In January, the mean temperature is 24° F in southeastern Iowa and 13° F in northwestern Iowa.

A gentle precipitation gradient exists generally from southeast to northwest, with an average of over 34 inches in the extreme southeast and east to less than 26 inches in extreme northwestern Iowa. The available moisture of eastern Iowa favors the growth of upland deciduous forest, an extension of the eastern deciduous woodland biome. These upland forests provide habitat for a variety of forest-dwelling birds that are missing in western Iowa. The dry conditions of western Iowa limit the distribution of trees, allowing mid- and tall-grass prairies to flourish and attracting some prairie birds associated with the dry western plains. The dry conditions reach their maximum in the Loess Hills of western Iowa. These hills, which were kept treeless prior to settlement by the hot, dry conditions and prairie fires, have become more forested in recent decades, resulting in a change in the avifauna.

There is considerable variation in the length of the growing season, from 135 days in northeastern and northwestern Iowa to 175 days in southeastern Iowa, with a state average of 158 days. The varying climatic conditions from north to south and east to west produce subtle but definite effects on Iowa's avifauna. Iowa is on the north–south or east–west edge of the range for a number of species, thus making the state an interesting location for bird study.

Geological history: The current habitats in Iowa are a product of the state's geologic past and the current climatic conditions. An understanding of Iowa's geologic history should give a person interested in birds a better understanding of why various habitats and their associated avifauna occur where they do. The geology of Iowa is described in easily understood terms in *Iowa's Natural Heritage* (Cooper and Hunt 1982). The state's landforms are described in more detail in *Landforms of Iowa* (Prior 1991). Both references are extensively illustrated and are recommended to anyone interested in understanding Iowa's geology.

Precambrian rock, formed on earth before life began, is found exposed only in the extreme northwestern corner of Iowa at Gitchie Manitou State Preserve. Otherwise, these ancient rocks are covered by thick layers of younger sedimentary rocks (up to a mile thick in southwestern Iowa), which were formed during the Paleozoic Era when early life forms flourished in seas covering Iowa. These seas waxed and waned during a span of millions of years, and the sediments deposited in them were compressed into shale, sandstone, limestone, and dolomite. These layers of sedimentary rock later became warped, so they now tilt from northeast to southwest. The result is that older sedimentary rocks are found in northeastern Iowa, younger rocks in southwestern Iowa.

In the Mesozoic (middle life) and Cenozoic (modern life) eras, North America gradually separated from the other continents and shifted from a tropical to a temperate location. There is little geologic evidence of the Mesozoic and early Cenozoic eras in Iowa, periods when erosion rather than deposition was the dominant agent at work. Although dinosaurs roamed the earth in Mesozoic times, only questionable traces of their fossils have been found in Iowa. In the late Mesozoic Era, volcanic activity in the western states produced some wind-blown ash deposits in Iowa. However, the major geological events that shaped Iowa's present land surface occurred late in the Cenozoic Era, during a period known as the Pleistocene (Ice) Age.

Glaciers, moving over Iowa from the north, covered the old, eroded bedrock surface and deposited hundreds of feet of glacial debris composed mainly of clay, boulders, sand, and gravel. Four major glacial periods are recognized, although recent evidence suggests that there were even more. The first glacial advances, the Nebraskan (beginning about 2,000,000 years ago) and the Kansan (spanning the period from 1,000,000 to 600,000 years ago), covered the entire state. In the northeastern corner, however, Paleozoic Era sedimentary rock remains near the surface and dominates the topography. The third glacial advance, the Illinoian, extended only a short distance into southeastern Iowa. The last glacial period, the Wisconsinan, brought a tongue-shaped ice mass into north-central Iowa as far south as the present site of Des Moines, hence the name "Des Moines Lobe."

During the Wisconsinan period, winds blew fine particles, known as loess, from sediments in the Missouri River floodplain eastward to cover much of the state. The greatest deposits of loess are present along the east side of the Missouri River valley and compose Iowa's well-known Loess Hills. The deposits thin to the east and are missing in the parts of the Des Moines Lobe that were still covered by the receding glacier.

The glacial deposits on the Des Moines Lobe are quite recent (14,000 to 12,500 years old) and thus are poorly drained and contain most of the state's natural lakes and potholes. The remainder of the state's older glacial deposits were subject to stream erosion for many thousands of years, producing a series of valleys without natural lakes. Where the rivers eroded deeply, portions of bedrock were exposed, such as at Dolliver State Park, Ledges State Park, Woodman Hollow State Preserve, Red Rock Reservoir, Lacey-Keosauqua State Park, and along the Maquoketa River in Jackson County and the Mississippi River in northeastern Iowa. These valleys are well suited for the development of artificial lakes and reservoirs.

After the last glacier receded, Iowa was forested with conifers typical of the cool, moist northern latitudes. Later the climate became warmer and dryer, and prairies eventually replaced most of the woodlands except for deciduous forests in the eastern part of the state. Decay from prairie and forest produced Iowa's famous topsoil. The deep roots of the prairie grasses, mixed with weathered deposits of loess and glacial till, formed this thick layer of rich soil. In the latter half of the 1800s, the forest and prairie were transformed into farmland, beginning in the east.

Currently, three-fourths of the land in Iowa is under cultivation. The lack of plant cover on these cultivated lands for much of the year exposes the soil to wind and water erosion, and the balance has shifted from a very slow buildup of topsoil beneath prairie to a rapid net loss of soil. Another recent change is the widespread use of chemicals to increase crop production. These chemicals have the potential for contaminating Iowa's abundant surface water as well as the underlying groundwater supplies that permeate much of the porous sedimentary rock beneath the state.

Natural regions: Iowa is divided into seven natural geologic regions, according to the distribution of bedrock, glacial deposits, loess deposits, and erosion by major rivers (see map on next page). These regions, based on the work of Prior (1991), will be briefly described.

Paleozoic Plateau: The Paleozoic Plateau in northeastern Iowa, the most scenic part of Iowa, is divided from the remainder of the state by the Niagaran (or Silurian) Escarpment. The rugged landscape with deep valleys and extensive woodlands provides some isolation for numerous woodland bird species. Much of the Paleozoic Plateau includes the Iowa portion of the Driftless Area, approximately 15,000 square miles of rugged terrain located mainly in Wisconsin, with lesser areas in Illinois, Minnesota, and Iowa. Here the bedrock controls the landscape, glacial influences are minimal, and extensive erosion has produced a varied landscape replete with caves, abundant rock outcrops, high bluffs, and deep valleys.

Iowan Surface: The Iowan Surface Region is situated between the young Des Moines Lobe on the west and the ancient Paleozoic Plateau on the east. This mature, rather homogeneous landscape with well-developed drainage systems is characterized by gently rolling topography, creating the "swell and swale" conformation. Boulders of Precambrian rocks, carried by glaciers from regions to the north and deposited in Iowa fields, are a prevalent feature, although they are steadily becoming scarcer. The southern portion of the Iowan Surface Region is characterized by somewhat steeper slopes and elongate, elliptical hills known as "paha." Paha are erosional remnants and have a distinct northwest to southeast orientation. They are covered by a cap of loess. The Wapsipinicon and Cedar rivers run nearly the full length of the Iowan Surface Region.

Des Moines Lobe: One of the youngest landform regions in Iowa is the tongue-shaped area in north-central Iowa left by the melting Wisconsin glacial ice some 13,000 years ago. This poorly drained region is generally flat, making it easily distinguishable from the rolling hills of the rest of the state. It contains ridges of glacial debris (moraines), the most prominent of which are Ocheyedan Mound in Osceola County, Pilot Knob in Hancock County, and Pilot Mound in Boone County. The Des Moines Lobe is a southern extension of the prairie pothole region of the Dakotas and western Minnesota. Many glacial marshes and lakes dot the surface. Larger lakes include Spirit Lake, West Okoboji, Storm Lake, and Clear Lake. The uplands contain some of the richest topsoil the world has known, originally covered by extensive tall-grass prairie. Because of the rich soil, this region is intensively farmed and has probably undergone the most alteration and disturbance of any region of Iowa. Though vastly diminished today, enough wetlands have been preserved to capture the feeling of the luxuriant diversity of the landscape prior to settlement. These wetlands contain rich areas for waterfowl production, including habitat for many marsh-dwelling birds.

In the northeastern Des Moines Lobe there is an area with glacial knobs partially or wholly surrounded by shallow marshes that contained the prairie fires and allowed scattered bur oaks to persist. These gentle ridges, dotted with large bur oaks under which tall-grass prairie species grew, formed an oak-savanna. The savanna, fairly widespread in Iowa, is especially noticeable in this area, particularly near Pilot Knob State Park. At one time, large areas of sedge swales and aspen bogs existed. Most have been drained and farmed, but a few are still mined for peat.

In the central part of the Des Moines Lobe are prominent glacial moraines, which are dry and often gravelly. These are especially visible in southwestern Wright County, southeastern Franklin County, and portions of Boone County. Small depressions ("kettleholes"), as well as potholes and marshes, result from the relatively recent glacial activity. This area contains more woodlands than are found farther north, and some species normally found in eastern or southern Iowa have outlying populations here, especially along the Des Moines River valley.

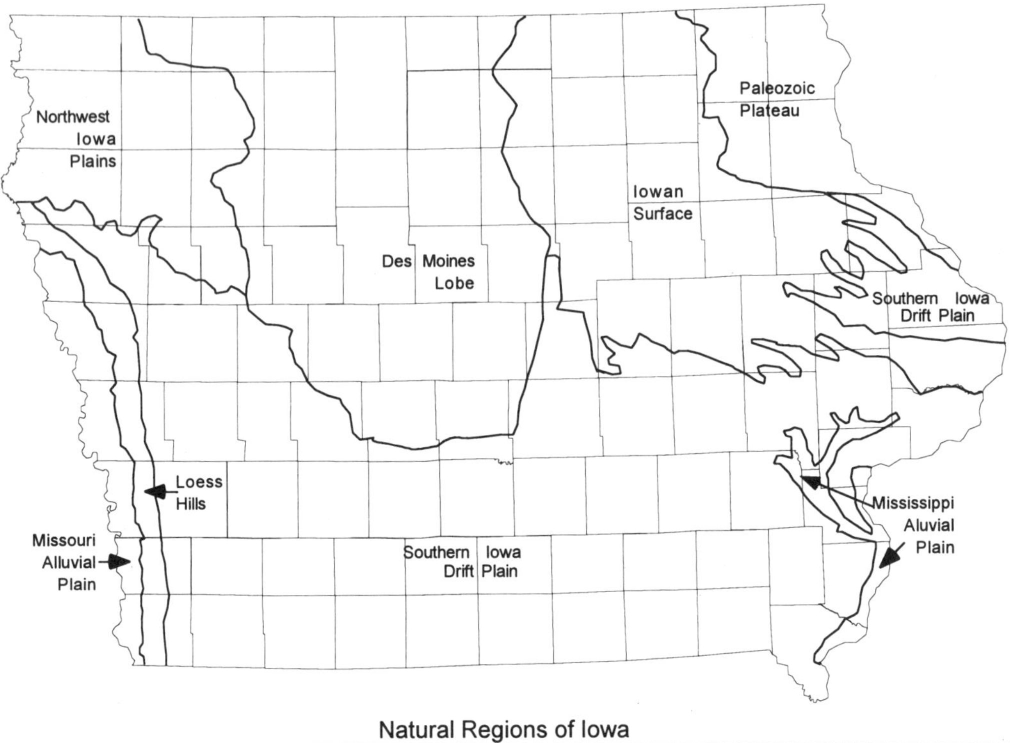

Natural Regions of Iowa

Southern Iowa Drift Plain: The southern half of Iowa was last covered by Kansan-age glaciation some 600,000 years ago. Prior to settlement, this part of Iowa was heavily wooded and today still contains a significant portion of the state's forest cover. The forest cover thins as one moves west across the region. The eroded, well-drained character of the landscape is shown by the absence of marshes and moraines and the steeply rolling topography. There are few flat uplands, and the principal flat-lying terrain occurs along the river valleys. The loess, deep in the far western edge, thins gradually as one travels east, and the hills become more undulating.

Loess Hills: In western Iowa, a relatively narrow tract of hills formed of wind-deposited loess parallels the floodplain of the Missouri River. These spectacular hills—steep, west-facing, and dry—are a unique feature of Iowa's landscape. Kept nearly treeless in the past by intermittent prairie fires and extreme climate, many are now heavily forested. Because of the steepness of their slopes, many of these areas have not been farmed, although grazing has often occurred. Wildfires are now controlled, and some of the grasslands are being invaded by trees.

Northwest Iowa Plains: The Northwest Iowa Plains Region is a largely treeless, gently rolling area of northwestern Iowa. Once tallgrass prairie, it has been largely converted to agriculture, and only small prairie remnants remain. Drainage is better developed there than in the Wisconsinan region to the east, and thus it lacks most of the prairie marshes of that region. This region has the lowest annual temperature, greatest altitude, and lowest annual precipitation in Iowa. In overall character, the landscape resembles the Iowan Surface Region.

Alluvial Plains: The character of the alluvial regions along Iowa's major rivers is much different that it was prior to settlement. Much of the floodplain forest and marsh has been converted to farmland.

Along the Mississippi River, the alluvial plain is composed of farmland with scattered tracts of forests and flooded backwaters and marshes. A section of the Mississippi Alluvial Plain extends along the Iowa and Cedar rivers in the area of prehistoric Lake Calvin, a glacial-age lake once thought to have formed, in part, when the Illinoian glacial advance blocked the lower Mississippi River; more recent evidence suggests possible formation at a later time.

The floodplain of the Missouri River, which is as much as 12 miles wide in places, has nearly all been converted to farmland. Old oxbows, reminders of the free-flowing river, are prominent features.

The character of both major rivers has been altered drastically, albeit in different ways. The Mississippi, with a series of 11 locks and dams, is largely a series of lake-like pools rather than a free-flowing river. In contrast, the Missouri, originally a shallow, wide river with extensive sandbar habitat, has been converted into a narrow, fast-flowing river. As a result, most of the oxbows are now dry and filled with vegetation, and the sandbars have essentially disappeared.

Birding areas: The locations of birds are often described in relation to counties, cities, water areas, and natural regions (see maps on insides of front and back covers). The state's 99 counties are fairly uniform in size and are laid out in rows and columns. We have divided them into the nine rectangular regions used by the Iowa Department of Agriculture and the state climatologist. In 1990, Iowa had 29 cities with over 10,000 population, 7 of them suburbs. Iowa's rivers, reservoirs, natural lakes, and Mississippi River dams also serve as landmarks for describing the occurrence of birds.

Many of the best birding areas of the state are located on public lands, which include national wildlife refuges, state parks, state preserves, state forests, state public hunting areas, and county parks and natural areas.

The "Iowa Official State Transportation Map," an excellent road map, is available free from the Iowa Department of Transportation (Office Supplies, 800 Lincoln Way, Ames, Iowa 50010, 1-515-239-1324) or at visitor's centers along interstate highways. County road maps for each county, in small, medium, and large sizes, are available from the Department of Transportation and individually from the various county courthouses at a reasonable cost. A convenient source of county maps and information on public areas for birding is the Iowa Sportsman's Atlas (Sportsman's Atlas Company, P. O. Box 132, Lytton, Iowa 50561, 1-800-568-8334). Maps of the four major reservoirs (Coralville, Rathbun, Red Rock, and Saylorville) are available at the reservoir headquarters or from the U.S. Army Corps of Engineers (Clock Tower Building, Rock Island, Illinois 61201).

The most popular birding areas in Iowa are water areas and wooded areas that are convenient to birders or have become popular because of rare birds found there. Many small parks and lakes are infrequently birded.

Perhaps the most consistently birded areas are the 4 major reservoirs, which are good for herons, waterfowl, raptors, shorebirds, gulls, and passerines. Shorebirds can be abundant when water conditions are low. Red Rock and Saylorville reservoirs are noted for their large concentrations of gulls, including many rarities first found at these locations.

The Missouri River itself does not provide many birding areas, but the broad flat river valley contains some of Iowa's best water areas, such as Riverton Area, Waubonsie Wildlife Area, and Forney Lake in Fremont County; Lake Manawa and the privately owned Power Plant Ponds in Pottawattamie County; De Soto National Wildlife Refuge in Harrison County; and Blue Lake in Monona County. These areas are noted for viewing the large flocks of geese that migrate in the Missouri River flyway, but are of more interest to birders for shorebirds, herons, and other water-associated birds. Although water conditions vary at these locations, Riverton Area at the confluence of the East and West Nishnabotna rivers is, on the average, the best location in Iowa for shorebirds, not only because of its habitat, but also because several species of shorebirds are most abundant in the Missouri River flyway. The Missouri River bottomlands are the best location to find Western Kingbirds and Blue Grosbeaks.

The Mississippi River valley differs from the Missouri valley in having 11 locks and dams with large pools above each and in having more heavily wooded bluffs, especially in northeastern Iowa. There are fewer wetlands along the Mississippi River, and they are less accessible. The Mississippi River pools have large concentrations of waterfowl, especially Pool 9 in Allamakee County in northeastern Iowa and Pool 19 in Lee County in southeastern Iowa. Pool 9 is noted for Tundra Swans in late fall, and both pools are staging areas for Canvasbacks. Winter birding on the Mississippi is noted for waterfowl, eagles, and gulls. The best viewing for winter gulls is in the Quad Cities in Scott County. The best shallow water areas for birding along the Mississippi River are the Louisa Unit of Mark Twain National Wildlife Refuge in Louisa County and Green Island Wildlife Area in Jackson County. Other noteworthy water areas in eastern Iowa that are not far from the Mississippi River include Cone Marsh in northwestern Louisa County and Goose Lake in northeastern Clinton County.

The Des Moines Lobe, with its extensively glaciated, flat farmland, attracts birders because of its glacial lakes and marshes, most of which are located at the periphery of the lobe. The largest lakes are Spirit Lake and West Okoboji in Dickinson County; Clear Lake in Cerro Gordo County; Storm Lake in Buena Vista County; and Black Hawk Lake in Sac County. These lakes are good areas to find waterfowl, gulls, and terns and are noted for pelicans and Franklin's Gulls in migration. The most heavily birded marshes are located in eastern Clay and western Palo Alto counties near the town of Ruthven and are sometimes referred to as "the Ruthven area." Other commonly birded water areas among the many that can be explored include the Kettleson Hogsback and Spring Run Wildlife Areas in Dickinson County, Union Slough National Wildlife Refuge in Kossuth County, Zirbel Slough in Cerro Gordo County, Snake Creek Marsh in Greene County, and Hendrickson Marsh in Story County. On the Des Moines Lobe, water accumulates readily in shallow fields after rains, and waterfowl and shorebirds may be found in these pools. The "Colo Ponds" are such an area that is frequently birded because of convenient location in eastern Story County.

The Paleozoic Plateau in northeastern Iowa, with its heavily wooded hills and valleys, is not heavily birded but is the best area of the state to find Golden Eagle, Ruffed Grouse, and Pileated Woodpecker. Birding locations include White Pine Hollow in Dubuque County; Pikes Peak State Park in Clayton County; and Yellow River Forest, Effigy Mounds National Monument, Pool 9, and the Upper Iowa River valley in Allamakee County.

The Iowan Surface Area, Southern Iowa Drift Plain, and Northwest Iowa Plains have rolling hills and valleys with few natural lakes and ponds. There are many small artificial lakes and ponds with surrounding woods that are good for general birding but are not much different from each other.

Wooded areas along the Mississippi and Des Moines rivers that are often birded for Eastern woodland species include the Croton Unit of Shimek Forest in Lee County, Lacey-Keosauqua State Park in Van Buren County, Wildcat Den State Park in Muscatine County, and Ledges State Park in Boone County. Major wooded parks in western Iowa along the Missouri River include Waubonsie State Park in Fremont County and Stone State Park in Woodbury County. Smaller areas that are known because they have been heavily birded include Brookside Park in Story County, Grammar Grove Wildlife Area in Marshall County, and Hickory Hill Park in Johnson County.

Chapter 3. **HISTORY OF IOWA ORNITHOLOGY**

The exploratory period: The eastern edge of Iowa was first explored by Marquette and Joliet in 1673. Scientific exploration of the western edge began with the Lewis and Clark expedition in 1804 and 1806. Their diaries have comments on some species, but there is no list of birds encountered (Moulton 1986, 1993). The first list of Iowa birds comes from the S. H. Long expedition, which stopped at Engineer Cantonment on the west bank of the Missouri River opposite Pottawattamie County, Iowa, and north of the present city of Omaha from 19 September 1819 to 6 June 1820. The biologist on this expedition was Thomas Say, later a famous entomologist. Say's list of species seen near Engineer Cantonment was published with the account of the expedition (James 1823; Thwaites 1905), but it is not clear which ones on the list were seen in Iowa rather than Nebraska. Say collected the first known Long-billed Dowitcher at Boyer River, which enters the Missouri River in northwestern Pottawattamie County. He listed several species that are now extinct (Passenger Pigeon and Carolina Parakeet), extirpated (Sharp-tailed Grouse) or accidental (Swallow-tailed Kite, Long-billed Curlew, Common Raven, Greater Prairie-Chicken, and Whooping Crane). He also reported Northern Hawk Owl, Brown Pelican, Laughing Gull, and Gull-billed Tern, which seem unlikely even for that day.

During the next 47 years there were no published contributions to Iowa ornithology except for brief notes left by two famous naturalists traveling the Missouri River on the state's western border. Maximilian, Prince of Wied, a German traveler and explorer, described his trip up the Missouri past Iowa in early May 1834 and his return in mid-May 1835 (Thwaites 1906a, 1906b). He was mostly interested in the Indians and only mentioned birds in passing. The only species mentioned that was later to be extirpated was Wild Turkey.

In the twilight of his career, John James Audubon made an expedition up and down the Missouri River, passing Iowa in mid-May and early October 1843. He was accompanied by Edward Harris, a patron of scientific men, for whom Audubon named the Harris's Sparrow and Harris's Hawk; by Isaac Sprague, an artist interested in birds, for whom Audubon named the pipit they discovered in North Dakota; and by John Bell, a naturalist-taxidermist, for whom Audubon named Bell's Vireo. Audubon left a detailed log of this trip, which was published by his granddaughter with annotations by Elliot Coues (Audubon and Coues 1897; Petersen 1971a, 1971b). Audubon gave the most definitive account of the Carolina Parakeet in Iowa, noting that this species was plentiful at least as far north as the area of Council Bluffs. Other birds of significance noted by Audubon were Swallow-tailed Kite, Wild Turkey, Sandhill Crane, Pileated Woodpecker (near the present site of Sioux City), Common Raven, and Lark Bunting.

Three eastern ornithologists, J. A. Allen, T. Martin Trippe, and John Krider, made early surveys of bird life in Iowa. Allen—who later founded the American Ornithologists' Union, edited the *Auk,* and was curator of birds and mammals at the American Museum of Natural History—visited Iowa from July to September 1867 when he was about 29 years old. He traveled in Boone, Crawford, Sac, Greene, Dallas, Guthrie, Audubon, and Carroll counties, where he listed 108 species (Allen 1868). Swallow-tailed Kite, Greater Prairie-Chicken, Ruffed Grouse, and Long-billed Curlew were common, and he saw Wild Turkey and Sandhill Cranes in small numbers but was told that the cranes were common in migration. During his trip he was helped by C. A. White, the director of the Iowa State Geological Survey, and was asked to develop a list of state birds for Iowa to be published as an appendix to White's *Report on the Geological Survey of the State of Iowa* (Allen 1870). Allen does not state how he developed this first state list of 283 Iowa species, except for noting the ones he had seen on his trip to Iowa. Many of the birds on the list must have been "hypothetical" in the sense of being postulated to occur, as there were very few sources of data on Iowa birds at the time.

T. Martin Trippe, a New Yorker in his early twenties, spent 2 years (years not given) in Mahaska and Decatur counties (Trippe 1873). He listed 162 species, of which he thought 92 were breeding. Greater Prairie-Chickens were abundant, and he saw Long-billed Curlews in Decatur County. He listed secondhand reports of Great Gray Owl and Carolina Parakeet. His Rock Wren report, later published separately, was considered dubious by the Records Committee.

John Krider was a collector from Philadelphia who spent time in Hancock County and wrote a book on birds he saw in Iowa and the East (Krider 1879). His data were sketchy, and his records cannot be considered as accurate as those of Allen and Trippe. A Red-tailed Hawk that Krider collected in Hancock County was described as a new subspecies and named for him (Hoopes 1873).

Early Iowa ornithologists: The first report from a local birder appears to be that of H. W. Parker (1871) from Poweshiek and Jasper counties, who added 54 species to Allen's 1868 list of 108 species. These were collected, and most were "preserved in the cabinet of Iowa College, Grinnell." Passenger Pigeon and Whooping Crane were included.

In the winter of 1881-1882, Wells W. Cooke attempted to secure the assistance of Iowa ornithologists to study bird migration (Cooke 1888). However, Cooke moved from Iowa and enlarged his study to cover the whole Mississippi valley. In 1882 he received reports from 13 observers, with 2 from Iowa, and in 1883 there were 26 observers, with 4 from Iowa. In the fall of 1883, at the first meeting of the American Ornithologists' Union, a committee on the "migration of birds" was appointed to cooperate with Cooke, and the area of reporting was enlarged to include the United States and Canada. In the spring of 1884 there were 27 Iowa observers reporting from 18 locations, and in the spring of 1885 there were reports from 19 locations with 15 new observers listed. Some of those observers who contributed much to the rapid development of ornithology in Iowa included William Praeger of Keokuk, C. R. Keyes of Des Moines and Iowa City, Lynds Jones of Grinnell, H. Osborn of Ames, C. F. Henning of Boone, and G. D. and Morton Peck of La Porte City. Following the publication of the "Report on Bird Migration in the Mississippi Valley in the Years 1884 and 1885" (Cooke 1888), the literature on Iowa ornithology developed rapidly.

Keyes and Williams (1889) published an annotated list of 262 species, most of which were based on specimens taken by the authors near Charles City, Des Moines, and Iowa City. This list is quite solid and can be considered the first authentic list of the birds of the state. Only a few species listed on the basis of secondhand information are questionable. Osborn (1891) published a condensed version of the Keyes and Williams list.

In the early developmental period of Iowa ornithology, the 1880s and 1890s, transportation was limited, so bird observations focused on the major geographic and governmental unit, the county. It is not surprising that a series of county lists were published over the 50-year period from 1881 to 1931. Pierce (1933a) described many of these early lists. The published county lists including 4 since 1931 are shown in the table (see next page).

Early organizations and publications: The late 1880s and early 1890s was a period of formation of ornithological organizations and publications. Burns (1915) described the early ornithological journals, and Pierce (1933b) outlined those that related to Iowa. On 15 June 1894 the Iowa Ornithological Association, Iowa's first state bird organization, was formed and with it came a substantial journal, *The Iowa Ornithologist.* The organization lasted for 5 years, with a peak membership of 89 in 1898. The journal was edited by David L. Savage through its 15 issues. Pierce (1933b) speculated that the demise of the organization and the journal were due to the war of 1898, loss of members to other fields, and financial matters. Many early records and much of the early history of Iowa ornithology can be found in the journal pages. *The Western Ornithologist*, published by C. C. Tryon of

Avoca, attempted to continue the efforts of *The Iowa Ornithologist* in 1900, but lasted for only 3 issues. It was quickly succeeded by *The Bittern*, published by Glen M. Hawthorn of Cedar Rapids, but this journal was also short-lived—only 4 issues in 1900-1901.

Published County and Regional Lists

County	Author (year)
Fremont	Anon. [Todd] (1881)
Johnson	Anon. [Shimek] (1883)
Jasper/ Poweshiek	Jones (1889)
Buena Vista	Crone (1890)
Poweshiek	Kelsey (1891)
Franklin	Shoemaker (1896) (See Ducey 1983)
Allamakee/ Winneshiek	Bartsch (1897)
Winnebago/ Hancock	Anderson (1897)
Boone	Henning (1900)
Scott	Wilson (1906)
Polk	Fagan (1909)
Cass	Pellet (1913)
Clay	Gabrielson (1914)
Clay/Palo Alto	Tinker (1914)
Floyd	Fenton (1916)
Clay/O'Brien	Gabrielson (1917)
Sac	Spurrell (1917, 1919, 1921)
Marshall	Gabrielson (1918, 1919)
Story	Cole (1920)
Buchanan	Pierce (1921)
Story	Paulson (1922)
Floyd	Fenton (1923-24)
Wapello	Spiker (1924)
Keokuk	Nauman (1926)
Buchanan	Pierce (1930)
Polk	DuMont (1931)
Woodbury	Bennett (1931)
Scott	Hodges (1959)
Black Hawk	Schlicht (1973)
Polk	Dinsmore (1995)
Story	Dinsmore and Zaletel (1996)

From 1901 to 1924 there was no periodical specific to Iowa ornithology. Rudolph M. Anderson collected lists and notes from observers in 34 counties and combined these with all published accounts for his doctoral dissertation, "The Birds of Iowa," which was published in the *Proceedings of the Davenport Academy of Sciences* (Anderson 1907) and represents the first "book" on Iowa birds. Anderson's account of 353 species and 24 hypothetical species is a masterpiece for its completeness and accuracy of citations. Anderson was aided by the master's degree thesis of Paul Bartsch (1899), "The Literature of Iowa Birds," which listed all publications relevant to Iowa ornithology from 1804 to 1899 and cited the references in which each species was mentioned. Anderson, unlike his successor DuMont, made little attempt to evaluate the accuracy of some of the reports he received.

In 1906, Bert Heald Bailey published *200 Wild Birds of Iowa: A Handbook for Use in Schools and as a Guide in Identification for All Who Desire to Become Acquainted with Our Common Birds.* At the end of the book, Bailey listed 300 species, giving data on frequency and season supplied by contributors from 10 locations. Earliest and average migration dates were compiled by high school classes in Cedar Rapids from 1902 to 1905. In a second edition (Bailey 1910), a complete list of 352 species for the state was appended. Bailey graduated from Rush Medical College in 1900 at age 25. Because a heart condition prevented his becoming a medical missionary, he accepted a position as chairman of zoology and curator of the museum at Coe College in Cedar Rapids until his death 17 years later. He was just completing a doctoral dissertation, "The Raptorial Birds of Iowa" (Bailey 1918), when he died.

Another physician who did not practice medicine, Thomas C. Stephens, was a prominent leader in Iowa ornithology for many years. Stephens became a professor of biology at Morningside College in Sioux City in 1906 and contributed to ornithology until his death in 1948. Stephens was president of the Wilson Ornithological Club in 1914 and editor of the *Wilson Bulletin* from 1925 to 1939. He continued the work of Bartsch, which was published after his death as "An Annotated Bibliography of Iowa Ornithology" (Stephens 1957), covering the years 1898 to 1947.

Ira N. Gabrielson graduated from Morningside College in 1912 and did graduate work at the Lakeside Laboratory of the University of Iowa at West Okoboji in the summers of 1911 and 1913. After teaching biology at Marshalltown High School for 3 years, he entered the service of the federal government, where he carried out many ornithological studies in the West and later became the first director of the Fish and Wildlife Service. While in Iowa, Gabrielson produced nesting studies of several species and lists for 3 counties.

During the period 1900 to 1930, many Iowa ornithological contributions appeared in the *Wilson Bulletin*, *Auk,* and *Proceedings of the Iowa Academy of Sciences*. These took the form of reports on interesting observations, county lists, and several seasonal compilations. Winter season reports from the upper Missouri valley were published for the years 1916 to 1930 and 1938 to 1941 (Stephens 1917, 1918, 1920, 1930; Spiker 1926; Youngworth 1931; Laffoon 1941).

The Iowa Ornithologists' Union: At a meeting of the Iowa Conservation Association in Ames on 28 February 1923, T. C. Stephens chaired a meeting that resulted in the formation of the Iowa Ornithologists' Union (Rosene 1932). The first 3 annual meetings were held in February/March, but subsequent meetings were switched to May in order to include a spring field trip. Besides Stephens, Walter Rosene, president for the first 3 years, and A. J. Palas, president for the next 3 years, were important leaders in the new organization. During the first 7 years of the Iowa Ornithologists' Union, a series of 24 mimeographed letters were circulated at irregular intervals (Pierce 1936). In 1929 and 1930, the letters became *The Bulletin*, edited by F. L. R. Roberts.

In 1931, *Iowa Bird Life* was started as the quarterly publication of the Iowa Ornithologists' Union. The journal, edited by Fred J. Pierce from 1931 to 1960, by Peter C. Petersen from 1961 to 1985, by Thomas H. Kent from 1986 to 1989, and by James J. Dinsmore from 1990 to present, rapidly became the repository for information on Iowa birds. Until 1961 most of the reports were in the form of short notes and articles except for publication of the Christmas Bird Count starting in 1937 and spring counts from 1943 through 1948. In 1961, reports submitted by various observers were compiled into General Notes Reports, which became Field Reports in 1963 (compiled by Woodward H. Brown from 1961 to 1976, by Nicholas S. Halmi from 1976 to 1979, and by Thomas H. Kent and others since 1979).

Books on Iowa Birds: Although the inception of *Iowa Bird Life* in 1931 marked the beginning of the modern era of Iowa ornithology, the reports in the period from Anderson's publication in 1907 to 1933 were incorporated in another landmark publication, "A Revised List of the Birds of Iowa" by Philip A. DuMont (1933). DuMont was a very active field observer from Des Moines who examined most of the specimens in the state in the process of compiling the second major book on Iowa birds. It is interesting that both Anderson and DuMont compiled county lists, Anderson (1897) in Winnebago and Hancock counties and DuMont (1931) in Polk County, prior to undertaking work at the University of Iowa on the state's birds.

Woodward H. Brown (1971) provided a major summary of Iowa bird records, updating the work of DuMont. Several other books on Iowa birds besides those already mentioned (Anderson 1907; Bailey 1906, 1910, 1918; DuMont 1933; Stephens 1957) include the following: *How to Know the Wild Birds of Iowa and Nebraska*, by Dietrich Lange (1906), is an identification guide, apparently for schoolchildren, and contains little specific information on Iowa bird distribution and frequency. *Bird Notes from the Journal of a Nature Lover*, by William G. Ross (1938), is the posthumous diary of a lawyer who birded with his family from his home in Fairfield, mostly between 1898 and 1910. Ross gave lucid glimpses of bird life at that time. Interestingly, there is no hint of contact with other birders. *Birds of an Iowa Dooryard*, by Althea R. Sherman (1952), is another posthumous collection of bird studies carried out at a single location, National, in Clayton County. Sherman is most noted for her pioneering studies of the nesting of Chimney Swifts in an especially constructed tower, but she also described in detail other birds she observed in the area over many years. *Birding in Eastern Iowa*, by Frederick W. Kent and Thomas H. Kent (1975), details yearly and seasonal distribution of birds seen in eastern Iowa by the authors over a period of 25 years and displays their photographs. *Birds of Iowa* and *Iowa Birdlife*, by Gladys Black (1979, 1992), are collections of popular accounts of some Iowa birds, many of which were previously published in the *Des Moines Register*. *Waterfowl in Iowa*, by Jack W. and Mary R. Musgrove (1977), was first published in 1943, the fifth edition appearing in 1977. The Musgroves covered Iowa's waterfowl in detail, including identification, distribution, frequency, and specific Iowa records. Two Iowa books covered the biology of single species: *The Blue-winged Teal: Its Ecology and Management*, by Logan J. Bennett (1938a), and *The Ring-necked Pheasant in Iowa*, by Allen L. Farris, Eugene D. Klonglan, and Richard C. Nomsen (1977). The only book on birding localities, *Birding Areas of Iowa*, edited by Peter C. Petersen (1979a), is a compilation of articles by various authors published in *Iowa Bird Life*.

Surveys and projects: The first Christmas Bird Count in Iowa was at Decorah in 1903. One or more counts have been made in the state yearly since 1906, and there are reviews of the data from 1903 to 1936 (Dinsmore 1993) and from 1937 to 1956 (Brown 1957). Human and environmental factors affecting Iowa Christmas Bird Counts from 1958 to 1978 were evaluated (Legg and Frye 1981). Wind speed was the only environmental factor found to affect counts; human factors were important in affecting the degree of coverage and thus the number of species seen. Christmas Bird Count data have been used to evaluate population trends of hawks (Koenig 1975), woodpeckers (Koenig 1977), and Black-capped Chickadee and Tufted Titmouse (Brown 1975). In addition, Christmas Bird Count data, especially from 1960 to 1995, have been used extensively in preparing species accounts for this book.

The Breeding Bird Survey, which monitors the breeding bird populations of the United States and Canada, was initiated in 1966 (Robbins and Van Velzen 1969). The Breeding Bird Survey is based on randomly selected routes using public roads, along which volunteers record the number of birds seen or heard. Each route is 24.5 miles long and consists of fifty 3-minute stops spaced at half-mile intervals. At each stop the observer records the number of each species heard or seen during the 3-minute period. The same routes are covered each year in June, starting one-half hour before local sunrise on a day that is neither foggy nor rainy and with wind speed less than 12 miles per hour. The data are sent to the Migratory Bird Research Laboratory, National Biological Service, Laurel, Maryland.

Surveys on the 34 Iowa routes (see map on next page) are a source of quantitative data on breeding bird populations, which is frequently referred to in the species accounts in this book. Since the routes follow public roads, the Breeding Bird Surveys sample only the bird populations of roadside habitats. Nocturnal species, species inhabiting deep woods and marshes, and shy and secretive species are not well sampled by this technique and are poorly represented in survey results.

From 1985 to 1990, under sponsorship of the Iowa Department of Natural Resources and the Iowa Ornithologists' Union, the distribution of Iowa's breeding birds was extensively studied. Random and selected 3-by-3-mile blocks were surveyed for evidence of nesting (Jackson et al. 1996). A more quantitative and locally intensive breeding bird survey of public lands near the Coralville Reservoir was conducted from 1991 to 1994 (Kent et al. 1994).

Iowans have been banding birds since the 1930s. Myrle Jones banded over 14,000 birds between 1933 and 1966, mostly in Iowa, and Peter C. Petersen banded more than 80,000 in Iowa from 1958 to 1981. *Iowa Bird Life* has included summaries of birds banded in Iowa from 1961 to 1983, with the first 11 summaries by Dean Roosa and the next 12 by Keith and Irene Layton. The summaries include the number of each species banded and the total birds banded by each bander, but do not usually include dates and locations for rare birds.

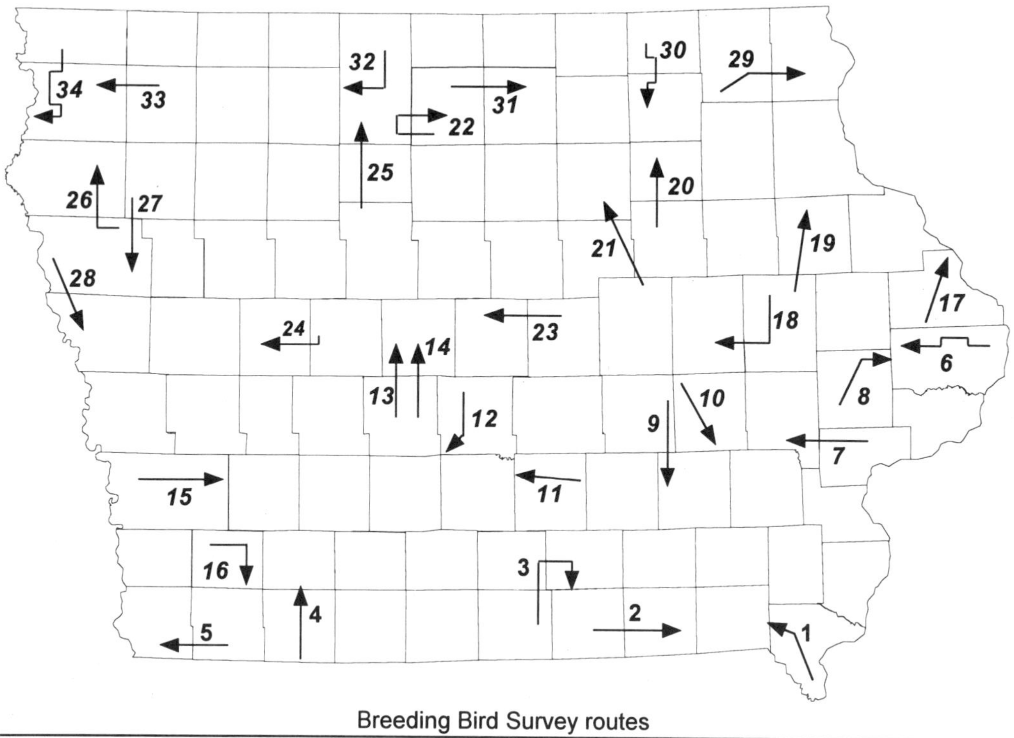

Breeding Bird Survey routes

Various types of bird surveys have been conducted in Iowa from time to time. There are published accounts of the ornithological component of summer forays in Fremont (Silcock 1977), Allamakee (Koenig 1979), and Lee (Petersen 1979b) counties. There are published accounts of winter raptor surveys from 1978 to 1980 (Roosa and Bartelt 1977; Roosa 1978; Roosa et al. 1979).

Weller (1962) started a program aimed at collecting data on individual bird nests with the intent of better understanding the distribution and nesting habits of breeding birds in Iowa. This program was eventually dropped due to lack of support. In 1976, a second program was started at Iowa State University in conjunction with the North American Nest Record Card Program. Nest records generated within the state are copied and later entered into a computer for storage and retrieval. The data on 2,117 cards for 104 species covering nest records from 1961 to 1981 has been summarized (Newhouse 1982). Mourning Dove is the most frequent species represented, with 349 nests. This project has been inactive since the mid-1980s.

A survey of nesting colonies of herons, egrets, and cormorants was started in 1993 by the Wildlife Diversity Program of the Iowa Department of Natural Resources (Hemesath 1994).

Institutional involvement: Ornithological contributions from the University of Iowa have centered around the Museum of Natural History, which first began as the "cabinet" of natural history in the Old Capitol building in 1858 (Schrimper 1982). The museum, the second oldest natural history museum west of the Mississippi River, was largely developed under the curatorship of Charles C. Nutting from 1886 to 1927. Museum training and preparation and display of ornithological specimens were fostered by succeeding curators Homer Dill (1927-1949), Walter C. Thietje (1949-1971), and George D. Schrimper (1971-present). The major collectors of Iowa ornithological specimens were Samuel Calvin, Daniel H. Talbot, Charles Nutting,

Paul Bartsch, Rudolf M. Anderson, Frank Bond, Ira N. Gabrielson, Alfred M. Bailey, Homer Dill, Walter Thietje, and John R. Rohner. Most of Iowa's bird species are displayed in Bird Hall on the third floor of Macbride Hall on the University of Iowa campus in Iowa City.

In the 1930s, Iowa State College (now Iowa State University) became another center of ornithological work in Iowa. At that time, Logan Bennett, Paul Errington, George Hendrickson, and their students began intensive studies of various game species, including waterfowl, Mourning Dove, Northern Bobwhite, and Ring-necked Pheasant. Although most of these studies had a management orientation, they provided much basic biological information. This study orientation was continued in the 1950s by Ed Kozicky, in the 1960s and 1970s by Milton Weller, and currently by Louis Best, James Dinsmore, and Erwin Klaas. Recent studies have focused more attention on nongame species and on habitats in general.

Many of Iowa's colleges have contributed to the study of ornithology in Iowa, although in recent years this contribution has much diminished because of changing educational priorities. Ornithological activities at Iowa's colleges centered around interested professors and small museums. Some of the most active individuals were Bert H. Bailey at Coe College from 1900 to 1918, Thomas C. Stephens at Morningside College from 1906 to 1946, J. Harold Ennis, a sociology professor who taught ornithology, at Cornell College from 1938 to 1965, and Martin L. Grant at the University of Northern Iowa (formerly Iowa State Teachers College) from 1936 to 1968. More recently, Neil Bernstein at Mount Mercy College, Tex Sordahl at Luther College, and Jill Trainer at the University of Northern Iowa have continued work on Iowa birds.

Specimens: Most of the specimens of Iowa birds were obtained many years ago. Some were sent to national museums, but most are housed in Iowa. The Iowa collections are mostly Iowa birds. However, the University of Iowa collection does contain numbers of specimens from other geographic areas. The collections are used for education, answering puzzling identification problems, and documenting the occurrence of vagrant species in Iowa. The locations of many of the specimens of accidental species are noted in the Species Accounts. The five largest Iowa collections are briefly described below and the others listed, along with some of the more important rare specimens.

The Museum of Natural History at the University of Iowa in Iowa City is the largest of the state collections, with 3,975 specimens from Iowa. It includes the Iowa collections of D. H. Talbot, Paul Bartsch, R. M. Anderson, and I. N. Gabrielson. Rarities include King Eider, Black Vulture, Swallow-tailed Kite, Greater Prairie-Chicken, Sharp-tailed Grouse, Whooping Crane, Long-billed Curlew, Ruff, Parasitic Jaeger, Long-tailed Jaeger, Sabine's Gull, Passenger Pigeon, Clark's Nutcracker, and Black-billed Magpie (Kent and Schrimper 1996).

The Iowa State University collection at Ames contains 2,660 specimens with about 1,600 from Iowa. Included is the O. P. Allert collection of 700 birds (Hendrickson 1944) and the Philip A. DuMont collection. Most Iowa species are represented, with emphasis on waterfowl. Rarities include Red-necked Grebe, Cattle Egret, Snowy Egret, Black-bellied Whistling-Duck, Ross's Goose, Eurasian Wigeon, King Eider, Greater Prairie-Chicken, Yellow Rail, Purple Gallinule, Sandhill Crane, Long-billed Curlew, Red Knot, Burrowing Owl, Great Gray Owl, Rufous Hummingbird, Black-billed Magpie, Blue Grosbeak, Smith's Longspur, and Chestnut-collared Longspur (Dinsmore 1992).

The Coe College Biology Department collection in Cedar Rapids contains 2,000 skins, 300 mounted birds, and 400 egg sets. Rarities include Swallow-tailed Kite, Whooping Crane, and Smith's Longspur.

The Putnam Museum in Davenport contains 625 skins, 570 mounted birds, and 1,500 egg sets. Most of the material is from eastern Iowa and western Illinois. The Iowa Wesleyan College collection is included. Rarities include Pacific Loon, King Eider, Black Scoter, Swallow-tailed Kite, Greater Prairie-Chicken,

Eskimo Curlew, Long-billed Curlew, Sabine's Gull, and Passenger Pigeon.

The Iowa Historical Society collection in Des Moines consists of several hundred skins mostly collected by Jack W. Musgrove. The major emphasis is waterfowl but many raptors and shorebirds are included. Rarities are Harlequin Duck, Prairie Falcon, Common Raven, and Pine Grosbeak.

Other smaller collections are as follows, with rarities in parentheses: Calhoun County Historical Society at Rockwell City, composed of the former Odebolt High School collection (Trumpeter Swan, Swallow-tailed Kite, Long-billed Curlew, and Clark's Nutcracker); Central College at Pella; Cornell College at Mount Vernon, including the Morningside College collection; Iowa Conservation Commission Education Center at Springbrook State Park; Luther College at Decorah; Museum of History and Science at Waterloo; Sanford Museum at Cherokee; Sioux City Public Museum; Sogers Museum at Maquoketa; Saint Ambrose College at Davenport; University of Northern Iowa at Cedar Falls; Wartburg College at Waverly; and Westmar College at Le Mars.

Public organizations: The Iowa Department of Natural Resources (previously the Iowa Conservation Commission) is the major conservation agency in Iowa and as such has a major impact on bird populations. Historically, the major concern of the commission has been hunted species, such as waterfowl, snipe, woodcock, rails, and upland game birds. Over the years it has conducted numerous studies and surveys of these species, both to better understand their basic biology and to assess populations in order to set suitable hunting seasons. Northern Bobwhite and Ring-necked Pheasant are some of the most studied birds in Iowa. The commission has also played a major role in the reintroduction of Wild Turkey, Canada Goose, Ruffed Grouse, Greater Prairie-Chicken, and Peregrine Falcon.

In 1977, with the adoption of the state endangered species list, the Iowa Conservation Commission was given authority to work with nongame wildlife. In fact, the commission, through habitat acquisition and management programs, had been benefiting nongame wildlife for many years. The Iowa Department of Natural Resources manages thousands of acres of wildlife habitat, including much of the native marsh habitat left in Iowa, and thus has a major impact on all wildlife. Likewise, most of the state parks, again under their management, have woodlands that are important habitat for thrushes, vireos, warblers, tanagers, and other woodland species.

Employees of the Iowa Department of Natural Resources constitute the largest group of trained field biologists working in Iowa. Several are active in ornithological groups in the state and contribute to the Field Reports in *Iowa Bird Life.* Several employees of the commission have made extensive contributions to Iowa ornithology. Carl Fritz Henning, custodian of the Ledges State Park from 1921 to 1941, contributed reports on Iowa birds since the 1880s and was an active member of the Iowa Ornithological Association. Bruce F. Stiles began his career with the commission as a conservation officer in 1938 and was its director from 1948 to 1959. Myrle L. Jones, after an early teaching career, served in naturalist and park officer positions at Ledges, Dolliver, Waubonsie, Fort Defiance, and Bellevue state parks from 1938 to 1965. He and his wife were active birders and banders. Dean Roosa, who was ecologist for the State Preserves Board, initiated a number of surveys of raptors and nesting birds.

Beginning in the 1960s, county conservation boards were established and are now present in all 99 counties. The counties collectively now manage more public land than the Iowa Department of Natural Resources. A number of county conservation board employees are active in reporting bird sightings.

Chapter 4. **SPECIES ACCOUNTS**

This chapter contains accounts of all wild birds that have been accepted by the Records Committee of the Iowa Ornithologists' Union as having occurred in Iowa through 1995 (Kent 1996) plus 1 additional species (Neotropic Cormorant) that was accepted in 1996. See Chapter 1 for more details on the state list. Other species that have been reported in Iowa are annotated in Appendix A.

The purpose of the species accounts is to describe the distribution and frequency of birds that occur in Iowa based on all available information through 1995 and selectively through the summer of 1996. For species that breed or winter in Iowa, we describe where Iowa fits into their overall range. For migrants or transients, we describe both the breeding and winter ranges. For species that are not Regular in Iowa (Casual and Accidental species), we describe in some detail when, where, and how frequently they stray from their regular range. For species that no longer occur in Iowa (Extirpated) or no longer occur anywhere (Extinct), we provide a historical summary of their occurrence in Iowa.

The numbers and distribution of some species have changed over the years or are currently in a state of flux. Detection of these changes is difficult, and those changes that are detected may be part of a normal fluctuation in population or may be an aberration of the method used to detect the change, so we tread lightly in making statements about population changes. The main sources of information on numbers came from Breeding Bird Survey and Christmas Bird Count data from Iowa.

It is not the intent of this book to deal with bird identification except to point out where identification problems may affect the reliability of data on frequency and distribution. There are many excellent field guides on identification as well as detailed works on individual species. We also do not provide full details on the habitat of species that occur in Iowa, but habitat is often mentioned when it affects the distribution of birds in Iowa and the changes in their location over time.

The species accounts are grouped by orders and families, and sometimes by subfamilies. A brief description of the major features of birds in each order is given. Each family account begins by defining the number of species in the family that occur in the world, North America, and Iowa. The number of species in each family for the world is taken from *Birds of the World* (Clements 1991) and usually agrees closely with the number listed in *A World Checklist of Birds* (Monroe and Sibley 1993). The number of "North American" species is taken from the *ABA Checklist: Birds of the Continental United States and Canada, Fifth Edition* (Checklist Committee of the American Birding Association 1996). The number of species in Iowa is taken from the "Official Checklist of Iowa Birds, 1996 Edition" (Kent 1996).

Also in the family introduction, we summarize the status of the species in Iowa and give some general characteristics of the family. In some cases we also make comparisons on the occurrence and distribution of species in the group.

Each species account begins with the common and scientific names, followed by the status of the species and whether it nests. Names correspond with those in the *Check-list of North American Birds*, 6th Edition (American Ornithologists' Union 1983) and supplements published in the journal *Auk* through 1995. The status is taken from the "Official Checklist of Iowa Birds, 1996 Edition" (Kent 1996).

The timelines were prepared by the authors based on analysis of data and personal experience. The rarer the species at any time of year, the more the timeline representation is based on actual data. The frequency representations on the timelines are plotted by one-third of months (early for days 1-10, middle for days 11-20, and late for days 21-31).

The perception of abundance is a function of observer activity, skill, time spent in the field, and travel. It is also influenced by habitat specificity and flocking. In some instances we have used terms such as "fairly common" or "uncommon to common" to modify the frequency descriptions.

In a very crude fashion, the frequency codes can be translated as follows:

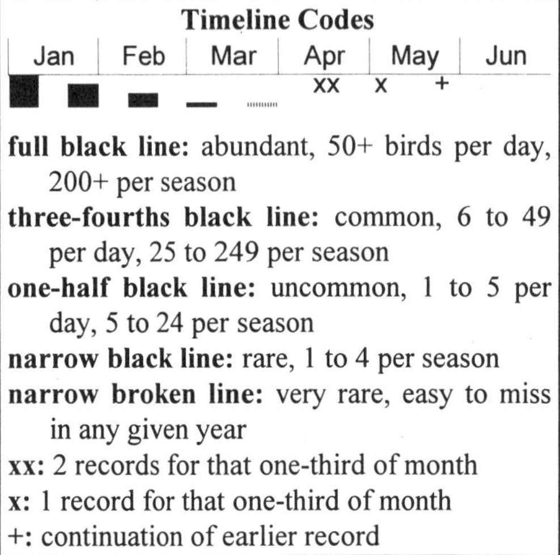

full black line: abundant, 50+ birds per day, 200+ per season
three-fourths black line: common, 6 to 49 per day, 25 to 249 per season
one-half black line: uncommon, 1 to 5 per day, 5 to 24 per season
narrow black line: rare, 1 to 4 per season
narrow broken line: very rare, easy to miss in any given year
xx: 2 records for that one-third of month
x: 1 record for that one-third of month
+: continuation of earlier record

Listed below the timeline for many species are early and late arrival and departure dates, arranged in 4 columns from left to right as follows: early spring (listed under January), late spring (listed under April), early fall (listed under July), and late fall (listed under October). The earliest dates are listed at the top of columns 1 and 3 and the latest dates at the bottom of columns 2 and 4.

The seasons are defined by the migration times of the birds, not by arbitrary dates for each season. Thus late fall migrants for some species may occur in January. Sometimes lingering birds obscure the dates for departure and arrival. For example, there are no late spring or early fall dates for several shorebirds, because there are scattered records throughout June. In general, early and late dates are given if there is a break of at least 2 to 3 weeks without any records. When there are only a few winter or summer records, the dates of these records are listed separately.

The dates listed represent the 3 earliest or latest *birds*. When there is a tie for the day of the month, the earliest year takes precedence. For example, a bird seen on 4 April 1946 is treated as earlier than one seen on 4 April 1947, and 4 June 1946 is later than 4 June 1947. When the date/year are the same, birds were seen at different locations on that day.

The authors have exercised some discretion in selecting these dates. We have given preference to records that are published and/or well documented. We have omitted many unpublished records that appeared in *Iowa Birds* (Dinsmore et al. 1984) and secondhand records that appeared in previous works on Iowa birds (Anderson 1907, DuMont 1933, Brown 1971). Many of Brown's dates were not cited as to year and location, and some were found to be incorrect. We also looked carefully at all dates that were well outside of the expected date range based on other Iowa records and records from surrounding states. The more difficult the identification and the less likely the date, the more we tended to leave the record out. It should be emphasized that many of the unusual date records are very well substantiated. We cannot claim to have been entirely consistent in excluding some early and late date records, only that we used our own judgment. In order to make the early and late dates more readable and compact, we have not included the references as was done in *Iowa Birds* (Dinsmore et al. 1984). We do, however, have this information on a database. Most of the references for date records are easily found in the corresponding Field Reports in *Iowa Bird Life* or in the previous general references on Iowa birds.

It is interesting to compare the early and late dates in *Iowa Birds* (Dinsmore et al. 1984) with the current records. In many instances the dates have less spread, which suggests that as more data accumulate, the closer the dates approach the biological potential for a given species. In some cases, however, species have shown more potential to linger between seasons. The number of new early and late records has slowed only slightly in recent years. The list will continue to evolve. Most impressive is the amount of data on migration intervals that has accumulated since the publication of *Iowa Birds* in 1984. The authors hope that *Birds in Iowa* will continue this trend. Any bird outside the early and late date range listing in this book is worthy of being substantiated by written details or photographs and reported. In fact, any bird seen at a time not represented by a solid line on the timeline is worth reporting.

For Accidental species and for rare nesting species, full citations are given for each record in the box beneath the **Status**. P-numbers refer to the accession number of photographs, videotapes, or recordings in the Iowa Ornithologists' Union Photo File.

The information and generalizations given under **Occurrence** are based on a number of sources. Previous works on Iowa birds (Anderson 1907, DuMont 1933, Brown 1971, Dinsmore et al. 1984) provide the starting point. For many species, especially the less common species, we plotted data from Field Reports and articles in *Iowa Bird Life* by year, time of month, and county. The plots were then used to describe the distribution and seasonal occurrence and to construct the timelines and maps. For distribution we often refer to the 9 areas of the state used by the state climatologist (see inside front or back cover). References to areas of the state are often generalizations, not exact limitations.

Other sources of data that we used heavily include Breeding Bird Surveys, Christmas Bird Counts, winter feeder surveys for 1984 and 1985 (Hollis 1984, 1986), *The Iowa Breeding Bird Atlas* (Jackson et al. 1996), and a survey of breeding birds at the Coralville Reservoir in Johnson County (Kent et al. 1995). The complete file of the Iowa Ornithologists' Union Records Committee was available for use in preparation of accounts on Accidental and some previously Accidental species. For Accidental species, we list all of the Accepted records. Previous references (Anderson 1907, DuMont 1933, Dinsmore et al. 1984) attempted to cite all reports of these species. We decided to end that practice, but we do try to indicate when there are unaccepted records cited in earlier works on Iowa birds.

Information on species' distribution in relation to Iowa is presented in the **Comment** section. Winter and breeding ranges are condensed and paraphrased based on maps in various field guides, books on families of birds, and the *Check-list of North American Birds*, 6th Edition (American Ornithologists' Union 1983). Information on distribution of vagrants is mostly from a database developed by one of the authors (Kent) using a variety of sources, such as books on state birds, *Distributional Checklist of North American Birds* (DeSante and Pyle 1986), and seasonal reports in *American Birds/Field Notes*. Some of the most recent records may not be included, and it was not feasible to check the acceptance of all of the records by state committees. We know that there will be a few vagrant records that we have not cited, but this should not detract from our goal, which is to define the pattern of vagrancy for species that do not normally occur in Iowa.

We often compare early and late dates in Iowa with those cited for Minnesota (Janssen 1987), Wisconsin (Robbins 1991), Illinois (Bohlen 1989), and Missouri (Robbins and Easterla 1992). For most species, allowing for differences in latitude, there is close agreement on migration intervals among these states. The comparative data help define the rarity of some records in Iowa.

Maps are used to show the county distribution of Accidental species and most Casual species. Maps are used for Regular species if their distribution does not include the entire state. For nesting species, we often shade the counties that have June and July records and add an "N" to indicate that there is a confirmed nesting record for the county. For rare and local nesting species, we sometimes use a "+" to indicate counties for which the only records are for migrants.

We follow the practice used in *Iowa Birds* (Dinsmore et al. 1984) for references. Those specific to the species are included in the species account under **References**; more general references are in Literature Cited at the end of the book. For references to specific bird records in the Field Reports and Christmas Bird Counts sections of *Iowa Bird Life* we reference the volume and page within our text using the abbreviation *IBL*. We include the county location with each bird record cited. In addition to the state map with county names and areas, other maps on the inside of the front and back covers show cities; rivers, reservoirs, and major lakes; and natural regions.

ORDER GAVIFORMES

Loons (Family Gaviidae)

Loons, the only family in the order, comprise 5 species, with 5 from North America and 3 from Iowa. They have pointed bills, webbed feet, and legs placed far back on the body that aid them in diving for fish. They cannot take off from land, and must paddle to take off from water. Once airborne they are strong flyers. Their loud voices are unique.

Loons nest on shallow ponds and lakes of the northern Holarctic. They winter on sea coasts. Red-throated and Pacific loons have been found more frequently in Iowa in recent years, changing their status from Accidental to Casual (almost Regular). Arctic Loon, which was recently split from Pacific Loon, occurs in Eurasia and northwestern Alaska and has strayed to California. Yellow-billed Loon, which is similar in appearance to Common Loon, breeds in the western Nearctic and winters in the Pacific. It has strayed to Minnesota, Illinois, Missouri, Tennessee, and Texas.

Red-throated Loon (*Gavia stellata*)

Status: Casual

By year since 1960 (also 1996)

60	63	66	69	72	75	78	81	84	87	90	93
				1				1 1 1	1 2	2 1	2 4

By month -- all records

Jan	Feb	Mar	Apr	May	Jun	Jul	Aug	Sep	Oct	Nov	Dec
		1	+ 1 2	1				1	1	3 4 2	1

31 Mar 1984	24 Apr 1995	2 Sep 1972	25 Nov 1994
19 Apr 1996	30 Apr 1989	29 Oct 1995	30 Nov 1985
	9 May 1994	4 Nov 1990	1 Dec 1986

Occurrence: Of 17 Accepted records through 1995, 5 are from spring and 12 are from fall. The early spring bird remained at Cedar Lake in Linn County from 31 Mar to 20 April 1984 (Bendorf 1984). The fall records are from late October to early December, except for the first Accepted record of 3 birds on a small pond at Jester Park in Polk County from 2 to 4 September 1972. The latter record may have been a family group, as 2 of the birds were in alternate plumage and the other appeared to be an immature bird (Burns and Burns 1972). The only other record involving more than 1 bird was of 2 at Lake Manawa in Pottawattamie County from 27 to 30 April 1989 (Myers 1989). One of these birds was in partial molt to alternate plumage.

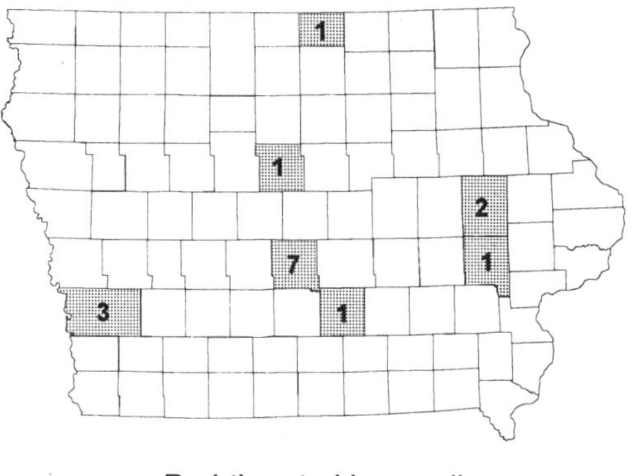

Red-throated Loon, all

All other records are of birds in basic plumage. Except for the September birds, all birds were on reservoirs or large lakes.

There are 12 reports from 1873 to 1977 that lack sufficient information to judge their accuracy (Dinsmore et al. 1984, Kent 1995). One of these records (28 Apr 1873, near Ottumwa) was reevaluated and changed from Accepted to Not Accepted. A specimen at the University of Iowa previously accepted as Arctic (Pacific) Loon was reexamined and found to be a Red-throated Loon in basic plumage taken ca. 1895 on the Illinois side of the Mississippi River near Burlington. There is another Illinois record on the Mississippi opposite Clinton from 6 November 1970 (Bohlen 1978).

Comment: Red-throated Loons migrate from their Holarctic nesting grounds to coastal wintering grounds. In North America, most winter on the Atlantic and Pacific coasts, but some remain on the Great Lakes, and a few reach the Gulf Coast. The nesting grounds nearest to Iowa are around Hudson Bay. The numbers found in other Midwestern states away from the Great Lakes are similar to the Iowa experience.

The increased number of reports of this species in recent years can be attributed in part to extensive coverage of Iowa's reservoirs by birders. It is likely that more were missed in the past, but the reservoirs seem to have provided stop-over places for migrating loons.

References:

Bendorf, C. J. 1984. Red-throated Loon at Cedar Lake. *Iowa Bird Life* 54:52-54.

Burns, S., and S. Burns. 1972. Red-throated Loons at Jester Park, Des Moines. *Iowa Bird Life* 42:71-72.

Myers, R. K. 1989. Red-throated Loons at Lake Manawa. *Iowa Bird Life* 59:117.

Pacific Loon (*Gavia pacifica*)

Status: Casual

By year since 1960 (also 1895, 1948)

60 63 66 69 72 75 78 81 84 87 90 93

1 (1981) 1 (1986) 1 2 2 1 1 (1988–1992) 2 5 (1994–1995)

By month -- all records

Jan	Feb	Mar	Apr	May	Jun	Jul	Aug	Sep	Oct	Nov	Dec
			1			1 +	+ +	+ +	7 5	1 2	+ 1

28 Apr 1981 — 29 Apr 1981

22 Oct 1989 — 21 Nov 1995

23 Oct 1988 — 6 Dec 1986

23 Oct 1990 — 12 Dec 1948

summer: 13 Jul to 16 Sep 1994

Occurrence: Of the 18 Accepted records, 1 is from spring, 1 is from summer, and 16 are from fall. The bird from 28 April 1981 that stopped overnight at Amana Lake in Iowa County was in alternate plumage (Bendorf 1981). All other birds, including 1 that summered at Anderson Lake in Hamilton County from 13 July to 16 September 1994 (Dinsmore 1995), were in basic plumage, except for the latest bird on 11 to 12 December 1948 at Des Moines in Polk County (Berkowitz 1949), which was described as being in alternate plumage. All records are of single birds, although more than 1 may have been present at

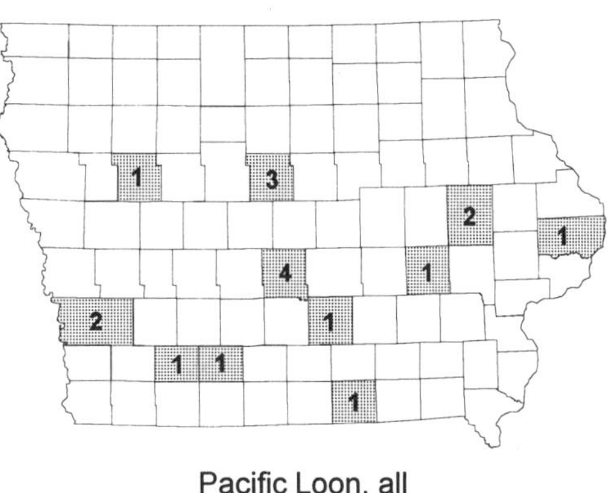

Pacific Loon, all

Saylorville Reservoir in Polk County in 1986 (Dinsmore 1987). The sightings are from lakes and reservoirs across the state, except for the first record on the Mississippi River at Sabula in Jackson County on 16 November 1895 (Giddings 1896, DuMont 1933).

Historically, 4 specimen-associated reports and 5 other reports without details (Dinsmore et al. 1984, Kent 1994) are Not Accepted. The 1 extant specimen (ca. 1895, Burlington) was reexamined and found to be a Red-throated Loon with label reading "Burlington, Illinois side."

Comment: Pacific Loons nest in the Arctic from western Hudson Bay to eastern Siberia and winter on the West Coast south to Baja California and south to Japan. Very few migrate to the East and Gulf coasts. This species has been recorded in all states west of the Mississippi River, but has not been found in many eastern states, especially southeastern states. In contrast to Red-throated Loon, Pacific Loon is less frequent in the Midwest (Iowa being an exception), not attracted to the Great Lakes, and more likely to be found in fall than spring. In western Alaska, the range overlaps with that of the very similar Arctic Loon, a species that breeds across the Palearctic and winters south to Japan and Spain.

The increase in Iowa records since 1986 may be due in part to increased awareness of this species and efforts to find it among the greatly increased number of Common Loons that linger in Iowa in the fall.

In Iowa, Pacific Loons are most likely to be in basic or juvenal plumage and can be difficult to separate from Common Loon. Juveniles have scaly scapulars and wing coverts and appear browner and paler than adults. Separation from the smaller, slimmer Red-throated Loon with its upturned bill is easier than separation from the highly variable Common Loon. Details of body structure and plumage should be recorded and checked carefully (Walsh 1988, Kaufman 1990).

References:

Bendorf, C. J. 1981. Arctic Loon at Amana Lake. *Iowa Bird Life* 51:76.

Berkowitz, A. C. 1949. Pacific Loon and other water birds at Des Moines impounding reservoir. *Iowa Bird Life* 19:19.

Dinsmore, S. 1987. Pacific Loons at Saylorville Reservoir. *Iowa Bird Life* 57:59-60.

Dinsmore, S. J. 1995. First summer record of Pacific/Arctic Loon for Iowa. *Iowa Bird Life* 65:55-56.

DuMont, P. A. 1933. The Iowa specimen of Pacific Loon reexamined. *Wilson Bull.* 45:89-90.

Giddings, J. 1896. *Urinator arcticus* in Jackson Co. *Iowa Ornithologist* 2:73.

Walsh, T. 1988. Identifying Pacific Loons: some old and new problems. *Birding* 20:12-28.

Common Loon (*Gavia immer*)

Status: Regular; formerly nested

Jan	Feb	Mar	Apr	May	Jun	Jul	Aug	Sep	Oct	Nov	Dec
	X	X									

8 Mar 1987
16 Mar 1991
17 Mar 1945
winter: 17 Feb 1976
nesting record: 1893, Rice L., Winnebago Co. (Anderson 1907)

3 Jan 1987
6 Jan 1986
10 Jan 1987

Occurrence: This fairly common migrant is usually found from early April to early May and from mid-October to mid-November on larger lakes, reservoirs, or rivers but also may occur on ponds and gravel pits. In most summers, a few are found, usually in northern Iowa or on a large reservoir. Summer birds may be in either basic or alternate plumage, suggesting that both nonbreeding adult and subadult birds may summer in Iowa. A few remain in Iowa into early or mid-December, usually at the large reservoirs and along the Mississippi River. The only January records are from 3 January 1987 at Keokuk in Lee County (*IBL* 57:52), up to 6 January 1986 at Iowa City in Johnson County (*IBL* 56:57), and 10 January 1987 at Saylorville Reservoir in Polk County (*IBL* 57:52). One at Lake Macbride in Johnson County on 17 Feb 1976 (*IBL* 46:55) could have been either an early migrant or a wintering bird.

There are a few summer reports from northern Iowa prior to 1900 and 1 report of eggs taken from a nest on a muskrat house at Rice Lake in Winnebago County in 1893 (Anderson 1907). There is a secondhand report of nesting up to 1900 in Sac County (Spurrell 1917).

Comment: The winter range is along the coasts of North America from southern Canada south to northern Mexico. The nesting range extends across much of Canada south into the northern United States. In Minnesota, Common Loons currently nest south to the Twin Cities (Janssen 1987).

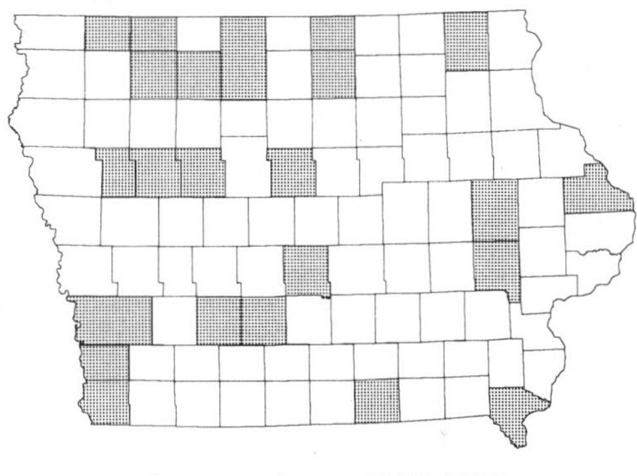

Common Loon, 1960-1995
June-July

ORDER PODICIPEDIFORMES

Grebes (Family Podicipedidae)

Grebes, the only family in the order, comprise 22 species, with 7 from North America and 6 from Iowa. Of the Iowa species, 5 are Regular and 1 is Accidental.

Grebes are elongated, rotund, short-tailed birds with strong legs placed at the rear for use in diving and with moderately long necks and pointed beaks. The feet are partially webbed with paddle-like lobes on the toes. Grebes nest in tropical and temperate wetlands that have emergent vegetation, but may be found on large bodies of water in migration. Grebes feed by diving for fish and aquatic invertebrates. They are seldom seen in flight and are able to submerge slowly when alarmed.

Pied-billed Grebe (*Podilymbus podiceps*)

Status: Regular; nests

Jan	Feb	Mar	Apr	May	Jun	Jul	Aug	Sep	Oct	Nov	Dec

Occurrence: This common migrant and fairly common summer resident is found on lakes and ponds throughout Iowa from mid-March to late November. It is a summer resident of marshes with dense emergent vegetation throughout Iowa but is most common in northwestern and north-central Iowa. Nesting begins in late April and peaks in late May and early June (Glover 1953).

In fall, a few linger where there is open water. Pied-billed Grebes were reported from 1 to 5 locations on Christmas Bird Counts in 26 of 36 years from 1960 to 1995. Mid-winter birds are unusual, except at the artificially heated Cedar Lake in Linn County where birds were present every winter from 1989 to 1995. The only other records between mid-January and late February are from Davenport in Scott County on 15 February 1970 (*IBL* 40:18), Coralville Reservoir in Johnson County on 7 February 1978 (*IBL* 48:47), Brown's Lake in Woodbury County on 3 February 1991 (*IBL* 61:53), and Red Rock Reservoir in Marion County on 18 February 1995 (*IBL* 65:45).

Historically, nesting populations declined with the loss of wetlands (DuMont 1933), and that trend has probably continued, although census data are lacking.

Comment: This species is a resident of North and South America except for the coldest regions. The North American population winters in the United States (except the north-central portions south to central Missouri) and Middle America. The breeding range includes the winter range and extends north through the Canadian provinces. The breeding range in Iowa is limited only by the availability of suitable habitat.

Reference:

Glover, F. A. 1953. Nesting ecology of the Pied-billed Grebe in northwestern Iowa. *Wilson Bull.* 65:32-39.

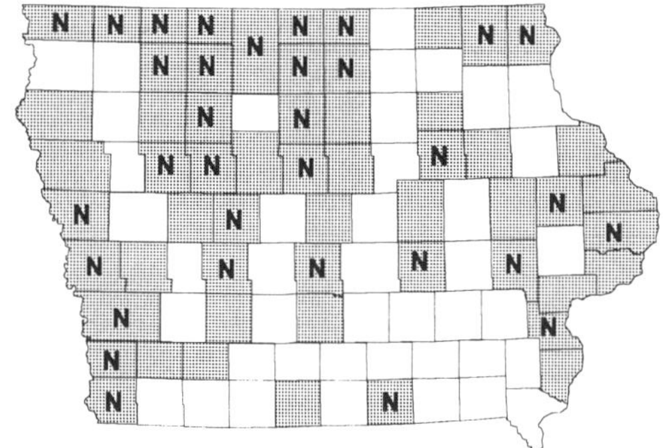

Pied-billed Grebe, 1960-1995
June-July and nesting (N)

Horned Grebe (*Podiceps auritus*)

Status: Regular

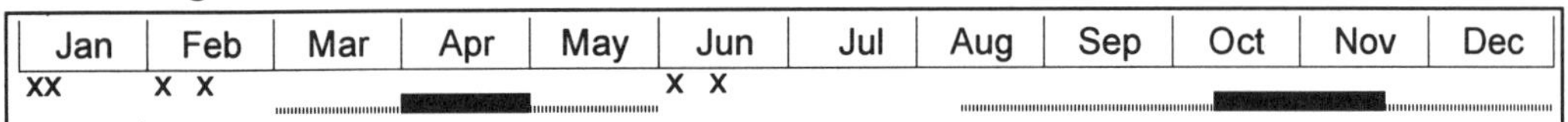

Jan	Feb	Mar	Apr	May	Jun	Jul	Aug	Sep	Oct	Nov	Dec
XX	X X				X X						

5 Mar 1983	24 May 1986	13 Aug 1995	22 Dec 1965
8 Mar 1988	9 Jun 1965	16 Aug 1984	1 Jan 1973
9 Mar 1992	11 Jun 1928	16 Aug 1987	7 Jan 1987

winter: 10 Feb 1951, 12 Feb 1986, Feb 1994

Occurrence: This uncommon migrant is usually found in April and from mid-October to mid-November. In recent years there have been several reports of late migrants remaining until early or mid-December, most often on large reservoirs. There are only 3 reports from Christmas Bird Counts from 1960 to 1995. The January records are from the artificially heated Cedar Lake in Linn County, where there were 3 on 1 January 1973 (*IBL* 43:25) and 1 from 30 December 1986 to 7 January 1987 (*IBL* 57:52). Winter records include 1 at Davenport in Scott County on 10 February 1951 (Morrissey et al. 1952), 1 found in a chicken coop in Madison County on 12 February 1986 (*IBL* 56:57), and 1 at Dubuque in Dubuque County in February 1994 (*IBL* 64:45).

Comment: The winter range is along the coasts from Alaska to California and from the Maritime Provinces of Canada south to Florida and west to Texas. The nesting range is from Alaska and northern Canada south to eastern Washington, northern Montana, North Dakota, and northern Minnesota. Horned Grebes also nest in northern Europe and Asia. They formerly nested in southern Minnesota within 25 miles of the Iowa border (Janssen 1987), but there are no known nesting records for Iowa.

Reference:

Morrissey, T., T. J. Feeney, and E. C. Greer. 1952. Records of unusual birds from the Davenport area during 1951. *Iowa Bird Life* 22:45-46.

Red-necked Grebe (*Podiceps grisegena*)

Status: Regular; possible nesting

By year since 1960

60			63			66			69			72			75			78			81			84			87			90			93		
				1	1	2			1			1				1			1		2	1		3	3	6	2	5	1	3	3	1	4	6	5

By month -- all records

Jan			Feb			Mar			Apr			May			Jun			Jul			Aug			Sep			Oct			Nov			Dec		
							1	2	8	9	4	7	4	1	3		1		1		1		1	1	2	2	1	2	3	3	6	4		2	

11 Mar 1990	21 May 1984	9 Sep 1928	24 Nov 1986
28 Mar 1995	24 May 1996	11 Sep 1955	15 Dec 1953
30 Mar 1957	27 May 1994	20 Sep 1982	17 Dec 1939

summer: 6 Jun 1928, 6 Jun 1929, 23 Jun 1965, 20 Jul 1966, 4 Aug 1988, 28 Aug 1990
possible nesting: 9 Jun 1993, Emmet Co. (IBL 63:94)

Occurrence: The 69 records of this species are about equally divided between spring and fall, and there are a few summer records. The few birds that have been found in Iowa have been spread over a wide range of dates in both spring and fall.

Nesting has not been proven for Iowa; however, a pair was seen building a nest on 9 June 1993 in Emmet County, but were gone the next day after a storm (*IBL* 63:94). The records from 4 August 1988 at Zirbel Slough in Cerro Gordo County (*IBL* 59:8) and from 28 August 1990 at Union Slough National Wildlife Refuge in Kossuth County (*IBL* 61:17) were of juveniles, raising the possibility that they were hatched in Iowa. A migrating family group of 2 adults and 2 immatures was north of Ames in Story County on 19 Oct 1985 (*IBL* 55:121).

Most of the records are from the wetland areas of north-central Iowa or from large reservoirs, especially Saylorville Reservoir. There are few records from the western and southern edges of the state.

Historically, there is no evidence that this species bred in the wetlands of northern Iowa. The first acceptable record is from 25 April 1926 at Independence in Buchanan County (Pierce 1930). There are only 16 records prior to 1960.

Comment: This Holarctic species nests in wetlands of the northern hemisphere and winters in coastal waters. The nearest nesting areas for this relatively uncommon species are in central Minnesota and eastern South Dakota. Migrants are commonly found on Lake Superior and must continue their eastward migration well to the north, as Illinois, Indiana, and Ohio have about as few sightings as Iowa. We do not know whether Iowa birds winter on the East or West Coast, although the former seems more likely. This species is even rarer in states to the south of Iowa, and is very rare on the Gulf Coast in winter.

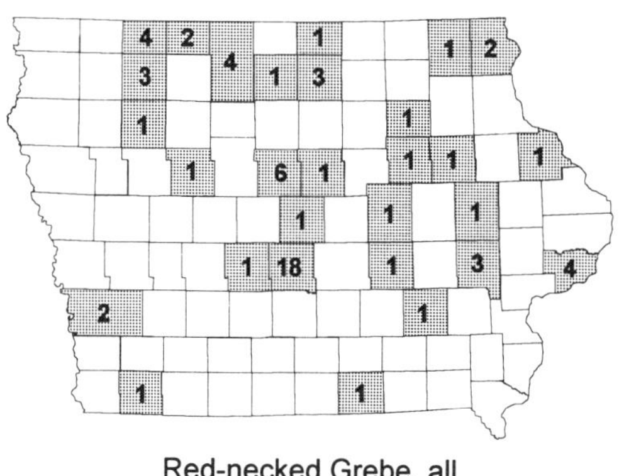

Red-necked Grebe, all

Eared Grebe (*Podiceps nigricollis*)

Status: Regular; occasionally nests

Jan	Feb	Mar	Apr	May	Jun	Jul	Aug	Sep	Oct	Nov	Dec
x											x

14 Mar 1986
14 Mar 1992
15 Mar 1984

20 Dec 1990
23 Dec 1967
2 Jan 1966

Occurrence: This uncommon migrant in western Iowa and rare migrant in eastern Iowa is usually seen from mid-April through May and from late September to late October. It occasionally nests on wetlands with thick stands of emergent vegetation in northwestern Iowa. Courting Eared Grebes were seen in Palo Alto County and at Little Wall Lake in Hamilton County in June 1990 (*IBL* 60:101) and at Silver Lake in Worth County in May 1992 (*IBL* 62:74). The only confirmed nestings since 1966 were near Center Lake and at Grover's Lake in Dickinson County in 1993 (*IBL* 63:94, 64:10) and at Eagle Lake in Emmet County on 28 July 1981 (*IBL* 51:99). At the latter location there were 25 adults and 25 young.

Eared Grebes occasionally remain in Iowa until freeze-up. They were reported on Christmas Bird Counts in 5 of 36 years from 1960 to 1995, with the latest at Cedar Rapids in Linn County on 2 January 1966 (*IBL* 36:4).

Historically, Eared Grebe was considered locally common and nested at Eagle Lake in Hancock County (Anderson 1907). Small colonies were found in Clay County near Ruthven from 1933 to 1936 (Friley and Hendrickson 1937), and broods were seen at West Swan Lake in Emmet County in 1965 and 1966 and at Rush Lake in Osceola County in 1966 (Brown 1971). Two Eared Grebes banded as young in Emmet County in 1965 and 1966 were recovered in winter, 1 on the Gulf Coast of Texas and 1 in central Mexico (Jehl and Yochem 1986).

Comment: In North America, the winter range of this Holarctic species is along the Pacific Coast from British Columbia and inland from Nevada and Utah south to Guatemala. Most Eared Grebes winter on the Gulf of California and at the Salton Sea in southern California. The nesting range covers much of western North America from southern Canada south to the southwestern United States. Iowa is at the eastern edge of the nesting range. This Holarctic species occurs across Eurasia, where it is known as Black-necked Grebe. Most of North America's Eared Grebes gather at Mono Lake in California and the Great Salt Lake in Utah before moving to wintering grounds (Jehl 1988).

References

Friley, C. E., and G. O. Hendrickson. 1937. Eared Grebes nesting in northwest Iowa. *Iowa Bird Life* 7:2-3.

Jehl, J. R. 1988. Biology of the Eared Grebe and Wilson's Phalarope in the nonbreeding season: a study of adaptations to saline lakes. *Studies in Avian Biology*, No. 13.

Jehl, J. R., and P. K. Yochem. 1986. Movements of Eared Grebes indicated by banding recoveries. *J. Field Ornithology* 57:208-212.

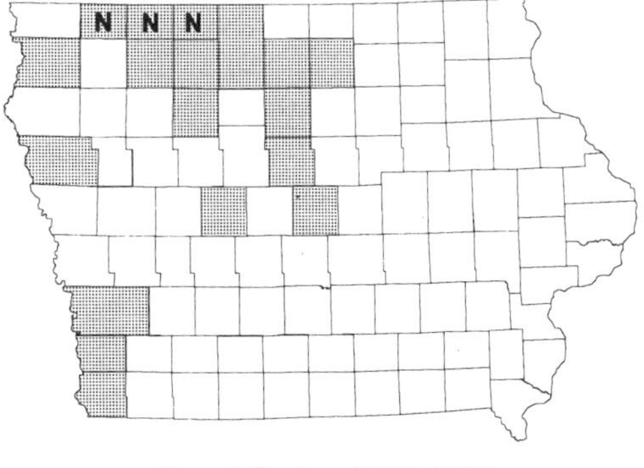

Eared Grebe, 1960-1995
June-July and nesting (N)

Western Grebe (*Aechmophorus occidentalis*)

Status: Regular; occasionally nests

Jan	Feb	Mar	Apr	May	Jun	Jul	Aug	Sep	Oct	Nov	Dec
		X	XX								XX X

29 Mar 1938	1 Dec 1987
9 Apr 1984	6 Dec 1994
9 Apr 1992	16 Dec 1990

nesting records:

29 Jun 1981, Rush L., Osceola Co., 4 yg. (Kent 1981)

15, 23 Jul, 11 Aug 1984, Rush L., Osceola Co., 2 yg. (*IBL* 54:80, 108)

12, 22 Jun 1988, Rush L., Osceola Co., nest with eggs, 1 yg. (*IBL* 58:107, photo)

28 Jun 1992, Silver L., Worth Co., 2 yg. (*IBL* 62:105)

Occurrence: This rare migrant and summer resident is most common from late April to mid-May and from mid-October to late November in western and central Iowa. In migration it is found on lakes and reservoirs and in summer on marshes with dense stands of emergent vegetation.

Nesting was first confirmed in 1981 when a pair with 4 young was seen at Rush Lake in Osceola County (Kent 1981). Since then, nesting has been confirmed again at Rush Lake in 1984 and 1988 and at Silver Lake in Worth County in 1992.

Historically, there were only a few records prior to 1930 (Anderson 1907, DuMont 1933). The first definite date was 8 August 1926 in Dickinson County (DuMont 1933). Western Grebe did not become regular in Iowa until 1970, and there has been a steady increase in records since then, averaging 2 per year in the 1970s, 5 per year in the 1980s, and 13 per year in the 1990s.

Comment: The winter range is along the Pacific Coast from British Columbia south to Baja California and the Gulf of California. The nesting range extends from the Prairie Provinces of Canada south through the Dakotas and western Minnesota and west to southern California and northern Mexico. Northern Iowa is at the eastern edge of its nesting range.

Reference:

Kent, T. H. 1981. Western Grebe breeding in Osceola County. *Iowa Bird Life* 51:105.

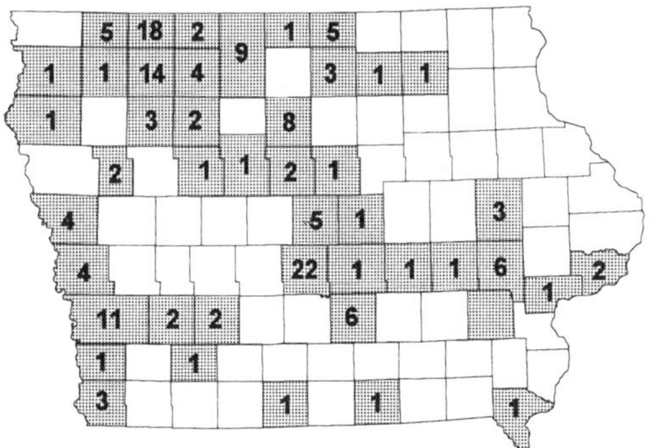

Western Grebe, 1960-1995

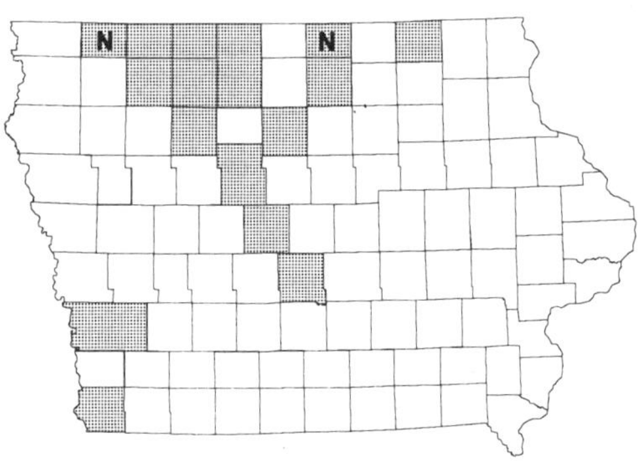

Western Grebe, 1960-1995
June-July and nesting (N)

Clark's Grebe (*Aechmophorus clarkii*)

Status: Accidental

By year since 1960

60	63	66	69	72	75	78	81	84	87	90	93
							1	1 1			2 1

By month -- all records

Jan	Feb	Mar	Apr	May	Jun	Jul	Aug	Sep	Oct	Nov	Dec
				2 1					1	1 1	

5 May 1983, Cone Marsh, Louisa Co. (*IBL* 53:48, 54:38)
6 Oct 1985, Big Creek S.P., Polk Co. (S. Dinsmore 1986)
7 May 1986, Hendrickson M., Story Co. (*IBL* 56:82, 57:77)
13 May 1994, Trumbull L., Clay Co. (Brewer 1995)
25 Nov 1994, South Twin L., Calhoun Co. (P-0433, Dinsmore 1995)
12 to 13 Nov 1995, Pleasant Creek L., Linn Co. (*IBL* 66:17)

Occurrence: There are 6 records, 3 from spring and 3 from fall. One was photographed. The first record was documented before Clark's and Western grebes were split in 1985.

Comment: Clark's and Western grebes overlap in range (Ratti 1981). All states touching Iowa have at least 1 record. The eastward vagrancy pattern, however, is poorly understood at present, because birders have been trying to identify this species for only a few years.

In 1994, Clark's Grebes nested in southern Minnesota at Minnesota Lake in Faribault County, which is just north of Winnebago County in north-central Iowa (Janssen 1994). The most consistent field mark is the yellow-orange bill of Clark's compared to green-yellow of Western, but this mark may be difficult to see. A Clark's in alternate plumage will have white entirely around the eye and a Western will have the eye completely within the black; however, in fall the facial features are more variable. The paler sides of the Clark's may help in picking out a likely bird, but this mark is not conclusive. Voice differences are not helpful in Iowa, where the birds are silent. Several articles present more detailed analysis of field marks (J. J. Dinsmore 1986, Ratti 1981, Storer and Nuechterlein 1985, Kaufman 1990).

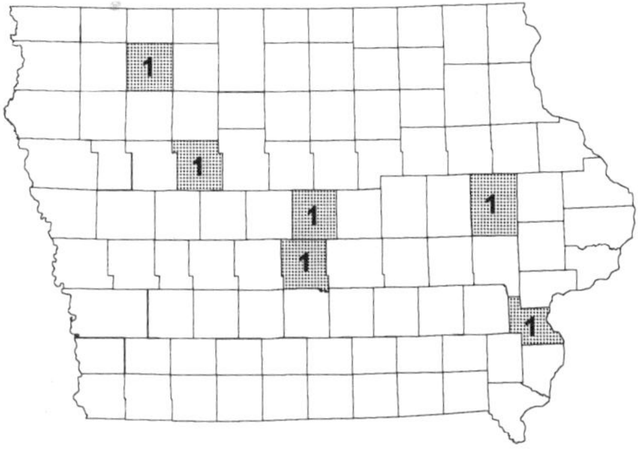

Clark's Grebe, all

References:

Brewer, M. M. 1995. Clark's Grebe in Clay County. *Iowa Bird Life* 65:23.

Dinsmore, J. J. 1986. Identification of Western and Clark's grebes. *Iowa Bird Life* 56:104-106.

Dinsmore, S. 1986. Clark's Grebe at Big Creek State Park. *Iowa Bird Life* 56:31.

Dinsmore, S. J. 1995. Clark's Grebe in Calhoun County. *Iowa Bird Life* 65:86-87.

Janssen, R. B. 1994. Possible breeding for Clark's Grebes in Minnesota. *Loon* 66:208.

Ratti, J. T. 1981. Identification and distribution of Clark's Grebe. *Western Birds* 12:41-46.

Storer, R. W., and G. L. Nuechterlein. 1985. An analysis of plumage and morphological characters of the two color forms of the Western Grebe (*Aechmophorus*). *Auk* 102:102-119.

ORDER PELICANIFORMES

The families in this order include tropicbirds, boobies and gannets, pelicans, cormorants, darters (anhingas), and frigatebirds. They are all large fish-eating birds with webbed feet. The webs uniquely include all four toes. They have long beaks, rudimentary or absent nostrils, and throat pouches (except for tropicbirds). Their short legs and large wings are adapted for flying. Many of the species in these families live at sea. Only 4 of the 6 families are represented in Iowa, and, of the 5 species, 2 are Regular and 3 are Accidental.

Pelicans (Family Pelecanidae)

Pelicans comprise 8 species, with 2 from North America and 2 from Iowa. They are well known for their long bills and huge gular pouches. American White Pelicans occur in fresh waters where they flock and feed communally by herding fish. Brown Pelicans frequent marine waters and feed by plunge-diving. This is a very old family, with skeletal remains dating back 20 million years.

American White Pelican (*Pelecanus erythrorhynchos*)

Status: Regular; possible nesting

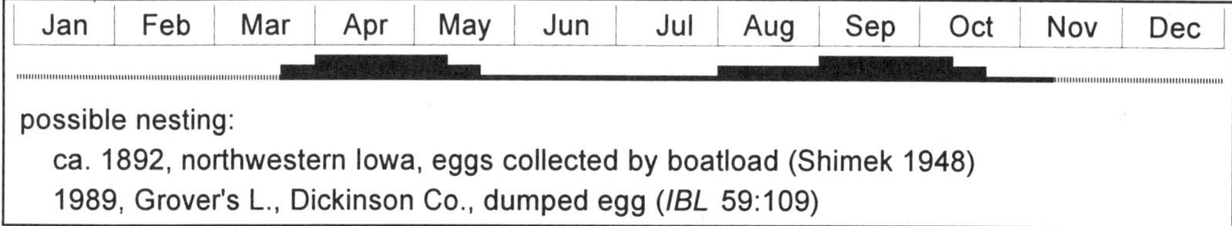

Jan
Feb
Mar
Apr
May
Jun
Jul
Aug
Sep
Oct
Nov
Dec
possible nesting:
ca. 1892, northwestern Iowa, eggs collected by boatload (Shimek 1948)
1989, Grover's L., Dickinson Co., dumped egg (*IBL* 59:109)

Occurrence: This common migrant arrives in late March and departs by early November. In spring, peak numbers are present in April and early May, and in fall the peak is in September and early October when thousands may be found at some sites. Until the late 1980s, it was reported most often from western and central Iowa and was rare in eastern Iowa, but in recent years, increasing numbers have been reported from eastern Iowa.

A few nonbreeders remain throughout the summer, but by mid- to late July, migrants begin arriving as they move south from breeding colonies. The 500 pelicans in the Grover's/Hottes lake area in Dickinson County in June 1989 (*IBL* 59:109), 500 at Union Slough National Wildlife Refuge in Kossuth County on 30 June 1991 (*IBL* 61:113), and 700 at Runnells Wildlife Area on 28 June 1992 (*IBL* 62:105) were large concentrations for mid-summer while 850 at Rice Lake in Winnebago and Worth counties on 16 July 1989 (*IBL* 59:109) probably included migrants. Although summering birds in Iowa sometimes have a knob near the tip of the bill that is typical of breeding birds, there are no confirmed nesting records for Iowa. A dumped egg was found at Grover's Lake in Dickinson County in the summer of 1989 (*IBL* 59:109).

American White Pelicans sometimes linger into early or mid-December, usually at one of the large reservoirs or along the Mississippi River. Often these are injured birds. Occasional birds are found in mid-winter such as 1 at Iowa City in Johnson County from 6 January to 1 February 1985 (*IBL* 55:24), 1 that remained at La Porte City in Black Hawk County until early February 1989 (*IBL* 59:48), 3 that wintered below Red Rock Reservoir dam in Marion County in 1993-1994 (*IBL* 64:45), and 1 at Keokuk in Lee County in 1994-1995 (*IBL* 65:45). Wintering birds that died include 2 at Red Rock Reservoir in Marion County on 20 January 1992 and 1 at Rathbun Reservoir in Appanoose County on 19 January 1992 (*IBL* 62:52).

Historically, pelican eggs were said to have been collected by the boatload in northwestern Iowa in 1882 (Shimek 1948). Later, the species was considered a rare and declining migrant (Anderson 1907).

Comment: The winter range is along the Gulf Coast from Florida to Texas and northern Mexico and from southern California and Arizona south along the coast of Mexico. The nesting range is from the Prairie Provinces of Canada east to western Ontario and south to California. Some also nest along the coast of Texas. Most colonies are in the northern Great Plains of the United States and southern Canada.

The closest nesting colony to Iowa is at Minnesota Lake in south-central Minnesota, about 35 miles north of the Iowa border (Fall and Hiemenz 1994). Pelican populations seem to have recovered from the depressed levels of a few decades ago, and far more are being reported in Iowa now than at any other time in this century. With the large number that now summer in Iowa, perhaps some might try to nest in Iowa, most likely in the Great Lakes region.

References:

Fall, B., and N. Hiemenz. 1994. Newly discovered American White Pelican colonies in southern Minnesota. *Loon* 66:111-113.

Shimek, B. 1948. The plant geography of Iowa. *Univ. Iowa Studies in Natural History*, Vol. 18, No. 4.

Brown Pelican (*Pelecanus occidentalis*)

Status: Accidental

By year since 1960 (also 1900, 1959)

60	63	66	69	72	75	78	81	84	87	90	93
			1				1			2	1

By month -- all records

Jan	Feb	Mar	Apr	May	Jun	Jul	Aug	Sep	Oct	Nov	Dec
		1	1	1 1 1		1			1		

Jul 1900, near Boone, Boone Co., specimen no longer extant (Henning 1901, DuMont 1933)
26 Apr 1959, Brenton Sl., Polk Co. (Peasley and Peasley 1960)
10 May 1969, near Montpelier, Muscatine Co. (Petersen 1972: photo)
18 Oct 1982, Keokuk, Lee Co. (*IBL* 52:118, 53:35)
21 Mar 1992, Rathbun Res., Appanoose Co. (*IBL* 62:74, 63:69)
6 to 11 May 1992, De Soto N.W.R., Harrison Co. (P-0327, P-0328, P-0329, *IBL* 62:74, 63:69, *Amer. Birds* 46:444)
30 to 31 May 1993, Rathbun Res., Appanoose Co. (P-0384, P-0387, *IBL* 63:72)

Occurrence: Of the 7 records, 5 are from spring, 1 from summer, and 1 from fall. There is 1 Not Accepted report that lacks details (*IBL* 33:86; 61:83).

Comment: Brown Pelicans are resident in coastal areas from northern South America to the mid-Atlantic states and California. They straggle northward to Canada on both coasts, and more northerly birds migrate south in winter. The Brown Pelican population was greatly diminished beginning in the 1950s due to pesticides (DDT) that affected the calcification of egg shells, but they have gradually recovered and are now doing well. Vagrancy to inland states prior to the population decline involved only a few birds in most states. The number of Midwestern vagrants has increased with the population recovery. Although there is a coastal post-breeding dispersal of this species, inland records are most common in April, followed closely by May, June, and July. There are 3 or fewer Midwestern records each from March, August, September, October, and November. Brown Pelican is not a common vagrant to interior Midwestern states. Iowa has as many records as any state in the area.

References:

Henning, C. F. 1901. A southern bird in central Iowa. *Annals of Iowa (3rd series)* 5:62-63.

Peasley, H. R., and Mrs. H. R. Peasley. 1960. Brown Pelican record near Des Moines. *Iowa Bird Life* 30:47.

Petersen, P. C. 1972. Brown Pelican in Muscatine County. *Iowa Bird Life* 42:51.

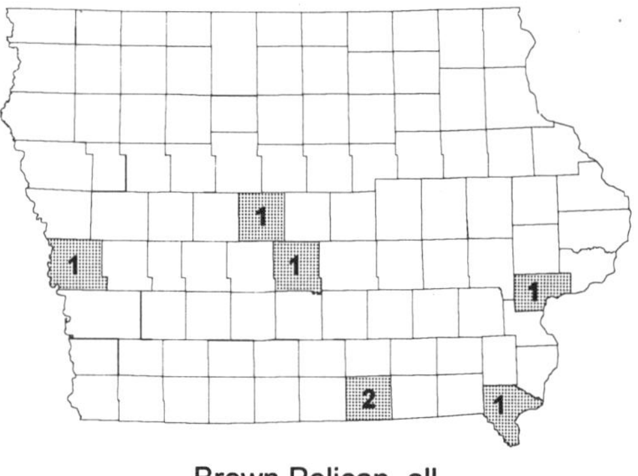

Brown Pelican, all

Cormorants (Family Phalacrocoracidae)

Cormorants comprise 37 species, with 6 from North America and 2 from Iowa. Cormorants are diving birds with dark plumage, hooked bills, colored eyes and facial skin, and often crests. They often perch on dead trees or posts over water. They nest in colonies in trees, on ledges, or on the ground. Cormorants occur on coasts and on inland waters worldwide.

Double-crested Cormorant (*Phalacrocorax auritus*)

Status: Regular; nests

Jan	Feb	Mar	Apr	May	Jun	Jul	Aug	Sep	Oct	Nov	Dec

Occurrence: This fairly common migrant and rare nesting species is found on lakes, rivers, and marshes throughout Iowa. Migrants arrive in late March with the peak of migration in late April and early May. Fall migration peaks in October and most are gone by the end of November. The only nesting colonies in recent years have been on the Mississippi River and at Coralville Reservoir in Johnson County. The colony near Sabula in Clinton County is the largest with about 689 nests in 1995 (*IBL* 65:96). The Coralville Reservoir colony had about 10 nests in 1991 (*IBL* 61:113) and 1994 (*IBL* 64:107), but many of the nest trees have fallen and the colony has declined. Cormorants attempted to nest at Union Slough National Wildlife Refuge in Kossuth County from 1991 to 1993 but were unsuccessful (*IBL* 61:113, 62:105, 63:94). Nonbreeding birds are present in small numbers in summer.

A few cormorants remain in Iowa in December every year and are reported on Christmas Bird Counts, most often at reservoirs or along the Mississippi River. Rarely they attempt to winter such as 2 at Lock 14 in Scott County in 1980-1981 (*IBL* 51:31), 1 at Bettendorf in Scott County in 1986-1987 (*IBL* 57:52), 3 at Davenport in Scott County until 19 February 1989 (*IBL* 59:48), 1 at Cedar Lake in Linn County in 1992-1993 and 1993-1994 (*IBL* 63:46, 64:45), and 1 or 2 below Red Rock Reservoir dam in Marion County in 1994-1995 (*IBL* 65:45).

Anderson (1907) called the cormorant a fairly common migrant and noted that it had formerly nested in northern Iowa but he was unaware of any nesting sites. The cormorant is much more abundant in Iowa now than it was even 20 years ago. Flocks of 100 were unusual in the late 1970s, while groups of more than 1,000 have been reported in migration in recent years.

Comment: The winter range extends coastally from the Aleutians and New England south to the West Indies and Mexico and inland in the lower Mississippi Valley. The breeding range includes much of the coastal winter range extending north to Newfoundland and south-central Canada and north- central United States. Increased numbers have been especially noticeable in the Great Lakes and Great Plains regions, and they are considered a pest in some areas.

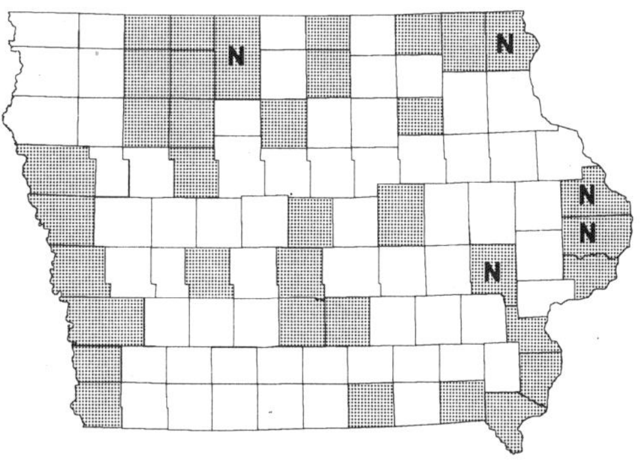

Double-crested Cormorant, 1960-1995
June-July and nesting (N)

Neotropic Cormorant (*Phalacrocorax brasilianus*)

Status: Accidental

4 May 1996, Little River R. A., Decatur Co., ad. (P-0505, *IBL* 66:100)

Occurrence: There is 1 spring record.

Comment: The permanent range is from southern Louisiana and Texas south to the West Indies, Middle America, and South America. This species is casual to Arizona, New Mexico, Colorado, Oklahoma, Kansas, and Mississippi. There are several records in the 1990s north to Nebraska, Missouri, Illinois, and Minnesota. Vagrant records occur from April to October.

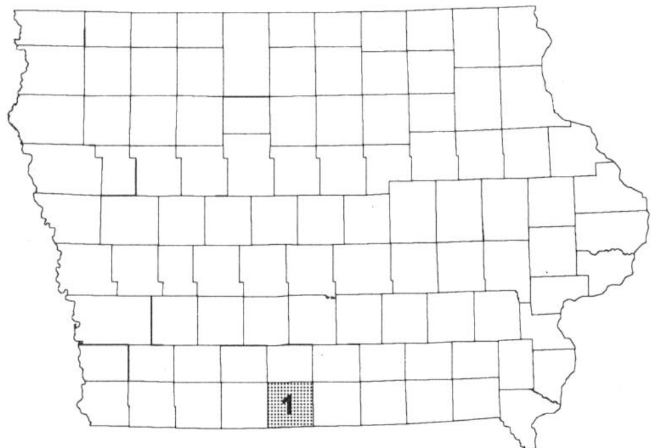

Neotropic Cormorant, all

Darters (Family Anhingidae)

Darters comprise 4 species, with 1 from North America and 1 from Iowa. Darters are found on wooded rivers and lakes throughout the world. They can swim with just their heads exposed, and they use their long, pointed bills to spear fish. Darters have a special hinge mechanism on the eighth cervical vertebra that allows muscles to dart the bill forward to spear fish. They hold their wings out when perched. These strange waterbirds also take to the air and soar.

Anhinga (*Anhinga anhinga*)

Status: Accidental

18 to 31 Oct 1953, near Riverton, Fremont Co. (Collins 1953)

Occurrence: There is 1 fall sight record. There are 2 other Not Accepted reports (Dinsmore et al. 1984).

Comment: Anhinga is found from Argentina to Gulf Coastal areas, moving north in breeding season to eastern Texas, Louisiana, Mississippi, and up the Mississippi River to Tennessee and historically to southern Illinois and southeastern Missouri. Spring vagrancy records, which are about equally divided between April and May, outnumber fall (September-October) records by about 2 to 1, with a few also in summer. Fewer than 5 have been recorded in Wisconsin, Ontario, Ohio, Indiana, Nebraska, and Colorado. Most of the records have occurred since 1960. A bird at Fontenelle Forest south of Omaha in Nebraska from 2 to 5 May 1987 was just across the Missouri River from Iowa (Molhoff 1989).

Anhingas are found in swampy areas, swimming or sitting on branches. They often soar, but soaring cormorants may be mistaken for Anhingas, as apparently happened in Minnesota (Eckert 1989).

References:

Collins, Mrs. W. H. 1953. A sight record of the Anhinga in Fremont County. *Iowa Bird Life* 23:72.

Eckert, K. R. 1989. Proceedings of the Minnesota Ornithological Records Committee. *Loon* 61:10-13.

Molhoff, W. J. 1989. Second report of the N.O.U. Records Committee. *Nebr. Bird Review* 57:42-47.

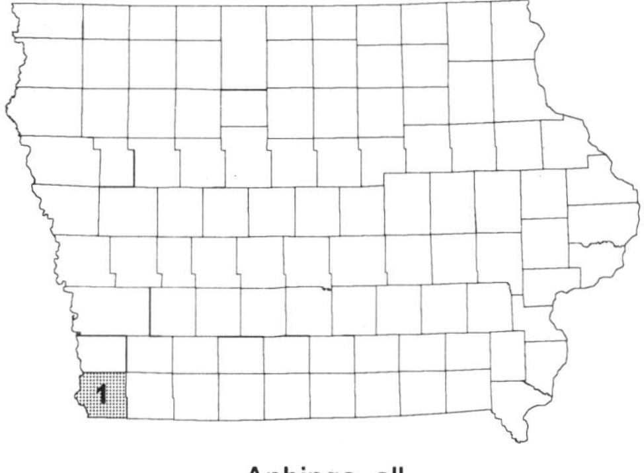

Anhinga, all

Frigatebirds (Family Frigatidae)

Frigatebirds comprise 5 species, with 3 from North America and 1 from Iowa. These large birds of tropical and subtropical marine waters have long, pointed wings, deeply forked tails, and long, hooked bills. These superb flyers can glide on air currents or maneuver adeptly to steal fish from boobies and terns. They are adapted to feed and drink on the wing and have limited mobility on land or water.

Magnificent Frigatebird (*Fregata magnificens*)

Status: Accidental

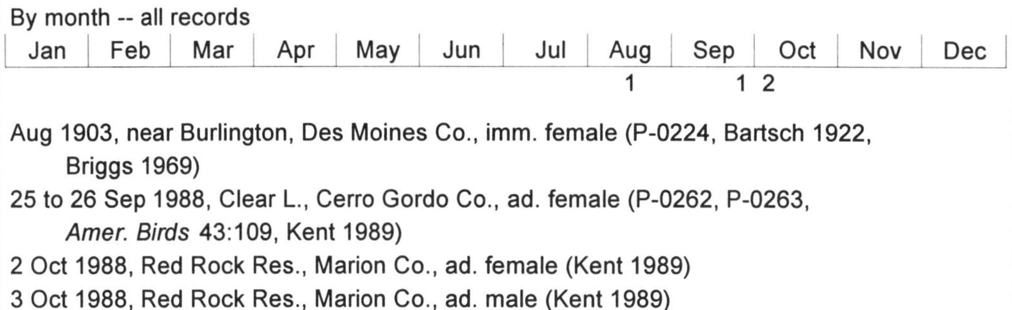

By month -- all records

Jan	Feb	Mar	Apr	May	Jun	Jul	Aug	Sep	Oct	Nov	Dec
							1	1	2		

Aug 1903, near Burlington, Des Moines Co., imm. female (P-0224, Bartsch 1922, Briggs 1969)
25 to 26 Sep 1988, Clear L., Cerro Gordo Co., ad. female (P-0262, P-0263, *Amer. Birds* 43:109, Kent 1989)
2 Oct 1988, Red Rock Res., Marion Co., ad. female (Kent 1989)
3 Oct 1988, Red Rock Res., Marion Co., ad. male (Kent 1989)

Occurrence: The specimen photographed by Bartsch (Briggs 1969) was reevaluated by the Records Committee and accepted. The other 3 records all followed hurricane Gilbert in 1988. There are 3 Not Accepted reports (Dinsmore et al. 1984, Kent 1989).

Comment: The breeding range is coastal, north to the Florida Keys and Baja California and south to Peru and Brazil. East Coast records are scattered from April to September, with a few from October to February, and are not usually storm associated (Kent 1989). West Coast records are usually of immature birds in July and August. Inland records in the Midwest are most commonly storm associated, occur from August to October, and involve immatures and adults. Almost half of the Midwest records are from September. There are also records from April, June, July, and December. The Midwest records are widely scattered with only a few north of Iowa. The greatest number occurred after hurricane Gilbert in September 1988, when there were at least 22 inland records from 14 states and Ontario (*Amer. Birds* 43:52).

Males, females, and immatures can be easily separated, but separation from the very unlikely Great Frigatebird and Lesser Frigatebird is more difficult (Kent 1989).

References:

Bartsch, P. 1922. An inland record of the Man-o'-war-bird. *Auk* 39:249-250.

Briggs, S. 1969. Some notes on an early Iowa record and Paul Bartsch. *Iowa Bird Life* 39:85-87.

Kent, T. H. 1989. Magnificent Frigatebirds in Iowa. *Iowa Bird Life* 59:56-62.

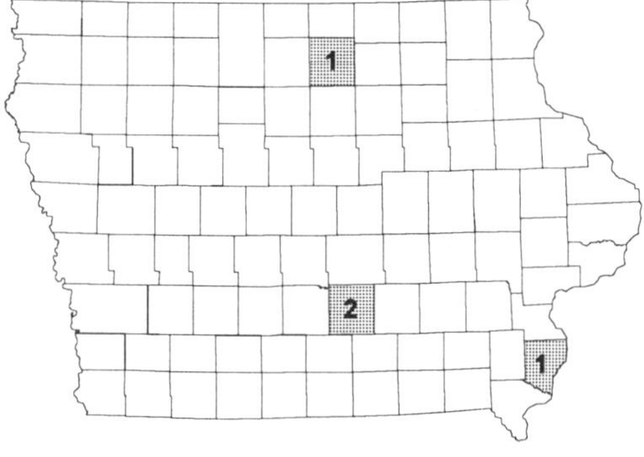

Magnificent Frigatebird, all

ORDER CICONIIFORMES

The families in this order include bitterns and herons, ibises and spoonbills, storks, and 2 other single-species families found only in Africa. They are long-legged, long-necked waders that often nest in colonies. This ancient group is found worldwide.

Bitterns and Herons (Family Ardeidae)

Herons and bitterns comprise 65 species, with 16 from North America and 12 from Iowa. Herons have long legs, necks, and bills with short tails and broad wings. Bitterns are more squat and make booming calls. A special articulation of the sixth vertebra accounts for the kinked neck. Most herons and bitterns are found near water where they feed on fish, insects, and small vertebrates.

Of the Iowa species, 10 are Regular and 2 Accidental. Several species disperse widely after the breeding season and can be found wherever there is suitable wetland habitat. Species that nest mainly south of Iowa, such as Snowy Egret and Little Blue Heron, also exhibit northward dispersal in spring. Tricolored Heron, which is Accidental in Iowa, is typically a spring over-migrant.

American Bittern (*Botaurus lentiginosus*)

Status: Regular; nests

Jan	Feb	Mar	Apr	May	Jun	Jul	Aug	Sep	Oct	Nov	Dec
+ x		XX								X	X + +

24 Mar 1979 — 14 Nov 1987
28 Mar 1987 — 17 Nov 1979
2 Apr 1991 — 21 Nov 1987
winter: 4 Dec 1954 to 2 Jan 1955, 15 Jan 1892

Occurrence: This rare migrant and nesting species occurs in wetlands with dense emergent vegetation throughout Iowa. Migrants arrive in mid-April and depart by mid-November. Most recent nesting reports are from northwestern and north-central Iowa. Nesting begins in late April or early May and extends into June (Provost 1947). The only winter reports are near Des Moines in Polk County from 4 December 1954 to 2 January 1955 (Brown 1971) and at Burlington in Des Moines County on 15 January 1892 (University of Iowa specimen #16121).

In the early 1900s, this was a fairly common nesting species in Iowa (Anderson 1907), but the loss of wetlands and associated wet prairies has removed much of its nesting habitat. There is some indication that it nests only on larger wetlands (Brown and Dinsmore 1986), a further limitation to its ability to thrive in Iowa.

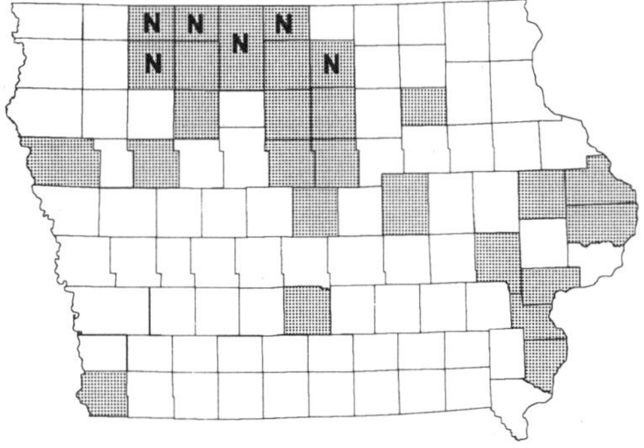

American Bittern, 1960-1995
June-July and nesting (N)

Comment: The winter range is the southern United States and Middle America. The breeding range includes most of the Canadian provinces, the United States south to central Missouri and locally to Texas and Mexico.

References:

Brown, M., and J. J. Dinsmore. 1986. Implications of marsh size and isolation for marsh bird management. *J. Wildlife Management* 50:392-397.

Provost, M. W. 1947. Nesting of birds in the marshes of northwest Iowa. *Amer. Midland Naturalist* 38:485-503.

Least Bittern (*Ixobrychus exilis*)

Status: Regular; nests

Jan	Feb	Mar	Apr	May	Jun	Jul	Aug	Sep	Oct	Nov	Dec
			XX						X X	X	

28 Apr 1984	8 Oct 1951
30 Apr 1981	18 Oct 1980
1 May 1986	12 Nov 1981

Occurrence: This rare summer resident occurs in marshes and edges of lakes where there is thick emergent vegetation. It is seldom seen unless disturbed. Migrants arrive in early to mid-May and probably depart in September, but there are few data on arrival and departure dates. Nesting starts in late May or early June and extends into July (Kent 1951, Weller 1961). Most nesting reports are from north-central and northwestern Iowa.

Historically, Least Bittern was considered less common and more local than the American Bittern (Anderson 1907). With the loss of wetlands since then, it undoubtedly is less abundant now.

Comment: The winter range is from Florida, coastal Texas, and Baja California south to the Greater Antilles and most of South America. The breeding range includes most of the winter range and includes the eastern United States, north to the Canadian border, west to the central Great Plains, and south to the Gulf Coast of northern Mexico. A western population breeds north to central California and in other isolated locations.

References:

Kent, T. 1951. The Least Bitterns of Swan Lake. *Iowa Bird Life* 21:59-61.

Weller, M. W. 1961. Breeding biology of the Least Bittern. *Wilson Bull.* 73:11-35.

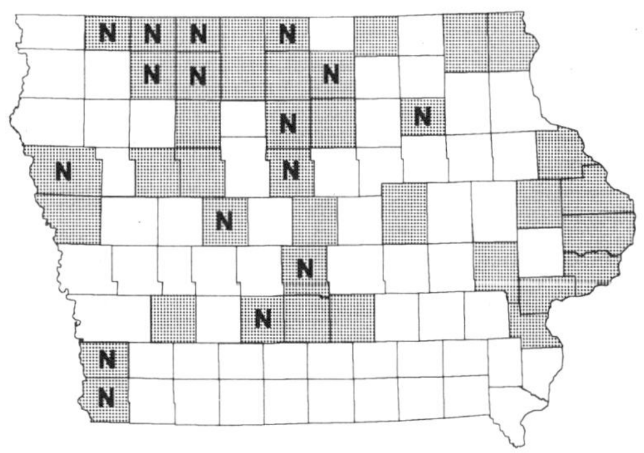

Least Bittern, 1960-1995
June-July and nesting (N)

Great Blue Heron (*Ardea herodias*)

Status: Regular; nests

Jan	Feb	Mar	Apr	May	Jun	Jul	Aug	Sep	Oct	Nov	Dec

Occurrence: This, the best-known of Iowa's herons, is a common migrant and fairly common summer resident statewide. Migrants arrive in early March, and most depart by early December. On Christmas Bird Counts, the number of counts reporting Great Blue Herons has dramatically increased, averaging 1 per year in the 1960s, 2 in the 1970s, 10 in the 1980s, and 17 in the 1990s. The highest counts have been along the Mississippi River in the southern half of the state, especially in Louisa and Des Moines counties. Other common Christmas Bird Count locations are along major rivers and reservoirs, but a few are also reported in all areas of the state, especially in mild winters. From 1983 to 1995, 1 to 5 birds were reported in January and February in 11 of 13 years.

Great Blue Herons usually nest in colonies that are near rivers or lakes and that usually contain fewer than 100 nests. Rarely, solitary nests are found. In Iowa, most nests are placed high in large trees such as cottonwoods (Zeutenhorst 1990).

Historically, Great Blue Heron was considered fairly common in Iowa, but there were few specific nesting records (Anderson 1907, DuMont 1933). There is evidence that some nesting populations were adversely affected by environmental chemicals in the 1970s (Konermann et al. 1978), but they seem to have recovered in recent years.

Comment: The winter range is from southern Alaska, the central United States, and New England south to the West Indies and northern South America. The winter range extends north to approximately central Missouri, but it is not unusual to find birds farther north. The breeding range includes the winter range and extends north to the central parts of the Canadian provinces.

References:

Konermann, A. D., L. D. Wing, and J. J. Richard. 1978. Great Blue Heron nesting success in two Iowa reservoir ecosystems. In: A. Sprunt, IV, J. C. Ogden, and S. Winckler, eds. Wading birds. *National Audubon Society Research Report*, No. 7.

Zeutenhorst, K. L. 1990. Nest sites of the Great Blue Heron in central Iowa. *Iowa Bird Life* 60:6-8.

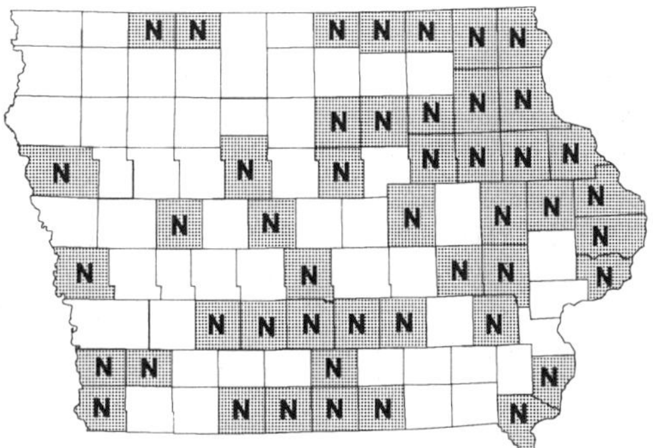

Great Blue Heron, 1960-1995
Nest colonies (N)

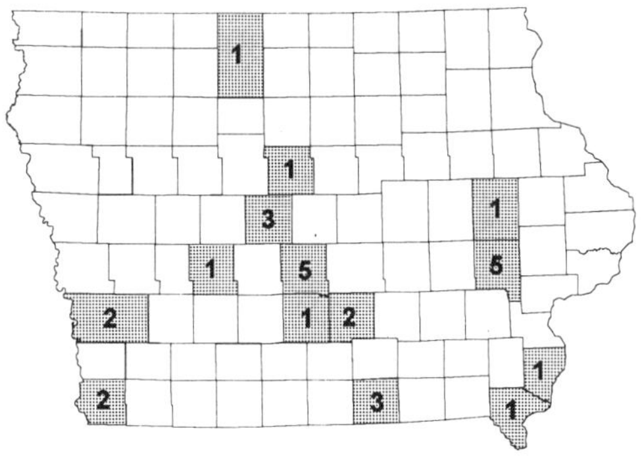

Great Blue Heron, 1960-1995
January-February records

Great Egret (*Ardea alba*)

Status: Regular; nests

Jan	Feb	Mar	Apr	May	Jun	Jul	Aug	Sep	Oct	Nov	Dec
		x x								xx	
7 Mar 1966										19 Nov 1984	
17 Mar 1963										21 Nov 1992	
20 Mar 1994										26 Nov 1961	

Occurrence: This uncommon to common migrant and rare summer resident is found along lakes, rivers, and ponds throughout Iowa. Migrants arrive in late March and depart by late October. Most of the nesting colonies are along the Mississippi River where this species often nests with Great Blue Herons. In 1991, nests away from the Mississippi River were in Great Blue Heron colonies, with 2 nests at West Swan Lake in Emmet County and 4 nests below Saylorville Reservoir Dam in Polk County (*IBL* 61:113). Great Egrets rarely nest along the Missouri River, most recently in 1994 when there were 3 nests at Blue Lake in Monona County (*IBL* 64:72). A colony near Sabula in Clinton County contained 180 nests in 1995 (*IBL* 65:96). In late summer, post-breeding concentrations are often obvious throughout Iowa such as 135 at Union Slough National Wildlife Refuge in Kossuth County on 28 Aug 1994 (*IBL* 65:11).

Historically, the Great Egret was rare in Iowa, probably as a result of plume hunting that decimated its populations throughout North America. After an absence of 20 years, birds returned to the state around 1930 (DuMont 1933), and after that the first report of nesting was in 1942 near Sabula in Jackson County (Harlan 1943).

Comment: This world-wide species retreats in winter to coastal United States south from North Carolina and northern California. The nesting range in the central part of North America extends north to extreme southern Canada with widespread post-breeding dispersal.

Reference:

Harlan, J. R. 1943. An Iowa nesting colony of the American Egret. *Iowa Bird Life* 13:58-62.

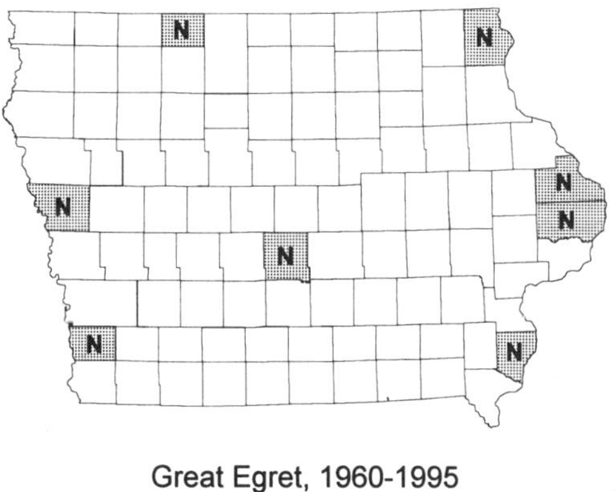

Great Egret, 1960-1995
Nesting (N)

Snowy Egret (*Egretta thula*)

Status: Regular

By year since 1960 (also 10 records 1930 to 1959)

60			63			66			69			72			75			78			81			84			87			90			93		
				1	1					1				1	2	2	1	2		3	2	3		5	7	7	5	9	4	4	4		3	7	8

By month -- all records

Jan			Feb			Mar			Apr			May			Jun			Jul			Aug			Sep			Oct			Nov			Dec		
								2	1	6	7	6	7	9		1	2	2	5	8	1	7	5	2	3	4		1							

27 Mar 1985	27 Sep 1995
29 Mar 1988	29 Sep 1985
6 Apr 1976	18 Oct 1987

Occurrence: This rare migrant is usually found from mid-April to late May and from mid-July to late September. There are only a few records in June and early July. Records have been from all areas of the state with the most common location being along the Missouri River in the southern half of the state. There are no nesting records.

There are only 7 reports prior to 1930 (Anderson 1907, DuMont 1933). In August 1930, 30 were reported in Des Moines County (Holland 1930). On 24 July 1934, 2 were collected in Clay County but misidentified as Little Blue Herons (Bennett 1935, Dinsmore et al. 1984). There were only 10 records from 1930 to 1959. After that, there were reports from 2 years in the 1960s, from 6 years in the 1970s, from 9 years in the 1980s, and all but 1 year from 1990 to 1995. The average number of reports per year was 1.5 from 1974 to 1983, but increased to 5 per year from 1984 to 1995.

Comment: The winter range is in central California and along the coasts from California and South Carolina to southern South America. Snowy Egrets nest through much of Middle America and in all but southernmost South America. In United States, the breeding range extends along the coasts to northern California and Maine and in the interior north to southern Idaho and Montana, to central Kansas, and to southern Missouri and Illinois. Nests have been found in eastern South Dakota since 1972 (South Dakota Ornithologists' Union 1991), irregularly in southwestern and once in eastern Minnesota (Janssen 1987), and in 1975 in northeastern Wisconsin (Robbins 1991). The first Minnesota record was in 1950, and the species became regular in the late 1970s (Janssen 1987), a pattern not unlike that for Iowa. Nesting in Iowa is possible and would most likely occur at a site with other herons.

References:

Bennett, L. J. 1935. Little Blue Herons in Iowa. *Iowa Bird Life* 5:13.

Holland, H. M. 1930. Snowy Egrets in Des Moines County, Iowa. *Wilson Bull.* 42:289.

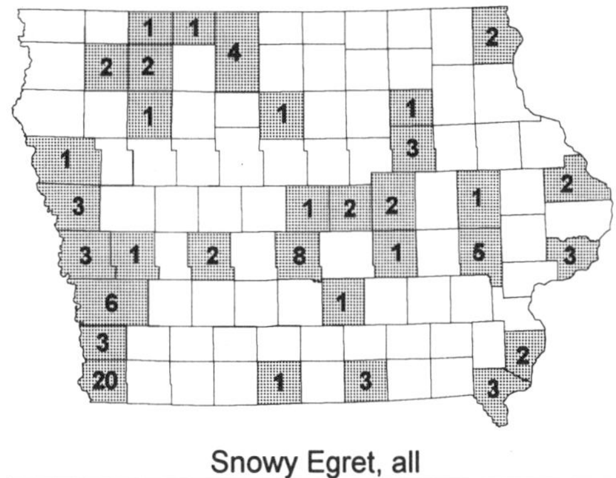

Snowy Egret, all

Little Blue Heron (*Egretta caerulea*)

Status: Regular; possible nesting

Jan	Feb	Mar	Apr	May	Jun	Jul	Aug	Sep	Oct	Nov	Dec

x x .... x x x

31 Mar 1967 — 26 Sep 1992
6 Apr 1971 — 2 Oct 1987
11 Apr 1981 — 11 Oct 1977
possible nesting: 1, 5 Jul 1984, Folsom L., Mills Co. (Silcock 1984)

Occurrence: This rare migrant is usually found from mid-April to late May and from mid-July to early September. There are only a few records in June and early July. It is found on lakes and marshes throughout Iowa with the most records from the southwestern and southeastern corners and from central Iowa. Spring birds are almost all adults, and most fall birds are all-white juveniles. Only an occasional "calico" first-summer bird has been noted: 30 April 1982 in Louisa County (*IBL* 52:53), 3 May 1988 in Pottawattamie County (*IBL* 58:78), and 4 August 1994 in Fremont County *IBL* 65:11).

The only report of nesting is from 1984 at Folsom Lake in Mills County at a large nesting colony of Cattle Egrets (Silcock 1984). On 1 July, 30 Little Blue Herons, some carrying nesting material, were observed and, on 5 July, an incubating bird was flushed from a nest. Little Blue Herons were not seen at the colony later in the summer.

There are only a few reports prior to 1900 (Anderson 1907) and apparently none between 1903 and 1925 (DuMont (1933). There were irregular reports from 1925 to 1960, and regular reports since 1960, except for 1 year. The number of reports per year has increased, averaging 2 in the 1960s, 3 in the 1970s, and 9 in the 1980s. An unusual concentration of 125 birds was reported from Lee County in September 1934 (DuMont 1935, Youngworth 1935). An invasion was also noted in Wisconsin that year (Robbins 1991). There are no specimens and only 1 photograph (P-0068).

Comment: The winter range is from Baja California, South Carolina, and the Gulf Coast south to Uruguay. The nesting range includes the winter range and extends north to southern California, southeastern Missouri, and along the East Coast to Maine. Nesting has occurred in North Dakota, South Dakota, Minnesota, and possibly Wisconsin. Immature birds seen in late summer are assumed to have wandered north after fledging, but the origin of these birds is unknown. Reports of this species should include the plumage (adult, all white, or calico).

References:

DuMont, P. A. 1935. The American Egret and Little Blue Heron in Iowa. *Iowa Bird Life* 5:43.

Silcock, R. 1984. First nesting of Cattle Egret and Little Blue Heron for Iowa. *Iowa Bird Life* 54:101-103.

Youngworth, W. 1935. Notes on the American Egret and Little Blue Heron in Iowa. *Wilson Bull.* 47:73-74.

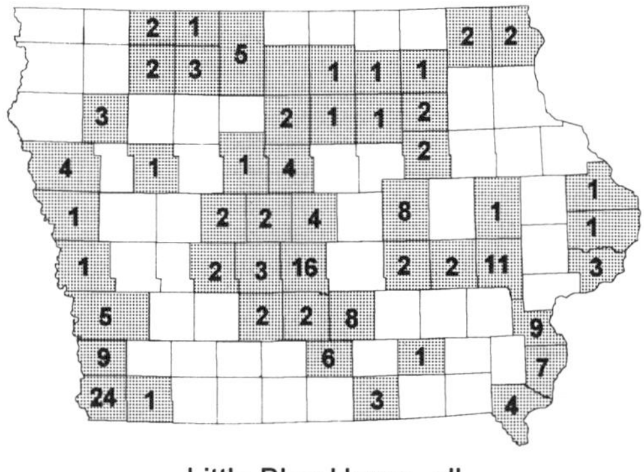

Little Blue Heron, all

Tricolored Heron (*Egretta tricolor*)

Status: Accidental

29 Apr 1989, Cone M., Louisa Co. (Kent 1991)
4 May 1991, Power Plant Ponds, Pottawattamie Co. (Greer 1992)

Occurrence: The 2 sight records are from spring.

Comment: This species breeds along the Gulf Coast and Atlantic Coast of the United States and from central Baja California south on both coasts to northern South America. In winter, there is some movement south, especially along the Atlantic Coast. In spring, this species occurs at many inland locations, the most consistent being in the St. Louis and Chicago areas and at the eastern end of Lake Ontario. There are fewer late summer and fall records, and many of these are explained by birds that have lingered from spring. It would be interesting to know whether the spring dispersal to the Midwest involves first-summer or adult birds. Little information is available on aging of herons, and most sightings do not mention the age of the bird. Nesting occurred in North Dakota at Long Lake National Wildlife Refuge in 1978 (*Amer. Birds* 32:1176) and in Kansas at Cheyenne Bottoms in 1976 and most subsequent years (Thompson and Ely 1991).

Based on records from surrounding states, Iowa should have more records of Tricolored Heron. The 2 spring sightings may be of birds that were headed north and only stopped briefly in Iowa.

References:

Greer, J. G. 1992. Tricolored Heron in Pottawattamie County. *Iowa Bird Life* 62:88-89.

Kent, T. H. 1991. Tricolored Heron at Cone Marsh. *Iowa Bird Life* 61:1-4.

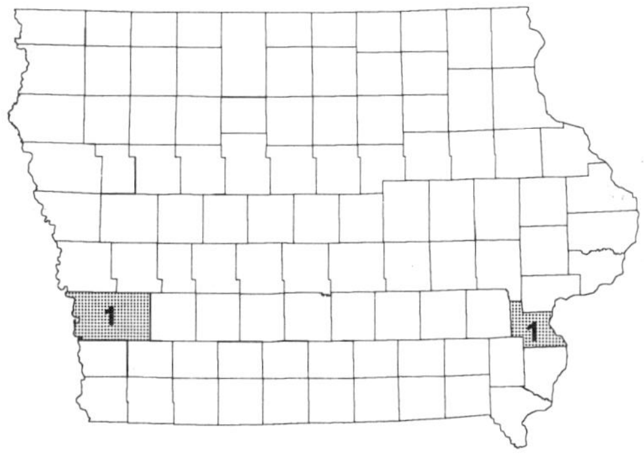

Tricolored Heron, all

Reddish Egret (*Egretta rufescens*)

Status: Accidental

5 to 8 Sep 1993, near Colfax, Jasper Co., juvenile (P-0406, Schantz 1996)

Occurrence: This unexpected visitor was a juvenile that came north in the year of the great Midwest floods.

Comment: This species, which stays close to salt water, inhabits the Gulf Coast, the West Indies, and Central America. It reaches Venezuela in winter and a few have wandered up the East Coast as far as Nova Scotia.

Inland records are exceedingly rare and include the following: August 1875, Colorado Springs, El Paso County, Colorado, immature, specimen (Andrews and Richter 1992); 30 September 1951, Marais Temps Clair, St. Charles County, Missouri (Robbins and Easterla 1992); 3, 9 November 1963, Osage County, Oklahoma (Wood and Schnell 1984); 1 September 1978, Louisville, Jefferson County, Kentucky (Monroe et al. 1988); 27 to 29 May 1991, Blue Lake, Bent County, Colorado, sub-adult (Andrews and Richter 1992); 11 June 1993, Amercian Falls Reservoir, Idaho (*Amer. Birds* 47:1128); 2 August 1993 in Monroe County Michigan, immature (*Amer. Birds* 48:111, Friscia 1994); 21 to 28 August 1993, northwestern Indiana, immature (*Amer. Birds* 48:114); 14 August to 2 October 1993, Lake Calumet, Cook County, Illinois, immature (*Amer. Birds* 48:114, Friscia 1994); and 29 May 1995, Jackson, Wyoming (*Field Notes* 49:280).

References:

Friscia, S. 1994. Reddish Egret first confirmed state record. *Meadowlark* 3:45-47.

Schantz, T. 1996. Reddish Egret in Jasper County. *Iowa Bird Life* 66:63-64.

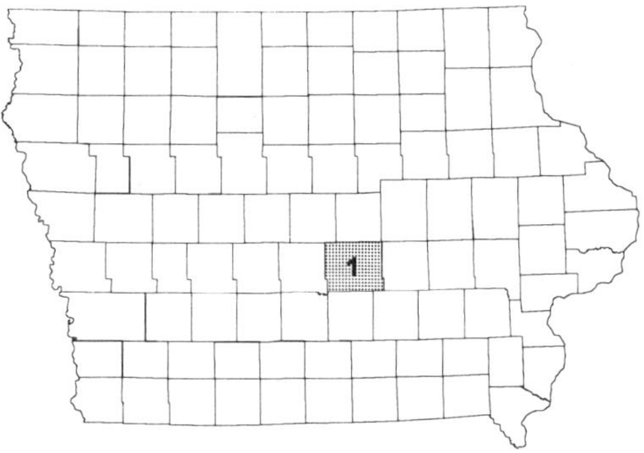

Reddish Egret, all

Cattle Egret (*Bubulcus ibis*)

Status: Regular; occasionally nests

Jan	Feb	Mar	Apr	May	Jun	Jul	Aug	Sep	Oct	Nov	Dec

20 Mar 1977
26 Mar 1966
27 Mar 1988

late Nov 1970
20 Nov 1982
26 Nov 1982

nesting records:
1984, Folsom L., Mills Co., 135 nests (Silcock 1984)
1993, near Marshalltown, Marshall Co. (*IBL* 64:10)
1993, Blue L., Monona Co. (Lisa Hemesath)

Occurrence: This uncommon migrant and rare summer resident is found on pastures, wet meadows, and near wetlands throughout Iowa. Spring migrants arrive in late April and depart by the end of May. A few may remain through the summer. Fall migrants arrive in late August, and most depart by the end of September; a few have lingered into November.

Cattle Egrets have been reported nesting in Iowa 3 times. In 1984, at least 135 nests were found at Folsom Lake in Mills County (Silcock 1984). In 1993, several pairs nested near Marshalltown (*IBL* 64:10). That same year, another colony was reported near Blue Lake in Monona County (Lisa Hemesath, personal communication).

The first Cattle Egret in Iowa was collected at Little Wall Lake in Hamilton County on 21 April 1961 (Weller 1961). By 1977, there were reports from 41 counties (Dinsmore 1978). In the summers of 1984, 1988, and 1993, large numbers were found in southwestern Iowa. On 18 July 1993, more than 1,000 were seen in Fremont County (*IBL* 63:95). A large colony in northeastern South Dakota is probably the source of many of the birds seen in western Iowa.

Comment: The winter range is from Florida south into the West Indies and northern South America. The breeding range extends from southern Ontario and the northern United States to South America. This Old World species apparently reached South America on its own in the late 1800s and Florida in 1941. From there, its populations increased rapidly and by the late 1960s, it had occupied much of eastern United States (Telfair 1983).

References:

Dinsmore, J. J. 1978. Cattle Egrets in Iowa, 1961-1977. *Iowa Bird Life* 48:119-126.

Silcock, R. 1984. First nesting of Cattle Egret and Little Blue Heron for Iowa. *Iowa Bird Life* 54:101-103.

Telfair, R. C. 1983. *The Cattle Egret: A Texas Focus and World View.* Texas Agricultural Experiment Station, Texas A&M Univ., College Station, TX.

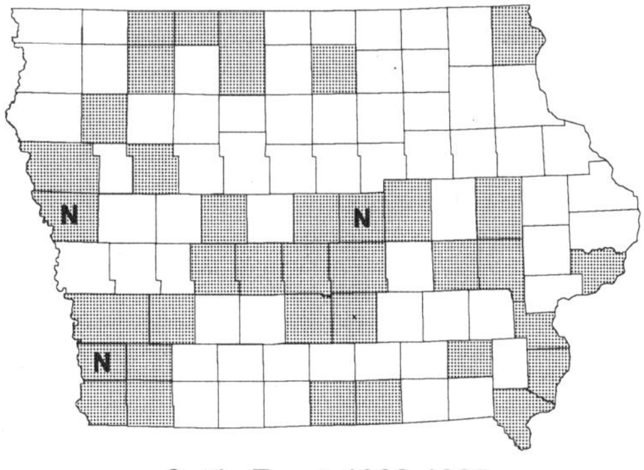

Cattle Egret, 1960-1995
June-July and nesting (N)

Green Heron (*Butorides virescens*)

Status: Regular; nests

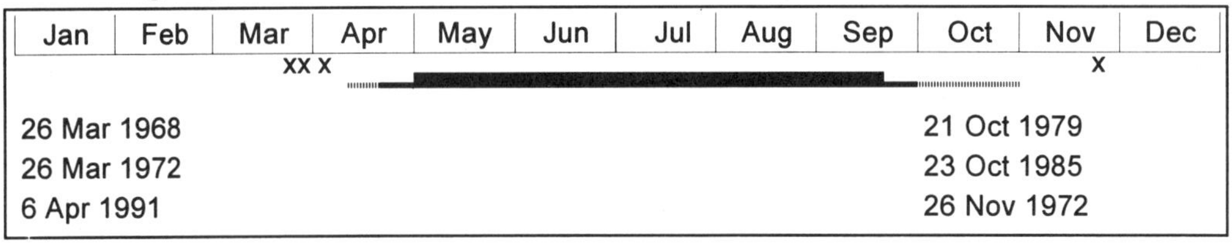

Jan	Feb	Mar	Apr	May	Jun	Jul	Aug	Sep	Oct	Nov	Dec
		XX X								X	

26 Mar 1968
26 Mar 1972
6 Apr 1991

21 Oct 1979
23 Oct 1985
26 Nov 1972

Occurrence: This uncommon summer resident is found from May to mid-September along wooded wetlands and rivers. Nesting starts in May and extends into June or early July. Green Herons, which are less conspicuous than other herons because of their habitat and solitary nature, can be found in all areas of Iowa.

Comment: The winter range is from Florida, the Gulf Coast, and southwestern United States south to northern South America. The breeding range is from the Canadian border south throughout eastern and parts of western United States to the West Indies and Middle America.

Black-crowned Night-Heron (*Nycticorax nycticorax*)

Status: Regular; nests

Jan	Feb	Mar	Apr	May	Jun	Jul	Aug	Sep	Oct	Nov	Dec
	x	x									x

17 Mar 1986	11 Nov 1995
24 Mar 1982	11 Nov 1994
26 Mar 1916	12 Nov 1995
winter: 29 Dec 1957, 16 Feb 1960	

Occurrence: This uncommon migrant and rare summer resident arrives in mid-April and departs by late September. Migrants are found at lakes and marshes. Winter records are from Cedar Rapids in Linn County on 29 December 1957 (*IBL* 28:14) and Davenport in Scott County on 16 and 21 Feb 1960 (*Audubon Field Notes* 14:312).

Several large nesting colonies have been discovered such as the 150 nests at Goose Lake in Greene County in July 1966 (Faaborg 1967) and 140 nests at West Hottes Lake in Dickinson County on 21 June 1977 (Nigus 1977). Most nesting colonies have been in dense stands of cattail or bulrush over water in thickly vegetated marshes (Nigus 1977). In recent years, the only colony that has been reported regularly is in the Grover's/Hottes Lake area of Dickinson County.

Historically, Black-crowned Night-Heron was considered a fairly common migrant and nesting species with several known breeding colonies (Anderson 1907, DuMont 1933). It appears to have been more common then than now.

Comment: This world-wide species breeds north throughout most of the United States and parts of southern Canada. The winter range includes coastal United States from New England and Oregon south and scattered inland locations.

References:

Faaborg, J. 1967. Observations among the night herons. *Iowa Bird Life* 37:27-29.

Nigus, T. A. 1977. A marsh nesting colony of Black-crowned Night Herons. *Iowa Bird Life* 47:108-109.

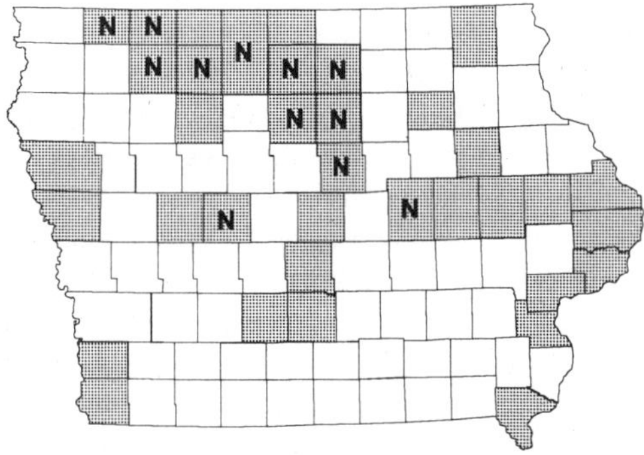

Black-crowned Night-Heron, 1960-1995
June-July and nesting (N)

Yellow-crowned Night-Heron (*Nyctanassa violacea*)

Status: Regular; occasionally nests

Jan	Feb	Mar	Apr	May	Jun	Jul	Aug	Sep	Oct	Nov	Dec
		X							X XX		
31 Mar 1963									4 Oct 1953		
1 Apr 1963									11 Oct 1985		
3 Apr 1963									14 Oct 1960		

Occurrence: This rare migrant and summer resident is found from early April to late September with most reports from mid-April through May and late June to mid-August. It is seen most often in wooded wetlands along major rivers and in large cattail marshes. It has been found in all areas of the state with the most records from southeastern and southwestern Iowa and from Polk County. Reports averaged 5 per year from 1976 to 1995. A road-killed bird from Story County on 26 April 1981 is at Iowa State University (#1678, Dinsmore 1992).

The first nests were found at Des Moines in Polk County on 5 May 1956 (Brown 1956) and nests were found at that location in 1957, 1959, 1960, and 1961 (Brown 1961). In 1960, nests were found at Sny Magill Area in Clayton County and at Springbrook State Park in Guthrie County (Brown 1961). Since then there have been no confirmed reports of nesting, but adults and immatures have been seen regularly in late summer and fall. The number of Yellow-crowned Night-Herons may be underestimated because their habitat is often inaccessible.

Historically, this species was first recorded by John James Audubon near Council Bluffs in Pottawattamie County on 10 May 1843 (Audubon and Coues 1897). There were only 9 additional reports up to 1952, but from 1952 to 1995 there were only 2 years in which this species was not reported.

Comment: The winter range is from Florida, the Gulf Coast, and Baja California south to northern South America. The breeding range includes the winter range and eastern United States north to southern Minnesota and southern New England.

References:

Brown, W. H. 1956. Yellow-crowned Night Heron nesting in the city of Des Moines. *Iowa Bird Life* 26:57-59.

Brown, W. H. 1961. Yellow-crowned Night Heron in Iowa. *Iowa Bird Life* 31:26-27.

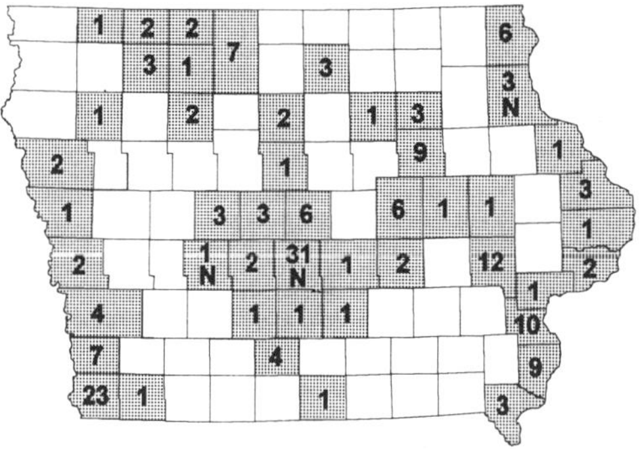

Yellow-crowned Night-Heron, all Records and nesting (N)

Ibises and Spoonbills (Family Threskiornithidae)

Ibises and spoonbills comprise 33 species, with 5 from North America and 4 from Iowa. Ibises have long decurved bills used for probing in mud for food, while spoonbills have flat bills that are expanded at the end and used to sift small organisms from water. These social nesters are often found in heron colonies.

Of the Iowa species, 3 are Accidental and 1 Casual. The Casual species, White-faced Ibis, would be Regular if the unidentified dark ibises seen in Iowa were considered to be this species, which would not be an unreasonable assumption.

White Ibis (*Eudocimus albus*)

Status: Accidental

5 to 16 Sep 1995, Coralville Res., Johnson Co., imm. (P-0464, *IBL* 66:18, 66(1) cover)

Occurrence: The only record is of an immature bird in fall that remained for 12 days.

Comment: The range of this resident species is coastal from North Carolina and Baja California south to northern South America. Individuals stray northward on a fairly regular basis, from May to September, and have been found as far north as North Dakota and Minnesota. Many of the late summer and fall birds are immatures.

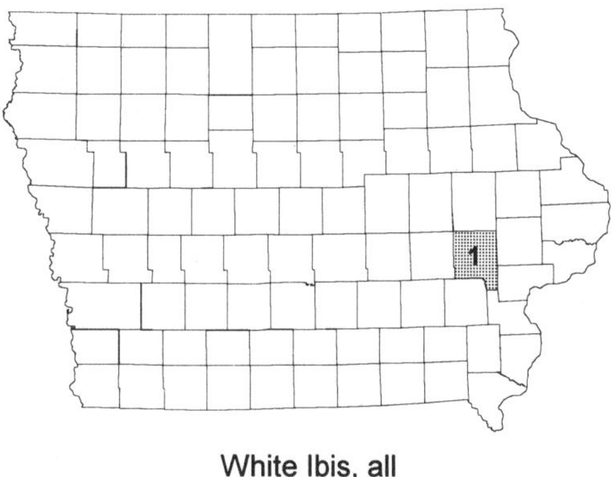

White Ibis, all

Glossy Ibis (*Plegadis fulcinellus*)

Status: Accidental

4 to 5 May 1992, Kossuth Co. (P-0338, P-0339, Kenne 1994)
18 to 22 May 1995, Riverton A., Fremont Co. (P-0452, Kent et al. 1995)

Occurrence: On 4 and 5 May 1992, a bird in alternate plumage was photographed next to a White-faced Ibis in spring in north-central Iowa (Kenne 1994), not far south of the location of Minnesota's first record and just a year later (Janssen 1992). On 18 May 1995, 2 Glossy Ibises were photographed with a White-faced Ibis in southwestern Iowa (Kent et al. 1995). Other reports of Glossy Ibis (Dinsmore et al. 1984) have not been convincing enough to be accepted.

Comment: Glossy Ibis is an Old World species of Eurasia, Africa, and Australia that also occurs in the West Indies and the southeastern United States. It breeds and winters from Florida west to Louisiana and north along the East Coast. Like other ibises, it wanders to inland locations across eastern United States. The boundary zone of wandering White-faced and Glossy ibises runs from Louisiana to Lake Michigan, but individual birds may stray in either direction. The problem is telling them apart, which requires a close view and birds in alternate plumage. There are few records of Glossy Ibis west of the Mississippi River. It is accidental in Texas, but has bred in northeastern Arkansas and southeastern Missouri. There is 1 other record from Missouri. There are single records from Oklahoma, Minnesota, and Saskatchewan and 3 records from Colorado. Most of the identifiable dark ibises are found in April and May.

The field marks that help identify a Glossy Ibis in breeding plumage include plumbaceous facial skin with a pale blue border broken behind the eye, dark eye, and carmine leg color limited to ankles (Pratt 1976, Kaufman 1990). Alternate plumage is acquired in late winter and is retained until August. Adult plumage is not attained until the second summer. Immatures are not identifiable as to species. Birds in basic plumage that have a gray or blue edge to the facial skin and dark eye are Glossy Ibis, but a very close view is required to confirm these characteristics.

References:

Janssen, R. B. 1992. A Glossy Ibis in Minnesota. *Loon* 64:5-10.

Kenne, M. 1994. Glossy Ibis in Kossuth County. *Iowa Bird Life* 64:83-84.

Kent, T. H., J. L. Fuller, and A. R. Tetrault. 1995. Glossy Ibis in Fremont County. *Iowa Bird Life* 65:87-88.

Pratt, H. D. 1976. Field identification of White-faced and Glossy ibises. *Birding* 8:1-5.

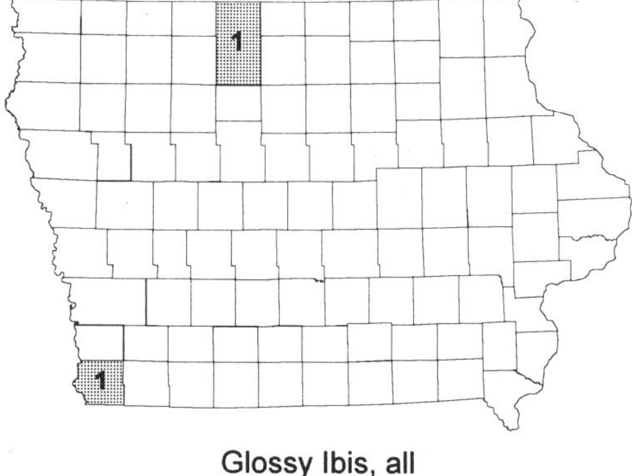

Glossy Ibis, all

White-faced Ibis (*Plegadis chihi*)

Status: Regular; occasionally nests

White-faced Ibis and *Ibis sp. -- by year since 1960

60			63			66			69			72			75			78			81			84			87			90			93		
																	1				4	2		2		4	1			4	2	1		1	6
*1			1													1	1	3			2	1	2	2	1	6	2	5	1	3	1	2		1	5

By month -- all records

Jan			Feb			Mar			Apr			May			Jun			Jul			Aug			Sep			Oct			Nov			Dec		
										1	8	3	8	4	1		1				1				1										
*									1	2	3	6	4			1				1	2	1	1	5	3	7	4		3						

6 Apr 1986*	21 Oct 1995*
13 Apr 1986*	22 Oct 1990*
15 Apr 1995	25 Oct 1995*

nesting: 5, 13 Jun 1986, Jemmerson Sl., Dickinson Co. (Dinsmore and Dinsmore 1986)

Occurrence: This rare migrant and once-nesting species has been found most often from late April through May. Most fall ibises have not been identifiable as to species (White-faced versus Glossy) and have been found from August to October. Records have been from all areas of the state with over two-thirds from the western half of the state.

The only nesting record involved 1 nest on 5 June and 2 more nests with eggs on 13 July 1986 at Jemmerson Slough in Dickinson County (Dinsmore and Dinsmore 1986). No birds or nests were found on 9 August, suggesting that nesting was unsuccessful.

Historically, the first record involves 1 of 13 shot in Greene County in April 1891 by B. H. Osborn (University of Iowa specimen #04839, Kent and Schrimper 1996). The next definite White-faced Ibis record did not occur until 1977, when 1 was found in Clay County on 18 May (Ryan 1977). There are 7 other reports of Ibis species prior to 1960. Two of these involved specimens: September 1905 from McGregor in Clayton County (Iowa State University specimen, DuMont 1935a, b) and 21 August 1954 from Swan Lake in Johnson County (University of Iowa specimen #32541, Meyer 1954).

Comment: The winter range is from southern California and Texas south to Argentina. The breeding range includes the winter range and extends north to southern Oregon, Idaho, and North Dakota. The Iowa nesting report is the most easterly for the species. For many years this species was considered conspecific with the Glossy Ibis. The 2 species are similar appearing, especially in basic and immature plumages.

References:

Dinsmore, S., and J. J. Dinsmore. 1986. White-faced Ibis nesting in Dickinson County. *Iowa Bird Life* 56:120-121.

Meyer, A. W. 1954. Glossy Ibis at Swan Lake. *Iowa Bird Life* 24:80.

Ryan, M. R. 1977. Spring and summer observations of herons in northwest Iowa, 1977. *Iowa Bird Life* 47:96-98.

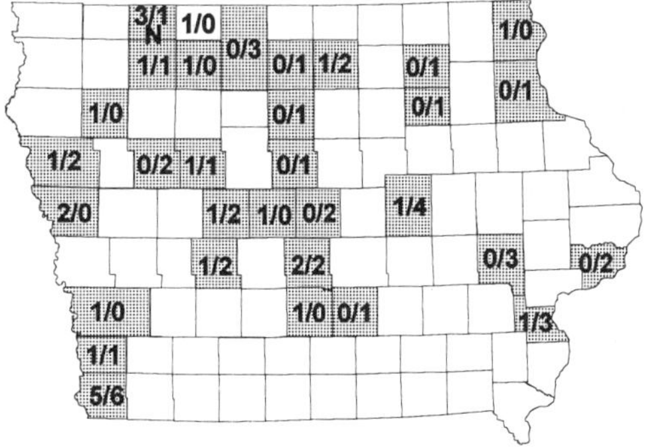

White-faced Ibis/Ibis species, all Records and nesting (N)

Roseate Spoonbill (*Ajaia ajaja*)

Status: Accidental

16 Aug 1960, Union Slough N.W.R., immature (P-0039, Burgess 1960)

Occurrence: An immature bird was caught in flight on a short, blurred, 8-mm movie film sequence in mid-August in north-central Iowa (Burgess 1960).

Comment: This species inhabits the Gulf Coast from Florida to Texas and the Pacific Coast from Mexico to Chile. It strays north to California and Arizona and very rarely to the Midwest. There are 1 to 3 records in states as far north as Utah, Colorado, Nebraska, Iowa, Wisconsin, Illinois, and Ohio. Northward strays have been recorded from April to November, but about two-thirds have been from August and September.

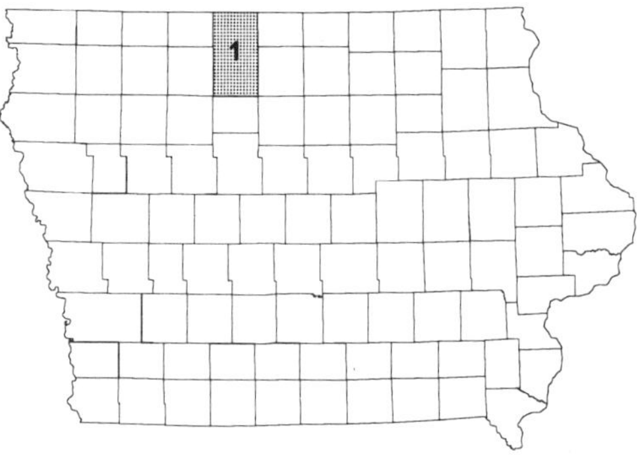

Roseate Spoonbill, all

Reference:

Burgess, H. H. 1960. Roseate Spoonbill observed at Union Slough. *Iowa Bird Life* 30:67-68.

Storks (Family Ciconiidae)

Storks comprise 19 species, with 2 from North America and 1 from Iowa. They are large birds with long necks, short tails, and long, stout bills with surface grooves. Most species are tropical. They feed while walking in wet or dry areas.

Wood Stork (*Mycteria americana*)

Status: Accidental

25 Sep 1977, Mississippi River bottoms, Louisa Co. (documentation by M. A. Thwaits)

Occurrence: The 1 sight record of this species is from fall in southeastern Iowa. There are 2 other reports that are Not Accepted (Dinsmore et al. 1984, *IBL* 63:69).

Comment: The range of this declining coastal species includes the Atlantic Coast south from South Carolina and the Gulf Coast west to eastern Texas. It occurs on the Pacific Coast of Mexico south to South America. Birds disperse inland in the coastal states and more rarely to inland states farther north. Since 1960 there have been 1 or more records from Montana, South Dakota, Iowa, Wisconsin, Michigan, Indiana, Illinois, Missouri, Kansas, and Oklahoma. Wood Storks have been recorded in the Midwest from February to November, but most records are evenly scattered from May to September.

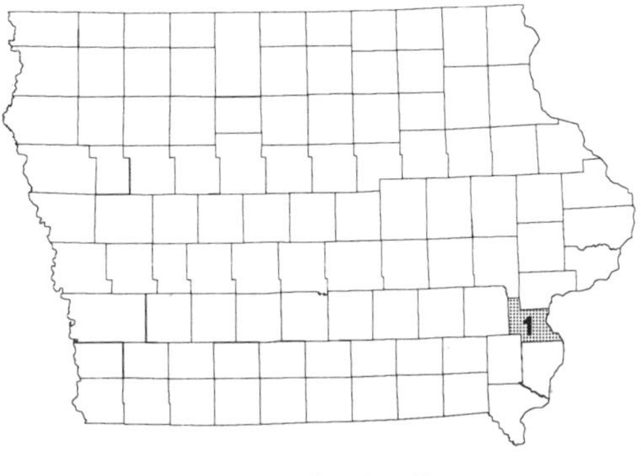

Wood Stork, all

ORDER ANSERIFORMES

Swans, Geese, and Ducks (Family Anatidae)

Swans, geese, and ducks (waterfowl) comprise 154 species, with 60 from North America and 41 from Iowa. The only other family in this order comprises 3 species of screamers in South America. Waterfowl occur in all areas of the world, and many species occur in more than one hemisphere. Most are highly aquatic, feeding on plants, invertebrates, and fish, but some are largely terrestrial, feeding on grains and plants. They have heavy bodies, webbed feet, and flat bills. They are gregarious but not colonial nesters.

Of the Iowa species, 32 are Regular and 9 are Accidental. Common nesting species in Iowa include Canada Goose, Wood Duck, Mallard, and Blue-winged Teal. More localized and less common regular nesting species include Northern Pintail, Northern Shoveler, Redhead, Hooded Merganser, and Ruddy Duck. Irregular nesting species include Green-winged Teal, Gadwall, Canvasback, and Ring-necked Duck. There are also nesting records for American Black Duck, American Wigeon, Lesser Scaup, and Bufflehead.

Extensive areas for nesting waterfowl in Iowa were converted to farmland as the state was settled, but remnants remain, especially in the glaciated area of the Des Moines Lobe. Habitat for wintering waterfowl increased with the construction of 11 locks and dams along the Mississippi River and 4 large reservoirs and with the invention of combines that leave considerable grain in farm fields. Far more ducks and geese winter in Iowa now than a few decades ago.

Black-bellied Whistling-Duck (*Dendrocygna autumnalis*)

Status: Accidental

By year since 1960

60	63	66	69	72	75	78	81	84	87	90	93
					1				1 1		2

By month -- all records

Jan	Feb	Mar	Apr	May	Jun	Jul	Aug	Sep	Oct	Nov	Dec
				1	1				2	1	

8 May 1977, Zirbel Sl., Cerro Gordo Co. (P-0169, Barrett 1977, *IBL* 64:69)
29 May 1987, Boone Co. (P-0223, *IBL* 57:119, *IBL* 64:69)
23 Oct 1988, Ingham L., Emmet Co. (*IBL* 64:69)
24 Oct 1993, Blue L., Monona Co. (Iowa State Univ. specimen #2611, P-0409, *IBL* 64:11)
1 Nov 1993, Big M., Butler Co. (Iowa State Univ. specimen #2612, P-0457, *IBL* 65:82)

Occurrence: Of the 5 records, 2 are from spring and 3 from fall. Two were shot by hunters and preserved as specimens, and 1 was captured and photographed during a waterfowl research project (Barratt 1977).

Comment: The range of this mostly resident species of northern and eastern South America and Middle America extends to southern Texas and southern Arizona. Classically, the species was migratory at the northern edge of its range, with most birds leaving the United States in winter. In recent years, the range has expanded in southern Texas and extended north as far as Dallas (Schneider et al. 1993). There are 1 to a few reports each from California, Nevada, New Mexico, Colorado, Oklahoma, Kansas, Nebraska, Louisiana, Arkansas, Missouri, Iowa, Minnesota, Tennessee, Illinois, Michigan, Ontario, Pennsylvania, and West Virginia. The Midwestern records are from May to November.

In Iowa, Black-bellied Whistling-Ducks are much less common in captivity than Fulvous Whistling-Ducks (Francis Moore, personal communication). Some states treat these species as vagrants and others consider them possible escapees. The Records Committee of the Iowa Ornithologists' Union classified Black-bellied Whistling-Duck as a vagrant based on the apparent range expansion and recent increase in extralimital records that are mostly from spring and fall.

References:

Barratt, B. 1977. Black-bellied Whistling Duck, a new species for Iowa. *Iowa Bird Life* 47:104-106.

Schneider, J. P., T. C. Tacha, and D. Lobpries. 1993. Breeding distribution of Black-bellied Whistling Ducks in Texas. *Southwestern Naturalist* 38:383-385.

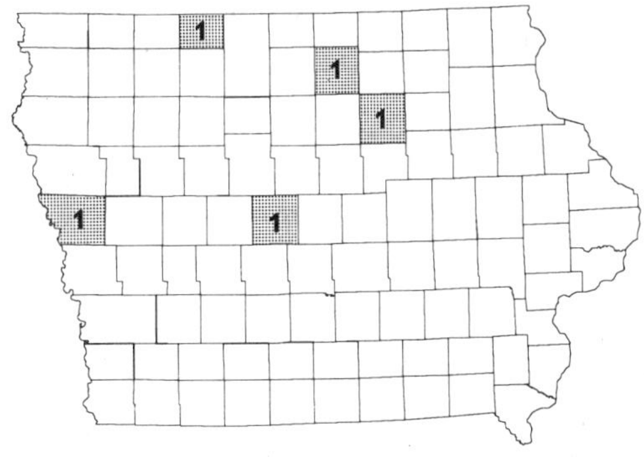

Black-bellied Whistling-Duck, all

Tundra Swan (*Cygnus columbianus*)

Status: Regular

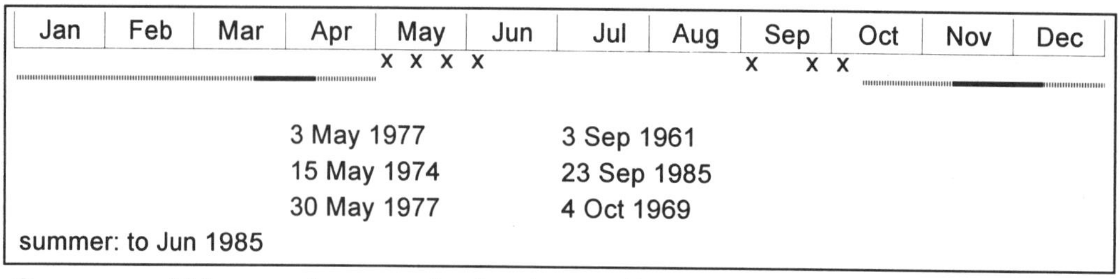

Jan	Feb	Mar	Apr	May	Jun	Jul	Aug	Sep	Oct	Nov	Dec
				x x x x				x	x x		
			3 May 1977			3 Sep 1961					
			15 May 1974			23 Sep 1985					
			30 May 1977			4 Oct 1969					

summer: to Jun 1985

Occurrence: This rare migrant can be found anywhere in Iowa, but is only regular in fall on the Mississippi River in northeastern Iowa, especially above Lock and Dam 9 in Allamakee County. Fall migrants arrive in mid-November and depart in early December. In spring, most records are from late March and early April and average about 5 reports per year. The numbers in spring vary from 1 to 200, but in fall more than 1,000 may be seen in Allamakee County.

The only summer record is of a bird that lingered at Union Slough National Wildlife Refuge in Kossuth County in June 1985 and eventually died (*IBL* 55:89). Tundra Swans were found on Christmas Bird Counts in 7 of 13 years from 1983 to 1995, usually along the Mississippi River. The few mid-winter reports include 2 that wintered near Princeton in Scott County in 1989-1990 (*IBL* 60:50), 1 in Fremont County on 12 January 1992 (*IBL* 62:52), 1 at Iowa City in Johnson County from 2 January through February 1991 (*IBL* 61:54), 1 on 3 January and 2 on 8 February 1991 at Keokuk in Lee County (*IBL* 61:54), and singles at Red Rock Reservoir in Marion County on 19 January 1982 (*IBL* 52:25) and in the winter of 1994-1995 (*IBL* 65:46). Up to 10 were in Scott County from 2 to 24 February 1988 (*IBL* 59:48).

Historically, Tundra Swan was also an uncommon migrant (Anderson 1907, DuMont 1933).

Comment: The winter range in the West is along the coast from Washington to California and at interior locations from California and Utah south to New Mexico. The winter range in the east is mainly from Chesapeake Bay south to North Carolina, and less commonly on the Gulf Coast and in the interior of the Midwest. The breeding range is along the coastal plain of Alaska and Canada east to Hudson Bay. The Eurasian subspecies, Bewick's Swan, *C. c. bewickii*, breeds in northern Russia and winters south to Great Britain and Japan.

Most of the Iowa birds probably winter on Chesapeake Bay and migrate northwest in spring and southeast in fall, which accounts for their occurrence in greater numbers in northeastern Iowa and relatively late spring arrival time compared to other waterfowl.

Trumpeter Swan (*Cygnus buccinator*)

Status: Regular; formerly nested

Jan	Feb	Mar	Apr	May	Jun	Jul	Aug	Sep	Oct	Nov	Dec

Occurrence: The first documented occurrence of this species in Iowa since the 1800s was at Otter Creek Marsh in Tama County on 23 December 1984 when 9 adults were photographed (P-0157, *IBL* 58:120). Using neck tag numbers, it was determined that these birds, part of a reintroduced population, left Carver Park Reserve in Hennepin County, Minnesota, on 12 December 1984, and at least 1 wintered in Oklahoma and returned to marshes near St. Cloud, Minnesota (L. N. Gillette, letter to T. H. Kent). From 1984 to 1994 there were 1 to 5 reports per year of Trumpeter Swans in Iowa from late November to late April and from all areas of the state.

By 1995, Trumpeter Swans had been released at 15 sites throughout Iowa with more releases planned (Andrews 1995). At least 2 broods hatched in 1996. In winter, birds with various neck collars, wing tags, and leg bands migrate into Iowa from Minnesota and Wisconsin. Less is known about migration of birds into Iowa from the longer-established South Dakota and Nebraska populations. If the present trend continues, this species will be well established in Iowa in a few years.

Historically, Trumpeter Swans nested in Iowa, but the extent of their occurrence is not well documented. They disappeared from the Midwest in the late 1800s. The last dated record for Iowa was 20 September 1897 (Anderson 1907). The only definite nesting record was from Hancock County in 1883, although nesting was said to occur at the headwaters of the Des Moines River as late as 1875 (Anderson 1907). Another nest was reported in Oakland Valley in Franklin County in 1871 (Banko 1960). The only known specimen is undated from Sac County and collected by H. B. Smith (P-0078, DuMont 1933). The Records Committee reviewed all of the historical references to this species, and the only acceptably documented record, besides those from Hancock and Sac counties, is a description of specimens (undated) from Webster County (Anderson 1907).

Comment: The natural breeding range, which once extended from the Arctic south to Indiana and Missouri, is now contracted to central and southern Alaska and isolated locations in western Canada and the northwestern United States. Introduced populations were started in South Dakota in 1960, in Minnesota in 1966, in Wisconsin in 1987, and more recently in other Midwestern states. The Alaska population winters from southern Alaska to Washington. Interior populations winter on breeding grounds or move south to find open water.

References:

Andrews, R. 1995. Trumpeting the cause for wetlands. *Iowa Conservationist* 54(3):36-40.

Banko, W. E. 1960. The Trumpeter Swan. *U.S. Fish and Wildlife Service, North American Fauna*, No. 63.

Mute Swan (*Cygnus olor*)

Status: Regular

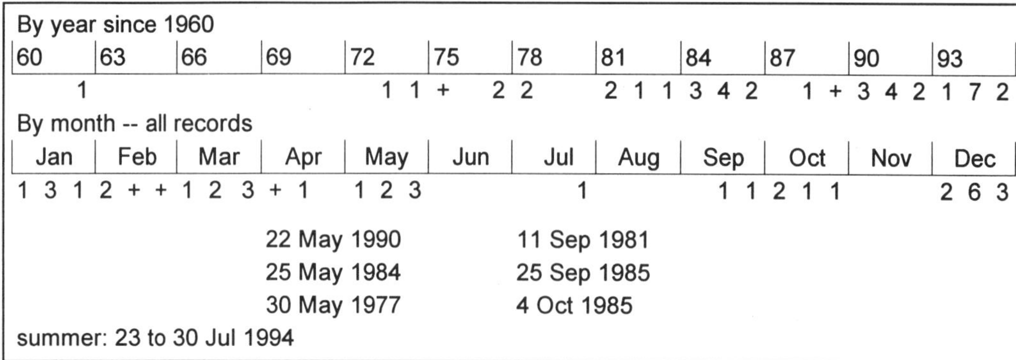

By year since 1960

60	63	66	69	72	75	78	81	84	87	90	93

1 1 1 + 2 2 2 1 1 3 4 2 1 + 3 4 2 1 7 2

By month -- all records

Jan	Feb	Mar	Apr	May	Jun	Jul	Aug	Sep	Oct	Nov	Dec

1 3 1 2 + + 1 2 3 + 1 1 2 3 1 1 1 2 1 1 2 6 3

22 May 1990 11 Sep 1981
25 May 1984 25 Sep 1985
30 May 1977 4 Oct 1985

summer: 23 to 30 Jul 1994

Occurrence: Since 1973, from 1 to 4 (except for 7 in 1994) have been reported per year except for 4 years when none were reported. Of 40 reports, 27 are from eastern, 9 from central, and 4 from western Iowa. Some of the reported birds may not have been feral (see Comment). The reports are scattered from mid-September to late May. Of those birds where age was indicated, 18 percent were immatures.

The first record is of 1 shot on the Mississippi River in Muscatine County in November 1962 (Musgrove and Musgrove 1977). The next record was of a "feral" pair that appeared at the New London Country Club in Henry County on 24 March 1973 and nested (*IBL* 43:46). This nest, as well as a nest at Maripesa Park in Jasper County in 1974 (Dorrow 1974) were flooded out. Another pair said to be "feral" nested at Moorehead Park in Ida County in the summer of 1994 (*IBL* 64:107). No color-marked Mute Swans have been reported, so it is not possible to determine the origin of most birds. It appears likely that the number of records will increase and nesting birds could become established.

Comment: This species, which is native to temperate Eurasia, has been widely introduced in other areas of the world. Birds were introduced in New York in the late 1880s (Zeranski and Baptist 1990). The East Coast population, which occurs from Massachusetts to Virginia, has expanded rapidly since the 1950s. A pair introduced in Charlevoix County in 1919 is thought to be responsible for the well-established Michigan population, which has expanded more rapidly since the 1970s and doubled from 1985 to 1991 (McPeek and Adams 1994). The first migrant in Wisconsin was noted in 1958, and the first nest was found in northern Wisconsin in 1975 (Robbins 1991). Breeding birds are established in Ashland County, Wisconsin. Nesting also occurs regularly in Ontario, Ohio, and Illinois and has been reported in Indiana and Missouri.

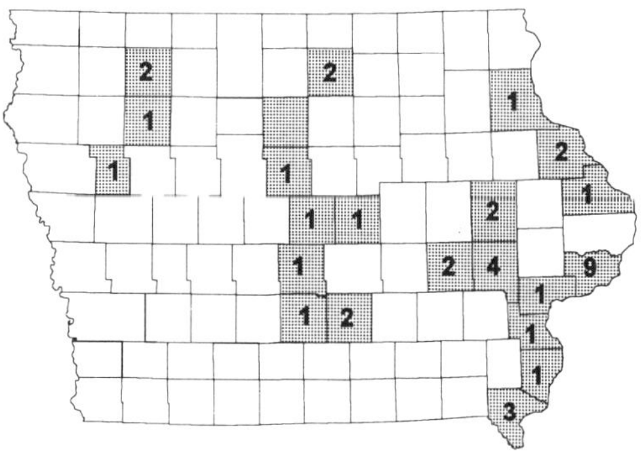

Mute Swan, all.

Mute Swans remain on breeding grounds in winter if open water is available; otherwise, they move south in family groups or as individuals. First-year birds may have more tendency to wander. The fact that Mute Swans are often domesticated and kept in parks and on ponds makes it difficult to determine whether an individual swan is feral or not. The pattern of occurrence, spreading out from nesting areas around the Great Lakes, suggests that many of the birds seen on rivers and lakes in Iowa are feral. Any swan that is not obviously of domestic origin should be reported. Reports should indicate whether the bird is an immature or adult. Immatures should be described, because they are difficult to distinguish from immature Tundra and Trumpeter swans (Peterjohn 1986). Swans reach maturity in their first year, but the changes in body and bill color occur at different rates for the 3 species.

References:

Dorrow, H. 1974. Our birds have problems too. *Iowa Bird Life* 44:106-108.

Peterjohn, B. 1986. Identification of immature swans. *Iowa Bird Life* 56:9-10.

Bean Goose (*Anser fabalis*)

Status: Accidental

29 Dec 1984 to 10 Jan 1985, De Soto N.W.R., Harrison Co. (Wilson 1985, Wright and Grenon 1985).

Occurrence: The only record is of a bird seen by many and photographed on the Iowa-Nebraska line (Wilson 1985, Wright and Grenon 1985). It was thought to be of the race *A. f. middendorffii*, which is the largest race and has a long, deep-based, black bill with orange restricted to a sub-terminal band (Madge and Burn 1988). The fact that the bird was of an eastern Siberian race was an important factor in the acceptance as a wild bird, because eastern races are extremely rare in captivity and, like other Siberian species, could follow North American species into the Midwest (Wilson 1985).

Comment: This species breeds across northern Europe and Asia and winters in southern Europe and Asia. Strays occur regularly in Alaska, but the only record in the United States south of Alaska prior to the Iowa-Nebraska bird was in Washington from March to 6 April 1984 (*Amer. Birds* 38:949). Subsequently, a bird identified as *A. f. middendorfii* was in Quebec from 14 to 15 Oct 1987 (*Amer. Birds* 42:46). The only other record of Bean Goose from Canada was also in Quebec, from 14 to 21 October 1982. It was shot and found to be of the European race, *A. f. rossicus* (*Amer. Birds* 37:159).

References:

Wilson, B. 1985. Bean Goose in the Midlands. *Iowa Bird Life* 55:83-86.

Wright, R., and A. Grenon. 1985. Three species of Siberian geese seen in Nebraska. *Nebr. Bird Review* 53:3-4.

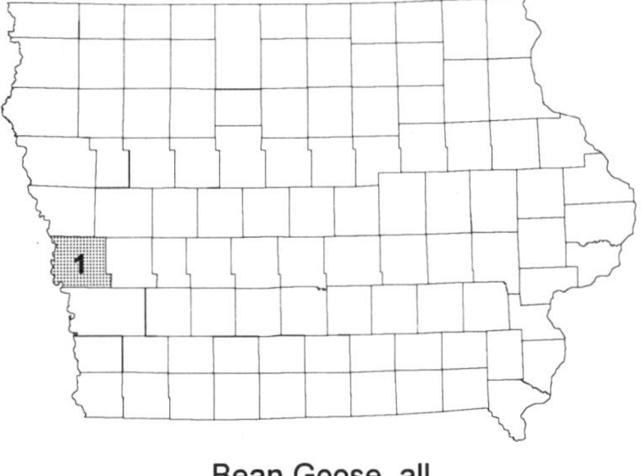

Bean Goose, all

Greater White-fronted Goose (*Anser albifrons*)

Status: Regular

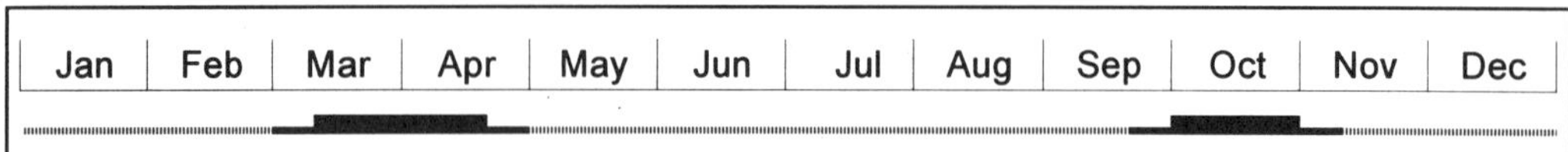

Occurrence: This uncommon migrant is most common from early March to late April and from late September to early November. It is much more common in western Iowa, but in recent years it has been found increasingly often in central and eastern Iowa. Rarely birds linger into summer including 1 at Tomahawk Marsh in Sac County in 1994 (*IBL* 65:12), 2 at Union Slough National Wildlife Refuge in Kossuth County until 11 July 1989 (*IBL* 59:109), 1 at Eagle Lake in Hancock County on 16 June 1985 (*IBL* 55:89), and 1 at Saylorville Reservoir in Polk County from 11 to 13 June 1985 (*IBL* 55:89). These are likely sick or injured birds such as the bird with a broken wing that summered at the Power Plant ponds in Pottawattamie County in 1986 (*IBL* 56:114).

A few also remain into December, most commonly in southwestern Iowa. On Christmas Bird Counts, this species was reported in 16 of 36 years from 1960 to 1995 and every year since 1986. Two wintered at Ida Grove in Ida County in 1992-1993 (*IBL* 63:46). Other recent mid-winter records include 1 at Swan Wildlife Area in Marion County on 11 January 1992 (*IBL* 62:52), 4 at Keokuk in Lee County on 21 January 1989 (*IBL* 59:49), 37 in Fremont County on 30 January 1988 (*IBL* 58:54), and 3 in Guthrie County until 8 January 1987 (*IBL* 57:52). The 30 at Bays Branch Wildlife Area in Guthrie County on 11 February 1990 (*IBL* 60:50) may have been early migrants.

Comment: This Holarctic species breeds on the Arctic tundra, winters in coastal states from Texas and Washington south to central Mexico and at inland locations in California, the Great Basin, and New Mexico. In the United States, much of the population migrates through the central Great Plains with most of the birds passing to the west of Iowa.

Snow Goose (*Chen caerulescens*)

Status: Regular

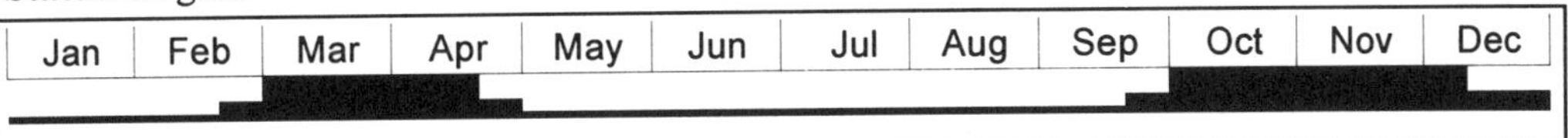

Occurrence: This abundant migrant arrives in late February or March, and most depart by late April. Fall migrants arrive in late September, and most depart by mid- or late December. Although Snow Geese spend much of their time on wetlands, migrants typically feed on uplands, especially in harvested grain fields. A few linger through the summer, especially along the Missouri River. Usually these are singles or small groups, but 35 summered at Badger Lake in Monona County in 1988 (*IBL* 58:108). In fall, large flocks may linger into late December, especially in southwestern Iowa when there is little snow cover and food is available. These late flocks move south if there is a major snowstorm but may return in mid-winter if the snow cover melts. In 1988-1989, 153,000 were still at De Soto National Wildlife Refuge in Harrison County on 10 January, and they left with a cold spell in early February (*IBL* 59:49). Snow Geese were reported on Christmas Bird Counts in 32 of 36 years from 1960 to 1995, most commonly near the Missouri River.

Although large flocks move through Iowa in both spring and fall, in recent years, the spring flocks have been somewhat smaller as the birds have tended to migrate through central Nebraska (*IBL* 63:73). The largest flocks occur in November or early December along the Missouri River Valley, especially at De Soto National Wildlife Refuge in Harrison County and at Riverton Area and Forney Lake in Fremont County. Migration peaks there typically number in the hundreds of thousands and provide the greatest wildlife spectacle to be seen in Iowa. In the past decade, fewer Snow Geese have been seen in eastern Iowa, a reflection of the recent shift of this species' migration pathways to the west.

Both Anderson (1907) and DuMont (1933) considered this species a common migrant, noting that the blue form was less abundant than the white form, a ratio between the two color forms that still prevails. This species may be the most abundant migrant waterfowl in Iowa.

Comment: The winter range is from Puget Sound and the central Valley of California to New Mexico and northern Mexico, from Missouri and Kansas south to the Gulf of Mexico, and locally on the East Coast, mainly Chesapeake Bay. The breeding range is along the Arctic Coast from northeastern Siberia and northern Alaska to western Greenland and south to James Bay.

One seen at De Soto National Wildlife Refuge on 22 November 1994 had been color marked on Wrangel Island in Russia (*IBL* 65:12). Increasingly in recent years, many have wintered farther north as their natural wintering grounds have been altered and they have shifted to agricultural crops as a winter food supply.

Based on winter surveys, Snow Goose populations have increased greatly in the past several decades. There is growing concern that these populations are altering the nesting habitat to the detriment of this and other species and that Snow Geese may suffer dramatic population declines due to disease, food shortage in the breeding season, or severe weather.

Ross's Goose (*Chen rossii*)

Status: Regular

Jan	Feb	Mar	Apr	May	Jun	Jul	Aug	Sep	Oct	Nov	Dec

x x + + + + + + + + + + x x x

17 May 1991 — 25 Sep 1994
20 May 1994 — 4 Oct 1987
23 May 1992 — 15 Oct 1989

Summer: Jun to Oct 1988

Occurrence: This rare migrant is usually found from mid-March to early April and from early November to early December. A few linger into December with the flocks of Snow Geese in southwestern Iowa. This species was reported on Christmas Bird Counts in 8 of 13 years from 1983 to 1985. Most depart by the end of December, but a few have remained into January, including 12 at De Soto National Wildlife Refuge in Harrison County on 6 January 1989 (*IBL* 59:49), 1 collected at Riverton Area in Fremont County on 14 January 1983 (*IBL* 53:24), and 1 there on 17 February 1984 (*IBL* 54:16). One wintered in Webster County in 1994-1995 (*IBL* 65:71). Three at Riverton Area on 26 February 1982 (*IBL* 52:25) were early migrants. There is a summer record from Bays Branch Wildlife Area in Guthrie County in 1988 (*IBL* 58:108).

This species was first reported in Iowa in 1945 when 1 was found in Clinton County (Brown 1971). In 1968 and 1969, it was estimated that Ross's Geese made up about 0.08 percent of the flocks of Snow Geese at De Soto National Wildlife Refuge (Prevett and MacInnes 1972). Since then, as birders and biologists have learned to identify this species, it has been found to make up almost 1 percent of the birds in the flocks of Snow Geese in western Iowa, especially at De Soto National Wildlife Refuge, Forney Lake, and Riverton Area (Robinson 1982, Frederick and Johnson 1983). Priebe (1987) reported that Ross's Geese comprised 0.14 percent of the geese (39 Ross's and 28,365 Snow Geese) taken at those 3 hunting areas from 1972 to 1985. Although the first state record was from eastern Iowa, most reports are from western Iowa. In recent years, a few have been found almost every year in eastern Iowa. The most dependable way to find this species is to look for individuals or family groups along the edges of large flocks of Snow Geese.

Comment: Most winter in the Central Valley of California, in New Mexico, and along the Gulf Coast, a distribution similar to that of Snow Goose. The breeding range is along the Arctic Coast from the Northwest Territories to Hudson Bay. This species' populations have increased greatly in recent decades.

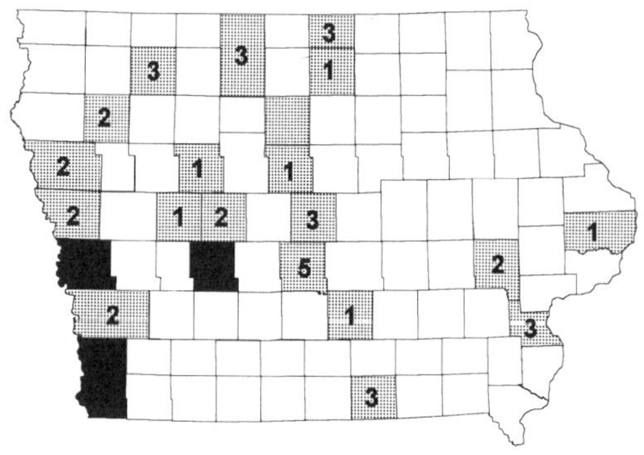

Ross's Goose, all
More than 10 (black)

References:

Frederick, R. B., and R. R. Johnson. 1983. Ross' Geese increasing in central North America. *Condor* 85:257-258.

Prevett, J. P., and C. D. MacInnes. 1972. The number of Ross' Geese in central North America. *Condor* 74:431-438.

Priebe, C. 1987. Ross' Goose in southwest Iowa. *Iowa Bird Life* 57:9-10.

Robinson, J. C. 1982. Mid-continent observations of Ross' Geese. *Iowa Bird Life* 52:3-5.

Brant (*Branta bernicla*)

Status: Accidental

By year since 1960

60	63	66	69	72	75	78	81	84	87	90	93
						1	1		1 1 +		

By month -- all records

Jan	Feb	Mar	Apr	May	Jun	Jul	Aug	Sep	Oct	Nov	Dec
+									1	1 1	1 +

2 Nov 1980, De Soto N.W.R., Harrison Co., mounted bird of eastern race (P-0094, Dinsmore et al. 1981)

18 Nov 1983, near Riverton A., Fremont Co., imm., western race, shot by hunter (*IBL* 53:98, 54:38)

4 Oct 1987, Red Rock Res., Marion Co., imm., eastern race, caught by hunters (P-0244, Dinsmore 1988)

12 Dec 1988 to 3 Jan 1989, De Soto N.W.R., Harrison Co., eastern race (P-0274, Silcock 1989)

Occurrence: There are 4 well-substantiated records, 3 of the eastern race, *B. b. hrota*, and one of the western race, *B. b. nigricans*. There are numerous old reports, most of which are likely incorrect (Dinsmore et al. 1984). Some of the early reports of "brant" probably refer to "blue geese" or small races of Canada Goose.

Comment: Brant breed on Arctic tundra and winter on coastal estuaries and plains. They are rare but regular transients through the Midwest. Most are found from October to December, but some are seen from March to June. Brant have been seen in all states.

The nominate race *B. b. bernicla*, which has a dark belly and flanks, breeds in western Siberia and Europe and winters in Europe. The eastern race, *B. b. hrota*, which has a white belly and flanks, breeds in Canada and on North Atlantic islands and winters on the East Coast. The western race, *B. b. nigricans*, which has a black belly and white flanks, breeds in eastern Siberia and western Canada and winters on the Pacific Coast and to some extent in Asia. Juveniles lack the white neck patch until mid-winter and have white edging to wing coverts.

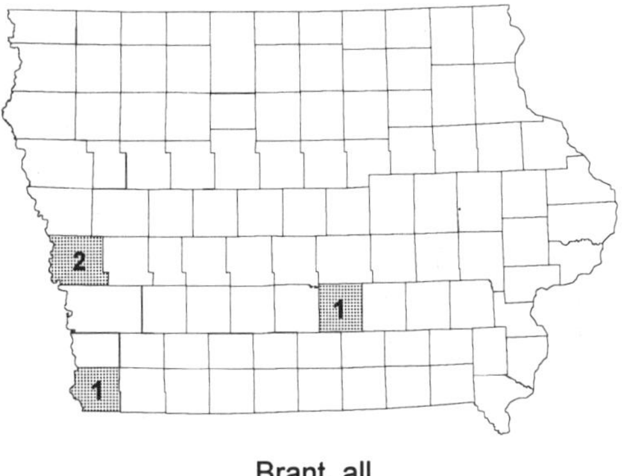

Brant, all

References:

Dinsmore, J. J. 1988. Brant at Red Rock Reservoir. *Iowa Bird Life* 58:24-25.

Dinsmore, J. J., S. Dinsmore, and M. Dinsmore. 1981. Brant specimen from Iowa. *Iowa Bird Life* 51:125-126.

Silcock, W. R. 1989. Brant at De Soto N.W.R. *Iowa Bird Life* 59:88.

Canada Goose (*Branta canadensis*)

Status: Regular; nests

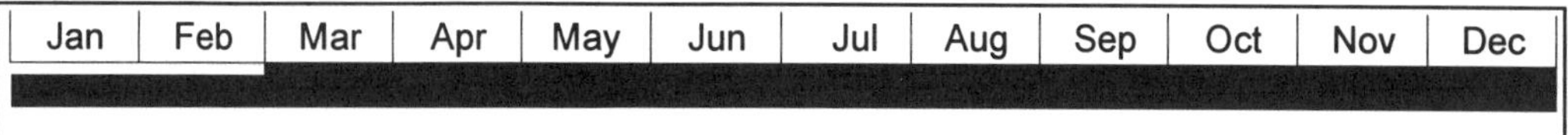

Occurrence: This abundant permanent resident and migrant inhabits lakes, ponds, and other wetlands throughout Iowa. The largest nesting populations are in the wetlands of northwestern Iowa. In the past 2 decades the nesting range has expanded to cover the entire state. Nesting starts in late March or early April and most eggs hatch in early or mid-May (Nigus and Dinsmore 1980). Large flocks of migrants move through Iowa, in spring from mid-February through early April and in fall from mid-October through late December. Thousands of them winter in Iowa. Canada Geese are reported on more than half of the Christmas Bird Counts in the state.

This was a common nesting species, especially on the prairie wetlands of north-central and northwestern Iowa in the 1800s. Because of habitat loss and excessive hunting, those populations declined rapidly and Canada Goose disappeared as a nesting species in Iowa around 1900 (Dinsmore 1994). In 1964, the Iowa Conservation Commission began a restocking program, first near Estherville, Spirit Lake, Ruthven, and Lake Mills, and later throughout the state. As a result, Canada Goose nesting populations became established in Iowa and by 1990 Canada Geese were nesting in nearly every county in the state (Bishop 1978, Zenner and LaGrange 1991).

Comment: The winter range is from the northern United States south to northern Mexico. The breeding range extends from northern Canada and Alaska south to include the northern half of the United States.

Historically, the nesting Canada Geese in Iowa were Giant Canada Geese (*B. c. maxima*), a race that was nearly extirpated. Through the use of breeding stock from aviculturists, birds of this race were released in Iowa and southern Minnesota and eventually became established in the Midwest. Several other subspecies of Canada Geese migrate through Iowa.

References:

Bishop, R. 1978. Giant Canada Geese in Iowa. *Iowa Conservationist* 37(10):5-12.

Nigus, T. A., and J. J. Dinsmore. 1980. Productivity of Canada Geese in northwestern Iowa. *Proc. Iowa Acad. Sci.* 87:56-61.

Zenner, G. G., and T. G. LaGrange. 1991. Land of the giants. *Iowa Conservationist* 50(6):28-31.

Wood Duck (*Aix sponsa*)

Status: Regular; nests

Jan	Feb	Mar	Apr	May	Jun	Jul	Aug	Sep	Oct	Nov	Dec

Occurrence: This common summer resident arrives in early March and departs by mid-November. A few have been found on Christmas Bird Counts in 32 of 36 years from 1960 to 1995 with the most along the Mississippi River. From 1980 to 1995, birds have over-wintered at 1 to 4 locations, usually where there are flocks of Mallards and often at urban locations.

Historically, this was a fairly common species, especially in eastern Iowa, but by the early 1900s, its numbers were already greatly reduced (Anderson 1907). Due to excessive hunting, its numbers declined rapidly and by the 1930s it was rare in Iowa. The combination of more restrictive hunting seasons and programs to provide nest boxes led to a rapid population turnaround and placed the Wood Duck among the most abundant waterfowl species in Iowa. It is especially common in flooded timber along rivers and streams in eastern Iowa, but it also nests in isolated woodlots and trees in the farmlands of north-central and northwestern Iowa. An example of its adaptability is the large nesting population at Union Slough National Wildlife Refuge in Kossuth County, where several hundred pairs nest in boxes in a region that historically probably had few if any Wood Ducks (Fleskes et al. 1990).

Comment: The eastern population winters from Missouri and New England south to Cuba and northeastern Mexico and breeds throughout this area (except for the southwestern portion) north to southern Canada as far west as Saskatchewan. The western population that winters from British Columbia to northern Mexico breeds from central California to southern Canada and east to Montana.

Reference:

Fleskes, J. P., J. A. Guthrie, and G. L. Welp. 1990. Raising Wood Ducks on a prairie marsh: The story of Union Slough. In: L. H. Fredrickson, G. V. Burger, S. P. Havera, D. A. Graber, R. E. Kirby, and T. S. Taylor, eds. *Proc. 1988 North American Wood Duck Symposium.*

Green-winged Teal (*Anas crecca*)

Status: Regular; occasionally nests

Jan	Feb	Mar	Apr	May	Jun	Jul	Aug	Sep	Oct	Nov	Dec

Occurrence: This common migrant is most abundant from early March to mid-May and from mid-September to early December. A few remain until late December, with reports on Christmas Bird Counts in 30 of 36 years from 1960 to 1995, most commonly along the Missouri River. Most mid-winter reports are of 1 or 2 individuals, but 78 were seen in Fremont County on 30 January 1988 (*IBL* 58:54).

A few summer in Iowa every year and occasionally nest, usually in northwestern or north-central Iowa. Nests were found in 3 years from 1962 to 1974 at Dewey's Pasture in Clay and Palo Alto counties (Weller 1979).

Comment: In North America, the winter range of this Holarctic species extends from Mexico north to Alaska, central Missouri (occasionally farther north), and the Maritime Provinces. The breeding range is from the Arctic south to Colorado, southern Minnesota, and Maine. This species is a rare nesting species throughout Minnesota (Janssen 1987), more common in Wisconsin (Robbins 1991), and irregular in Iowa. The Eurasian subspecies (*A. c. crecca*) has not been documented as occurring in Iowa.

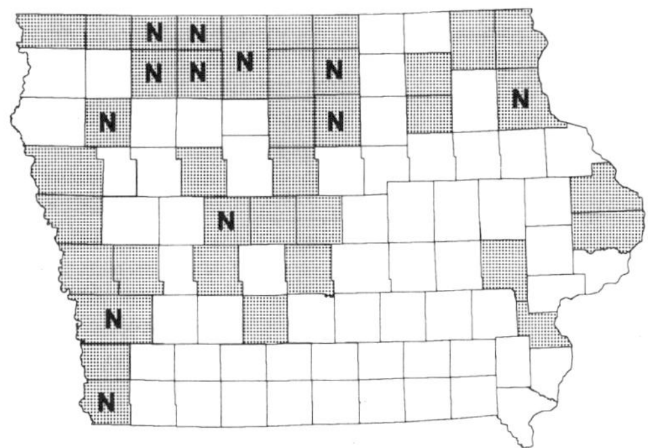

Green-winged Teal, 1960-1995
June-July and nesting (N)

American Black Duck (*Anas rubripes*)

Status: Regular; occasionally nests

Jan	Feb	Mar	Apr	May	Jun	Jul	Aug	Sep	Oct	Nov	Dec

Nesting:

1888, Buena Vista Co., 2 nests (Crone 1890)
Jun 1933, Trumbull L., Clay Co., nest (Bennett 1934)
prior to 1943, Mississippi R., ad. with yg. (Musgrove and Musgrove 1943)
13 Jun 1980, near Ruthven, Palo Alto Co., ad. with 3 yg. (Schaufenbuel 1981)
7 May 1991, Scott Co., 2 yg. (*IBL* 61:90)

Occurrence: This rare migrant and winter resident arrives in early November and departs by early April and is more common in eastern than western Iowa. Individual birds or pairs can often be found by scanning flocks of Mallards. A few winter in Iowa every year, especially along the Mississippi River.

The 5 nesting records span over 100 years with 3 from northwestern Iowa and 2 from the Mississippi River. Other recent summer reports include 1 at Dan Green Slough in Clay County on 5 June 1980 (*IBL* 50:74), 1 at Mud Lake in Clay County on 1, 3 July 1989 (*IBL* 59:109), 1 at Big Wall Lake in Wright County on 4 June 1988 (*IBL* 58:108), and 2 at Hendrickson Marsh in Story County on 20 June 1985 (*IBL* 55:89).

Historically, this species was at least as uncommon as it is today (Anderson 1907, DuMont 1933).

Comment: The winter range is from southeastern Minnesota and southern Wisconsin east to New Brunswick and Nova Scotia, south to the Gulf Coast states and west to eastern Oklahoma and Kansas. The breeding range includes eastern Canada and the eastern United States south to northeastern (occasionally southern) Minnesota and southern Wisconsin.

Mallard (*Anas platyrhynchos*)

Status: Regular; nests

Occurrence: This abundant permanent resident is found on virtually all types of wetlands throughout Iowa. Migrants move through from late February to early April and again in October and November.

Mallards are abundant nesting ducks in Iowa. Nesting starts in mid-April and peaks in late April or early May (Humburg et al. 1978). At Union Slough National Wildlife Refuge in Kossuth County, nest losses were high with many nests lost to predators, especially red fox (Fleskes and Klaas 1991).

Mallards are commonly found on Christmas Bird Counts throughout Iowa, most abundantly along the Missouri River. Many of these remain through the winter, and it is the most widespread and abundant wintering waterfowl in Iowa.

Comment: In North America, the winter range of this Holarctic species extends from southern Canada south to central Mexico and Cuba. The breeding range is from central Alaska south and east to the Maritime Provinces and then south in the East to the central

United States and in the West to central Mexico.

Reference:

Humburg, D. D., H. H. Prince, and R. A. Bishop. 1978. The social organization of a Mallard population in northern Iowa. *J. Wildlife Management* 42:72-80.

Northern Pintail (*Anas acuta*)

Status: Regular; nests

Occurrence: This common migrant and rare nesting species is found throughout Iowa. Spring migrants arrive in early March and depart in mid-May; fall migrants arrive in late August and depart in early December. Pintails are among the first waterfowl to arrive in spring, and, in mild winters, some may appear in mid- or late February, such as 700 at Runnells Wildlife Area in Marion County on 22 February 1992 (*IBL* 62:52).

A few nest in most years, mainly in northwestern and north-central Iowa. Since 1960, the only other confirmed nesting records are from near Mondamin in Harrison County in 1961 (Department of Natural Resources banding records) and from Lakin Slough in Guthrie County in 1988 (*IBL* 58:108).

A few remain until late December with reports on Christmas Bird Counts in 34 of 36 years from 1960 to 1995, most commonly along the Missouri River. Most leave when the last open water freezes in late December or early January, but in most years a few attempt to overwinter such as 44 in Fremont County on 30 January 1988 (*IBL* 58:54).

Comment: In the New World, the winter range of this Holarctic species is from coastal Alaska and New England and central Missouri in the interior south to the West Indies and extreme northern South America. The breeding range is from the Arctic Coast south to the Great Lakes, northern Iowa, and southern New Mexico. Iowa is near the southern edge of its nesting range and just north of the usual winter range.

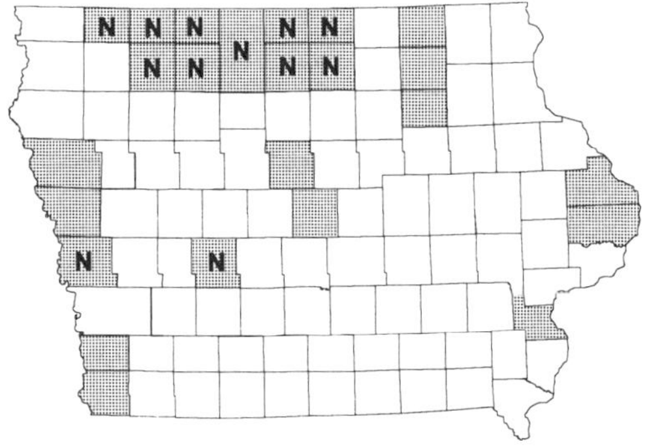

Northern Pintail, 1960-1995
June-July and nesting (N)

Garganey (*Anas querquedula*)

Status: Accidental

11 May 1991, northwestern Woodbury Co., male (*IBL* 61:90, 62:70)

Occurrence: There is 1 sight record of a male from spring.

Comment: This species breeds in freshwater wetlands across Europe and central Asia and is a long-distance migrant to wintering grounds in the northern tropics of Asia and central Africa. Vagrants are found in the spring in Alaska, in the fall and winter in Hawaii, and in the spring on the East Coast, Midwest, and West Coast. Birds found on the East Coast and inland could be birds that overshoot Africa in the fall (Spear et al. 1988). There are at least 32 records from central North America including records from Arizona, Texas, Oklahoma, Arkansas, Colorado, Tennessee, Illinois, Iowa, Minnesota, North Dakota, Montana, Idaho, Alberta, Saskatchewan, Manitoba, Yukon, and Ontario (Backstrom 1993). All are from spring and correspond with Blue-winged Teal migration (April and May for Iowa's latitude).

Most of the birds that are recognized are males in alternate plumage, a plumage that they wear for only a few months in spring. Fall migrants would likely be missed because of their similarity to other teal. The identification of females is difficult, but not impossible (Jackson 1992).

References:

Backstrom, P. 1993. Minnesota's second record of Garganey. *Loon* 65:55-57.

Jackson, G. D. 1992. Field identification of teal in North America: Female-like plumages—Part II. *Birding* 24: 214-223.

Spear, L. B., M. J. Lewis, M. T. Myres, and R. L. Pyle. 1988. The recent occurrence of Garganey in North America and the Hawaiian Islands. *Amer. Birds* 42: 385-392.

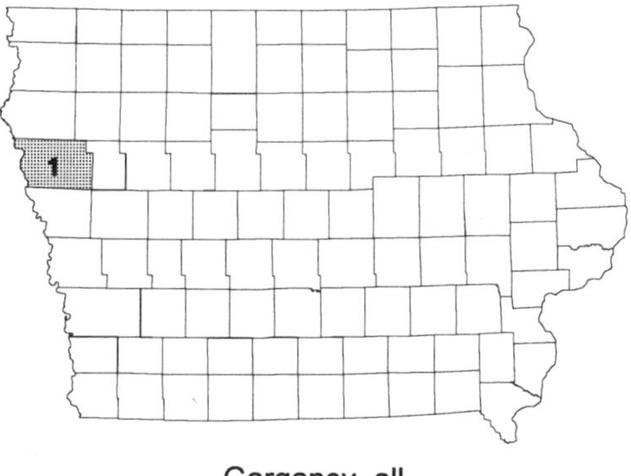

Garganey, all

Blue-winged Teal (*Anas discors*)

Status: Regular; nests

Jan	Feb	Mar	Apr	May	Jun	Jul	Aug	Sep	Oct	Nov	Dec

3 Mar 1991	2 Jan 1966
3 Mar 1991	2 Jan 1966
5 Mar 1990	3 Jan 1965

Occurrence: This common migrant and summer resident arrives in mid-March and departs by mid-October. It nests throughout Iowa, although most nesting reports are from the prairie pothole region of northwestern and north-central Iowa, where it is the most abundant nesting duck. Nesting starts in mid-May and extends into June with a peak of hatching in mid- to late June (Bennett 1938a). At Union Slough National Wildlife Refuge in Kossuth County, nest losses were high with many nests lost to predators, especially red fox (Fleskes and Klaas 1991). Among the regular waterfowl in Iowa, this is the least hardy species.

Blue-winged Teal were reported on Christmas Bird Counts in 13 of 36 years from 1960 to 1995, but at only 1 or 2 sites, and with 9 of those years from 1963 to 1971. There are no mid-winter records.

Comment: The winter range is from North Carolina and southern California and the southern edge of the United States to northern South America. The breeding range extends north to the Yukon in the west and central Canada in the east, south to North Carolina, central Louisiana, and New Mexico. There are only a few mid-winter records from nearby states.

Cinnamon Teal (*Anas cyanoptera*)

Status: Regular

By year since 1960

60 63 66 69 72 75 78 81 84 87 90 93

1 1 2 1 1 1 2 2 1 2 2 3 3 1 2 6 1 6 2 2 4 7 4 5 3 4 7

Jan	Feb	Mar	Apr	May	Jun	Jul	Aug	Sep	Oct	Nov	Dec
				x	x x	x		xx	xx	x	

5 Mar 1976	19 May 1986	7 Sep 1980	16 Oct 1941
6 Mar 1991	19 May 1984	7 Sep 1985	19 Oct 1980
6 Mar 1992	21 May 1989		30 Nov 1994

Summer: 21 Jun 1942, 3 Jul 1973, 17 Jul 1986

Occurrence: This rare spring migrant and occasional fall migrant has been seen every year since 1976 with an average of 5.5 reports per year from 1986 to 1995. Spring records extend from early March to mid-May, but most are in April. Most of the 75 records from 1960 to 1995 are from western and central Iowa, with only 10 percent from eastern Iowa. Most records are of single males, but females have been noted with males on occasion.

There are 3 summer records: 21 June 1942 at Grover's Lake in Dickinson County (King 1944); near Des Moines on 3, 4 July 1973 (Brown 1973a); and 17 July 1986 at New Lake in Woodbury County (*IBL* 56:114). The 5 fall records were of single males except for 1 with 2 males; 2 birds were shot by hunters and others were well described by birders. There is another undocumented fall report (Brown 1971).

Historically, this species was reported irregularly (Anderson 1907, DuMont 1933, Brown 1971). It has been seen every year since 1967 except for 1971 and 1975. The increase in sightings could be entirely due to increased birding activity.

Comment: The northern population of this New World species winters from central California and central Texas south to northern South America. The breeding range is from Mexico north to southern Canada and east to the western part of the Great Plains. There are resident populations in both northern and southern South America. The pattern of occurrence in Missouri and Minnesota is similar to Iowa, but the number of records drops off in Wisconsin and Illinois and even more so in states that are farther east.

Reference:

King, R. L. 1944. Summer birds of the Okoboji region 1938-1942. *Proc. Iowa Acad. Sci.* 51:467-470.

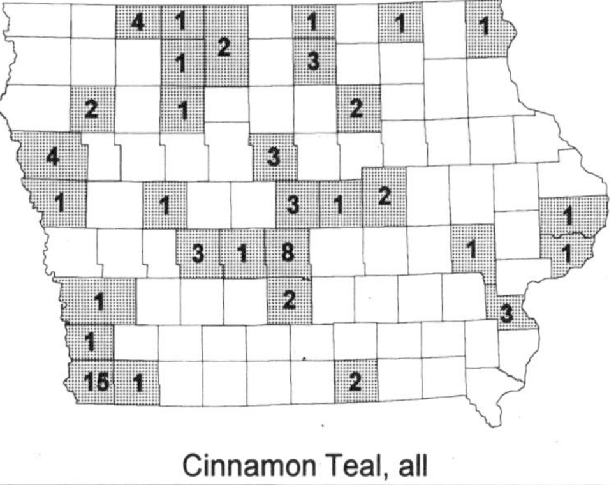

Cinnamon Teal, all

Northern Shoveler (*Anas clypeata*)

Status: Regular; nests

Jan	Feb	Mar	Apr	May	Jun	Jul	Aug	Sep	Oct	Nov	Dec

Occurrence: This common migrant and rare summer resident is found on lakes and marshes throughout Iowa. Migrants arrive in mid-March and depart by the end of November. A few nest in Iowa in most years, usually in northwestern and north-central Iowa. Nests were found in 5 of 13 years from 1962 to 1974 at Dewey's Pasture in Clay and Palo Alto counties, where it was the fifth most common waterfowl (Weller 1979). In some years this species may be fairly common, such as 1989 when 12 to 15 nests were found at Union Slough National Wildlife Refuge in Kossuth County (*IBL* 59:110).

Northern Shovelers very rarely overwinter, although a few were found on Christmas Bird Counts in 20 of 36 years from 1960 to 1995. A few have remained into early January, and returning birds have been noted in late February. There are 5 reports of birds between mid-January and mid-February from 1984 to 1995, most at locations with open water and other wintering waterfowl.

Comment: In the New World, the winter range of this Holarctic species is from the southern United States north coastally to British Columbia and South Carolina and south through the West Indies and Middle America. The breeding range is predominantly west of the Great Lakes and from northern Colorado to northern Alaska, and casually east and south of this range. Iowa is on the southeastern corner of the nesting range.

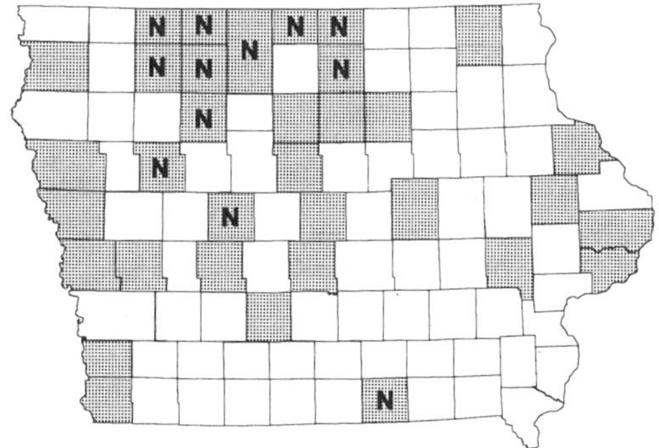

Northern Shoveler, 1960-1995
June-July and nesting (N)

Gadwall (*Anas strepera*)

Status: Regular; occasionally nests

Jan	Feb	Mar	Apr	May	Jun	Jul	Aug	Sep	Oct	Nov	Dec

Occurrence: This common migrant is most common from mid-March to late May and from early September to mid-December. Some linger until late December, especially along the Missouri River. This species was reported on Christmas Bird Counts in 29 of 36 years from 1960 to 1995. A few over-winter nearly every year.

A few remain every summer, mainly in northwestern and north-central Iowa, and occasionally nest. At Dewey's Pasture in Clay and Palo Alto counties, 7 nests were found from 1962 to 1974 (Weller 1979). Since then, the only specific nesting records are 2 at Union Slough National Wildlife Refuge in Kossuth County in 1984 (*IBL* 54:81). A brood was found on Dewey's Pasture in Palo Alto County in 1939 (Low 1941).

Comment: In the New World, this Holarctic species winters from Mexico and the West Indies north to the southern Great Lakes and in the west to southern Alaska. The breeding range includes the Great Lakes Region, the northern Great Plains, in the West from California to coastal Alaska, and in the East in the Maritime Provinces. It nests largely in the Prairie Pothole region of southern Alberta, Saskatchewan, and Manitoba south through northern Montana, the Dakotas, and western Minnesota. Iowa is at the southern edge of its nesting range.

Reference:

Low, J. B. 1941. Gadwall and Franklin's Gull nesting in Iowa. *Iowa Bird Life* 11:31-32.

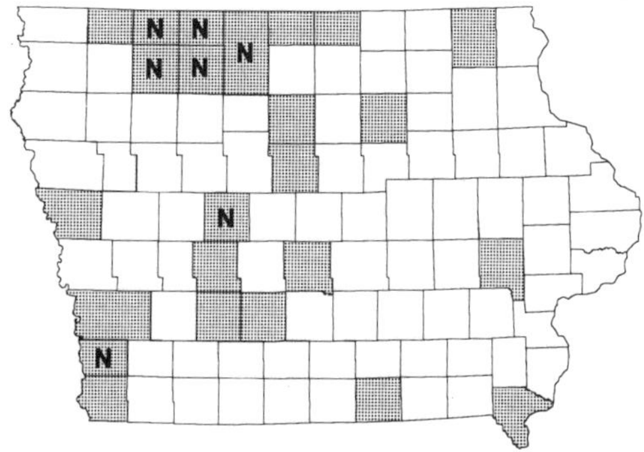

Gadwall, 1960-1995
June-July and nesting (N)

Eurasian Wigeon (*Anas penelope*)

Status: Accidental

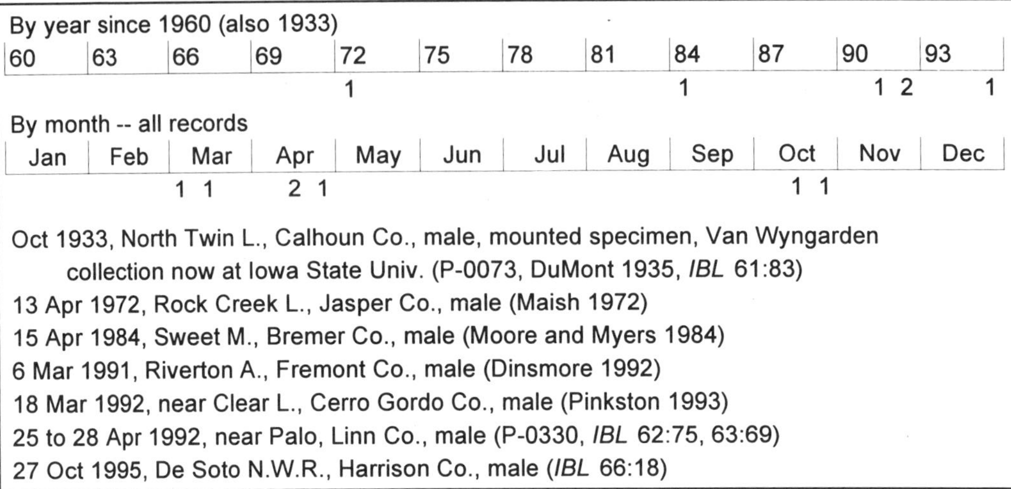

By year since 1960 (also 1933)

60	63	66	69	72	75	78	81	84	87	90	93
				1				1		1 2	1

By month -- all records

Jan	Feb	Mar	Apr	May	Jun	Jul	Aug	Sep	Oct	Nov	Dec
		1 1	2 1						1 1		

Oct 1933, North Twin L., Calhoun Co., male, mounted specimen, Van Wyngarden collection now at Iowa State Univ. (P-0073, DuMont 1935, *IBL* 61:83)
13 Apr 1972, Rock Creek L., Jasper Co., male (Maish 1972)
15 Apr 1984, Sweet M., Bremer Co., male (Moore and Myers 1984)
6 Mar 1991, Riverton A., Fremont Co., male (Dinsmore 1992)
18 Mar 1992, near Clear L., Cerro Gordo Co., male (Pinkston 1993)
25 to 28 Apr 1992, near Palo, Linn Co., male (P-0330, *IBL* 62:75, 63:69)
27 Oct 1995, De Soto N.W.R., Harrison Co., male (*IBL* 66:18)

Occurrence: All 7 records are of single males, 5 from spring and 1 from fall. In addition, on 1 to 2 April 1985, west of Spirit Lake in Dickinson County, LaVonne Foote found 3 male and 2 female Eurasian Wigeon. The Records Committee accepted the identification, but, after receiving conflicting opinions from 2 experts, was undecided as to whether these might be escaped birds (*IBL* 55:61).

Comment: Eurasian Wigeon breeds from Iceland all the way across Europe and Asia and winters to the south in temperate areas. Of the Eurasian waterfowl that visit North America, Eurasian Wigeon is the most common. Some migrate and winter on East and West coasts every year. In the interior, most records are from spring and most are males. It is likely that females are overlooked.

The vagrancy pattern of this species has been known for many years (Hasbrouck 1944), with an apparent increase in the number coming from the west (Edgell 1984). Compared to Iowa, there are many more records along the front range of the Rocky Mountains (Montana, Wyoming, and Colorado) and along the west side of the Great Lakes (Minnesota, Wisconsin, and Illinois). More Iowa records can be expected.

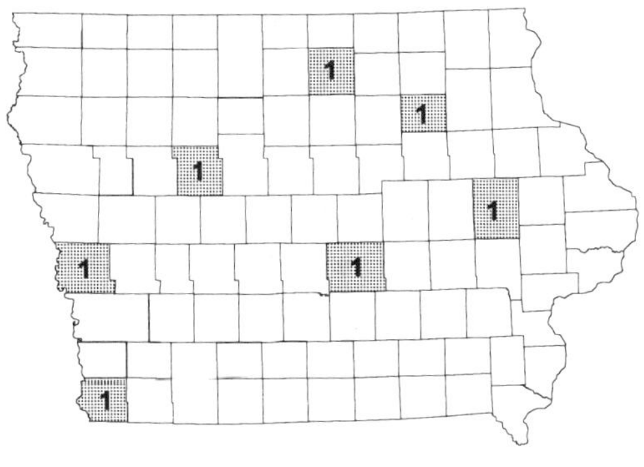

Eurasian Wigeon, all

References:

Dinsmore, S. J. 1992. Eurasian Wigeon at Riverton Wildlife Area. *Iowa Bird Life* 62:83.

DuMont, P. A. 1935. Specimen of European Widgeon taken in northwestern Iowa. *Wilson Bull.* 47:236.

Edgell, M. C. R. 1984. Trans-hemispheric movements of Holarctic Anatidae: The Eurasian Wigeon (*Anas penelope* L.) in North America. *J. Biogeography* 11:27-39.

Hasbrouck, E. M. 1944. Apparent status of the European Widgeon in North America. *Auk* 61:93-104.

Maish, Mrs. J. 1972. European Widgeon in central Iowa. *Iowa Bird Life* 42:49.

Moore, F. L., and B. Myers. 1984. Eurasian Wigeon at Sweet Marsh. *Iowa Bird Life* 54:54.

Pinkston, R. 1993. Eurasian Wigeon in Cerro Gordo County. *Iowa Bird Life* 63:23-24.

American Wigeon (*Anas americana*)

Status: Regular; occasionally nests

Jan	Feb	Mar	Apr	May	Jun	Jul	Aug	Sep	Oct	Nov	Dec

Nesting:

1961, Union Slough N.W.R., Kossuth Co., nest with eggs (Trauger 1962)
1965, Worth Co. (Musgrove and Musgrove 1977)
1982, Willow Sl., Mills Co., female with brood (*IBL* 52:119)
1989, Union Slough N.W.R., Kossuth Co., nest (*IBL* 59:110)
1992, near Graettinger, Palo Alto Co., brood (*IBL* 62:106)
1992, Russ W.A., Winnebago Co., brood (*IBL* 62:106)

Occurrence: This common migrant is most common from mid-March to late May and from early September to late November. Wigeon were reported on Christmas Bird Counts in 31 of 36 years from 1960 to 1995. Most leave by the end of December, although there have been from 1 to 3 reports in mid-winter from 1981 to 1995, but few before that.

A few are found in summer in most years, mainly in northwestern or north-central Iowa, but most of these probably are nonbreeders. Of the 6 confirmed nesting records, 5 are from northern Iowa and 1 from southwestern Iowa.

Comment: The winter range of this New World species is from Middle America and the West Indies north to the southern United States and coastally to southern Alaska and the Maritime Provinces. The breeding range is from central Alaska south and east to northern Nevada and Colorado, South Dakota, and southern Ontario. This species breeds regularly in north-central Minnesota and only sporadically elsewhere in Minnesota and Wisconsin.

Reference:

Trauger, D. L. 1962. American Widgeon nests at Union Slough National Wildlife Refuge. *Iowa Bird Life* 32:26-27.

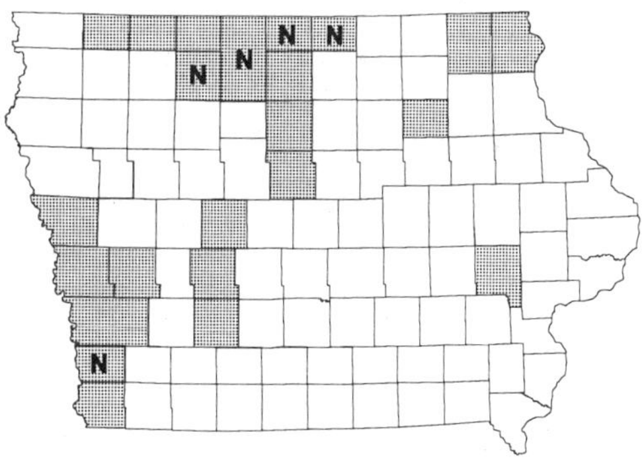

American Wigeon, 1960-1995
June-July and nesting (N)

Canvasback (*Aythya valisineria*)

Status: Regular; occasionally nests

Jan | Feb | Mar | Apr | May | Jun | Jul | Aug | Sep | Oct | Nov | Dec

Occurrence: This common migrant and rare summer resident occurs most commonly from early March to mid-April and from mid-October to late November.

Canvasbacks were not known to nest in Iowa prior to the 1930s (Anderson 1907, DuMont 1933). The first nesting record in 1937 in Clay County was of a nest containing eggs of both Redhead and Canvasback (Bennett 1937). There have been nesting records in 3 or 4 years per decade from the 1960s through the 1990s. From 1962 to 1972, only 1 nest was found at Dewey's Pasture in Clay and Palo Alto counties (Weller 1979).

A few apparently nonbreeding birds are found in summer, usually in June and most often in northwestern or north-central Iowa. From 1980 to 1995, there were 6 reports from July, 3 from August, and none from September. At Pool 19 in Lee County, Canvasbacks arrive in mid-October and peak about 20 November, and peak numbers may exceed 150,000 (Serie et al. 1983).

This species was reported on Christmas Bird Counts in 34 of 36 years from 1960 to 1995, usually along the Mississippi River and especially on pool 19 near Keokuk in Lee County. If the river stays open, those birds may remain well into January. The dynamic nature of their movements is illustrated by counts made near Keokuk in 1992: the 4,000 present on 10 January dwindled to 200 in mid-January but increased to 5,000 in early February and 25,000 by 21 February (*IBL* 62:53). In 1994-1995, counts there showed a similar pattern: 21,000 on 29 December, 1,000 on 30 January, and 10,000 on 2 February (*IBL* 65:47). One at Ottumwa in Wapello County on 7 February 1993 (*IBL* 63:46) was far from its normal winter range.

Comment: The winter range is from southern British Columbia south through the Central Valley of California to southern California and Arizona, and from southeastern Iowa, southern Michigan, western New York, and Connecticut south to the Gulf of Mexico and central Mexico. The breeding range is from central Alaska south and east to northern Nevada, South Dakota, and western Minnesota. Pool 19 in southeastern Iowa is a major migration stopover location for this species.

References:

Bennett, L. J. 1937. Canvasback breeding in Iowa. *Auk* 54:534.

Low, J. B. 1941. Nesting of ruddy duck in Iowa. *Auk* 58:506-517.

Serie, J. R., D. L. Trauger, and D. E. Sharp. 1983. Migration and winter distributions of Canvasbacks staging on the Upper Mississippi River. *J. Wildlife Management* 47: 741-753.

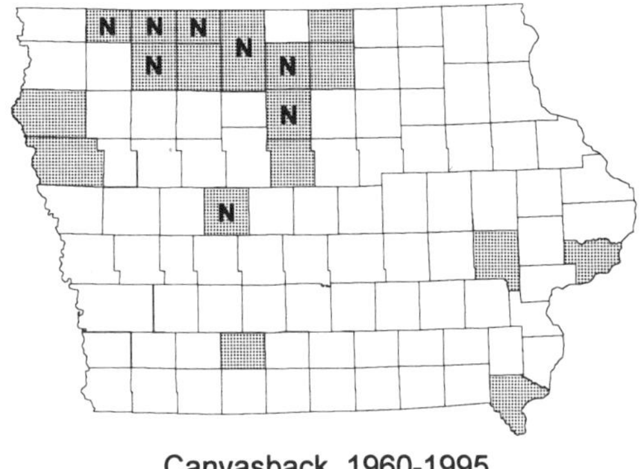

Canvasback, 1960-1995
June-July and nesting (N)

Redhead (*Aythya americana*)

Status: Regular; nests

Jan	Feb	Mar	Apr	May	Jun	Jul	Aug	Sep	Oct	Nov	Dec

Occurrence: This uncommon migrant and rare summer resident is found in migration from early March to mid-May and from late September to mid-November. A few nest regularly in north-central and northwestern Iowa and rarely elsewhere. Nesting begins in early May and peaks in mid- and late June (Low 1940, 1945).

A few remain in Iowa in December. Redheads have been reported on Christmas Bird Counts in 31 of 36 years from 1960 to 1995, mainly along the border rivers. Most depart by late December, and there are only 12 reports from mid-January to mid-February from 1981 to 1996.

A small breeding population was found in Clay County in 1933 (DuMont 1933) that was not known to previous observers (Anderson 1907). Broods were observed in that area in 12 of 13 years from 1962 to 1974 (Weller 1979). Redheads continue to nest regularly in northwestern and north-central Iowa and occasionally in southwestern Iowa. In June 1995, 26 pairs were seen at Spring Run Wildlife Area in Dickinson County (*IBL* 65:96).

Comment: The winter range is from central California, northern Arizona and New Mexico, southeastern Iowa, Lake Erie, and Connecticut south to southern Mexico. The breeding range is from northern Alberta and Saskatchewan south to northwestern Iowa, southern Colorado, northern Utah, and the Central Valley of California. Iowa is at the southeastern corner of its breeding range.

References:

Low, J. B. 1940. Production of the Redhead (*Nyroca americana*) in Iowa. *Wilson Bull.* 52:153-164.

Low, J. B. 1945. Ecology and management of the Redhead, *Nyroca americana*, in Iowa. *Ecological Monographs* 15:35-69.

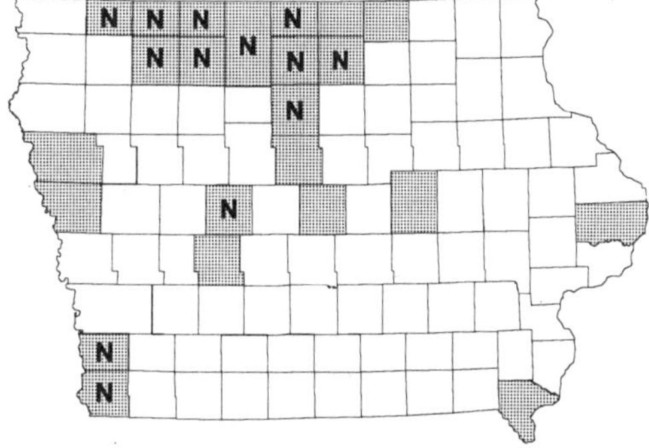

Redhead, 1960-1995
June-July and nesting (N)

Ring-necked Duck (*Aythya collaris*)

Status: Regular; occasionally nests

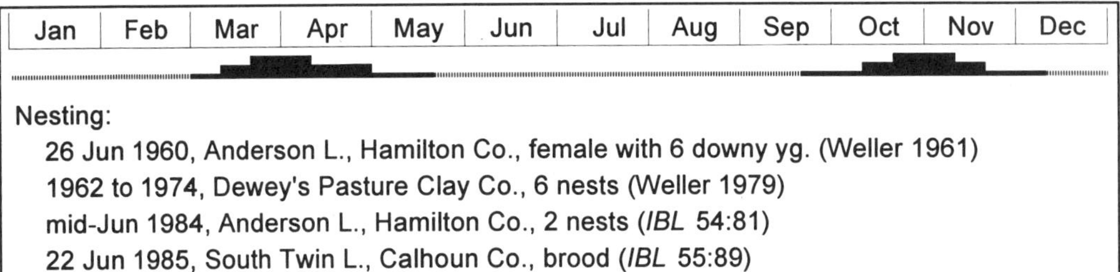

Nesting:

26 Jun 1960, Anderson L., Hamilton Co., female with 6 downy yg. (Weller 1961)
1962 to 1974, Dewey's Pasture Clay Co., 6 nests (Weller 1979)
mid-Jun 1984, Anderson L., Hamilton Co., 2 nests (*IBL* 54:81)
22 Jun 1985, South Twin L., Calhoun Co., brood (*IBL* 55:89)

Occurrence: This common migrant and rare summer resident is found in migration from early March to mid-May and from late September to early December. A few remain into December. This species was reported on Christmas Bird Counts in 29 of 36 years from 1960 to 1995, most commonly along the border rivers. Most leave by late December, but a few over-winter in most years, especially along the Mississippi River in southeastern Iowa. These birds may leave and return during mid-winter thaws, such as the 100 that appeared in Lee County on 24 January 1986 (*IBL* 56:58).

A few, mostly nonbreeders, are found in Iowa in most summers, but occasionally nest. There are records of 10 nests in 4 years from 3 locations, all since 1960. There is an old indefinite reference to nesting at Clear Lake in Cerro Gordo County ca. 1884 (Cooke 1888).

Comment: The winter range is from the southern United States north coastally to Alaska and New England and south to the West Indies and Middle America. It extends north along the Mississippi River to southern Missouri. The breeding range is in the northern United States, the Canadian provinces, Mackenzie, and locally in eastern Alaska. The breeding range of Ring-necked Duck in Minnesota extends almost to the southern border, and it is the third most common nesting duck in that state (Janssen 1987). Compared to the Lesser Scaup, Ring-necked Ducks tend to inhabit marshes more than open lakes.

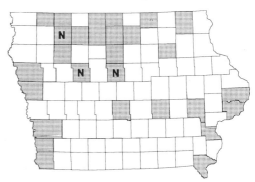

Ring-necked Duck, 1960-1995
June-July and nesting (N)

Greater Scaup (*Aythya marila*)

Status: Regular

Jan	Feb	Mar	Apr	May	Jun	Jul	Aug	Sep	Oct	Nov	Dec
				x	x x	x			xx x		

24 May 1990 — 5 Oct 1987
6 Jun 1982 — 10 Oct 1945
15 Jun 1988 — 13 Oct 1985

Summer: 9 Jul 1988

Occurrence: This rare migrant and winter resident has been reported every year from 1975 to 1995, but only rarely before that. Reports averaged over 10 per year from 1984 to 1995. Most records are from November to early January and March to mid-April, with a few earlier and later.

A few were reported on Christmas Bird Counts in 11 of 13 years from 1983 to 1985, but in only 3 years from 1960 to 1982. A few migrants are found in early January and late February, and from 1983 to 1995 there were 11 reports from mid-January to mid-February.

The only June and July records are 2 at New Lake in Woodbury County on 6 June 1982 (*IBL* 52:89), 1 at the Power Plant ponds in Pottawattamie County from 9 to 15 June 1988 (*IBL* 58:108), and 1 on the Mississippi River near Montrose in Lee County on 1, 9 July 1988 (*IBL* 58:108).

Although early observers considered this species common (Anderson 1907), a later observer found only 1 specimen and considered it to be a rare migrant (DuMont 1933). Two old nest reports (Anderson 1907) are likely incorrect. As birders have become familiar with the field characteristics of this species and have been able to identify it (Kent and Shires 1979, Kaufman 1990), it has been reported far more frequently, although it is still rare and difficult to identify.

Comment: In North America, the winter range of this Holarctic species is along the Pacific Coast from southern Alaska to southern California, along the Atlantic Coast from Newfoundland to Florida, and, to a much lesser extent, along the Gulf Coast. It also winters on the southern Great Lakes and north in the Mississippi and Ohio river valleys to central Missouri and southern Ohio. The breeding range is from Alaska east to Hudson Bay. It also nests in Iceland and northern Eurasia.

Reference:

Kent, T. H., and T. K. Shires. 1979. Greater Scaup in Iowa—a challenge. *Iowa Bird Life* 49:35-39.

Lesser Scaup (*Aythya affinis*)

Status: Regular; occasionally nests

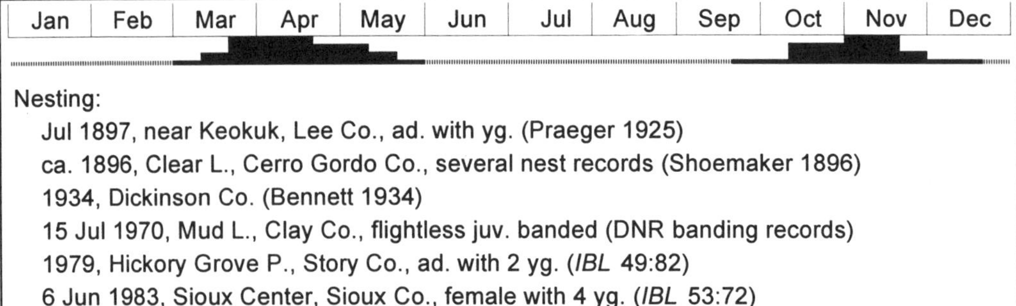

Nesting:

Jul 1897, near Keokuk, Lee Co., ad. with yg. (Praeger 1925)
ca. 1896, Clear L., Cerro Gordo Co., several nest records (Shoemaker 1896)
1934, Dickinson Co. (Bennett 1934)
15 Jul 1970, Mud L., Clay Co., flightless juv. banded (DNR banding records)
1979, Hickory Grove P., Story Co., ad. with 2 yg. (*IBL* 49:82)
6 Jun 1983, Sioux Center, Sioux Co., female with 4 yg. (*IBL* 53:72)

Occurrence: This species, the most abundant migrant diving duck in Iowa, is most common from early March to late May and from late September to mid-December. Spring migrants often linger into early June and occasionally spend the summer, but there are only 6 definite nesting records spread over 86 years.

In 1969, large numbers arrived on Pool 19 in Lee County in late October, and peak numbers were present in early November (Thornburg 1973). In late fall, birds often linger into December. Some are reported on Christmas Bird Counts every year, most commonly along the Mississippi River. Most of those birds leave in late December or early January, and some return by late February. From 1983 to 1996, reports from mid-January to mid-February averaged 2 per year and included birds on the Mississippi River in southeastern Iowa and birds wintering with Mallard flocks. The largest mid-winter concentration was 300 on the Mississippi River at Montrose in Lee County on 31 January 1988 (*IBL* 58:54).

Comment: The winter range is from British Columbia east to Massachusetts and south to the West Indies and northern South America. Southeastern Iowa is on the northern edge of the winter range. The breeding range is from central Alaska and the western shore of Hudson Bay south to southern British Columbia, Montana, and northeastern South Dakota. The regular nesting range is much farther from Iowa than for Ring-necked Duck, but there are occasional nest records to the east and south of the normal range. For such an abundant species, it is not surprising that nonbreeding birds would linger into summer. Molting Lesser Scaup and Ring-necked Ducks can be very difficult to distinguish from each other.

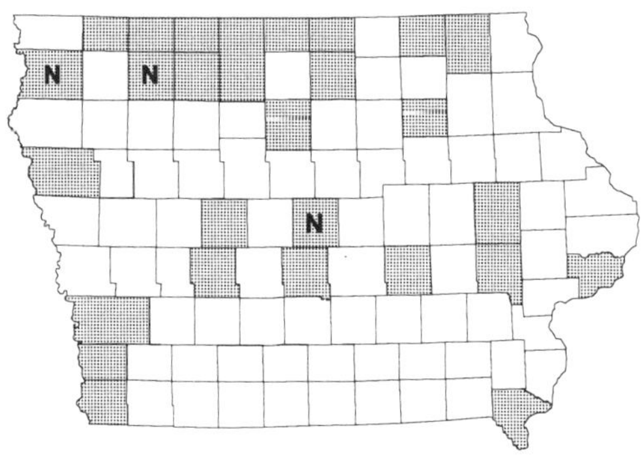

Lesser Scaup
June-July 1960-1995, all nesting (N)

Common Eider (*Somateria mollissima*)

Status: Accidental

1 Nov 1901, near Sioux City, Woodbury Co. (DuMont 1934)
27 Jan to 7 Apr 1995, Red Rock Res., Marion Co., female (P-0442, P-0443, *IBL* 65:47, 71)

Occurrence: The first record is Accepted as a sight record based on DuMont's examination of a specimen, now missing. DuMont records only a few bits of description along with notes and measurements made by Guy Rich. Rich listed it as a male (Anderson 1907), but DuMont described it as "in low plumage" (DuMont 1933). DuMont's re-examination of the specimen convinced him that it was not a King Eider and was of the Pacific subspecies, *S. m. v-nigra.*

The second record was of a female present from mid-winter to early spring below the dam at Red Rock Reservoir in Marion County. Photographs allowed identification as *S. m. v-nigra* based on bill characteristics.

Four other reports are Not Accepted (Dinsmore et al. 1984).

Comment: Common Eider is a bird of the Arctic and Subarctic coasts from Maine and southern Alaska northward. It also occurs in northern Europe and eastern Siberia. Subspecies may be determined on the basis of bill shape. The Iowa records are of the subspecies *S. m. v-nigra,* which breeds from eastern Siberia to western Canada. Three more of the 6 races are found in North America: *S. m. borealis* in Baffinland and Greenland, *S. m. dresseri* on the Atlantic Coast, and *S. m. sedenteria* in Hudson Bay. Although the Common Eider breeds farther south coastally than King Eider, it is much less frequent as a vagrant to the interior. Vagrants occur down the East Coast, to the Great Lakes, and rarely farther west to Kansas, Nebraska, South Dakota, North Dakota, and Iowa. There are no records in United States west of the central Great Plains states and south of Alaska. Dates for vagrants are spread evenly from October to April, except for November, which has about half of the records.

Eiders do not visit the Midwest in bright male breeding plumage. Determining the age, sex, and species (Common vs. King) may be quite difficult and demands a close look, photographs, or a specimen. Head shape and bill characteristics are particularly important.

Reference:

DuMont, P. 1934. Iowa specimen of the "American Eider" re-determined as the Pacific Eider. *Wilson Bull.* 46:203.

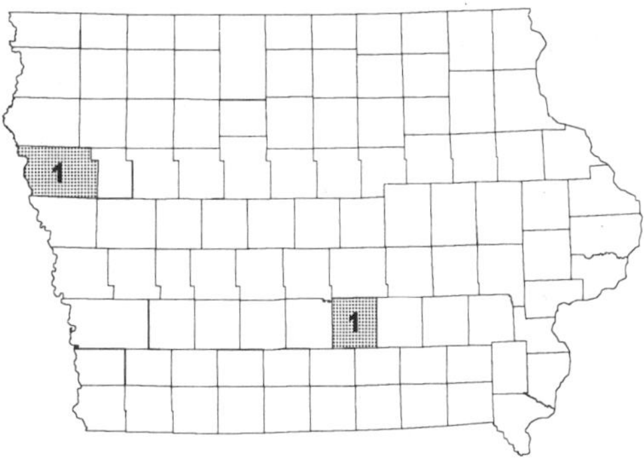

Common Eider, all

King Eider (*Somateria spectabilis*)

Status: Accidental

By year since 1960

60	63	66	69	72	75	78	81	84	87	90	93
			1 1					1 1			

By month -- all records

Jan	Feb	Mar	Apr	May	Jun	Jul	Aug	Sep	Oct	Nov	Dec
										3 1 +	

8 Nov 1970, L. Odessa, Louisa Co., female or imm. (Univ. of Iowa specimen #33585, Newlon and Kent 1981)

8 Nov 1971, Ingham L., Emmet Co., imm. female, status of mounted specimen unknown (P-0226, Petersen 1972, Kent 1987)

10 to 24 Nov 1985, De Soto N.W.R., Harrison Co., imm. male and imm. female (P-0194, Kent 1987)

17 Nov 1986, Clear L., Cerro Gordo Co., second-year male, imm. female (Iowa State Univ. specimens #2386, P-0206, Hansen 1987, Kent 1987)

Occurrence: The 4 records are from November and involve 6 immature birds. There are 2 Not Accepted records of specimens taken on the Mississippi River that could be either Iowa or Illinois records: a first-winter male shot opposite the city of Keokuk on 10 November 1894 (University of Iowa specimen #25003, P-0050, Praeger 1925) and an immature male shot on the "outer basin" of the Mississippi near New Boston, Illinois (Putnam Museum specimen examined by Morrissey, Morrissey 1951).

Comment: This Holarctic species breeds across the High Arctic and winters coastally about as far south as Common Eiders breed. Some birds, especially immatures, migrate farther south along the East and West coasts and a few have even reached the Gulf Coast. Most Midwest records are from the Great Lakes, but a few have reached Iowa, Nebraska, and Kansas. Dates range from October to May, with about two-thirds in November and December.

Juvenal plumage is retained into fall. Juveniles and females are best identified by head shape and bill characteristics, which require a close view, photographs, or a specimen. First-year males develop white fronts and light-colored bills by mid-winter and retain this appearance at least into the second year.

References:

Hansen, J. L. 1987. King Eiders at Clear Lake. *Iowa Bird Life* 57:94.

Kent, T. H. 1987. Eiders in Iowa. *Iowa Bird Life* 57:88-93.

Morrissey, T. 1951. Another Iowa record of the King Eider. *Iowa Bird Life* 21:41-42.

Newlon, M. C., and T. H. Kent. 1981. Fifth record of the King Eider for Iowa. *Iowa Bird Life* 51:126-129.

Petersen, P. C. 1972. Another King Eider record for Iowa. *Iowa Bird Life* 42:50.

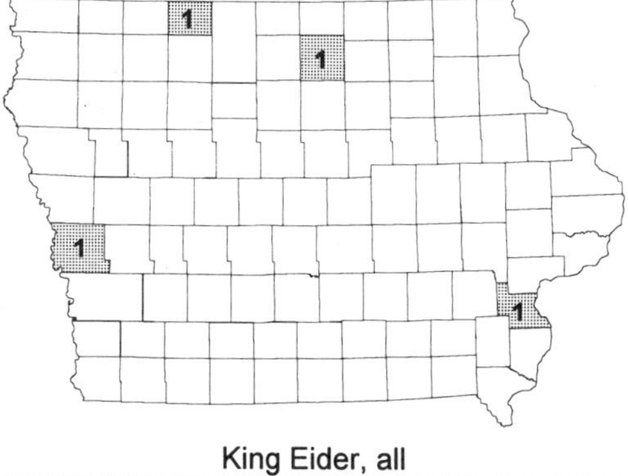

King Eider, all

Harlequin Duck (*Histrionicus histrionicus*)

Status: Accidental

27 Dec 1932, near Adelphi, Polk Co., alternate male, State Historical Museum specimen now missing (DuMont 1934)
31 Oct 1976, Big Creek L., Polk Co. (State Historical Museum specimen, P-0138, Musgrove and Musgrove 1977).

Occurrence: The 2 records are from central Iowa in fall. There are 5 other old reports with insufficient documentation (Dinsmore et al. 1984).

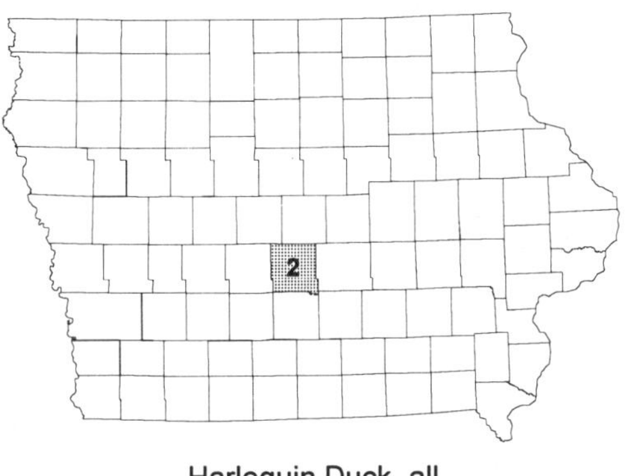

Harlequin Duck, all

Comment: This species breeds along mountain streams and rocky coasts from eastern Siberia to Yellowstone Park and from Iceland to the Gaspe Peninsula, and winters coastally south to California and North Carolina. A few are found on the Great Lakes each winter. This species has been found in most eastern and western mountainous states and rarely in plains states including Iowa, Missouri, and Nebraska. Most records are from October to January and March to April.

Reference:

DuMont, P. A. 1934. The Western Harlequin Duck in central Iowa. *Wilson Bull.* 46:63-64.

Oldsquaw (*Clangula hyemalis*)

Status: Regular

By year since 1960

60	63	66	69	72	75	78	81	84	87	90	93

1 2 1 1 1 3 2 1 1 1 1 3 1 1 1 4 6 3 2 7 4 7 8 9 8 9 9 8 8 8 13

Jan	Feb	Mar	Apr	May	Jun	Jul	Aug	Sep	Oct	Nov	Dec
				x		x			x		

7 May 1996 — 11 Oct 1985

8 May 1992 — 24 Oct 1959

12 May 1992 — 24 Oct 1987

Summer: 29 Jul 1990

Occurrence: This rare migrant and winter resident is found from late October to early May. It has been seen every year from 1978 to 1995, with an average of 9 reports per year from 1986 to 1995. Prior to 1978 it was reported in most but not all years, with 0 to 3 per year. Just over half of the reports are from November and December.

There are a number of winter reports including several birds that seemed to be wintering: 2 on the Mississippi River in Lee County on 16 February 1995 (*IBL* 65:47), 1 at Red Rock Reservoir in Marion County from 24 December 1992 to 30 January 1993 (*IBL* 63:47), 3 at Saylorville Reservoir in Polk County from 3 December 1988 to 4 February 1989 (*IBL* 59:50), 1 at Red Rock Reservoir in Marion County from 19 December 1982 to 14 January 1983 (*IBL* 53:24), and 1 at Cherokee in Cherokee County in 1995-1996 (*IBL* 66:55). Other late winter birds at Sandusky in Lee County on 15 February 1992 (*IBL* 62:53), near Burlington in Des Moines County on 9 February 1986 (*IBL* 56:58), and 3 at Saylorville Reservoir on 16 February 1990 (*IBL* 60:51) may have been early migrants or previously undetected wintering birds. The only summer record is 1 at Rice Lake in Winnebago County on 29 July 1990 (*IBL* 60:102), which probably was the same bird present there on 11 May (*IBL* 60:66).

Most reports are from large lakes, reservoirs, and the Mississippi River. Most are immatures but rarely a male in bright winter plumage is seen.

Comment: In North America, the winter range of this Holarctic species is coastal from the Bering Sea to central California and from Greenland south to North Carolina and inland on the Great Lakes and sporadically elsewhere. The breeding range is along the coastal plain of Alaska and northern Canada east to Labrador and Greenland. It also breeds on Iceland and across northern Eurasia.

Black Scoter (*Melanitta nigra*)

Status: Regular

By year since 1960

60	63	66	69	72	75	78	81	84	87	90	93

1 4 1 2 1 1 2 1 1 2 4 6 2 8 3 1 3 5 6 4

Jan	Feb	Mar	Apr	May	Jun	Jul	Aug	Sep	Oct	Nov	Dec
	x		x x x	x					xx		x

30 Mar 1991	13 Apr 1994	12 Oct 1994	18 Dec 1993
30 Mar 1996	25 Apr 1992	16 Oct 1989	20 Dec 1986
31 Mar 1979	19 May 1989	24 Oct 1995	26 Dec 1959

winter: 15 Feb 1948

Occurrence: This rare migrant is found from late October through mid-December. There are only 7 spring reports. The winter report from 15 February 1948 at Credit Island in Scott County involved 2 males and a female (Hodges 1948).

This is the least common of the 3 scoters in Iowa. It has been seen every year from 1983 to 1995 with an average of 4 reports per year from 1986 to 1995. From 1960 to 1982 it was reported in only 7 of 23 years. Most reports are of birds in immature/female plumage, but an occasional adult male is noted.

The first documented record is based on a specimen at the Putnam Museum that was taken on the Mississippi River in Louisa County on 23 November 1952 (Morrissey 1954). There are about 12 previous reports (Dinsmore et al. 1984). Other specimens include 1 from Willow Slough in Mills County from 4 November 1960 (University of Iowa #33207) and 1 from Big Creek Lake in Polk County (Iowa State University #2393, Dinsmore 1992).

Comment: In North America, the winter range of this Holarctic sea duck is from southern Alaska to southern California, from Newfoundland to Florida, and on the Great Lakes. The breeding range is in western Alaska and in northern Quebec and western Labrador. The increased number of reports of this species may be due to increased observer effort and to the increased number of lakes and reservoirs; however, there were few reports of this species in Wisconsin prior to 1935 (Robbins 1991). Nearby states also have few spring records.

References:

Hodges, J. 1949. Notes on the bird life in the Mississippi Valley. *Proc. Iowa Acad. Sci.* 56:343-345.

Morrissey, T. 1954. Another record for the American Scoter in Iowa. *Iowa Bird Life* 24:15.

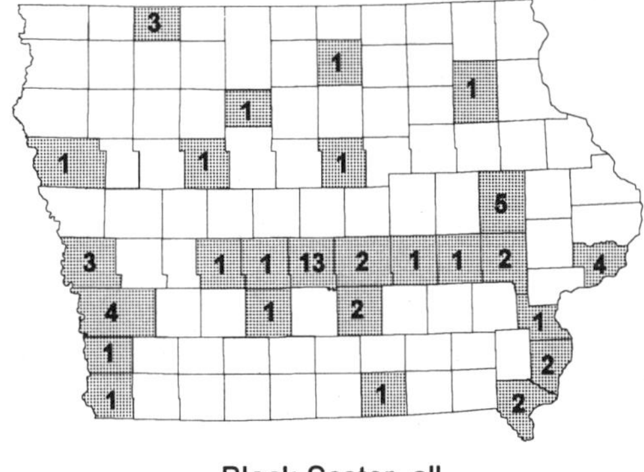

Black Scoter, all

Surf Scoter (*Melanitta perspicillata*)

Status: Regular

Jan	Feb	Mar	Apr	May	Jun	Jul	Aug	Sep	Oct	Nov	Dec
		x x	x	x				x			

14 Mar 1986	19 May 1975	23 Sep 1991	17 Dec 1994
28 Mar 1893	19 May 1972	2 Oct 1988	20 Dec 1994
9 Apr 1984	22 May 1988	5 Oct 1980	20 Dec 1992

Occurrence: This rare migrant is found from mid-April to mid-May and October to mid-December, with fall records outnumbering spring records by almost 3 to 1. Fall birds are most commonly found on large bodies of water. More than half of the spring records are from early and mid-May, and many of these records are from small ponds and marshes. There are more spring records for Surf Scoter than for the other scoters, and it is the only scoter with a preponderance of spring records from May. Most reports are of birds in immature/female plumage.

This species has been seen every year from 1983 to 1995, with an average of 6 reports per year from 1986 to 1995. From 1960 to 1982 it was reported in 11 of 23 years.

Prior to 1960, there are scattered records in each decade, and 8 specimens were mentioned by DuMont (1933). The first specimen was from Burlington in Des Moines County from 28 March 1893 (University of Iowa #16077, Anderson 1907). There are 6 specimens at Iowa State University (Dinsmore 1992) and 4 at the University of Iowa (THK).

Comment: The winter range of this New World species is mainly coastal from the Aleutian Islands south to Baja California, from Nova Scotia to Florida, and to a lesser extent on the Great Lakes and Gulf Coast. The breeding range is from central Alaska south and east through northern British Columbia, Alberta, and Saskatchewan to Hudson Bay. It also nests in eastern Quebec and western Labrador.

A gradual increase in the number of reports has also been noted in Wisconsin (Robbins 1991). Spring birds in northern and western Wisconsin (away from Lake Michigan) tend to be found in May rather than April.

White-winged Scoter (*Melanitta fusca*)

Status: Regular

Jan	Feb	Mar	Apr	May	Jun	Jul	Aug	Sep	Oct	Nov	Dec
x x	x	xx x		x x xx	x				x		

14 Mar 1987	22 May 1994	8 Oct 1932	27 Dec 1975
16 Mar 1980	24 May 1996	12 Oct 1985	27 Dec 1969
23 Mar 1977	5 Jun 1988	12 Oct 1994	29 Dec 1984
winter: 12 to 16 Jan 1991, 26 Jan 1975, 21 Feb 1987			

Occurrence: This rare migrant is most common (85 percent of reports) in fall from mid-October to late December. Spring records are scattered from mid-March to late May, with 1 lingering to 5 June 1988 on the Mississippi River in Lee County (*IBL* 58:108). Mid-winter reports are from Keokuk in Lee County on 26 January 1975 (*IBL* 45:21), from Davenport in Scott County from 12 to 16 January 1991 (*IBL* 61:55), and from Rathbun Reservoir in Appanoose County on 21 February 1987 (*IBL*

57:54). Most of the reports involve birds in immature/female plumage.

White-winged Scoter is the most common of the scoters. It has been seen every year from 1977 to 1995 with an average of 7 reports per year from 1986 to 1995. From 1960 to 1976 it was reported in only 3 of 17 years. Historically, this species was also the most common of the scoters (Anderson 1907, DuMont 1933).

Comment: In North America, the winter range of this Holarctic species is from the Aleutian Islands south to Baja California, from Newfoundland to North Carolina, and on the Great Lakes. The breeding range is from central Alaska south and east to southern British Columbia, southern Saskatchewan, southern Manitoba, and western Ontario.

Common Goldeneye (*Bucephala clangula*)

Status: Regular

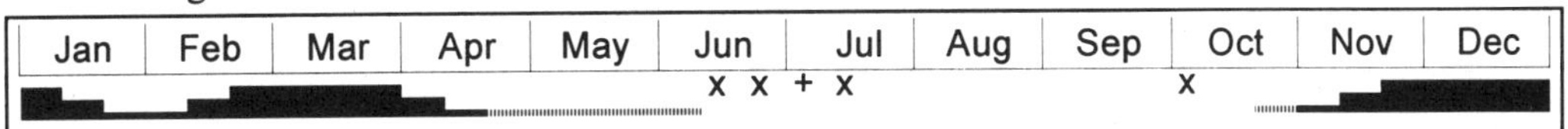

Jan	Feb	Mar	Apr	May	Jun	Jul	Aug	Sep	Oct	Nov	Dec
					x x	+ x			x		

10 Jun 1986	8 Oct 1981
13 Jun 1990	24 Oct 1980
20 Jun 1990	25 Oct 1994

Summer: 16 Jun to 17 Jul 1982

Occurrence: This common migrant and winter resident arrives in early November and departs in mid-April. More than most other ducks, it is found on the large rivers and reservoirs. The only summer records are 1 at Davenport in Scott County from 16 June to 17 July 1982 (*IBL* 52:89), 1 at Dunbar Slough in Greene County until 10 June 1986 (*IBL* 56:84), 1 until 20 June 1990 at Cardinal Marsh in Winneshiek County (*IBL* 60:102), 1 until 13 June 1990 at Union Slough National Wildlife Refuge in Kossuth County (*IBL* 60:102), and 1 on 4 June 1991 at Princeton Marsh in Scott County (*IBL* 61:114). Goldeneyes regularly stay in Iowa until the last open water freezes, and many over-winter, most commonly along the Mississippi River in Scott County south of the nuclear power plant at Cordova, Illinois. The largest wintering concentration was 3,250 at Montrose in Lee County on 29 January 1995 (*IBL* 65:47). Common Goldeneyes are reported on Christmas Bird Counts every year.

Comment: In North America, the winter range of this Holarctic species is from the Aleutian Islands and southeastern Alaska to southern California, from the Maritime Provinces to the Gulf Coast, along the Great Lakes, and in most of continental United States to northern Mexico. The breeding range is across the Canadian provinces and extends into northern states, the Northwest Territories, and central Alaska.

Barrow's Goldeneye (*Bucephala islandica*)

Status: Accidental

Jan	Feb	Mar	Apr	May	Jun	Jul	Aug	Sep	Oct	Nov	Dec
1		1 1 +	+							1 1	1 1

7 Mar to 6 Apr 1984, Forney L., Fremont Co., male (P-0163, Silcock 1984)
14 Mar 1987, De Soto N.W.R., Harrison Co., male (*IBL* 57:81, 58:75, 64:69)
2 to 6 Jan 1989, De Soto N.W.R., Harrison Co., male (P-0276, Silcock 1989)
12 to 15 Nov 1989, Power Plant Ponds, Pottawattamie Co., male (Grenon 1990)
27 to 28 Nov 1994, Terra L., Johnston, Polk Co., male (P-0434, *IBL* 65:12)
9 Dec 1995, Red Rock Res., Marion Co., male (*IBL 66:55*)
18 Dec 1995, Montrose, Lee Co., male (*IBL* 66:55)

Occurrence: Of the 2 spring and 5 fall/winter records, 4 are from western, 2 from central, and 1 from eastern Iowa. Five old records are unsubstantiated or incorrect (Dinsmore et al. 1984).

Comment: This species breeds on lakes and ponds from central Alaska to northwestern Wyoming and from northeastern Quebec to Iceland, wintering coastally south to central California and to New York and locally in the interior of western North America. Most Midwest records are from the Great Lakes, but some are reported inland. Most vagrants are seen from November to March with a few from April to May.

Males are easily identified by the white facial crescent, steep forehead, and black wing coverts enclosing a series of white spots that extend anteriorly to the water line. Females should be separated with caution from Common Goldeneye, but may be identified by head and bill shape, especially when the 2 species are together. Female Barrow's Goldeneyes from the western population often have all-yellow bills, but this feature can occasionally be seen on a female Common Goldeneye. Hybrids with Common Goldeneye are also possible to identify (Martin and Di Labio 1994).

References:

Grenon, A. G. 1990. Barrow's Goldeneye in Pottawattamie County. *Iowa Bird Life* 60:74.

Martin, P. R., and B. M. Di Labio. 1994. Identification of Common x Barrow's Goldeneye hybrids in the field. *Birding* 26:104-105.

Silcock, W. R. 1984. Barrow's Goldeneye in Fremont Co. Iowa and an analysis of interior vagrancy patterns. *Iowa Bird Life* 54:75-77.

Silcock, W. R. 1989. Barrow's Goldeneye at De Soto N.W.R. *Iowa Bird Life* 59:89-90.

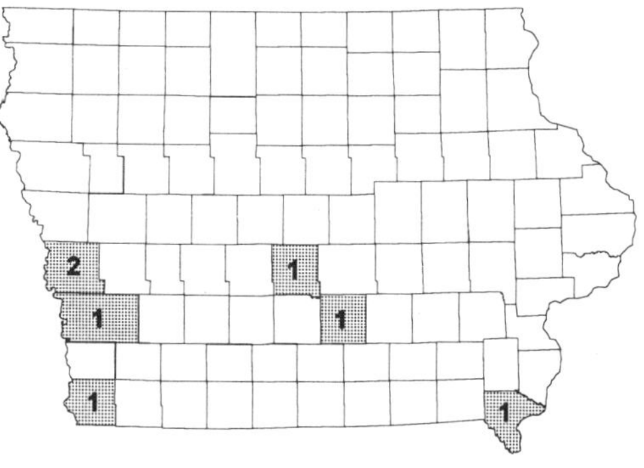

Barrow's Goldeneye, all

Bufflehead (*Bucephala albeola*)

Status: Regular; occasionally nests

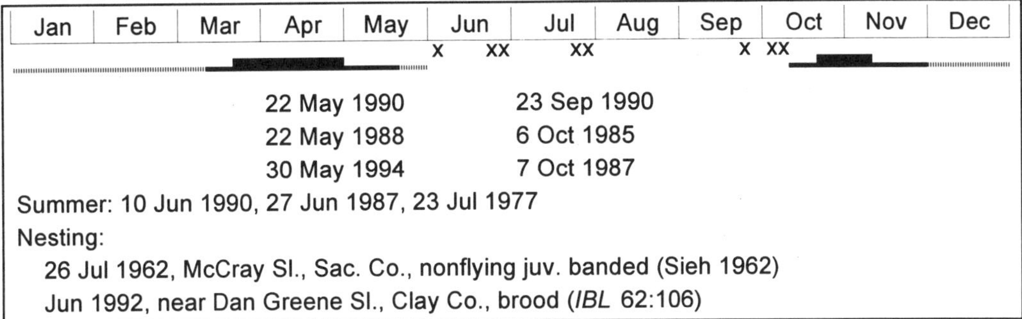

Occurrence: This common migrant is found from mid-March to mid-May and from mid-October to late November. A few linger into December every year. There were reports on Christmas Bird Counts in 28 of 36 years from 1960 to 1995, most commonly along the Mississippi River. Most of these depart in late December or early January. From 1981 to 1995, there were 8 reports from mid-January to mid-February.

Beside the 2 breeding records, there are 3 other summer records: 23 July 1977 at Goose Lake in Clinton County (*IBL* 47:100), 27 June 1987 near Brandon in Buchanan County (*IBL* 57:119), and until 10 June 1990 at West Okoboji in Dickinson County (injured bird, *IBL* 60:102).

Comment: The winter range is from the Aleutian Islands south to Baja California, Nova Scotia south to central Florida, and across the southern United States and north centrally to northern Illinois, southern Michigan, and Lake Erie. The breeding range is from central Alaska south to the southern border of Canada and northern Montana. Iowa is far south of the usual breeding range.

Reference:

Sieh, J. 1962. Bufflehead breeding in Iowa. *Iowa Bird Life* 32:85.

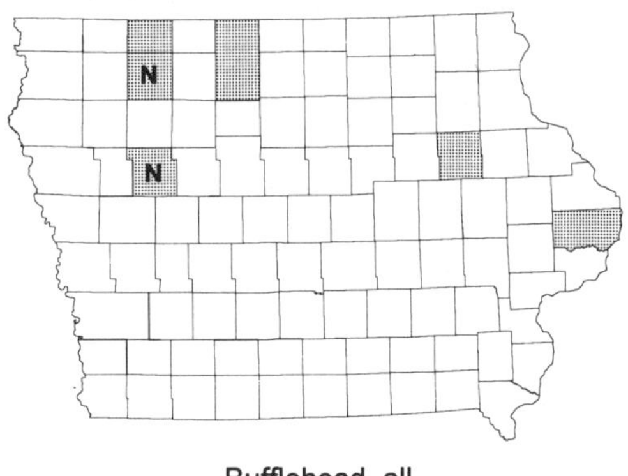

Bufflehead, all
June-July and nesting (N)

Hooded Merganser (*Lophodytes cucullatus*)

Status: Regular; nests

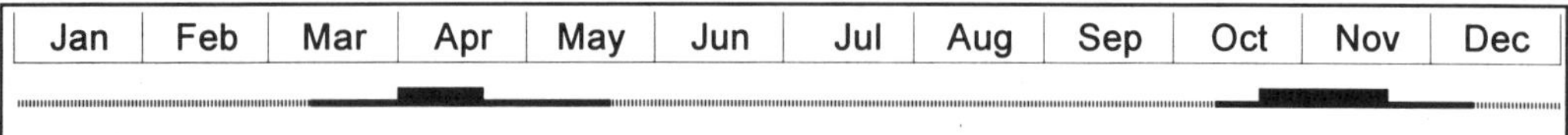

Occurrence: This uncommon migrant and rare summer and winter resident is most commonly found from mid-March to mid-May and from mid-October to early December. It is a rare summer resident throughout Iowa, most commonly in the flooded timber along the Mississippi River. There is also a small population nesting in Wood Duck nest boxes at Union Slough National Wildlife Refuge in Kossuth County.

A few regularly linger into December. Hooded Mergansers were reported on Christmas Bird Counts in 31 of 36 years from 1960 to 1995, with the most along the Mississippi River. A few over-winter, again most commonly along the Mississippi River or at urban lakes that receive warm-water outflows, such as Cedar Lake in Linn County and Terra Lake in Polk County.

Historically, this species was considered to be a fairly common migrant and rare nester with few specific nesting records (Anderson 1907, DuMont 1933). More recently, it has probably benefited from the nest boxes provided for Wood Ducks.

Comment: The winter range is mainly in coastal states from southeastern Alaska to southern California and from New England to Texas. The western population breeds from Oregon to southeastern Alaska, and the eastern population breeds from Arkansas north to Manitoba and east to the Maritime Provinces. Iowa lies on the west edge of the eastern population's range.

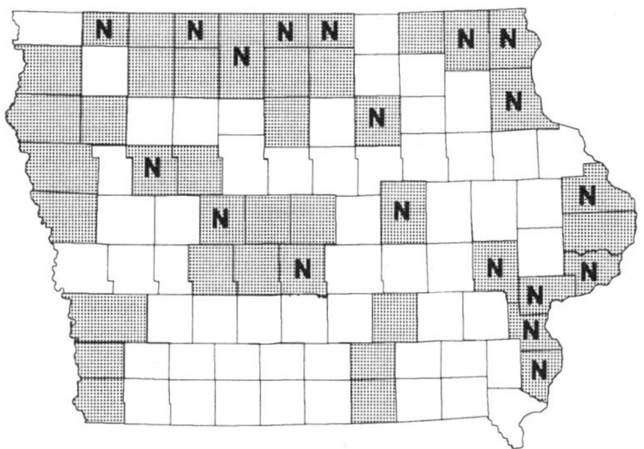

Hooded Merganser, 1960-1995
June-July and nesting (N)

Common Merganser (*Mergus merganser*)

Status: Regular

Jan | Feb | Mar | Apr | May | Jun | Jul | Aug | Sep | Oct | Nov | Dec

x + + xx   x x

5 Aug 1995   19 Oct 1988
10 Sep 1995   28 Oct 1991
10 Sep 1965   4 Nov 1995

Occurrence: This common migrant and winter resident arrives in November and departs by early May. Occasional birds straggle into early June, and there are 12 reports from mid-June to early September.

Iowa is near the northern edge of this species' wintering range and thus wintering populations fluctuate almost daily with changing ice conditions. For example, the 10,000 at Red Rock Reservoir in Marion County on 1 January 1995 had declined to 500 on 4 January and all departed soon thereafter (*IBL* 65:47). That same year, 600 were on the Mississippi River at Montrose in Lee County on 29 January but 3,000 were present on 2 February (*IBL* 65:47).

This species is apparently more common than it once was (Anderson 1907, DuMont 1933), probably because of the more extensive open water below the locks and dams on the Mississippi River and on the large reservoirs, where large numbers congregate in late fall and open water allows birds to over-winter.

Comment: In North America, the winter range of this Holarctic species includes most of the continental United States and parts of northern Mexico and southern Canada. The breeding range covers most of the Canadian provinces, the northern parts of the eastern United States, and in the West extends north to southern Alaska and south to New Mexico. In winter, unlike the Red-breasted Merganser, this species favors freshwater habitat on rivers, large lakes, and reservoirs.

Red-breasted Merganser (*Mergus serrator*)

Status: Regular

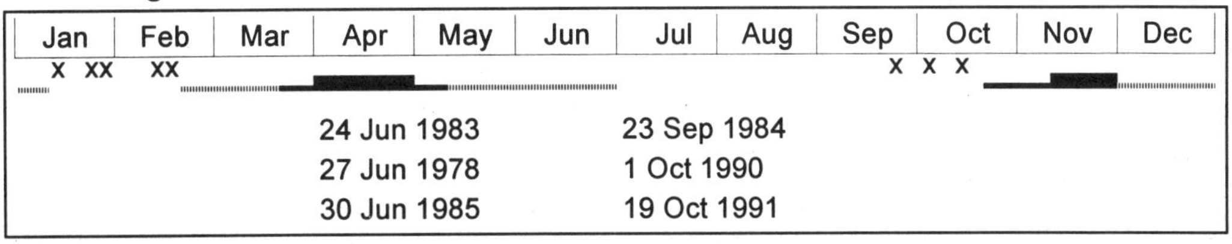

Jan	Feb	Mar	Apr	May	Jun	Jul	Aug	Sep	Oct	Nov	Dec
X XX	XX							X	X X		
			24 Jun 1983			23 Sep 1984					
			27 Jun 1978			1 Oct 1990					
			30 Jun 1985			19 Oct 1991					

Occurrence: This uncommon migrant is most common from late March to early May and from late October to late November. This species is the least likely of the 3 mergansers to be found in winter. On Christmas Bird Counts, it has been found in 30 of 36 years from 1960 to 1995, most commonly along the Mississippi River. There are 6 reports from mid-January to mid-February. There are no reports of birds remaining throughout the summer, but there are 10 reports from June.

Comment: In North America, the winter range of this Holarctic species is mainly on the coasts from the Aleutian Islands to Baja California and from the Maritime Provinces to the Gulf Coast. The breeding range includes Alaska and northern Canada, and in the east dipping south to the Great Lakes.

Ruddy Duck (*Oxyura jamaicensis*)

Status: Regular; nests

Jan	Feb	Mar	Apr	May	Jun	Jul	Aug	Sep	Oct	Nov	Dec

xx x xx

18 Feb 1996	2 Jan 1995
20 Feb 1994	3 Jan 1987
22 Feb 1992	6 Jan 1995

winter: 23 Jan 1996, 29 Jan 1995, 1 Feb 1996

Occurrence: This common migrant and rare summer resident arrives in mid-March and departs by early December. A few regularly nest in marshes with thick emergent vegetation in northwestern and north-central Iowa. Nests were found at Dewey's Pasture in Clay and Palo Alto counties in 10 of 13 years from 1962 to 1974 (Weller 1979). Outside of that region, there are reports of broods at Swan Lake in Johnson County in 1960 (Kent 1960), at Cardinal Marsh in Winneshiek County in 1990 (*IBL* 60:102), and at Blue Lake in Monona County in 1994 (*IBL* 64:108). Nesting starts in early May and extends into July (Low 1941).

This species is uncommon on Christmas Bird Counts with reports in 16 of 36 years from 1960 to 1995, mostly along the Missouri or Mississippi rivers. There are only 3 reports from mid-January to early February.

Comment: Ruddy Duck is a New World species, except for an introduced population in England. It is found as a resident in western South America and in the West Indies. The North American population winters in the southern United States south to northern Central America and north coastally to British Columbia and Massachusetts. The breeding range is from northern Alberta and Saskatchewan south to southern California and in the Great Plains to Texas. This species formerly bred in eastern United States and southern Canada and is considered sporadic there now. Iowa is at the southeastern edge of the nesting range.

References:

Kent, F. W. 1960. Spring and summer notes from the Iowa City region. *Iowa Bird Life* 30:65-66.

Low, J. B. 1941. Nesting of the Ruddy Duck in Iowa. *Auk* 58:506-517.

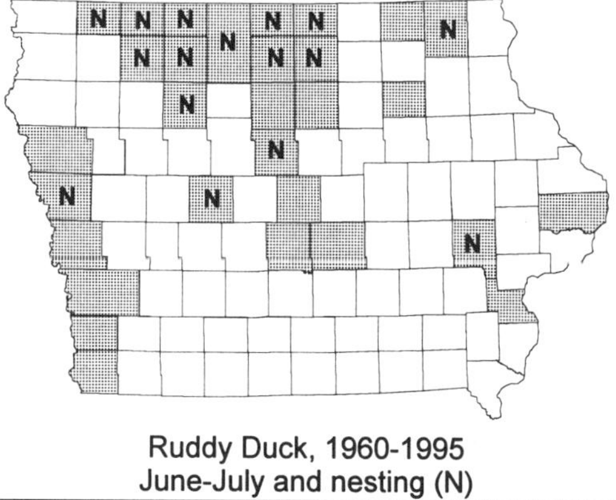

Ruddy Duck, 1960-1995
June-July and nesting (N)

ORDER FALCONIFORMES

The families in this order include American vultures; kites, eagles, hawks, and allies; caracaras and falcons; and Secretary-bird. There is some evidence that American vultures are more closely related to storks than to hawks. Osprey is sometimes treated as a separate family. The Secretary-bird is a single species found in Africa. Birds in this order have strong, hooked bills with sharp edges and fleshy cere at the base. Except for American vultures, the species in this order have sharp, curved talons and an opposable hind toe. Their strong flight and keen vision aid in hunting.

American Vultures (Family Cathartidae)

American vultures comprise 7 species, with 3 from North America and 2 from Iowa. These large, mostly black-brown birds with bare heads often have a strong sense of smell and eat carrion. They nest in caves, hollow trees, buildings, and other birds' nests. They differ from Old World vultures (which are hawks) in having a completely perforated nasal septum. Their long, poorly hooked claws are too weak for grasping.

Black Vulture (*Coragyps atratus*)

Status: Accidental

17 Sep 1933, Dallas Co. (Univ. of Iowa specimen, Dill 1933)
29 Aug 1959, Winnebago Co., shot but not preserved (Burgess 1959)

Occurrence: The 2 records are from late summer. Another report lacks details (Dinsmore et al. 1984).

Comment: This species breeds from northern Argentina north to southern Arizona, Texas, and the southeastern United States. In the Midwest, nesting occurs north to northern Texas, eastern Oklahoma, and the extreme southern portions of Missouri, Illinois, Indiana, and Ohio, with some but not all of the birds moving south in winter. Along the East Coast, nesting occurs to southern Pennsylvania.

Vagrants occur along the East Coast to the Maritime Provinces at almost any time of year. Vagrants are very uncommon in the Midwest, even in the northern parts of the states in which they nest. There are a few records north to Nebraska, Iowa, and Wisconsin. There are practically no vagrant records from the western United States, but there are single reports from British Columbia and the Yukon (Godfrey 1986). Midwest vagrants have been found in every month except February, but are most likely from March to July and in September to October.

References:

Burgess, H. H. 1959. Black Vulture in Winnebago County. *Iowa Bird Life* 29:98.

Dill, H. R. 1933. The Black Vulture in Dallas County Iowa. *Wilson Bull.* 45:203.

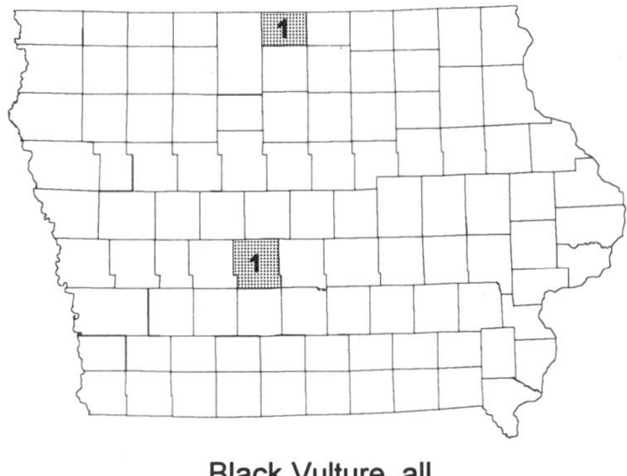

Black Vulture, all

Turkey Vulture (*Cathartes aura*)

Status: Regular; nests

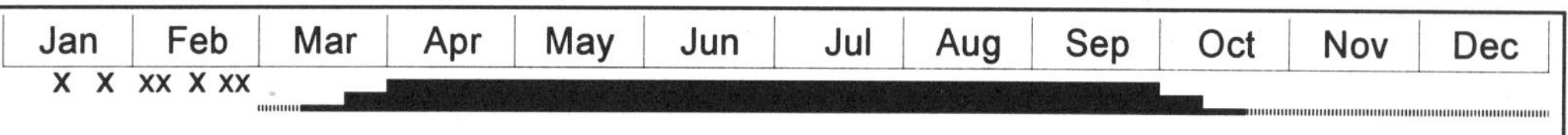

Occurrence: This common summer resident arrives in mid-March and departs by mid-October. Most nesting reports are from south-central Iowa, but occasionally nests are found near the eastern and western borders of Iowa. Numbers may be increasing in northwestern Iowa (*IBL* 63:95, 64:108).

Vultures rarely remain into December. There are 14 reports on Christmas Bird Counts from 1960 to 1995. In addition to the Christmas Bird Count records, there are 7 winter records from January and February.

Comment: The breeding range is from southern Canada south throughout South America. The winter range is from northern California and Arizona east to Maryland and south throughout the breeding range. In the Midwest, birds winter in southern Illinois and southern Missouri, rarely farther north.

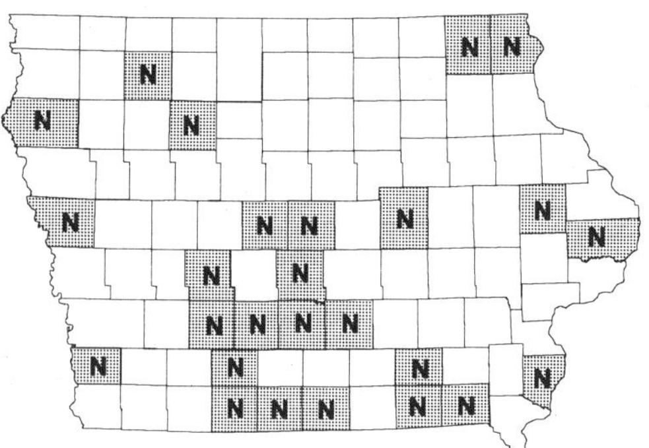

Turkey Vulture, 1960-1995
Nesting (N)

Kites, Eagles, Hawks, and Allies (Family Accipitridae)

Kites, eagles, hawks, and allies comprise 238 species, with 28 from North America and 15 from Iowa. Species in this large, varied, widespread family are carnivorous and feed by day. They have hooked bills, acute vision, and powerful feet and claws. They are unique among raptors in having the inside of their eggs greenish and in defecating forcefully. All build their own nests, usually in trees. Osprey is a world-wide species that is often treated as a separate family or subfamily. Its outer toe is large and can face backward as in owls.

Osprey (*Pandion haliaetus*)

Status: Regular

Jan	Feb	Mar	Apr	May	Jun	Jul	Aug	Sep	Oct	Nov	Dec
XX		XX X									X

4 Mar 1981
6 Mar 1992
17 Mar 1971

27 Dec 1964
16 Jan 1977
17 Jan 1980

Occurrence: This uncommon migrant is found from early April to mid-May and from late August to late October. From 1988 to 1995, 1 to 7 Ospreys were reported per year in June and July. Prior to that there were very few summer records. There are no documented reports of nesting. Summer birds may be nonbreeders or early migrants.

Historically, the only report of nesting, which was near Cedar Rapids in Linn County, is stated as follows: "George H. Berry collected a single addled egg from a nest in which there were three young, May 16, 1892" (Bailey 1918). Not all of Berry's reports were reliable and this date for young birds would be very unusual. There is also a report of Ospreys nesting along the Missouri River in Douglas or Washington county, Nebraska, just across the river from Pottawattamie County, Iowa, prior to 1900, but no details are provided (Bruner 1901).

A few Ospreys linger in fall into early December. There were reports from Christmas Bird Counts in 6 years from 1960 to 1995. The only mid-winter reports are 3 at Red Rock Reservoir in Marion County on 15 to 16 January 1977 (*IBL* 47:19) and 1 at Riverton Area in Fremont County on 17 January 1980 (*IBL* 50:25).

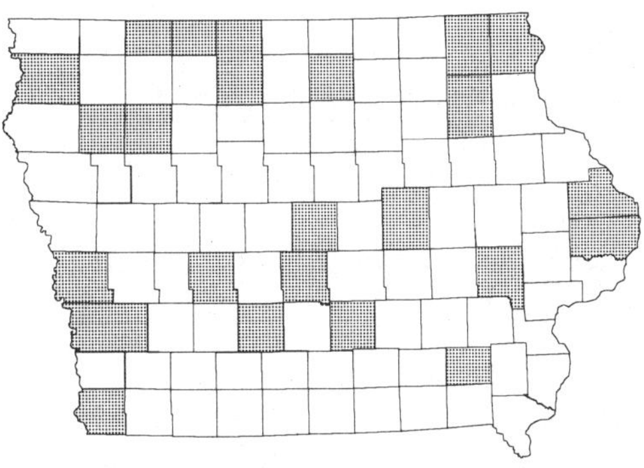

Osprey, 1960-1995
June-July

Comment: In the New World, the winter range is from southern Florida, southern Texas, and southern California south to southern South America. The breeding range is from tree line in Alaska and Canada south through the Rocky Mountain states to New Mexico, to southern Saskatchewan, and to the Great Lakes, and also coastally on the Atlantic and Gulf coasts. Ospreys have a broad breeding range that includes Europe, Asia, Africa, and Australia. Ospreys currently nest along the Wisconsin River in central Wisconsin about 75 miles northeast of the Iowa border (Robbins 1991). There is seemingly suitable nesting habitat along the Mississippi River in northeastern Iowa, and it seems plausible that this species might sometime nest in Iowa.

Reference:

Bruner, L. 1901. Birds that nest in Nebraska. *Proc. Nebr. Ornithologists' Union* 2:48-61.

Swallow-tailed Kite (*Elanoides forficatus*)

Status: Accidental; formerly nested

13 Jul 1867, Denison, Crawford Co., nests with young (Allen 1868, Anderson 1907)
25 Aug 1872, Creston, Union Co. (Museum of Comparative Zoology, Harvard, *IBL* 65:82)
3, 17 Jun 1875, Black Hawk Co., nest with 2 and 3 eggs (Peck 1913)
8 Apr 1883, Woodbury Co. (Univ. of Iowa #29688, P-0041, DuMont 1933)
12 Sep 1896, near Boone, Boone Co., shot (Henning 1896)
fall 1901, Jasper Co., specimen no longer extant (DuMont 1932, 1933)
20 Sep 1903, Cedar Rapids, Linn Co. (Coe College specimen, P-0069, Bailey 1918, DuMont 1933)
Sep 1907, Poweshiek Co., specimen no longer extant (DuMont 1933)
summer 1910, Sigourney, Keokuk Co., shot (Nauman 1924)
1913, Jefferson Co., specimen no longer extant (DuMont 1933)
prior to 1917, Ida Co. (specimen at Rockwell City, P-0079, Spurrell 1917, DuMont 1933)
early Jul 1931, near Oakland, Pottawattamie Co., specimen to Swenk (Swenk 1932, DuMont 1933)
14 to 15 May 1992, Cedar Falls, Black Hawk Co. (*IBL* 62:75, 63:69).

Occurrence: Since 1931, there is 1 spring sight record. Although there are only 12 Accepted early records, the additional reports (Anderson 1907) and data from surrounding states (Palmer 1988) suggest that the species was a fairly common summer resident until about 1880, when it rapidly declined.

Comment: In the United States, this species is a summer resident in Florida and along the Gulf and East coasts from Louisiana to South Carolina. A southern subspecies, *E. f. yatapa*, breeds from northern Argentina to southern Mexico. Birds arrive in Florida by late February and farther north by March. Most leave by early September to winter in South America, but a few have remained into October and November.

Historically, the range of this species extended from eastern Texas north to west-central Minnesota and along the Mississippi and Ohio rivers (Palmer 1988). The last nesting in Minnesota was in 1907, and after 1910 the range was reduced to states where nesting occurs now. A modest recovery in numbers has occurred since the 1950s.

Vagrants now occur in the East north to New England, in the Midwest in states where nesting once occurred, and in Colorado. The number of vagrants per year has increased from 4 in 10 states in the 1960s, to 9 in 21 states and Ontario in the 1970s, to 15 in 21 states and Ontario in the 1980s (Palmer 1988). Vagrants are most common in May with about equal numbers in other months from April to September.

References:

Henning, C. F. 1896. Notes and news. *Iowa Ornithologist* 2:85.

Nauman, E. D. 1924. Birds of early Iowa. *Palimpsest* 5:133-138.

Swenk, M. H. 1932. The Swallow-tailed Kite in Pottawattamie County, Iowa. *Wilson Bull.* 44:182.

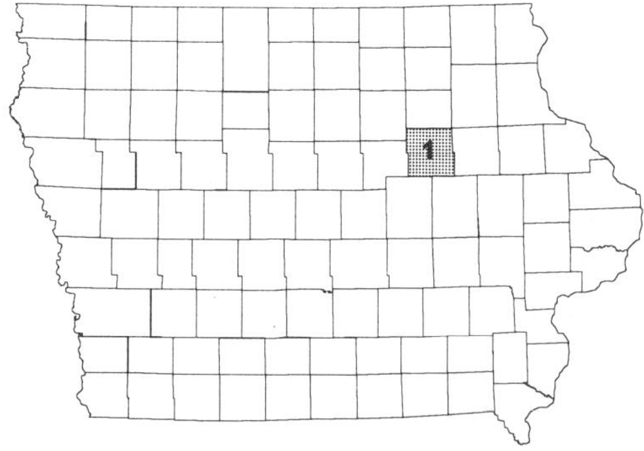

Swallow-tailed Kite, 1960-1995

Mississippi Kite (*Ictinia mississippiensis*)

Status: Regular; occasionally nests

Jan	Feb	Mar	Apr	May	Jun	Jul	Aug	Sep	Oct	Nov	Dec
								x xx			
12 May 1992									13 Sep 1995		
14 May 1980									23 Sep 1994		
14 May 1993									26 Sep 1994		

Occurrence: This species has recently returned to Iowa after being absent since at least 1907. The first 4 Accepted modern records were as follows: 29 May 1978 at Cardinal Marsh in Winneshiek County (*IBL* 48:72, 55:56); 14 May 1980 at Waubonsie State Park in Fremont County (*IBL* 50:46, 52:41, 64:69); 5 to 9 June 1989 at Dudgeon Lake in Benton County (P-0284, P-0289, Conrads et al. 1989); and 19 May 1990 at Coralville Reservoir in Johnson County (Kent 1992).

Since 1991, several adults summered in Clive in Polk County and in 1995 a nest was found and young fledged (Walsh 1996). They may have nested there for several years before being discovered.

Additional records away from the Polk County location include: 16 May 1992 at Cedar Falls in Black Hawk County (*IBL* 62:75); 17 May 1994 at Iowa City in Johnson County (*IBL* 64:74); 22 May 1994 in Story County (*IBL* 64:74); 23 September 1994 in Pottawattamie County (*IBL* 65:13); and 26 September 1994 in Marshall County (*IBL* 65:13). The latter 2 sightings were at hawk watches. Several other recent records were Not Accepted by the Records Committee, but may have been correct.

There are 2 old records that are Accepted: 26 August 1884 near Burlington in Des Moines County (2 specimens now lost, Bailey 1918, DuMont 1933) and prior to 1907 at Fort Dodge in Webster County (1 shot, Anderson 1907). There are 2 other old records with dates and several other indefinite references to this species that suggest that it occurred in Iowa prior to 1900 (Dinsmore et al. 1984). There is no definite evidence that Mississippi Kite was ever common in Iowa, and no specimens are known to exist.

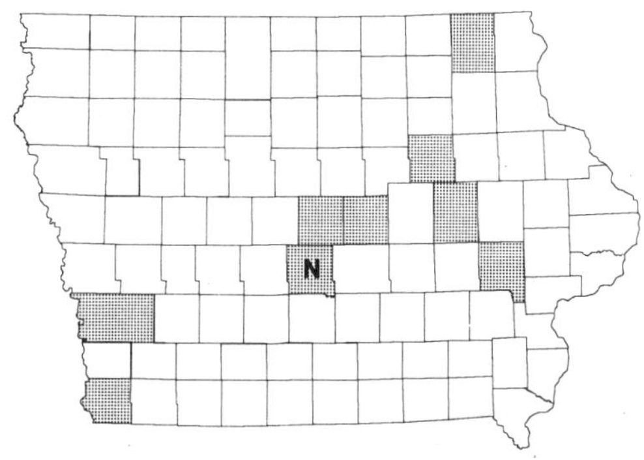

Mississippi Kite, 1960-1995
County locations and nesting (N)

Comment: The breeding range is in the southern United States from Arizona to North Carolina except for southern Texas and southern Florida. The range extends north to southwestern and central Kansas and western Nebraska and from Arkansas up along the Mississippi River to southern Missouri and along the Ohio River to Indiana. The birds occupy riparian habitat and often nest in colonies. They often feed and roost away from nest sites, which may be hard to locate. Nesting may have occurred in Iowa prior to 1900.

The winter range is in southern South America. The first spring migrants arrive in the United States in late March and reach more northerly locations by late April to early May (Palmer 1988). Most leave the United States by late September with a few lingering to October. Winter records have been recorded from South Carolina and Texas (Palmer 1988) and Florida (*Amer. Birds* 41:273).

In the Midwest, birds wander north to Wyoming, Saskatchewan, South Dakota, Minnesota, Wisconsin, Michigan, and Ontario. About half of extralimital records for the Midwest are from May, and about one-fourth are from June. Most fall records are from September with some in August. The earliest date is 17 March 1957 from northwestern Missouri (Robbins and Easterla 1992), and the latest is 31 October 1982 from southeastern Minnesota (Janssen 1987).

Historically, Mississippi Kite populations declined in the early 1900s and began to recover in the 1950s. There were few reports from the central Mississippi Valley between 1910 and 1950 (Parker and Ogden 1979).

References:

Conrads, D. J., M. Phelps, and T. H. Kent. 1989. Mississippi Kite at Dudgeon Lake. *Iowa Bird Life* 59:118-120.

Kent, T. H. 1992. Mississippi Kite at Coralville Reservoir. *Iowa Bird Life* 62:23-24.

Parker, J. W., and J. C. Ogden. 1979. The recent history and status of the Mississippi Kite. *Amer. Birds* 33:119-129.

Walsh, P. J. 1966. Notes on a Mississippi Kite nest in central Iowa. *Iowa Bird Life* 66:1-10.

Bald Eagle (*Haliaeetus leucocephalus*)

Status: Regular; nests

Jan	Feb	Mar	Apr	May	Jun	Jul	Aug	Sep	Oct	Nov	Dec

Occurrence: This rare summer resident and common migrant and winter resident is found throughout Iowa. Fall migrants begin to arrive in mid-September and peak in November, about the time rivers and lakes freeze. In most years, more than 1,000 over-winter in Iowa, especially along the Mississippi River. There they congregate near open water below the dams. Concentrations of 100 or more eagles are routine near several of these dams from December through late February. Bald Eagles were reported on 81 percent of Christmas Bird Counts from 1990 to 1995. Bald Eagle has replaced the Red-tailed Hawk as the most common raptor on those counts. Spring migrants appear with the first open water, usually in late February or March. Most have departed by early April.

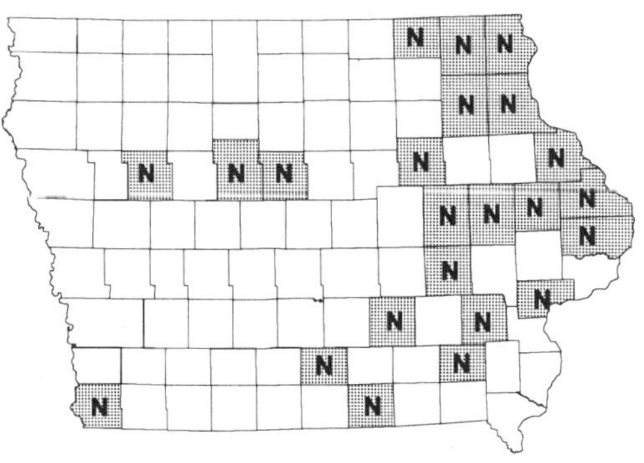

Bald Eagle, 1960-1995
Nesting (N)

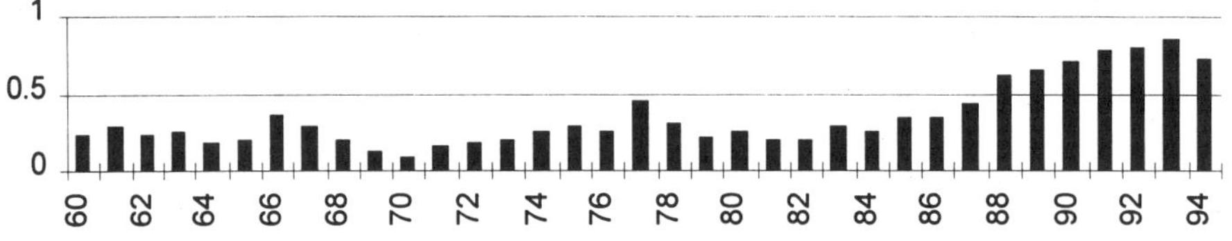

Bald Eagle, 1960-1994
Christmas Bird Counts, number per party-hour

Nesting starts in March, and young usually leave the nest in June. Most reports of nesting have been in eastern Iowa, especially along the Mississippi River, but in recent years the nesting range has expanded to include other river valleys in eastern Iowa and western Iowa.

Historically, the Bald Eagle was an uncommon migrant and rare nesting species (Anderson 1907, DuMont 1933). The last Bald Eagle nest site in Allamakee County was said to have been deserted in the 1860s (Orr 1937). Bailey (1918) said that a nest near Waubeek in Linn County in 1892 was the only authentic nest he knew of. There is also a report of a nest in Jasper County in 1905 (DuMont 1934).

The first Bald Eagle nest in modern times was found in northeastern Iowa in 1977 (Roosa and Stravers 1989). Since then, the number of nests reported has risen steadily and reached 43 in 1995 (B. Ehresman, personal communication).

Comment: The winter range includes southern Canada and most of the United States. The breeding range covers most of the United States and Canada north to the tree line.

The recovery of Bald Eagle populations in Iowa has been remarkable. This is reflected both in the increase in the breeding population and in the number wintering in Iowa. The number of active nests and the areas of the state that they encompass have increased greatly in recent years. Likewise, the number that winter in Iowa has increased dramatically, and the areas of Iowa that they occupy in winter has also increased. Wintering eagles usually concentrate near open water where they can feed on dead fish or waterfowl. Thus their numbers and the area they occupy fluctuate between years and even within a winter depending upon the severity of the weather. Even so, the open water below the dams along the Mississippi River, especially at Keokuk and Davenport, is a dependable winter site for Bald Eagles. Eagles may be found in open country, especially in northeastern Iowa, where they may feed on carrion.

References:

DuMont, P. A. 1934. The Bald Eagle as an Iowa bird. *Iowa Bird Life* 4:3-4.

Orr, E. 1937. Notes on the nesting of the Bald Eagle in Allamakee County, Iowa. *Iowa Bird Life* 7:18-19.

Northern Harrier (*Circus cyaneus*)

Status: Regular; occasionally nests

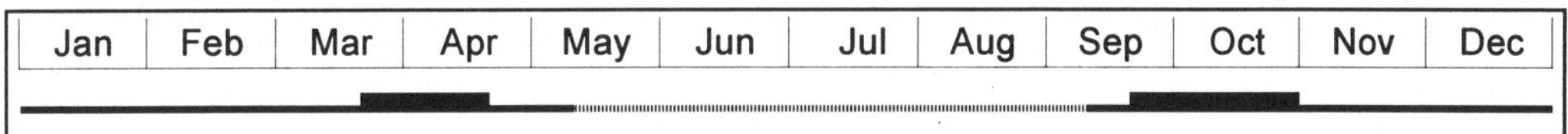

Occurrence: This uncommon to common migrant and winter resident and rare summer resident is most common in migration from mid-March to mid-April and from mid-September to late October. A few winter in Iowa every year, especially in winters with little snow cover and high numbers of voles, their preferred food. They are reported on about half of the Christmas Bird Counts, most often in southern Iowa. A few probably nest in Iowa nearly every summer, but there are few specific nesting reports. In most summers there are reports of a few harriers in July; these probably include both early migrants and birds dispersing after the nesting season.

Northern Harrier, 1960-1995
Nesting (N)

Ornithologists working in Iowa in the early 1900s considered this a common nesting species on grasslands (Gabrielson 1917, Tinker 1914). Numerous nests were found in northwestern Iowa in 1933 and 1934 (Bennett 1934). The breeding population has declined greatly since then. From 1957 to 1989, nesting was reported in only 7 counties (Roosa and Stravers 1989), and there are nesting reports from only 12 counties from 1960 to 1995. An intensive search in 1993 for nesting Northern Harriers in the Iowa Great Lakes region, which contains some of the best remaining nesting habitat, produced only 1 confirmed and 2 probable nests in Emmet and Palo Alto counties (Hemesath 1993).

Comment: In the New World, the winter range of this Holarctic species is from all but the northernmost United States south to northern South America. The breeding range is from Alaska east to southern Quebec and south through the northern half of the United States in the East and almost to Mexico in the West.

Reference:

Hemesath, L. 1993. Northern Harriers and Short-eared Owls in northwestern Iowa. *Nongame News* 9(2 & 3):6-8.

Sharp-shinned Hawk (*Accipiter striatus*)

Status: Regular; occasionally nests

Jan	Feb	Mar	Apr	May	Jun	Jul	Aug	Sep	Oct	Nov	Dec

Occurrence: This common migrant and uncommon winter resident is most common from late March to mid-May and from late August to late October. At peak times, 100 or more may pass by a concentration point in a day, for example, 134 at Grammer Grove Wildlife Area in Marshall County on 1 October 1995 and 109 there on 17 October 1995 (*IBL* 66:19). Sharp-shinned Hawks are reported on about one-third of the Christmas Bird Counts, and a few winter in Iowa every year. They occasionally winter near bird feeders and catch sparrows and other birds as they come to the feeder.

This species is rarely found in summer, but it may nest occasionally. There are 2 nest records in the Twentieth Century—2 recently fledged young in Monona County in the Loess Hills in 1978 (Roosa and Stravers 1989) and a juvenile along the Iowa River near Steamboat Rock in Hardin County on 16 July 1989 (*IBL* 60:13, 61:85). There are 5 other summer reports from 1960 to 1995.

Both Anderson (1907) and DuMont (1933) called this species a common migrant and an uncommon summer resident in northern Iowa. Bailey (1918) mapped nesting records from 10 counties. Most of his references do not substantiate nesting of this species; however, Bartsch (1897) described nests on cliffs in Allamakee and Dubuque counties and implied nesting at other sites in northeastern Iowa.

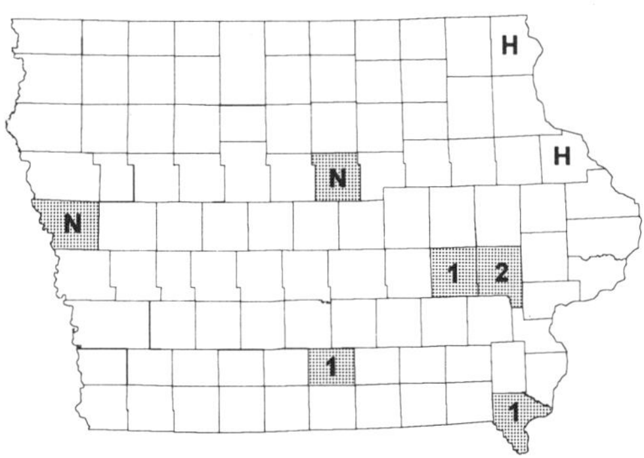

Sharp-shinned Hawk, 1960-1995
June-July, nesting (recent N, historical H)

Comment: The winter range includes all of the United States except the north-central portions south to Central America. Iowa is on the northern edge of the winter range, but there are casual records north to Minnesota (Janssen 1987). The breeding range is from Alaska east to Newfoundland and south to the Great Lakes states, northern Arizona and New Mexico, and northern Georgia in the Appalachians. A resident subspecies is found in the Greater Antilles and in Central and South America.

Sharp-shinned Hawks nest in small numbers, mainly in conifers, in the Ozarks of Missouri (Robbins and Easterla 1992) and in southeastern Wisconsin (Bielefeldt and Rosenfield 1994). The main nesting areas in Wisconsin and Minnesota are in the north.

Reference:

Bielefeldt, J., and R. N. Rosenfield. 1994. Summer birds of conifer plantations in southeastern Wisconsin. *Passenger Pigeon* 56:123-135.

Cooper's Hawk (*Accipiter cooperii*)

Status: Regular; nests

Jan	Feb	Mar	Apr	May	Jun	Jul	Aug	Sep	Oct	Nov	Dec

Occurrence: This uncommon migrant and rare winter and summer resident is most common from mid-March to early May and from mid-September to early October. Most nesting reports are from large wooded tracts in eastern and southern Iowa. Nesting starts in April and extends into June. Cooper's Hawks are found on about one-fourth of Christmas Bird Counts and are most common in central and southern Iowa.

Both Anderson (1907) and DuMont (1933) called this a common or fairly common permanent resident, and its status has probably changed little since then. Bailey (1918) said it was common throughout Iowa. Roosa and Stravers (1989) showed nesting records from 11 counties, mainly in eastern and southern Iowa. Cooper's Hawks have been found nesting in several other counties since then, but again in that same general area of the state.

Comment: The winter range includes most of the United States from southern Minnesota to northern Central America. The breeding range is from southern Canada south to northern Mexico and Florida.

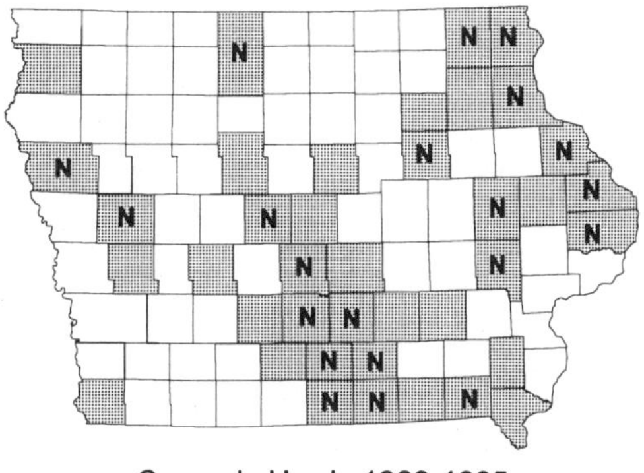

Cooper's Hawk, 1960-1995
June-July and nesting (N)

Northern Goshawk (*Accipiter gentilis*)

Status: Regular

Jan	Feb	Mar	Apr	May	Jun	Jul	Aug	Sep	Oct	Nov	Dec
								XX			
			19 Apr 1984			6 Sep 1980					
			20 Apr 1984			9 Sep 1966					
			21 Apr 1996			16 Sep 1966					

Occurrence: This rare winter resident occurs from September to mid-April. From 1960 to 1980, there were 0 to 6 reports per year with an average of 2. In contrast, from 1981 to 1994, there were 5 to 22 reports per calendar year with an average of 12. Records are scattered throughout the state and throughout the seasons. A few are reported on Christmas Bird Counts every year, most often in northern or central Iowa.

This species is known for periodic invasions when large numbers move south from their usual wintering grounds north of Iowa. The most recent invasion in Iowa was in 1985-1986 when about 30 were reported (*IBL* 56:58). There is an undocumented summer report (*IBL* 34:64).

Comment: In the New World, the breeding range of this Holarctic species is from tree line in Alaska east to Newfoundland and into the northern United States south to Pennsylvania and northern Minnesota in the East and in the mountains south to northern Mexico in the West. The winter range includes the breeding range and extends south into the northern United States and east from the mountains into the western Great Plains. Iowa is near the southern edge of its usual wintering range, although some go farther south, especially in invasion years.

Red-shouldered Hawk (*Buteo lineatus*)

Status: Regular; nests

Jan	Feb	Mar	Apr	May	Jun	Jul	Aug	Sep	Oct	Nov	Dec

Occurrence: This rare permanent resident occurs throughout Iowa, but most reports are from heavily wooded riparian areas in eastern Iowa, especially near the Mississippi River in northeastern Iowa. A few winter in the state, again most commonly near the Mississippi River. Migrants arrive in March and depart in September or October. There are few reports from western Iowa—1 that hit a door in Hull in Sioux County in winter 1993-1994 (*IBL* 64:47) and 1 at Hitchcock Nature Area in Pottawattamie County on 17 September 1994 (*IBL* 65:13).

Both Anderson (1907) and DuMont (1933) called this a fairly common summer resident, especially in southern Iowa. Red-shouldered Hawk populations declined rapidly, apparently in the 1950s and 1960s (Brown 1964, 1971), and it is much less common now than it was 50 years ago.

On Christmas Bird Counts, Red-shouldered Hawks declined sharply in the mid-1960s. From 28 to 36 birds were seen per year from 1960 to 1964, and 2 to 9 were seen per year from 1965 to 1969. In only 4 years since then (1970, 1988, 1994, and 1995) have there been 10 or more birds seen on Christmas Bird Counts, and in 3 years (1973, 1980, and 1984) none were seen.

Habitat loss, forest fragmentation, or perhaps competition from Red-tailed Hawks have all been suggested as possible reasons for the decline (Brown 1964, Bednarz and Dinsmore 1981). In 1993, 21 nest sites were known for eastern Iowa (Stravers and McKay 1993). Nesting starts in April and eggs usually hatch in May (Bednarz and Dinsmore 1982).

Comment: The winter range is from New England west to Iowa and south to the Gulf Coast. The breeding range is from southern Canada south to Florida and west to Minnesota and eastern Texas. An isolated population is permanently resident in California.

References:

Bednarz, J. C., and J. J. Dinsmore. 1981. Status, habitat use, and management of Red-shouldered Hawks in Iowa. *J. Wildlife Management* 45:236-241.

Bednarz, J. C., and J. J. Dinsmore. 1982. Nest-sites and habitat of Red-shouldered and Red-tailed hawks in Iowa. *Wilson Bull.* 94:31-45.

Brown, W. H. 1964. Population changes in the Red-shouldered and Red-tailed hawks. *Iowa Bird Life* 34:82-88.

Brown, W. H. 1971. Winter population trends in the Red-shouldered Hawk. *Amer. Birds* 25:813-817.

Stravers, J., and K. McKay. 1993. Red-shouldered Hawk reproductive success in Iowa during 1993. *Iowa Bird Life* 63:91-92.

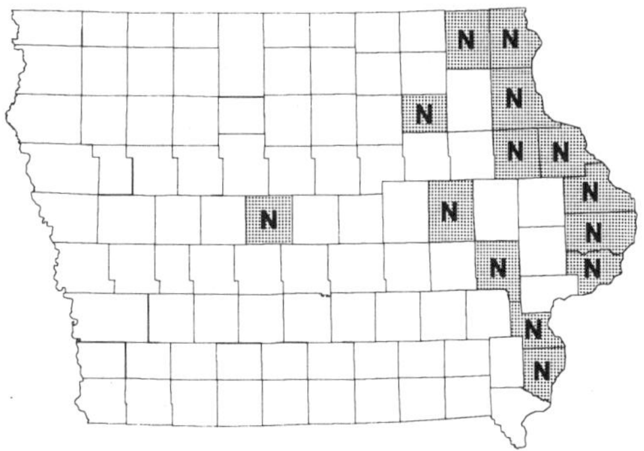

Red-shouldered Hawk, 1960-1995
Nesting (N)

Broad-winged Hawk (*Buteo platypterus*)

Status: Regular; nests

Jan	Feb	Mar	Apr	May	Jun	Jul	Aug	Sep	Oct	Nov	Dec

6 Apr 1965 16 Oct 1921
7 Apr 1984 21 Oct 1995
11 Apr 1978 29 Oct 1983

Occurrence: This common migrant and rare summer resident is most common from mid-April to early May and from mid- to late September. Broad-winged Hawks often migrate in large flocks. Flights numbering in the thousands have been reported: 1,085 at Algona in Kossuth County on 21 September 1993 (*IBL* 64:12), 1,026 at Grammar Grove Wildlife Area in Marshall County on 18 September 1994 (*IBL* 65:13), 2,000 to 3,000 on 22 September 1911 near Cedar Rapids in Linn County (Bailey 1912), and 5,000 at Waterloo in Black Hawk County on 26 September 1965 (*IBL* 35:89). Broad-winged Hawks roost in woods at night and by mid-morning they can rise on thermals as they form loosely organized migrating flocks. Spring flocks tend to be smaller and more widespread.

This species has nested in all areas of the state, but it is most commonly found in large wooded tracts, especially near rivers and streams in eastern Iowa. There are reports of nesting from 12 counties from 1960 to 1989, most in a broad band from southwestern to northeastern Iowa. A few Broad-winged Hawks are reported every summer, and presumably most of these represent nesting pairs.

Comment: The winter range is from Guatemala south through much of northern South America. Some winter in southern Florida. The breeding range includes southern Canada from Alberta east to the Maritime Provinces and south to Texas and Florida. There is also a resident population in the West Indies.

Broad-winged Hawks do not linger in fall nor arrive early in spring. Winter records north of Florida, such as the 13 reported on Christmas Bird Counts in Iowa from 1960 to 1982, are suspect, and acceptance would require convincing evidence such as a specimen or photographs.

Reference:

Bailey, B. H. 1912. A remarkable flight of Broad-winged Hawks. *Proc. Iowa Acad. Sci.* 19:195-196.

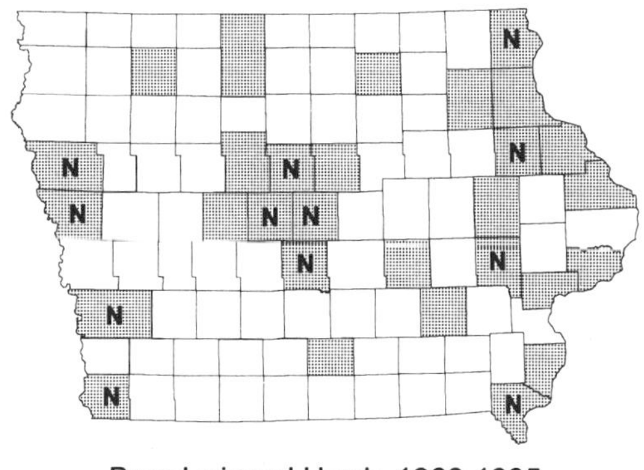

Broad-winged Hawk, 1960-1995
June-July and nesting (N)

Swainson's Hawk (*Buteo swainsoni*)

Status: Regular; nests

Jan	Feb	Mar	Apr	May	Jun	Jul	Aug	Sep	Oct	Nov	Dec
		XX									

18 Mar 1972	3 Nov 1985
18 Mar 1992	10 Nov 1973
23 Mar 1994	11 Nov 1972

Occurrence: This rare migrant and rare summer resident arrives in mid-April and departs by early October. The distribution of both migrants and summer residents is predominantly in western and northern Iowa. Nesting was reported in 13 counties from 1960 to 1989 (Roosa and Stravers 1989). Some nest sites have been occupied repeatedly for many years, such as 1 near Allendorf in Osceola County from 1978 to 1996 and 1 near Cedar Falls from 1977 to 1982.

Anderson (1907) considered this species a fairly common migrant and summer resident in the central and northern parts of Iowa. DuMont (1933) called it an uncommon migrant and very local breeder, a statement that matches its current status.

Like the Broad-winged Hawk, Swainson's Hawks often migrate in groups. Several large concentrations have been reported in Iowa including more than 300 found in Cherokee County on 19 April 1992 (Bierman 1992) and 200 to 300 that roosted along the Little Sioux River in Dickinson County on 5 October 1940 (Williams 1941).

Comment: The winter range is on the Pampas of southern South America and irregularly north to central America and the extreme southern United States. The breeding range is in the West from northern Mexico to the Yukon east to Minnesota, Iowa, and Missouri. The nesting range has a peculiar extension across northern Iowa, southern Minnesota, and locally in northern Illinois.

Swainson's Hawks arrive a little earlier and leave a little later than Broad-winged Hawks, but are not expected from late fall to early spring. Winter records north of the extreme southern United States, such as the 9 reported on Christmas Bird Counts in Iowa from 1960 to 1982 and in 1991, are suspect (Browning 1974), and acceptance would require convincing evidence such as a specimen or photographs. Swainson's Hawks in juvenal and first-basic plumages (including first-summer birds) are difficult to identify (Browning 1974).

References:

Bierman, D. 1992. Swainson's Hawk fallout in Cherokee County. *Iowa Bird Life* 62:117-118.

Browning, M. R. 1974. Comments on the winter distribution of the Swainson's Hawk (*Buteo swainsoni*) in North America. *Amer. Birds* 28:865-867.

Williams, N. J. 1941. Migration of Swainson's Hawks in western Iowa. *Iowa Bird Life* 11:35.

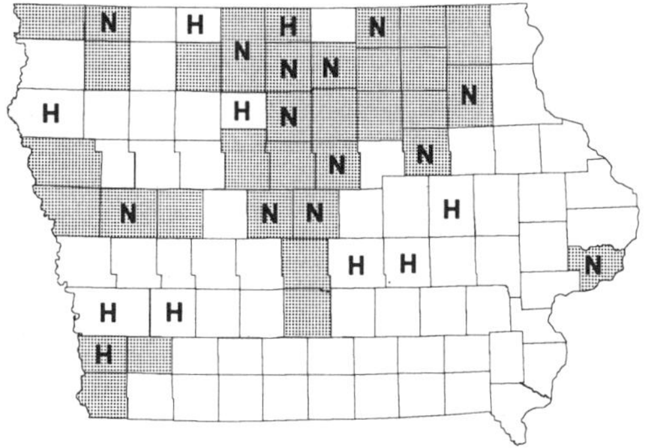

Swainson's Hawk, 1960-1995
June-July and nesting (recent N, historical H)

Red-tailed Hawk (*Buteo jamaicensis*)

Status: Regular; nests

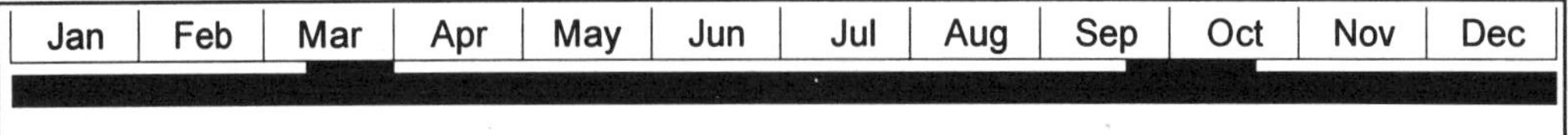

Occurrence: Red-tailed Hawks are abundant in migration, common in winter and uncommon to common in summer. They are most abundant on the wooded edges of agricultural land in eastern and southern Iowa. Migrants are most obvious in March and early April and from late September through late October.

Red-tailed Hawks are reported on 95 percent of the Christmas Bird Counts, including nearly all of the counts in central and southern Iowa.

Anderson (1907) considered the Red-tailed Hawk a common summer resident and DuMont (1933) called it fairly common. It is still a common nesting species throughout Iowa except in very open agricultural regions.

Comment: The breeding range is across most of North America from the northern limit of the boreal forest south through Central America and the West Indies. The winter range is from southern Canada south throughout the breeding range.

Four subspecies of red-tails are known from Iowa (DuMont 1933). The breeding birds are the subspecies *B. j. jamaicensis*. The western subspecies, *B. j. calurus,* is a fairly common migrant, especially in western Iowa. Both the dark-colored Harlan's Red-tailed Hawk, *B. j. harlani,* and the light-colored Krider's Red-tailed Hawk, *B. j. krideri,* are occasionally found during migration or winter. The Krider's form was originally described from a specimen taken in Winnebago County in 1872 (Hoopes 1873). Both it and the Harlan's subspecies are said to have formerly nested in Iowa. Little is known about the relative abundance of the various subspecies in Iowa and whether the birds that breed in Iowa remain here in winter or move south and are replaced by birds from the north.

Red-tailed Hawks are extremely variable and easily confused with other species. There are many gradations from dark to light morphs, from immatures to adults, and from one subspecies to another.

Reference:

DuMont, P. A. 1933. The Iowa Red-tailed Hawks. *Iowa Bird Life* 3:5-7.

Ferruginous Hawk (*Buteo regalis*)

Status: Accidental

28 Oct 1973, Shenandoah, Page Co., adult (*IBL* 43:104, Wilson 1988)
27 Oct 1977, near Pocahontas, Pocahontas Co., immature, banded in North Dakota, road kill (Gilmer 1985, Wilson 1988)
26 Oct 1983, near Shenandoah, Page Co., adult (*IBL* 53:99, 54:38, Wilson 1988)
22 Sep 1984, near Liscomb, Marshall Co., immature, wing-tagged in North Dakota (Proescholdt 1985, Wilson 1988)
22 Mar 1995, Mark Twain N.W.R., Louisa Co., dark phase adult (*IBL* 65:72, 66:96)

Occurrence: Of the 5 Accepted records, 4 are from fall and 1 from spring. They involve 3 adults (1 dark phase) and 2 immatures. Numerous other reports, many of which were reviewed by Wilson (1988), are Not Accepted. There is a specimen of an immature bird at the University of Iowa said to have been from 21 August 1936 at Tiffin in Johnson County, but no other information to substantiate that it came from there is available. Most of the early reports are without description, and later reports are often associated with poor views, incomplete descriptions, or features that could apply equally well to the various plumages of Red-tailed Hawk.

Comment: This species inhabits dry, open, tall-grass habitat. It breeds from the panhandle of Texas and northern Arizona north to western Washington and southern Saskatchewan, and as far east as the central Dakotas and western Nebraska. It winters from western Nebraska to the Pacific Coast and northern Mexico. It is considered a rare but regular migrant in western Minnesota (Janssen 1987).

Fall migration begins in late September and early October. In spring, adults arrive in the north by late March to early April, with year-old birds following later (Palmer 1988).

The Ferruginous Hawk has the smallest range of any buteo north of Mexico (Palmer 1988). The pattern of vagrancy to the east is very limited, and its determination is compounded by well-established identification problems (Bohlen 1986, Eckert 1982, Robbins and Easterla 1992). In Wisconsin, there are 4 old specimen records and 8 recent records from fall-winter, 1 from spring, and 1 from summer (Robbins 1991). In Michigan, there are 7 well-documented records from fall, winter, and spring (McPeek and Adams 1994). In Indiana, 2 of 5 records were of birds examined in the hand (Keller et al. 1978). In Illinois, identification problems make it hard to tell how many records are valid (Bohlen 1989). In Missouri, there are 6 fall records and 1 possible spring record (Robbins and Easterla 1992). Other states east of the Mississippi River with records are Mississippi, Florida, Virginia, and New Jersey (DeSante and Pyle 1986).

References:

Bohlen, H. D. 1986. The status of the Ferruginous Hawk in Illinois. *Illinois Birds and Birding* 2:40-41.

Eckert, K. R. 1982. Field identification of the Ferruginous Hawk. *Loon* 54:161-164.

Gilmer, D. S., D. L. Evans, P. M. Konrad, and R. E. Stewart. 1985. Recoveries of Ferruginous Hawks banded in south-central North Dakota. *J. Field Ornithology* 56:184-187.

Proescholdt, B. 1985. Ferruginous Hawk in central Iowa. *Iowa Bird Life* 55:74-75.

Wilson, B. L. 1988. Records of Ferruginous Hawk in Iowa. *Iowa Bird Life* 58:95-100.

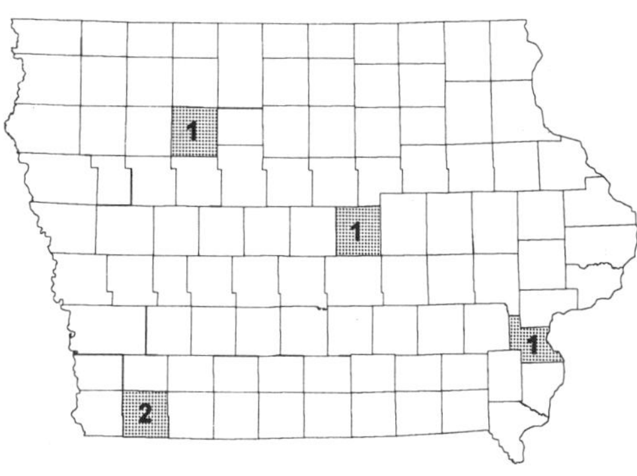

Ferruginous Hawk, all

Rough-legged Hawk (*Buteo lagopus*)

Status: Regular

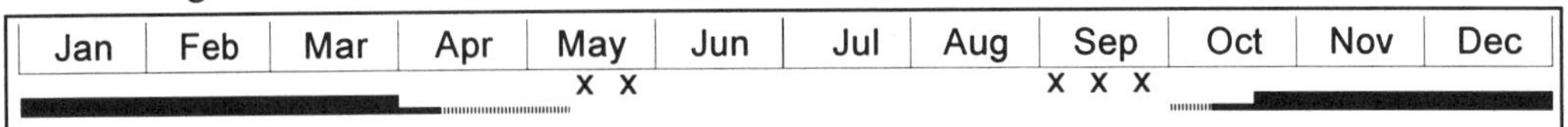

Jan	Feb	Mar	Apr	May	Jun	Jul	Aug	Sep	Oct	Nov	Dec
				x x				x x x			

20 May 1991 — 1 Sep 1981
24 May 1992 — 12 Sep 1977
31 May 1996 — 23 Sep 1990

Occurrence: This uncommon migrant and winter resident is usually found from mid-October to late March. It is found on about three-fourths of the Christmas Bird Counts. The occurrence is uniform across Iowa, but numbers vary considerably from year to year.

There is a possible summer record from 13 June 1982 in Pocahontas County (*IBL* 52:89) and another undocumented summer report (Dinsmore et al. 1984).

Both Anderson (1907) and DuMont (1933) called this species a fairly common winter resident indicating little change in its numbers since then.

Comment: In North America, the winter range of this Holarctic species is from southern Canada south throughout the United States except for the southeastern states, and to northern Mexico. The breeding range is on the Arctic tundra from Alaska east to Labrador. There are only a few June-July reports from northern Minnesota and northern Wisconsin.

Golden Eagle (*Aquila chrysaetos*)

Status: Regular

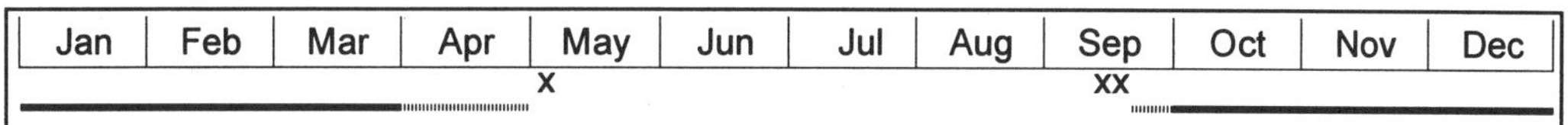

Jan	Feb	Mar	Apr	May	Jun	Jul	Aug	Sep	Oct	Nov	Dec
				x				xx			

30 Apr 1990 15 Sep 1914
30 Apr 1963 17 Sep 1985
10 May 1992 22 Sep 1993

Summer: Jun 1930

Occurrence: This rare migrant and winter resident is found in all areas of the state, usually along wooded, hilly river valleys and sometimes near large bodies of water. The reports of this species are rather uniformly spread from early October and to late March, with a few records in September and April. Many of the winter records are from the wooded river valleys of northeastern Iowa, especially along the Upper Iowa River, but there are scattered winter records from other areas of the state. The average number reported per year has risen steadily with 2.2 in the 1960s, 3.1 in the 1970s, 7.1 in the 1980s, and 11.0 in the 1990s. The increase can probably be accounted for by increased birding activity and reporting and by discovery of the wintering population in northeastern Iowa. Most of the birds that have been aged are immatures, but adults are seen regularly in northeastern Iowa in winter.

The only summer report is of 1 killed near Spencer in Clay County in June 1930 (Youngworth 1933). There is no suggestion that the frequency of this species has changed over time (Anderson 1907, DuMont 1933).

Comment: In North America, this Holarctic species breeds from northern Mexico north to north-central Alaska and east across Canada. In winter it retracts from the far north and can be found across most of the eastern United States south to the Gulf Coast as well as in its permanent range in the West.

Reference:

Youngworth, W. 1933. Migration records of eagles and Snowy Owls in the Upper Missouri valley. *Wilson Bull.* 45:32-33.

Caracaras and Falcons (Family Falconidae)

Caracaras and falcons comprise 63 species, with 10 from North America and 5 from Iowa. Of the Iowa species, 4 are Regular and 1 is Accidental. Falcons are similar to hawks, but they have long, pointed wings, are fast flyers, and often kill prey by breaking their necks. The inside of their egg shells is buff, and they defecate while perched.

American Kestrel (*Falco sparverius*)

Status: Regular; nests

Jan	Feb	Mar	Apr	May	Jun	Jul	Aug	Sep	Oct	Nov	Dec

Occurrence: American Kestrel is common in winter and summer, but may be abundant in migration from mid-March to early April and from mid-September to early October.

This species was found on 95 percent of the Christmas Bird Counts from 1990 to 1995 with the highest numbers in southern Iowa, especially those bordering the large rivers. The fewest are found in north-central Iowa. The Christmas Bird Count data illustrate the recovery from depressed numbers in the 1960s. The number per party-hour has increased four-fold from 0.1 to 0.4 from 1960 to 1994 (chart), and the percent of counts with kestrels increased from 57 to 94 during that period.

The American Kestrel is now a common nesting species throughout Iowa, although there was concern that populations were declining in the 1960s and 1970s. The numbers found on Breeding Bird Surveys averaged 9.3 per year from 1967 to 1976 and 30.0 per year from 1985 to 1994.

In 1983, the Iowa Department of Natural Resources began a nest-box program for kestrels along interstate highways. More than half of the 700 boxes are used (Jackson et al. 1996). Based on a study of nest boxes along an interstate highway in central Iowa, incubation usually started in late April and the median fledging date was 20 June (Varland and Loughin 1993). At least one young fledged from 69 percent of the nests.

Comment: The winter range is from the northern United States south to Central America and the West Indies. The breeding range is from Alaska east to Newfoundland and south to the Gulf Coast, Mexico, and the West Indies. There is also a South American population.

Reference:

Varland, D. E., and T. M. Loughin. 1993. Reproductive success of American Kestrels nesting along an interstate highway in central Iowa. *Wilson Bull.* 105:465-474.

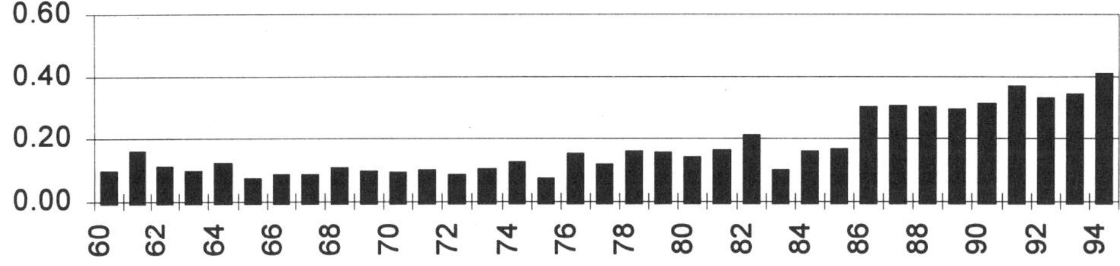

American Kestrel, 1960-1994
Christmas Bird Counts, number per party-hour

Merlin (*Falco columbarius*)

Status: Regular; formerly nested

Jan	Feb	Mar	Apr	May	Jun	Jul	Aug	Sep	Oct	Nov	Dec
				XX X	X X		X XX				

17 May 1995	14 Aug 1939
18 May 1991	21 Aug 1975
21 May 1995	30 Aug 1989

Summer: 3 Jun 1990, 14 Jun 1963

Occurrence: This rare migrant and rarer winter resident is most common from late March to early May and in September. The numbers found on Christmas Bird Counts have steadily increased with birds found on 2 counts in 2 years in the 1960s, 4 counts in 4 years in the 1970s, 23 counts in 8 years in the 1980s, and 33 counts in every year from 1990 to 1995. Of the Merlins found on Christmas Bird Counts, 75 percent are from counts along the Missouri and Mississippi rivers and counts that include large reservoirs, and only 10 percent are from the northern third of the state. Beginning in 1986, 1 to 12 Merlins have been seen in January-February each year at locations that are more widely scattered than the Christmas Bird Count reports.

Both Anderson (1907) and DuMont (1933) considered the Merlin an uncommon migrant, the latter noting that occasionally 1 remained until December or January. There are 2 old records of nesting (Bailey 1918). According to Bailey, Lynds Jones found a nest with 4 eggs near Grinnell in Poweshiek County on 28 April, but Jones (1889) only lists the species as nesting. Bailey examined 2 eggs taken by George Berry on 27 April 1908 east of Marion in Linn County. There are no other nest records. There are summer reports from 14 June 1963 at Sioux City in Woodbury County (Youngworth 1963) and from 3 June 1990 in Chickasaw County (*IBL* 60:103).

Comment: In the New World, the winter range of this Holarctic species is from British Columbia, the central United States, and New England south to northern South America. Winter records have also increased in Minnesota since the late 1970s (Janssen 1987).

The breeding range is from Alaska east to Labrador and south into the Great Lakes states, the northern Great Plains, and Washington. The closest nesting area to Iowa is in northern Minnesota.

Two subspecies of Merlins have been reported in Iowa, the eastern form *F. c. columbarius* and the paler western Richardson's form *F. c. richardsonii*. Presumably, the western form is most often found in western Iowa but there are no good data to document that.

Reference:

Youngworth, W. 1963. The Pigeon Hawk in western Iowa. *Iowa Bird Life* 33:72-73.

Peregrine Falcon (*Falco peregrinus*)

Status: Regular; formerly nested, reintroduced

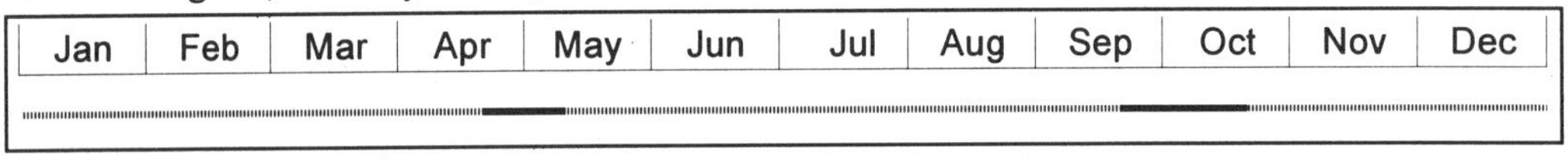

Jan	Feb	Mar	Apr	May	Jun	Jul	Aug	Sep	Oct	Nov	Dec

Occurrence: This rare permanent resident is most often seen in migration, mainly from late April to early May and from mid-September to October.

Peregrine Falcons are less common in winter than Merlins. On Christmas Bird Counts, there were reports from 3 counts in the 1960s, 2 in the 1970s, and 3 in the 1980s; however, there were reports from 1 count each year from 1991 to 1994 and from 2 counts in 1995. There were 1 to 3 reports from January-February each year from 1991 to 1995, but only in only 2 years from 1981 to 1990.

From 1989 to 1992, 44 young Peregrine Falcons were released at Cedar Rapids, Des Moines, and Muscatine. Four of these birds have returned to nest in Cedar Rapids and Des Moines, and 8 have nested in other states (Andrews et al. 1995). In Des Moines, peregrines fed largely on Rock Doves and a variety of small birds (Myers and Pease 1995).

Prior to the DDT era, the Peregrine Falcon was a regular but rare nesting species (Anderson 1907). DuMont (1933) said it was extirpated as a nesting species, but a few pairs continued to nest on bluffs along the Mississippi River in northeastern Iowa. The last nesting report from that area was in 1967 (Roosa and Stravers 1989). Reintroduction programs began in the Midwest in the mid-1980s (Redig and Tordoff 1991). Birds from those releases undoubtedly account for some of the increase in the number of migrants seen in Iowa in the late 1980s and 1990s. In Iowa, young peregrines were released in Cedar Rapids in 1989 (4) and 1990 (13), Des Moines in 1991 (19), and Muscatine in 1992 (8). Peregrines nested in both Cedar Rapids and Des Moines in 1992, 1993, 1994, and 1995, the first nesting attempts in Iowa in about 25 years. A pair also apparently attempted to nest at Davenport in 1992 and 1993, but those attempts were unsuccessful. Birds released in Iowa have dispersed widely and have been reported nesting in Winnipeg, St. Louis, Omaha, Topeka, La Crosse, and Minnesota (Andrews et al. 1995).

Comment: In the New World, the winter range of this Holarctic species is in the southern United States south through most of South America. Historically, the Peregrine Falcon nested across most of North America from the Arctic south to central Mexico. As a result of nesting failures caused by pesticides, its nesting range was greatly reduced in the 1960s and 1970s, but in the past decade it has been reestablished over large parts of that range. The Peregrine Falcon is a cosmopolitan species that nests on all continents except Antarctica.

References:

Myers, L. M., and J. L. Pease. 1995. Analysis of Peregrine Falcon (*Falco peregrinus*) food habits. *Iowa Bird Life* 65:25-29.

Redig, P. T., and H. B. Tordoff. 1991. Peregrine Falcon restoration in the Midwest and Upper Great Lakes. In: B. G. Pendleton, and D. L. Krahe, eds. Proceedings of the Midwest Raptor Management Symposium and Workshop. *National Wildlife Federation Scientific and Technical Series* 15:243-251.

Gyrfalcon (*Falco rusticolus*)

Status: Accidental

27 Mar 1992, northwestern Kossuth Co., imm. gray morph (P-0351, Bolduan 1994)
25 Sep 1993, near Spirit L., Dickinson Co., imm. gray morph (Silcock 1994)

Occurrence: Both Iowa records are of immature gray-morph birds found at marshy areas in northern Iowa, 1 in spring and 1 in fall. The identification of the spring bird is based on excellent photographs, and the fall bird was seen by a group of experienced birders. There are 3 old reports (Dinsmore et al. 1984) and 3 recent ones that are Not Accepted.

Comment: The breeding range is in the Holarctic south to the northern parts of the boreal forest. In winter, birds move south as far as the northern edge of the United States. The number moving south in winter varies with food supply, and most of the more southerly birds are immatures. The most southerly records are from Colorado, Kansas, Oklahoma, Missouri, and Virginia. Records close to Iowa include southern Minnesota (Janssen 1987), a specimen on 22 November 1981 in South Dakota just across from Akron, Iowa (Dinsmore et al. 1984), a sight record on 18 December 1977 at Squaw Creek National Wildlife Refuge in northwestern Missouri (Robbins and Easterla 1992), and an immature female specimen on 3 November 1971 south of Galena in northwestern Illinois (Bohlen 1989).

Records in the Midwest are distributed from October through March, but there are a few records in September and April, with extreme dates of 8 September 1949 in South Dakota (South Dakota Ornithologists' Union 1991) and 17 April in Minnesota (Janssen 1987).

Most records from the Midwest are of gray-phase immatures, but white- and dark-phased birds have been reported. Identification of Gyrfalcon is difficult because of the plain features and because viewing time is often very limited. The Iowa records fit the expected pattern—immature, gray-phase birds hunting waterfowl at the early and late extremes of migration. Wintering birds may have territories with roosting sites and hunting areas, or they may be seen only in passing.

References:

Bolduan, B. 1994. Gyrfalcon in Kossuth County. *Iowa Bird Life* 64:21-22.

Silcock, R. 1994. Gyrfalcon in northwestern Iowa. *Iowa Bird Life* 64:115-116.

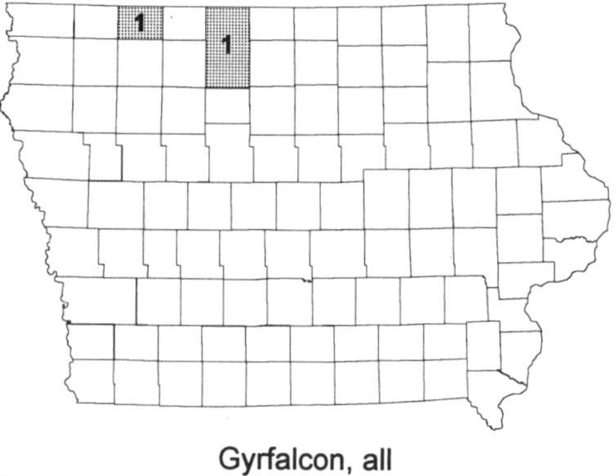

Gyrfalcon, all

Prairie Falcon (*Falco mexicanus*)

Status: Regular

By year since 1960

60 63 66 69 72 75 78 81 84 87 90 93

1 2 1 2 1 1 1 4 4 2 7 2 5 6 1 8 6 5 3 7 6

Jan Feb Mar Apr May Jun Jul Aug Sep Oct Nov Dec

x xx

24 Apr 1992	23 Aug 1963
26 Apr 1979	31 Aug 1949
1 May 1978	5 Sep 1988

Occurrence: Reports of this rare winter resident have dramatically increased since 1981, when there were 5 well-substantiated records in that year. There are 4 reports from the 1960s, 4 from the 1970s, 41 from the 1980s, and 35 from 1990 to 1995. The records are fairly evenly distributed from mid-October to late February, but there are a few beginning in late August and extending to early May.

Of the records since 1960, 58 percent are from western, 40 percent from central, and 2 percent from eastern Iowa. The western Iowa records are evenly distributed from north to south, while the central records are mostly in the central area from north to south.

Of 27 reports from 1927 to 1958, 26 are from northwestern Iowa from Kossuth County west and Woodbury County north; the other is from the southwest (Dinsmore et al. 1984). Three specimens taken in the 1880s (Anderson 1907) are not available (DuMont 1933). DuMont examined specimens taken in Dickinson County in 1925 and about 1927 and another from Story County from fall 1927. One was collected in Clay County on 6 January 1935 (Iowa State University specimen #2002, DuMont 1935, Dinsmore 1992). A specimen from 25 September 1943 taken in Dickinson County is at the State Historical Museum (Musgrove 1944, Dinsmore et al. 1984).

Comment: The breeding range is in the western United States from New Mexico to southern Canada and east to eastern Colorado and western North Dakota. The winter range includes all except the most northerly part of the breeding range and extends to central Mexico and onto the Great Plains. States to the east of Iowa as far as Ohio have progressively fewer records compared to Iowa.

References:

DuMont, P. A. 1935. Prairie Falcon records from northwestern Iowa. *Wilson Bull.* 47:162-163.

Musgrove, J. W. 1944. Prairie Falcon collected in Dickinson County. *Iowa Bird Life* 14:76.

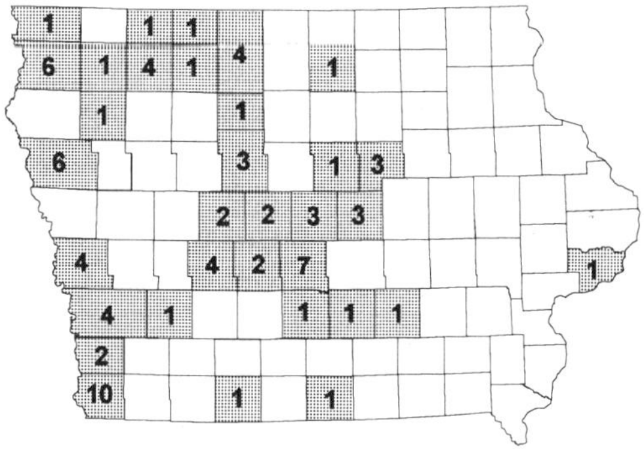

Prairie Falcon, 1960-1995

ORDER GALLIFORMES

Of the several families of gallinaceous birds, only one occurs in Iowa. Birds in this order are vegetarian and have short, stout beaks, rounded wings, and well-developed tails. They have strong feet for scraping and running and have strong breast muscles. They are often gregarious, nest on the ground, and have precocious young. Many are game birds, and some have been domesticated.

Partridges, Grouse, Turkeys, and Quail (Family Phasianidae)

Partridges, grouse, turkeys, and quail comprise 174 species, with 21 from North America and 7 from Iowa. Partridge and pheasants have heavy builds with short, rounded wings; short, rounded bills with upper mandible overhanging the lower; and stout legs with spurs except in native American species. Grouse are northerly birds with feathered legs and elaborate mating rituals. Turkeys are large New World birds with bare head and neck. Quail are small, short-tailed birds with brightly colored males.

Of the 5 Regular Iowa species, 2 are introduced (Gray Partridge, Ring-necked Pheasant), 1 is reintroduced (Wild Turkey), and 2 are native (Ruffed Grouse, Northern Bobwhite). One formerly abundant species is now Accidental (Greater Prairie-Chicken). Finally, one species whose former status is unknown is now extirpated from the state (Sharp-tailed Grouse).

Gray Partridge (*Perdix perdix*)

Status: Regular; nests

Jan	Feb	Mar	Apr	May	Jun	Jul	Aug	Sep	Oct	Nov	Dec

Occurrence: This uncommon permanent resident has occurred in all areas of the state, but is much more common in northern and east-central Iowa. Numbers and distribution fluctuate, with few or none in most areas of southern Iowa. Gray Partridge inhabit open agricultural fields and roadside ditches, and they tend to survive better than Ring-necked Pheasants in intensively farmed areas. They often come to roadsides early and late in the day, and pairs are often seen there in late May or early June.

The first successful introduction of Gray Partridges in Iowa was in 1905 in Palo Alto County. Several additional releases resulted in established populations in north-central and northwestern Iowa (Leopold 1933, Spiker 1929). Birds stocked in southwestern Iowa from 1969 to 1972 led to the establishment of a population there, and releases in southeastern Iowa in 1979 had similar success. In the 1980s, the range of this species in Iowa expanded rapidly and reached northern Missouri, but in the early 1990s numbers declined and Gray Partridge disappeared from much of southern Iowa.

Comment: Gray Partridge are found from central Alberta and Manitoba south to Montana, the Dakotas, western Minnesota, and Iowa. They also occur in southern Wisconsin and northern Illinois, southern Ontario, and in Washington, Oregon, Idaho, and northern

Nevada. This introduced species is native to Europe and western Asia.

References:

Leopold, A. 1933. Report of the Iowa game survey. The Hungarian Partridge in Iowa. *Outdoor America* (Feb-Mar):6-8, 21.

Spiker, C. J. 1929. The Hungarian Partridge in northwest Iowa. *Wilson Bull.* 41:24-29.

Ring-necked Pheasant (*Phasianus colchicus*)

Status: Regular; nests

Jan	Feb	Mar	Apr	May	Jun	Jul	Aug	Sep	Oct	Nov	Dec

Occurrence: This abundant permanent resident throughout Iowa prospers on agricultural land, especially where there are hayfields and pastures. Pheasants were first introduced to Iowa in 1900 when 2,000 birds escaped from a game farm at Cedar Falls in Black Hawk County. Additional birds were released in other counties, and by about 1920 they were well-established in northern Iowa, which remained their main range for many years. It was not until the 1960s and 1970s that pheasant populations became well-established in southern Iowa (Farris et al. 1977). The Ring-necked Pheasant is the top game species in Iowa, with more than one million taken by hunters yearly.

Comment: Ring-necked Pheasants are found from British Columbia and Washington east to New England and New Jersey, north to Alberta and south to Colorado and Kansas. They are native to China.

Reference:

Farris, A. L., E. D. Klonglan, and R. C. Nomsen. 1977. *The Ring-necked Pheasant in Iowa.* Iowa Conservation Commission, Des Moines.

Ruffed Grouse (*Bonasa umbellus*)

Status: Regular; nests

Jan	Feb	Mar	Apr	May	Jun	Jul	Aug	Sep	Oct	Nov	Dec

Occurrence: This uncommon permanent resident of second-growth forest is found in northeastern Iowa. Its populations undergo periodic cycles, and in some years it is very difficult to locate.

Historically, Ruffed Grouse were found in woodlands over much of Iowa, but with heavy hunting pressure and the loss of habitat, disappeared from most of the state. By the mid-1930s, it was confined to northeastern Iowa (Dinsmore 1994), where it now is found in about 8 counties.

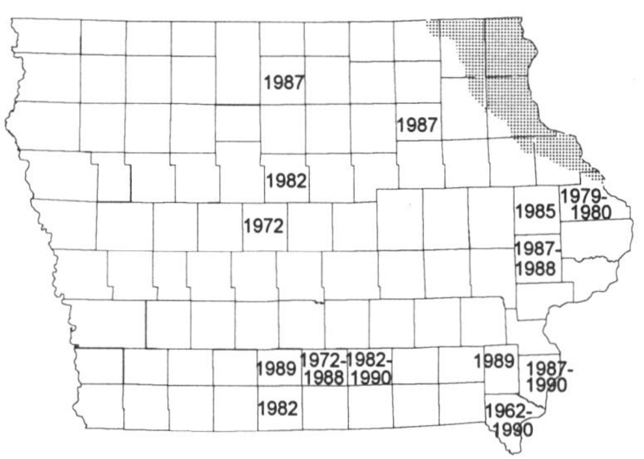

Ruffed Grouse
Natural range and introduction sites (years)

Since 1962, the Department of Natural Resources has released about 1,300 Ruffed Grouse in 14 counties in eastern and central Iowa with mixed success (Andrews et al. 1995). At Shimek Forest in Lee County and Stephens Forest in Lucas County, grouse were reported for several years after they were released (Little and Sheets 1982, *IBL* 64:74; 65:48; 66:20), while other releases were unsuccessful. One found in Page County in 1990 was far from any release site and may have come from Missouri (*IBL* 61:19). Ruffed Grouse are still a game species in Iowa, but in most years only a few thousand are taken by hunters.

Comment: The range of this permanent resident is from Alaska east to Labrador and south to northern California, Utah, the Great Lakes states, Tennessee, and North Carolina. Iowa is near the southern edge of its range in the Midwest.

Reference:

Little, T. W., and R. Sheets. 1982. Transplanting Iowa Ruffed Grouse. *Proc. Iowa Acad. Sci.* 89:172-175.

Greater Prairie-Chicken (*Tympanuchus cupido*)

Status: Accidental; formerly nested

By year since 1960

60	63	66	69	72	75	78	81	84	87	90	93
2 1	1					1		1		1	1

By month -- all records

Jan	Feb	Mar	Apr	May	Jun	Jul	Aug	Sep	Oct	Nov	Dec
2 1 1	1 + +	+ + +	+							1	1

28 Jan 1960, Buchanan Co. (Bordner 1960)
1960, Mills Co. (Stemple and Rodgers 1961)
13 Jan 1962, Sioux City, Woodbury Co. (Youngworth 1962)
late Nov 1965, Fremont Co. (*IBL* 36:19)
7 Feb 1979, Harrison Co. (Schaufenbuel 1979)
2 Jan 1984, Osceola Co. (Spengler 1984)
11 Dec 1992, near Larchwood, Lyon Co. (Iowa State Univ. #2578, Eby 1993)
4 Jan to 5 Apr 1994, Cherokee, Cherokee Co. (Bierman 1994)

Occurrence: This rare winter visitor to northern and western Iowa was once an abundant resident throughout the state and is now being reintroduced into southern Iowa. The most recent records from northwestern Iowa are likely winter visitors from the Dakotas or Minnesota.

When settlers arrived, prairie chickens were common over all but northwestern Iowa. Populations increased rapidly as settlers created a patchwork of pastures and croplands within the native prairie that covered much of Iowa. In the 1870s and 1880s, this species was abundant and hunted extensively. In winter, Iowa populations were augmented by migrants from the north. As a result of the hunting pressure and the rapid loss of most native prairies, the population declined rapidly in the late

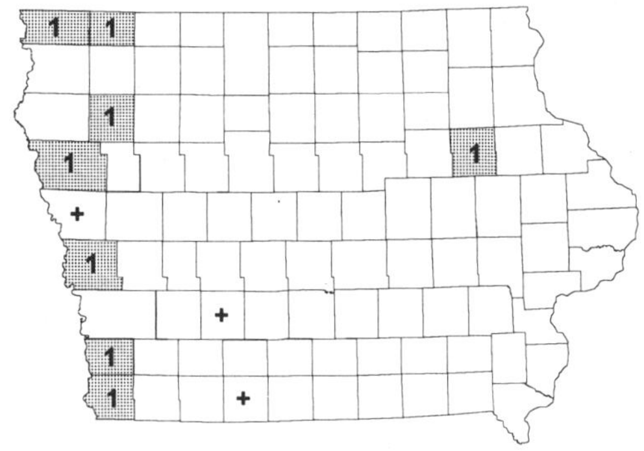

Greater Prairie-Chicken, 1960-1995
Records and introduction sites (+)

1800s and early 1900s (Dinsmore 1994). Although hunting was banned in 1917, the few remaining populations gradually disappeared. The last nesting population, which was in Appanoose County, disappeared in the 1950s (Stempel and Rodgers 1961).

The first attempts to restock Greater Prairie-Chickens in Iowa were in 1980 and 1982 when 53 and 49 were released in the Loess Hills near Onawa in Monona County. A brood was seen there in 1982, but those birds disappeared in a few years. From 1987 to 1994, 445 prairie chickens were released in Ringgold County. In 1993 and 1994, 115 more were released in nearby Adair County in an attempt to start a second population (Andrews et al.). Although the Ringgold County population shows some signs of being established, it is still too early to know if either of those populations will be self-sustaining.

Comment: The current range of this partially migratory species includes scattered areas across the eastern Dakotas, western Minnesota, central Nebraska, and central and eastern Kansas. Isolated populations are found in Wisconsin, Illinois, Missouri, and Texas. Originally the range was much greater, extending to New England and covering much of the Midwest.

References:

Bierman, D. 1994. Greater Prairie-Chicken in Cherokee County. *Iowa Bird Life* 64:115.

Bordner, Mrs. R. I. 1960. Records from several localities in Iowa. *Iowa Bird Life* 30:61-62.

Eby, M. 1993. Greater Prairie-Chicken in Lyon County. *Iowa Bird Life* 63:55.

Schaufenbuel, J. 1979. Greater Prairie Chicken in Harrison County. *Iowa Bird Life* 49:26-27.

Spengler, R. 1984. Greater Prairie Chicken in Osceola County. *Iowa Bird Life* 54:21.

Stempel, M. E., and S. Rodgers. 1961. History of prairie chickens in Iowa. *Proc. Iowa Acad. Sci.* 68:314-322.

Youngworth, W. 1962. A prairie hen in Sioux City. *Iowa Bird Life* 32:20.

Sharp-tailed Grouse (*Tympanuchus phasianellus*)

Status: Extirpated

ca. 1850, Des Moines, Polk Co. (Amer. Museum of Natural History, DuMont 1933)
10 Feb 1883, Hardin Co. (Univ. of Iowa #29088, P-0059, Kent and Schrimper 1996)
20 Mar 1903, Whittemore, Kossuth Co. (Chicago Acad. Sci. #11138)

Occurrence: There are 3 Iowa specimens of this extirpated species. There are no other records for which the identification can be verified. Some early observers may have confused this species with the very similar appearing Greater Prairie-Chicken. There is some evidence that this species was the common prairie grouse in northwestern Iowa when explorers first arrived (Hayden 1863, Johnsgard and Wood 1968). The prairie-chicken seems to have been better adapted to live in the agricultural landscape that was created with settlement, and the sharp-tail rapidly disappeared from Iowa. A brood reported in northern Kossuth County in 1931 and 2 birds seen in the same area in June 1934 (DuMont 1935) seem to be the last reports of Sharp-tailed Grouse in Iowa.

The Department of Natural Resources has made several attempts to reintroduce Sharp-tailed Grouse into western Iowa in recent years. The first, of 37 birds near Onawa in Monona County in 1990, seems to have been a failure. It is too early to assess the most recent release of 69 birds near Mapleton in Monona County in March 1995 (Weiner 1995).

Comment: The range of this resident species is from central Alaska east to James Bay and south to northern Michigan, north-central Minnesota, central Nebraska, central Colorado, and eastern Oregon. Some of the populations are isolated. The closest populations to Iowa are in Nebraska and South Dakota.

References:

DuMont, P. A. 1935. Additional breeding birds in Iowa. *Oologist* 52:83-84.

Hayden, F. V. 1863. On the geology and natural history of the Upper Missouri. *Transactions American Philosophical Society* 12:1-218.

Johnsgard, P. A., and R. E. Wood. 1968. Distributional changes and interaction between Prairie Chickens and Sharp-tailed Grouse in the Midwest. *Wilson Bull.* 80:173-188.

Weiner, E. 1995. 1995 sharptail release summary. *Wildlife Notes* 14(2):1-3.

Wild Turkey (*Meleagris gallopavo*)

Status: Regular; nests

Jan	Feb	Mar	Apr	May	Jun	Jul	Aug	Sep	Oct	Nov	Dec

Occurrence: This fairly common permanent resident occurs throughout the state. It is most abundant in southern and eastern Iowa but is found sparingly even along wooded valleys in the largely agricultural regions of northwestern Iowa.

Wild Turkeys were common in Iowa when settlers arrived. Due to excessive hunting and habitat loss, they were extirpated from Iowa by the early 1900s (Dinsmore 1994). After several attempts, Wild Turkeys were successfully reintroduced into Shimek and Stephens state forests in southern Iowa in the 1960s. During the 1970s and 1980s, birds from those populations were moved to other sites, and by about 1989, wild populations were established in virtually every county of Iowa (Jackson 1991). A limited hunting season for turkeys was opened in 1974, and by 1989 the entire state was open to hunting.

Comment: The Wild Turkey is a permanent resident from the northern United States south to the Gulf Coast and northern Mexico and east to the Atlantic Coast. Its populations are more scattered in the western third of its range. Due to excessive hunting and habitat loss, its range was greatly reduced in the late 1800s and early 1900s. Recently it has been restocked in many states, and it now occupies a range that is more extensive than it was prior to settlement.

Reference:

Jackson, D. 1991. The final chapter: restoring the Wild Turkey in Iowa. *Iowa Conservationist* 50(4):7-10.

Northern Bobwhite (*Colinus virginianus*)

Status: Regular; nests

Jan	Feb	Mar	Apr	May	Jun	Jul	Aug	Sep	Oct	Nov	Dec

Occurrence: This fairly common permanent resident of southern Iowa is uncommon to rare in northern Iowa. It typically is found along hedgerows or in grassy areas with scattered shrubs. Currently, bobwhite are primarily found in the southern 2 or 3 rows of counties. Populations have traditionally fluctuated widely, increasing during years with mild winters and favorable nesting conditions and then dropping abruptly, usually after a severe winter. In addition to these somewhat predictable year-to-year fluctuations in quail populations, there has been a gradual but steady long-term decline in numbers, apparently in response to the steady loss of the brushy habitat that this species favors.

Historically, bobwhites were common in all parts of the state and may have increased in numbers after settlement (Anderson 1907), but by the 1930s, they were much less abundant and common only in southern Iowa (DuMont 1933).

Comment: The range of this resident species is from Massachusetts west to southern South Dakota and south to the Gulf Coast, eastern Mexico, Guatemala, and Cuba. Iowa is at the northwestern edge of the Northern Bobwhite's range.

ORDER GRUIFORMES

Gruiformes are a very diversified ancient order with many fossil and recently extinct forms. There are about 200 living species in 11 families, with representatives of 3 families in North America and 2 in Iowa. They are united by similarities of skeletal and muscular structure. They have short tails, rounded wings, long necks, and long legs. Most are aquatic, but some live in plains, deserts, or forest. Hind toes are elevated in most. Feet are unwebbed, but coots have lobed toes. Some are large and strong flyers; others are smaller and weak flyers or flightless.

Rails, Gallinules, and Coots (Family Rallidae)

Rails, gallinules, and coots comprise 132 species, with 14 from North America and 8 from Iowa. Of the Iowa species, 6 are Regular and 2 Accidental. These marsh dwelling birds have large legs and feet; short, rounded wings; and short tails. They are poor flyers and migrate at night. Rails have long, decurved bills; coots and gallinules have short, rounded bills and frontal shields.

Yellow Rail (*Coturnicops noveboracensis*)

Status: Regular

By year since 1960

60	63	66	69	72	75	78	81	84	87	90	93

1 1 1 1 2 3 2 3 5 2 3 4 5 6 2 3 1 3 2 4 3 2

Jan	Feb	Mar	Apr	May	Jun	Jul	Aug	Sep	Oct	Nov	Dec
			X				X		X X X		

4 Apr 1991	21 May 1985	31 Aug 1970	20 Oct 1987
13 Apr 1983	26 May 1979	13 Sep 1982	22 Oct 1993
15 Apr 1886	27 May 1892	19 Sep 1992	early Nov 1964

Occurrence: This rare migrant is most commonly found from late April to mid-May and from late September to early October. There are 59 reports since 1960 and 22 before that. Most records are of birds flushed from the edges of marshes or from grassy fields and are identified by seeing the white area on the trailing edge of the wing. Locations of sightings reflect where birders walk marshy edge or known stopover locations, such as Snake Creek Marsh in Greene County. There are, however, relatively few records from western and north-central Iowa, where most water-associated birds are plentiful. Owing to its secretive nature, this species is undoubtedly more common than the records reflect, and the locations and dates reflect observer bias.

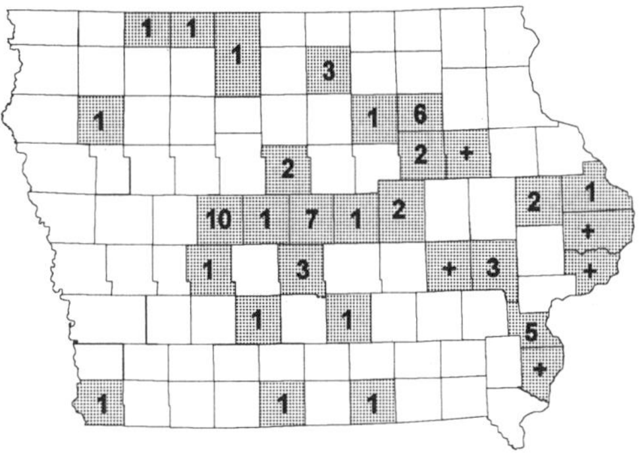

Yellow Rail, all
1960-1995 and historical (+)

Unlike other rails, Yellow Rails have only been heard a few times in Iowa (personal communications to T. Kent). Other unusual modes of discovery include the following: caught inside the Armory at Iowa City in Johnson County on 18 May 1933 (University of Iowa specimen #25591); tower kill at Alleman in Polk County on 1 October 1973 (Iowa State University specimen #1533, Mosman 1975) and 21 September 1985 (Iowa State University specimen #1897, *IBL* 55:124, Dinsmore et al. 1987); found dead at the fairgrounds at Cherokee in Cherokee County on 20 October 1987 (Iowa State University specimen #2424, Dinsmore 1992); found dead in Marshall County on 4 April 1991 (Iowa State University specimen #2544, Dinsmore 1992); caught by a dog in Emmet County on 13 September 1982 (Iowa State University specimen #1780, Dinsmore 1992); caught by a dog at Big Marsh in Butler County on 21 September 1980 (P-0008, *IBL* 51:27); injured by a mower and banded in Jackson County in early November 1964 (*IBL* 35:25); netted at Muskrat Slough in Jones County on 19 May 1963 (Petersen 1963); and caught in a yard after a snow storm at Ames in Story County on 13 April 1983 (P-0101, *IBL* 53:49). There are several old references to birds that were shot. Most noteworthy are birds collected at Burlington in Des Moines County on 15 April 1886 (DuMont 1933) and in Johnson County on 27 May 1892 (Anderson 1907). These unusual modes of discovery account for most of the early and late dates.

Comment: The winter range is near the Atlantic and Gulf coasts in the southeastern United States and near the Pacific Coast in central California. The breeding range extends from the Rocky Mountains east across southern Canada to the Atlantic Ocean, dipping south into the northern United States from North Dakota east to northern Michigan. The known nesting area nearest to Iowa is in northern Minnesota. This species is a local permanent resident in Mexico.

Reference:

Petersen, P. 1963. Banding at Muskrat Slough. *Iowa Bird Life* 33:32-33.

Black Rail (*Laterallus jamaicensis*)

Status: Accidental

By year since 1960 (also 1899, 1952, 1959)

60	63	66	69	72	75	78	81	84	87	90	93
1							1 1		2	1	1

By month -- all records

Jan	Feb	Mar	Apr	May	Jun	Jul	Aug	Sep	Oct	Nov	Dec
			2 +	3		2	1		1		

11 Jul 1899, Fort Dodge, Webster Co. (Anderson 1907)
17 May 1952, Fisher's L., Polk Co. (McCabe 1952)
summer 1959, Plymouth Co. (Bryant 1962)
13 May 1961, Cone M., Louisa Co. (*IBL* 31:66)
29 Aug 1981, Cone M., Louisa Co. (*IBL* 51:115, 117; 52:42)
24 Apr and 1 May 1982, Hendrickson M., Story Co. (*IBL* 52:56; 53:35)
15 May 1989, Zirbel Sl., Cerro Gordo Co. (*IBL* 59:78, 81; 61:85)
8 Oct 1989, Dickinson Co. (Hansen 1991)
26 Apr 1992, near Ankeny, Polk Co., 2 (Kraemer and Miller 1993)
12 Jul 1994, State Line M., Kossuth Co. (*IBL* 64:108, 65:81)

Occurrence: Of 10 Accepted records, 5 are from spring, 4 from summer, and 1 from fall. There are 11 old Not Accepted records (Dinsmore et al. 1984) and 4 recent ones, many of which could well have been this species.

Comment: Black Rails are found on the Gulf, Atlantic, and Pacific coasts north to northern California and New England, at inland locations north of the Gulf of California and in the central United States. They also occur from Central America south to Chile. Thus, Black Rail populations are often geographically isolated.

In the Midwest, records range north to east-central Minnesota and central Wisconsin. The pattern of records for almost all interior states is very similar to Iowa—records scattered over many years and locations, many questionable records, and evidence of nesting lacking. There are nesting records for Kansas, Illinois, and possibly Indiana. About half of the records are from May with fewer from April, September, and October and only a few from summer. Extreme dates are 20 April 1963 in northwestern Missouri (Robbins and Easterla 1992) and 19 October 1952 in northeastern Arkansas (James and Neal 1986).

The occurrence of Black Rails in the Midwest is an enigma. Are most of the birds strays from coastal populations? Or is there widespread nesting throughout the Midwest that has gone undetected? Although this species is secretive, it does call and sometimes flushes, so why is it not detected more often? Many sources mention its nocturnal habits as a reason for the lack of records, but, at least in Arizona, birds with radio transmitters are sedentary at night (Flores 1991).

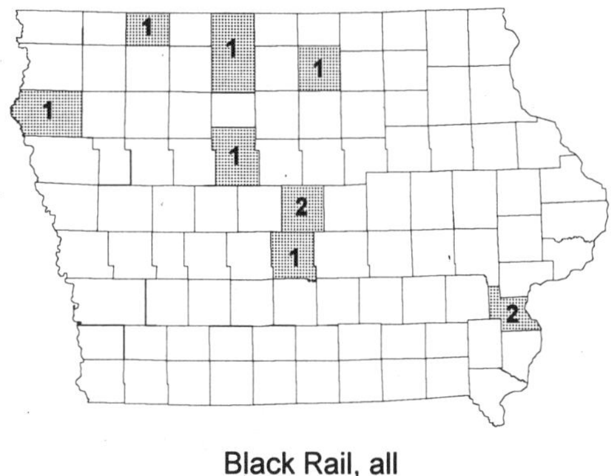

Black Rail, all

References:

Bryant, E. J. 1962. Black Rail in western Plymouth County. *Iowa Bird Life* 32:87.

Flores, R. E. 1991. Ecology of the California Black Rail in southwestern Arizona. Master's thesis, Univ. of Rhode Island, Kingston.

Hansen, J. L. 1991. Black Rail in Dickinson County. *Iowa Bird Life* 61:26-27.

Kraemer, D., and B. Miller. 1993. Black Rail sighting in Polk County. *Iowa Bird Life* 63:105.

McCabe, O. 1952. A record of the Black Rail near Des Moines. *Iowa Bird Life* 22:42-43.

King Rail (*Rallus elegans*)

Status: Regular; nests

By year since 1960

60	63	66	69	72	75	78	81	84	87	90	93
1 3 5	5 2 1	2	1 3 1		1	1	2 2 2	4 6 3	9 3 3 3	1 4	3 2

Jan	Feb	Mar	Apr	May	Jun	Jul	Aug	Sep	Oct	Nov	Dec

x (Jan); x (Oct)

15 Apr 1909
17 Apr 1921
18 Apr 1953
winter: 9 Jan 1966

6 Oct 1929
7 Oct 1894
14 Oct 1962

Occurrence: This rare migrant and summer resident has been reported most commonly from late April through July, with fewer fall records and 1 winter record. The most reported in any year is 9 in 1986, with 1 to 4 reported in most years. Most reports are either from near the Mississippi River or from the prairie pothole region of north-central and northwestern Iowa. The only winter record is from Goose Lake in Greene County on 9 January 1966 (*IBL* 36:22).

Nesting starts in mid-May and extends into June (Tanner and Hendrickson 1956). The only verified nesting records from 1980 to 1995 are in northwestern Iowa at Dewey's Pasture in Clay County in June 1981 (*IBL* 51:100) and near the Mississippi River in Dubuque County in July 1986 (*IBL* 57:120), near Maquoketa in Jackson County in July 1987 (*IBL* 57:120), at Green Island Wildlife Area in Jackson County in July 1992 (*IBL* 62:107), and in Des Moines County (Jackson et al. 1996).

The King Rail was considered fairly common in appropriate habitat at the beginning of the Twentieth Century (Anderson 1907). By the 1930s, it was considered greatly reduced as a breeding species (DuMont 1933); however, it was still a fairly common nesting species in Clay and Palo Alto counties (Bennett 1934, Bennett and Hendrickson 1939). In the early 1950s, 6 nests were found in Clay County (Tanner and Hendrickson 1956). Since 1960, despite extensive field work in that area, it has been reported there only a few times.

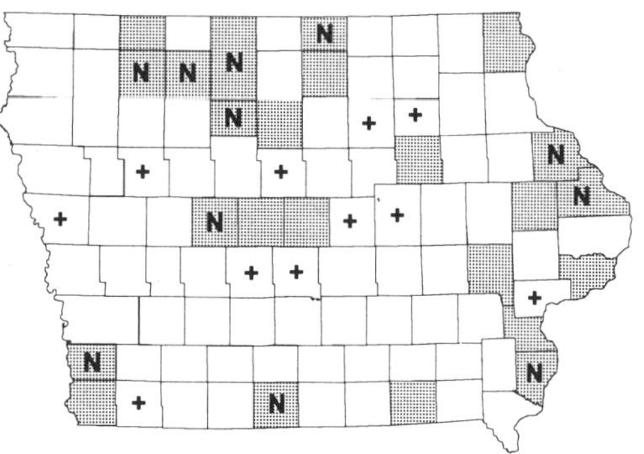

King Rail, 1960-1995
June-July, nesting (N), and spring/fall (+)

Comment: The winter range is near the coast from New Jersey south to central Mexico and in the Mississippi River Valley north to Arkansas. The breeding range is from the eastern Dakotas south to eastern Texas and east to Massachusetts and Florida. This species also occurs in the Greater Antilles. A winter record from a Quad Cities Christmas Bird Count on 26 December 1960 is listed as from Rock Island (Bohlen 1989). There is another winter record from Illinois and 3 December records from Wisconsin (Robbins 1991), but no winter records from Missouri (Robbins and Easterla 1992). Most experts believe that populations of this species are declining (Reid et al. 1994).

References:

Bennett, L. J., and G. O. Hendrickson. 1939. Adaptability of birds to changed environment. *Auk* 56:32-37.

Reid, F. A., B. Meanley, and L. H. Fredrickson. 1994. King Rail. In: T. C. Tacha, and C. E. Braun, eds. *Migratory Shore and Upland Game Bird Management in North America.* International Association of Fish and Wildlife Agencies, Washington, D.C.

Tanner, W. D., and G. O. Hendrickson. 1956. Ecology of the King Rail in Clay County, Iowa. *Iowa Bird Life* 26:54-56.

Virginia Rail (*Rallus limicola*)

Status: Regular; nests

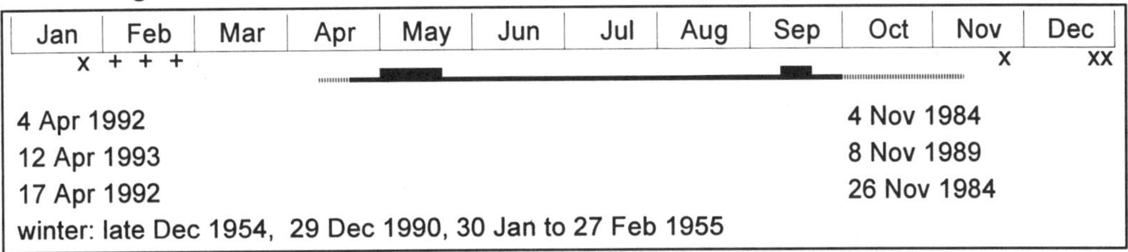

Occurrence: This uncommon migrant and rare nesting species arrives in late April and most are gone by late September. In migration it may be found in all areas of the state, but its nesting range is in north-central and northwestern Iowa. Nesting begins in mid-May with the peak in late May through mid-June (Tanner and Hendrickson 1954).

The winter birds involve 1 that was taken inside and died prior to 26 December 1954 at Des Moines in Polk County (Brown 1956), 1 that stayed in open water at Camp Dodge in Polk County from 30 January to 27 February 1955 (Brown 1956), and 1 near open water at Brown's Lake in Woodbury County on 29 December 1990 (*IBL* 61:56). The 26 November 1984 record is of an injured bird found in a turkey brooder house in Buena Vista County (*IBL* 54:112).

With the loss of wetlands, this species is probably much less abundant now than it was a century ago.

Comment: The winter range follows the coasts of the United States and extends into Mexico. Wintering also occurs at interior locations in the southwestern United States. There are a few winter records from Minnesota, Wisconsin, and Illinois. The breeding range is from southern Canada east of the Rocky Mountains south to northern Missouri and Maryland; in the West, it nests from southern British Columbia south into northern Mexico. Virginia Rails are also found in South America from Colombia to Chile.

Virginia Rail, 1960-1995
June-July and nesting (N)

References:

Brown, W. H. 1956. Winter record of the Virginia Rail in Polk County. *Iowa Bird Life* 26:19.

Tanner, W. D., and G. O. Hendrickson. 1954. Ecology of the Virginia Rail in Clay County, Iowa. *Iowa Bird Life* 24:65-70.

Sora (*Porzana carolina*)

Status: Regular; nests

Jan	Feb	Mar	Apr	May	Jun	Jul	Aug	Sep	Oct	Nov	Dec
		x								xx x	xx

31 Mar 1990
1 Apr 1988
4 Apr 1948
winter: 29 Dec 1985, 30 Dec 1982

12 Nov 1989
17 Nov 1986
22 Nov 1987

Occurrence: This common migrant and uncommon summer resident arrives in late April and leaves by late September. In summer, it is most common in marshes with thick emergent vegetation in north-central and northwestern Iowa, but nests sparingly elsewhere. Nesting starts in mid-May and extends into late June or early July (Tanner and Hendrickson 1956).

Winter records are from Ventura Marsh in Cerro Gordo County on 30 December 1982 (*IBL* 53:25) and from Muscatine in Muscatine County on 29 December 1985 (*IBL* 56:19, 58).

Sora, the most common rail in Iowa, was once considered abundant and nested primarily in the northern half of the state (Anderson 1907). Its nesting range is probably much reduced from 100 years ago.

Comment: The winter range is from the southern United States to the West Indies and northern South America. The breeding range extends from northern Canada to the central United States. Iowa is on the southern edge of the breeding range. There are December records from Minnesota and Illinois and 2 midwinter records from Wisconsin.

Reference:

Tanner, W. D., and G. O. Hendrickson. 1956. Ecology of the Sora in Clay County, Iowa. *Iowa Bird Life* 26:78-81.

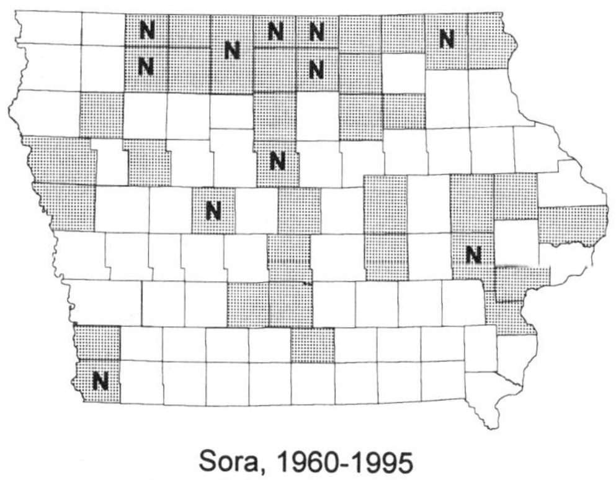

Sora, 1960-1995
June-July and nesting (N)

Purple Gallinule (*Porphyrula martinica*)

Status: Accidental

By year since 1960 (also 1937)

60	63	66	69	72	75	78	81	84	87	90	93
	1					1	1		1		1

By month -- all records

Jan	Feb	Mar	Apr	May	Jun	Jul	Aug	Sep	Oct	Nov	Dec
				1 2 3	+ + +						

13 May 1937, Cedar Falls, Black Hawk Co. (Dix 1937)

7 May 1964, northwestern Louisa Co. (P-0400, Kent 1964)

22 May 1978, Ames, Story Co. (Iowa State Univ. #1648, P-0113, Dinsmore and Graham 197 Dinsmore 1992)

16 May to 7 June 1983, near South Amana, Iowa Co. (P-0100, P-0104, P-0133, Haldy 1983)

late May to 31 Jun 1988, near Burlington, Des Moines Co. (P-0258, Cecil 1988)

24 May to 14 Jun 1994, Sweet M., Bremer Co. (Stone 1995)

Occurrence: All 6 records are of birds first discovered in May. There are 7 additional reports that lack details (Dinsmore et al. 1984).

Comment: This species winters from southern Florida, Louisiana, and Texas and the Pacific Coast of Mexico south to Argentina and Chile. In summer it moves north to southeastern Tennessee and the Carolinas. It also occurs in areas bordering the Mediterranean and Caspian seas. Purple Gallinules are notorious vagrants, occurring north as far as Wyoming, Nebraska, Minnesota, Ontario, Quebec, and Labrador, and occasionally nesting in Illinois, Ohio, and Delaware. About three-fourths of Midwest vagrants are found from April to June and the rest scattered in all months except January. This species is usually found climbing in the understory around wooded ponds.

References:

Cecil, R. 1988. Purple Gallinule in Des Moines County. *Iowa Bird Life* 58:115.

Dinsmore, J. J., and D. L. Graham. 1979. Purple Gallinule in Ames. *Iowa Bird Life* 49:87-88.

Dix, Mrs. R. S. 1937. Purple Gallinule in Black Hawk County. *Iowa Bird Life* 7:34.

Haldy, L. 1983. Purple Gallinule in Iowa County. *Iowa Bird Life* 53:58.

Kent, F. W. 1964. A Purple Gallinule in Iowa. *Iowa Bird Life* 34:50-51.

Stone, T. 1995. Purple Gallinule in Bremer County. *Iowa Bird Life* 65:52.

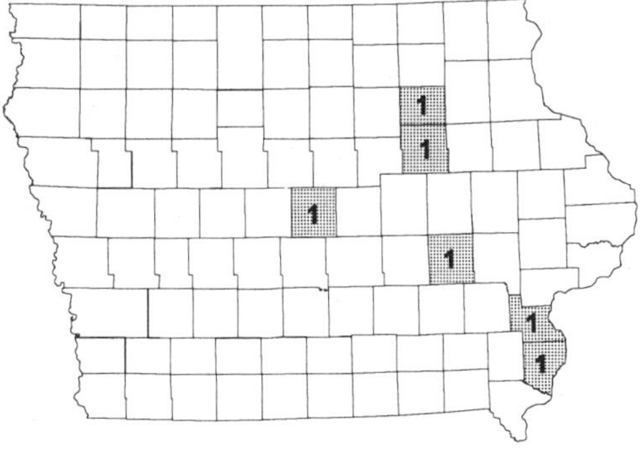

Purple Gallinule, all

Common Moorhen (*Gallinula chloropus*)

Status: Regular; nests

Jan	Feb	Mar	Apr	May	Jun	Jul	Aug	Sep	Oct	Nov	Dec
			x x								

Spring	Fall
5 Apr 1942	21 Oct 1986
20 Apr 1991	23 Oct 1982
21 Apr 1986	29 Oct 1984

Occurrence: This rare migrant and summer resident arrives in late April and departs by late September. Most reports of nesting are at several large wetlands with thick emergent cover in north-central Iowa and near the Mississippi River. Nesting starts in mid-May and peaks in early June (Fredrickson 1971). Moorhens are most obvious when broods leave the nest and associate with adults in open water in July or August.

Historically, this species was not common (Anderson 1907). In the late 1960s, 19 nests were found near Ruthven in Clay and Palo Alto counties (Fredrickson 1971), but it seems to have disappeared from that area since then. In recent years, Big Wall Lake in Wright County, Goose Lake in Clinton County, and Green Island Wildlife Area in Jackson County have been the most reliable places to find this species. The 27 adults and 33 young reported at Big Wall Lake in Wright County in June 1986 (*IBL* 56:115) is the largest concentration reported in Iowa.

Comment: The winter range is from southern United States south through the West Indies and South America and in Eurasia and Africa. The breeding range includes the winter range and extends north in the eastern United States to southern Minnesota.

Reference:

Fredrickson, L. H. 1971. Common Gallinule breeding biology and development. *Auk* 88:914-919.

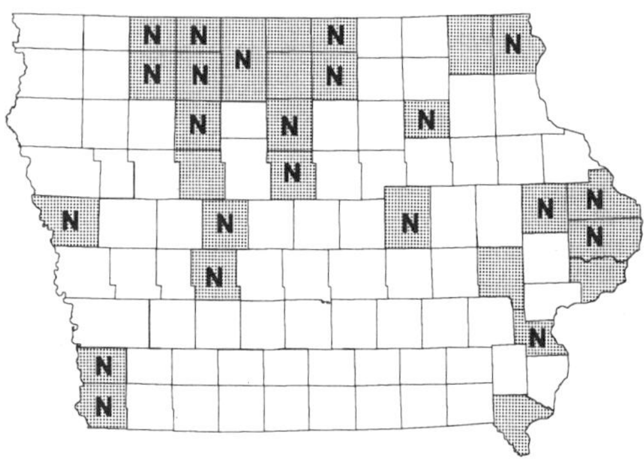

Common Moorhen, 1960-1995
June-July and nesting (N)

American Coot (*Fulica americana*)

Status: Regular; nests

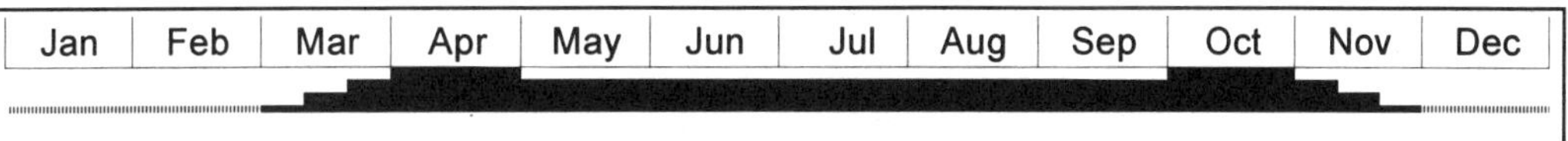

Occurrence: This abundant migrant and common summer resident occasionally over-winters. It is found statewide on all types of open water, but during the nesting season is most often found on wetlands with good inter-spersion of open water and stands of thick emergent vegetation. Migrants start arriving in early March and usually peak in April. Fall migration usually peaks in October but a few may linger until late November or December. Coots often congregate in large flocks during migration.

Coots nest at least occasionally throughout the state but are most abundant in northwest-ern and north-central Iowa. Nesting generally starts in early May and continues into June (Provost 1947, Fredrickson 1970).

From 1980 to 1996, there have been 1 to 3 reports of coots per year from January to mid-February. Wintering birds are usually found with wintering waterfowl at artificially heated areas such as Cedar Lake in Linn County and at Rock Valley in Sioux County. In some years, the first spring migrants appear in late February.

Comment: The winter range is from northern United States to the West Indies and Middle America, and the breeding range extends from there north across the Canadian provinces. American Coots also inhabit the mountains of South America and the Hawaiian Islands.

References:

Fredrickson, L. H. 1970. The breeding biology of American Coots in Iowa. *Wilson Bull.* 82:445-457.

Provost, M. W. 1947. Nesting of birds in the marshes of northwest Iowa. *Amer. Midland Naturalist* 38:485-503.

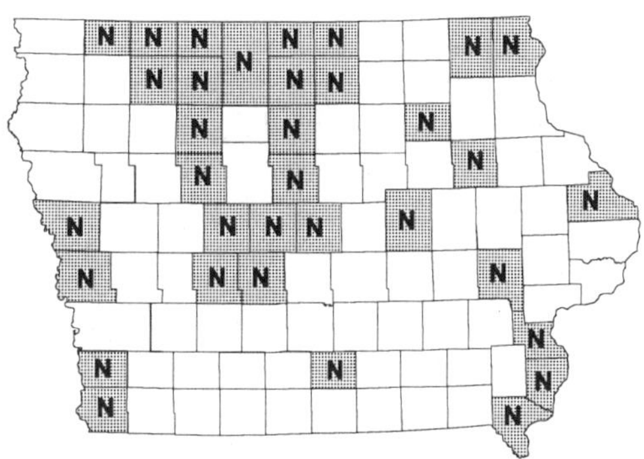

American Coot, 1960-1995
Nesting

Cranes (Family Gruidae)

Cranes comprise 15 species, with 3 from North America and 2 from Iowa. They are found on open habitats on all continents except Antarctica and South America. Both of the Iowa species nested in Iowa prior to settlement. The Whooping Crane is classified as Accidental based on 1 record in the last 50 years. The Sandhill Crane was originally more common in Iowa but was rare in the state until the late 1970s when increasing numbers were reported. It began nesting in Iowa again in 1992.

Cranes are large birds with long legs, necks, and bills. They occupy upland habitats. The loud trumpet-like calls of the cranes carry long distances and are a good way to locate them.

Sandhill Crane (*Grus canadensis*)

Status: Regular; nests

Jan	Feb	Mar	Apr	May	Jun	Jul	Aug	Sep	Oct	Nov	Dec

Occurrence: This rare migrant and summer resident is usually found on open habitats such as wetlands and wet grasslands. Migrants arrive in March and leave in November or early December. Most spring migrants are found in March, but singles at Amana in Iowa County on 10 February 1987 (*IBL* 57:55) and Saylorville Reservoir in Polk County on 21 February 1990 (*IBL* 60:51) were probably early migrants.

The first recent Iowa summer report was of 2 at Lylah's Marsh in Howard County on 23 July 1988 (*IBL* 58:109). A few have been found nearly every summer since then, and in 1992, 2 broods were found at Otter Creek Marsh in Tama County, the first known nesting in Iowa since 1894 (Poggensee 1992). Cranes nested successfully at Otter Creek Marsh in 1993, 1994, and 1995 (*IBL* 63:96, 65:14, 97) and at Sweet Marsh in Bremer County in 1995 (*IBL* 65:97). A nest at Green Island Wildlife Area in Jackson County in 1993 was flooded (*IBL* 63:96).

Cranes sometimes linger into December and have been reported on Christmas Bird Counts several times in recent years. Winter records include the following: mid-November 1979 to early January 1980 near Randalia in Fayette County (Schaufenbuel 1980) and at Riverton Area in Fremont County in 1980-1981 (*IBL* 51:32). One was seen near Moravia in Appanoose County from December 1980 to 13 February 1981 (Dinsmore 1989). In the winter of 1988-1989, 1 near Saylorville Reservoir in Polk County and 3 near Burlington in Des Moines County apparently over-wintered (*IBL* 59:51). One wintered in the Bays Branch and Lake Icaria region in 1994-1995—it was seen repeatedly with 2 neck-collared geese at both locations (*IBL* 65:48).

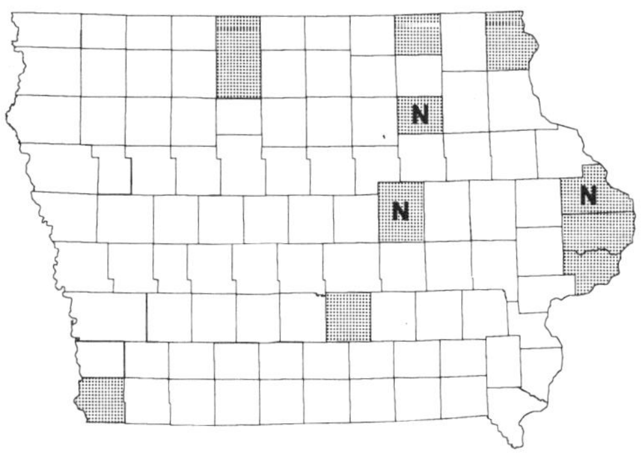

Sandhill Crane, 1960-1995
June-July and nesting (N)

In the 1800s, the Sandhill Crane was a fairly common nesting species on the wet prairies of northern Iowa. Habitat loss and excessive hunting led to its rapid disappearance (Dinsmore 1994). The last recorded nest was near Eagle Lake in Hancock County in 1894

(Anderson 1894). The number of Sandhill Cranes reported in Iowa increased greatly in the late 1970s and 1980s (Dinsmore 1989), culminating in their return as a nesting species. Nesting birds derive from populations in Wisconsin, which increased greatly in the 1970s and 1980s (Robbins 1992) and eventually spilled over into Iowa. These birds winter in Florida and Georgia. The huge flocks that gather in central Nebraska nest in the Arctic. Those flocks are probably the source of most cranes seen in western Iowa.

Most reports of cranes in Iowa are of individuals or groups of fewer than 10 birds; the only large flocks reported were 250 seen near Inwood in Lyon County on 10 April 1982 (*IBL* 52:55), 90 at Brown's Lake in Woodbury County on 27 October 1994 (*IBL* 65:14), and 75 to 80 at Estherville on 6 November 1948 (Wolden 1948).

Comment: The winter range is in central California and from southern United Sates to northern Mexico. The breeding range extends across much of northern Canada, Alaska, and Siberia south into the northern Rocky Mountains and Great Lakes states. Isolated populations nest in Florida and southern Georgia, southern Mississippi, and Cuba. Sandhill Crane populations have generally thrived in recent years, even with a limited hunting season. Overall, their populations total about 650,000 birds (Tacha et al. 1994). With the recent rapid growth of the Great Lakes populations, it seems likely that Sandhill Crane numbers in Iowa will increase and that they will reoccupy additional portions of their original range.

References:

Anderson, R. M. 1894. Nesting of the Whooping Crane. *Oologist* 11:263-264.

Dinsmore, J. J. 1989. The return of Sandhill Cranes to Iowa. *Iowa Bird Life* 59:71-74.

Poggensee, D. 1992. Nesting Sandhill Cranes at Otter Creek Marsh, Tama County. *Iowa Bird Life* 62:112-113.

Schaufenbuel, J. 1980. Sandhill Crane wintering in Fayette County. *Iowa Bird Life* 50:54.

Tacha, T. C., S. A. Nesbitt, and P. A. Vohs. 1994. Sandhill Crane. In: T. C. Tacha, and C. E. Braun, eds. *Migratory Shore and Upland Game Bird Management in North America.* International Association of Fish and Wildlife Agencies, Washington, D.C.

Wolden, B. O. 1948. Sandhill Cranes at Estherville. *Iowa Bird Life* 18:68.

Whooping Crane (*Grus americana*)

Status: Accidental; formerly nested

31 Oct 1972, near Clinton, Clinton Co. (Petersen 1972)

Occurrence: The only modern record is from fall in eastern Iowa after a storm. Reasonable secondhand details from a single observer are available (Petersen 1972). Three other reports since 1963 are Not Accepted (Dinsmore et al. 1984).

Whooping Cranes formerly nested on some of the larger marshes of northern Iowa and also migrated through the state (Allen 1952). There are nesting records from 11 counties (Dinsmore 1994). The last nest was found in Hancock County in 1894 (Anderson 1894). The only records from the early 1900s were from 24 March 1904 in Sac County (Spurrell 1917) and 9 April 1911 near Webb in Clay County (Gabrielson 1917).

There are 4 specimens at the University of Iowa taken at Holly Springs in Woodbury County in 1887 (#5395, #5399 [P-0062], #5400, #5403, Kent and Schrimper 1996) and 1 at Coe College taken in Linn County in 1880 (#492, P-0070). Three including a downy young were at the Philadelphia Academy of Sciences, and 4 others were in private collections (DuMont 1933).

Comment: The remaining population of this species winters at Aransas National Wildlife Refuge on the coast of Texas and breeds at Wood Buffalo National Park in Alberta. From a low of 21 birds in 1944-1945, with protection, the population grew to 165 in the wild and another 145 in captivity in 1995.

The breeding range formerly extended south to Iowa and locally in southeastern Texas and southern Louisiana, and the winter range extended on the Gulf Coast to Florida and to northern Mexico.

A few are seen in migration in Nebraska each year. More unusual are records in Holt County in northwestern Missouri from 13 to 15 October 1958 (Robbins and Easterla 1992), in Pike County in west-central Illinois just south of Iowa from 16 October to 5 November 1958 (Bohlen 1989), in Waukesha County in southeastern Wisconsin on 17 April 1959 (Robbins 1991), at Rice Lake National Wildlife Refuge in Aiken County in east-central Minnesota on 7 November 1951 (Janssen 1987), and in Mahnomen County in northwestern Minnesota on 12 October 1985 (Janssen 1987).

References:

Allen, R. P. 1952. The Whooping Crane. *National Audubon Society Research Report*, No. 3.

Anderson, R. M. 1894. Nesting of the Whooping Crane. *Oologist* 11:263-264.

Petersen, P. C. 1972. Whooping Crane in Clinton County. *Iowa Bird Life* 42:98.

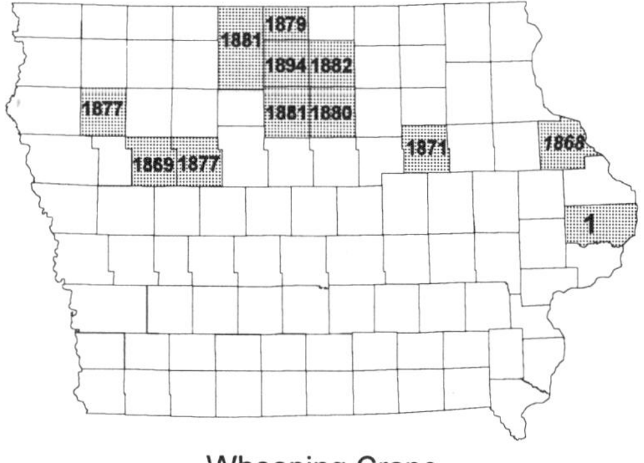

Whooping Crane
Last nesting year and recent record (1)

ORDER CHARADRIIFORMES

Charadriiformes comprise several families and subfamilies of birds associated with seashores and inland water areas. Most have compact plumage and many have webbed toes. They are strong flyers and long-distance migrants. Many breed in colonies and have precocial young. Families represented in Iowa include plovers; stilts and avocets; sandpipers and phalaropes; skuas, gulls, terns, and skimmers; and auks, murres, and puffins.

Plovers (Family Charadriidae)

Plovers comprise 66 species, with 16 from North America and 6 from Iowa. Plovers are stocky shorebirds with relatively thick, short bills that are swollen at the tip. They have moderately long legs and wings, short tails, and dark and white markings. They feed on animal food picked or probed from the surface. Most plovers lay 4 eggs in a simple scrape on the ground and depend on cryptic colors of the eggs to hide them from predators.

Of the Iowa species, 5 are Regular and 1 is Accidental. Of the 2 breeding species, 1 is common and 1 is rare. The 3 Regular migrants are long-distance migrants, breeding in the Arctic and wintering far to the south.

Black-bellied Plover (*Pluvialis squatarola*)

Status: Regular

Jan	Feb	Mar	Apr	May	Jun	Jul	Aug	Sep	Oct	Nov	Dec
			x		x x						

18 Apr 1976	5 Jun 1992	1 Aug 1982	23 Nov 1990
21 Apr 1985	10 Jun 1985	1 Aug 1995	25 Nov 1991
24 Apr 1983	19 Jun 1985	3 Aug 1988	28 Nov 1992
summer: 26, 27 Jun 1973			

Occurrence: This species is a relatively late migrant in both spring and fall. The majority of spring birds are seen in mid-May, while the fall migration is spread over several months. Most are found singly or in small groups on mudflats, but they may also be found in wet fields. High counts for spring and fall are 32 at Saylorville Reservoir in Polk County on 19 May 1994 (*IBL* 64:75) and 110 at Spirit Lake in Dickinson County on 11 October 1989 (*IBL* 60:13).

Comment: This Holarctic species winters coastally in the United States and southward throughout the world and breeds near the Arctic Coast. The black axillaries, white rump, and prominent white wing stripe seen on flying birds distinguish this species from American Golden-Plover.

American Golden-Plover (*Pluvialis dominicus*)

Status: Regular

Jan	Feb	Mar	Apr	May	Jun	Jul	Aug	Sep	Oct	Nov	Dec
						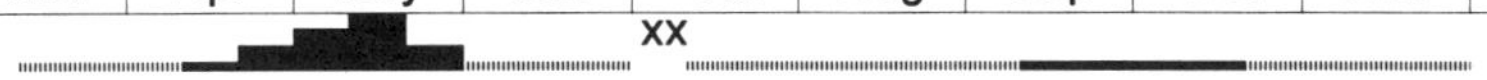 XX					

13 Mar 1982 — 22 Nov 1980
14 Mar 1987 — 23 Nov 1988
15 Mar 1996 — 27 Nov 1995

Occurrence: This species is one of the most abundant spring migrants in Iowa, but many flocks flying over or present in farm fields go unnoticed. They also occur in and near wetlands. Although the large flocks usually occur in May, a few birds arrive in March and some may linger through the summer. Many fewer pass through Iowa in fall as singles or in small flocks. High counts for spring and fall are 2,500 at Colo in Story County on 21 May 1983 (*IBL* 53:50) and 700 at Big Wall Lake in Wright County on 7 October 1990 (*IBL* 61:19).

Historically, in the late 1800s, golden plovers were even more abundant than now, but they were marketed along with Eskimo Curlews, a species with similar habitat and migration pattern. Numbers plummeted, but, unlike those for the curlew, have recovered considerably (Dinsmore 1994).

Comment: This species winters in the east-central portions of South America. In spring, most migrate through the Midwest. Breeding occurs over most of the Arctic in North America. In fall, most migrate to the East Coast and over the Atlantic Ocean to the wintering grounds. Pacific Golden-Plover (*Pluvialis fulva*) is a similar and recently separated species that breeds in Siberia and western Alaska and winters in southeastern Asia, Pacific islands, and California. It is too early to know whether *fulva*, like some other Asiatic shorebirds, will be found in the Midwest.

In early spring, summer, and fall, birds in basic and juvenal plumages have been confused with other plovers.

Snowy Plover (*Charadrius alexandrinus*)

Status: Accidental

By year since 1960 (also 1996)

60	63	66	69	72	75	78	81	84	87	90	93
									2	1 2	

By month -- all records

Jan	Feb	Mar	Apr	May	Jun	Jul	Aug	Sep	Oct	Nov	Dec
			1	3 1 1							

6 to 7 May 1988, Bays Branch W.A., Guthrie Co. (P-0251, Dinsmore and Fix 1988)
22, 25 May 1988, Dunbar Sl., Greene Co. (P-0246, Dinsmore and Fix 1988)
28 Apr 1990, near Burlington, Des Moines Co. (*IBL* 60:67; 62:21)
10 to 12 May 1992, Riverton A., Fremont Co., male (P-0331, P-0332, *IBL* 62:76, 63:69)
13 May 1992, Riverton A., Fremont Co., female (*IBL* 62:76, 63:69)
3 May 1996, Saylorville Res., Polk Co., male (P-0504, *IBL* 66:102)

Occurrence: The 6 records are all from spring. The first 2 records are possibly of the same bird, and the 2 at Riverton Area in Fremont County may have been a pair traveling together.

Comment: The Snowy Plover (known in Europe as the Kentish Plover) has a worldwide distribution in the temperate and tropical zones of both Northern and Southern hemispheres. In North America it is found year around on Gulf and Pacific coasts, and it migrates to the southern Great Plains and Great Basin for nesting. There were very few extralimital records in the Midwest prior to 1960, but since then there are more than 40 records in widely scattered locations north and east to Montana, Saskatchewan, South Dakota, Nebraska, Minnesota, Wisconsin, Michigan, Ontario, Pennsylvania, Illinois, Indiana, Missouri, Tennessee, and Arkansas.

About half of the extralimital records are from May, with the others spread evenly from March to September. Extreme dates are 25 March 1967 in northwestern Missouri (Robbins and Easterla 1992) and 9 September 1985 in northwestern Tennessee (Robinson 1990).

Reference:

Dinsmore, S. J., and A. S. Fix. 1988. Snowy Plovers in central Iowa. *Iowa Bird Life* 58:86-87

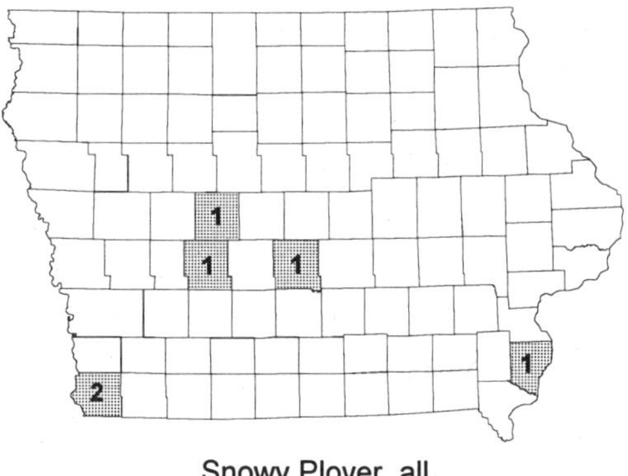

Snowy Plover, all

Semipalmated Plover (*Charadrius semipalmatus*)

Status: Regular

Jan	Feb	Mar	Apr	May	Jun	Jul	Aug	Sep	Oct	Nov	Dec
										XX X	
1 Apr 1991			14 Jun 1978			1 Jul 1989			3 Nov 1990		
3 Apr 1982			15 Jun 1985			3 Jul 1986			6 Nov 1970		
9 Apr 1989			15 Jun 1985			6 Jul 1986			28 Nov 1989		

Occurrence: This fairly common small plover is found over a wide range of dates and locations, usually on mudflats. High counts for spring and fall are 180 at Coralville Reservoir in Johnson County on 13 May 1980 (*IBL* 50:47) and 64 at Union Slough National Wildlife Refuge in Kossuth County on 6 August 1989 (*IBL* 60:14).

Comment: This Nearctic species winters coastally from the central United States to southern South America and breeds from Newfoundland across northern Canada and Alaska.

Piping Plover (*Charadrius melodus*)

Status: Regular; nests

Jan	Feb	Mar	Apr	May	Jun	Jul	Aug	Sep	Oct	Nov	Dec
11 Apr 1977									15 Sep 1994		
11 Apr 1990									17 Sep 1991		
14 Apr 1985									19 Sep 1991		

Occurrence: This species is a very rare and intermittent breeder along the Missouri River and rare migrant at other locations. A few pairs have nested on fly-ash deposits near the power plants south of Council Bluffs since 1983 (Wilson et. al. 1983) and south of Sioux City starting in 1985 (Williams 1985). The total nesting population is usually fewer than 5 pairs. Nesting begins in May, and most eggs hatch from late May to mid-June.

Historically, although nesting was suspected along Missouri River, it was not until 1940 that the first nests were found in Pottawattamie County at Lake Manawa (Stiles 1940) and at Carter Lake (Moser 1940). From 1968 to 1973 evidence of nesting was reported at De Soto National Wildlife Refuge in Harrison County (*IBL* 38:88, 39:62, 42:69, 43:75).

Reports of migrants, which average about 3 per year from 1980 to 1995, are from widely scattered locations, usually of single birds, and usually from mid-April to mid-May and mid-August to early September. More than one-third are from the 4 large reservoirs in Polk, Marion, Appanoose, and Johnson counties.

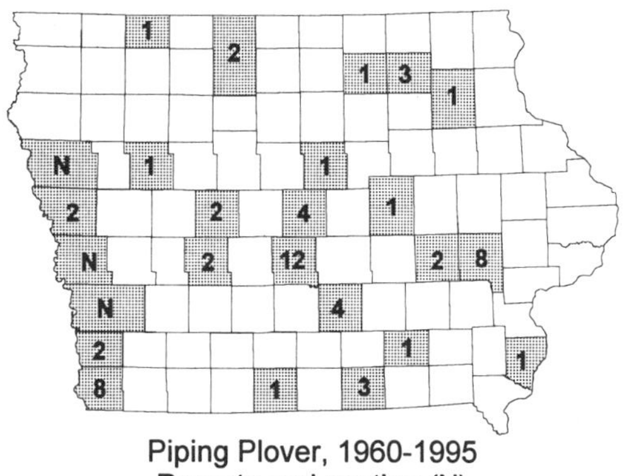

Piping Plover, 1960-1995
Reports and nesting (N)

Comment: Piping Plovers winter along the Gulf Coast, the southern Atlantic Coast, and locally to Cuba. They breed along the northern Atlantic Coast, Great Lakes, and Missouri River from Iowa north, and across northern Minnesota and the Prairie Provinces. They nest on sandy areas near water, where they are easily disrupted by human activities. The total interior population was estimated at 2,440 pairs in 1991 (Haig and Plissner 1993).

References:

Haig, S. M., and J. H. Plissner. 1993. Distribution and abundance of Piping Plovers: Results and implications of the 1991 international census. *Condor* 95:145-156.

Moser, R. A. 1940. The Piping Plover and Least Tern nesting in Omaha. *Nebr. Bird Review* 8:92-94.

Stiles, B. F. 1940. Nesting of the Piping Plover in Iowa. *Iowa Bird Life* 10:48-49.

Williams, R. D. 1985. Nesting observations of the Piping Plover near Sioux City. *Nebr. Bird Review* 53:74-76.

Wilson, B. L., L. Padelford, and B. Padelford. 1983. Piping Plover nests in Pottawattamie Co. *Iowa Bird Life* 53:69-70.

Killdeer (*Charadrius vociferus*)

Status: Regular; nests

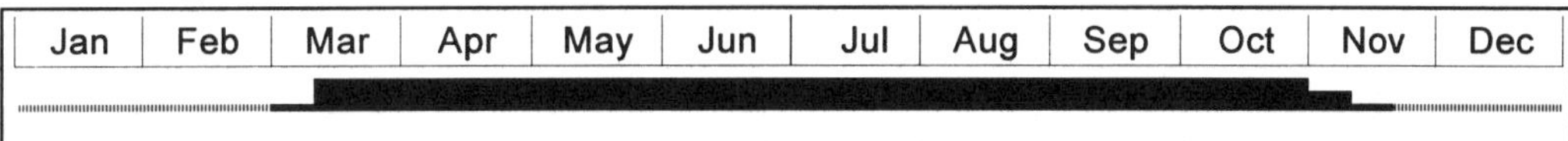

Occurrence: Killdeer is a common nesting species throughout Iowa, easily the most common nesting shorebird. Numbers on Breeding Bird Surveys average from 8.8 per count in the southern parts of the state to 15.7 in the northeast, with no evidence of change from 1967 to 1991. Nesting begins in mid-April and extends well into the summer, probably with many pairs producing 2 broods.

Migrants can appear with the first mild weather in February, but are more typically seen in March. Spring migrants are more dispersed and move through over a shorter period than in fall. In fall, large numbers often congregate near shallow water or in grassy fields. High counts for spring and fall are 500 at Riverton Area in Fremont County on 28 March 1991 (*IBL* 61:92) and 408 at Polk City in Polk County on 27 July 1986 (*IBL* 56:115).

A few typically linger into December. They are found on 12 percent of Christmas Bird Counts (north 4 percent, middle 12 percent, south 17 percent). In most years, there are 1 to 3 reports from mid-January to early February from varied locations where there is open water.

Comment: The regular winter range is about 1 state to the south of Iowa and extends to northwestern South America. The breeding range is from Mexico to southern Alaska and the northern edge of the Canadian provinces. Killdeer have adapted well to agricultural landscapes that dominate Iowa. They nest in fields, on roads, in parks, and other habitats created by humans.

Stilts and Avocets (Family Recurvirostridae)

Stilts and avocets comprise 10 species, with 3 from North America and 2 from Iowa. These long-legged, long-billed shorebirds are found mainly in tropical and subtropical areas of the world.

Black-necked Stilt (*Himantopus mexicanus*)

Status: Casual

By year since 1960 (also 1996)

60	63	66	69	72	75	78	81	84	87	90	93
								1		1 1	1 1

By month -- all records

Jan	Feb	Mar	Apr	May	Jun	Jul	Aug	Sep	Oct	Nov	Dec
			1 +	3 +	1			1			

1, 2 Jun 1984, Union Slough N.W.R., Kossuth Co., 2 (P-0143, P-0144, *IBL* 54:82; 55:57)
6 to 14 Apr 1991, Snyder Bend P., Woodbury Co. (Huser 1992)
12 May 1992, Riverton A., Fremont Co. (P-0333, Johnson and Allen 1994)
20 to 21 May 1993, Amana L., Iowa Co., 2 (P-0386, Kent 1994)
5 Sep 1994, Storm L., Buena Vista Co., 2 (*IBL* 65:14, 81)
18, 19 May 1996, Washington Co., 3 (P-0501, *IBL* 66:103)

Occurrence: Of the 6 recent well-substantiated records, 5 are from spring and 1 from fall. Old, Not Accepted records include 2 unlabeled specimens and 6 sightings at specified locations from 1890 to 1954 (Dinsmore et al. 1984). Based on the ease of identification and likelihood of occurrence, these reports are probably correct.

Comment: This species breeds coastally from Oregon and Delaware south to Argentina and Chile, but also migrates inland to nest in western states as far east as Idaho, Wyoming, Kansas, and Texas. It is closely related to the White-winged Stilt, *Himantopus himantopus*, of the Old World, which also has a tropical and temperate zone permanent range and additional northward breeding range in the Northern Hemisphere.

Extralimital records of Black-necked Stilts began to increase in the 1960s and continued in the 1970s and 1980s. There are records for almost all states and provinces. First state nesting records occurred in southeastern Missouri in 1990 (Jacobs 1991) and in southwestern Illinois in 1994 (McKee and Fink 1995). This species is as rare in states bordering Iowa as it is in Iowa.

About one-third of the extralimital records are from May, followed by June, July, and August and then by April, September, and October. Extreme dates are 21 March 1988 in southeastern Tennessee and 4 November 1985 in north-central Tennessee (Robinson 1990).

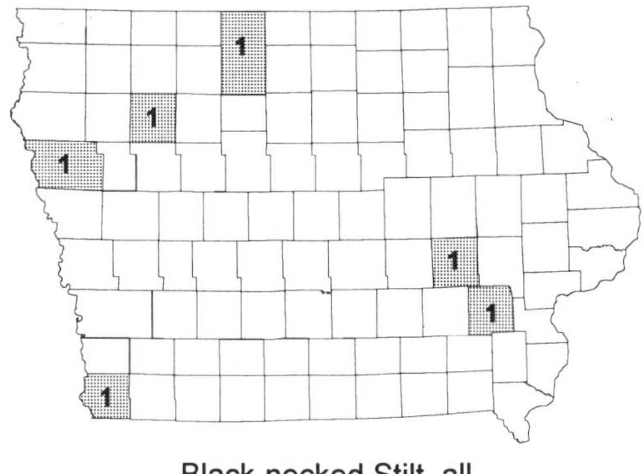

Black-necked Stilt, all

References:

Huser, B. 1992. Black-necked Stilt in Woodbury County. *Iowa Bird Life* 62:84-85.

Jacobs, B. 1991. First state nesting record for Black-necked Stilts, *Himantopus mexicanus*. *Bluebird* 58:7-11.

Johnson, A., and P. Allen. 1994. Black-necked Stilt at Riverton Area. *Iowa Bird Life* 64:20-21.

Kent, T. H. 1994. Black-necked Stilt at Amana Lake. *Iowa Bird Life* 64:53.

McKee, C., and T. Fink. 1995. First confirmed nesting of Black-necked Stilt in Illinois. *Meadowlark* 4:6-7.

American Avocet (*Recurvirostra americana*)

Status: Regular

Jan	Feb	Mar	Apr	May	Jun	Jul	Aug	Sep	Oct	Nov	Dec

8 Apr 1991	28 May 1990	26 Jun 1987	6 Nov 1994
12 Apr 1992	30 May 1992	6 Jul 1973	9 Nov 1956
13 Apr 1993	6 Jun 1983	7 Jul 1982	10 Nov 1931
Summer: to 3 Jul 1986			

Occurrence: Avocets are rare migrants that are found singly or in small flocks. The number of reports has increased in recent years, which is due at least in part to increased birding activity. Birds may be found across the state, but southwestern Iowa is the most consistent location, especially in spring. High counts for spring and fall are 50 in Fremont and Mills counties on 26 April 1986 (*IBL* 56:86) and 35 near Chariton in Lucas County on 23 October 1966 (*IBL* 36:104).

The 2 or 3 birds that were south of Sioux City up to 3 July 1986 exhibited behavior suggestive of nesting (*IBL* 56:115). Berry reported collecting a set of 4 eggs east of Hawarden on 2 June 1902 (Anderson 1907), but some of Berry's reports have been questioned.

Comment: This species winters coastally in the southern United States, Mexico, and the West Indies and breeds on the East Coast and throughout the western United States and the Prairie Provinces. Iowa is close to the breeding range in South Dakota, and there is an extralimital nesting record from 1977 in Faribault County in south-central Minnesota near Iowa (Janssen 1987). Nesting in Iowa is a possibility.

Sandpipers, Phalaropes, and Allies (Family Scolopacidae)

Sandpipers and phalaropes comprise 87 species, with 63 from North America and 33 from Iowa. Of 7 species that have nested in Iowa, 3 are regular nesters (Spotted Sandpiper, Upland Sandpiper, American Woodcock), 2 are irregular nesters (Common Snipe, Wilson's Phalarope), and 2 are former nesters (Marbled Godwit, Long-billed Curlew). The other 26 species are strictly migrants, of which 3 are Casual (Whimbrel, Red Knot, Red Phalarope), 4 are Accidental (Long-billed Curlew, Sharp-tailed Sandpiper, Curlew Sandpiper, Ruff), and 1 is Extirpated (Eskimo Curlew). Most of the migrants are equally common in spring and fall, but Hudsonian Godwit and White-rumped Sandpiper are rare in fall because they migrate to the East Coast and then south over the Atlantic Ocean.

Sandpipers generally are found in open habitats, especially on mudflats, flooded fields, and shorelines, where they feed on various invertebrates. Most of the species are cryptically colored and lay their eggs in a simple ground nest. Most are long-distance migrants. Many of the New World species winter in South America or on coasts and breed in the Arctic or Subarctic. They may fly hundreds of miles in a day and stop only where there is suitable feeding habitat. Migrants may be seen in Iowa from March to early December. Sandpipers found in June may be early or late migrants or nonbreeding birds that are lingering south of the nesting grounds. For several species, southbound migrants regularly arrive in Iowa in early July, making shorebirds the earliest of fall migrants.

With few exceptions (e.g., Hudsonian Godwit, Ruff, phalaropes), sexes are not distinguishable in the field. Plumages (juvenal, basic, alternate) are, however, recognizable for most species and are of considerable aid in identification of sandpipers. In spring, birds may arrive in basic (winter) plumage and show all gradations of molt to alternate (breeding) plumage. In fall, adults return first in worn alternate plumage and later show variable molt to basic plumage. Juveniles return later and, with time, show all stages of molt to first-basic plumage (which may include retained juvenal feathers).

Greater Yellowlegs (*Tringa melanoleuca*)

Status: Regular

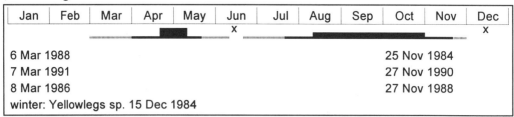

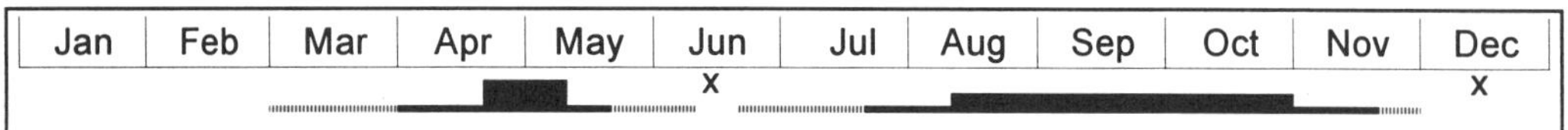

Jan	Feb	Mar	Apr	May	Jun	Jul	Aug	Sep	Oct	Nov	Dec

6 Mar 1988 — 25 Nov 1984
7 Mar 1991 — 27 Nov 1990
8 Mar 1986 — 27 Nov 1988
winter: Yellowlegs sp. 15 Dec 1984

Occurrence: This species is a fairly common migrant, usually seen as singles or small flocks. Only in late fall are Greater Yellowlegs likely to outnumber Lesser Yellowlegs. The increasing number of late June records could represent lingering birds or early fall migrants. A yellowlegs found on a Christmas Bird Count at Saylorville Reservoir in Polk County on 15 December 1984 (*IBL* 55:12, 27, 58) was most likely a Greater. High counts for spring and fall are 82 in Guthrie County on 14 April 1985 (*IBL* 55:63) and 176 at Runnells Area on 29 October 1989 (*IBL* 60:14).

Comment: Greater Yellowlegs winter throughout South America, Middle America, and the West Indies north to coastal areas of United States and breed in the Subarctic zone of North America. Greater Yellowlegs are relatively easy to identify by size and longer, slightly upturned bill when standing next to a

Lesser Yellowlegs. When seen alone, identification is not as easy, but can be based on the bill, thick knees, markings on underparts that extend posteriorly to the legs (alternate plumage), and the harsher 3- to 5-note call.

Lesser Yellowlegs (*Tringa flavipes*)

Status: Regular

Jan	Feb	Mar	Apr	May	Jun	Jul	Aug	Sep	Oct	Nov	Dec
										XX	

5 Mar 1955	19 Nov 1991
8 Mar 1994	22 Nov 1989
10 Mar 1986	25 Nov 1988

Occurrence: This species is one of the most common migrant sandpipers in Iowa and may occur in very large numbers. It is widespread and may be found singly or in loose flocks wherever shorebirds are encountered. Many of the birds found in June may be early or late migrants, but some may be lingering nonbreeding birds, such as the 1 to 5 at Hendrickson Marsh in Story County from 9 to 22 June 1985 (*IBL* 55:91). High counts for spring and fall are 1,500 at Riverton Area in Fremont County on 9 May 1987 (*IBL* 57:82) and 6,000 at Union Slough National Wildlife Refuge in Kossuth County on 28 August 1988 (*IBL* 59:12).

Comment: Lesser Yellowlegs have a winter range similar to Greater Yellowlegs, which includes South America, Middle America, the West Indies, and the southern coastal United States. The breeding range, however, extends farther north than the range of the Greater Yellowlegs to include both Subarctic and Arctic North America and is limited to areas west of James Bay. Solitary birds in early March, June, and November should be carefully distinguished from Greater Yellowlegs.

Solitary Sandpiper (*Tringa solitaria*)

Status: Regular

Jan	Feb	Mar	Apr	May	Jun	Jul	Aug	Sep	Oct	Nov	Dec

4 Apr 1986	24 May 1988	23 Jun 1961	11 Oct 1981
5 Apr 1981	26 May 1989	24 Jun 1989	13 Oct 1995
7 Apr 1988	28 May 1972	26 Jun 1977	13 Oct 1991

Occurrence: This fairly common migrant does not linger late in spring and is usually the earliest returning sandpiper in fall. It can be found as early as late June. It is found singly or in small loosely associated groups, often in ponds, streams, and backwaters. Occasionally larger numbers are encountered. High counts for spring and fall are 66 at Riverton Area in Fremont County on 29 April 1989 (*IBL* 59:81) and 202 at Coralville Reservoir in Johnson County on 20 July 1991 (*IBL* 61:115).

Comment: The winter range is in South America east of the Andes, in eastern Middle America to the southern tip of Texas, and in the West Indies. Breeding occurs in the boreal forests of Canada and Alaska and rarely to northern Minnesota. This tree nester often uses old songbird nests.

Willet *(Catoptrophorus semiplamatus)*

Status: Regular

Jan	Feb	Mar	Apr	May	Jun	Jul	Aug	Sep	Oct	Nov	Dec
		x						x	xx		

27 Mar 1994	1 Jun 1979	22 Jun 1988	15 Sep 1991
2 Apr 1972	2 Jun 1962	23 Jun 1989	19 Oct 1974
3 Apr 1986	3 Jun 1984	23 Jun 1995	20 Oct 1984

Occurrence: This rare migrant is found singly or in small numbers in the same habitat as yellowlegs. Early fall migrants in small flocks may be encountered in late June or early July, especially in western Iowa. High counts for spring and fall are 85 in central Iowa on 26 April 1986 (*IBL* 56:86) and 100 at Coralville Reservoir in Johnson County on 9 August 1975 (*IBL* 45:93).

Historically, Berry reported shooting a female and taking a set of 4 eggs near Hawarden in Sioux County on 2 June 1900 (Anderson 1907), but some of Berry's reports have been questioned. Cooke (1888) cites a less definite report: "Mr. Preston reported it as a rare breeder near Newton, Iowa." These old references were not judged sufficient to classify this species as an extirpated nester in Iowa; however, it seems plausible that this species may have nested along with other prairie birds that formerly bred in Iowa.

Comment: Willets winter coastally in United States and south to northern South America. Birds that breed in the Great Basin and the northern Great Plains are highly migratory, while birds that breed along the Gulf and East coasts and in the West Indies are much less so. Many adults depart from northern breeding areas before young have fledged, which accounts for the early arrival in western Iowa of birds that could be coming from nearby nesting areas in the Dakotas and north-central Nebraska.

Spotted Sandpiper (*Actitis macularia*)

Status: Regular; nests

Jan	Feb	Mar	Apr	May	Jun	Jul	Aug	Sep	Oct	Nov	Dec
+ +			x						x x	x	x + +

2 Apr 1981	31 Oct 1989
17 Apr 1986	2 Nov 1986
18 Apr 1982	16 Nov 1953
winter: 7 Dec 1976 to 14 Jan 1977	

Occurrence: Although this nesting species can be considered uncommon in terms of numbers encountered, it is widespread and present in appropriate habitat. Most arrive by early May and leave by late September. They are found along rivers, wooded ponds, dikes, and roadways near water. Spotted Sandpipers do not usually associate with other shorebirds and are usually seen in pairs or family groups, except in fall, when they may be found on mudflats with other shorebirds.

There are few published nesting reports in the last decade, which reflects their scattered distribution and difficulty in locating nests. They probably nest throughout the state (Jackson et al. 1996). Two nests with eggs were found on 27 June 1913 at West Okoboji in Dickinson County and followed to fledging (Smith 1914). The only winter record is from

Dubuque County from 7 December 1976 to 14 January 1977 (Rooks and Heathcote 1977).

Comment: The winter range is on the West Coast and from the southern United States south to northern Argentina. The breeding range is from northern Arkansas north to southern Arctic areas. Females may bond successively with up to 5 males (polyandry), leaving the males to care for the eggs and young (Oring et al. 1983). The Iowa winter record is quite unusual. There is a January record from Wisconsin (Robbins 1991) and several winter records from Tennessee (Robinson 1990).

References:

Oring, L. W., D. B. Lank, and S. J. Maxson. 1983. Population studies of the polyandrous Spotted Sandpiper. *Auk* 100:272-285.

Rooks, J. D., and P. Heathcote. 1977. Wintering Spotted Sandpiper at E. B. Lyons Prairie-Woodland Preserve, Dubuque. *Iowa Bird Life* 47:22.

Smith, A. F. 1914. Notes on the Spotted Sandpiper. *Wilson Bull.* 26:81-86.

Upland Sandpiper (*Bartramia longicauda*)

Status: Regular; nests

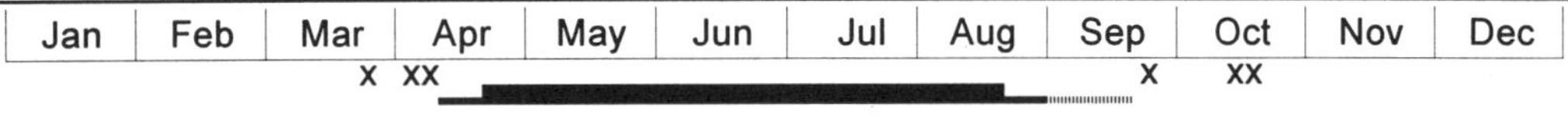

Jan	Feb	Mar	Apr	May	Jun	Jul	Aug	Sep	Oct	Nov	Dec
		x	xx					x	xx		

26 Mar 1968	29 Sep 1983
7 Apr 1963	13 Oct 1976
10 Apr 1992	15 Oct 1978

Occurrence: This species is an uncommon to rare nesting species in grassland areas. Most arrive in mid- to late April and leave in August. Birds are detected across the state on Breeding Bird Survey routes, averaging 1 per route, and with no change in numbers from 1967 to 1991. Birds frequently return to preferred grassy areas year after year, where they are most easily detected early or late in the day sitting on posts or by hearing their melodious whistle overhead. Nesting occurs from late April to early June. High counts include 40 in Adair County in the summer of 1988 (*IBL* 58:109) and 23 near Lamoni in Decatur County on 16 July 1984 (*IBL* 54:82).

Upland Sandpiper is one of the most typical species of tall-grass prairie, which once covered most of Iowa. It was reported as common by early Iowa ornithologists, but market hunting and plowing of the prairie led to a rapid decline in numbers (Dinsmore 1994). By the 1930s, it was considered uncommon (DuMont 1933). Brown (1960) summarized information and opinions about the status of this species up to 1960. Breeding Bird Surveys from 1967 to 1991 suggest that the population is stable.

Comment: Upland Sandpipers are long-distance migrants, wintering on the pampas of east-central South America and breeding from Oklahoma diagonally north to the Maritime Provinces in the east and British Columbia and southern Alaska in the west.

Reference:

Brown, W. H. 1960. Former abundance and present status of the Upland Sandpiper in Iowa: A cooperative study. *Iowa Bird Life* 30:31-37.

Eskimo Curlew (*Numenius borealis*)

Status: Extirpated

spring 1866, northwestern Iowa, thousands (Hough 1901)
5 Apr 1893, Burlington, Des Moines Co., specimen location uncertain (Univ. of Iowa #16803, Anderson 1907, DuMont 1933, 1933a)
10 Apr 1900, Grinnell, Poweshiek Co., 3 specimens at Harvard Univ. (Hahn 1963)
3 May 1901, Davenport, Scott Co., specimen not examined (Charleston Museum, SC; Hodges 1950)

Occurrence: Although the above records are the only Accepted ones, there is circumstantial evidence indicating that this species was once an abundant spring migrant in Iowa (Dinsmore 1994).

Comment: Eskimo Curlews wintered in east-central South America and migrated through Central America and the Great Plains to nesting grounds in the Northwest Territories. In fall, they flew to the East Coast and south over the Atlantic Ocean to South America. The period of rapid decline, due to market hunting, loss of habitat, or, perhaps, climatic change (Banks 1977), was from 1870 to 1885. Eskimo Curlews traveled with American Golden-Plovers, and both were heavily slaughtered during the eastern fall migration in New England and at other East Coast locations in years in which their flights were pushed ashore by bad weather. They were also hunted in spring as they moved north through the Great Plains (Gollop et al. 1986). The early pioneer ornithologists in Iowa may have missed this species because of its limited migration interval in April and May, its upland habitat preference, and probable occurrence mostly in western Iowa, which was largely unsettled at that time. There is evidence that a remnant population of this species may be breeding in the Northwest Territories and migrating through central United States in spring.

References:

Banks, R. C. 1977. The decline and fall of the Eskimo Curlew, or why did the curlew go extaille? *Amer. Birds* 31:127-134.

Gollop, J. B., T. W. Barry, and E. H. Iversen. 1986. Eskimo Curlew, a vanishing species? *Saskatchewan Natural History Society Special Publication*, No. 17.

Hahn, P. 1963. *Where is That Vanished Bird?* Royal Ontario Museum, Toronto.

Hodges, J. 1950. Specimen of the Eskimo Curlew for Iowa discovered. *Iowa Bird Life* 20:26.

Hough, E. 1901. The dough bird again. *Forest and Stream* 56:146.

Whimbrel (*Numenius phaeopus*)

Status: Casual

By year since 1960 (also 1895, 1943, 1952, 1958, 1996)

60	63	66	69	72	75	78	81	84	87	90	93
1 1	1 1 1	1		1			1 2	1	3 1	1 3	1 4

By month -- all records

Jan	Feb	Mar	Apr	May	Jun	Jul	Aug	Sep	Oct	Nov	Dec
			3	1 1 8	1		1 1	1 1	1		

22 Apr 1961	26 May 1992	1 Aug 1987	3 Sep 1987
24 Apr 1992	26 May 1960	27 Aug 1995	14 Sep 1952
25 Apr 1987	27 May 1994		1 Oct 1995

summer: 26 Jun 1988

Occurrence: Of the 29 records, 23 are from spring, 1 from summer, and 5 from fall. Most are late spring migrants (19 from mid- to late May). The bird at Algona on 26 June 1988 (*IBL* 58:109) is one of few late June records for the Midwest.

Comment: This Holarctic species winters coastally from California and Virginia south to all tropical coasts of the world and into the southern temperate zone. Breeding occurs in Arctic Alaska and Northwest Territories, on western Hudson Bay, from Iceland to western Siberia, and very locally in other areas of Siberia. Most migrants follow coastal routes, but some move overland through central United States, especially in spring, where most are detected as migrating flocks along the Great Lakes, with only scattered birds away from these large bodies of water.

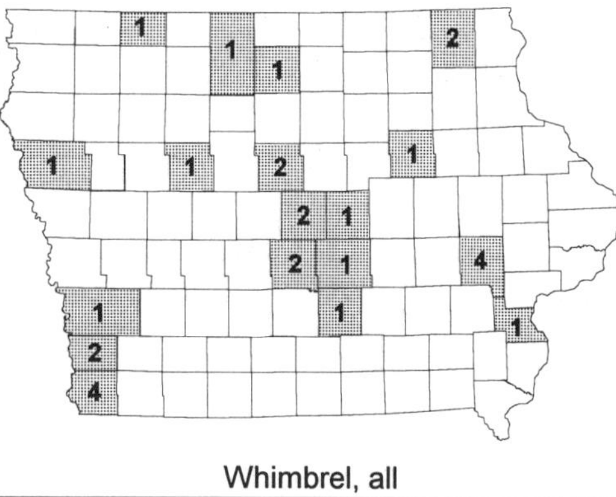

Whimbrel, all

Long-billed Curlew (*Numenius americanus*)

Status: Accidental; formerly nested

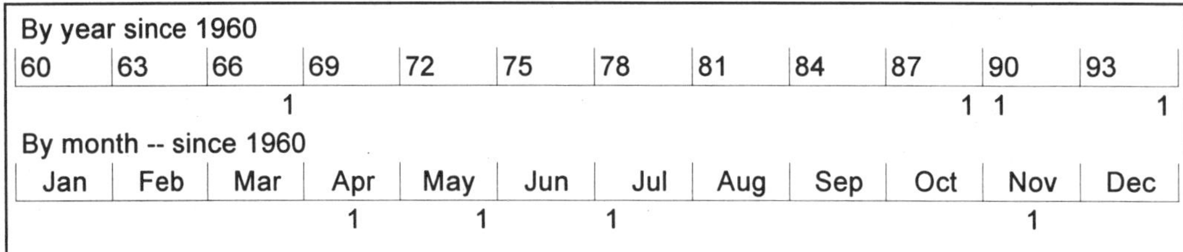

By year since 1960
60 63 66 69 72 75 78 81 84 87 90 93
1 1 1 1
By month -- since 1960
Jan Feb Mar Apr May Jun Jul Aug Sep Oct Nov Dec
1 1 1 1

ca. 1876, Sac Co. (specimen at Rockwell City, P-0080, Spurrell 1917, DuMont 1933)
ca. 1880, Kossuth Co. (Preston 1893, Anderson 1907)
10 Jun 1881, Dickinson Co., specimen at Philadelphia Academy of Sciences not examined (Oberholser 1918, DuMont 1933)
8 Apr 1884, Wolf Creek Sl., Woodbury Co. (Univ. of Iowa #10662, P-0052, DuMont 1933)
31 Mar 1893, near Hornick, Woodbury Co. (Iowa State Univ. #2520, Dinsmore 1992)
prior to 1933, Jefferson Co., specimen no longer extant (DuMont 1933)
15 May 1932, near Ogden, Boone Co. (DuMont 1933)
12 Nov 1968, Emmet Co. (Iowa State Univ. #2496, Priebe 1990, Dinsmore 1992)
11 Apr 1989, Riverton A., Fremont Co. (Priebe 1990)
4 Jul 1990, Power Plant Ponds, Pottawattamie Co. (Silcock 1991)
22 May 1995, Black Hawk L., Sac Co. (*IBL* 65:73)

Occurrence: The 4 records from 1960 to 1995 are from early and late spring, summer, and late fall. The other Accepted record from the 1900s is from late spring 1933. There are 5 records from the 1800s and 1 of unknown date that are Accepted and several other old reports (Anderson 1907, DuMont 1933, Dinsmore 1994).

Historically, comments of early ornithologists (Preston 1893, Anderson 1907, Dinsmore 1994) suggest that this species was a fairly common nester in the northern and western parts of Iowa. Habitat loss probably led to its disappearance. The last mentioned nesting date was about 1885 (Spurrell 1917).

Comment: This species winters in California and Texas south coastally in Mexico. The eastern population breeds in the western Great Plains and the Rocky Mountains north to the Prairie Provinces, and the western population breeds from the Great Basin north into British Columbia. Long-billed Curlews inhabit grasslands and wet meadows, but may also be found on shorelines. The nearest breeding area to Iowa is in north-central Nebraska.

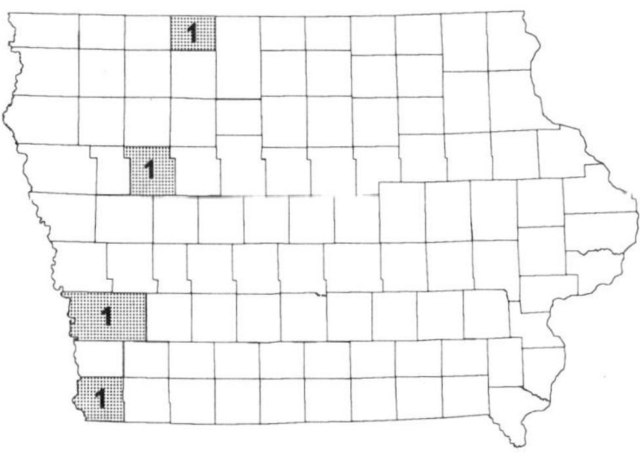

Long-billed Curlew, 1960-1995

References:

Oberholser, H. C. 1918. Notes on the subspecies of *Numenius americanus* Bechstein. *Auk* 35:188-195.

Preston, J. W. 1893. Some prairie birds. *Ornithologist and Oologist* 18:82-83.

Priebe, C. 1990. Long-billed Curlew in southwestern Iowa. *Iowa Bird Life* 60:20.

Silcock, W. R. 1991. Long-billed Curlew in Pottawattamie County. *Iowa Bird Life* 61:120-121.

Hudsonian Godwit (*Limosa haemastica*)

Status: Regular

Jan	Feb	Mar	Apr	May	Jun	Jul	Aug	Sep	Oct	Nov	Dec
		X	XX						XX		

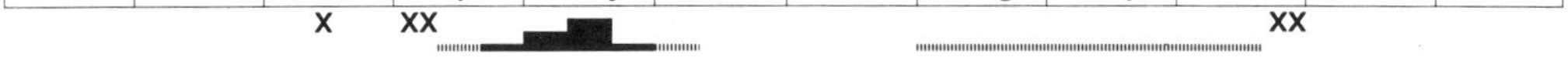

20 Mar 1976	4 Jun 1978	4 Aug 1979	20 Oct 1988
3 Apr 1970	5 Jun 1986	4 Aug 1984	23 Oct 1966
8 Apr 1991	8 Jun 1986	4 Aug 1987	30 Oct 1994

Occurrence: This species is a rare to uncommon spring migrant in most parts of the state, except in western Iowa where small to large flocks can be expected in mid-May at areas where shorebirds concentrate such as Riverton Area in Fremont County. Flocks of more than 100 may be present, with a high count of 284 in Greene County on 10 May 1988 (*IBL* 58:81). Hudsonian Godwits are rare and irregular in fall.

Comment: The winter range is in the temperate zone of southeastern South America. The breeding grounds are discontinuous and include Hudson Bay, the Northwest Territories, the Anchorage area, and northwestern Alaska. In spring, Hudsonian Godwits migrate north through central United States. In fall, almost the entire population stages around Hudson and James bays. Apparently, most fly nonstop from there to South America, although some stop along the East Coast and a few pass through the Midwest.

Spring birds display a variety of plumages from basic to alternate, and females are paler with much less chestnut color on the underparts. Hudsonian Godwits, at least in spring, are more likely to occur in flocks than Marbled Godwits. Even experienced observers can confuse these 2 species if not flushed. Hudsonians have a white rump, white wing stripe above and below, and dark underwing coverts. The latter mark also distinguishes Hudsonian from Black-tailed Godwit, a Eurasian species that is a vagrant to the East Coast and western Alaska.

Marbled Godwit (*Limosa fedoa*)

Status: Regular; formerly nested

Jan	Feb	Mar	Apr	May	Jun	Jul	Aug	Sep	Oct	Nov	Dec
					X			X XX	X		

3 Apr 1982	27 May 1978	16 Jun 1991	23 Sep 1973
5 Apr 1981	30 May 1994	23 Jun 1985	29 Sep 1995
6 Apr 1991	31 May 1995	29 Jun 1991	1 Oct 1984

Occurrence: Marbled Godwit is a rare migrant in Iowa. It is most often found singly in typical shorebird habitat anywhere in the state. It is an early migrant in spring and fall, with the most sightings from mid- to late April. High counts for spring and fall are 21 at Bays Branch Wildlife Area in Guthrie County on 20 April 1988 (*IBL* 58:81) and 20-25 at Blue Lake in Monona County on 19 August 1973 (*IBL* 43:75).

Historically, there is evidence of nesting in Iowa until about 1890 (Anderson 1907, Dinsmore 1994). At that time, the prairies were being plowed as northwestern Iowa was settled, and both Marbled Godwit and Long-billed Curlew ceased to nest in Iowa.

Comment: This species winters on coastal beaches from southern Oregon and Virginia south to Panama and breeds in the northern Great Plains and in an isolated area around

James Bay. The nesting area nearest to Iowa is in northeastern South Dakota. Because this species is a relatively short-distance migrant and breeds close to Iowa, it is not surprising that it is an early spring and fall migrant. This common bird of the Gulf Coast in winter is not very common east of the Great Plains and not very gregarious.

Marbled Godwits are much less variable in plumage than Hudsonians. Their tawny brown color is not as distinctive as their cinnamon wing linings and lack of white rump and wing stripes as seen in flight.

Ruddy Turnstone (*Arenaria interpres*)

Status: Regular

Jan	Feb	Mar	Apr	May	Jun	Jul	Aug	Sep	Oct	Nov	Dec
	X								X		

1 May 1996	11 Jun 1928	23 Jul 1995	29 Sep 1986
6 May 1956	15 Jun 1966	26 Jul 1985	29 Sep 1973
7 May 1967	16 Jun 1988	29 Jul 1988	11 Oct 1992
winter: Feb 1980			

Occurrence: This species is a rare but regular migrant that may be found on mud flats or on sandy or rocky beaches. Most are singles. Ruddy Turnstones are late spring migrants—they are not unusual in early June. In fall, however, they are unlikely to be very early or very late. High counts for spring and fall are 30 at Elk Creek Marsh in Worth County on 20 May 1966 (Sutter 1966) tied by 30 at Big Creek Lake in Polk County on 27 May 1994 (*IBL* 64:75) and 13 at Hendrickson Marsh in Story County on 29 July 1988 (*IBL* 58:109).

The winter record is of a bird photographed on the lock at Keokuk in Lee County in February 1980 (P-0004, *IBL* 50:47).

Comment: This Holarctic species winters coastally throughout the tropics and temperate zones of both hemispheres. It breeds coastally all around the Arctic Ocean. Most migrate along the coasts rather than through the central United States. First-year birds remain on the wintering grounds. There is a winter record from Ohio (Peterjohn 1989).

Reference:

Sutter, B. 1966. A twist in turnstone feeding tactics. *Iowa Bird Life* 36:57.

Red Knot (*Calidris canutus*)

Status: Casual

By year since 1960 (also 1934, 1937)

60	63	66	69	72	75	78	81	84	87	90	93
								2 1 1	1 2	1 2	1 4

By month -- all records

Jan	Feb	Mar	Apr	May	Jun	Jul	Aug	Sep	Oct	Nov	Dec
				2 1		1	2 1 1	4 3 +	2		

12 May 1994		22 Jul 1995	27 Sep 1984
13 May 1992		5 Aug 1986	1 Oct 1995
	21 May 1934	5 Aug 1988	8 Oct 1992

Occurrence: There are 14 fall and 3 spring records. Three other reports lack details (Dinsmore et al. 1984). The first record from 21 May 1934 at Lost Island Lake in Palo Alto County was of 14 birds in alternate plumage (Bennett (1935, 1938b). The mid-May birds at Riverton Area in Fremont County on 13 May 1992 (*IBL* 62:77) and at Blue Lake in Monona County on 12 May 1994 (Ernzen 1994) exhibited only slight evidence of molt to alternate plumage and could easily have been overlooked. The first record from fall was a juvenile at Anderson Lake in Hamilton County from 6 to 10 September (Iowa State University specimen #520, P-0117, Scott 1938).

Of the early fall records, 4 were of birds in alternate plumage: 22 July 1995 at Rathbun Reservoir in Appanoose County (*IBL* 66:20); 5 to 6 August 1986 at Saylorville Reservoir in Polk County (3 birds, Dinsmore 1987); and 5 August 1988 (*IBL* 59:13) and 31 August 1989 (*IBL* 60:14) at Union Slough National Wildlife Refuge in Kossuth County. The later fall records are of 1 or 2 birds in basic or juvenal plumage, except for the latest on 8 October 1992 at Rathbun Reservoir in Appanoose County that involved 4 birds (Scott 1993, date incorrect in *IBL* 63:18).

Comment: This Holarctic breeder winters coastally from the Atlantic and Pacific coasts and Europe south to the southern parts of South America, Africa, Australia, and New Zealand. Although this species has been found in all states and provinces except West Virginia, most migrate in a few large flocks and stop at localized areas along the East Coast. It is regular but rare in the Midwest. This long-distance migrant may fly over Iowa on its way to and from the Gulf Coast or arrive there via the Atlantic flyway. Early spring and fall birds in basic or juvenal plumages are easy to overlook; however, efforts in recent years have been successful in finding them. Sightings of this species deserve careful study and documentation.

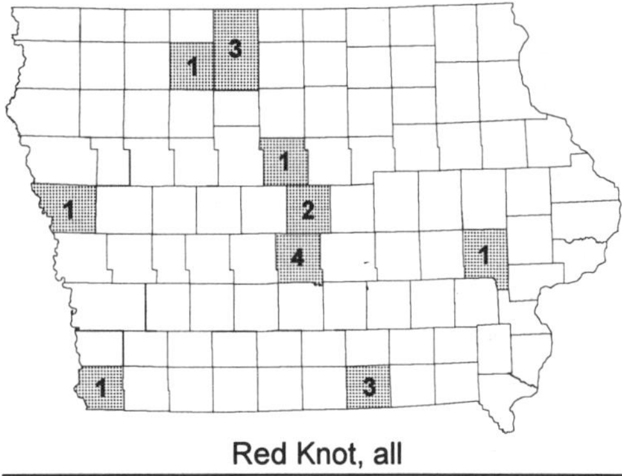

Red Knot, all

References:

Dinsmore, S. 1987. Red Knot at Saylorville Reservoir. *Iowa Bird Life* 57:24.

Ernzen, P. 1994. Red Knot in Monona County. *Iowa Bird Life* 64:85.

Scott, C. 1993. Red Knots at Rathbun Reservoir. *Iowa Bird Life* 63:104.

Scott, T. G. 1938. American Knot in Iowa. *Auk* 55:275-276.

Sanderling (*Calidris alba*)

Status: Regular

Jan	Feb	Mar	Apr	May	Jun	Jul	Aug	Sep	Oct	Nov	Dec
			x xx							x	

8 Apr 1981	3 Jun 1983	15 Jul 1990	10 Nov 1986
13 Apr 1992	5 Jun 1985	15 Jul 1994	10 Nov 1963
19 Apr 1990	7 Jun 1988	20 Jul 1989	11 Nov 1989

Occurrence: This rare migrant is most consistently found in mid- to late May on mud or sandy flats where it exhibits its typical running behavior. High counts for spring and fall are 30 at Coralville Reservoir in Johnson County on 23 May 1979 (*IBL* 49:60) and 49 at Big Creek Lake in Polk County on 11 September 1986 (*IBL* 57:16).

The plumage of spring birds varies from basic to varying degrees of molt to alternate. Early fall birds, which are not frequent in Iowa, may be in worn alternate plumage; most are in basic or juvenal plumage.

Comment: This Holarctic species is a typical wintering bird of ocean beaches from southern Alaska and Maritime Provinces to the tropics and temperate zones of both hemispheres. The breeding range is more limited in High Arctic of northern Canada, Greenland, and central Siberia. The late spring and fall migration fits with other species that nest far north in the Arctic. Most of the migration for this species is coastal or pelagic, but small numbers move through the central United States.

Semipalmated Sandpiper (*Calidris pusilla*)

Status: Regular

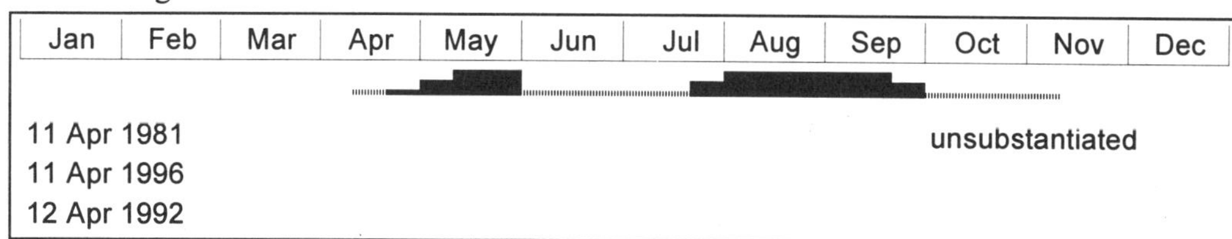

Occurrence: This common migrant tends to be a late spring and average fall migrant. In mid- to late May it may be the most common sandpiper if extensive mudflats are available. Late fall records are not well substantiated. In the field, it is difficult, and sometimes impossible, to distinguish between Western and Semipalmated sandpipers in basic plumage. High counts for spring and fall are 4,000 at Riverton Area in Fremont County on 23 May 1992 (*IBL* 62:77) and 550 at Union Slough National Wildlife Refuge in Kossuth County on 29 July 1985 and 9 August 1988 (*IBL* 55:91, 59:13).

Comment: This Nearctic species winters in tropical northeastern South America, the West Indies, and southern Central America and breeds in the High Arctic from Alaska to Labrador. It is an uncommon migrant on the West Coast, but common centrally and abundant on the East Coast.

Semipalmated Sandpiper exemplifies identification problems with "peeps." Plumage differences are hard to detect in this overall gray, black-legged species. This species sometimes runs on mudflats and at a distance can be confused with Sanderling. Some authorities say that basic-plumaged birds can not be distinguished in the field from Western Sandpiper, others are willing to make the distinction based on a typical bill—short and tubular in Semipalmated; long, pointed, and drooped in Western (Kaufman 1990). It has been determined that wintering birds in southeastern United States are Westerns, not Semipalmated (Phillips 1975). In Iowa, a few recent, well-studied black-legged peeps in October have been identified as Westerns; older reports of late Semipalmateds are less well substantiated.

Reference:

Phillips, A. R. 1975. Semipalmated Sandpiper: Identification, migrations, summer, and winter ranges. *Amer. Birds* 29:799-806.

Western Sandpiper (*Calidris mauri*)

Status: Regular

Jan	Feb	Mar	Apr	May	Jun	Jul	Aug	Sep	Oct	Nov	Dec
			X	X	X				X X	X X	
unsubstantiated			unsubstantiated			1 Jul 1987			15 Oct 1895		
						8 Jul 1988			28 Oct 1994		
						8 Jul 1989			6 Nov 1994		

Occurrence: About three-fourths of the records of this rare migrant are from fall. Fall records span July through September, with a few later records. Most reports are of juveniles in late August and early September. The early and late dates for spring are undocumented.

Returning adults in worn alternate plumage are found in July or early August, and birds in basic plumage (with or without retained juvenile feathers) have been substantiated for October and early November. Most of the 110 reports for this species are not well substantiated. Many of the spring birds have been in alternate plumage, but the earliest and latest dates are of birds that have not been well documented. There are 2 published photographs of August birds (Petersen and Lonnecker 1966, Kent 1987). The 3 juveniles taken at Burlington in Des Moines County on 15 October 1895 by Paul Bartsch are at the University of Iowa (#16362, #16363, #16363, P-0481, Anderson 1907, DuMont 1933, Kent and Schrimper 1996).

Comment: Western Sandpipers winter coastally from California and Virginia south to the West Indies and northern South America. The breeding range is limited to northern Alaska and the tip of Siberia. It is an abundant species on the West Coast, and lesser numbers migrate eastward to winter on the East Coast (Senner and Martinez 1982). Most adults either bypass or fly over the Midwest; juveniles are more likely to stop on their way south.

Our knowledge of the occurrence of this species is hampered by difficulty in identification, especially of early spring and late fall birds, and by failure of observers to provide detailed descriptions. Experience with this species in other states in the Midwest is similar to Iowa's.

References:

Kent, T. H. 1987. Bird identification quiz. *Iowa Bird Life* 57:124-126.

Petersen, P., and W. Lonnecker. 1966. Western Sandpipers at Davenport. *Iowa Bird Life* 36:87.

Senner, S. E., and E. F. Martinez. 1982. A review of Western Sandpiper migration in the interior of North America. *Southwestern Naturalist* 27:149-159.

Least Sandpiper (*Calidris minutilla*)

Status: Regular

Jan	Feb	Mar	Apr	May	Jun	Jul	Aug	Sep	Oct	Nov	Dec
										x x x	

14 Mar 1986	7 Jun 1989	23 Jun 1988	17 Nov 1986
16 Mar 1985	8 Jun 1992	24 Jun 1992	23 Nov 1982
19 Mar 1977	9 Jun 1985	26 Jun 1977	2 Dec 1990

Occurrence: This small, yellow-legged peep is common to abundant on mudflats and wet fields and has a broad migration interval in both spring and fall. High counts for spring and fall are 150 at Coralville Reservoir in Johnson County on 9 May 1990 (*IBL* 60:68) and 600 at Union Slough National Wildlife Refuge in Kossuth County on 17 August 1988 (*IBL* 59:13).

Comment: The winter range is from southern United States to the northern half of South America, and it breeds from Newfoundland across northern Canada to Alaska.

White-rumped Sandpiper (*Calidris fuscicollis*)

Status: Regular

Jan	Feb	Mar	Apr	May	Jun	Jul	Aug	Sep	Oct	Nov	Dec
			xx			x xx					

27 Apr 1990	25 Jun 1985	21 Jul 1992	20 Oct 1983
29 Apr 1989	27 Jun 1988	29 Jul 1985	22 Oct 1994
2 May 1976	1 Jul 1989	2 Aug 1991	7 Nov 1913

Occurrence: This late spring migrant occurs in small flocks with other shorebirds across the state; however, in mid- to late May in western Iowa it may rival Semipalmated Sandpiper as the most common shorebird. The high count for spring is 2,000 at Riverton Area in Fremont County on 19 May 1989 (*IBL* 59:82). White-rumped Sandpipers are usually found into early June, and a few have lingered into late June.

This species is rare in fall, with about 15 reports from 1960 to 1995, and some are not well substantiated.

Comment: The winter range is in the temperate zone of southern South America. The breeding range is in the High Arctic from the northern shore of Alaska to Baffin Island. Spring migration is through the Midwest, and the fall route is to the East Coast and over water to South America. The late spring migration fits with the long-distance migration pattern. It appears that a few birds may linger in Iowa in summer. Fall sightings of this species deserve careful study and documentation.

Baird's Sandpiper (*Calidris bairdii*)

Status: Regular

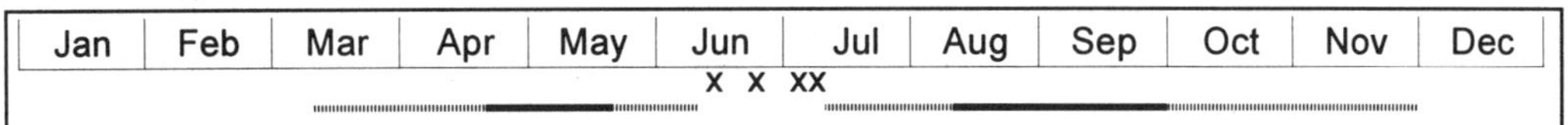

Jan	Feb	Mar	Apr	May	Jun	Jul	Aug	Sep	Oct	Nov	Dec
					x x	xx					

11 Mar 1991	6 Jun 1981	28 Jun 1992	21 Nov 1982
13 Mar 1988	9 Jun 1985	7 Jul 1986	24 Nov 1992
16 Mar 1989	11 Jun 1985	8 Jul 1992	26 Nov 1989

Occurrence: This species is a rare migrant over most of the state, although it is often common in southwestern Iowa. It has a very wide migration interval in both spring and fall. High counts for spring and fall are 400 at Riverton Area in Fremont County on 27 April 1991 (*IBL* 61:92) and 70 at Union Slough National Wildlife Refuge in Kossuth County on 28 August 1988 (*IBL* 59:13).

Comment: Wintering grounds are in southern and western South America north to the equator. Breeding grounds in the High Arctic extend from northwestern Greenland to the eastern tip of Siberia. The migration route for both spring and fall is mainly through central United States to the west of Iowa.

Pectoral Sandpiper (*Calidris melanotos*)

Status: Regular

Jan	Feb	Mar	Apr	May	Jun	Jul	Aug	Sep	Oct	Nov	Dec
	x										x

19 Feb 1983	21 Nov 1982
4 Mar 1990	25 Nov 1976
5 Mar 1977	1 Dec 1987

Occurrence: Pectorals are among the most abundant of Iowa's shorebirds and have been found in every month except January. A few arrive in early March, and by late April and early May, areas with extensive mudflats are covered with them. Flocks are also found in wet, grassy fields. June birds may be early or late migrants or lingering summer birds. A few hardy birds remain until winter. High counts for spring and fall are 2,500 at Coralville Reservoir in Johnson County on 7 May 1985 (*IBL* 55:64) and 11,800 at Union Slough National Wildlife Refuge in Kossuth County on 5 August 1988 (*IBL* 59:13).

Comment: Wintering grounds are in southern South America and also in Australia and New Zealand. Breeding grounds are from western Hudson Bay along the Arctic Coast to central Siberia. All birds are said to leave the United States in winter, so the record from Cone Marsh in Louisa County on 19, 26 February 1983 (*IBL* 53:25) is quite unusual and may be a very early spring migrant.

Sharp-tailed Sandpiper (*Calidris acuminata*)

Status: Accidental

By year since 1960

60	63	66	69	72	75	78	81	84	87	90	93
				1					1	1	1

By month -- all records

Jan	Feb	Mar	Apr	May	Jun	Jul	Aug	Sep	Oct	Nov	Dec
				1				1	1 1		

3 Oct 1974, Coralville Res., Johnson Co., juv. (Halmi 1974, 1989)
30 Sep 1988, Credit Is., Scott Co., juv. (Petersen 1989)
14 Oct 1990, Coralville Res., Johnson Co., juv. (Kent 1991)
15 May 1994, Riverton A., Fremont Co., alt. (P-0439, P-0465, *IBL* 65:81)

Occurrence: Of the 4 records, 3 are sight records of juveniles in fall, and 1 is of a spring bird in alternate plumage that was photographed and tape recorded. The photographs and recording of this unexpected spring bird were reviewed by an expert on shorebirds (Noble Proctor). The locations of the 1974 and 1990 birds were within one-half mile of each other.

Comment: This species nests near the Arctic Coast of central Siberia and winters in Australia and New Zealand. It is a regular vagrant to the West Coast and occasional vagrant to the Midwest, East Coast, and Europe. Most records are of juveniles in September and October with some in August and November. Records from the Midwest include 1 to 3 from Wyoming, Colorado, Texas, Iowa, Illinois, and Ohio. The few spring records are from Texas, Massachusetts, Connecticut, Saskatchewan, and Alberta.

Sharp-tailed Sandpiper resembles Pectoral Sandpiper in appearance and behavior and is usually found with pectorals. Careful study is required for identification of this Asian vagrant.

References:

Halmi, N. S. 1974. Sight record of Sharp-tailed Sandpiper near Iowa City. *Iowa Bird Life* 44:106.

Halmi, N. S. 1989. Sharp-tailed Sandpiper. *Iowa Bird Life* 59:128 [drawing].

Kent, T. H. 1991. Sharp-tailed Sandpiper at Coralville Reservoir. *Iowa Bird Life* 61:122-123.

Petersen, P. C. 1989. Sharp-tailed Sandpiper at Davenport. *Iowa Bird Life* 59:90-91.

Sharp-tailed Sandpiper, all

Dunlin (*Calidris alpina*)

Status: Regular

Jan	Feb	Mar	Apr	May	Jun	Jul	Aug	Sep	Oct	Nov	Dec
					x x	x xx					

2 Apr 1981	9 Jun 1983	11 Jul 1986	2 Dec 1990
8 Apr 1995	10 Jun 1986	16 Jul 1989	2 Dec 1986
10 Apr 1993	15 Jun 1985	27 Jul 1975	9 Dec 1988
summer: 22 Jun 1988			

Occurrence: Dunlin is an uncommon to common late migrant in both spring and fall. It is among the few shorebirds typically found in late fall. High counts for spring and fall are 150 at Sweet Marsh in Bremer County on 12 May 1984 (*IBL* 54:46) tied by 150 in Kossuth County on 28 May 1985 (*IBL* 55:64) and 140 at Coralville Reservoir in Johnson County on 14 October 1990 (*IBL* 61:20).

Comment: This Holarctic species winters coastally from southern Alaska and New England south to northern Mexico and from England south to northern Africa and southern Asia. It breeds from eastern Greenland east across the Arctic Coast to western Alaska and in more isolated areas from Hudson Bay north.

Curlew Sandpiper (*Calidris ferruginea*)

Status: Accidental

10 May 1985, Nashua, Chickasaw Co. (P-0154, Moore 1985)
13 May 1988, Coralville Res., Johnson Co. (P-0252, Bendorf and Kent 1988)

Occurrence: The 2 spring records are of birds in alternate plumage that were photographed.

Comment: This species has a limited breeding area in the Arctic coastal region of central Siberia and a wide migration path to wintering areas from western Africa to New Zealand. It is a regular vagrant along the East Coast and somewhat less common on the West Coast and in the Midwest. Records from the Rocky Mountain states and Great Plains are from Alberta, Manitoba, North Dakota, and Kansas. Most records from the central United States are east of the Mississippi River and along the Gulf Coast. Although this species has been found in every month of the year, the distribution of records generally follows that of other shorebirds with peaks in May to June, July to August (adults), and September to October (juveniles). About two thirds of the records are from fall, except on the West Coast where there are even fewer spring records.

References:

Bendorf, C. J., and T. H. Kent. 1988. Curlew Sandpiper at Coralville Reservoir. *Iowa Bird Life* 58:87-89.

Moore, F. L. 1985. Curlew Sandpiper at Cedar Lake, Nashua, Chickasaw County. *Iowa Bird Life* 55:72.

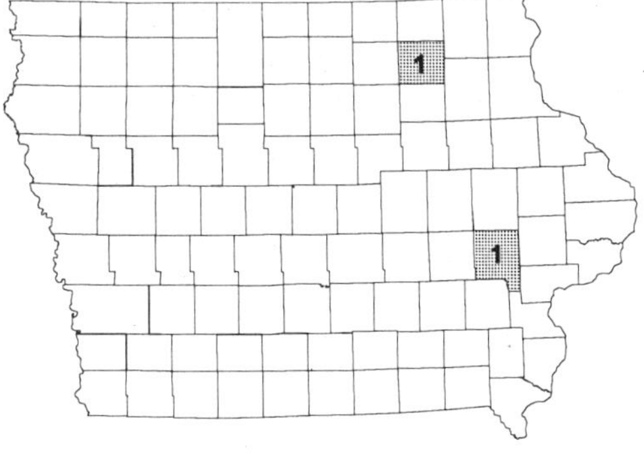

Curlew Sandpiper, all

Stilt Sandpiper (*Calidris himantopus*)

Status: Regular

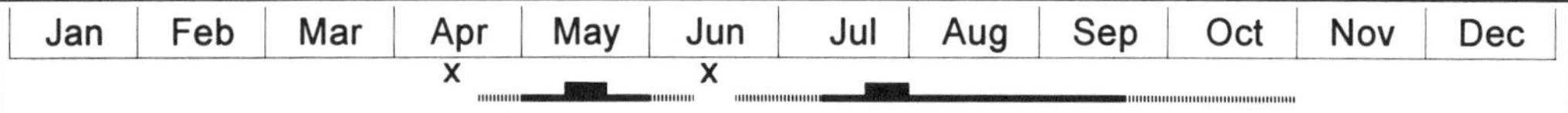

Jan	Feb	Mar	Apr	May	Jun	Jul	Aug	Sep	Oct	Nov	Dec

13 Apr 1988	6 Jun 1990	23 Jun 1991	23 Oct 1982
21 Apr 1986	10 Jun 1979	26 Jun 1993	25 Oct 1983
22 Apr 1969	12 Jun1994	27 Jun 1985	28 Oct 1989

Occurrence: This migrant has an average spring and fall migration interval and is usually uncommon, although large concentrations may occur in fall. High counts for spring and fall are 75 at Coralville Reservoir in Johnson County on 13 May 1988 (*IBL* 58:81) and 1,500 at Union Slough National Wildlife Refuge in Kossuth County on 10 September 1963 (*IBL* 33:88).

Comment: Most winter in central South America, but some remain in southern California, Texas, and Florida. Most migrate through the central flyway to breeding grounds that extend from western Hudson Bay to the northern coast of Alaska.

Buff-breasted Sandpiper (*Tryngites subruficollis*)

Status: Regular

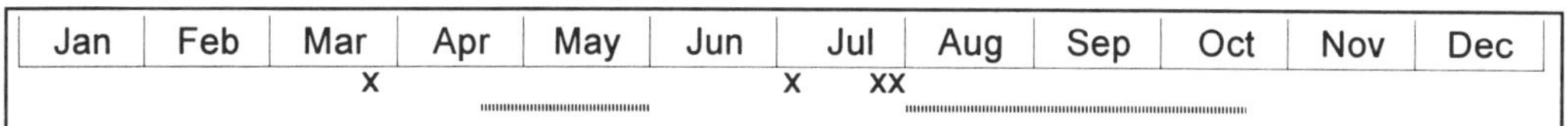

Jan	Feb	Mar	Apr	May	Jun	Jul	Aug	Sep	Oct	Nov	Dec

29 Mar 1996	20 May 1984	8 Jul 1992	13 Oct 1989
24 Apr 1985	25 May 1992	22 Jul 1980	13 Oct 1973
26 Apr 1981	26 May 1991	26 Jul 1984	18 Oct 1990

Occurrence: This rare migrant that is more common in western Iowa, prefers grassy areas, which are usually, but not always, near water. High counts for spring and fall are 40 in Osceola County on 24 April 1985 (*IBL* 55:64) and 257 at Riverton Area in Fremont County on 2 August 1987 (*IBL* 58:19).

Comment: This species winters on the pampas of southeastern South America and breeds in the High Arctic from northern Alaska to the Northwest Territories. Most migrate through central United States, but there is also an eastward fall movement similar to that of several other shorebirds that winter in southern South America.

Ruff (*Philomachus pugnax*)

Status: Accidental

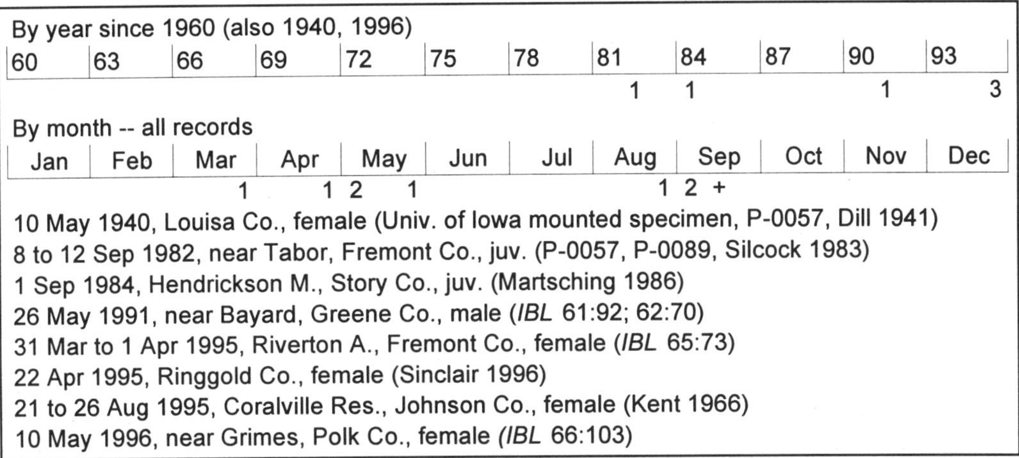

By year since 1960 (also 1940, 1996)

60 63 66 69 72 75 78 81 84 87 90 93

1 1 1 3

By month -- all records

Jan Feb Mar Apr May Jun Jul Aug Sep Oct Nov Dec

1 1 2 1 1 2 +

10 May 1940, Louisa Co., female (Univ. of Iowa mounted specimen, P-0057, Dill 1941)
8 to 12 Sep 1982, near Tabor, Fremont Co., juv. (P-0057, P-0089, Silcock 1983)
1 Sep 1984, Hendrickson M., Story Co., juv. (Martsching 1986)
26 May 1991, near Bayard, Greene Co., male (*IBL* 61:92; 62:70)
31 Mar to 1 Apr 1995, Riverton A., Fremont Co., female (*IBL* 65:73)
22 Apr 1995, Ringgold Co., female (Sinclair 1996)
21 to 26 Aug 1995, Coralville Res., Johnson Co., female (Kent 1966)
10 May 1996, near Grimes, Polk Co., female (*IBL* 66:103)

Occurrence: Of 8 records, 5 are from spring and 3 from fall. The 1 male found in May was in partial molt to alternate plumage. The other records include 5 females and 2 juveniles.

Comment: This Palearctic shorebird breeds across northern Eurasia, and most birds winter in Africa; however, nesting has occurred in Alaska, and migrants and wintering birds have been found in most areas of the world. It is a regular vagrant on the East and West coasts and in the Midwest, but there are only a few records from the Rocky Mountain and Great Plains states. Iowa has fewer records than states to the north, south, and east. There are slightly more records from spring than fall on the East Coast and Midwest, while most of the West Coast records are from fall and winter. Early records and migration patterns were analyzed by Peakall (1965).

References:

Dill, H. R. 1941. Ruff in Iowa in spring. *Auk* 58:257.

Kent, T. H. 1996. Ruff at Coralville Reservoir. *Iowa Bird Life* 66:112-113.

Martsching, P. 1986. Ruff in Story County. *Iowa Bird Life* 56:64.

Peakall, D. B. 1965. The status of the Ruff in North America. *Wilson Bull.* 77:294-296.

Silcock, W. R. 1983. A Ruff (*Philomachus pugnax*) in southwest Iowa. *Iowa Bird Life* 53:87-90.

Sinclair, J. 1996. Ruff in Ringgold County. *Iowa Bird Life* 66:65-66.

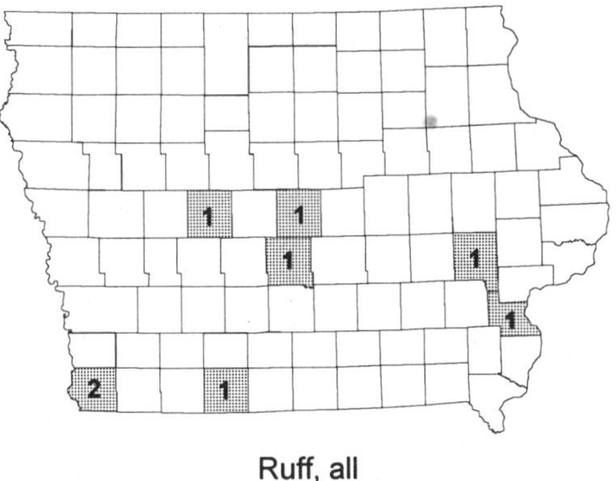

Ruff, all

Short-billed Dowitcher (*Limnodromus griseus*)

Status: Regular

Jan	Feb	Mar	Apr	May	Jun	Jul	Aug	Sep	Oct	Nov	Dec
					x x						

26 Apr 1986	8 Jun 1992	26 Jun 1988	21 Sep 1995
26 Apr 1988	8 Jun 1986	2 Jul 1988	21 Sep 1980
27 Apr 1985	13 Jun 1985	3 Jul 1986	22 Sep 1990

Occurrence: This fairly common migrant is relatively late in spring and early in fall compared to Long-billed Dowitcher. Spring birds are usually in alternate plumage, as are the early returning fall adults. By August, juveniles predominate. Dowitchers are found feeding in shallow water, usually in small flocks. High counts for spring and fall are 300 at Riverton Area in Fremont County on 11 May 1991 (*IBL* 61:92) and 95 at Union Slough National Wildlife Refuge in Kossuth County on 29 July 1985 (*IBL* 55:92).

Comment: Short-billed Dowitchers winter coastally from northern California and North Carolina south to the West Indies and northern South America. Three separate breeding ranges correspond to the 3 subspecies: east of Hudson Bay (*L. g. griseus*), west of Hudson Bay (*L. g. hendersoni*), and southern Alaska (*L. g. caurinus*). *L. g. hendersoni* is the subspecies that migrates through Iowa. There are several detailed references on identification and plumages of dowitchers (Pitelka 1950, Newlon and Kent 1980, Wilds and Newlon 1983, Jaramillo et al. 1991). Sightings of dowitchers outside of their usual time periods deserve careful study and documentation.

References:

Jaramillo, A., R. Pittaway, and P. Burke. 1991. The identification and migration of breeding plumaged dowitchers in southern Ontario. *Birder's J.* 1:8-25.

Newlon, M. C., and T. H. Kent. 1980. Speciation of dowitchers in Iowa. *Iowa Bird Life* 50:59-68.

Pitelka, F. A. 1950. Geographic variation and the species problem in the shore-bird genus *Limnodromus*. *Univ. of California Publications in Zoology* 50:1-108.

Wilds, C., and M. Newlon. 1983. The identification of dowitchers. *Birding* 15:151-165.

Long-billed Dowitcher (*Limnodromus scolopaceus*)

Status: Regular

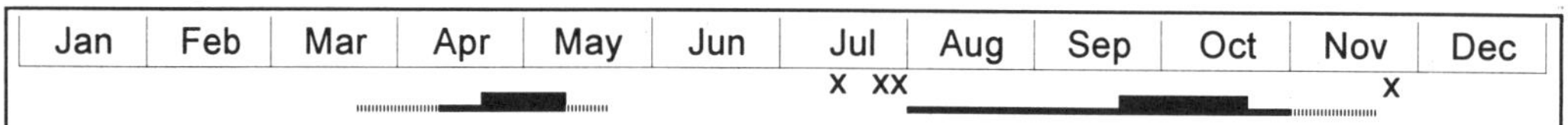

Jan	Feb	Mar	Apr	May	Jun	Jul	Aug	Sep	Oct	Nov	Dec
						x xx				x	

23 Mar 1986	14 May 1994	18 Jul 1987	16 Nov 1990
23 Mar 1991	14 May 1990	25 Jul 1992	19 Nov 1987
25 Mar 1984	16 May 1985	29 Jul 1985	25 Nov 1994

Occurrence: A few Long-billed Dowitchers in basic plumage may show up by late March, but most are found in late April or early May in variable degrees of molt to alternate plumage. Adults in worn alternate plumage appear in late July or early August. By September, most are juveniles, and late fall birds are in first-basic plumage, usually with some retained juvenal feathers. High counts for spring and fall are 72 at Rush Lake in Palo Alto County on 7 May 1986 (*IBL* 56:87) and 94 at Bays Branch Wildlife Area in Guthrie County on 12 October 1985 (*IBL* 55:125).

Comment: The winter range is on the West Coast and the southern United States south through Mexico. Long-billed Dowitchers are more likely than Short-billeds to be found near fresh water. The breeding range is far north and west in the Northwest Territories, northwestern Alaska, and eastern Siberia. Long-billeds have much farther to travel than Short-billeds, so it is not surprising that they leave earlier in the spring and return later in the fall. Sightings of dowitchers outside of their usual time periods deserve careful study and documentation. See references under Short-billed Dowitcher.

Common Snipe (*Gallinago gallinago*)

Status: Regular; occasionally nests

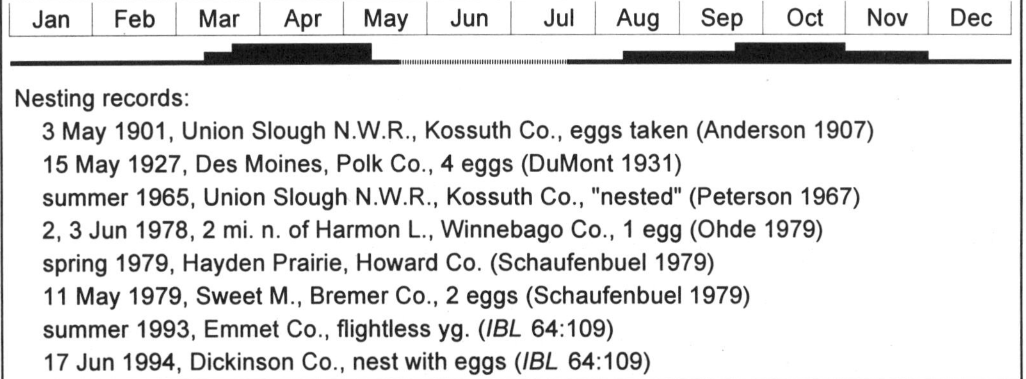

Nesting records:

3 May 1901, Union Slough N.W.R., Kossuth Co., eggs taken (Anderson 1907)
15 May 1927, Des Moines, Polk Co., 4 eggs (DuMont 1931)
summer 1965, Union Slough N.W.R., Kossuth Co., "nested" (Peterson 1967)
2, 3 Jun 1978, 2 mi. n. of Harmon L., Winnebago Co., 1 egg (Ohde 1979)
spring 1979, Hayden Prairie, Howard Co. (Schaufenbuel 1979)
11 May 1979, Sweet M., Bremer Co., 2 eggs (Schaufenbuel 1979)
summer 1993, Emmet Co., flightless yg. (*IBL* 64:109)
17 Jun 1994, Dickinson Co., nest with eggs (*IBL* 64:109)

Occurrence: This species is a common early spring and late fall migrant. Some birds winter along open ditches and waterways. It is a rare nesting species. The 6 specific nesting records are listed above. There is an indefinite reference of nesting from Winnebago County circa 1875 (Krider 1879). High counts for spring and fall are 400 at Cone Marsh in Louisa County on 5 April 1994 (*IBL* 64:76) and 400 at Riverton Area in Fremont County on 15 October 1988 (*IBL* 59:13).

Snipe were found on 27 percent of Christmas Bird Counts (north 14 percent, middle 31 percent, and south 29 percent). Wintering birds are often found at the same locations year after year. Spring-fed ditches and streams are favorite locations. A winter bird at Hawarden in Sioux County on 5 January 1990 (*IBL* 60:52) was unusual for northwestern Iowa.

Comment: This Holarctic species winters in southern temperate and tropical areas of the northern hemisphere and breeds across northern temperate and southern Arctic areas in North America and Eurasia. Although the winter range is often depicted as extending to central Missouri, some birds normally overwinter north to Minnesota and Wisconsin, but rarely to South Dakota.

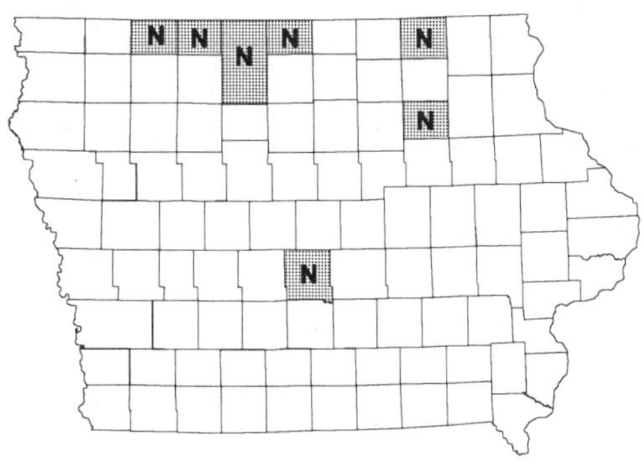

Common Snipe, 1960-1995
nesting (N)

Northern Iowa is on the edge of the breeding range, but we really do not know how consistently this species nests in Iowa. The fluttering sound of male birds in flight display is often heard in spring, but this does not provide definite evidence of nesting; however, the 3 early May nesting dates cited above suggest that some of the displaying males heard in early May could be on territory.

Several thousand snipe are taken legally by hunters each year in Iowa.

References:

Ohde, B. 1979. Common Snipe nesting in Winnebago County. *Iowa Bird Life* 49:91-92.

Peterson, D. 1967. Summer shorebird migration at Union Slough National Wildlife Refuge. *Iowa Bird Life* 37:23.

American Woodcock (*Scolopax minor*)

Status: Regular; nests

Jan	Feb	Mar	Apr	May	Jun	Jul	Aug	Sep	Oct	Nov	Dec
x	xx									x	x x

30 Jan 1995	27 Nov 1977
15 Feb 1987	8 Dec 1984
17 Feb 1990	20 Dec 1987

Occurrence: This widespread nesting species is more common in eastern Iowa because it is associated with woodland edge habitat. We do not have good estimates of the frequency of this species in Iowa. It is most easily detected by listening for displaying territorial males at dawn or dusk. Broods have been seen as early as mid-April, indicating that nesting can start as early as late March.

Several thousand are taken each fall since a hunting season was reopened in 1972. Data on wings submitted by hunters suggests that the peak fall migration in Iowa is late October to early November (Smith and Barclay 1978). Historically, woodcock were apparently common at the time of settlement (Dinsmore 1994). Market hunters, some of whom claimed to have killed several thousand in a year, were considered responsible for a plummeting population, and this species was afforded protection from hunting.

Comment: American Woodcock winter in southeastern United States from Texas to Arkansas to New Jersey. They breed across all but the very southern portions of this range north to southern Canada. The range has expanded west of Iowa into the eastern parts of Oklahoma, Kansas, and the Dakotas (Smith and Barclay 1978). Although woodcock may be very early or very late migrants, they apparently do not overwinter as far north ás Iowa. They are very unusual in winter in southern Missouri and southern Illinois. Breeding bird counts in eastern United States and Canada indicate a decline from 1970 to 1988 (Sauer and Bortner 1991).

References:

Sauer, J. R., and J. B. Bortner. 1991. Population trends from the American Woodcock singing-ground survey, 1970-88. *J. Wildlife Management* 55:300-312.

Smith, R. W., and J. S. Barclay. 1978. Evidence of westward changes in the range of the American Woodcock. *Amer. Birds* 32:1122-1127.

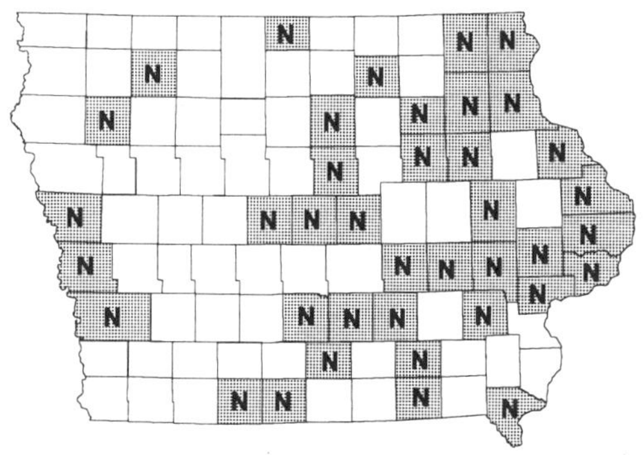

American Woodcock, 1960-1995
Nesting (N)

Wilson's Phalarope (*Phalaropus tricolor*)

Status: Regular; occasionally nests

Jan	Feb	Mar	Apr	May	Jun	Jul	Aug	Sep	Oct	Nov	Dec
		x x	x x					xx			

13 Mar 1983 — 19 Sep 1983
28 Mar 1991 — 24 Sep 1969
1 Apr 1995 — 28 Sep 1986

Recent nesting records:

1965, Union Slough N.W.R., Kossuth Co., adults all summer, yg. in Aug (Peterson 1967)
2 Jun 1968, Dewey's Pasture, Clay Co., 4 eggs later destroyed (Bergman et al. 1968)
18 Jun 1968, Oppedahl Tract, Palo Alto Co., 4 hatched by 1 July (Bergman et al. 1968)
6 Jun 1984, e. of New Albin, Allamakee Co., 4 eggs (Koenig 1984)
7, 27 Jun, 11 Jul 1992, Coralville Res., Johnson Co., male defending territory (*IBL* 62:108)
31 May 1996, Harrier M., Boone Co., male on nest (*IBL* 66:104)

Occurrence: This uncommon migrant is currently an irregular nesting species. High counts for spring and fall are 400 in southwest Iowa on 28 April 1984 (*IBL* 54:46) and 27 at Union Slough National Wildlife Refuge in Kossuth County on 28 August 1988 (*IBL* 59:13).

In addition to the 5 nesting records listed above, another suggestive record is of 2 adults on 2 July and a juvenile and female on 15 July 1983 at Riverton Area in Fremont County (*IBL* 53:73). Historically, it was a common nesting species in the 1800s (Anderson 1894, 1907), but withdrew as a nesting species about 1900 (DuMont 1933).

Comment: This Nearctic species winters in southern and western South America and breeds in western United States and Canada and discontinuously around the Great Lakes. It is a frequent vagrant to Europe. It is abundant in the west, but seems to be less common in Iowa in recent years (T. Kent, personal observation).

References:

Anderson, R. M. 1894. Nesting of the Whooping Crane. *Oologist* 11:263-264.

Bergman, R. D., L. C. Bates, and D. K. Voigts. 1968. Wilson's Phalaropes nesting in northwest Iowa. *Iowa Bird Life* 38:132-133.

Koenig, D. 1984. A Wilson's Phalarope nest in Allamakee County. *Iowa Bird Life* 54:123.

Peterson, D. 1967. Summer shorebird migration at Union Slough National Wildlife Refuge. *Iowa Bird Life* 37:23.

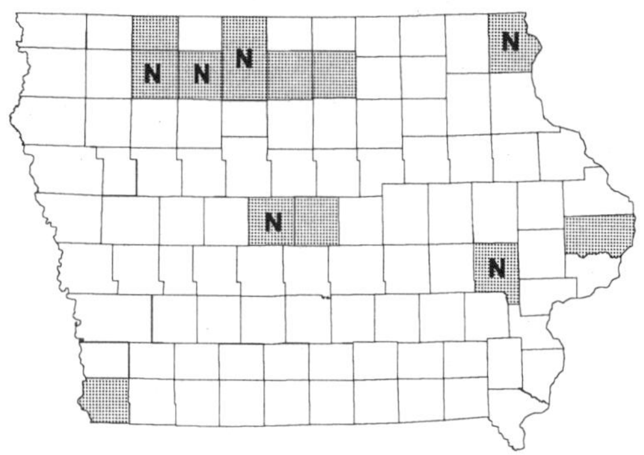

Wilson's Phalarope, 1960-1995
June-July and nesting (N)

Red-necked Phalarope (*Phalaropus lobatus*)

Status: Regular

Jan	Feb	Mar	Apr	May	Jun	Jul	Aug	Sep	Oct	Nov	Dec

26 Apr 1980 | 2 Jun 1977 | 26 Jul 1988 | 7 Oct 1982
27 Apr 1996 | 3 Jun 1984 | 4 Aug 1991 | 21 Oct 1991
30 Apr 1978 | 4 Jun 1983 | 11 Aug 1985 | early Nov 1969
summer: 22 Jun 1983

Occurrence: This rare migrant averages about 5 reports per year, equally divided between spring and fall, and occurring across the state in typical shorebird habitat. It is a late spring and relatively late fall migrant with peaks from mid- to late May and late August to early September. The June record may have been a late migrant. The 110 at East Okoboji in Dickinson County on 13 September 1934 (DuMont 1935) is a very large concentration for this species.

Comment: This largely pelagic Holarctic species winters at sea in tropical waters of the Pacific and Indian oceans and breeds around the Arctic Ocean and locally south to the Aleutians. Birds in Iowa and other inland locations are seen at the time most of the population is migrating at sea.

Reference:

DuMont, P. A. 1935. Northern Phalaropes in northwestern Iowa. *Wilson Bull.* 47:72.

Red Phalarope (*Phalaropes fulicaria*)

Status: Accidental

By year since 1960

60	60	66	69	72	75	78	81	84	87	90	93
									1	3 1	1 2

By month -- all records

Jan	Feb	Mar	Apr	May	Jun	Jul	Aug	Sep	Oct	Nov	Dec
							1	1 2 +	2 1	1	

30 Sep to 3 Oct 1988, Saylorville Res., Polk Co. (P-0260, P-0268, Dinsmore and Engebretsen 1989)
4 Aug 1991, Saylorville Res., Polk Co. (P-0308, Dinsmore 1992)
25 to 29 Sep 1991, Saylorville Res., Polk Co. (P-0299, P-0309, P-0343, *IBL* 62(2) cover, Proescholdt 1992)
26 Oct 1991, Saylorville Res., Polk Co. (Proescholdt 1992)
8 to 9 Nov 1992, Rathbun Res., Appanoose Co. (P-0344, Kent 1993)
29 Nov 1994, Spirit L., Dickinson Co. (P-0421, Schoenewe 1966)
19 Sep 1995, Saylorville Res. (Dinsmore 1966)
22 to 26 Oct 1995, Saylorville Res. (Dinsmore 1966)

Occurrence: There are 8 fall records of birds in basic plumage or juveniles molting to basic. There is 1 report of 3 females in breeding plumage at Amana Lake in Iowa County on 17 May 1940 (Serbousek 1940) that is Not Accepted for lack of description.

Comment: This Holarctic pelagic species breeds across northern Asia, North America, Greenland, and Iceland. Asian breeders migrate eastward and are abundant on the Pacific Coast on their way to and from wintering grounds off of Chile. North American breeders migrate eastward to wintering grounds off of Africa; therefore, this species is not as abundant on the East Coast as it is on the West Coast. Vagrants have been found around the world at coastal locations as well as inland in the Northern Hemisphere. Red Phalaropes have been found in all states and provinces and are regular migrants through the interior in small numbers. Records extend from March to December but the vast majority are from September to November with a much smaller peak in May.

References:

Dinsmore, S. J. 1992. A second Red Phalarope at Saylorville Reservoir. *Iowa Bird Life* 62:86-87.

Dinsmore, S. J. 1996. Red Phalaropes at Saylorville Reservoir. *Iowa Bird Life* 66:113-114.

Dinsmore, S. J., and B. Engebretsen. 1989. Red Phalarope at Saylorville Reservoir. *Iowa Bird Life* 59:19.

Kent, T. H. 1993. Red Phalarope at Rathbun Reservoir. *Iowa Bird Life* 63:82.

Proescholdt, M. 1992. Two more Red Phalaropes at Saylorville Reservoir. *Iowa Bird Life* 62:87-88.

Schoenewe, L. A. 1996. Red Phalarope at Spirit Lake. *Iowa Bird Life* 66:111-112.

Serbousek, L. 1940. Shore birds at Amana Lake. *Iowa Bird Life* 10:27.

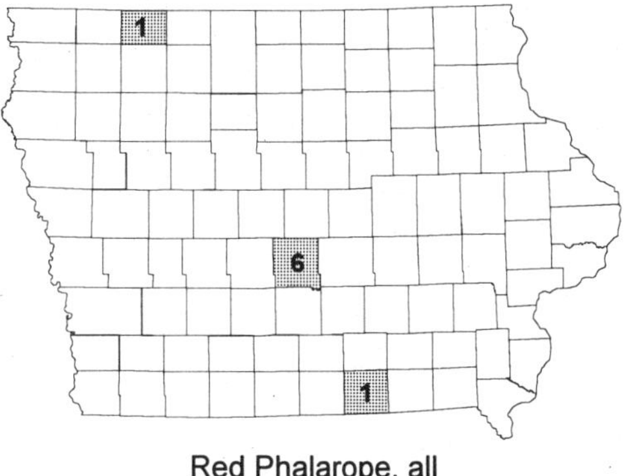

Red Phalarope, all

Skuas, Gulls, Terns, and Skimmers (Family Laridae)

Skuas, gulls, terns, and skimmers comprise 104 species, with 57 from North America and 27 from Iowa. Only 4 species have nested in Iowa, 3 regularly (Forster's, Least, and Black terns) and 1 for the first time in 1994 (Ring-billed Gull). There are 14 Regular species, 4 Casual species, and 9 Accidental species. This family has the most Casual and Accidental species of any family of birds in Iowa.

Skuas, which include the 3 species of jaegers, have hooked bills and long pointed wings and are known for their predatory behavior. They have a fleshy cere across the base of the upper mandible. Away from their breeding grounds, they are pelagic birds that occasionally migrate through the central United States, especially immature birds. Parasitic Jaeger is by far the most likely to occur in Iowa.

Gulls and terns lack the cere of skuas. They are long-winged birds that frequent coastal and inland waters. Gulls are larger and bulkier with stout bills that are down-curved at the tip. Terns have narrower, more pointed wings and thinner, sharp-pointed bills.

The number and variety of gulls in Iowa has undergone a dramatic increase over the last 30 years. Ring-billed Gulls are found by the thousands on Iowa's reservoirs and major rivers in spring and fall and by the hundreds on smaller bodies of water. Many first-year birds linger during the summer, and now this species is beginning to nest. Herring and Bonaparte's gulls are also much more numerous. Franklin's Gull was always common in western Iowa, so it is hard to judge whether it has increased. These common gulls have brought with them almost all of the vagrant gulls that could be expected to occur in Iowa. Some of these occur during migration and others during winter, especially along the Mississippi River. Of the 19 species of gulls reported in Iowa, 10 were added to the state list since 1982, which gives Iowa more gull species than some coastal states.

The terns have undergone less dramatic changes in recent years. Least Tern is barely hanging on as a nesting species in western Iowa.

Pomarine Jaeger (*Stercorarius pomarinus*)

Status: Accidental

28 Sep to 2 Oct 1988, Saylorville Res., Polk Co., 2 juv. (P-0264, P-0265, P-0266, Dinsmore 1989)

Occurrence: The only record is of 2 fall juveniles that allowed close approach by boat and were photographed.

Comment: This Holarctic pelagic species breeds north of the Arctic Circle and winters from California and the Carolinas to south of South America, Africa, and Australia. Most of the Midwestern records are from the Great Lakes, but there are scattered other records from most inland states.

Many jaegers are not identified as to species, so this species is probably a bit more common than the verified records indicate. Light- and dark-phase birds in immature and adult plumages are reported. Most are found from September to November, with fewer from May to August and in December.

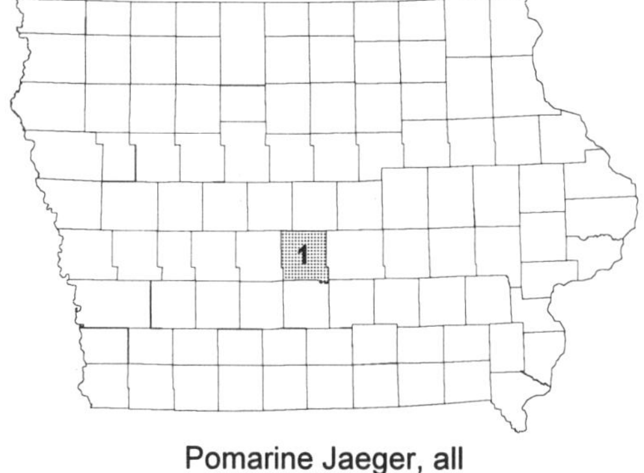

Pomarine Jaeger, all

Reference:
Dinsmore, S. J. 1989. Pomarine Jaegers at Saylorville Reservoir. *Iowa Bird Life* 59:20-21.

Parasitic Jaeger (*Stercorarius parasiticus*)

Status: Accidental

By year since 1960 (also 1896, 1905)

60	63	66	69	72	75	78	81	84	87	90	93
	1	1			1			1	1 3 1	1	1 1

By month -- all records

Jan	Feb	Mar	Apr	May	Jun	Jul	Aug	Sep	Oct	Nov	Dec
								3 1 4	1 1 2	1	1

Records of Parasitic Jaeger

- 6 Oct 1896, near Keokuk, Lee Co., juv. (Univ. of Iowa #25004, P-0054, Praeger 1925)
- 20 Sep 1905, Eagle L., Hancock Co., imm., Coe College specimen no longer extant (Anderson 1907, DuMont 1933)
- 13 to 17 Oct 1985, Saylorville Res., Polk Co., juv. (Myers 1986)
- 29 to 30 Sep 1988, Saylorville Res., Polk Co., juv. (*IBL* 59:13, 77)
- 3 Sep 1990, Saylorville Res., Polk Co., juv. (*IBL* 61:20, 62:21)

Records of Jaeger species

- 6 to 8 Dec 1963, Lock and Dam 14, Scott Co., imm. (Petersen 1964)
- 4 Sep 1966, Rice L., Winnebago Co., ad. (Sutter 1966)
- 4 Sep 1976, L. Manawa, Pottawattamie Co., dark ad. (Hoffman 1976)
- 27 Oct 1987, Saylorville Res., Polk Co., juv. (*IBL* 58:19, 74)
- 28 Sep 1988, Saylorville Res., Polk Co., imm. (*IBL* 59:13, 77)
- 19 Nov 1988, Saylorville Res., Polk Co., imm. (*IBL* 59:13, 77)
- 29 Oct 1989, Algona, Kossuth Co., 2 imm. (*IBL* 60:14)
- 22 Sep 1994, Saylorville Res., imm. (*IBL* 65:15, 81)
- 24 Sep 1995, L. Manawa, Pottawattamie Co., imm. (*IBL* 66:21)

Occurrence: There are 5 fall records of immature Parasitic Jaegers and 9 other fall-winter records of Jaeger species that are most likely Parasitic. There are also 2 spring reports that lack details (Dinsmore et al. 1984). Most of the records since 1985 have come from Saylorville Reservoir in Polk County where there are many gulls and birders.

Comment: This Holarctic pelagic species breeds farther south than Pomarine and Long-tailed jaegers and is a more frequent visitor to inland locations. It winters at sea from northern temperate waters south throughout southern oceans.

In the Midwest, this species has been seen in almost all states, but is most likely on the Great Lakes. Almost all records are from fall with peak in September to October. Most are immatures.

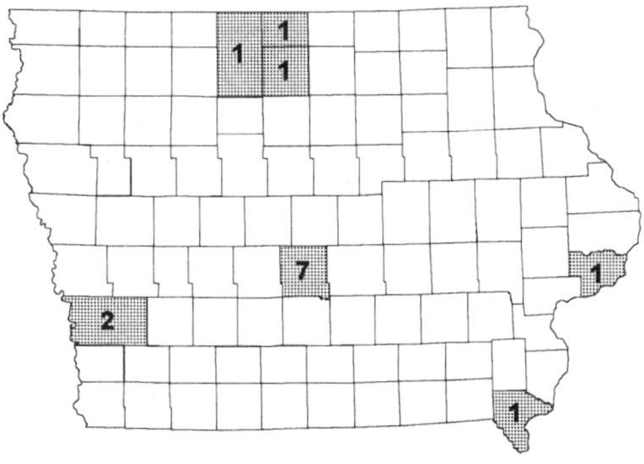

Parasitic Jaeger and Jaeger Species, all

References:

Hoffman, T. A. 1976. Parasitic (?) Jaeger at Lake Manawa Iowa. *Nebr. Bird Review* 44:58-59.

Myers, B. 1986. Parasitic Jaeger at Saylorville Reservoir. *Iowa Bird Life* 56:31.

Petersen, P. 1964. Parasitic Jaeger in Eastern Iowa. *Iowa Bird Life* 34:26.

Sutter, B. E. 1966. Parasitic Jaeger in Winnebago County. *Iowa Bird Life* 36:109-110.

Long-tailed Jaeger (*Stercorarius longicaudus*)

Status: Accidental

15 Jun 1907, near Lone Tree, Johnson Co., ad. female (Univ. of Iowa mounted specimen, P-0053, Anderson 1908, Kent and Schrimper 1996)
4 to 13 Sep 1994, Tomahawk M./Black Hawk L., Sac Co., ad. (P-0423, Ernzen 1996)

Occurrence: The 2 records are of adults in summer and fall. The first bird was shot while flying with pigeons on a farm and captured alive. The second bird was seen by many observers over a marsh and at a medium-sized lake.

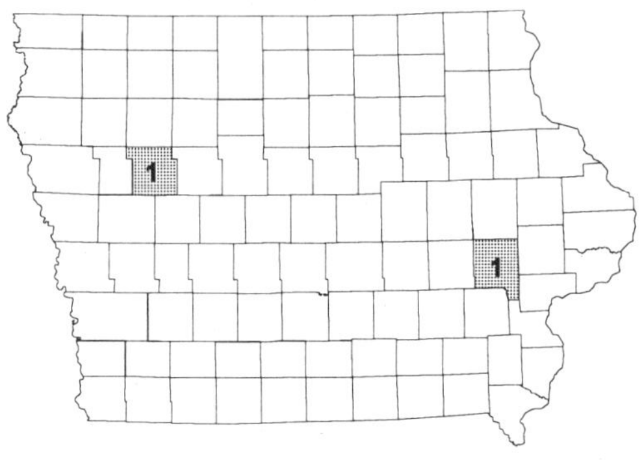

Long-tailed Jaeger, all

Comment: This Holarctic pelagic species nests mostly above the Arctic Circle and winters at unknown locations in the Atlantic and Pacific in the Southern Hemisphere. It is even more pelagic than the other 2 jaegers, yet it is almost uncanny that there are 1 to 5 records from most inland states.

Most inland records are from late August to October, but there is a small peak from late May to late June, which includes the first Iowa bird.

References:

Anderson, R. M. 1908. An addition to the birds of Iowa. *Auk* 25:215.

Ernzen, P. 1996. Long-tailed Jaeger in Sac County. *Iowa Bird Life* 66:26-27.

Laughing Gull (*Larus atricilla*)

Status: Casual

By year since 1960

60	63	66	69	72	75	78	81	84	87	90	93
									3	1 3 1	1 3 5

By month -- all records

Jan	Feb	Mar	Apr	May	Jun	Jul	Aug	Sep	Oct	Nov	Dec
			1	1		1 2 2	1 2 1	2 1 1	2 +		

Occurrence: Since the first Accepted records in 1989 (Kent 1991), there have been 15 records involving 16 birds, with 2 from spring and the rest from mid-summer to early fall. Of the 16 birds, 9 were juveniles, 3 were second-year birds, and 2 were adults. One previously Accepted record (Dinsmore et al. 1984) as well as 10 other old and recent records are Not Accepted. An adult molting to basic plumage at Lake Manawa in Pottawattamie County on 9 Sep 1990 was established as an escapee from the Henry Doorly Zoo in Omaha, Nebraska.

Comment: The breeding range is on the East Coast north to the Maritime Provinces, on the Gulf Coast, in the Caribbean south to northern South America, and on the West Coast of Mexico. The winter range extends from the Carolinas to Peru and Brazil.

Laughing Gulls regularly stray to the Great Lakes, especially the southern parts. They occur with diminishing frequency to the west of the Mississippi River, but have reached Saskatchewan and Manitoba and a number have been seen in Colorado. Most arrive in May, a few earlier, and most leave by September, but a few have remained to January. A female attempted to nest in Ohio (Peterjohn 1989). Spring birds may be adults or immatures. Juveniles, which may appear in August and September as they have in Iowa, must be birds that have dispersed from breeding grounds along the Gulf Coast.

Juvenile Laughing Gulls are easy to identify compared to second-summer and adult birds that may occur in Iowa. Separation of adult Laughing Gull from first- and second-summer Franklin's Gull is a notorious diagnostic challenge (Goetz 1983, W.S.O. Records Committee 1984, Lehman 1994).

References:

Goetz, R. 1983. Spring identification of Laughing Gulls and Franklin's Gulls. *Illinois Audubon Bull.* 204:33-36.

Kent, T. H. 1991. Laughing Gulls in Des Moines County. *Iowa Bird Life* 61:29-32.

Lehman, P. 1994. Franklin's vs. Laughing Gulls—a "new" problem arises. *Birding* 26:126-127.

W.S.O. Records Committee. 1984. Status and identification of Laughing Gulls in Wisconsin. *Passenger Pigeon* 46:134-136.

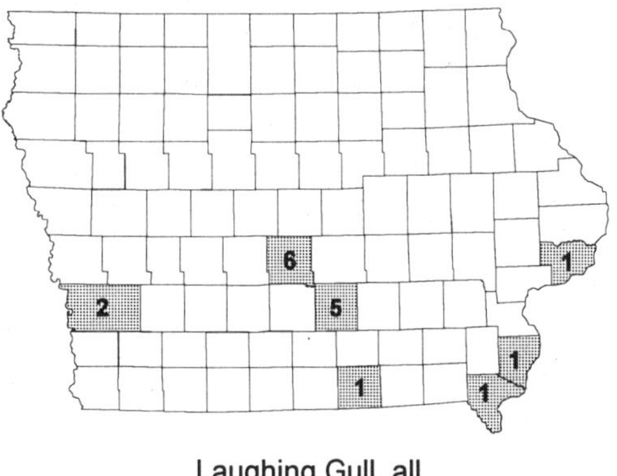

Laughing Gull, all

Franklin's Gull (*Larus pipixcan*)

Status: Regular; occasionally nests

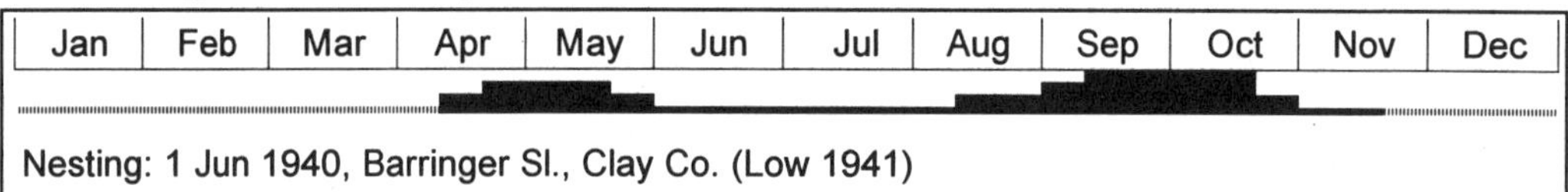

Nesting: 1 Jun 1940, Barringer Sl., Clay Co. (Low 1941)

Occurrence: This species is a common to abundant migrant in western and central Iowa, often occurring in large flocks. In spring, birds may be seen in fields and standing water, as well as on lakes and reservoirs. In fall, they are more concentrated on large bodies of water and stay longer. This species is found less consistently and in much smaller numbers in eastern Iowa.

Some birds are found in summer, particularly in northwestern Iowa; however, there is only 1 confirmed nesting record. On 1 June 1940, at Barringer Slough in Clay County, 800 were present, and on 6 June 3 nests were found, 1 of which hatched eggs (Low 1941).

Prior to 1987, there were only 3 winter records, all from December. Since 1987, except for 1994-1995, from 1 to 3 adults in alternate plumage have been found each winter with dates evenly distributed from December through February.

Comment: This species winters on the Pacific Coast from southern Central America to Chile. The breeding range is from eastern South Dakota and western Minnesota, north through the Prairie Provinces, south to southern Oregon. Nesting occurs sporadically at Heron Lake in Minnesota, which is only 20 miles north of the Iowa Great Lakes region. It is surprising that there are not more nesting records from Iowa.

Franklin's Gull is an unusual 3-year gull in that it undergoes 2 complete molts each year. Molt to alternate plumage occurs in early winter, usually in South America, but the few wintering birds that have occurred north to Missouri, Iowa, and South Dakota have also been in alternate plumage. First- and some second-alternate plumaged birds lack the white area between the wing tip and mantle, which can make them difficult to distinguish from Laughing Gull.

Reference:

Low, J. B. 1941. Gadwall and Franklin's Gull nesting in Iowa. *Iowa Bird Life* 11:31-32.

Little Gull (*Larus minutus*)

Status: Accidental

By year since 1960 (also 1996)

60	63	66	69	72	75	78	81	84	87	90	93
									1 1	1	1

By month -- all records

Jan	Feb	Mar	Apr	May	Jun	Jul	Aug	Sep	Oct	Nov	Dec
			2						1 1	1	

27 Oct, 1 Nov 1988, Saylorville Res., Polk Co., first-basic (*IBL* 59:14, 77; 65:83)
8 Oct 1989, Saylorville Res., Polk Co., ad. basic (P-0369, P-0370, Dinsmore et al. 1990)
23 Apr 1992, s of Council Bluffs, Pottawattamie Co., ad. alt. (P-0334, *IBL* 62:77; 63:69; *Amer. Birds* 46:430)
14 to 20 Nov 1994, Big Creek S.P., ad. basic (Dinsmore 1995)
21 to 22 Apr 1996, Black Hawk L., Sac Co., ad. alt. (*IBL* 66:104)

Occurrence: The 5 records are of single birds, with 2 in spring and 3 in fall. All were adults except for 1 fall bird.

Comment: The Little Gull is a Eurasian species of temperate climates that has invaded North America and now breeds sparingly along the Great Lakes and winters along the Atlantic Coast. Nesting was first noted on Lake Michigan in Wisconsin in 1972. More unusual was a nest in 1986 at Heron Lake in Minnesota (Schladweiler 1986), which is about 20 miles north of Spirit Lake in Dickinson County.

This species is a vagrant to widely scattered locations including the Pacific and Gulf Coasts, Prairie Provinces, Colorado, Kansas, Oklahoma, and Missouri. Most records are from August to November with a small peak in April to May, but this species can occur at any time of year.

References:

Dinsmore, S. J. 1995. Little Gull at Big Creek Lake. *Iowa Bird Life* 65:85-86.

Dinsmore, S. J., P. Allen, and R. Allen. 1990. Little Gull at Saylorville Reservoir. *Iowa Bird Life* 60:77.

Schladweiler, J. 1986. First state nesting record for the Little Gull. *Loon* 58:166-170.

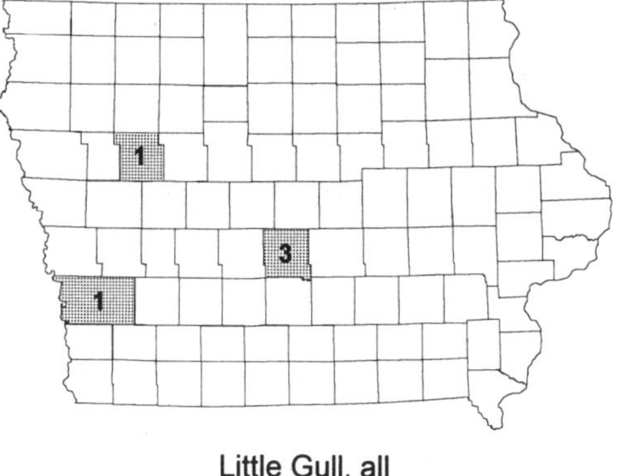

Little Gull, all

Black-headed Gull (*Larus ridibundus*)

Status: Accidental; possible nesting

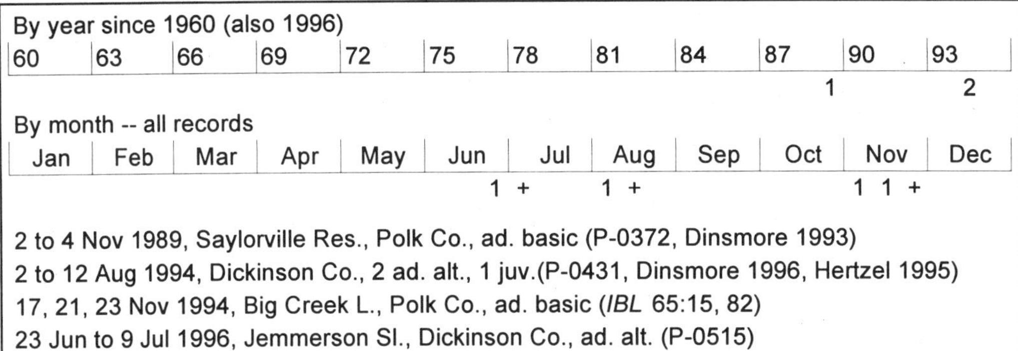

By year since 1960 (also 1996)

60	63	66	69	72	75	78	81	84	87	90	93
									1		2

By month -- all records

Jan	Feb	Mar	Apr	May	Jun	Jul	Aug	Sep	Oct	Nov	Dec
					1	+	1 +			1 1 +	

2 to 4 Nov 1989, Saylorville Res., Polk Co., ad. basic (P-0372, Dinsmore 1993)
2 to 12 Aug 1994, Dickinson Co., 2 ad. alt., 1 juv.(P-0431, Dinsmore 1996, Hertzel 1995)
17, 21, 23 Nov 1994, Big Creek L., Polk Co., ad. basic (*IBL* 65:15, 82)
23 Jun to 9 Jul 1996, Jemmerson Sl., Dickinson Co., ad. alt. (P-0515)

Occurrence: There are 2 fall records of adults in basic plumage and 2 summer records. On 2 August 1994, an adult in alternate plumage was at the northwestern end of Spirit Lake in Dickinson County. A short time later, and about 3 miles away at Kettleson Waterfowl Production Area, another adult in alternate plumage was feeding a juvenile (Dinsmore 1996). It seems likely that these birds nested in Dickinson County or in southern Minnesota. An adult was present from 28 May to July 1986 at Heron Lake in Jackson County, Minnesota (Janssen 1986), which is about 25 miles away from where the Iowa birds were found in 1994. In June and July 1996, an adult was reported in northern Dickinson County about 2 miles south of the 1994 location.

Comment: This Eurasian species of temperate climates has invaded North America and bred in the Maritime Provinces. It winters from there south to the Carolinas in small numbers. Vagrants occur regularly in western Alaska and occasionally on the West Coast. States bordering the Great Lakes have a number of records, and there are a few records from other states including Wyoming, Colorado, Nebraska, Oklahoma, Texas, Mississippi, Missouri, Tennessee, and Iowa. Vagrant records are scattered over all months with about two thirds in the second half of the year.

References:

Dinsmore, S. J. 1993. Common Black-headed Gull at Saylorville Reservoir. *Iowa Bird Life* 63:53-54.

Dinsmore, S. J. 1996. Probable breeding of Black-headed Gulls in northwestern Iowa. *Iowa Bird Life* 66:27-29.

Hertzel, A. 1995. Common Black-headed Gull along the Minnesota-Iowa border. *Loon* 67:54-56.

Janssen, R. B. 1986. Minnesota's first Common Black-headed Gull. *Loon* 58:104-107.

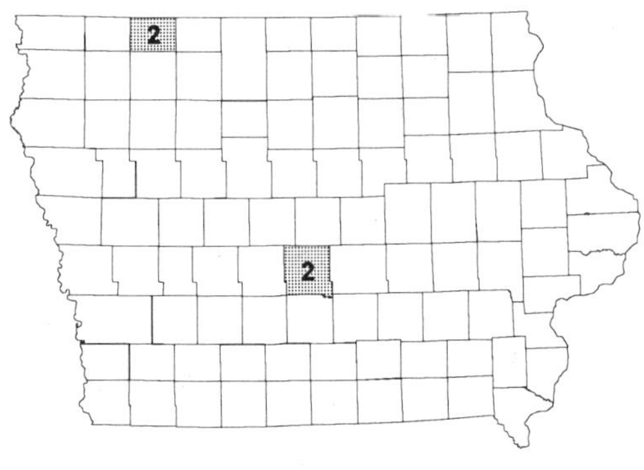

Black-headed Gull, all

Bonaparte's Gull (*Larus philadelphia*)

Status: Regular

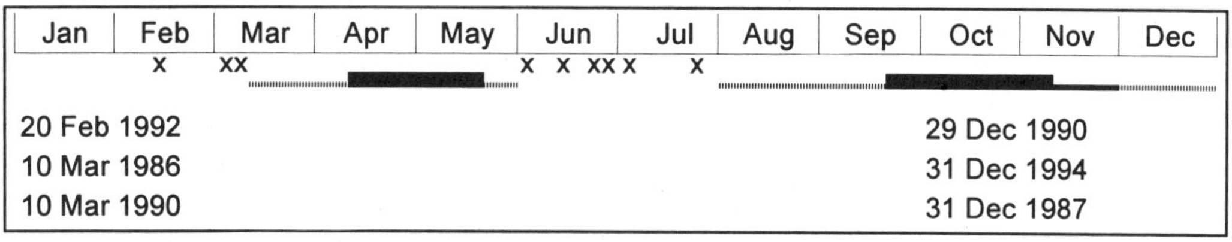

Jan	Feb	Mar	Apr	May	Jun	Jul	Aug	Sep	Oct	Nov	Dec
	X	XX			X X XX X	X					

20 Feb 1992	29 Dec 1990
10 Mar 1986	31 Dec 1994
10 Mar 1990	31 Dec 1987

Occurrence: This fairly common migrant has become more frequent over the last 20 years, with more remaining into December and a few occurring in summer. An unusually late concentration were 400 at Red Rock Reservoir in Marion County on 1 December 1990 with 175 still there on 16 December (*IBL* 61:57).

Prior to 1985, there were 3 summer records: 6 June 1928 at Long Pond in Dallas County (DuMont 1932), 13 June 1933 at Spirit Lake in Dickinson County (Roberts 1933), and 23 June 1958 at Cedar Lake in Linn County (Serbousek 1958). Several of the more recent summer birds have been in first-alternate plumage (*IBL* 59:112; 60:104; 65:98).

Comment: This species winters coastally from New England and Washington south to northern South America, and sparingly on the southern parts of the Great Lakes in mild winters. It breeds from western Quebec across Canada to British Columbia and north to the Northwest Territories and Alaska.

References:

DuMont, P. A. 1932. Notes from central Iowa. *Wilson Bull.* 44:170-177.

Roberts, F. L. R. 1933. June notes. *Iowa Bird Life* 3:39.

Serbousek, L. 1958. Notes from Cedar Rapids. *Iowa Bird Life* 28:64.

Mew Gull (*Larus canus*)

Status: Accidental

By year since 1960

60	63	66	69	72	75	78	81	84	87	90	93
							1				2 1

By month -- all records

Jan	Feb	Mar	Apr	May	Jun	Jul	Aug	Sep	Oct	Nov	Dec
+											1 3 +

19 to 31 Dec 1982, Lock and Dam 14, Scott Co., second-basic (P-0175, P-0176, Kent 1983)
19 to 21 Dec 1993, Red Rock Res., Marion Co., first-basic (Johnson 1995)
20 Dec 1993, Saylorville Res., Polk Co., ad. basic (Dinsmore 1995)
11 Dec 1994 to 1 Jan 1995, Red Rock Res., Marion Co., first-basic (Dinsmore and Sinclair 1995)

Occurrence: The 4 records are all from December and involve 2 in first-basic, 1 in second-basic, and 1 in adult basic plumage. Three of the birds were of the North American race, *L. c. brachrhynchus*, but the other may have been of the Eurasian race, *L. c. canus* (Johnson 1995).

Comment: This species breeds across Eurasia, Alaska, and northwestern Canada as far east as northern Saskatchewan and Manitoba. The Eurasian subspecies, *L. c. canus*, known as Common Gull, is a vagrant to the northern parts of the East Coast. The eastern Siberian subspecies, *L. c. kamtschatschensis*, is a vagrant to western Alaska. The North American subspecies, *L. c. brachrhynchus*, winters on the Pacific Coast and is a rare vagrant to Rocky Mountain states. The few records from Minnesota, Iowa, Wisconsin, Illinois, Michigan, and Ohio include birds of the North American race.

References:

Dinsmore, S. J. 1995. Mew Gull at Saylorville Reservoir. *Iowa Bird Life* 65:103-104.

Dinsmore, S. J., and J. Sinclair. 1995. Another Mew Gull at Red Rock Reservoir. *Iowa Bird Life* 65:104-105.

Johnson, A. 1995. Mew Gull at Red Rock Reservoir. *Iowa Bird Life* 65:53-55.

Kent, T. H. 1983. Mew Gull at Lock and Dam 14. *Iowa Bird Life* 53:45-46.

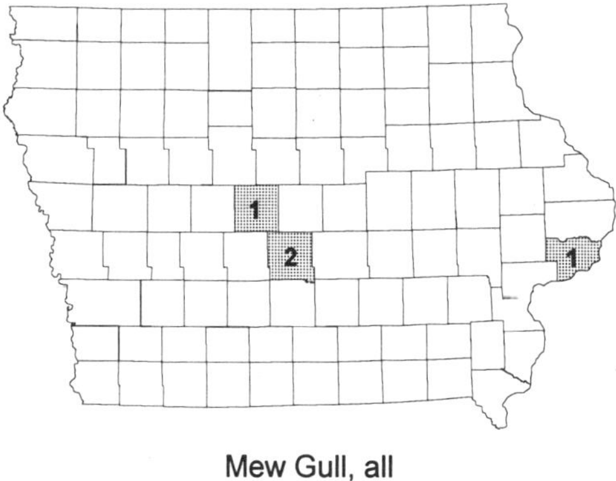

Mew Gull, all

Ring-billed Gull (*Larus delawarensis*)

Status: Regular; occasionally nests

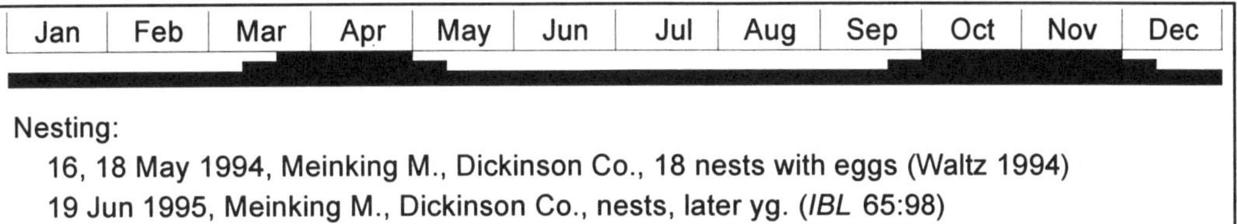

Nesting:

16, 18 May 1994, Meinking M., Dickinson Co., 18 nests with eggs (Waltz 1994)

19 Jun 1995, Meinking M., Dickinson Co., nests, later yg. (*IBL* 65:98)

Occurrence: This species is an abundant migrant in Iowa, and some linger in summer and winter. The largest concentrations are found at Red Rock and Saylorville reservoirs where flocks number in the tens of thousands. Smaller numbers, however, can be found anywhere in the state and in a variety of habitats including plowed fields and sanitary landfills.

First-alternate plumaged birds, along with occasional older birds, remain on larger bodies of water throughout the state in summer. In 1994, this species nested for the first time in Dickinson County, but the 18 nests with eggs were apparently destroyed by a predator (Waltz 1994). Nesting occurred at the same location in 1995 with young birds present in late June (*IBL* 65:98).

Most leave in mid-winter when the rivers and lakes are frozen, but they quickly return as the ice melts. A few may be found with Herring Gulls along the Mississippi River in mid-winter. The number found on Christmas Bird Counts varies with the amount of open water. This species is found on 63 percent of counts along the Mississippi River, 11 percent along the Missouri River, and 17 percent of those away from the 2 rivers. The high count for December is 35,000 at Saylorville Reservoir on 8 December 1990, with 10,000 still there on 19 December (*IBL* 61:57).

Historically, DuMont (1933) considered this species fairly common. Brown (1971) indicated that there were no July records. Kent and Kent (1975) showed more spring than fall records from 1949 to 1973, whereas today it would be difficult to make a fall field trip without seeing this species. The average number seen per year on Christmas Bird Counts has risen from 964 in the years 1973 to 1982 to 12,597 in the years 1983 to 1992. Ring-billed Gulls now outnumber Herring Gulls on Christmas Bird Counts.

Comment: This species winters coastally from British Columbia and Maritime Provinces south to the West Indies and Panama, and centrally along the Great Lakes and from central Missouri south. Ring-billed Gulls breed in colonies, which can be in Labrador, along the Great Lakes, or in the West from northern South Dakota to southern Oregon and north to northern Alberta. In the West, there are isolated colonies south of this range. The nearest colony to Iowa is near Watertown in South Dakota, about 130 miles northwest of Spirit Lake.

Reference:

Waltz, T. J. 1994. Ring-billed Gulls nesting in Dickinson County. *Iowa Bird Life* 64:117.

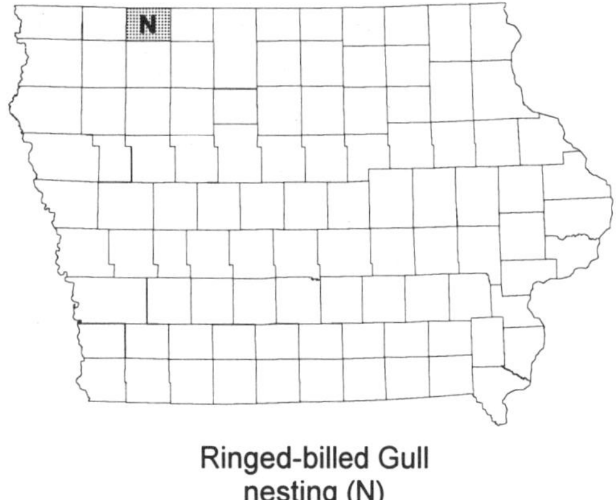

Ringed-billed Gull
nesting (N)

California Gull (*Larus californicus*)

Status: Casual

By year since 1960

60	63	66	69	72	75	78	81	84	87	90	93
									1	2	2 1

By month -- all records

Jan	Feb	Mar	Apr	May	Jun	Jul	Aug	Sep	Oct	Nov	Dec
								2 + +	+ + 1	2	1 +

23 to 24 Nov 1989, Credit Is., Scott Co., ad. (Petersen 1991)
8 Sep to 14 Oct 1990, Saylorville Res., Polk Co., ad. (Dinsmore 1992)
27 to 28 Oct 1990, Coralville Res., Johnson Co., first-basic (Kent 1991)
21 Nov 1993, Carter L., Pottawattamie Co., ad. (P-0414, Bray 1994)
6, 19 Dec 1993, Saylorville Res., Polk Co., first-basic (Pinkston 1994)
3 to 6 Sep 1995, Runnells W.A. and Red Rock Res., Marion Co., first-basic (P-0477, Dinsmore and Sinclair 1996)

Occurrence: The 6 fall records include 3 adults and 3 first-winter birds.

Comment: This North American gull breeds from northern California, northern Utah, and northeastern South Dakota north through the Prairie Provinces to southern Mackenzie and winters on the Pacific Coast. Considering that this species nests in North Dakota, it is surprising that there are only a few records (fewer than 10 in most states) from states south and east of there including Nebraska, Kansas, Oklahoma, Texas, Minnesota, Iowa, Missouri, Wisconsin, Illinois, Indiana, Michigan, Ohio, and New York. Vagrant spring birds are found from March to May, and fall records extend from July to January with the peak in October-November.

References:

Bray, T. E. 1994. California Gull at Carter Lake, Pottawattamie County. *Iowa Bird Life* 64:82-83.

Dinsmore, S. J. 1992. California Gull at Saylorville Reservoir. *Iowa Bird Life* 62:24-25.

Dinsmore, S. J., and J. Sinclair. 1996. California Gull at Runnells Wildlife Area. *Iowa Bird Life* 66:110.

Kent, T. H. 1991. First-winter California Gull at Coralville Reservoir. *Iowa Bird Life* 61: 123-124.

Petersen, P. C. 1991. California Gull at Davenport, first accepted Iowa record. *Iowa Bird Life* 61:121-122.

Pinkston, R. 1994. First-winter California Gull at Saylorville Reservoir. *Iowa Bird Life* 64:114.

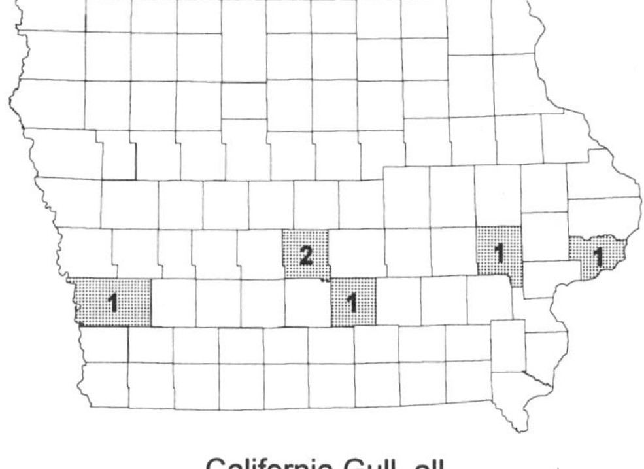

California Gull, all

Herring Gull (*Larus argentatus*)

Status: Regular

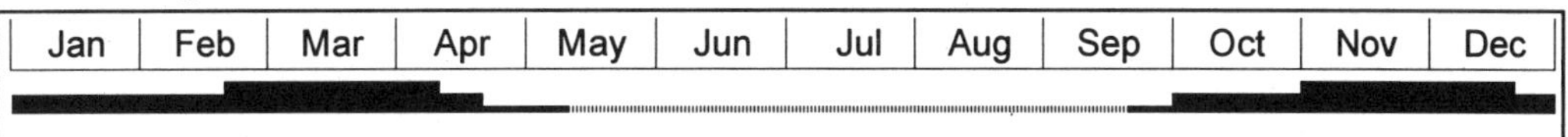

Occurrence: This common migrant is greatly outnumbered by Ring-billed Gull except in winter when Herrings remain longer along major rivers and reservoirs. Some usually remain along the lower Mississippi River below the dams except in the severest of conditions. This species is found on 74 percent of Christmas Bird Counts along the Mississippi River, 6 percent along the Missouri River, and 17 percent of those away from the 2 rivers. The average number seen per year on Christmas Bird Counts has risen from 1,317 in the years 1973 to 1982 to 4,161 in the years 1983 to 1992. Even though the number of Herring Gulls in mid- to late December has increased, it is no longer the commonest gull at this time of year due to the much greater increase in Ring-billed Gulls.

Most Herring Gulls follow the melting ice north in spring, but a few, usually first-basic birds, remain into May. There were 3 June-July records from 1973 to 1982 (Dinsmore et al. 1984) and 10 more from 1983 to 1995. Half of the summer records are from the Mississippi River and the others from large reservoirs and northern lakes. Early fall birds may be immatures or adults, but most birds do not arrive until ice forms. In winter, immature birds are relatively less common than in migration. Late spring and summer birds are mostly immatures, but an occasional adult has been noted.

Comment: In North America, the winter range of this Holarctic species is from southern Alaska, the Great Lakes, and Newfoundland south to northern Mexico and the West Indies. The breeding range is along the East Coast from North Carolina north, along the Great Lakes, and throughout most of Canada and Alaska, except for the prairie regions and southern Alaska. Up to 10 subspecies of Herring Gull are found in the northern hemisphere.

Thayer's Gull (*Larus thayeri*)

Status: Regular

By year since 1960

60 63 66 69 72 75 78 81 84 87 90 93

1 5 1 2 4 1 6 4 6 4 6

Jan	Feb	Mar	Apr	May	Jun	Jul	Aug	Sep	Oct	Nov	Dec
		x x							x x		

15 Mar 1991	24 Oct 1991
16 Mar 1988	29 Oct 1989
31 Mar 1996	4 Nov 1995

Occurrence: The first Accepted record of this species was a first-basic bird at Red Rock Reservoir on 10 December 1985 (Bendorf 1986). Since then Thayer's Gull has been found every year with about 40 records through 1995. A number of reports have not been accepted by the Records Committee, and in some instances it is difficult to determine whether reports pertain to the same or different birds or how many birds were present.

About 75 percent of the records are from November and December. Almost all of the records are from large rivers and reservoirs and associated with concentrations of Herring Gulls. Most are in first-basic plumage, but at least 7 adults and 1 second-basic have been identified.

Comment: Most Thayer's Gulls winter from southern Alaska to Baja California, but in recent years increasing numbers were reported across the United States from the East Coast and south to Texas. The breeding range is in north-central Canada and islands of the Arctic Ocean.

First-basic Thayer's Gulls vary in darkness of coloration. Darker birds may be difficult to tell from Herring Gull, and lighter birds may resemble Iceland Gull. In adults, the wing tip pattern and eye color are used to separate Thayer's from these same 2 species. It is likely that Thayer's and Iceland gulls will be combined into 1 species.

Reference:

Bendorf, C. J. 1986. Thayer's Gull at Red Rock Reservoir. *Iowa Bird Life* 56:94.

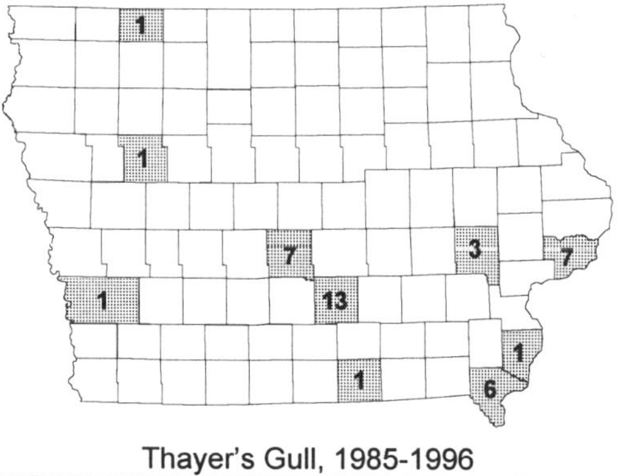

Thayer's Gull, 1985-1996

Iceland Gull (*Larus glaucoides*)

Status: Casual

By year since 1960

60	63	66	69	72	75	78	81	84	87	90	93
										2 3	3 1

By month -- all records

Jan	Feb	Mar	Apr	May	Jun	Jul	Aug	Sep	Oct	Nov	Dec
2 1 1	+ 1 1	1								1	1

13 to 16 Mar 1991, Red Rock Res., Marion Co., first or second year (P-0320, Kent 1992)
31 Dec 1991 to 2 Jan 1992, Lock and Dam 14, Scott Co., first-basic (Kent 1992)
4 Jan to 9 Feb 1992, Scott Co., first-basic (P-0324, P-0326, Kent 1992)
4 Jan 1992, Lock and Dam 14, Scott Co., second-basic (P-0235, Kent 1992)
29 Feb 1992, Saylorville Res., Polk Co., first-basic (P-0336, Kent 1992)
16 to 30 Jan 1993, Iowa City, Johnson Co., first-basic (P-0355, *IBL* 63:49)
31 Jan 1993, Lock and Dam 14, Scott Co., adult (*IBL* 63:49)
14 Feb 1993, Credit Is., Scott Co., first-basic (*IBL* 63:49)
17, 18 Nov 1995, Saylorville Res., Polk Co., first-basic (P-0473, P-0479, Dinsmore 1996)

Occurrence: The 9 records have been from mid-November to mid-March and have involved 6 first-year, 1 second-year, 1 adult, and 1 that could have been either a first- or second-year bird. Several old (Dinsmore et al. 1984) and recent records have not been accepted by the Records Committee, but may have been this species.

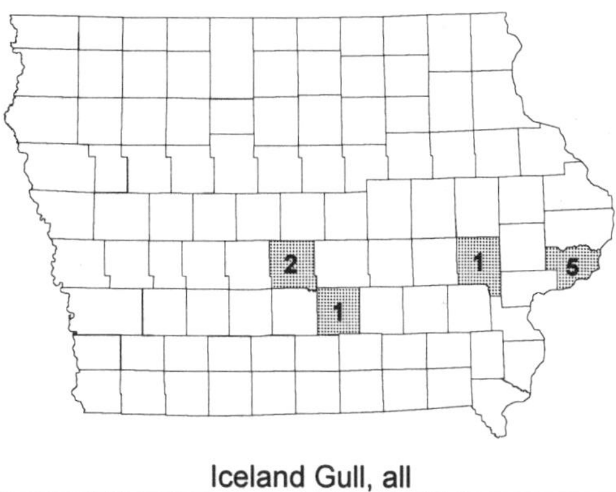

Iceland Gull, all

Comment: Iceland Gulls winter in Europe and from Labrador to Virginia and casually to the Great Lakes. Breeding occurs on Greenland and Baffin Island. The more westerly birds, known as Kumlien's Gull (*L. g. kumlieni*), have some dark in the wing tip and are thought to interbreed with Thayer's Gull.

References:

Dinsmore, S. J. 1996. Iceland Gull at Saylorville Reservoir. *Iowa Bird Life* 66:66-67.

Kent, T. H. 1992. Iceland Gulls in Iowa. *Iowa Bird Life* 62:95-98.

Lesser Black-backed Gull (*Larus fuscus*)

Status: Regular

By year since 1960

60	63	66	69	72	75	78	81	84	87	90	93
								1	3 2 2	2 1 2	4 4 2 3

By month -- all records

Jan	Feb	Mar	Apr	May	Jun	Jul	Aug	Sep	Oct	Nov	Dec
2 1 1	2 1	1	1				1		1 1	1 2	3 5 3

19 Feb 1990 — 19 Aug 1989
10 Mar 1991 — 5 Oct 1989
16 Apr 1993 — 20 Oct 1986

Occurrence: The first record was from Red Rock Reservoir in Marion County from 1 to 5 December 1984 (P-0147, P-0152, P-0144, Kent and Bowles 1985). There are 1 to 4 records per year from 1986 to 1995. These 26 records are scattered from August to April with most from winter. All except 2 were adults. The records are from reservoirs and large rivers in eastern and central Iowa. The August record was an adult at Saylorville Reservoir in Polk County on 19 August 1989 (*IBL* 60:15, 61:85).

Comment: This European species winters south to Africa and the Middle East and increasingly west to North America. There are few records before 1960, a few in the 1960s, and many more in the 1970s and 1980s. Most records are from the East Coast, Gulf Coast (especially Texas), and the Great Lakes region. Iowa has a surprising number of records considering that records to the west of Iowa are limited to California, Colorado, Oklahoma, and Texas. This species is found from October to March with a few lingering to June, so the August record from Iowa is quite unusual. The breeding range is in western Europe from Spain to Norway and Iceland.

Reference:

Kent, T. H., and J. Bowles. 1985. Lesser Black-backed Gull at Red Rock Reservoir. *Iowa Bird Life* 55:21-22.

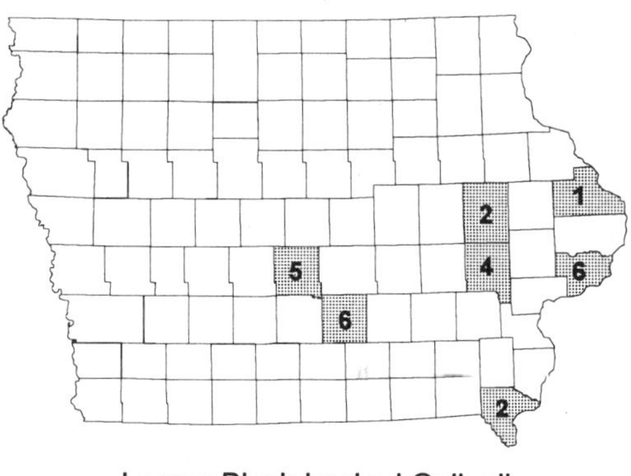

Lesser Black-backed Gull, all

Slaty-backed Gull (*Larus schistisagus*)

Status: Accidental

12 to 21 Feb 1989, Scott Co., ad. (P-0277, P-0278, Fuller 1989)

Occurrence: The 1 record is from winter on the Mississippi River.

Comment: This species breeds and winters on the west coast of the Bering Sea south to Japan. Only a few wander to western Alaska, making it even more incredible that single birds have wandered to British Columbia, Alton Dam north of St. Louis, and the Quad Cities area. There have been subsequent records from Texas, Ontario, Oregon (2), Ohio, and Indiana (Brock 1994). The difficulties in identification are discussed by Goetz et al. (1986).

References:

Brock, K. J. 1994. A Slaty-backed Gull sight record for Indiana. *Meadowlark* 3:47.

Fuller, J. 1989. Slaty-backed Gull in Scott County. *Iowa Bird Life* 59:121-123.

Goetz, R. E., W. M. Rudden, and P. B. Snetsinger. 1986. Slaty-backed Gull winters on the Mississippi River. *Amer. Birds* 40:207-216.

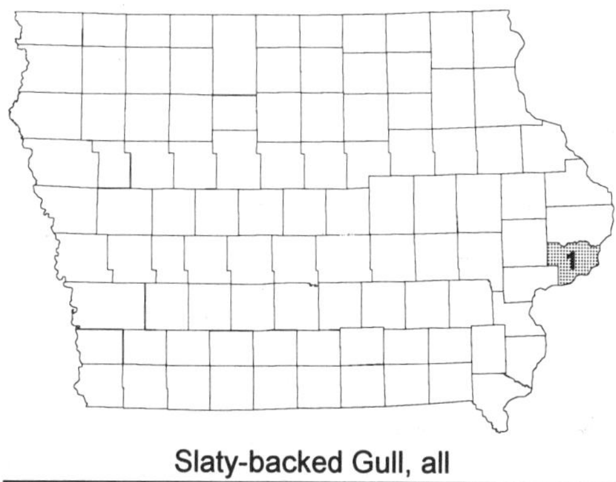

Slaty-backed Gull, all

Glaucous Gull (*Larus hyperboreus*)

Status: Regular

Jan	Feb	Mar	Apr	May	Jun	Jul	Aug	Sep	Oct	Nov	Dec
										x	

3 Apr 1996 — 9 Nov 1991
4 Apr 1983 — 12 Nov 1995
5 Apr 1988 — 14 Nov 1995

Occurrence: There are about 90 records of this rare winter visitant, and most are rather uniformly distributed from late November to late March, with fewer reports from February when some of the birds move to the south of Iowa. Almost all have been found along the Mississippi and Missouri rivers or at large reservoirs.

The first record was of 1 collected at Lake Manawa in Pottawattamie County on 27 March 1941 (Stiles 1941). The number of records has steadily increased, with 5 before 1960, 3 in the 1960s, 6 in the 1970s, and 42 in the 1980s. This species has been found every year since 1977, and in the 1990s averaged 6 reports per year. Most birds are in first-basic plumage, but a few adults and occasional birds in second-basic plumage have been noted.

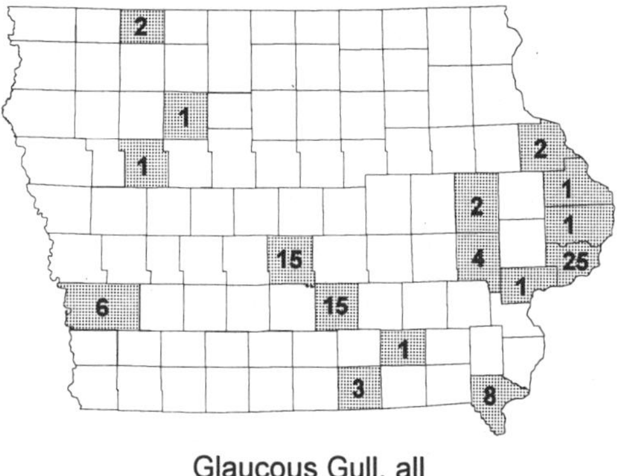

Glaucous Gull, all

Comment: This Holarctic species winters from the Subarctic south coastally to northern California and the Carolinas and to the Great Lakes and upper Midwest. It breeds in coastal areas of the Arctic in both hemispheres.

Reference:

Stiles, B. F. 1941. The Glaucous Gull is taken in Iowa. *Iowa Bird Life* 11:36.

Great Black-backed Gull (*Larus marinus*)

Status: Regular

By year since 1960

60	63	66	69	72	75	78	81	84	87	90	93
						1	1	3	2 1 1	2 2	2 1 3

By month -- all records

Jan	Feb	Mar	Apr	May	Jun	Jul	Aug	Sep	Oct	Nov	Dec
1 1	2 1	1	1			1				1 1	3 3 3

28 Feb 1993	14 Jul 1982
7 Mar 1982	7 Nov 1987
30 Apr 1987	30 Nov 1986

Occurrence: Of the 19 records, 17 are from November to early March, with the others from late April and mid-July. All records are from the Mississippi River or at Red Rock and Saylorville reservoirs except the first 2, which were in western Iowa. A first-basic bird was found at Lake Manawa on 6, 7 December 1978 (Green 1979) and an adult was at West Okoboji on 14 July 1982 (P-0088, Harr 1982). Unlike Lesser Black-backed Gulls in Iowa, which are mostly adults, Great Black-backed Gulls have been represented by 8 first-year, 4 second-year, and 7 adult birds. A second-year bird provided an identification problem (Kent 1992).

Comment: This North Atlantic species breeds from North Carolina north to Iceland, and from eastern Russia south to the British Isles. Numbers along the East Coast have steadily increased over many decades, and wintering birds are now regular south to Florida and on the Great Lakes. West of Iowa, there are records from Texas, Kansas, Colorado, Nebraska, and Saskatchewan. Most occur on partially frozen rivers and reservoirs, but there are occasional records from summer and early fall, including the July record from Iowa.

References:

Green, R. C. 1979. Great Black-backed Gull near Omaha. *Nebr. Bird Review* 47:39-40.

Harr, D. C. 1982. Great Black-backed Gull in the Iowa Lakes Region. *Iowa Bird Life* 52:127-128.

Kent, T. H. 1992. Second-year Great Black-backed Gull on the Mississippi River. *Iowa Bird Life* 62:89-90.

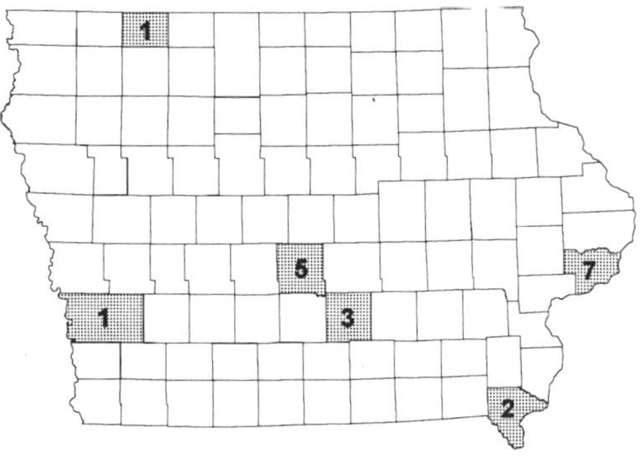

Great Black-backed Gull, all

Black-legged Kittiwake (*Rissa tridactyla*)

Status: Regular

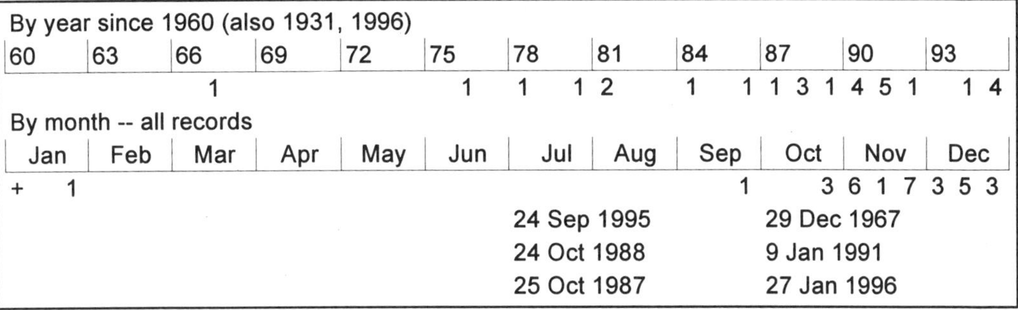

By year since 1960 (also 1931, 1996)
60 63 66 69 72 75 78 81 84 87 90 93
1 1 1 1 2 1 1 1 3 1 4 5 1 1 4
By month -- all records
Jan Feb Mar Apr May Jun Jul Aug Sep Oct Nov Dec
+ 1 1 3 6 1 7 3 5 3
24 Sep 1995
24 Oct 1988
25 Oct 1987
29 Dec 1967
9 Jan 1991
27 Jan 1996

Occurrence: There are 29 records from fall–winter. All were immature birds with 28 being typical first-basic birds in late fall (late October through December with 2 lingering into January). There are 2 reports of 2 birds and one of 4 birds; all others were singles. The early fall bird at Lake Manawa in Pottawattamie County from 24 to 28 September 1995 was molting from first-alternate to second-basic plumage (P-0466, P-0472, P-0467, *Field Notes* 50:62, Padelford and Padelford 1996).

There was a 36-year hiatus between the first record, a specimen taken in Polk County on 22 November 1931 (DuMont 1933), and the second record, a bird in Scott County from 17 to 29 December 1967 that was photographed (Petersen 1968).

Comment: This Holarctic pelagic species winters in northern temperate waters of oceans and breeds on cliffs of the Arctic and Subarctic coasts of the northern hemisphere. Some first-winter birds migrate through central North America in fall. The Iowa pattern is quite similar to other Midwestern states, including the increased number of records in recent years. Adults and spring sightings are unusual and should be carefully substantiated.

References:

DuMont, P. A. 1933. The Atlantic Kittiwake taken in central Iowa. *Auk* 50:102-103.

Padelford, B., and L. Padelford. 1996. Black-legged Kittiwake in Pottawattamie County. *Iowa Bird Life* 66:115.

Petersen, P. 1968. Black-legged Kittiwake at Davenport. *Iowa Bird Life* 38:20-21.

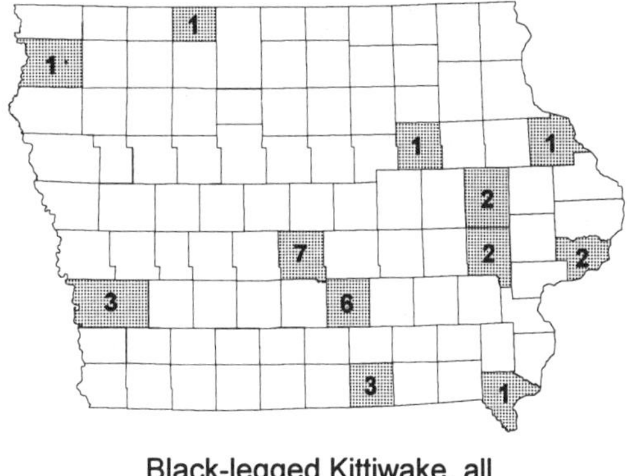

Black-legged Kittiwake, all

Ross's Gull (*Rhodostethia rosea*)

Status: Accidental

31 Oct to 1 Nov 1993, Red Rock Res., Marion Co. (P-0407, P-0413, *Amer. Birds* 48:116, Fuller 1994)

Occurrence: The 1 fall record is the earliest for the lower 48 states.

Comment: This high Arctic species breeds in isolated areas in Siberia, northern Canada, Greenland, and Spitsbergen. In Alaska, it migrates east to Point Barrow and back in fall. It has become a regular winter visitant to the British Isles. The wintering grounds are unknown, but suspected to be in Arctic waters. The increasing number of records from the lower 48 states have been from Oregon, Colorado, Nebraska, North Dakota, Minnesota, Iowa, Missouri, Illinois, Indiana, Tennessee, Maryland, New Jersey, New York, Connecticut, and Massachusetts. The nearest breeding area is a small colony at Churchill, Manitoba.

Records in the United States and in Europe peak in November to December and April to May (Bledsoe and Sibley 1985, Scarpulla 1991). Where these birds are going or where they come from is not known.

References:

Bledsoe, A. H., and D. Sibley. 1985. Patterns of vagrancy of Ross' Gull. *Amer. Birds* 39:219-227.

Fuller, J. 1994. Ross's Gull found at Red Rock Reservoir. *Iowa Bird Life* 64:113.

Scarpulla, E. J. 1991. First record of Ross' Gull for Maryland. *Maryland Birdlife* 47:31-37.

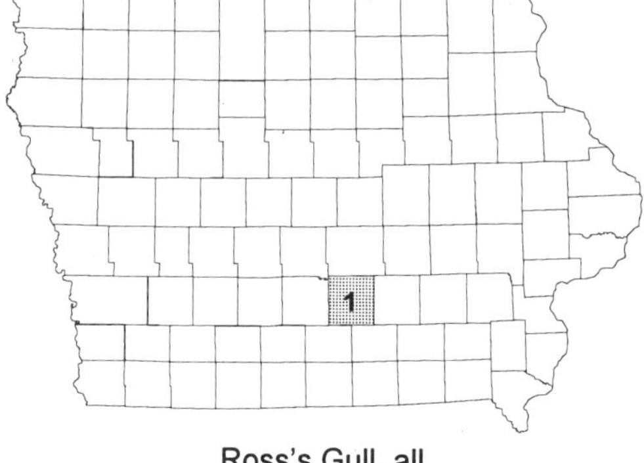

Ross's Gull, all

Sabine's Gull (*Xema sabini*)

Status: Casual

By year since 1960 (also 1891, 1894)

60	63	66	69	72	75	78	81	84	87	90	93
							1	1	1 2	1	1 1 4

By month -- all records

Jan	Feb	Mar	Apr	May	Jun	Jul	Aug	Sep	Oct	Nov	Dec
								2 1 3	1 4 2	1 + +	

5 Sep 1994	23 Oct 1993
6 Sep 1995	26 Oct 1991
14 Sep 1995	23 Nov 1983

Occurrence: Of the 14 records, 13 are from September and October and 1 from November. The first 2 records are specimens taken at Burlington in Des Moines County on 15 October 1891 and 12 October 1894 (University of Iowa specimens #15981, #15982, Bartsch 1899, Kent and Schrimper 1996). The next record was not until 10 to 23 November 1983 at Saylorville Reservoir (P-0112, P-0160, Kent 1983). From 1983 to 1995, Sabine's Gulls have been found in 8 of 13 years, with at least 6 birds at 4 locations in 1995. The only other record with 2 birds was of a juvenile and the only adult seen in Iowa at the Quad Cities in Scott County from 13 to 26 October 1991 (*IBL* 62(1) cover, Pinkston 1992).

Comment: This pelagic species is a circumpolar breeder in the high Arctic. Migration is in the eastern Pacific to wintering grounds off of South America and in the eastern Atlantic to wintering grounds off of Africa. There is also a regular but small migration through the interior. Most of the interior birds are in juvenal plumage. Unlike other gulls, molt to first-basic plumage does not occur until birds reach wintering grounds.

Almost all states have records of Sabine's Gull, and the number found in Iowa is about average. Three-fourths of the inland records occur in September and October. There are a few fall stragglers to January. The few birds that have been found in April to May and July are presumably spring and fall migrating adults.

References:

Bartsch, P. 1899. *Xema sabinii* and *Chordeiles virginianus sennetti*—two additions to the Iowa avifauna. *Auk* 16:86.

Kent, T. H. 1983. Sabine's Gull at Saylorville Reservoir. *Iowa Bird Life* 53:105-106.

Pinkston, R. 1992. Sabine's Gulls at the Quad Cities. *Iowa Bird Life* 62:114-116.

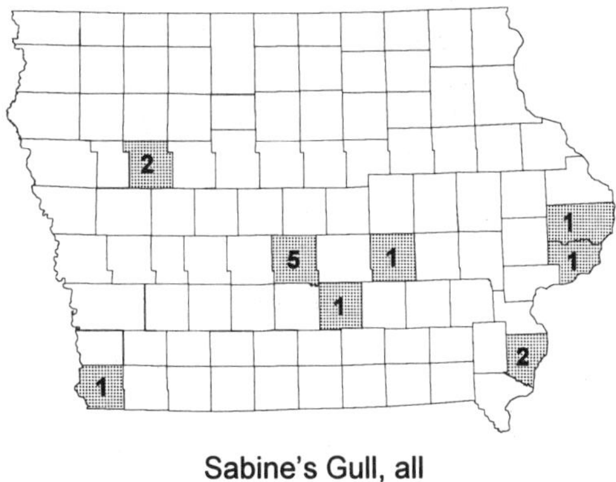

Sabine's Gull, all

Ivory Gull (*Pagophila eburnea*)

Status: Accidental

20 Dec 1975, Rathbun Res., Appanoose Co. (Ayres 1976)
24 Dec 1990 to 1 Jan 1991, Red Rock Res., Marion Co. (*IBL* 61(2) cover photo, Dinsmore 1991)

Occurrence: The 2 December records are of birds in first-basic plumage.

Comment: This circumpolar species of the High Arctic winters on the ice pack and rarely moves very far south. In winter, it reaches the Maritime Provinces but not New England or any eastern state. In the West, it has been found south to Oregon. Most of the inland records are from Minnesota (9) with others from Colorado, Montana, Iowa, Wisconsin, and Ohio. Most but not all have been first-year birds and have occurred from December to early April. An adult was recorded in Minnesota on 28 October 1970 (Janssen 1987). Records from late May in Montana (Skaar et al. 1985) and July in Wisconsin (Robbins 1991) are difficult to explain.

References:

Ayres, C. C. 1976. A rare Ivory Gull at Rathbun Lake. *Iowa Bird Life* 46:15-16.

Dinsmore, S. J. 1991. Ivory Gull at Red Rock Reservoir. *Iowa Bird Life* 61:110-111.

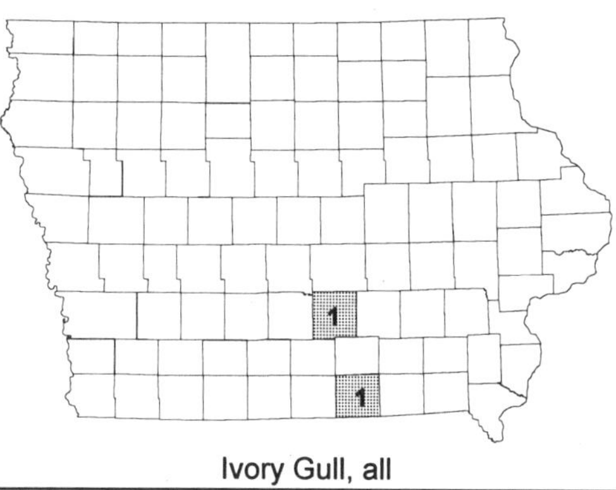

Ivory Gull, all

Caspian Tern (*Sterna caspia*)

Status: Regular

Jan	Feb	Mar	Apr	May	Jun	Jul	Aug	Sep	Oct	Nov	Dec
									x	xx	

19 Apr 1988	28 Oct 1990
19 Apr 1990	1 Nov 1965
19 Apr 1992	7 Nov 1983

Occurrence: This uncommon migrant is usually found on large bodies of water. A few are reported in most summers, and they occasionally linger at 1 location all summer, such as those at Power Plant Ponds in Pottawattamie County in 1985 (*IBL* 55:92) and Saylorville Reservoir in Polk County in 1986 (*IBL* 56:116). In fall, adults have been seen feeding juveniles, although there is no evidence that this species has ever nested in Iowa (Peck 1972).

Comment: This species breeds throughout the world in both northern and southern hemispheres and at coastal and widely separated inland locations. North American birds winter along the Gulf Coast and from southern California south to the equator. The nesting grounds nearest to Iowa are along the Great Lakes and in southern Manitoba.

Reference:

Peck, M. E. 1972. An unusual observation of Caspian Terns. *Iowa Bird Life* 42:101.

Common Tern (*Sterna hirundo*)

Status: Regular

Jan	Feb	Mar	Apr	May	Jun	Jul	Aug	Sep	Oct	Nov	Dec
									x x x		

14 Apr 1952	7 Oct 1995
18 Apr 1986	13 Oct 1985
20 Apr 1980	27 Oct 1985

Occurrence: Common Tern is rare in Iowa with 10 or fewer reports per year. Adults are easily mistaken for the much more common Forster's Tern. Although most records are from the Mississippi and Missouri rivers and large reservoirs, others are scattered across the state. Spring reports outnumber fall reports by about 2 to 1, and there are scattered reports throughout the summer.

Comment: This Holarctic species winters south to Argentina with only a few remaining in southern California and Florida in winter. Most first-summer birds remain on the wintering grounds. Breeding occurs on the East Coast from Florida north and at inland locations across the northern United States and Canada from Newfoundland to Alberta.

More data are needed to obtain a clear picture of the occurrence of this species in Iowa. Observers are urged to gain more experience in identifying terns when visiting states where Common Terns are more common, and to carefully describe birds that are reported in Iowa.

Forster's Tern (*Sterna forsteri*)

Status: Regular; nests

Jan	Feb	Mar	Apr	May	Jun	Jul	Aug	Sep	Oct	Nov	Dec

7 Apr 1986	2 Nov 1989
7 Apr 1995	5 Nov 1985
10 Apr 1987	9 Nov 1977

Occurrence: This uncommon species is widespread in small numbers during migration and is a localized colonial nester in north-central to northwestern Iowa. Forster's Terns tend to be more colonial than Black Terns. Iowa colonies have contained as many as 30 to 40 nests (Bergman et al. 1970). Nesting occurs from late May to mid-June, with nests placed on a mat of marsh vegetation or a muskrat house. Migrants begin to appear away from the nesting range by late June.

Comment: This species winters coastally from California and Virginia south to Central America. Nesting areas include the East Coast and marshy areas from the Great Lakes west to California.

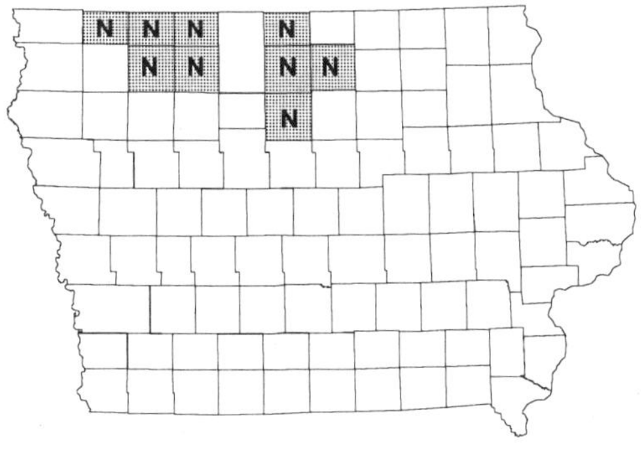

Forster's Tern, 1960-1995
Nesting (N)

Reference:

Bergman, R. D., P. Swain, and M. W. Weller. 1970. A comparative study of nesting Forster's and Black terns. *Wilson Bull.* 82:435-444.

Least Tern (*Sterna antillarum*)

Status: Regular; nests

Jan	Feb	Mar	Apr	May	Jun	Jul	Aug	Sep	Oct	Nov	Dec
			x	....	....	....	....	x			

Spring	Fall
22 Apr 1978	8 Sep 1932
11 May 1986	8 Sep 1959
13 May 1986	13 Sep 1974

Occurrence: Nesting records of this rare species are limited to the Missouri River, while records of migrants are widely scattered across the state. Currently, the only nesting sites are on fly-ash deposits at the power plants south of Council Bluffs in Pottawattamie County and at Port Neal in Woodbury County. Nesting was first reported at the Pottawattamie County plant in 1984 (*IBL* 54:83) and has continued there in most years since, averaging 10 nests per year. They did not nest in 1990 when a Peregrine Falcon was in the area (*IBL* 60:103, 104), and there was only 1 nest in 1992 (*IBL* 62:108). Nesting occurred south of Sioux City in 1986 (*IBL* 56:116) and in 1995 (*IBL* 65:98, 66:22). Nesting starts in late May and extends into June, with young still at the site in July (Dinsmore et al. 1993).

Historically, Lewis and Clark found Least Terns on the Missouri River in August 1804 (Moulton 1986). The first report of nesting was from Sioux City in 1929 (Youngworth 1930). Nesting apparently occurred in Monona County in 1934 (Ducey 1985). Nests were found at De Soto National Wildlife Refuge in Harrison County from 1968 to 1973 (*IBL* 38:88, 43:75).

Comment: Least Terns winter in Central and northern South America and breed coastally in the West Indies and north to central California and Maine, and along the Mississippi River and its tributaries, extending up the Mississippi to St. Louis and up the Missouri to Montana.

References:

Dinsmore, S. J., J. J. Dinsmore, and D. L. Howell. 1993. Least Terns nesting on fly-ash deposits. In: Higgins, K. F., and M. R. Brashier, eds. *Proc. The Missouri River and Its Tributaries: Piping Plover and Least Tern Symposium.* South Dakota State Univ., Brookings.

Ducey, J. 1985. The historic breeding distribution of the Least Tern in Nebraska. *Nebr. Bird Review* 53:26-36.

Youngworth, W. 1930. Breeding of the Least Tern in Iowa. *Wilson Bull.* 42:102-103.

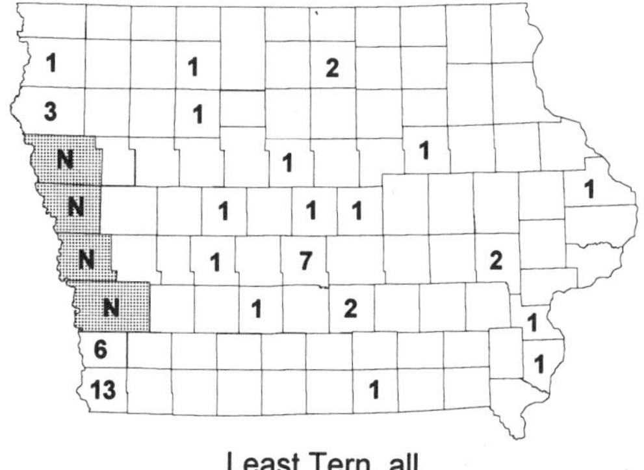

Least Tern, all
Nesting (N) and other records

Black Tern (*Chlidonias niger*)

Status: Regular; nests

Jan	Feb	Mar	Apr	May	Jun	Jul	Aug	Sep	Oct	Nov	Dec

Early dates	Late dates
12 Apr 1914	2 Oct 1983
29 Apr 1981	9 Oct 1983
29 Apr 1989	16 Oct 1994

Occurrence: This fairly common spring migrant is an uncommon nesting species in northwestern Iowa. Fall migration is less evident. In migration, small flocks are usually dispersed over the state in May, but in 1993 they were highly concentrated from 21 to 26 May, with an amazing 1,100 at Amana Lake in Iowa County on 26 May (*IBL* 63:76).

A few nest each year in north-central and northwestern Iowa. As recently as the 1960s, they also nested in central Iowa. Nests are built on flimsy floating platforms or on muskrat houses (Bergman et al. 1970). Nesting starts in late May and continues into July.

Comment: Black Terns breed in North America, Europe, and western Asia. In North America they nest from Iowa and Nebraska north to northern Manitoba, west to Oregon, and east to the Maritime Provinces. The North American population winters from Panama south to Chile and east to Surinam.

Reference:

Bergman, R. D., P. Swain, and M. W. Weller. 1970. A comparative study of nesting Forster's and Black terns. *Wilson Bull.* 82:435-444.

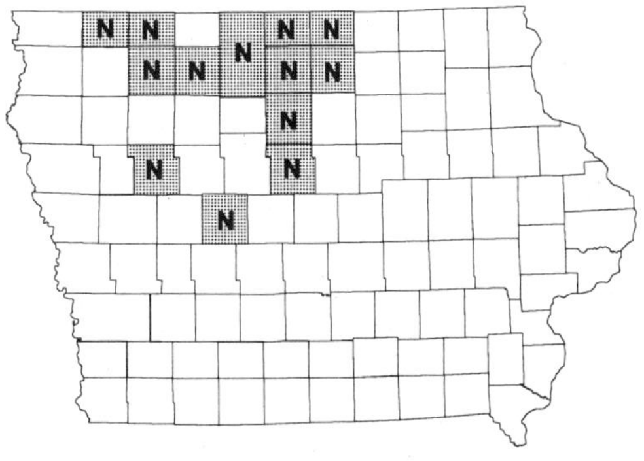

Black Tern, 1960-1995
Nesting (N)

Auks, Murres, and Puffins (Family Alcidae)

Auks, murres, and puffins, or alcids as they are commonly known, comprise 22 species, with 21 from North America and 3 from Iowa. These short-winged, marine diving birds live in cold coastal waters of the Northern Hemisphere and are not normally found inland. Iowa is unusual in having had 3 of these rare vagrants.

Thick-billed Murre (*Uria lomvia*)

Status: Accidental

16 Dec 1896, Atlantic, Cass Co., imm., specimen now lost (Brown 1897, Stephens 1932, DuMont 1933)
Jan 1897, Johnson Co., specimen now lost (Hoover 1897, Anderson 1907, DuMont 1933)

Occurrence: There are 2 records from the winter of 1896-1897, both based on specimens. The first was examined by Ludlow Griscom. The second specimen was mounted by Hoover, and, although we have no independent confirmation of the identification, it is Accepted based in part on the many inland records found at this time after a severe storm on the East Coast.

Comment: This Holarctic pelagic species nests on cliffs south on the West Coast to Kodiak in Alaska and on the East Coast to Newfoundland, wintering south to southeastern Alaska and New Jersey and casually to California and South Carolina.

A storm from Labrador in December 1896 dispersed many Thick-billed Murres south along the Atlantic Coast and west to Lake Erie with a few making it all the way to Indiana and Iowa (Peterjohn 1989, Gaston 1988). From 1893 to 1909 this species occurred almost annually in the eastern Great Lakes region with several records from Ohio and Michigan. There were also incursions in the mid-1920s with a record from Ohio (Peterjohn 1989) and in the early 1950s with a record from Michigan (Gaston 1988). It appears unlikely that this species will be found again in Iowa in the near future.

References:

Brown, J. H. 1897. An accidental visitor. *Iowa Ornithologist* 3:11.

Gaston, A. J. 1988. The mystery of murres: Thick-billed Murres, *Uria lomvia*, in the Great Lakes region, 1890-1986. *Canadian Field-Naturalist* 102:705-711.

Hoover, G. C. 1897. Notes and news. *Iowa Ornithologist* 3:24.

Stephens, T. C. 1932. Brunnich's Murre in Iowa. *Wilson Bull.* 44:239.

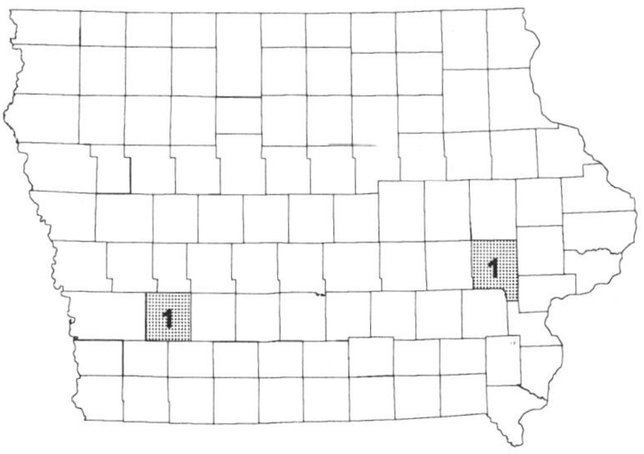

Thick-billed Murre, all

Marbled Murrelet (*Brachyramphus marmoratus*)

Status: Accidental

12 Dec 1991, Red Rock Res., Marion Co. (Dinsmore 1993)

Occurrence: The 1 sight record was of a bird with a bill suggestive of the Asiatic subspecies, *B. m. perdix*, which has a known vagrancy pattern in North America.

Comment: This species occurs in coastal waters of the North Pacific from northern California to Japan. Strangely, the 10 specimens from interior North America are of the Asiatic subspecies, *B. m. perdix* (Sealy et al. 1991). The 3 sight records cited by Sealy et al. (1991) and the Iowa record (Dinsmore 1993) also appear to be of the Asiatic subspecies. Records away from the West Coast are from Saskatchewan, Colorado, Iowa, Arkansas, Indiana (2), Quebec, Newfoundland, Massachusetts, North Carolina, and Florida and are scattered from July to December.

References:

Dinsmore, S. J. 1993. First record of a Marbled Murrelet for Iowa. *Iowa Bird Life* 63:1-2.

Sealy, S. G., H. R. Carter, W. D. Shuford, K. D. Powers, and C. A. Chase III. 1991. Long-distance vagrancy of the Asiatic Marbled Murrelet in North America, 1979-1989. *Western Birds* 22:145-156.

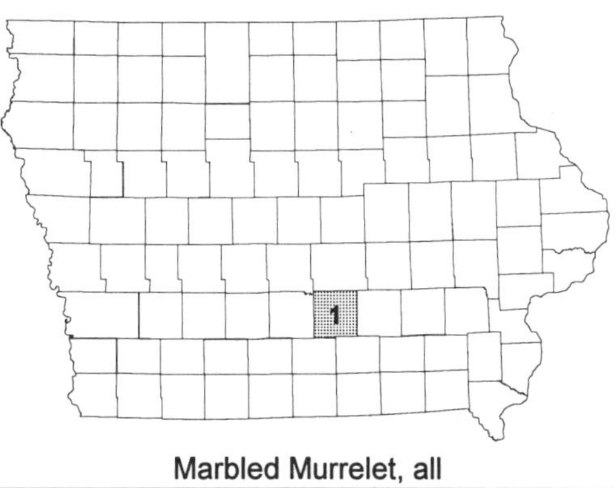

Marbled Murrelet, all

Ancient Murrelet (*Synthliboramphus antiquus*)

Status: Accidental

28 Oct 1987, Crystal L., Hancock Co. (Hansen 1988)

Occurrence: The 1 sight record is of a bird seen from a boat at close range for 30 minutes and heard to make a loud "krrreeep" call.

Comment: This pelagic species of the North Pacific breeds south to British Columbia and Korea and in winter may be found south to California and Formosa. Of the alcids, it is the most likely to stray to Iowa (Munyer 1965, Kent 1988). Records are scattered across northern states and provinces as far east as Quebec and Ohio and south to Indiana, Illinois, Iowa, New Mexico, and Utah with 1 aberrant record in Louisiana. The greatest number have been from Minnesota (6) and Wisconsin (5). Two-thirds of the vagrants records are from October to November. A few have been found in spring from March to May and at other odd dates.

References:

Hansen, J. L. 1988. Ancient Murrelet at Crystal Lake. *Iowa Bird Life* 58:59.

Kent, T. H. 1988. Mapping vagrants. *Iowa Bird Life* 58:101-105.

Munyer, E. A. 1965. Inland wanderings of the Ancient Murrelet. *Wilson Bull.* 77:235-242

Ancient Murrelet, all

ORDER COLUMBIFORMES

Pigeons and doves are the major family in this order. The other family of dodo and solitaires involves 3 extinct species.

Pigeons and Doves (Family Columbidae)

Pigeons and doves comprise 305 species, with 18 from North America and 4 from Iowa. Of the Iowa species, 2 are Regular, 1 is Accidental, and 1 is Extinct. Pigeons and doves are stout birds with short necks and short, slender, rounded bills, usually thickened toward the tip. They feed their young a milk-like material produced by the lining of the crop, and they drink by sucking rather than tipping the head backward. They are powerful flyers. Generally they lay 2 eggs in a poorly constructed nest. The larger species tend to be called pigeons.

Rock Dove (*Columa livia*)

Status: Regular; nests

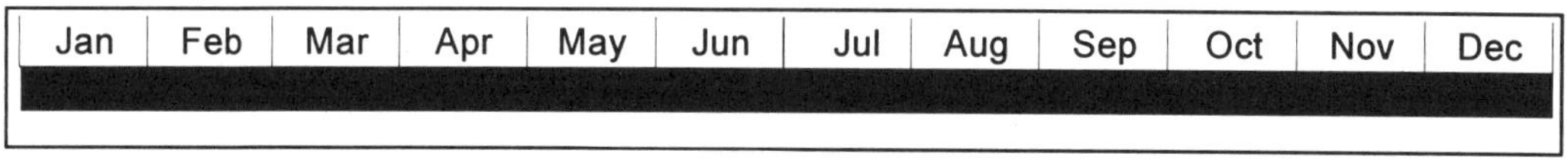

Jan	Feb	Mar	Apr	May	Jun	Jul	Aug	Sep	Oct	Nov	Dec

Occurrence: This abundant permanent resident is found in towns, on farms, on bridges, and occasionally near natural rock outcroppings. On Breeding Bird Surveys, Rock Doves average 17.8 per route with relatively few in the south (3.2) and the most in the northeast (31.8). The numbers were stable from 1967 to 1991. On Christmas Bird Counts, Rock Doves average 43.7 per 10 party hours (south 34.3, middle 52.0, north 40.6).

Historically, there is no record of how this introduced species spread to Iowa in the 1800s. It was not given full standing on the American Ornithologists' Union Check-list until 1931, and, until the 1960s, only birds using natural habitat were recognized as wild. Nesting occurred on the cliffs at Iowa Falls in Hardin County as early as 1917 (Spiker 1933, Ennis 1949). Other early nesting sites were near Stone City in Jones County (Spiker 1933, Ennis 1949) and near Mount Vernon in Linn County (Ennis 1949).

Comment: This Eurasian species has followed humans to all areas of the world except for extremely cold regions. It would be interesting to have more data on the distribution of this species in rural Iowa to confirm the subjective observation and data from Breeding Bird Surveys that suggest a high density in the hilly northeastern part of the state.

References:

Ennis, J. H. 1949. Rock Doves and Cliff Swallows at Iowa Falls. *Iowa Bird Life* 19:22.

Spiker, C. J. 1933. Naturalization of the Rock Dove in Iowa. *Iowa Bird Life* 3:10-11.

Mourning Dove (*Zenaida macroura*)

Status: Regular; nests

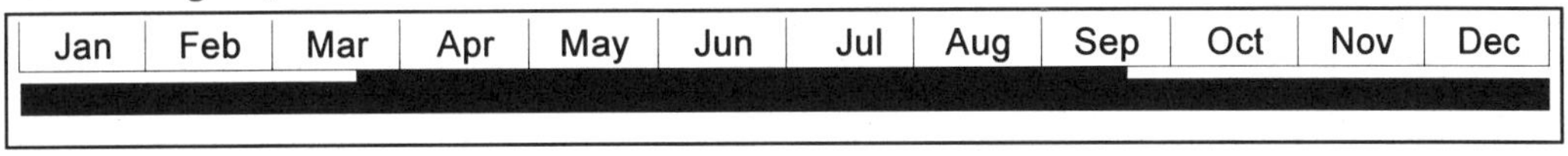

Jan	Feb	Mar	Apr	May	Jun	Jul	Aug	Sep	Oct	Nov	Dec

Occurrence: This abundant summer resident is also a fairly common winter resident. On Breeding Bird Surveys, Mourning Doves average 29.6 per route with relatively more in the south (45.5) and west (47.5). The numbers were stable from 1967 to 1991. Nesting occurs from late March to mid-September. Fledglings unable to fly were reported as late as 14 October 1963 at Goldfield in Wright County (*IBL* 33:88).

Mourning Doves are found on 77 percent of Christmas Bird Counts, with an average of 7.0 per 10 party-hours (south 5.3, central 9.6, north 2.1). They were reported by 13 percent of participants in the winter feeder surveys (Hollis 1986).

Comment: This species ranges throughout Central America and North America to southern Canada, with the winter range extending north into Minnesota. Most of the birds move south from the northern areas in winter, but increasing numbers winter at bird feeders in towns and around farms.

Passenger Pigeon (*Ectopistes migratorius*)

Status: Extinct; formerly nested

Occurrence: This formerly abundant woodland species was an abundant migrant and summer resident. Nesting records are predominantly from northeastern Iowa (Dinsmore 1994).

In migration, an estimated 600 million were seen at a single location in Dubuque County in one day (McGee 1910). McGee noted the decline in migration by the early 1860s, only occasional flocks and decreased nesting by the early 1870s, and disappeared by 1876. Bond (1921) witnessed intermittent flights in Johnson County from 1872 to 1876 and illustrated the vast extent of the flocks in a painting. Nauman (1933) described flocks in southeastern Iowa so dense that they obscured the sun and noted their disappearance by 1880.

Orr (1936) described colonial nesting in Winneshiek and Allamakee counties and recounted how the birds would leapfrog through the newly sown wheat fields extracting all of the seed. He described commercial trapping and the packing of birds in barrels for shipment to market. He noted that scattered pairs were fairly common in the 1870s with final disappearance in the late 1880s or early 1890s. DuMont (1933) lists all of the Iowa records after 1880 including sight records as late as 1903. Schorger (1955) lists a 1900 Ohio report as the last sighting of this species in the wild. The last verifiable Iowa record is 1 shot near Keokuk in Lee County in 1896 and now at the University of Michigan.

Comment: Passenger Pigeons wintered in southeastern United States from southern Missouri south and bred from Mississippi north to Canada and west to eastern Kansas. The last one died in captivity in Cincinnati in 1914. Clearing of forests and market hunting were factors in this species extinction.

References:

Bond, F. 1921. The later flights of the Passenger Pigeon. *Auk* 38:523-527.

DuMont, P. A. 1933. The Passenger Pigeon as a former Iowa bird. *Proc. Iowa Acad. Sci.* 40:205-211.

McGee, W. J. 1910. Notes on the Passenger Pigeon. *Science* 32:958-964.

Nauman, E. D. 1933. Iowa's vanishing hosts. *Iowa Bird Life* 3:47-48.

Orr, E. 1936. The Passenger Pigeon in northeastern Iowa. *Iowa Bird Life* 6:22-26.

Schorger, A. W. 1955. *The Passenger Pigeon. Its Natural History and Extinction.* Univ. of Wisconsin Press, Madison.

Common Ground-Dove (*Columbina passerina*)

Status: Accidental

19 Oct to 2 Nov 1991, Cedar Rapids, Linn Co. (P-0295, P-0312, Fuller 1992)

Occurrence: There is 1 fall record. An old undocumented report from Des Moines in Polk County on 10 June 1922 was considered by the observer to be an escapee (Pangburn 1922).

Comment: This species is resident from the southern portions of South Carolina, Texas, and California through Central America and the Caribbean to northern South America. It has a distinct fall vagrancy pattern north as far as Nevada, Utah, Wyoming, South Dakota, Iowa, Wisconsin, and Michigan, and on the East Coast to Massachusetts and Nova Scotia. Almost all records from the Midwest are from fall (90 percent), typically in October and November (60 percent). Most records of vagrants are from states to the south of Iowa.

References:

Fuller, J. 1992. Common Ground-Dove at Cedar Rapids. *Iowa Bird Life* 62:93-94.

Pangburn, C. H. 1922. The Ground Dove in central Iowa. *Auk* 39:566.

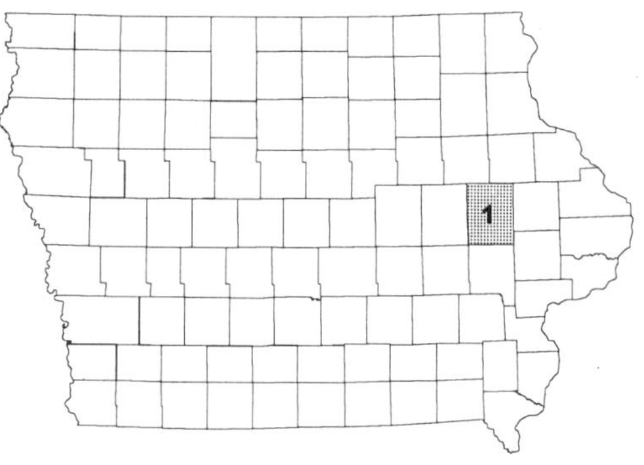

Common Ground-Dove, all

ORDER PSITTACIFORMES

Lories, Parakeets, Macaws, and Parrots (Family Psittacidae)

All of the species in this order are lumped into 1 family. Lories, parakeets, macaws, and parrots comprise 350 species, with 6 in North America, and 1 in Iowa. The extinct Carolina Parakeet is the only naturally occurring North American species, except, perhaps, for 1 or 2 species in the Southwest. Most of the parrots are inhabitants of tropical areas, with large concentrations in Central and South America and in the Australian region. They are brightly colored and have short, strongly hooked bills adapted to feeding on fruits.

Carolina Parakeet (*Conuropsis carolinensis*)

Status: Extinct

8 May 1843, southwestern corner of Iowa (Audubon and Coues 1897, Anderson 1907)

Occurrence: The evidence for the occurrence of this species in Iowa is meager, with only one Accepted record. It was listed as occurring along the Missouri River by Say in 1819-1820 (James 1823, DuMont 1933) and by Maximillian in 1934 (Anderson 1907). Other indefinite records are for Webster County in the 1850s and 1860s (McKinley 1965), in Decatur County prior to 1873 (Trippe 1873), and in Dickinson County (no date given, Bartsch 1895).

Comment: Iowa and eastern Nebraska apparently represented the northern and western edge of the range of this eastern woodland species that occurred south to central Florida. The last bird died in the Cincinnati Zoo in 1918. The records of this species in the upper Mississippi and Missouri river valleys are detailed by McKinley (1965). It probably disappeared from Iowa in the 1860s.

References:

Bartsch, P. 1895. Birds extinct in Iowa and those becoming so. *Iowa Ornithologist* 2:1-3.

McKinley, D. 1965. The Carolina Parakeet in the Upper Missouri and Mississippi river valleys. *Auk* 82:215-226.

ORDER CUCULIFORMES

This order is treated as 1 family with subfamilies (American Ornithologists' Union 1983), but others elevate the subfamilies to family level (Clements 1991). North American species include Old World cuckoos, New World cuckoos, anis, and ground-cuckoos. Species in this order are closely related to parrots but lack the heavy, hooked bills and have the outer hind toe reversible.

Cuckoos, Roadrunners, and Anis (Family Cuculidae)

Cuckoos, roadrunners, and anis comprise 142 species, with 8 from North America and 3 from Iowa. They are slender-bodied, long-tailed birds with stout, down-curved bills and short legs. Most are forest dwellers and feed on insect larvae.

Black-billed Cuckoo (*Coccyzus erythropthalmus*)

Status: Regular; nests

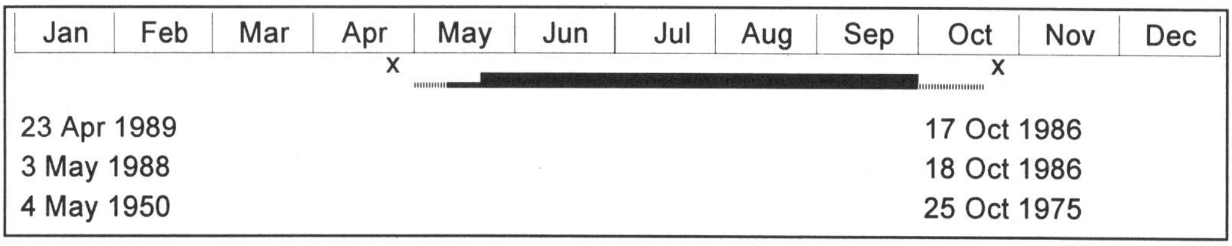

Jan	Feb	Mar	Apr	May	Jun	Jul	Aug	Sep	Oct	Nov	Dec
			X						X		

Earliest	Latest
23 Apr 1989	17 Oct 1986
3 May 1988	18 Oct 1986
4 May 1950	25 Oct 1975

Occurrence: This uncommon summer resident does not arrive until mid- or late May and most leave in September. The number on Breeding Bird Surveys averaged 0.6 per route with fewer in the northeast (0.1) and perhaps in the west (0.4), and no indication of change from 1967 to 1991. At the Coralville Reservoir, with predominantly heavily wooded areas, Yellow-billed Cuckoos outnumbered Black-billed by about 6:1 (Kent et al. 1994). The nesting season starts in late May and extends at least through June (Smith 1979) and probably into August.

Comment: This species winters from northern South America south to Bolivia. It breeds in the eastern United States and southern Canada north from the latitude of Oklahoma and Tennessee and west to the Rocky Mountains. Although both cuckoos are found in a variety of woodland and edge habitat, Black-billed Cuckoos avoid more densely wooded areas.

Comparison of the frequency and habitat of the 2 cuckoos in Iowa is complicated by their secretiveness and experience needed to identify them by voice. Views of cuckoos are often brief, and differences in voice can be confusing.

Reference:

Smith, L. M. 1979. Some aspects of cuckoo nesting ecology in Lucas County, Iowa. *Iowa Bird Life* 49:63-64.

Yellow-billed Cuckoo (*Coccyzus americanus*)

Status: Regular; nests

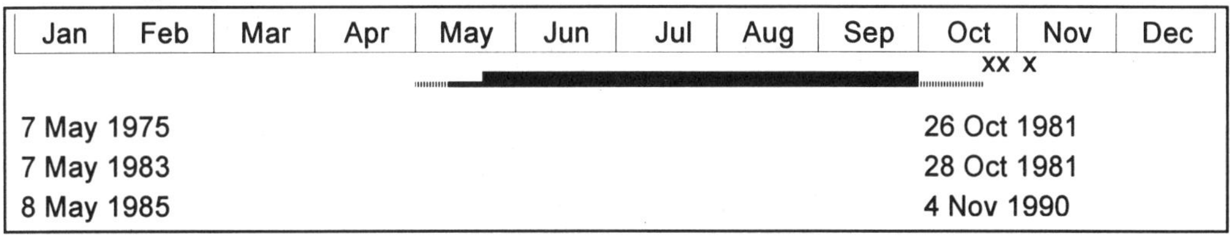

Jan	Feb	Mar	Apr	May	Jun	Jul	Aug	Sep	Oct	Nov	Dec
									XX	X	
7 May 1975									26 Oct 1981		
7 May 1983									28 Oct 1981		
8 May 1985									4 Nov 1990		

Occurrence: Yellow-billed Cuckoo is an uncommon summer resident, but slightly more common than Black-billed. The number on Breeding Bird Surveys averaged 1.0 per route in the period from 1967 to 1991, but this number varied from 0.5 to 2.1 in various years. There was little variation in numbers across the state. The nesting season starts in late May and extends at least through June (Smith 1979) and probably into August.

Comment: The winter range is similar to Black-billed Cuckoo, ranging from northern South America to northern Argentina. The breeding range, however, is more to the south and west, involving southern United States, northern Mexico, and southern California north to central Minnesota. Habitat preference overlaps with Black-billed Cuckoo, but Yellow-billed are more likely in woods with dense undergrowth. The population cycles of this species are correlated with outbreaks of tent caterpillars.

Reference:

Smith, L. M. 1979. Some aspects of cuckoo nesting ecology in Lucas County, Iowa. *Iowa Bird Life* 49:63-64.

Groove-billed Ani (*Crotophaga sulcirostris*)

Status: Accidental

22 Oct 1966, Cedar Rapids, Linn Co. (Dinsmore et al. 1984, *IBL* 64:70)
19 Oct to 25 Nov 1987, Jacob Krumm W.A., Jasper Co. (P-0231, P-0241, *Amer. Birds* 42:17, *IBL* 58(1) cover, Koenig 1988)

Occurrence: There are 2 records from fall. Another report of a specimen said to have been killed by a cat in Osceola County (Musgrove 1948) lacks details of description, date, and location.

Comment: This species is resident in southern Texas and southern Baja California south coastally to Chile and Guyana. Many move south from Texas in winter, but others wander northeast along the Gulf Coast to Florida and north to the Midwest as far north as Manitoba, Minnesota, Wisconsin, Michigan, and Ontario (Kent 1988). Others have been found in the Southwest to southern California and Nevada. Iowa has fewer records than any contiguous state. About 60 percent of the northern records are from October and most of the rest from September and November.

References:

Kent, T. H. 1988. Mapping vagrants. *Iowa Bird Life* 58:101-105.

Koenig, D. 1988. Groove-billed Ani in Jasper County. *Iowa Bird Life* 58:26.

Musgrove, J. W. 1948. The Groove-billed Ani and Mountain Bluebird specimens in Iowa collection. *Iowa Bird Life* 18:70.

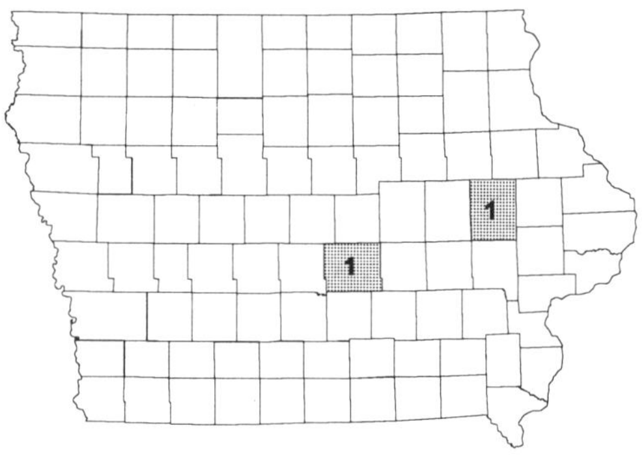

Groove-billed Ani, all

ORDER STRIGIFORMES

Owls are mostly nocturnal predators with large heads with feathered facial disks, large external ear openings with flaps, forward-facing eyes, and small hooked bills. Their feet are strong with sharp talons, and their soft, fluffy plumage allows for silent flight.

Barn Owls (Family Tytonidae)

Barn owls comprise 17 species, with 1 in North America and Iowa. Barn owls have long legs feathered to the feet, long wings, an elongated beak, a serrated talon on the middle toe, and a heart-shaped facial disc. The eyes are smaller than in typical owls and are black. They have barred or spotted plumages often rich in gold.

Barn Owl (*Tyto alba*)

Status: Regular; nests

By year since 1960

60			63			66			69		
2	2	3	3	3	1		2			2	

72			75			78			81		
	1	1	2		1	1	4	1	1		6

84			87			90			93		
6	4	3	7	3	2	2	1	4	2	5	10

By month -- all records

Jan			Feb			Mar			Apr			May			Jun		
2			2	1		2			2	5	3	4	1	1		1	2

Jul			Aug			Sep			Oct			Nov			Dec		
1		2	1	3	1	2	2	3	1	2	2			2	4	2	6

Occurrence: Barn Owl is a rare resident, with 10 or fewer reports per year, which are scattered over all months with the most records from southwestern, south-central, and central Iowa. Most of the nesting records are from the southern half of the state. In 1995, 4 nests were present at a farmstead in Taylor County (*IBL* 65:99). Some of the winter records are of birds that were found dead.

In an attempt to augment the population, the Department of Natural Resources released 427 birds from 1983 to 1987 (Ehresman et al. 1988). None of the released birds are known to have nested. Many were killed by Great Horned Owls. The number of reports seems to have increased during the years of release.

Historically, Anderson (1907) describes the Barn Owl as "a rather rare resident in the southern half of the state and very rarely appears north of the middle line of the state," and DuMont (1933) calls it "A rare resident in all parts of the state, somewhat more numerous in the southern and western portions."

Comment: This worldwide species of temperate and tropical areas reaches the northern edge of its range in Iowa. In states to the north of Iowa, it is a rare summer resident in southern South Dakota (South Dakota Ornithologists' Union 1991), irregular in southern Minnesota (Janssen 1987), and rare in summer and winter in southern Wisconsin (Robbins 1991).

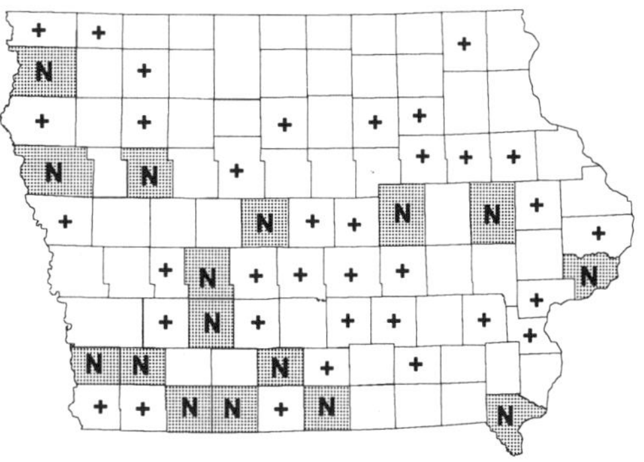

Barn Owl, 1960-1995
Nesting (N) and other records (+)

Although it appears that there may be a decline in the number of Barn Owls in Iowa and nearby states, this species was never common, and Iowa lies at the northern edge of where this species can breed. We do not have data on how many Barn Owls reside in Iowa or how much movement they undergo. Some obviously migrate south, such as 1 fledged in Davenport in 1967 and recovered on 9 January 1968 in Louisiana (Morrissey 1968). They are very nocturnal and not often seen. Compared to typical owls, they have large broods and a short life-span. They tend to wander, with some birds being found to the north of the usual breeding range. A bird released in Clayton County, Iowa, on 22 August 1984 was found dead 175 miles to the northeast in Waupaca County, Wisconsin, on 10 January 1985 (Wydeven 1986).

References:

Ehresman, B. L., D. A. Reeves, and K. P. Schlarbaum. 1988. Post release survival and movements of captively reared Common Barn-Owls in Iowa. *Annual Symposium of the National Wildlife Rehabilitation Association* 7:133-150.

Morrissey, T. J. 1968. Notes of birds in the Davenport area: Part III owls. *Iowa Bird Life* 38:107-118.

Wydeven, A. P. 1986. Iowa-banded Barn Owl in Waupaca County. *Passenger Pigeon* 48:79-80.

Typical Owls (Family Strigidae)

Typical owls comprise 160 species, with 20 from North America and 10 from Iowa. Of the Iowa species, 8 are Regular and 2 Accidental. Three species are common permanent residents, and 3 others nest irregularly.

Eastern Screech-Owl (*Otus asio*)

Status: Regular; nests

Jan	Feb	Mar	Apr	May	Jun	Jul	Aug	Sep	Oct	Nov	Dec

Occurrence: This permanent resident is probably fairly common, but the data to substantiate this are minimal. It is reported on two-thirds of Christmas Bird Counts from all areas of the state. It is likely that it could be found on more counts with sufficient effort. The number per square kilometer was estimated at 0.1 to 0.2 in Marion County (DeGeus and Bowles 1991). Most are found in small woodlands, farmsteads, or towns. They are quite nocturnal, but occasionally call during the day in response to a tape.

Comment: Eastern Screech-Owl is a permanent resident of the eastern United States north to southern Canada, west to eastern Colorado, and south to northeastern Mexico. Although sometimes heard calling spontaneously, particularly during the nesting season, most are reported by birders who have elicited responses to taped calls. Birders most often seek them out during Christmas Bird Counts or spring counts.

Reference:

DeGeus, D. W., and J. B. Bowles. 1991. Relative abundance of Eastern Screech-Owls in a south-central Iowa township. *J. Iowa Acad. Sci.* 98:91-92.

Great Horned Owl (*Bubo virginianus*)

Status: Regular; nests

Jan	Feb	Mar	Apr	May	Jun	Jul	Aug	Sep	Oct	Nov	Dec

Occurrence: This common species is found in all areas of the state in a variety of habitats. The average number on Breeding Bird Surveys is 0.3 per route and on Christmas Bird Counts 1.2 per 10 party-hours. Some may migrate into the state in winter, as evidenced by the occasional sightings and specimens of the Arctic race, *B. v. subarcticus,* and a western form, *B. v. occidentalis* (DuMont 1933). Great Horned Owls use a variety of nesting sites including old hawk nests, hollow trees, ledges, and buildings. Eggs may be laid by early February.

Comment: This species is a permanent resident of North, Central, and South America to the tree line. Some move south from the far north in winter. Great Horned Owls are often active at dawn and dusk, when they can be seen sitting in the open or heard calling. Otherwise, they are usually flushed from daytime roosts.

Snowy Owl (*Nyctea scandiaca*)

Status: Regular

Jan	Feb	Mar	Apr	May	Jun	Jul	Aug	Sep	Oct	Nov	Dec
			xx x						xx		
			2 Apr 1977			1 Oct 1963					
			18 Apr 1900			7 Oct 1961					
			28 Apr 1977			10 Oct 1992					

Occurrence: This rare winter visitant is found every year. There were 3 to 8 reports per year from 1983 to 1995 except for 10 in 1992 and 18 in 1993. There were 24 reports for the winter of 1993-1994, a winter in which 351 were reported in Minnesota (Schladweiler 1994). Snowy Owls are found in all areas of the state, but there is a gradient from north to south. From 1980 to 1995, 57 percent of reports were from northern, 24 percent from central, and 19 percent from southern Iowa. Most reports are from November through February, with a few earlier and later. Christmas Bird Counts average 1 record per year. Many reports have been of immature birds, but most often the age is not reported.

Eruptions occurred in the winters of 1974-1975 with 77 reports (Black 1975), 1976-1977 with 206 reports (*IBL* 47:60), and 1980-1981 with 35 reports (*IBL* 51:32). Historically, eruptions were noted more frequently than they are now (Dinsmore et al. 1984).

Comment: This Holarctic species of the Arctic tundra exhibits some southward movement in winter. It is regular south to Minnesota with a few birds reaching Iowa each year. During its irregular eruptions, which are associated with decreases in the lemming population, more birds are found farther south, reaching northern Missouri, with rare stragglers south to the Gulf Coast states.

In the eastern United States, invasions occurred about every 4 years and sometimes lasted for 2 years (Gross 1947). A predominance of young birds the first year and adults the second year has been noted (Robbins 1991). In Iowa, the invasion pattern appears to be less regular. Perhaps minor invasions are not readily detected as far south as Iowa.

First-year birds are heavily marked with black barring. Females have an intermediate amount of barring, which is often brownish. Males have the least marking; older birds may be nearly pure white. Unlike most other owls in Iowa, this species is active during daylight hours.

References:

Black, G. B. 1975. Snowy Owl sightings in Iowa, winter of 1974-1975. *Iowa Bird Life* 45:61-62.

Gross, A. O. 1947. Cyclic invasions of the Snowy Owl and the migration of 1945-1946. *Auk* 64:584-601.

Schladweiler, J. L. 1994. Minnesota Snowy Owl invasion 1993-94. *Loon* 66:160-165.

Northern Hawk Owl (*Surnia ulula*)

Status: Accidental

25 Dec 1981 to 25 Feb 1982, Waterloo, Black Hawk Co. (P-0035, P-0167, *Amer. Birds* 36:300, Myers 1982)

Occurrence: The 1 winter record is of a very cooperative bird that remained for 2 months. Three old reports (Dinsmore et al. 1984) are highly questionable.

Comment: This Holarctic, diurnal species of coniferous forests has a North American range almost confined to Alaska and Canada. It breeds north to the tree line and south to extreme northern Minnesota and Michigan. Most of the winter movement is to the southern portions of the breeding range. Rarely, wintering individuals have reached south to Oregon, Idaho, Wyoming, Nebraska, Iowa, Illinois, Ohio, Pennsylvania, and New Jersey, where they have been discovered from September to April.

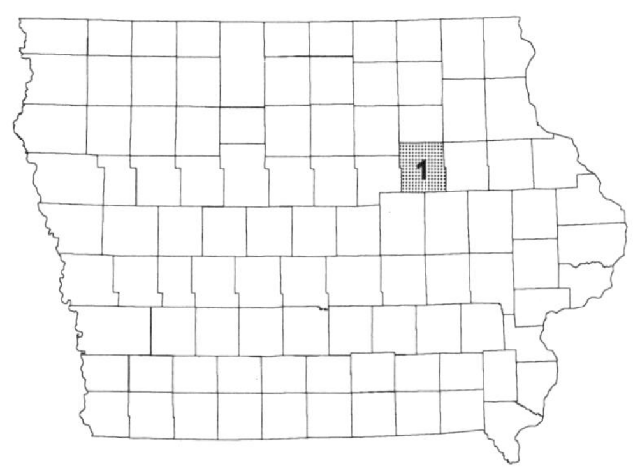

Northern Hawk Owl, all

Reference:

Myers, B. 1982. Iowa's first Hawk Owl (*Surnia ulula*). *Iowa Bird Life* 52:31-32.

Burrowing Owl (*Speotyto cunicularia*)

Status: Regular; occasionally nests

By year since 1960

60 63 66 69 72 75 78 81 84 87 90 93

2 1 2 1 1 1 2 2 4 1 1 3 1 3 3 2 5 1

By month -- all records

Jan	Feb	Mar	Apr	May	Jun	Jul	Aug	Sep	Oct	Nov	Dec
			5 6	1 1	2 2	2 1	1 2	2 3	1 1 1 1	+ +	1 +

20 Mar 1916 — 5 Oct 1924
29 Mar 1936 — 9 Oct 1956
1 Apr 1981 — 15 Oct 1964
winter: 20 to 28 Dec 1986

Occurrence: Migrants appear in early to mid-April, but most of the birds are discovered on nesting grounds during the summer. The winter record was 1 found during a Christmas Bird Count at Rathbun Reservoir in Appanoose County (*IBL* 57:46, 56). Nesting records are from western Iowa, especially northwestern Iowa. The most easterly nesting records are from Cerro Gordo County in 1987 (*IBL* 58:20) and Story County in 1923 (Birkeland 1933).

Historically, there were only 8 reports prior to 1910, but after that the 39 reports from 1911 to 1938 provided ample evidence of nesting in northwestern Iowa (Dinsmore et al. 1984). Suddenly Burrowing Owls disappeared, with only 2 reports from 1939 to 1959. They now appear to be reestablished, but the records are more widely dispersed than they were in the 1920s and 1930s.

Early reports mention the use of badger holes for nesting. Studies at a colony near Ruthven in Palo Alto and Clay counties revealed that the owls ate mice, frogs, ground squirrels, birds, and insects (Errington and Bennett 1935, Scott 1940). Two specimens taken on 13 July 1933 in Clay County (Youngworth 1958) are at Iowa State University.

Comment: The breeding range in western North America extends north to the southern parts of the Prairie Provinces, east to western Minnesota and Iowa, west to California and south to central Mexico. Other isolated populations are found in south Florida, the West Indies, and throughout South America. In winter, the western birds move south, where they may be found from western Texas to California. There are scattered records in states to the east of Iowa. The April to September span of dates is typical for nearby states, with a few records in late March or early October.

The reason for the decline in the late 1930s, which was also noted in Minnesota (Janssen 1987), is not clear. It could have been due to habitat loss, or, perhaps, it was a normal fluctuation in the range of this species.

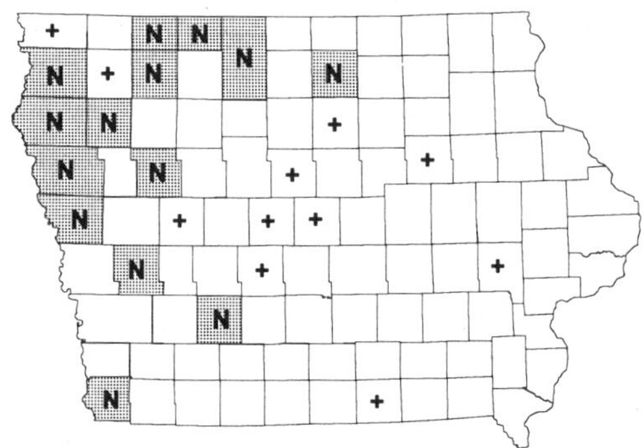

Burrowing Owl, 1960-1995
Nesting (N) and other records (+)

References:

Birkeland, H. 1933. The Burrowing Owl and other birds in Story County, Iowa. *Iowa Bird Life* 3:26.

Errington, P. L., and L. J. Bennett. 1935. Food habits of Burrowing Owls in northwestern Iowa. *Wilson Bull.* 47:125-128.

Scott, T. G. 1940. The western Burrowing Owl in Clay County, Iowa, in 1938. *Amer. Midland Naturalist* 24:585-593.

Youngworth, W. 1958. The Burrowing Owl as a vanishing species. *Iowa Bird Life* 28:56-57.

Barred Owl (*Strix varia*)

Status: Regular; nests

Jan	Feb	Mar	Apr	May	Jun	Jul	Aug	Sep	Oct	Nov	Dec

Occurrence: Barred Owls reside in river bottoms and upland forests, so it is not surprising that they are more common in eastern and southeastern Iowa and much less common in northwestern Iowa. They are nocturnal, but can be heard during the day, especially during the nesting season. There are no data on the numbers present other than Christmas Bird Counts, which show 0.5 birds per party hour (south 0.5, middle 0.6, north 0.2). Barred Owls eat a variety of birds, mammals, and insects (Errington and McDonald 1937). Few are found on Iowa Breeding Bird Surveys.

Comment: Barred Owls are found in eastern United States west to the central Great Plains, north to southern Canada, and across the Prairie Provinces to British Columbia and Washington. A separate population resides in central Mexico. Some of the northern birds migrate south.

Reference:

Errington, P. L., and M. McDonald. 1937. Conclusions as to the food habits of the Barred Owl in Iowa. *Iowa Bird Life* 7:47-49.

Great Gray Owl (*Strix nebulosa*)

Status: Accidental

15 Feb 1974, near Decorah, Winneshiek Co. (Berg 1974, photo)
11 to 26 Feb 1996, Big M., Butler Co. (*IBL* 66(2) cover)
1 Mar 1996, Des Moines, Polk Co. (Iowa State Univ. specimen #2643, P-0503, *IBL* 66:104)
10 Mar 1996, northwestern Fayette Co., Winneshiek Co. (P-0517, *IBL* 66:104)

Occurrence: There is 1 record from 1974 and 3 from 1996. Six old reports are Not Accepted (Dinsmore et al. 1984).

Comment: This Holarctic species of the northern forest has a range similar to the Northern Hawk Owl, except that its eastern range stops in Ontario, and in the west it lives in the Sierra Nevada Range to central California and in Rocky Mountains to northwestern Wyoming. It breeds in northern Minnesota and Wisconsin, but is more often recorded there in winter. It is a very rare vagrant as far south as Nebraska, Iowa, Indiana, Ohio, Pennsylvania, and New Jersey. The 1996 Iowa records were part of a massive invasion that was noted in Minnesota and Wisconsin.

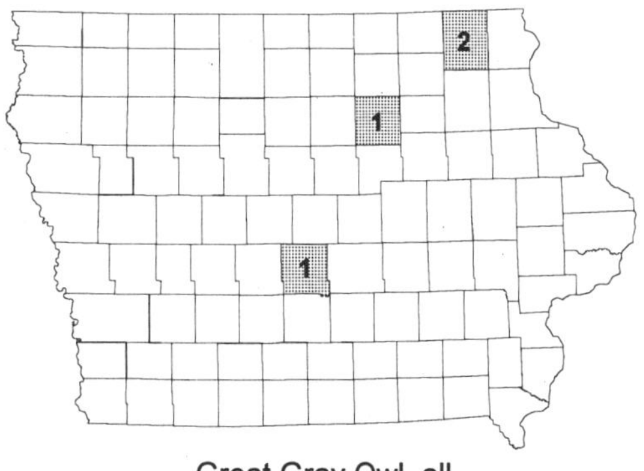

Great Gray Owl, all

Reference:

Berg, E. O. 1974. Great Gray Owl in N. E. Iowa. *Iowa Bird Life* 44:75.

Long-eared Owl (*Asio otus*)

Status: Regular; occasionally nests

Jan	Feb	Mar	Apr	May	Jun	Jul	Aug	Sep	Oct	Nov	Dec

Occurrence: Long-eared Owls are rare in winter and irregular nesters. Winter birds are usually found in thick conifer groves, often in the same locality year after year. They were found on 24 percent of Christmas Bird Counts (south 25 percent, middle 29 percent, north 8 percent). They feed almost exclusively on mice (Weller et al. 1963, Voight and Glenn-Lewin 1978). Nests are usually found in dense stands of conifers.

Comment: This Holarctic, nocturnal owl breeds from northern Texas to the Yukon. In winter, the range shifts south, ranging from southern Minnesota to central Texas with a dip into north-central Mexico. Although Iowa is well within the nesting range, nesting is rare, as it is in Illinois to the east and Missouri to the south. Numbers appear to have decreased in recent years, although there are few data to substantiate this.

Reference:

Voight, J., and D. C. Glenn-Lewin. 1978. Prey availability and prey taken by Long-eared Owls in Iowa. *Amer. Midland Naturalist* 99:162-171.

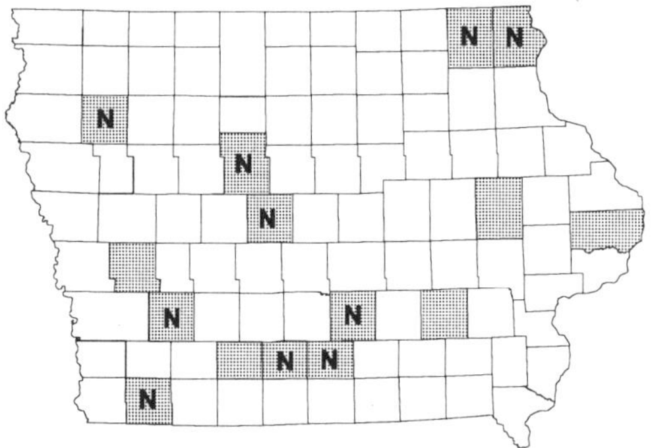

Long-eared Owl, 1960-1995
June-July and nesting (N)

Short-eared Owl (*Asio flammeus*)

Status: Regular; occasionally nests

Jan	Feb	Mar	Apr	May	Jun	Jul	Aug	Sep	Oct	Nov	Dec

Occurrence: Short-eared Owls are rare in winter and occasional nesters. In winter, they are typically found at dawn or dusk flying over grassy fields. They roost in groves, often in association with Long-eared Owls, or on the ground in dense grass. They were found on 17 percent of Christmas Bird Counts (south 17 percent, middle 22 percent, north 5 percent). Numbers reported fluctuate from year to year. They feed on small mammals, especially voles (Weller et al. 1963).

In addition to the confirmed nesting records, there are summer sightings of birds from 1965, 1974, 1975, 1977, 1979, 1988 (2), and 1990, which were likely nesting. Historically, it was recorded as nesting in several counties, mostly in northern Iowa (DuMont 1933). None were found during an intensive search in Dickinson, Emmet, and Palo Alto counties in the summer of 1993 (Hemesath 1993).

Comment: This widespread, Holarctic species breeds from Missouri and Illinois north to the Arctic coast. In winter, it ranges from southern Minnesota to southern Mexico. Historically, it was a more common nesting species in the Midwest, but now, for example, only occasional nests are found in Missouri and Illinois. The number of wintering birds appears to have decreased over the last 45 years (T. Kent, personal observation), which seems to be associated, at least in part, with a great decrease in pasture land and hayfields.

Reference:

Hemesath, L. 1993. Northern Harriers and Short-eared Owls in northwestern Iowa. *Nongame News* 9(3):6-8.

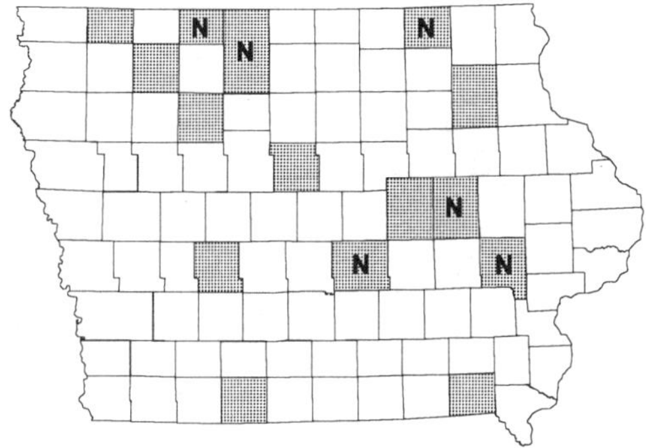

Short-eared Owl, 1960-1995
June-July and nesting (N)

Northern Saw-whet Owl (*Aegolius acadicus*)

Status: Regular

Jan	Feb	Mar	Apr	May	Jun	Jul	Aug	Sep	Oct	Nov	Dec
			x x	xx x							

11 Apr 1969 — 5 Oct 1959
22 Apr 1975 — 5 Oct 1985
4 May 1972 — 6 Oct 1977
summer: 6 May 1988, 28 May 1988

Occurrence: This rare little nocturnal owl is found in winter usually in groves of small conifers or in thickets with scattered conifers (Dinsmore 1990). Individual birds typically sit 6 to 20 feet from the ground and allow close approach. They were found on 8 percent of Christmas Bird Counts (2 percent south, 13 percent middle, 4 percent north). Some winter at the same locations over many years. They feed on small mammals, especially mice (Dinsmore and Clark 1991).

Although Iowa is often shown within the breeding range of this species, there are no known nesting records. In Allamakee County in 1988, birds were heard at Lansing Wildlife Area on 6 May and at Yellow River Forest on 28 May (*IBL* 58:82).

Comment: Northern Saw-whet Owl is a permanent resident from southern Canada and southern Alaska south in hilly and mountainous regions of United States and separately in central Mexico. The winter range extends south to Arkansas, the Great Plains, and northern Mexico.

In Missouri, evidence of nesting is based on a 1904 record from Montgomery County in east-central Missouri (Robbins and Easterla 1992). In Illinois, old and recent evidence of nesting is mainly from the northeast, but there is a record from 1890 in Marion County, which is in central Illinois at the level of St. Louis, and from 1951 on the Mississippi River near Quincy in Adams County (Bohlen 1989). In Wisconsin, the breeding range extends south to La Crosse (Robbins 1991). In Minnesota, nesting records are from the north, but there is a summer record from Winona County just north of La Crosse (Janssen 1987). The proximity of hilly northeast Iowa to the regular breeding range in Wisconsin, the similarity of habitat, and the birds heard in May in Allamakee County suggest that this species could be nesting in Iowa.

References:

Dinsmore, S. J. 1990. Locating Northern Saw-whet Owls. *Iowa Bird Life* 60:63.

Dinsmore, S. J., and W. R. Clark. 1991. Food habits of the Northern Saw-whet Owl in central Iowa: Effects of roost location. *J. Iowa Acad. Sci.* 98:167-169.

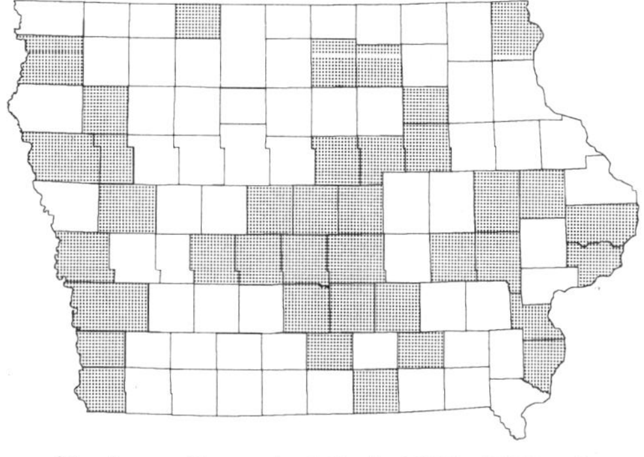

Northern Saw-whet Owl, 1960-1995, all

ORDER CAPRIMULGIFORMES

Birds in this order are active at night or twilight, have long pointed wings, small feet, small bills, and large gaping mouths for catching insects. Of the several families, only goatsuckers (nighthawks and nightjars) are found in North America.

Goatsuckers (Family Caprimulgidae)

Goatsuckers comprise 75 species, with 9 from North America and 3 from Iowa. They are known for their persistent calling at night. They normally rest during the day and are active from dusk to dawn. They have large mouths and long facial bristles, which are used to capture insects in flight. Feet and legs are small and of little use on the ground. They lay camouflaged eggs on the ground or other flat surfaces without constructing a nest.

Common Nighthawk (*Chordeiles minor*)

Status: Regular; nests

Jan	Feb	Mar	Apr	May	Jun	Jul	Aug	Sep	Oct	Nov	Dec
									XX		

Early dates	Late dates
24 Apr 1986	19 Oct 1986
25 Apr 1989	29 Oct 1986
26 Apr 1986	30 Oct 1994

Occurrence: Nighthawks are common summer residents. They are most often found in towns, where they nest on flat-topped roofs, but they may also be seen in rural areas, where they presumably nest on the ground. In late August and September, small groups of migrants are often seen in evenings, foraging as they move south. No data are available to determine their abundance or population changes over time.

Comment: The winter range is in South America to northern Argentina. The breeding range extends across North America from northern Mexico to the southern Yukon and southern Labrador.

Chuck-will's-widow (*Caprimulgus carolinensis*)

Status: Regular; nests

By year since 1960 (also 1933)

60	63	66	69	72	75	78	81	84	87	90	93
	1		2 2 2	2 1 2	3 1 1	2 5 3	3 2 2	2 2 1	1 8 4	2 4 3	4 3 4

Jan	Feb	Mar	Apr	May	Jun	Jul	Aug	Sep	Oct	Nov	Dec
			x				x	x			

24 Apr 1970
5 May 1990
7 May 1971

30 Jul 1974
13 Aug 1983
mid-Sep 1969

Occurrence: This rare summer resident has been found consistently at a few sites in southern Iowa, most often from early May to early July, with extremes of late April to mid-September at these sites. Of the 6 reports from the northern half of Iowa, 5 are from May and 1 from June. In the 1980s and 1990s, most reports were from near Waubonsie State Park in Fremont County, near Eddyville in Mahaska County, and at Big Sand Mound Preserve in Louisa County. Two nests were found at the latter location in 1990 (Brush 1990). Birds were also found at Stephens State Forest in Lucas County in 1994 and 1995 (*IBL* 64:110; 65:99).

Historically, the first record was from 17 June 1933 in Lee County, where a specimen was taken but not preserved (DuMont 1935). The second report was not until 9 May 1964 at Wildcat Den State Park in Muscatine County (Petersen 1964). One was banded at Camp Arrowhead in Wapello County in 1969, and a nest with 2 eggs was found there on 21 May 1970 (Ayres and Ayres 1970).

Comment: The winter range is on the Gulf Coast and from Florida south to the West Indies, Central America, and northern South America. The breeding range is in eastern North America from eastern Texas and eastern Kansas north to southern Iowa, central Illinois and New Jersey. There are records from 2 counties in South Dakota and Minnesota and 6 in Wisconsin. It is not known whether records from northern Iowa and states to the north represent nesting birds or strays. Some birds found in states to the north of Iowa were at the same location for more than 1 year. We do not know the extent of the population in southern Iowa. Surveying for this species, which usually sings at dawn and dusk, would be time-consuming and difficult.

References:

Ayres, C. C., and D. J. Ayres. 1970. A first banding and nesting record for Iowa, the Chuck-will's-widow. *Iowa Bird Life* 40:59-65.

Brush, T. 1990. Chuck-will's-widow nesting in eastern Iowa. *Iowa Bird Life* 60:107-108.

DuMont, P. A. 1935. Chuck-will's-widow collected in southeastern Iowa. *Wilson Bull.* 47:239.

Petersen, P. 1964. Chuck-will's-widow at Wildcat Den State Park. *Iowa Bird Life* 34:49-50.

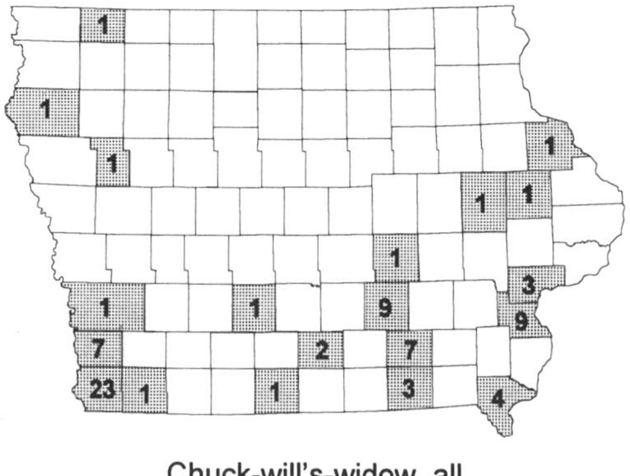

Chuck-will's-widow, all

Whip-poor-will (*Caprimulgus vociferus*)

Status: Regular; nests

Jan	Feb	Mar	Apr	May	Jun	Jul	Aug	Sep	Oct	Nov	Dec
										X	
11 Apr 1971									20 Oct 1973		
11 Apr 1988									20 Oct 1985		
12 Apr 1968									3 Nov 1984		

Occurrence: Whip-poor-wills are found in heavily wooded areas throughout Iowa. They are not often reported, making it difficult to quantify abundance and distribution. They sing mostly at dawn and dusk and are generally found at the same locations year after year. Migrants are occasionally encountered during the day.

The nesting records from 1960 to 1995 include a nest with 2 eggs at Yellow River Forest in Allamakee County in June 1987 (*IBL* 57:121), a fledgling in Poweshiek County in July 1987 (*IBL* 57:121), and a nest with 1 egg at Oskaloosa in Mahaska County in May 1993 (*IBL* 64:110). A fresh clutch was found in the Amana Woods in Iowa County on 25 June 1958 with hatching about 16 July (Kent and Vane 1958).

Comment: The winter range is from South Carolina, the Gulf Coast, and northern Mexico south to Panama. The breeding range is discontinuous: in the West from El Salvador north to west Texas, southern Nevada, and southern California, and in the East from Oklahoma and South Carolina north to southern Canada. Although the range barely reaches eastern Nebraska and South Dakota, this species is easily found in the Loess Hills on the western edge of Iowa.

Reference:

Kent, F. W., and R. F. Vane. 1958. A nesting of the Whip-poor-will in Iowa County. *Iowa Bird Life* 28:70-79.

ORDER APODIFORMES

Swifts and hummingbirds have small feet and specialized wing structure with a short, stout humerus and elongated elements beyond the elbow. They lay pure white eggs, and the young, which hatch naked and blind, must be able to fly when they leave the nest.

Swifts (Family Apodidae)

Swifts comprise 100 species, with 9 from North America and 1 from Iowa. They are gregarious, swallow-like birds with long, pointed wings, short tails and neck, and rapid flight. They capture insects in flight.

Chimney Swift (*Chaetura pelagica*)

Status: Regular; nests

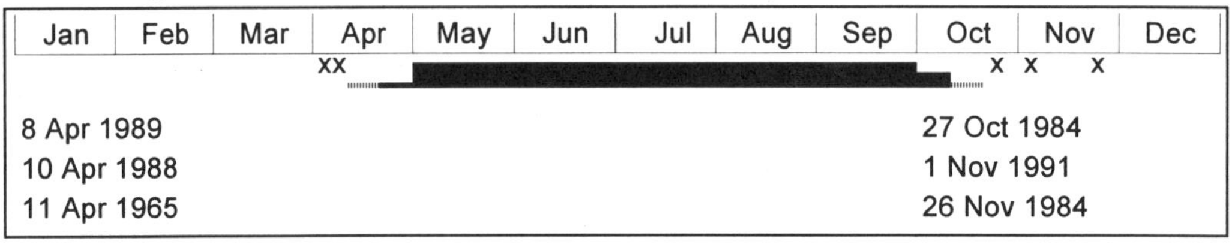

Jan	Feb	Mar	Apr	May	Jun	Jul	Aug	Sep	Oct	Nov	Dec
			XX							X X X	

8 Apr 1989 — 27 Oct 1984
10 Apr 1988 — 1 Nov 1991
11 Apr 1965 — 26 Nov 1984

Occurrence: This common summer resident is most often seen over cities. It is also widespread in rural areas as indicated by Breeding Bird Surveys, with an average of 6.7 per route from 1967 to 1991. Flocks often roost in large chimneys in fall with high counts of 6,000 in Ames in Story County on 29 September 1987 (*IBL* 58:20) and 4,000 at Fairfield in Jefferson County on 21 September 1990, 7 October 1991, and 2 October 1993 (*IBL* 61:21, 62:16, 64:13). These flocks build to a peak from mid-September to early October and then rapidly leave. The last are usually gone by 10 October.

A classic study of Chimney Swift nesting was carried on at National in Clayton County by Althea R. Sherman from 1918 to 1936 (Sherman 1952). She had a special tower constructed for her studies (Daubendiek 1969).

Comment: This species winters in the upper Amazon basin and breeds east of the Rocky Mountains in the United States and southern Canada. Surrounding states also have occasional November records.

Reference:

Daubendiek, M. S. 1969. The Sherman swift tower. *Iowa Bird Life* 39:46-48.

Hummingbirds (Family Trochilidae)

Hummingbirds comprise 320 species, with 23 from North America and 2 from Iowa. They are the smallest birds, with long needle-like bills used to sip nectar from flowers. They are very maneuverable flyers, being able to hover and move backwards. They feed mainly on nectar, but may take insects.

Ruby-throated Hummingbird (*Archilochus colubris*)

Status: Regular; nests

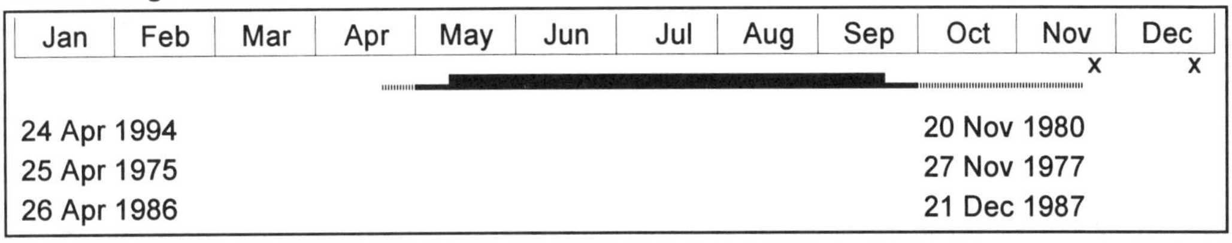

Jan	Feb	Mar	Apr	May	Jun	Jul	Aug	Sep	Oct	Nov	Dec
										x	x

24 Apr 1994	20 Nov 1980
25 Apr 1975	27 Nov 1977
26 Apr 1986	21 Dec 1987

Occurrence: This uncommon species is found around flowers and at feeders in migration and in or near deeply wooded areas in summer. Although it can be found anywhere in the state during nesting season, it is more common in the wooded areas of eastern Iowa. It is rarely detected on Breeding Bird Surveys, and there are no other data to substantiate its frequency. The unusually late record was of a bird captured on 21 December 1987 at Marshalltown in Marshall County and moved to a greenhouse where it died in late January 1988 (*IBL* 58:46, 48, 56, 74).

Comment: This species winters from south Texas to Costa Rica and breeds throughout the eastern United States and southern Canada east from Oklahoma, central Nebraska, and Alberta. There is a record from Wisconsin on 19 December 1980 (Robbins 1991). Late hummingbirds need to be carefully studied, because vagrants of other species tend to occur at this time.

Rufous Hummingbird (*Selasphorus rufus*)

Status: Accidental

By year since 1960

60	63	66	69	72	75	78	81	84	87	90	93
								1 1	2		1 1

By month -- all records

Jan	Feb	Mar	Apr	May	Jun	Jul	Aug	Sep	Oct	Nov	Dec
				1		1 1	+ 1	1	+	1 + +	

25 Sep to 2 Oct 1984, Chester, Howard Co., imm. male *Selasphorus* species (P-0146, Moore et al. 1984)

10 Jul 1986, St. Olaf, Clayton Co., male (P-0199, *IBL* 56(4) cover, Stone 1986)

29 Jul to 3 Aug 1987, St. Olaf, Clayton Co., male (P-0227, Stone 1988)

18 Aug 1987, Clear Lake, Cerro Gordo Co., male (P-0228, *IBL* 58:20, 74)

8, 9 May 1993, near Rippey, Boone Co., male (*IBL* 63:76)

4 to 25 Nov 1995, Cedar Rapids, Linn Co., imm. female (Iowa Sate Univ. specimen #2660, P-0474, P-0476, P-0500, *IBL* 66:22)

Occurrence: There are 4 records of adult males, 3 from fall and 1 from spring, and 1 late fall immature female that was captured and later died. In addition, there is a record of an immature male hummingbird classified as *Selasphorus* species. A male seen at the same feeder 2 years in a row may have been the same bird.

Comment: This species breeds in forested areas from extreme northern California east to western Montana and north to southern Alaska. Most winter in Mexico, but some remain on the California coast and from southern Arizona to Florida.

Rufous Hummingbird is a regular fall vagrant to eastern North America, with records in most states and provinces east and south of the breeding range. Records to the East Coast were detailed by Conway and Drennan (1979). The Iowa record is the only spring record for the Midwest, although there are mid-June records from Minnesota and Wisconsin. Males may arrive by July; females and immatures are more likely in September. Midwest records extend from June to November, with about two-thirds in August and September.

Female and immature Rufous and Allen's hummingbirds cannot be distinguished in the field. In the hand, they can be distinguished by careful analysis of tail feathers. This might be done by mist netting and taking measurements and close-up photographs of the spread tail feathers.

References:

Conway, A. E., and S. R. Drennan. 1979. Rufous Hummingbirds in eastern North America. *Amer. Birds* 33:130-132.

Moore, F. L., R. K. Myers, and T. H. Kent. 1984. Rufous Hummingbird in northeast Iowa. *Iowa Bird Life* 54:104-106.

Stone, L. 1986. Rufous Hummingbird in Clayton County. *Iowa Bird Life* 56:121-122.

Stone, L. 1988. Another Rufous Hummingbird in Clayton Co. *Iowa Bird Life* 58:27.

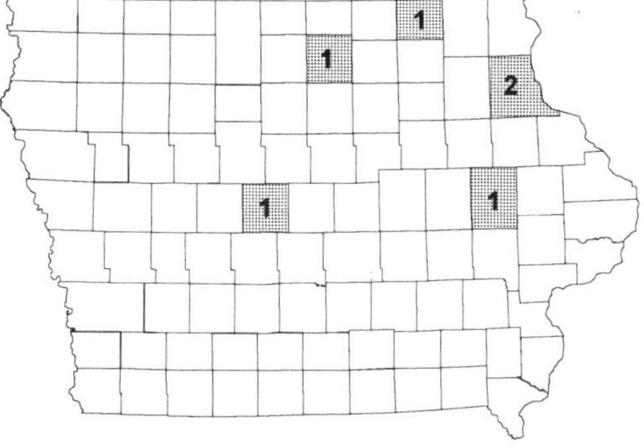

Rufous Hummingbird/*Selasphorus* species, all

ORDER CORACIIFORMES

This assemblage of several families, only 1 of which is found in North America, have their front 3 toes joined for part of their length (syndactyl). They are brightly colored cavity nesters with strong, prominent bills.

Kingfishers (Family Alcedinidae)

Kingfishers comprise 95 species, with 3 from North America and 1 from Iowa. They are large-headed birds with massive straight, pointed bills. Most are solitary and nest in burrows dug into embankments. They are usually found perched on exposed vantage points over water. The North American species feed mainly on fish.

Belted Kingfisher (*Ceryle alcyon*)

Status: Regular; nest

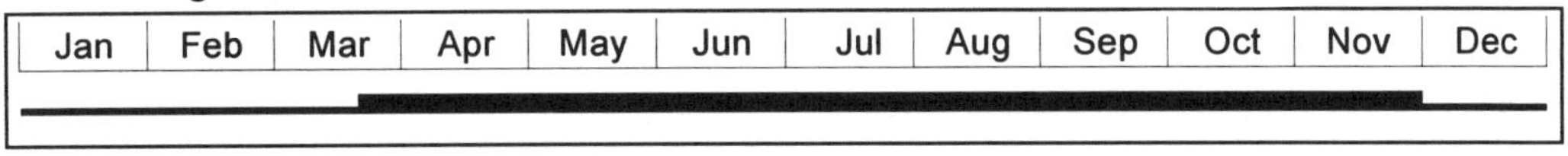

Jan	Feb	Mar	Apr	May	Jun	Jul	Aug	Sep	Oct	Nov	Dec

Occurrence: This uncommon species is found along rivers, streams, and lakes in summer and where there is open water in winter. Although Breeding Bird Surveys do not sample its habitat well, it was found on 27 percent of surveys with 0.4 birds per route.

Kingfishers were found on 64 percent of Christmas Bird Counts, with 0.4 per party-hour (south 0.4, middle 0.5, north 0.4). Later in the winter, most reports are from southeastern Iowa where there is open water below dams. Unusually far north were birds at Hawarden in Sioux County on 5 January 1989 (*IBL* 59:53) and 5 January 1990 (*IBL* 60:52) and at Mason City in Cerro Gordo County on 24 January 1989 (*IBL* 59:53) and 9 February 1992 (*IBL* 62:56).

Comment: This species breeds throughout the United States and Canada north to the timber line. It winters from southern Alaska and the level of central Minnesota south to northern South America. A few will winter as far north as they can find open water.

ORDER PICIFORMES

Members of the several families in this order have 2 front and 2 hind toes with a distinctive arrangement of thigh muscles and tendons. All are cavity nesters and inhabit forests and brushlands in tropical and temperate zones.

Woodpeckers and Allies (Family Picidae)

Woodpeckers comprise 213 species, with 25 from North America and 9 from Iowa. They are specialists in digging prey from wood or bark. They have long, pointed bills and a long protruding tongue, which is controlled by muscles attached to an enlarged hyoid bone. Their short legs, sharp nails, and stiff tails facilitate tree climbing. Woodpeckers feed as they move up and around tree trunks, and they have undulating flight. The most migratory species are those that probe the least; for example, Northern Flicker prefers ants and is migratory.

Of the Iowa species, 7 are Regular and 2 Accidental. All of the Regular species nest, and 3 are migratory (Red-headed Woodpecker, Yellow-bellied Sapsucker, Northern Flicker).

Lewis's Woodpecker (*Melanerpes lewis*)

Status: Accidental

By month -- all records

Jan	Feb	Mar	Apr	May	Jun	Jul	Aug	Sep	Oct	Nov	Dec
+ + +	+ + +	+ +							1	1 + 1	+ + +

28 Nov 1928 to 20 Mar 1929, Sioux City, Woodbury Co. (Bailey 1929, Youngworth 1929, 1931)

10 Nov 1935 to 10 Mar 1936, Clear Lake, Cerro Gordo Co. (Davis 1936a, 1936b)

14-18 Oct 1992, Cherokee Co. (P-0354, Brewer 1994)

Occurrence: There are 3 records of fall birds, with 2 remaining for the winter.

Comment: The breeding range is from southern British Columbia east to the Black Hills of South Dakota, south to northern New Mexico, and west to the Pacific Coast. The winter range is from Oregon and southern Colorado south to northern Mexico. Although this species is highly migratory within its range, it is a very rare vagrant, with only a few records east of the Great Plains in Minnesota, Iowa, Missouri, Arkansas, Wisconsin, Ontario, Massachusetts, and Rhode Island. About half of the records are from May to June and half from October to February, indicating a slight spring and fall vagrancy pattern.

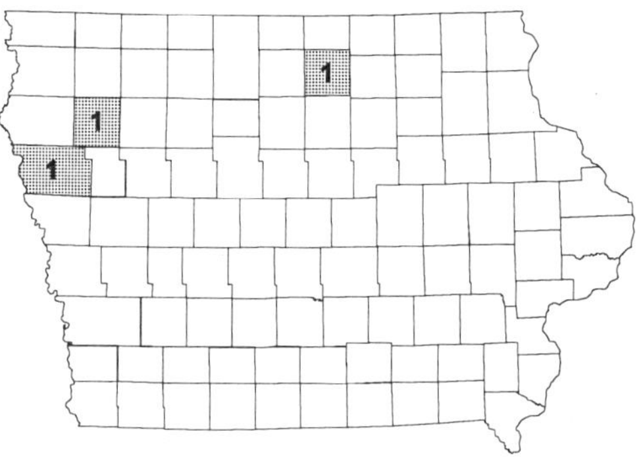

Lewis's Woodpecker, all

References:

Bailey, M. L. 1929. [no title]. *Bull. Iowa Ornithologists' Union* 7:3.

Brewer, M. M. 1994. Lewis's Woodpecker in Cherokee County. *Iowa Bird Life* 64:18.
Davis, F. H. 1936a. Lewis's Woodpecker at Clear Lake. *Iowa Bird Life* 6:12.
Davis, F. H. 1936b. Lewis's Woodpecker at Clear Lake. *Iowa Bird Life* 6:28.
Youngworth, W. 1929. [no title]. *Bull. Iowa Ornithologists' Union* 7:3.

Red-headed Woodpecker (*Melanerpes erythrocephalus*)

Status: Regular; nests

Jan	Feb	Mar	Apr	May	Jun	Jul	Aug	Sep	Oct	Nov	Dec

Occurrence: Red-headed Woodpecker is a common to abundant summer resident and uncommon winter resident. In summer, it is found in both wooded and open habitat across the state. In winter, it is more likely to be found in deep woods or near corn cribs.

Based on Breeding Bird Surveys, the summer population rose from 1969 to 1980 from 9 per route to 12 per route, then jumped to 16 per route in 1981. The sudden rise was followed by a sudden drop to 5 per route in 1982, with little recovery since. The cause for these changes is not known.

Winter populations also vary greatly, apparently due to the availability of mast (acorns and other nuts). On Christmas Bird Counts, the number per 10 party-hours per year has ranged from 0.3 to 3.9. The average was 1.9 (south 1.9, middle 2.6, north 0.8). In 1984 and 1985, Red-headed Woodpecker was reported at 22 and 13 percent of feeders in mid-winter (Hollis 1986).

Spring migrants arrive from mid-April to early May, and most leave from mid-August to early September.

Comment: This species breeds throughout the eastern United States and southern Canada to the Rocky Mountains. Most leave the northern and western parts of the range in winter.

Red-bellied Woodpecker (*Melanerpes carolinus*)

Status: Regular; nests

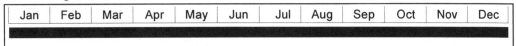

Jan	Feb	Mar	Apr	May	Jun	Jul	Aug	Sep	Oct	Nov	Dec

Occurrence: Red-bellied Woodpecker is a fairly common resident of woodland and riparian habitat. On Breeding Bird Surveys, the number per route averages 0.9, but varies from 2.1 in northeastern to 0.5 in western Iowa. On Christmas Bird Counts, the number per 10 party-hours averages 5.0 (south 5.4, middle 5.5, north 4.1). In 1984 and 1985, Red-bellied Woodpeckers were reported at 35 and 30 percent of feeders in mid-winter (Hollis 1986). Red-bellied is the second most common winter woodpecker (Downy is first) by both measures. There is no evidence of change in population density.

Comment: This species is a permanent resident in the eastern United States west to the panhandle of Oklahoma and north to central Minnesota and Wisconsin. In the early 1900s it was rare in northern Iowa (Anderson 1907), but gradually moved north and may be still expanding its range in Minnesota and Wisconsin.

Yellow-bellied Sapsucker (*Sphyrapicus varius*)

Status: Regular; nests

Jan	Feb	Mar	Apr	May	Jun	Jul	Aug	Sep	Oct	Nov	Dec

Occurrence: Sapsuckers are uncommon migrants, rare in winter, and rarely nest in northern Iowa, especially northeastern Iowa. Fall migration begins in late August, but most are found from late September to mid-October. Spring migration begins in late March and peaks in mid-April. A few linger into May.

Sapsuckers were found on 24 percent of Christmas Bird Counts (south 31 percent, middle 27 percent, north 6 percent). There are a few mid-winter reports each year. Unusually far north were birds at Algona in Kossuth County in early February 1993 (*IBL* 63:50) and at Mason City in Cerro Gordo County in the winter of 1990-1991 (*IBL* 61:58).

Sapsuckers nest in the lowlands of northeastern Iowa, especially in the Mississippi River floodplain. Nesting has also been confirmed in Kossuth and Sioux counties, and scattered other summer records suggest that it may occasionally nest away from northeastern Iowa.

Comment: This species winters from New Jersey, southern Missouri, and the Texas panhandle south to Panama. It breeds from Iowa and the eastern Dakotas north and west to the Yukon and east to the Appalachians and southern Labrador. Sapsuckers make characteristic holes in conifers and return to gather the sap. They do not frequent feeders.

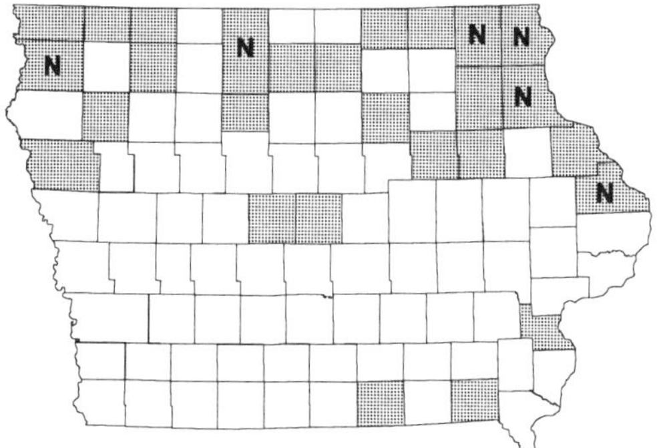

Yellow-bellied Sapsucker, 1960-1995
June-July and nesting (N)

Downy Woodpecker (*Picoides pubescens*)

Status: Regular; nests

Jan	Feb	Mar	Apr	May	Jun	Jul	Aug	Sep	Oct	Nov	Dec

Occurrence: This common permanent resident is widespread in a variety of habitats. On Breeding Bird Surveys, the number per route averages 0.9. At Coralville Reservoir in Johnson County, 7.4 per 10 party-hours were found on a breeding survey (Kent et al. 1994).

Downy is the most frequent woodpecker on Christmas Bird Counts with 10.7 per 10 party-hours (south 10.3, middle 12.6, north 8.5). It was reported at 60 percent of feeders in mid-winter (Hollis 1986).

Comment: Downy Woodpecker is a nonmigratory species found throughout the United States (except for the Southwest) and in Canada and Alaska north to the timberline.

Hairy Woodpecker (*Picoides villosus*)

Status: Regular; nests

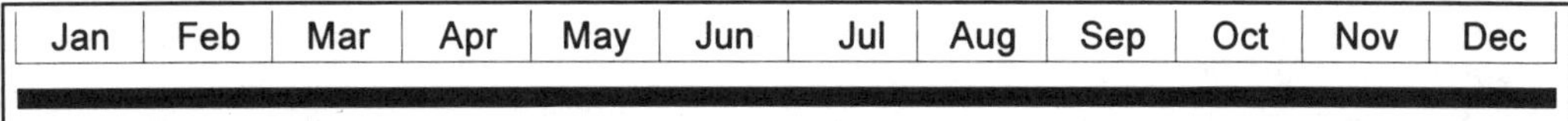

Occurrence: This uncommon permanent resident is widespread in a variety of wooded habitats, but is outnumbered by Downy Woodpecker by about 4 to 1. On Breeding Bird Surveys, the number per route averages 0.2. At Coralville Reservoir in Johnson County, 2.1 per 10 party-hours were found on a breeding survey (Kent et al. 1994).

On Christmas Bird Counts there were 2.4 per 10 party-hours (south 1.9, middle 2.7, north 3.3); however, the numbers have fluctuated from 0.03 to 4.10 per 10 party-hours in the years 1967 to 1991. Hairy Woodpeckers were reported at 31 and 29 percent of feeders in mid-winter in 1984 and 1985 (Hollis 1986).

Comment: This nonmigratory species has a range very similar to Downy Woodpecker, except that it extends into the Southwest and south to Panama. The Iowa data suggest that Hairy Woodpecker is more common in northern Iowa, and it may have a preference for more heavily wooded areas. Christmas Bird Count data from 1951 to 1975 suggest a decline in the number of Hairy Woodpeckers (Koenig 1977), while more recent data suggest an increase. The large fluctuation in numbers from year to year remains unexplained.

Black-backed Woodpecker (*Picoides arcticus*)

Status: Accidental

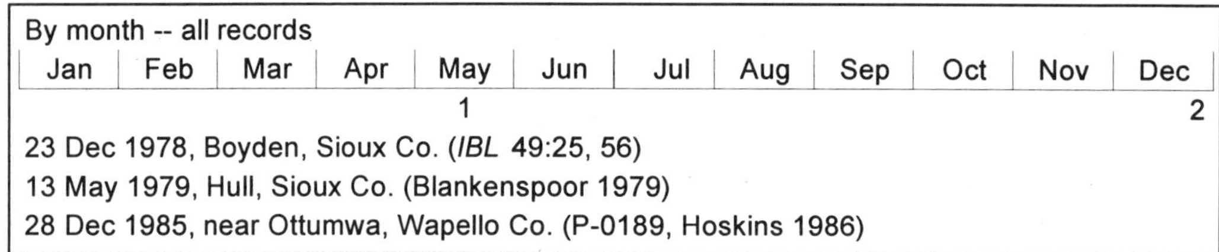

By month -- all records

Jan	Feb	Mar	Apr	May	Jun	Jul	Aug	Sep	Oct	Nov	Dec
				1							2

23 Dec 1978, Boyden, Sioux Co. (*IBL* 49:25, 56)
13 May 1979, Hull, Sioux Co. (Blankenspoor 1979)
28 Dec 1985, near Ottumwa, Wapello Co. (P-0189, Hoskins 1986)

Occurrence: Of 3 records, 2 are from winter and 1 from spring; however, the first 2 records, which were separated by a distance of about 5 miles and time of about 5 months, could have been the same bird. There are 3 old undocumented reports (Dinsmore et al. 1984).

Comment: This species of the coniferous forest of Alaska and Canada dips into the lower 48 states in the Sierra Nevada Range to central California, in the Rocky Mountains to northwestern Wyoming, in the Black Hills of South Dakota, and in the northern parts of Minnesota, Wisconsin, Michigan, New York, and the New England states. In Minnesota, fall migration is sometimes noted in the north, with some birds moving south to the Twin Cities region, and very few farther south (Janssen 1987). The southern limit of vagrants is in Nebraska, Iowa, Illinois, Indiana, Ohio, Pennsylvania, and Delaware. The very few records in these states are evenly distributed from September to May.

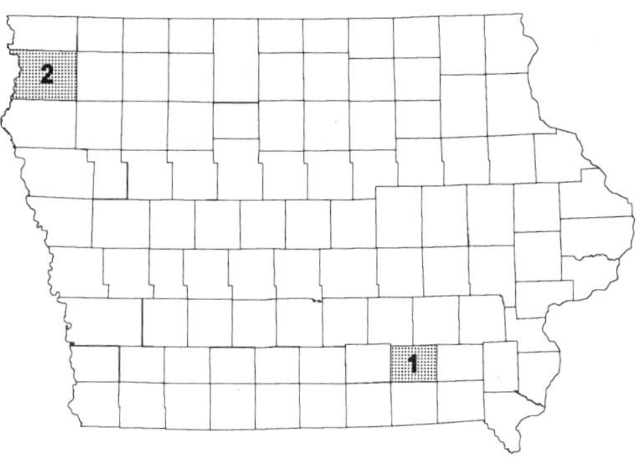

Black-backed Woodpecker, all

References:

Blankenspoor, G. W. 1979. Black-backed Three-toed Woodpecker in northwest Iowa. *Iowa Bird Life* 49:86.

Hoskins, N. R. 1986. Black-backed Woodpecker near Ottumwa. *Iowa Bird Life* 56:30.

Northern Flicker (*Colaptes auratus*)

Status: Regular; nests

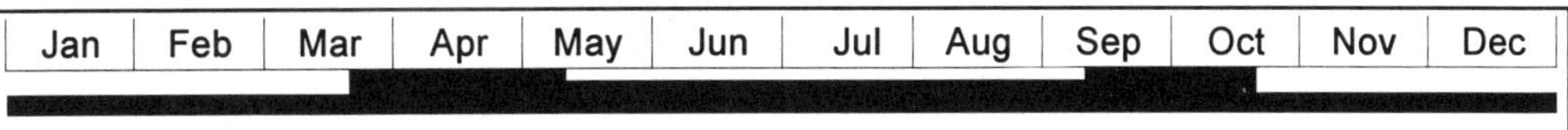

Occurrence: Flickers are present year around, but they vary from uncommon in winter to abundant in migration to common in summer. On Breeding Bird Surveys, the number per route averages 3.0. At Coralville Reservoir in Johnson County, 5.1 per 10 party-hours were found on a breeding survey (Kent et al. 1994).

On Christmas Bird Counts there were 3.0 per 10 party-hours (south 3.9, middle 3.3, north 1.3). Flickers are reported at 18 percent of feeders in mid-winter (Hollis 1986). In winter, there are scattered reports of the western red-shafted form.

Flickers are most conspicuous in migration, when they are found as individuals or loose flocks migrating across farmland, feeding on the ground in grassy areas, or along hedgerows.

Comment: Flickers breed in Central America and North America north to timberline. The winter range extends north to about central Minnesota.

Pileated Woodpecker (*Dryocopus pileatus*)

Status: Regular; nests

Jan Feb Mar Apr May Jun Jul Aug Sep Oct Nov Dec

Occurrence: The Pileated Woodpecker is a rare permanent resident. Most occur in river bottom timber in eastern Iowa. They are most common in the hilly and heavily wooded areas of northeastern Iowa. In recent years, a few have been seen regularly along the Des Moines River and its tributaries north to Polk, Clay, and Kossuth counties, and in the Cedar River drainage north to Clear Lake in Cerro Gordo County.

Pileated Woodpeckers are found on 94 percent of Christmas Bird Counts along the Mississippi River (0.6 per 10 party-hours) and rarely on other counts.

Comment: This species is a permanent resident in eastern United States and across Canada, dipping down into Idaho and northern California. The western edge of its southern range includes eastern Texas, Oklahoma, Missouri, eastern Iowa, Minnesota, and eastern North Dakota.

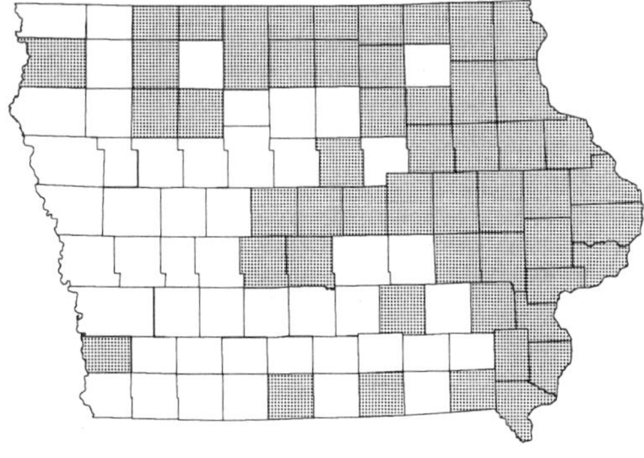

Pileated Woodpecker, 1960-1995

ORDER PASSERIFORMES

The passerines or perching birds comprise about 40 percent of the avian families and about 60 percent of the species. The characteristic feature of this order is 4 unwebbed toes that grip automatically when the bird falls backward. Passerines are also distinguished by structure of palate bones, reduced number of cervical vertebrae, and distinctive spermatozoa. The young hatch naked and helpless and are reared in the nest.

Many species in this order have evolved relatively recently, and differences in families are not great enough to allow easy classification. The more primitive suborders and families have 4 or fewer pairs of muscles to the voice box (syrinx) and are known as suboscines. Of these, only the New World or Tyrant Flycatchers occur in Iowa. All other passerines have more than 4 sets of syrinx muscles and are known as oscines or song birds, although not all of them sing well.

Tyrant Flycatchers (Family Tyrannidae)

Tyrant Flycatchers comprise 414 species, with 44 from North America and 16 from Iowa. Most of the Tyrant or New World flycatchers reside in the tropics, but some migrate north to nest. They are usually solitary and sally forth from exposed perches to catch insects. The sexes are alike, except in a few brightly colored species. Songs and call notes are usually distinctive and are the best means of identification of the small flycatchers of the genus *Empidonax*. Two of the front toes are partially joined at the base.

Of the Iowa species, 12 are Regular and 4 are Accidental. Of the Regular species, 8 nest regularly and 1 occasionally; the other 3 are migrants. One of the Accidental species, Say's Phoebe, was previously Regular and nested.

Olive-sided Flycatcher (*Contopus borealis*)

Status: Regular

Jan	Feb	Mar	Apr	May	Jun	Jul	Aug	Sep	Oct	Nov	Dec

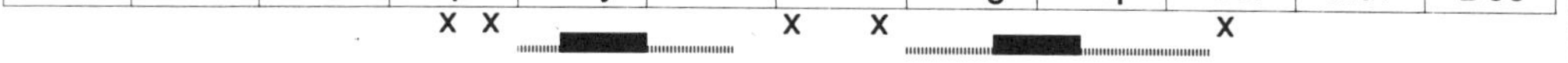

13 Apr 1988	11 Jun 1979	25 Jul 1977	7 Oct 1990
28 Apr 1965	12 Jun 1987	2 Aug 1985	9 Oct 1991
3 May 1978	13 Jun 1982	4 Aug 1978	20 Oct 1968
summer: 4 Jul 1962			

Occurrence: This uncommon migrant is usually found alone on the highest dead branch of a tall tree or in spring by its "quick-three-beers" song. It is a late spring migrant with a few remaining into June. Some return by the first week of August. The only summer record is from Clayton County in northeastern Iowa on 4 July 1962 (Koenig 1979).

Comment: This species winters in the mountains of South America south to southern Peru and irregularly in Central America and southern California. It breeds in the mountains of the eastern and western United States and in forested areas from central Minnesota north to timberline.

Western Wood-Pewee (*Contopus sordidulus*)

Status: Accidental

21 Jun 1979, Elm L., Wright Co. (Schaufenbuel 1979)

Occurrence: There is 1 sight record from June of a bird heard and seen by an experienced observer.

Comment: This species winters in South America from Colombia to Peru, and breeds in the west from Central America to Alaska east to the western edge of the Great Plains. Eastern and Western wood-pewees have minimal range overlap. In the field, they are considered indistinguishable except by voice.

Vagrants east of Nebraska have been reported from Minnesota, Iowa, Louisiana, Wisconsin, Illinois, Mississippi, Ontario, Maryland, and Massachusetts. There is a nesting record from northwestern Minnesota (Janssen 1987). Identification has been based on voice or specimen, and some authors consider the records "hypothetical". Reports are from May to June and August to September, plus 1 in early October.

Reference:

Schaufenbuel, J. 1979. First Western Pewee for Iowa. *Iowa Bird Life* 49:86.

Western Wood-Pewee, all

Eastern Wood-Pewee (*Contopus virens*)

Status: Regular; nests

Jan	Feb	Mar	Apr	May	Jun	Jul	Aug	Sep	Oct	Nov	Dec
			XX						X X		

26 Apr 1990	10 Oct 1973
30 Apr 1993	13 Oct 1982
1 May 1993	23 Oct 1983

Occurrence: This common summer resident is found in wooded areas across Iowa. A surprising number are recorded on Breeding Bird Surveys, with an average of 0.8 to 1.9 per route in all areas except the heavily wooded northeast, which had 4.4 per route. On the wooded bluffs of the Coralville Reservoir in Johnson County, pewees were found in every woods, with 1.1 per party-hour (Kent et al. 1994).

Pewees are late spring migrants. Fall birds are less evident because they are usually silent.

Comment: The winter range is in South America from Colombia to Peru. The breeding range is in the eastern United States and southern Canada west to the central Great Plains

Yellow-bellied Flycatcher (*Empidonax flaviventris*)

Status: Regular

Jan	Feb	Mar	Apr	May	Jun	Jul	Aug	Sep	Oct	Nov	Dec
					x		xx		x		

4 May 1977	7 Jun 1987	5 Aug 1981	7 Oct 1967
7 May 1972	8 Jun 1987	10 Aug 1987	10 Oct 1961
7 May 1988	12 Jun 1985	13 Aug 1968	12 Oct 1969

Occurrence: This migrant has been reported more frequently in recent years. Numbers are likely underestimated because this species occurs in dense understory and is difficult to identify. Old reports from summer are unsubstantiated (Dinsmore et al. 1984).

Comment: The winter range is from central Mexico to Panama. Migration is east of the central Great Plains to breeding grounds in the boreal coniferous forest from northern British Columbia to southern Labrador south to northern Minnesota and Wisconsin.

Acadian Flycatcher (*Empidonax virescens*)

Status: Regular; nests

Jan	Feb	Mar	Apr	May	Jun	Jul	Aug	Sep	Oct	Nov	Dec
			x								

27 Apr 1985	23 Sep 1991
3 May 1985	25 Sep 1963
3 May 1985	26 Sep 1964

Occurrence: This rare summer resident is found in heavily wooded river valleys of eastern and central Iowa. Birds are found in the lower canopy of small wooded streams and river bottoms. They tend to return to the same areas year after year and are easily identified by their song. In northeastern Iowa, 10 nests were found in June 1977 (Koenig 1979). Nonsinging birds in fall are difficult to identify. The late birds were netted and identified in the hand.

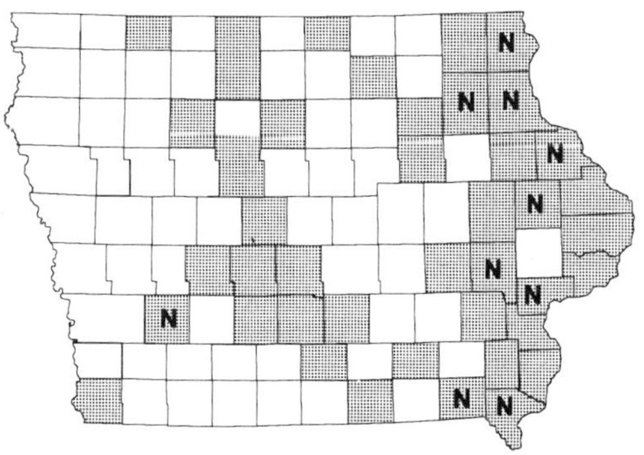

Acadian Flycatcher, 1960-1995
June-July and nesting (N)

Comment: Acadian Flycatchers winter in southern Central America and northern South America. They breed in the eastern United States north to southeastern Minnesota and west to eastern Nebraska.

Reference:

Koenig, D. 1979. Acadian Flycatcher and Veery nests. *Iowa Bird Life* 49:27-28.

Alder Flycatcher (*Empidonax alnorum*)

Status: Regular

Jan	Feb	Mar	Apr	May	Jun	Jul	Aug	Sep	Oct	Nov	Dec
							xx x				

12 May 1986	14 Jun 1989	see text	24 Aug 1985
13 May 1992	15 Jun 1983		29 Aug 1993
13 May 1995	18 Jun 1985		8 Sep 1983

Occurrence: Alder Flycatchers are late spring migrants and are identified by song. There is little evidence of their fall migration, because they cannot be distinguished from Willow Flycatcher in the field except by song, and fall birds rarely sing. There are a few reports from late June and July (Dinsmore et al. 1984, *IBL* 56:117, 59:113). Late July birds could be early migrants. More data are needed to determine whether this species summers in Iowa. The three late fall birds were singing.

Comment: This species, which has been rarely identified in winter, is presumed to winter in western South America. It breeds from Alaska and the Yukon across the Canadian provinces and south to central Minnesota and Wisconsin and south in the Appalachians. Nesting reports from northeastern Missouri are erroneous (Robbins and Easterla 1992). There are summer reports from isolated locations in southern Wisconsin (Robbins 1991), but not from Illinois (Bohlen 1989). In Ohio, early fall migrants have been noted in late July (Peterjohn 1989).

Willow Flycatcher (*Empidonax traillii*)

Status: Regular; nests

Jan	Feb	Mar	Apr	May	Jun	Jul	Aug	Sep	Oct	Nov	Dec
								x xx			

5 May 1964	4 Sep 1989
5 May 1965	21 Sep 1978
6 May 1966	25 Sep 1979

Occurrence: This uncommon and local summer resident breeds in swampy thickets in all areas of the state. A few are usually found in the same locations year after year. They are found on 30 percent of Breeding Bird Surveys with an average of 0.6 per route.

Comment: This species winters from central Mexico to Panama. It breeds mainly in the United States, south of the range for Alder Flycatcher, south to New Mexico and Arkansas. Historically, Traill's Flycatcher was split into Willow Flycatcher and Alder Flycatcher in 1973. Field identification is based on song or call note.

Least Flycatcher (*Empidonax minimus*)

Status: Regular; occasionally nests

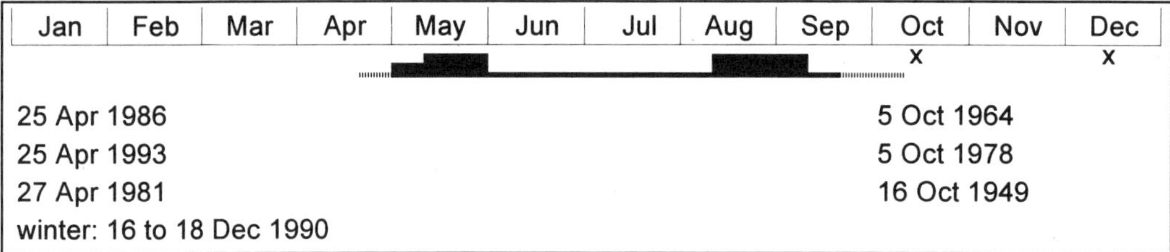

Occurrence: In migration, Least Flycatcher is the most common of the empidonax flycatchers. A few are reported each summer, especially in northeastern Iowa, where they probably nest. The only confirmed nesting records since 1960 are from Sweet Marsh in Bremer County on 5 July 1981 (*IBL* 51:101) and in Clayton County from the breeding bird atlas project (Jackson et al. 1996). Most of the summer records are in central and northeastern Iowa. The winter bird at Red Rock Reservoir in Marion County from 16 to 18 December 1990 was found on a Christmas Bird Count and identified by call note (Johnson 1992).

Historically, Least Flycatchers were said to be common summer residents in northern Iowa, and there were nesting records for Winnebago County (Anderson 1907) and Polk County (DuMont 1933).

Comment: The winter range is on the east and west slopes of Mexico south to Nicaragua, and casually north to southern California, Texas, and Florida. The breeding range is from southern Missouri and the Appalachians west to Idaho and north to the Yukon and the Maritime Provinces. In Missouri, there is only 1 recent nesting record and a few summer records (Robbins and Easterla 1992). In Illinois, there are only a few recent records suggestive of nesting (Bohlen 1989). In Minnesota, nesting extends to the southeastern corner, but summer birds are scarce to absent in the south-central to southwest (Janssen 1987).

In winter, Illinois has a record for 15 December 1973 and 2 November records (Bohlen 1989). Kentucky has 3 December records of unidentified empids (Monroe 1988). Late dates are in September and October for other nearby states.

Reference:

Johnson, A. 1992. An incredibly late Least Flycatcher. *Iowa Bird Life* 62:59-61.

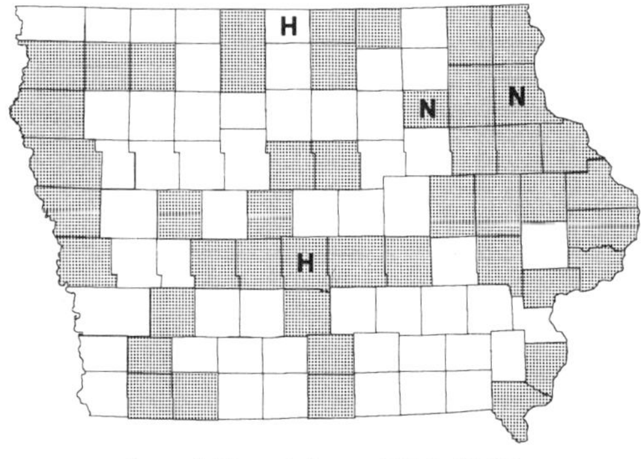

Least Flycatcher, 1960-1995
June-July, nesting (recent N, historical H)

Western Flycatcher species (*Empidonax* species)

Status: Accidental

14 to 15 November 1992, Lake Ahquabi, Warren Co. (P-0346, P-0347, P-0348, P-0389, *IBL* 64(1) cover, Johnson 1994)

Occurrence: The 1 fall record was well-substantiated by photographs and descriptions as Western Flycatcher sp., but was not identified to species.

Comment: The Western Flycatcher was split into Pacific-slope and Cordilleran flycatchers in 1989 (American Ornithologists' Union 1989) based on differences in voice and genetic studies. The Iowa bird was not heard while it was being watched, and, of course, could not be identified by its geographic location.

The Pacific-slope Flycatcher breeds in Pacific Coast states west of the Cascade and Sierra Nevada mountains from southeastern Alaska to Baja California and winters in Mexico and occasionally southern California. The Cordilleran Flycatcher breeds east of the Cascade and Sierra Nevada mountains from southern Alberta to Mexico and from eastern Washington to the Black Hills and winters in Mexico north to southern Arizona. The only vagrant records of these species east of Nebraska are from Pennsylvania Christmas Bird Count in Lancaster County on 16 December 1990 and 15 December 1991 (Johnson 1994). The recorded voice was identified as Pacific-slope Flycatcher. Empidonax flycatchers are extremely rare in the eastern United States in late fall and winter and are very difficult to identify.

References:

Johnson, A. 1994. Western Flycatcher at Lake Ahquabi. *Iowa Bird Life* 64:6-8.

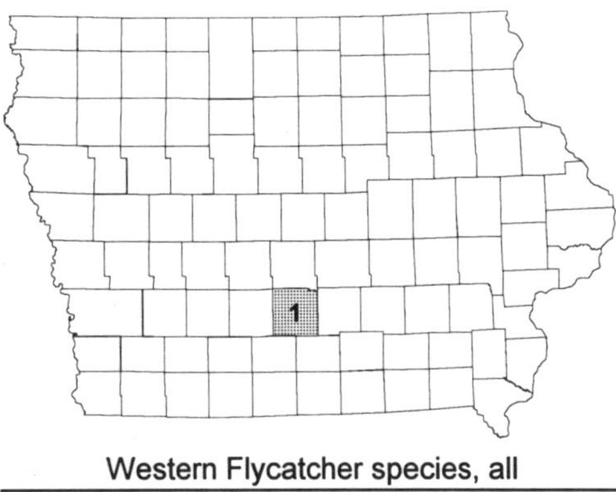

Western Flycatcher species, all

Eastern Phoebe (*Sayornis phoebe*)

Status: Regular; nests

Jan	Feb	Mar	Apr	May	Jun	Jul	Aug	Sep	Oct	Nov	Dec
x										x	x

15 Mar 1936 — 7 Nov 1990
15 Mar 1995 — 10 Nov 1991
18 Mar 1968 — 13 Nov 1988
winter: 27 Dec 1986, 3 Jan 1981

Occurrence: Eastern Phoebe is an uncommon summer resident. It nests under bridges, on rock outcroppings, and sometimes on buildings. It was found on 28 percent of Breeding Bird Surveys with an average of 0.5 per route. More are found on the Southern Iowa Drift Plain (1.2 per route) and northeastern hilly region (0.9 per route) than on the more recently glaciated Des Moines Lobe (0.2 per route).

More are seen in migration, especially in mid-April and late September to mid-October. Winter records are from Christmas Bird Counts at Glenwood in Mills County on 27

December 1986 (*IBL* 57:47) and Yellow River Forest on 3 January1981 (*IBL* 51:3).
Comment: The winter range is from Virginia, southern Missouri, and southern New Mexico south to east-central Mexico. The breeding range is in the United States from the northern part of Gulf coastal states and the Carolinas west to the central Great Plains and north across Canada from the Northwest Territories to the Maritime Provinces. Wisconsin and Illinois also have December and January records.

Say's Phoebe (*Sayornis saya*)

Status: Accidental; occasionally nests

By year since 1960

60	63	66	69	72	75	78	81	84	87	90	93
1 1 2	1 1 1	1 1 1	1	1	1 1	2 3 1	1 1 1		1		1

By month -- all records

Jan	Feb	Mar	Apr	May	Jun	Jul	Aug	Sep	Oct	Nov	Dec
		1	2 1	2 3	2 1 4	1	1 1	2 1			1 1

24 Mar 1963
7 Apr 1966
9 Apr 1964
winter: 22 Dec 1979, 17 Dec 1994

20 Sep 1964
20 Sep 1975
29 Sep 1963

Occurrence: This species nested in Plymouth and Sioux counties from 1960 to 1972 (Bryant 1969, *IBL* 43:75) and from 1977 to 1983 (Bryant 1977, 1984). The only record from those counties since 1987 was near Hawarden in Sioux County on 4 June 1987 (*IBL* 57:121). The nesting activity in Plymouth County was carefully studied (Bryant 1969, 1977, 1984; Bryant and Youngworth 1962). In one year, 21 nesting locations were found in Plymouth County and 2 in Sioux County (Bryant 1977).

Historically, Bryant's records are the first confirmed ones for Iowa. Old reports include a female shot by Berry near Hawarden in Sioux County in 1890 and an indefinite report from Mills County (Anderson 1907).

There are 6 records away from Plymouth and Sioux counties: 16 May 1972 in Fremont County (Silcock 1977); 20 September 1975 at West Okoboji in Dickinson County (*IBL* 46:23); 2 birds for several weeks beginning on 17 June 1978 west of Waubeek in Linn County (*IBL* 48:99); 2 birds on 25 August 1978 at Missouri Valley in Harrison County (*IBL* 48:139); 1 photographed on 22 December 1979 at St. Anthony in Marshall County (P-0001, *IBL* 50:26) and 1 in Appanoose County on 17 December 1994 (*IBL* 65:50).

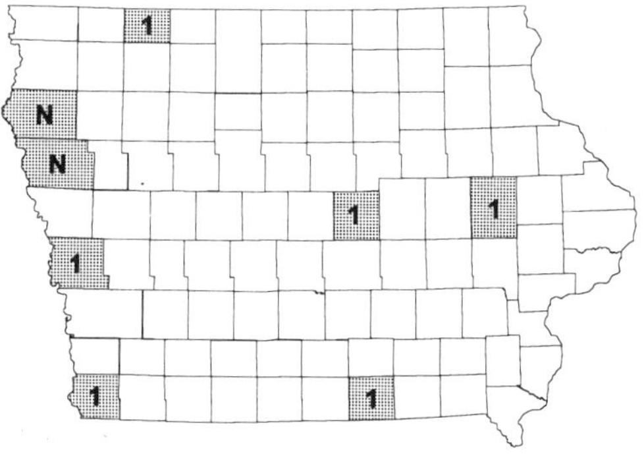

Say's Phoebe, all
Nesting (N) and other records

Comment: Say's Phoebe breeds from the Great Plains to the Pacific Coast and from Mexico to northern Alaska and the Yukon. It winters from western California, southern Arizona, and Texas south to central Mexico. The breeding range extends to central Nebraska and only rarely to eastern South Dakota, so the spread to northwestern Iowa appears to be discontinuous. Say's Phoebe prefers arid climate. The disappearance of nesting birds in the mid-1970s was associated with wetter conditions, and birds returned after several dryer years (Bryant 1977). Nicholson (1968) suggested that the small wooden bridges of

Plymouth County were more attractive than the steel and concrete bridges of nearby counties. Many of the older bridges in Plymouth County were replaced, and subsequently Say's Phoebe was found nesting in abandoned farm buildings (*IBL* 51:101, 119; Bryant 1984).

Say's Phoebe is an uncommon, but widespread vagrant east of Iowa with a few records from Nova Scotia to Florida and almost all intermediate states and provinces. Most are found from September to December and in May, with a few in January, March, April, and August.

References:

Bryant, E. 1969. Present status of the Say's Phoebe in Plymouth County. *Iowa Bird Life* 39:74-75.

Bryant, E. 1977. The Say's Phoebe returns to Plymouth County. *Iowa Bird Life* 47:110-111.

Bryant, E. J. 1984. The Say's Phoebe in Plymouth County. *Iowa Bird Life* 54:55.

Bryant, E. J., and W. Youngworth. 1962. Say's Phoebe in western Iowa. *Iowa Bird Life* 32:75-77.

Nicholson, B. 1968. Field trip May 19, 1968. *Iowa Bird Life* 38:62.

Vermilion Flycatcher (*Pyrocephalus rubinus*)

Status: Accidental

6 to 7 May 1983, near Sioux Center, Sioux Co., male (P-0130, Van Dyk 1983)
13 May 1988, Rice L., Worth Co., male (Anderson 1989)
25 Oct 1992, Rathbun Res., Appanoose Co., female (P-0349, P-0350, *Amer. Birds* 47:101, *IBL* 63(4) cover, Sinclair 1993)

Occurrence: There are 2 spring records of males and 1 fall record of a female.

Comment: The breeding range in the United States is mainly in southern parts of Arizona and New Mexico and southwestern Texas, but includes small parts of California, Nevada, and Oklahoma and extends south to southern South America. In the United States, birds migrate from the more northerly areas in fall, but some winter in the southern portions of the United States.

Vagrant records from the Midwest and Southeast decrease in number with distance from the normal range. Records extend north and east to North Dakota, Minnesota, Wisconsin, Ontario, Ohio, Kentucky, and North Carolina. About two-thirds of the vagrants to the north and east are from fall, with most in September and October, and one-third are from spring, with most in May.

References:

Anderson, G. 1989. Vermilion Flycatcher at Rice Lake. *Iowa Bird Life* 59:63.

Sinclair, J. 1993. Vermilion Flycatcher in Appanoose County. *Iowa Bird Life* 63:101-102.

Van Dyk, J. 1983. Vermilion Flycatcher in north-west Iowa. *Iowa Bird Life* 53:58-59.

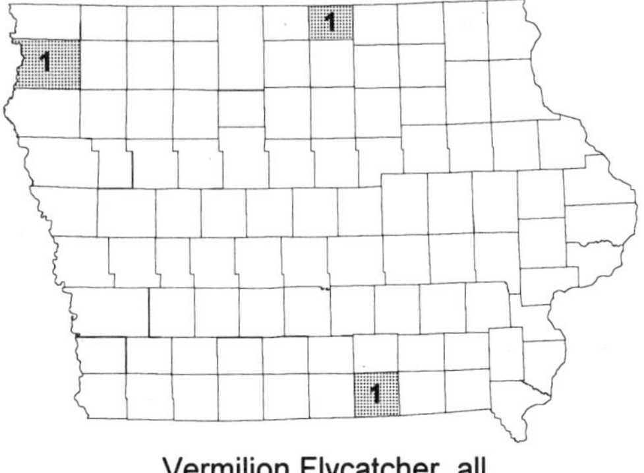

Vermilion Flycatcher, all

Great Crested Flycatcher (*Myiarchus crinitus*)

Status: Regular; nests

Jan	Feb	Mar	Apr	May	Jun	Jul	Aug	Sep	Oct	Nov	Dec
										X	

21 Apr 1989	3 Oct 1992
22 Apr 1979	9 Oct 1952
24 Apr 1994	8 Nov 1993

Occurrence: This common species of the woodlands, is most common in eastern Iowa. It was found on 58 percent of Breeding Bird Surveys with an average of 1.5 birds per route. On the wooded bluffs of the Coralville Reservoir in Johnson County, it was found in every woods with 1.2 per party-hour (Kent et al. 1994).

Comment: Great Crested Flycatcher winters from southern Florida, Cuba, and central Mexico south to northern South America. It breeds in the United States and southern Canada west to the central Great Plains. Based on late dates for surrounding states, a few more October records might be expected, but the record from 8 November 1993 at Effigy Mounds National Monument in Allamakee County (*IBL* 64:14) stretches the limit for the Midwest.

Western Kingbird (*Tyrannus verticalis*)

Status: Regular; nests

Jan	Feb	Mar	Apr	May	Jun	Jul	Aug	Sep	Oct	Nov	Dec
									XX	X	

21 Apr 1964	13 Oct 1967
28 Apr 1984	20 Oct 1985
28 Apr 1984	3 Nov 1984

Occurrence: This rare summer resident is regular in the Missouri River valley and irregular to central Iowa. The most easterly nesting records are from Grundy, Hamilton, and Polk counties, including the State Capitol grounds in 1992 and 1993 (*IBL* 62:109, 63:98). Migrants are occasionally seen in eastern Iowa.

Comment: The winter range is from central Mexico to Costa Rica and casually in the southern coastal United States. The breeding range is from northern Mexico throughout the western United States to southern Canada and from western Iowa and western Minnesota to the West Coast. Nesting occurs sporadically east to Wisconsin, Illinois, Michigan, and Ontario.

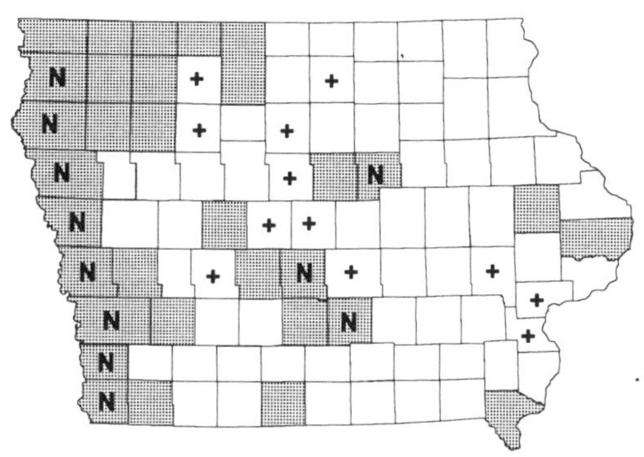

Western Kingbird, 1960-1995
June-July, nesting (N), and spring/fall (+)

Eastern Kingbird (*Tyrannus tyrannus*)

Status: Regular; nests

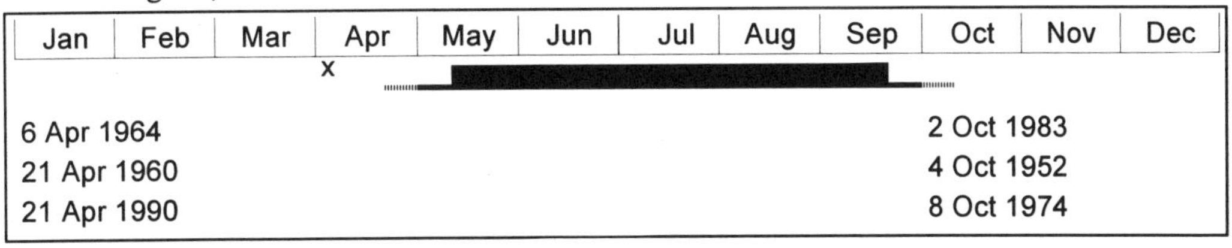

Jan	Feb	Mar	Apr	May	Jun	Jul	Aug	Sep	Oct	Nov	Dec
			x								

6 Apr 1964
21 Apr 1960
21 Apr 1990

2 Oct 1983
4 Oct 1952
8 Oct 1974

Occurrence: Eastern Kingbird is a common summer resident in open and edge habitat. On Breeding Bird Surveys the average number per route was 7.8 with no evidence of change from 1967 to 1991. In spring, a few may arrive by late April, but most arrive after the first week of May. In fall, kingbirds are seen in flocks on wires from late August to mid-September. The 500 in Sioux County on 16 August 1962 (*IBL* 32:83) was an unusually large concentration.

Comment: This species winters from Colombia to northern Argentina. It breeds in the United States and the Canadian provinces, except for extreme western and southwestern areas.

Scissor-tailed Flycatcher (*Tyrannus forficatus*)

Status: Regular; occasionally nests

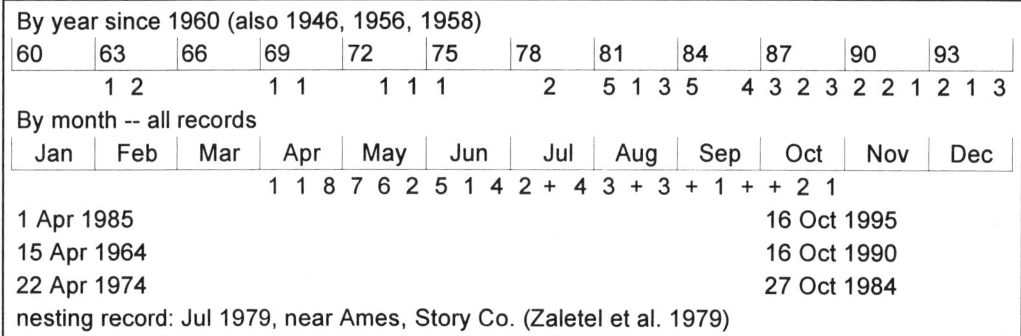

By year since 1960 (also 1946, 1956, 1958)

60 63 66 69 72 75 78 81 84 87 90 93

1 2 1 1 1 1 1 2 5 1 3 5 4 3 2 3 2 2 1 2 1 3

By month -- all records

Jan Feb Mar Apr May Jun Jul Aug Sep Oct Nov Dec

1 1 8 7 6 2 5 1 4 2 + 4 3 + 3 + 1 + + 2 1

1 Apr 1985 — 16 Oct 1995

15 Apr 1964 — 16 Oct 1990

22 Apr 1974 — 27 Oct 1984

nesting record: Jul 1979, near Ames, Story Co. (Zaletel et al. 1979)

Occurrence: From 1 to 5 Scissor-tailed Flycatchers are reported almost every year. Some appear to be spring migrants and others are discovered during the summer and fall. Some remain at the same location for several weeks. The 50 records are rather uniformly distributed in the state. A nest with 1 young was found near Ames in July 1979 (Zaletel et al. 1979).

Historically, the first record is from 18 May 1946 south of Belmont in Wright County (Brown 1946). A bird found dead at North Liberty in Johnson County on 1 April 1985 is a specimen (University of Iowa #35911, Kent and Schrimper 1996).

Comment: The winter range is from central Mexico to Costa Rica and in southern Florida. Almost all of the breeding range is in Texas, Oklahoma, and Kansas with extensions to southern Nebraska, southwestern Missouri, other touching states, and extreme northeastern Mexico. There are nesting records for Mississippi, Tennessee, and Iowa. This species is a regular vagrant with many records spanning the United States and Canada. The breeding range in Missouri has expanded to some extent in the 1900s (Robbins and Easterla 1992).

References:

Brown, H. M. 1946. A sight record of the Scissor-tailed Flycatcher in Wright County. *Iowa Bird Life* 16:68.

Zaletel, H., A. Thierman, and G. Burns. 1979. First nesting of Scissor-tailed Flycatcher in Iowa. *Iowa Bird Life* 49:77-78.

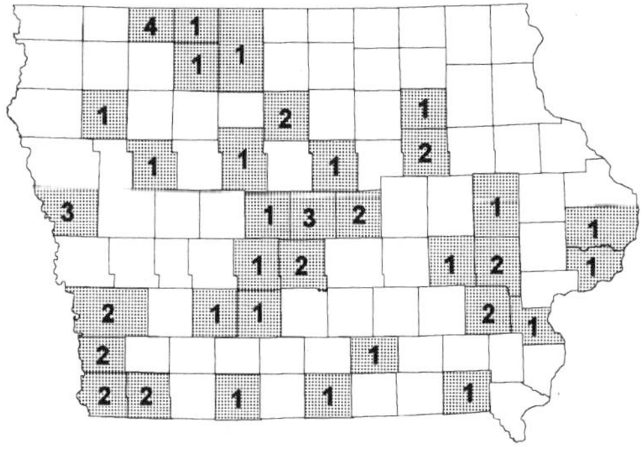

Scissor-tailed Flycatcher, all

Larks (Family Alaudidae)

Larks comprise 91 species, with 2 from North America and 1 from Iowa. These essentially Old World species, except for the more cosmopolitan Horned Lark, are small, dull colored terrestrial birds with inspired flight songs. They are a distinctive family of songbirds, because the tarsus is rounded in the back and scaled (instead of sharp and unsegmented) and because they have a five-muscled syrinx, which puts them at the primitive end of the songbirds.

Horned Lark (*Eremophila alpestris*)

Status: Regular; nests

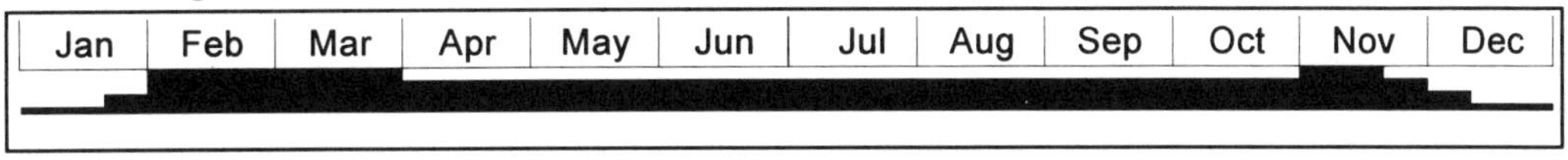

Jan	Feb	Mar	Apr	May	Jun	Jul	Aug	Sep	Oct	Nov	Dec

Occurrence: This common permanent resident and abundant migrant is found in open habitats throughout Iowa. In spring and summer it is usually found on croplands and pastures where it begins nesting in late March or early April. In winter, it occupies open fields but is most often seen when deep snow forces it to roadsides. Although Horned Larks are permanent residents in Iowa, there is considerable flux in the population. The nesting birds belong to the subspecies *E. a. praticola*, most of which leave Iowa in winter. In winter, they are replaced by birds from at least 2 other subspecies, *E. a. alpestris* and *E. a. hoyi* (Musgrove 1944). Migrants move through Iowa in November and in February and March.

Horned Larks are found on 75 percent of the Breeding Bird Surveys and 80 percent of Christmas Bird Counts. The number found on Christmas Bird Counts varies greatly from year to year, and the highest counts are in northern Iowa and near the Missouri River. Most of the Horned Larks leave the state in winter, but only briefly. Returning flocks are usually evident by early February.

Comment: The winter range is from southern Canada south to the southern United States and Mexico. The breeding range is from northern Alaska and Canada south to Mexico in the West and the southern United States in the East. This species also occurs in Colombia and across Europe, northern Asia, and northern Africa.

Reference:

Musgrove, J. W. 1944. The Horned Larks in Iowa. *Iowa Bird Life* 14:63-64.

Swallows (Family Hirundinidae)

Swallows comprise 88 species, with 14 from North America and 6 from Iowa. They have long wings and a short, broad, flattened bill with wide gape for catching insects on the fly. These world-wide species are gregarious and most are migratory and colonial nesters. Nests are in trees, in banks, or on cliffs or buildings, and the young must be able to fly when they leave the nest. There is no significant difference between swallows and martins. The 6 Iowa species are all relatively common and nest.

Tree Swallows are the earliest to arrive and the last to leave. Barn Swallows are second earliest and latest, while Cliff Swallows are the latest to arrive and, perhaps, the first to leave. In spring swallows are found near water, but in fall they may also congregate in huge mixed flocks along roadsides.

Purple Martin (*Progne subis*)

Status: Regular; nests

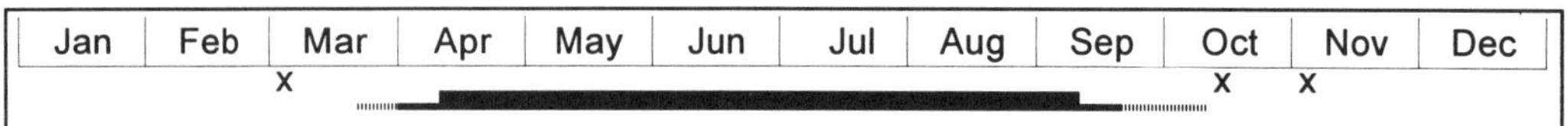

Jan	Feb	Mar	Apr	May	Jun	Jul	Aug	Sep	Oct	Nov	Dec
		x							x	x	

3 Mar 1983	10 Oct 1952
21 Mar 1991	14 Oct 1962
23 Mar 1964	2 Nov 1970

Occurrence: This uncommon summer resident arrives in early or mid-April and departs in September. It is usually found near fields, in towns, or near water. Although historically this colonial species nested in natural cavities, it now nests almost exclusively in birdhouses. Purple Martins are found on about one-quarter of the Breeding Bird Surveys, most commonly in western Iowa.

Like other swallows, large groups may congregate in migration, especially in fall. The largest group reported in Iowa was 9,000 in Lee County on 8 August 1985 (*IBL* 55:127).

Historically, this species was considered a common summer resident throughout Iowa (Anderson 1907, DuMont 1933). There are no data that would allow comparison of abundance in historic times versus now. It is the least common of the swallows and may be difficult to find on any given day.

Comment: The winter range is in South America south to southern Brazil. The breeding range is from southern Canada south to northern Mexico and the Gulf Coast.

Tree Swallow (*Tachycineta bicolor*)

Status: Regular; nests

Jan	Feb	Mar	Apr	May	Jun	Jul	Aug	Sep	Oct	Nov	Dec
											x

15 Mar 1983 — 15 Nov 1992
16 Mar 1996 — 17 Nov 1992
17 Mar 1992 — 5 Dec 1992

Occurrence: This abundant migrant and common summer resident occurs throughout Iowa. Many arrive by late March and remain until mid-October, which is much earlier and later than for other swallows.

Tree Swallows nest near water where there are dead trees and old woodpecker holes or in open areas where there are bluebird or other nest boxes and natural cavities. Following the construction of the large reservoirs in Iowa, there were many dead trees, which provided abundant nesting cavities for Tree Swallows, but most have fallen, and numbers of nesting Tree Swallows have diminished. Farm ponds also provide habitat for this species. This species was found on 15 percent of Breeding Bird Surveys, most commonly in northeastern Iowa; however, these surveys do not adequately sample this species' habitat.

In spring, most Tree Swallows are found over water, but in fall large flocks congregate along roadsides as well. The largest groups reported were 10,000 at Union Slough National Wildlife Refuge in Kossuth County on 28 August 1988 (*IBL* 59:15) and 8,000 at De Soto National Wildlife Refuge in Harrison County on 28 September 1985 (*IBL* 55:127). During warm falls, a few Tree Swallows may remain into November, and 1 remained until 5 December 1992 at Rathbun Reservoir in Appanoose County (*IBL* 63:50).

Comment: The winter range is from southern United States south through Mexico to Costa Rica. The breeding range is from Alaska east to Newfoundland and south almost to Mexico in the West and to northern United States in the East.

Northern Rough-winged Swallow (*Stelgidopteryx serripennis*)

Status: Regular; nests

Jan	Feb	Mar	Apr	May	Jun	Jul	Aug	Sep	Oct	Nov	Dec
									x x		

4 Apr 1981 — 11 Oct 1985
5 Apr 1984 — 16 Oct 1954
6 Apr 1985 — 25 Oct 1987

Occurrence: This common migrant and summer resident is usually found near water, and it nests in burrows in vertical banks along rivers, streams, and road cuts. It usually nests in loose colonies of a few pairs but often nests with Bank Swallows. Migrants arrive in late April or early May and depart by late September.

This species was found on 50 percent of Breeding Bird Surveys, most commonly in northeastern and western Iowa. Of the swallows, it is the most likely to be found at scattered locations along rivers.

Comment: The winter range is from the southern United States south through Central

America to Panama. The breeding range is from southern Alaska east to New Brunswick and south to the Gulf of Mexico and Costa Rica.

Bank Swallow (*Riparia riparia*)

Status: Regular; nests

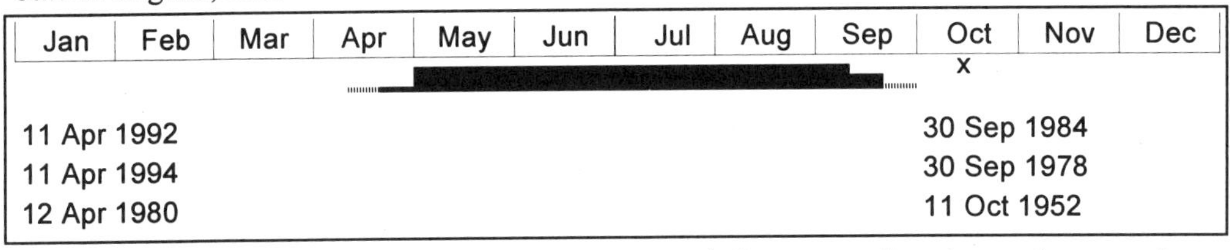

Jan	Feb	Mar	Apr	May	Jun	Jul	Aug	Sep	Oct	Nov	Dec
									X		

11 Apr 1992	30 Sep 1984
11 Apr 1994	30 Sep 1978
12 Apr 1980	11 Oct 1952

Occurrence: This common migrant and summer resident is usually found near water. It nests in vertical banks along rivers, streams, and road cuts. Bank Swallows typically nest in colonies, which may contain hundreds of nests. Migrants arrive in late April or early May and depart in mid- or late September.

Bank Swallows were found on about 20 percent of Breeding Bird Surveys, but numbers vary from year to year. They were reported far more often in northeastern Iowa than elsewhere in the state.

Comment: The winter range is from Panama south through much of South America. The breeding range is from Alaska east to Newfoundland and south to include all but the southernmost United States. Bank Swallows are also found across much of Europe and Asia.

Cliff Swallow (*Hirundo pyrrhonota*)

Status: Regular; nests

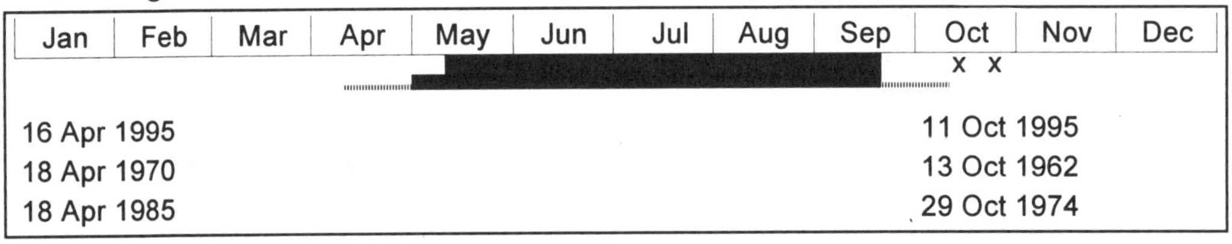

Jan	Feb	Mar	Apr	May	Jun	Jul	Aug	Sep	Oct	Nov	Dec
									X X		

16 Apr 1995	11 Oct 1995
18 Apr 1970	13 Oct 1962
18 Apr 1985	29 Oct 1974

Occurrence: This abundant summer resident arrives in mid-May and departs in mid-September. Of the swallows, it is the last to arrive in spring.

Its gourd-shaped nests are clustered on the sides of bridges, buildings, or cliffs. Some colonies may contain hundreds of nests. Cliff Swallows were found on 31 percent of the Breeding Bird Surveys from 1985 to 1994, but on only 10 percent from 1968 to 1977. They were found most frequently and in greatest numbers in eastern and northeastern Iowa and at scattered other locations.

Over the last 50 years, the number and distribution of nesting Cliff Swallows has increased greatly. In 1950, nesting Cliff Swallows were uncommon in eastern Iowa except on cliffs, such as those at Palisades-Kepler State Park (Kent and Kent 1974). Gradually, nesting areas expanded to include large bridges along major rivers and then small bridges in the countryside. Breeding Bird Survey data suggest that this species' nesting population is increasing rapidly in Iowa. Historically, the Cliff Swallow was considered a common resident throughout Iowa, although somewhat locally distributed (Anderson 1907, DuMont 1933).

Like other swallows, Cliff Swallows often form large post-breeding concentrations. The highest count was 5,000 at Sweet Marsh in Bremer County on 11 August 1985 (*IBL* 55:127).

Comment: The winter range is in southern South America. The breeding range is from Alaska east to Nova Scotia and south to northern Mexico in the West and almost to the Gulf Coast in the East.

Barn Swallow (*Hirundo rustica*)

Status: Regular; nests

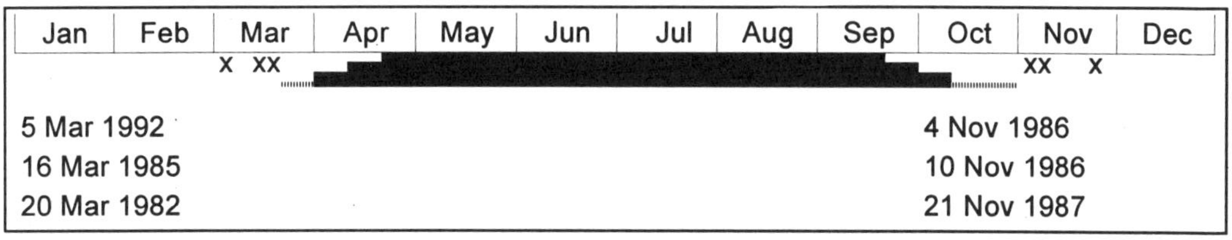

Jan	Feb	Mar	Apr	May	Jun	Jul	Aug	Sep	Oct	Nov	Dec
		x xx								xx x	
5 Mar 1992									4 Nov 1986		
16 Mar 1985									10 Nov 1986		
20 Mar 1982									21 Nov 1987		

Occurrence: This abundant resident arrives in April and departs in late September or early October. It is the most widely distributed and least colonial of the swallows. Mud nests are built on the outside or inside of buildings, bridges, or other man-made structures. The Barn Swallow is reported on nearly all of the Breeding Bird Surveys held in Iowa. The greatest numbers were reported in north-central and northwestern Iowa and the fewest in southern and northeastern Iowa.

The largest post-breeding concentration reported in Iowa was 5,000 at Sweet Marsh in Bremer County on 11 August 1985 (*IBL* 55:127). This may be the most abundant swallow in Iowa, although Tree, Bank, and Cliff swallows are usually seen in larger groups.

Comment: The winter range is from extreme southern United States south through Central America and much of South America. The breeding range is from Alaska east to Newfoundland and south to Mexico and northern Florida. It is also found in Eurasia and northern Africa.

Jays, Magpies, and Crows (Family Corvidae)

Jays, magpies, and crows comprise 113 species, with 20 from North America and 8 from Iowa. These 10-primaried oscines have strong, unnotched bills; nostrils covered by bristles; large, strong legs and feet; and tarsus scaled in front and terminated by a ridge. They are cosmopolitan, gregarious, intelligent, and omnivorous, but lack a musical song. Most pair for life and build bulky nests.

Of the Iowa species, 2 are abundant Regular species that are both resident and migratory, and 6 are Accidental. Of the Accidental species, 4 are from the West, 1 from the North, and 1 from the South.

Gray Jay (*Perisoreus canadensis*)

Status: Accidental

30 Oct 1976 to late Jan 1977, near Decorah, Winneshiek Co. (P-0012, Koenig 1977)
Nov 1976, Mason City, Cerro Gordo Co. (Halmi 1977)
Nov 1976, Cedar Falls, Black Hawk Co. (Halmi 1977)

Occurrence: The 3 records are all from northern Iowa and were found in the fall of 1976. There is an old specimen at the University of Iowa (#32540, P-0458), but its origin is in doubt (Kent and Schrimper 1996).

Comment: This boreal Nearctic species is found in the western mountains including the Black Hills, across Alaska and Canada, and barely into northern Minnesota, Wisconsin, Michigan, New York, and New England. In Minnesota, fall eruptions have been noted along Lake Superior from mid-September to November with associated fall-winter records farther south to about the Twin Cities (Janssen 1987). Eruptions occurred in 1929-1930, 1965-1966, 1974, 1976-1977, 1986, and 1995. The most southerly record for Minnesota is in the southeast within 1 county of Iowa. Janssen (1987) suggests that birds return northward by mid-December. In Wisconsin, Robbins (1991) notes 30 extralimital records since 1939, with most occurring from late October to January and most in central Wisconsin but at least 1 in the extreme southeast.

The Iowa birds appeared in a predictable pattern—in October and November of an invasion year in Minnesota and in northern counties near conifers. The likelihood of seeing more in Iowa is small; however, in a year when they are frequent at Duluth in October to November, one might occur again in northeastern Iowa.

References:

Halmi, N. 1977. More Gray Jays in Iowa. *Iowa Bird Life* 47:65.

Koenig, D. 1977. First Gray Jay record for Iowa. *Iowa Bird Life* 47:23.

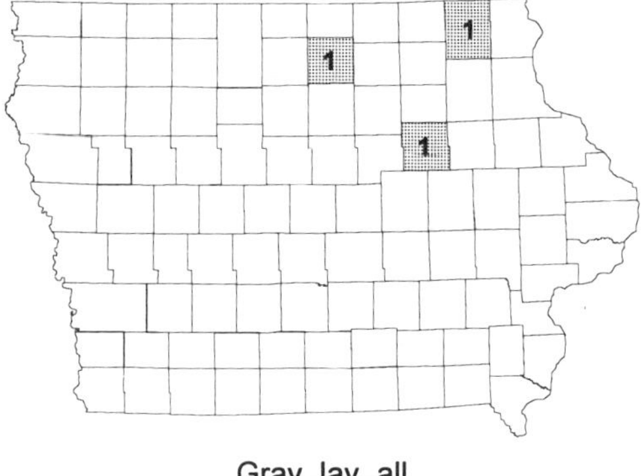

Gray Jay, all

Blue Jay (*Cyanocitta cristata*)

Status: Regular; nests

Jan	Feb	Mar	Apr	May	Jun	Jul	Aug	Sep	Oct	Nov	Dec

Occurrence: This abundant permanent resident prefers woodlands and urban areas but may be found in a variety of other habitats. Although it is found year-round, there is a noticeable migration of Blue Jays through Iowa. This migration is especially obvious in fall when small groups move south from mid-September through late October. Northbound birds are seen from April through early May. It is not clear whether the Blue Jays that winter in Iowa are local birds or birds from regions to the north.

Blue Jays are reported on all of the Christmas Bird Counts, with the greatest numbers found on counts near the Mississippi River. The number reported varies considerably from year to year.

Blue Jays were found on more than 90 percent of Breeding Bird Surveys with highest numbers in southern and northwestern Iowa.

Comment: The Blue Jay is a permanent resident east of the Rocky Mountains from central Canada south to the Gulf of Mexico. Birds in northern portions of the breeding range move south in winter.

An analysis of Christmas Bird Count data from 1962 to 1971 suggested that Blue Jays were less likely to migrate than in the past, perhaps because of winter bird feeding (Bock and Lepthien 1976). There is no recent analysis of those data to see if that trend is continuing.

Reference:

Bock, C. E., and L. W. Lepthien. 1976. Changing winter distribution and abundance of the Blue Jay, 1962-1971. *Amer. Midland Naturalist* 96:232-236.

Pinyon Jay (*Gymnorhinus cyanocephalus*)

Status: Accidental

17 Dec 1972 to early Jan 1973, Shenandoah, Page Co. (Zollars 1973)

Occurrence: There is 1 sight record of a bird at a feeder in southwestern Iowa in winter.

Comment: This species occupies pinyon-juniper habitat of the mountains and high plateaus of the western United States north to southern Montana, west to California, south to central New Mexico, and east to the Black Hills and the panhandle of Oklahoma. This species is notoriously nomadic and gregarious, with movements to the Pacific Coast, southern Canada, northern Mexico, and central Texas. The Iowa record, however, is aberrant in that it is the only record east of the Missouri River and it is away from pinyon–juniper habitat. Movements are likely related to the abundance of juniper berries.

Reference:

Zollars, R. 1973. Pinyon Jay in Shenandoah. *Iowa Bird Life* 43:28-29.

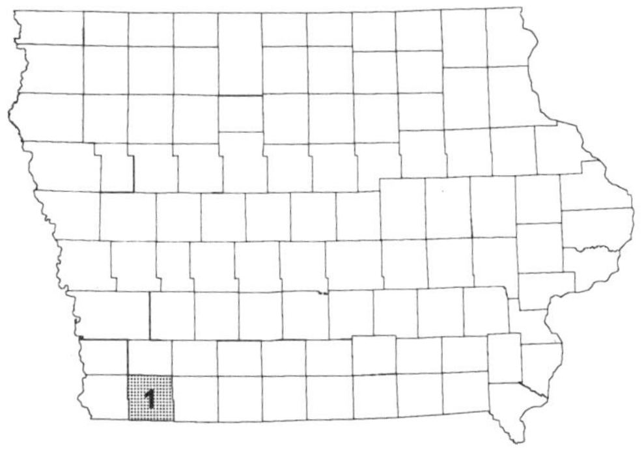

Pinyon Jay, all

Clark's Nutcracker (*Nucifraga columbiana*)

Status: Accidental

23 Sep 1894, near Boone, Boone Co. (Univ. of Iowa specimen #10753, P-0489, Nutting 1895, Henning 1895, Anderson 1907, Kent and Schrimper 1996)
prior to 1917, Sac Co. (specimen at Rockwell City, P-0081, Spurrell 1919)
27 Nov 1919, Tiffin, Johnson Co. (Univ. of Iowa mounted specimen #28401, P-0046, Stoner 1920, DuMont 1933)
14 to 15 Oct 1972, Ottumwa, Wapello Co. (P-0013, Ayres 1973)
16 to 19 Dec 1972, Pleasantville, Marion Co. (Dorow 1973, photo)

Occurrence: There are 3 old records based on specimens and 2 records from 1972 based on photographs, all from September to December. An invasion involving 33 sites was reported in 1972-1973 (Black 1973). Although only 2 of the reports were well-substantiated, this was clearly an invasion year (see below).

Comment: This species breeds in mountainous coniferous forest, migrating to lower elevations in winter. The breeding range extends to central British Columbia following the mountains south to southern New Mexico and northern Baja California. Clark's Nutcrackers wander irregularly to Alaska, the Yukon, the western Great Plains, Mexico, and the Pacific Coast. There are relatively few eastward vagrants to Minnesota, Ontario, Wisconsin, Michigan, Illinois, Missouri, and Arkansas. Incursions of 4 or 5 birds were noted in Minnesota in 1894, 1969, and 1972; these coincide with 3 of the 5 Iowa sightings. The fall of 1894 also produced records in Illinois and Missouri. In 1919, 3 specimens were taken in Nebraska. The fall-winter of 1972-1973 had the most notable invasion with vagrants noted in Texas (11 counties), Nebraska, Missouri, Iowa, Minnesota, Wisconsin, Illinois, and Ontario. Other eastward records are widely scattered over the years. Most of the eastern vagrant records are from September to January with the peak in November, and a few are from April to May.

References:

Ayres, C. G. 1973. First Clark's Nutcracker for Wapello County. *Iowa Bird Life* 43:14-17.

Black, G. B. 1973. Clark's Nutcracker sightings in Iowa, winter 1972-73. *Iowa Bird Life* 43:50-51.

Dorow, H. 1973. Another Clark's Nutcracker visits Iowa. *Iowa Bird Life* 43:27.

Henning, C. F. 1895. Clark's Crow or Nutcracker. *Iowa Ornithologist* 1:62-63.

Stoner, D. 1920. Bird records for the season 1919-1920 in the vicinity of Iowa City. *Proc. Iowa Acad. Sci.* 27:379-384.

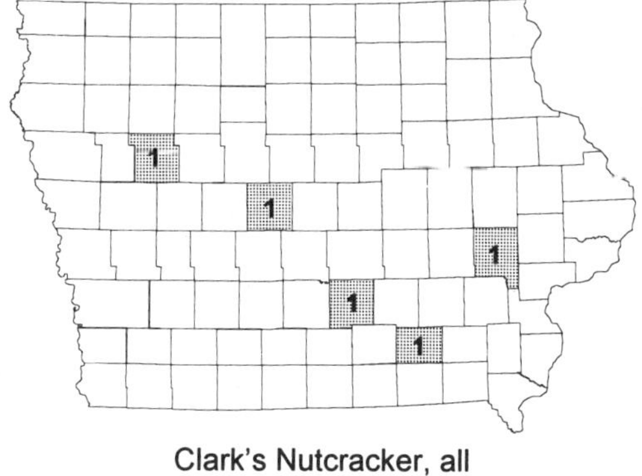

Clark's Nutcracker, all

Black-billed Magpie (*Pica pica*)

Status: Accidental; formerly nested

By year since 1960

60	63	66	69	72	75	78	81	84	87	90	93
				2 1	1	1		1		1	1

By month -- since 1960

Jan	Feb	Mar	Apr	May	Jun	Jul	Aug	Sep	Oct	Nov	Dec
				1	1		1		1 1	1 +	1

Records since 1960

spring 1972, Waubonsie S.P., Fremont Co. (*IBL* 42:40)
15 Aug 1972, Indianola, Warren Co. (*IBL* 42:70)
19 May 1973, Linn Co. (*IBL* 43:76)
24 Oct 1976, Cherokee Co. (*IBL* 46:114)
1 Jun 1980, Fairview Conservation A., Sioux Co. (Dinsmore et al. 1984)
6 Oct 1985, Hidden Bridge W.A., Lyon Co. (Harr 1986)
29 Dec 1990, Sioux City, Woodbury Co. (*IBL* 61:50, 58)
9, 19 Nov 1995, near Westfield, Plymouth Co. (*IBL* 66:23)

Nesting records: 1937, 1938, Bremer Co. (Dix 1937, 1938, Pierce 1939)

Occurrence: Of the 8 reports from 1960 to 1995, the first 5 are undocumented and the last 3 are typical fall-winter records from northwestern Iowa. The reports from June and August and those from central and eastern Iowa do not fit the usual pattern for this species.

Black-billed Magpies were first noted in Iowa by Thomas Say during the winter and until 23 March 1820 near what is now Pottawattamie County (James 1823). From that time until 1923 there were only 9 published reports of this species (Dinsmore et al. 1984). A few were found in northwestern Iowa in the fall-winter of 1914, 1915, and 1918, which were followed in 1921 by records in 16 counties, 5 of which were in central and eastern Iowa (Stoner 1922, Stephens 1930). Winter birds were noted in 3 counties from 1924 to 1926, but then there were no more records until 1934 when another massive fall-winter invasion occurred with birds in 20 counties (DuMont 1935). A smaller invasion in 1936 was followed by reports of 1 to 5 birds in the years 1937 to 1943. Over the next 16 years, the only reports were from Sioux City in Woodbury County in 1948, 1949, 1951, and 1958 (Dinsmore et al. 1984). During these periodic invasions, the earliest fall date was 20 September 1934 in Butler County (Iowa State Univ. specimen #667) and the latest spring date was 11 March 1940 in Union and Woodbury counties (Laffoon 1941).

A pair nested at a farm in Bremer County in 1937 and 1938, and the young were taken by farm children (Dix 1937, 1938). The pair first arrived in December 1936, and 1 was still there in January 1939, the other apparently having been shot (Pierce 1939).

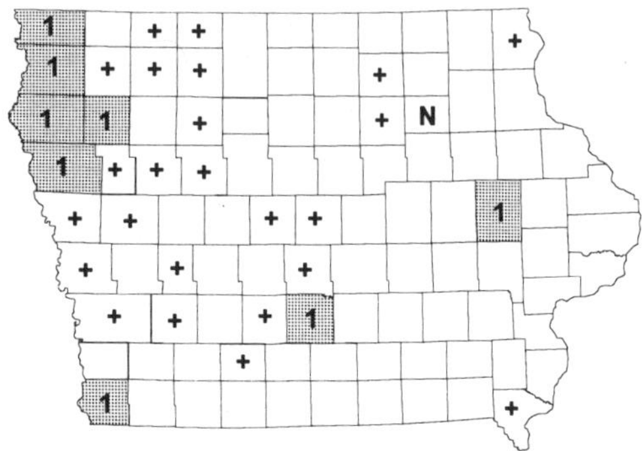

Black-billed Magpie, 1960-1995
Recent (shaded) and historical records (+, N)

Comment: This Holarctic species of open country is found from the Great Plains west to the mountains of California and from southwestern Alaska, the southern Yukon, and western Ontario on the north to northern New Mexico on the south. It also occurs across the temperate zone of Eurasia.

Magpies are regular in northwestern Minnesota and live in Nebraska and South Dakota within 100 miles of Iowa. In the Midwest, there are more records for Wisconsin than for Missouri, Illinois, Indiana, Ohio, and Michigan combined. There are also records from the East Coast from Newfoundland to North Carolina. Although some of these records may be of escaped birds, there is a seasonal pattern of sightings in the Midwest and the Northeast from October to January and April to May.

References:

Dix, Mrs. R. S. 1937. The nesting of the American Magpie (*Pica pica hudsonia*) in Bremer County, Iowa, summer of 1937. *Iowa Bird Life* 7:34.

Dix, Mrs. R. S. 1938. American Magpies nest in Bremer County, Iowa, the second successive year. *Iowa Bird Life* 8:56.

DuMont, P. A. 1935. The 1934-'35 magpie invasion into Iowa. *Iowa Bird Life* 5:46.

Harr, D. C. 1986. Black-billed Magpie in Lyon County. *Iowa Bird Life* 56:32.

Pierce, F. J. 1939. Further notes on the American Magpie in Bremer County, Iowa. *Iowa Bird Life* 9:10-11.

Stoner, D. 1922. On the eastward movement of magpies. *Wilson Bull.* 34:44-45.

American Crow (*Corvus brachyrhynchus*)

Status: Regular; nests

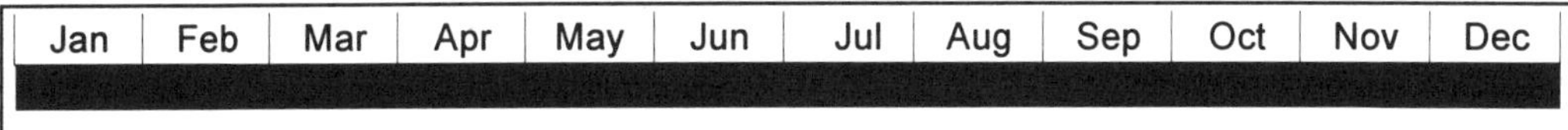

Occurrence: This abundant permanent resident is found in wooded areas, agricultural fields, farmsteads, and urban areas throughout Iowa. Iowa's resident crows are joined in October and early November by migrants from the north. They gather in large winter roosts, which may contain thousands of crows. A roost in Ames in Story County contained birds from as far north as southern Ontario as well as birds that nested locally (Schaefer 1983).

The American Crow is one of the most frequently reported species on Christmas Bird Counts. These counts are inflated by a few large winter roosts, such as 10,800 in Des Moines in Polk County in 1990, 9,200 in Ames in Story County in 1991, 30,000 in Keokuk in Lee County in 1990 and 1992, and an amazing 90,000 at Oakville in Louisa County in 1995 (*IBL* 66:47).

Crows are found on almost all Breeding Bird Surveys, with the highest counts in north-central Iowa and the fewest in western Iowa.

Comment: The breeding range is from southern Canada south to the southern United States and northern Mexico. In winter, most crows from the northern extremes of the breeding range move south into the northern or central United States.

Although concentrations of roosting crows are most noticeable in winter, some roost communally throughout the year; for example, 225 in Ames on 26 Jun 1993 (*IBL* 63:98) and 1,040 there on 3 Sep 1995 (*IBL* 66:23).

Reference:

Schaefer, J. M. 1983. The Common Crow as a sentinel species of rabies in wildlife populations. Ph.D. dissertation, Iowa State University, Ames.

Fish Crow (*Corvus ossifragus*)

Status: Accidental

8 May 1991, Big Sand Mound Preserve, Louisa-Muscatine county line (*IBL* 61:94, 62:71, 66:97)
25 Apr 1994, Big Timber Division, Mark Twain N.W.R., Louisa Co. (*IBL* 64:77; 65: 82; 66:97)
21 to 26 Apr 1995, Lake Odessa, Mark Twain N.W.R., Louisa Co. (*IBL* 65:74, 66:96)

Occurrence: The 3 records involve birds heard in spring in Louisa County from the upper end of Lake Odessa to the Muscatine County line.

Comment: This species is a permanent resident of coastal states from southern New England to the upper Texas Coast. A migratory population moves up the Mississippi Valley in spring to southern Missouri and southern Illinois, although some may overwinter in Missouri. The interior population appears to be gradually expanding, starting with expansion in Arkansas in the 1940s and with first documented records in Oklahoma in 1954, in Kentucky in 1959 (Monroe et al. 1988), in Illinois in 1962 (Bohlen 1989), and in Missouri in 1965 (Robbins and Easterla 1992). Expansion up the Ohio River to Kentucky and Indiana was noted in 1988 (*Amer. Birds* 42:1297) and along tributaries of the Arkansas River in eastern Oklahoma and Kansas in 1990 (*Amer. Birds* 44:456). Along the Mississippi River, this species has occurred north to Pike County in west-central Illinois and across the river in Pike County in northeastern Missouri.

In the interior, Fish Crow is a bird of floodplain forest and adjacent edge. It is identified by voice, which may be very similar to that of young American Crows. Birds heard after April should be interpreted with caution. The preliminary evidence suggests that this species will be expanding more into Iowa, but will continue to be an identification problem.

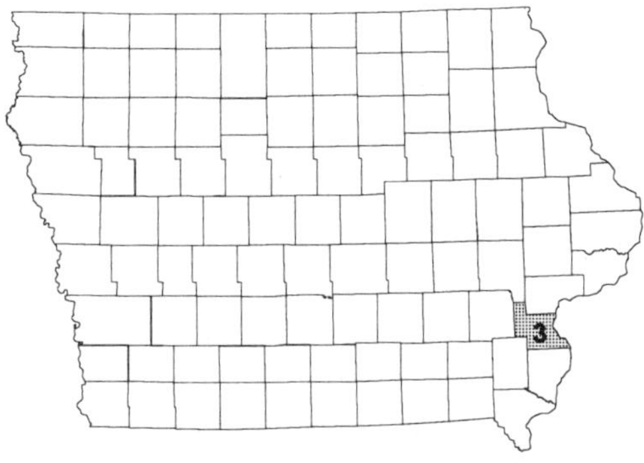

Fish Crow, all

Common Raven (*Corvus corax*)

Status: Accidental

7 Oct 1956, Potter's M., Dickinson Co. (State Historical Museum specimen, P-0139, P-0140, Sieh 1957)
18 Oct 1957, Union Slough N.W.R., Kossuth Co. (Burgess 1958)
20 Oct 1959, Silver L., Dickinson Co. (State Historical Museum specimen, P-0139, Sieh 1960)

Occurrence: The 3 Accepted records are all from northern Iowa in October in the late 1950s. The 4 other records from the 1950s and 1960s (Dinsmore et al. 1984) lacked sufficient detail to be accepted by the Records Committee. There is some evidence that this species was present along the Missouri River in the early 1800s but was gone from the state long before 1900 (Anderson 1907).

Comment: This Holarctic species occurs across northern North America. The range extends south in the mountains to Central America and to Georgia, but otherwise only to northern Minnesota, central Wisconsin, and New England. It is absent from most of the Great Plains, Midwest, and East. The range formerly extended south to Arkansas and Alabama. The most recent records from Nebraska, Illinois, Indiana, and Ohio are prior to 1954. In Minnesota, migrants are noted at Duluth from September through November; however, there only a few winter records south of the normal range in east-central Minnesota south to within 3 counties of Iowa. The Iowa records are farther west, a great distance from the normal range in Minnesota, which is in the northeast. The few old vagrant records for the Midwest are almost all from October or November.

References:

Burgess, H. H. 1958. Raven sighted at Union Slough Refuge. *Iowa Bird Life* 28:26-27.

Sieh, J. G. 1957. First authentic record of Raven in Iowa. *Iowa Bird Life* 27:21-22.

Sieh, J. G. 1960. Raven taken in Dickinson County. *Iowa Bird Life* 30:16.

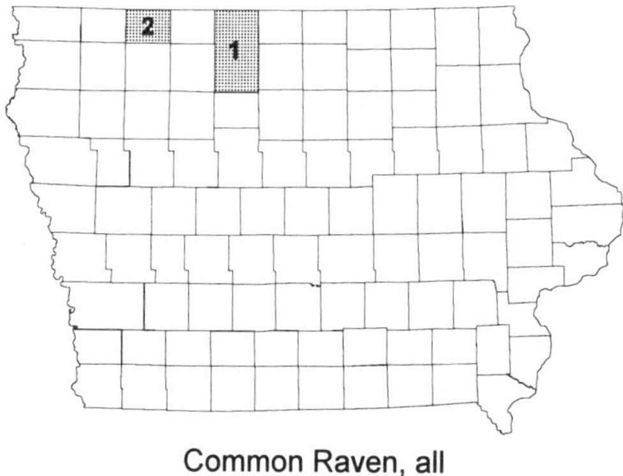

Common Raven, all

Titmice (Family Paridae)

Titmice comprise 54 species, with 10 from North America and 3 from Iowa. These closely related, mostly sedentary species are active, acrobatic, gregarious, woodland or scrubland birds. They have short bills, strong feet, and are arboreal. Nests are in holes or crevices with large clutches. Of the Iowa species, 2 are common permanent residents and 1 is Accidental.

Black-capped Chickadee (*Parus atricapillus*)

Status: Regular; nests

Jan	Feb	Mar	Apr	May	Jun	Jul	Aug	Sep	Oct	Nov	Dec

Occurrence: This abundant permanent resident is found in woodlands, urban areas, and riparian areas throughout Iowa and is one of the most conspicuous species in those habitats. It is reported on every Christmas Bird Count, with the greatest numbers from near the Mississippi and Missouri rivers and the fewest in northern Iowa. Chickadees were found on 60 percent of Breeding Bird Surveys, where they were most abundant in southern Iowa.

Comment: This species is a permanent resident from Alaska east to Newfoundland and south through the northern and central United States. The range has a sharp boundary with that of Carolina Chickadee in central Missouri and central Illinois.

Boreal Chickadee (*Parus hudsonicus*)

Status: Accidental

17 Nov 1976 to 7 Mar 1977, Des Moines, Polk Co. (P-0006, Brown 1976)
23 to 25 Nov 1978, Osage, Mitchell Co. (*IBL* 49:25)

Occurrence: Both records are of birds found in November; 1 remained for the winter. There are 2 other undocumented records (Dinsmore et al. 1984).

Comment: This species is well named—it lives in the boreal forest across Alaska and Canada dipping south into Montana, Minnesota, Wisconsin, and New England. In Minnesota, some birds move a short distance south beginning in late September, and there are occasional eruptions to central Minnesota (Janssen 1987). Across the United States the extent of southern movement, which includes only a few records for any state, is to Wyoming, South Dakota, Iowa, Illinois, Indiana, Ohio, West Virginia, and Virginia. Most southerly vagrants are found in November, but may remain for the winter. In most years there are no records from the states listed above, but in 1951, 1963, 1972, 1976, and 1977 there were records in 2 or 3 of these states.

Reference:

Brown, W. H. 1976. Boreal Chickadee in Des Moines. *Iowa Bird Life* 46:117.

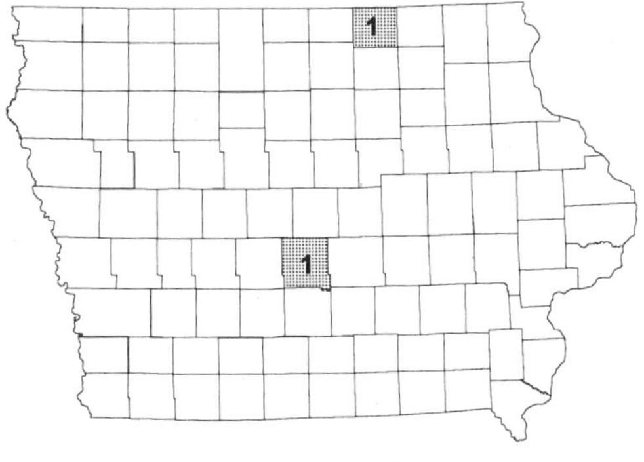

Boreal Chickadee, all

Tufted Titmouse (*Parus bicolor*)

Status: Regular; nests

Jan	Feb	Mar	Apr	May	Jun	Jul	Aug	Sep	Oct	Nov	Dec

Occurrence: This common permanent resident of woodlands and wooded river valleys in southern and eastern Iowa is absent from most of northwestern Iowa (Jackson et al. 1996, map). Tufted Titmice are found on about 70 percent of the Christmas Bird Counts with greatest numbers near the Mississippi River and fewest in northern and western Iowa. Tufted Titmice are found on about half of the Breeding Bird Surveys in southern and eastern Iowa and are rare elsewhere in the state.

At the beginning of the Twentieth Century, Tufted Titmice were rare permanent residents in southern Iowa with only a few records in northern Iowa (Anderson 1907). By the 1930s, this species was common in southern Iowa and expanding northward (DuMont 1933). The number per party on selected Christmas Bird Counts declined from 1955 to 1974 (Brown 1975).

Comment: The range of this permanent resident is from eastern Nebraska and southeastern Minnesota east to New England and south to the Gulf Coast and northeastern Mexico. In Wisconsin, the first titmouse was found in 1900, and there were population expansions in the 1920s and in the 1950s to early 1960s, followed by a probable decline since 1964 (Robbins 1991). In Minnesota, there was a northward expansion of range from the southeastern corner from the 1940s to the mid-1970s, followed by a retraction of the range (Janssen 1987). In both states, scattered records occur north of regular locations. There are only a few records from southeastern South Dakota and only 1 nesting record (South Dakota Ornithologists' Union 1991).

Reference:

Brown, W. H. 1975. Population changes in the Tufted Titmouse and Black-capped Chickadee. *Iowa Bird Life* 45:97.

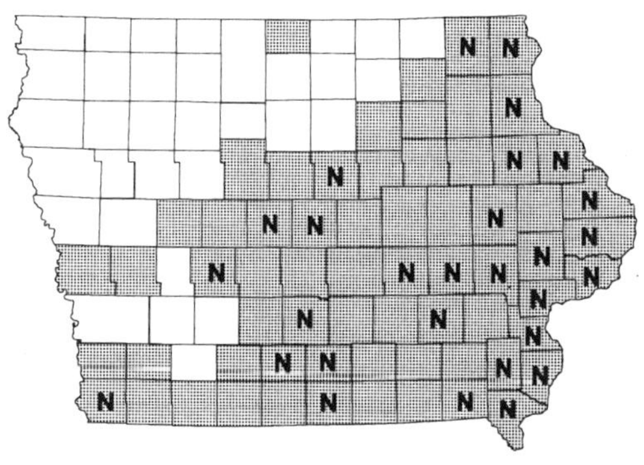

Tufted Titmouse
Summer and nesting (N)

Nuthatches (Family Sittidae)

Nuthatches comprise 25 species, with 4 from North America and 3 from Iowa. These small, plump arboreal birds have short tails, short legs, and long toes, features that allow them to climb in all directions. They nest in holes. Of the Iowa species, 1 is a common permanent resident, 1 is an eruptive migrant and winter resident, and 1 is Accidental.

Red-breasted Nuthatch (*Sitta canadensis*)

Status: Regular; occasionally nests

Jan	Feb	Mar	Apr	May	Jun	Jul	Aug	Sep	Oct	Nov	Dec

Summer: 9, 17 Jul 1978, 30 Jun to 25 Jul 1985, 7 Jul 1985, 15 Jul 1985, 29 Jun 1993
Nesting record: 20 to 26 May 1958, Des Moines, Polk Co., nest with yg. (Warters 1960)

Occurrence: This rare to uncommon winter resident is found in woodlands, especially conifer stands, and frequently comes to feeders. It usually arrives in late September or October and departs in late April or early May; however, some birds may arrive by mid-August and depart in late May, especially in invasion years. Red-breasted Nuthatches are found on about half of Iowa's Christmas Bird Counts. The number found is similar throughout the state but varies greatly from year to year. Many were found in 1983-1984, 1986-1987, 1989-1990, and 1995-1996.

The only nesting record is from Des Moines in Polk County, where adults were feeding young in a post from 20 to 26 May 1958 (Warters 1960, photo). Of the 5 June-July records, 3 were from 1985 (*IBL* 55:93). The 17 July 1978 record involved 3 birds at Des Moines in Polk County (*IBL* 48:99).

Comment: The winter range is across North America from southern Canada south to the central United States. The breeding range is in coniferous forest from central Canada south to the northern United States and south to North Carolina in the East and to southern Arizona and New Mexico in the West.

Based on Christmas Bird Count data, large numbers of Red-breasted Nuthatches invade the United States every 2 or 3 years, most likely in response to a crash of their normal food supply in the North (Bock and Lepthien 1972). The most recent such invasion in Iowa was in fall 1995 (*IBL* 66:23).

References:

Bock, C. E., and L. W. Lepthien. 1972. Winter eruptions of Red-breasted Nuthatches in North America, 1950-1970. *Amer. Birds* 26:558-561.

Warters, M. E. 1960. Red-breasted Nuthatches nest in Des Moines. *Iowa Bird Life* 30:17.

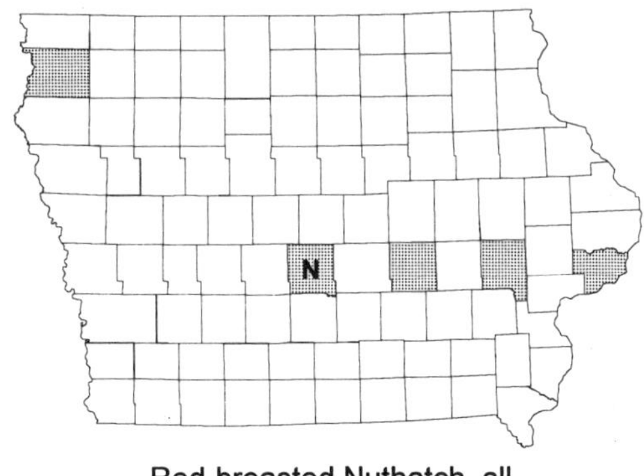

Red-breasted Nuthatch, all June-July and nesting (N)

White-breasted Nuthatch (*Sitta carolinensis*)

Status: Regular; nests

Jan	Feb	Mar	Apr	May	Jun	Jul	Aug	Sep	Oct	Nov	Dec

Occurrence: This common permanent resident is found in wooded habitats throughout Iowa. It is found on all Christmas Bird Counts, with highest counts in the middle third and lowest counts in southern Iowa. The number found per party hour increased steadily to 1986, peaked again in 1989, and then dropped steadily.

Comment: The range of this permanent resident is from southern Canada south to northern Mexico and the Gulf Coast. It is not found in parts of the southern Great Plains.

Pygmy Nuthatch (*Sitta pygmaea*)

Status: Accidental

26 Jan to 15 Apr 1977, Des Moines, Polk Co. (P-0014, Brooke 1977, Norris 1977, Petersen and Halmi 1977)

Occurrence: There is 1 winter record. Distinction from Brown-headed Nuthatch was based on gray-brown rather than brown cap, amount of white in wings and tail, voice, and response to taped calls.

Comment: This species inhabits Ponderosa pine and, less frequently, pinyon-juniper forests, in the mountainous west from British Columbia to central Mexico and east to the Black Hills, the Oklahoma panhandle, and mountains of western Texas. It seldom wanders from its nesting range, with 1 record from northeastern Texas (Oberholser 1974), 4 from eastern Kansas (Thompson and Ely 1992), and 1 from Iowa.

References:

Brooke, M. 1977. A new Iowa record: A Pygmy Nuthatch (*Sitta pygmaea*) in Des Moines. *Iowa Bird Life* 47:24.

Norris, B. 1977. Letter to P. C. Petersen.

Petersen, P. C., and N. S. Halmi. 1977. Editor's and Field Report Editor's comments on the Pygmy Nuthatch. *Iowa Bird Life* 47:24-25.

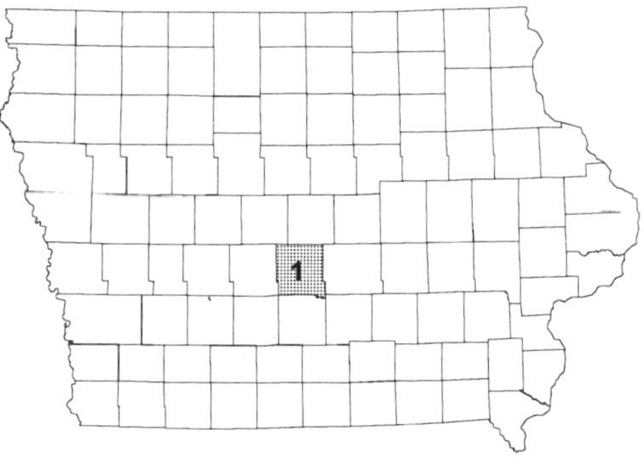

Pygmy Nuthatch, all

Creepers (Family Certhiidae)

Creepers comprise 7 species, with 1 in North America and Iowa. These small, brown birds with decurved bill, long claws, and stiff tail feathers creep upward on trunks and branches as they seek food. They nest in holes or behind lose bark.

Brown Creeper (*Certhia americana*)

Status: Regular; nests

Jan	Feb	Mar	Apr	May	Jun	Jul	Aug	Sep	Oct	Nov	Dec

Occurrence: This uncommon migrant and winter resident and rare summer resident is found in woodlands, especially bottomland woods. Fall migration is from late September to late October, and spring migration is from mid-April to early May. Brown Creepers are found on three-fourths of the Christmas Bird Counts. They are most commonly found near the Mississippi and Missouri rivers where they occurred on more than 90 percent of the counts. The number found varies greatly from year to year.

Most of the summer records are from the floodplain of the Mississippi River. Nesting was confirmed at 2 sites in Allamakee County in 1978 (Schaufenbuel 1979) and in Des Moines County in 1985 and 1987 (*IBL* 55:93, 57:122). Creepers have also nested in Boone and Bremer counties (Faaborg 1969, Schaufenbuel 1979). Birds in Johnson and Warren counties in July 1994 could have been nesting (*IBL* 64:110). A few probably nest along the Mississippi River and perhaps along some of its tributaries in most years. Historically, the only record of nesting was near Davenport in Scott County in 1891 (Wilson 1893).

Comment: The winter range includes most of the United States except for the northern Great Lakes and northern Rocky Mountains, and in the West, extends north to southern Alaska and the southern Prairie Provinces and south to northern Mexico. In the West, the breeding range and winter range overlap, but in the East, this species moves north to southern Canada and the northern edge of the United States. The breeding range includes northern Wisconsin and northeastern Minnesota, but in both states it extends as a narrow ribbon down along the Mississippi River to Iowa. Iowa is at the southern edge of its breeding range.

References:

Faaborg, J. 1969. Notes on the summer birds of Boone County. *Iowa Bird Life* 39:45.

Wilson, B. H. 1893. Nesting of the Brown Creeper. *Oologist* 10:260.

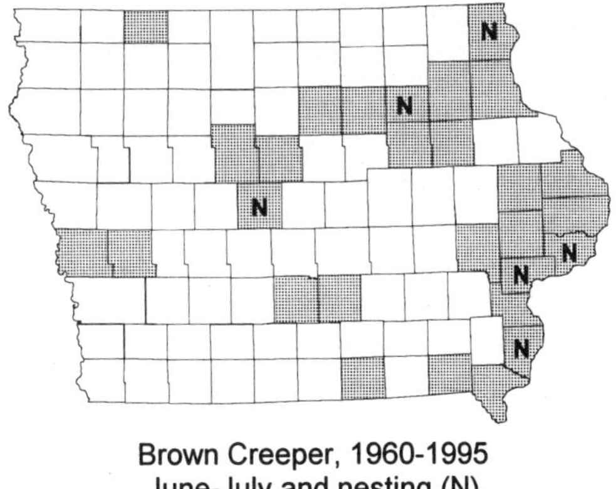

Brown Creeper, 1960-1995
June-July and nesting (N)

Wrens (Family Troglodytidae)

Wrens comprise 75 species, with 9 from North America and 7 from Iowa. These small, active, plain birds have a slender, curved bill adapted for probing; short legs with long claws; and short tails. All are confined to the New World except for Winter Wren, and most are tropical. Some species build multiple nests. They roost in a sheltered nook, socially in winter.

Of the Iowa species, 6 are Regular and 1 is Casual. Of the Regular species, 4 are summer residents and 1 is a permanent resident; and 2 are found in marshes or fields and 3 are woodland and edge species.

Rock Wren (*Salpinctes obsoletus*)

Status: Casual; formerly nested

By year since 1960 (also 1910)

60 63 66 69 72 75 78 81 84 87 90 93

1 2 1 1 1

By month -- all records

Jan	Feb	Mar	Apr	May	Jun	Jul	Aug	Sep	Oct	Nov	Dec

1 1 1 1 1 1 + 1 +

Records:

1 Apr 1910, Sioux City, Woodbury Co. (Bennett 1925)

21 May 1984, near Sioux City, Woodbury Co. (P-0402, Kent and Silcock 1984)

30 Oct 1986, Cedar Rapids, Linn Co. (Fye and Fye 1987)

22 Nov to 8 Dec 1986, Saylorville Res., Polk Co. (P-0207, Padelford and Padelford 1987)

8 to 28 Nov 1988, Saylorville Res., Polk Co. (P-0267, Dinsmore 1989)

17 Sep 1991, Red Oak, Montgomery Co., 2 (Carlisle 1992)

25 Apr 1993, Indianola, Warren Co. (P-0383, Johnson 1994)

Nesting record:

25 Jun 1898, Sioux City, Woodbury Co., nest with eggs (Anderson 1907, Bennett 1925)

Occurrence: There are 7 Accepted records, 3 from spring and 4 from fall. Birds have been found in rock outcroppings, bank cuts, rock facing, and in a garage.

There are also a number of old records from the Sioux City area in Woodbury County that, although undocumented, are likely correct. Guy Rich had notes on a nest that contained eggs that were about to hatch. The nest was taken near Riverside (western part of Sioux City) by Stanley Hills on 25 Jun 1898 (Bennett 1925). Rich also saw birds in 1899, 1900, 1901, and had measurements of 2 birds shot on 22 June 1898 (Anderson 1907).

Other likely, but Not Accepted records include 3 on 10 Aug 1941 east of Hornick in Woodbury County (Laffoon 1942) and a singing male north of Sioux City in Plymouth County on 16 June 1958 (Youngworth 1958). Three other old records are more questionable (Dinsmore et al. 1984).

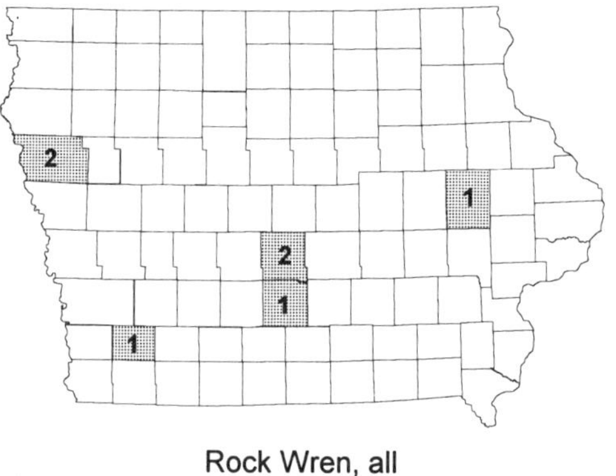

Rock Wren, all

Comment: This species of western, arid, rocky habitat breeds from southern British Columbia south to Central America, east to western North Dakota, and south to central Texas. In winter, it withdraws from the northeastern part of the range north of Oklahoma and east of Oregon.

Minnesota, Illinois, and Missouri have a vagrancy pattern similar to Iowa, but farther east there are only a few records from Ontario, Ohio, Kentucky, Tennessee, Alabama, Florida, Massachusetts, and Nova Scotia. There are vagrant records in all months, but three-fourths are from September to December with most in October, and there is a smaller peak in May. Nest building was noted in northwestern Minnesota in 1984 (Janssen 1987).

References:

Bennett, W. W. 1925. The Rock Wren in Iowa. *Wilson Bull.* 37:93.

Carlisle, D. 1992. Rock Wrens in Montgomery County. *Iowa Bird Life* 62:85-86.

Dinsmore, S. J. 1989. Rock Wren at Saylorville Reservoir. *Iowa Bird Life* 59:22.

Fye, D., and H. Fye. 1987. Rock Wren at Cedar Rapids. *Iowa Bird Life* 57:61.

Johnson, A. 1994. Rock Wren in Warren County. *Iowa Bird Life* 64:81-82.

Kent, T. H., and W. R. Silcock. 1984. Rock Wren in Woodbury County. *Iowa Bird Life* 54:37-38.

Laffoon, J. 1942. Some recent bird records in the Sioux City area. *Iowa Bird Life* 12:61.

Padelford, L., and B. Padelford. 1987. Rock Wren at Saylorville Reservoir. *Iowa Bird Life* 57:62.

Youngworth, W. 1958. Rock Wren near Sioux City. *Iowa Bird Life* 28:60.

Carolina Wren (*Thryothorus ludovicianus*)

Status: Regular; nests

Jan	Feb	Mar	Apr	May	Jun	Jul	Aug	Sep	Oct	Nov	Dec

Occurrence: This rare to locally uncommon permanent resident of wooded ravines and bottomland forest is most common in southern and eastern Iowa. The more northerly records are generally along major rivers. The Iowa population undergoes long cyclical changes. Most of the population may be wiped out during winters that are very cold or have deep snow cover, and many years may be required for recovery. The relatively few reports of nesting (map) underestimate the extent of nesting.

The cyclical population change is well illustrated by Christmas Bird Count data (chart). Only a few cycles are evident in 36 years. Most of Iowa's Carolina Wrens disappeared after the severe winters of 1978-1979 and again in 1984-1985. Since then, the population has increased steadily.

Comment: The Carolina Wren is a permanent resident from Nebraska and Iowa east to Massachusetts and south to the Gulf Coast and northern Central America. Iowa is at the northern edge of its range.

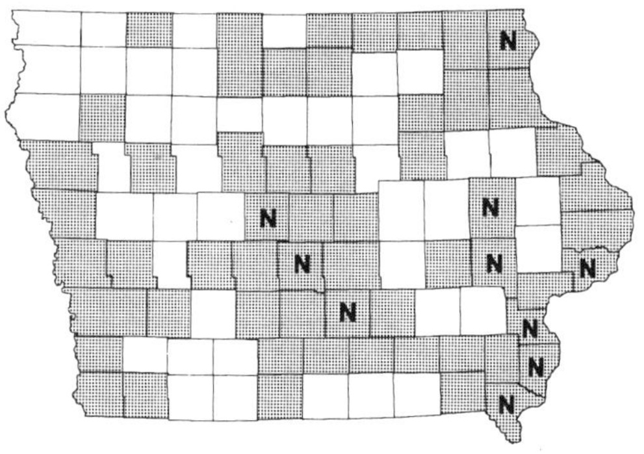

Carolina Wren, 1960-1995
Locations and nesting (N)

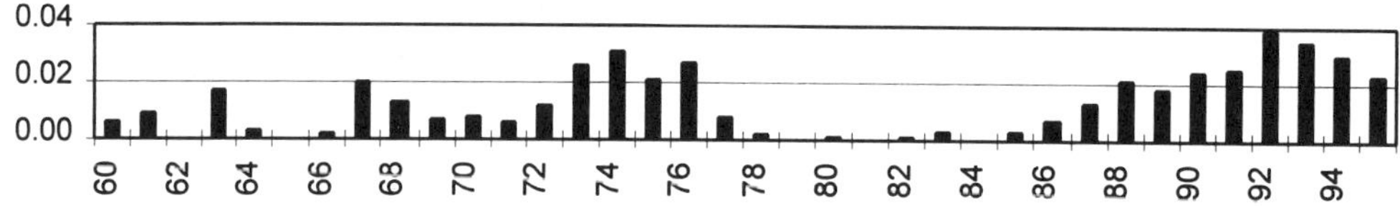

Carolina Wren, birds per party-hour on Christmas Bird Counts, 1960-1995

Bewick's Wren (*Thryomanes bewickii*)

Status: Regular; nests

By year since 1960 (49 records 1890 to 1959)

60	63	66	69	72	75	78	81	84	87	90	93
2 1 1	3	1 3	1 2	1 1 4	1 2 1	1	2 2 2	2 2	1 1	1 3 2	1 2

Jan	Feb	Mar	Apr	May	Jun	Jul	Aug	Sep	Oct	Nov	Dec
		x							x		xx

15 Mar 1939
21 Mar 1953
23 Mar 1964

29 Oct 1925
late Dec 1960
28 Dec 1973

Occurrence: This rare summer resident is found in thick brushy habitats mainly in southeastern Iowa. Some may arrive by late March, and they probably leave by September; however, there are few records after June. The record from 15 Mar 1939 at Fairfield in Jefferson County is of a bird that was fluttering at a door at 5:00 a.m. and was let inside and captured (Dole 1939). A report from 28 February 1953 at Iowa City in Johnson County by Peter P. Laude (Serbousek 1959) cannot be verified, but this species was resident near his home in the 1950s. There are 2 winter reports: at Cedar Falls in Black Hawk County until at least 28 December 1973 (Konig 1974) and at Davenport in Scott County in late December 1960 (*IBL* 31:10).

The pattern of records since the 1890s has been rather consistent—scattered records in each decade with only a few in any year, mostly from southeastern Iowa, with a few in other areas of the state. The first nests were found at Burlington in Des Moines County in 1892 and 1893 (Bartsch 1897, Anderson 1907), and nesting has been confirmed since then for 8 additional counties, the most recent in Iowa County in 1995 (*IBL* 65:99). The only known specimen from 19 Apr 1895 at Hillsboro in Henry County is at the American Museum of Natural History (DuMont 1933, M. LeCroy 1995—personal communication). There are photographs of a bird at a nest in Johnson County on 25 June 1950 (Kent 1950) and of a bird netted at Pioneer Ridge Park in Wapello County in May 1982 (*IBL* 52:92).

Currently, the most reliable location for this species is near the Croton Unit in Lee County, although it can be found at other locations and, undoubtedly, occurs at locations where it is not discovered. There was a small resident population at Iowa City in Johnson County from 1949 to 1961 that abruptly disappeared (Kent and Kent 1974).

Comment: The breeding range in the West is from the central United States to central Mexico with a northward coastal extension to southern British Columbia. In the East, the breeding range is across central states east to Pennsylvania. This species is regular in the Ozarks and irregular or casual north to Minnesota and Wisconsin. In the West, the winter range overlaps much of the breeding range. In the East, birds move south to the Gulf Coast states, although a few may winter north to the Ozarks. There has been a general decline in this species across eastern United States in the past several decades (Robbins et al. 1986).

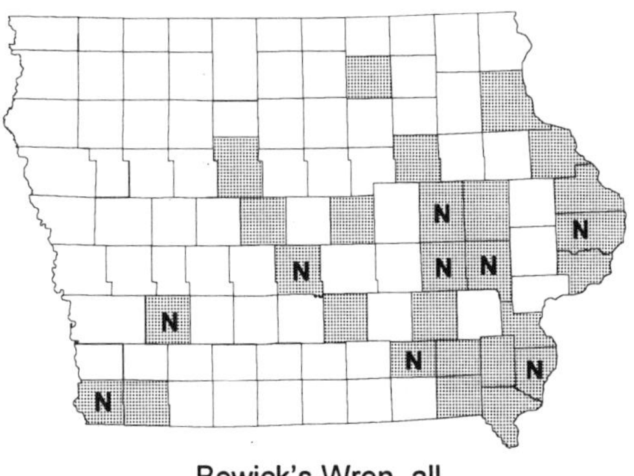

Bewick's Wren, all Locations and nesting (N)

References:

Bartsch, P. 1897. The wrens of Burlington, Iowa. *Iowa Ornithologist* 3:21-23.

Dole, J. W. 1939. Bewick's Wren at Fairfield in March. *Iowa Bird Life* 9:28.

Kent, F. W. 1950. Nesting Bewick's Wren near Iowa City. *Iowa Bird Life* 20:62.

Konig, M. E. 1974. A wintering Bewick's Wren in Cedar Falls. *Iowa Bird Life* 44:25.

House Wren (*Troglodytes aedon*)

Status: Regular; nests

Jan	Feb	Mar	Apr	May	Jun	Jul	Aug	Sep	Oct	Nov	Dec
x									x	x	x

7 Apr 1980
7 Apr 1991
9 Apr 1986
winter: 22 Dec 1979, 4 Jan 1975

25 Oct 1971
31 Oct 1980
7 Nov 1974

Occurrence: This abundant summer resident is found in wooded areas with thick underbrush throughout Iowa. Migrants arrive in late April or early May and depart in mid- or late September. House Wrens were found on nearly all of the Breeding Bird Surveys, with the greatest numbers in northeastern and western Iowa.

The only winter records are from Yellow River Forest in Allamakee County on 22 December 1979 (*IBL* 50:11) and from Keokuk in Lee County on 4 January 1975 (*Amer. Birds* 29:699).

Comment: The winter range is from the southern United States south through Mexico. The breeding range is from southern Canada to the southern United States and south into Mexico. Another form is resident in Central and South America and the West Indies.

Winter Wren (*Troglodytes troglodytes*)

Status: Regular; occasionally nests

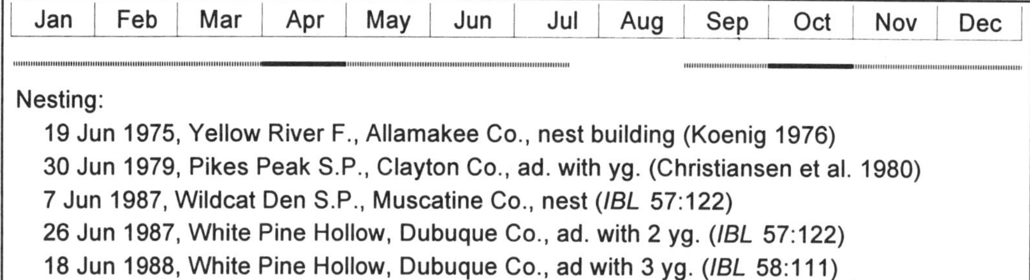

Jan | Feb | Mar | Apr | May | Jun | Jul | Aug | Sep | Oct | Nov | Dec

Nesting:
19 Jun 1975, Yellow River F., Allamakee Co., nest building (Koenig 1976)
30 Jun 1979, Pikes Peak S.P., Clayton Co., ad. with yg. (Christiansen et al. 1980)
7 Jun 1987, Wildcat Den S.P., Muscatine Co., nest (*IBL* 57:122)
26 Jun 1987, White Pine Hollow, Dubuque Co., ad. with 2 yg. (*IBL* 57:122)
18 Jun 1988, White Pine Hollow, Dubuque Co., ad with 3 yg. (*IBL* 58:111)

Occurrence: This uncommon migrant and rare summer and winter resident is found in wooded habitats throughout Iowa. Most migrants are seen in April and October. In addition to the nesting reports listed above, there are only a few other summer records (map).

The Winter Wren is reported on about 20 percent of Christmas Bird Counts, most commonly near the Mississippi River where it was found on about half of the counts. The number found varies greatly from year to year.

From 1960 to 1995, there were 15 reports from January and February at widely scattered locations. The most reliable winter location is at the base of the rocky bluffs at Burlington in Des Moines County, where this species was first noted to over-winter in the 1890s (Bartsch 1897). Over-wintering birds may be more common than the data indicates, and some are known to go unreported.

Comment: The winter range is from southern Alaska east to Massachusetts and south to southern United States. The breeding range is from Alaska east to Newfoundland and south to the northern United States. Winter Wren is also found in much of Europe, Asia, and northern Africa.

The breeding range in Minnesota and Wisconsin is in the northern parts of those states, although there are summer records in southeastern Minnesota and southwestern Wisconsin.

References:

Bartsch, P. 1897. The wrens of Burlington, Iowa. *Iowa Ornithologist* 3:21-23.

Christiansen, P., H. Hadow, and E. Hinman. 1980. *Natural resources inventory of Pikes Peak/Point and State Park, Clayton County, Iowa.* Report submitted to the Iowa Conservation Commission, Des Moines.

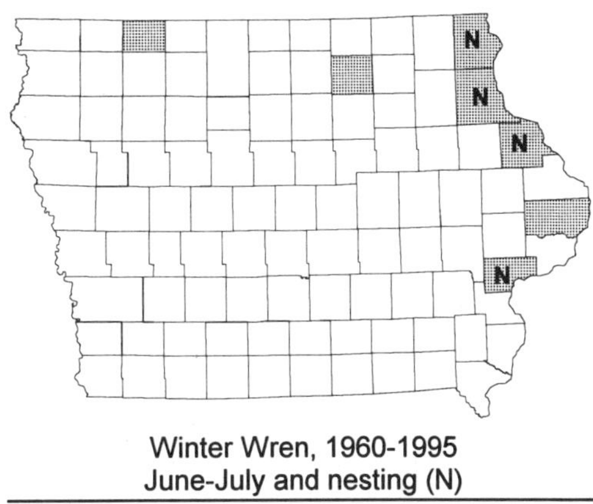

Winter Wren, 1960-1995
June-July and nesting (N)

Sedge Wren (*Cistothorus platensis*)

Status: Regular; nests

Jan	Feb	Mar	Apr	May	Jun	Jul	Aug	Sep	Oct	Nov	Dec
									XX	X	XX

20 Apr 1990 — 26 Oct 1989
25 Apr 1982 — 30 Oct 1982
25 Apr 1996 — 15 Nov 1977
winter: 20 Dec 1980, 20 Dec 1986, 26 Dec 1932

Occurrence: This uncommon migrant and summer resident is found in sedge meadows, wet prairies, and thick grass cover throughout Iowa. Migrants arrive in early May and depart in late September. Although this species may be locally conspicuous, there are few actual nests reported, and the time of egg laying is among the most unusual of all Iowa birds. Many nests are started in June (Crawford 1977) but more often, territorial birds are still active in July or August, making this among the latest nesting species in Iowa.

There are 3 winter records, all found on Christmas Bird Counts: at Des Moines in Polk County on 26 December 1932 (*Bird-Lore* 35:45) and at Cedar Rapids in Linn County on 20 December 1980 (*IBL* 51:3) and on 20 December 1986 (*IBL* 57:46, 47).

Comment: The winter range is in coastal states from the mid-Atlantic Coast and the Gulf Coast south to northern Mexico. The breeding range is from Saskatchewan east to New England and south to the central United States. Another population is resident in southern Mexico, Central America, and parts of South America.

There are occasional December records in nearby states, but 1 in Mower County in Minnesota, which is on the Iowa border, was very late on 25 January 1981 (Janssen 1987).

Reference:
Crawford, R. D. 1977. Polygynous breeding of Short-billed Marsh Wrens. *Auk* 94:359-362.

Marsh Wren (*Cistothorus palustris*)

Status: Regular; nests

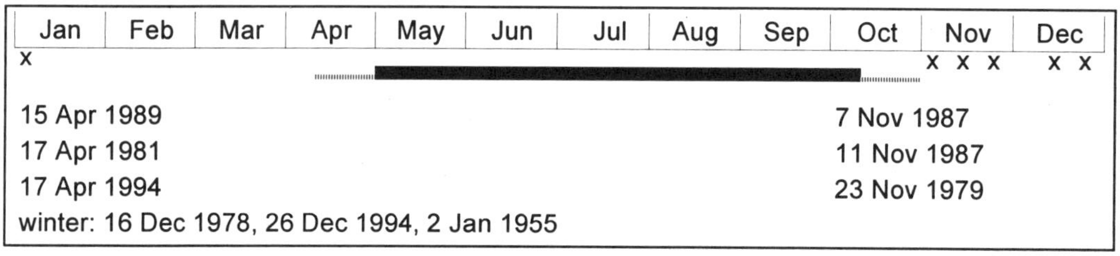

Jan	Feb	Mar	Apr	May	Jun	Jul	Aug	Sep	Oct	Nov	Dec
x										x x x	x x

15 Apr 1989 — 7 Nov 1987
17 Apr 1981 — 11 Nov 1987
17 Apr 1994 — 23 Nov 1979
winter: 16 Dec 1978, 26 Dec 1994, 2 Jan 1955

Occurrence: This uncommon migrant and summer resident is found in wetlands with thick stands of emergent vegetation throughout Iowa. Migrants arrive in early May and depart in early October. Marsh Wrens are locally common in north-central and northwestern Iowa and nest sparingly elsewhere. At Swan Lake in Johnson County, nests were active into early August (Kent 1952).

The 3 late birds were singles found on Christmas Bird Counts: 2 January 1955 at Des Moines in Polk County (*IBL* 25:7), 16 December 1978 on the Shenandoah count (*IBL* 49:10, 17), and 26 December 1994 at Riverton Area in Fremont County (*IBL* 65:50). Another on 2 January 1994 at Brown's Lake in Woodbury County was probably of this species (*IBL* 64:50, 65:82).

Comment: The winter range is from the western and southern United States to northern Mexico. The breeding range is from southern Canada south to the southern United States and northern Mexico. There are a few winter records from nearby states.

The song patterns of Marsh Wrens in eastern and western North America are different. The western form is found as far east as central Nebraska (Kroodsma 1989). It is possible that the western form may rarely migrate through or even nest in western Iowa.

References:
Kent, F. W. 1952. Notes on the Prairie Marsh Wren at Swan Lake in 1951. *Iowa Bird Life* 22:12-13.
Kroodsma, D. E. 1989. Two North American song populations of the Marsh Wren reach distributional limits in the central Great Plains. *Condor* 91:332-340.

Muscicapids (Family Muscicapidae)

This large family can be divided into several subfamilies, 2 of which have representatives in Iowa; however, gnatcatchers and kinglets are separated from Old World warblers and from each other in recent world lists (Clements 1991, Monroe and Sibley 1993). Old World warblers, Old World flycatchers, and thrushes are very large families or subfamilies, with several North American vagrants in each group, especially to Alaska.

Old World Warblers, Kinglets, and Gnatcatchers (Subfamily Sylviinae)

Kinglets comprise 6 species, with 2 from North America and 2 from Iowa. Gnatcatchers comprise 15 species, with 5 from North America and 1 from Iowa. The Old World warblers comprise 267 species, with 5 from North America and none from Iowa.

Golden-crowned Kinglet (*Regulus satrapa*)

Status: Regular

Jan	Feb	Mar	Apr	May	Jun	Jul	Aug	Sep	Oct	Nov	Dec
				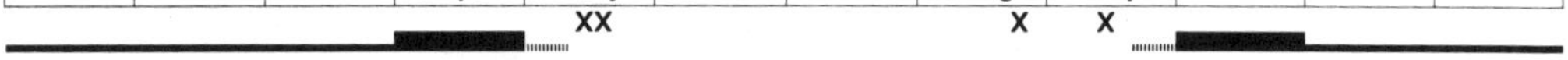 XX			X	X			

8 May 1983	31 Aug 1972
12 May 1987	18 Sep 1986
15 May 1960	21 Sep 1969

Occurrence: This uncommon migrant and rare winter resident arrives in early October and most depart by early November. In spring, migrants arrive in early April and depart in late April. In spring, males tend to arrive before females (Crim 1976).

This species is reported on about half of the Christmas Bird Counts, most commonly from near the Mississippi and Missouri rivers where it is found on about 80 percent of the counts. The number found varies greatly from year to year with almost none some years and fair numbers in others. Golden-crowned Kinglets are reported from January to March, but the data are sketchy and make it difficult to judge how many birds over-winter in Iowa.

Comment: The winter range is from southern Canada south to the Gulf Coast and northern Central America. The breeding range is from Alaska east to Newfoundland south in the mountains to North Carolina and Central America, but, otherwise, south only to northern Minnesota and Wisconsin.

Ruby-crowned Kinglet (*Regulus calendula*)

Status: Regular

Jan	Feb	Mar	Apr	May	Jun	Jul	Aug	Sep	Oct	Nov	Dec
XX	X				X	X	X X				

22 Mar 1980	27 May 1990	6 Aug 1986	23 Dec 1984
22 Mar 1987	27 May 1989	16 Aug 1965	1 Jan 1981
26 Mar 1985	29 May 1974	24 Aug 1977	10 Jan 1964

summer: 24-25 Jun and 24 Jul 1972, 23-24 Jul 1972
winter: 11 Feb 1986

Occurrence: This common migrant is usually found from mid-April to mid-May and mid-September to late October. In spring, most birds seen through mid-April were males, while later arrivals were predominantly females (Crim 1976).

Ruby-crowned Kinglets were reported on Christmas Bird Counts in 27 of 36 years from 1960 to 1995, with an average of 2 counts per year in those years. They were seen on 4 to 6 counts in 1962, 1973, 1974, 1984, and 1993. From 1 to 5 were reported per count, most often 1. There are only 2 reports from January and 1 from February.

The only summer reports are singles at Shenandoah in Page County on 24, 25 June and 24 July 1972 and at Iowa City in Johnson County on 23, 24 July 1972 (*IBL* 42:70).

Comment: The winter range is from the southern United States south to northern Central America. The breeding range is from Alaska east to Newfoundland and south to the northern United States. In the West, it breeds south almost to Mexico. In northern Minnesota and Wisconsin, the breeding range is similar to that of the Golden-crowned Kinglet.

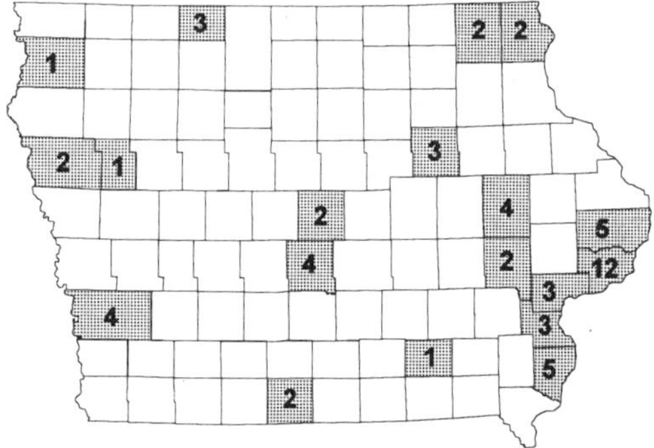

Ruby-crowned Kinglet, 1960-1995
Christmas Bird Counts, years found

Blue-gray Gnatcatcher (*Polioptila caerulea*)

Status: Regular; nests

Jan	Feb	Mar	Apr	May	Jun	Jul	Aug	Sep	Oct	Nov	Dec
										x	

Early dates	Late dates
5 Apr 1981	24 Sep 1978
9 Apr 1988	26 Sep 1993
9 Apr 1996	13 Nov 1964

Occurrence: This fairly common migrant and summer resident may be found in thick woodlands in most areas of the state, but is more common in eastern and central Iowa. It arrives in late April and departs in early or mid-September. It is much less common in northwestern Iowa, where it occurs only in large wooded tracts.

Comment: The winter range is from the southern United States to the West Indies and northern Central America. The breeding range is from Oregon east to New England and south to the Gulf coast and southern Mexico. It breeds north to central Wisconsin and east-central Minnesota. There are November records from Missouri and Wisconsin.

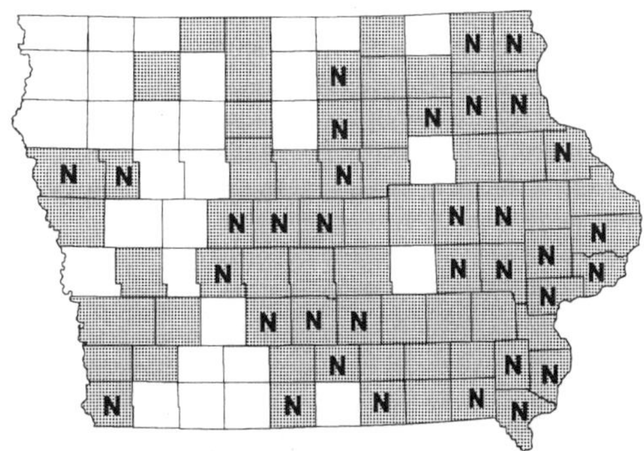

Blue-gray Gnatcatcher, 1960-1995
June-July and nesting (N)

Solitaires, Thrushes, and Allies (Subfamily Turdinae)

Thrushes comprise 177 species, with 21 from North America and 10 from Iowa. Thrushes tend to be larger and plumper than Old World warblers and flycatchers. They eat a varied diet and are often found on the ground. Juveniles are spotted.

Of the Iowa species, 9 are Regular and 1 is Casual. There are 4 nesting species (Eastern Bluebird, Veery, Wood Thrush, American Robin), 2 that are only seen in migration (Gray-cheeked and Swainson's thrushes), and 6 that may be found in winter (Eastern and Mountain bluebirds, Townsend's Solitaire, Hermit Thrush, American Robin, Varied Thrush).

Of the plain-gray to brown thrushes, only Hermit is expected to occur in winter, and only Veery and Wood Thrush are expected to occur in summer. Gray-cheeked and Swainson's thrushes are strictly migrants. Birds seen out of season, or even at early or late dates, need to be very well substantiated, if that is possible. Mid-summer or mid-winter birds may need a specimen, a netted bird with photographs and measurements, or a recording of call notes or song to be accepted as a valid record. For example, Florida has no acceptable mid-winter records of Veery or Gray-cheeked Thrush, and only 1 of Swainson's Thrush—a dead bird that had been banded in Massachusetts (Stevenson and Anderson 1994). Most of the thrushes have eastern and western subspecies that differ in color, which makes field identification difficult.

Eastern Bluebird (*Sialia sialis*)

Status: Regular; nests

Occurrence: This species is a common migrant and summer resident and a rare winter resident. Migrants may arrive as early as late February and depart as late as November. Eastern Bluebirds are found on about half of the Breeding Bird Surveys, most often from northeastern and southern Iowa. The number found on these routes increased from 11.6 per year from 1975 to 1984 to 38.2 per year from 1985 to 1994.

Eastern Bluebirds are reported on about 25 percent of the Christmas Bird Counts, with numbers varying greatly from year to year. Most are found near the Missouri and Mississippi rivers and in southern Iowa, and although many of these may leave the state after the count, at least a few over-winter.

Historically, the Eastern Bluebird was considered a common summer resident throughout Iowa (Anderson 1907, DuMont 1933). By the mid-1970s, numbers had declined considerably, making it uncommon. Since then, numbers have increased considerably, at least in part due to the numerous nest boxes that have been provided. In 1986, 36 percent of 2,447 nest boxes in 54 counties were occupied (Reeves and Efta 1987).

Comment: The winter range for migratory birds is from southern Iowa east to southern New England south to the Gulf Coast. The breeding range is from southern Saskatchewan east to Nova Scotia and south to the Gulf of Mexico and Nicaragua. Iowa is at the northern edge of the winter range. Birds in the southern part of the range are nonmigratory.

Reference:

Reeves, D. A., and R. Efta. 1987. Iowa bluebird nest box program for 1986. *Iowa Bird Life* 57:36-38.

Mountain Bluebird (*Sialia currucoides*)

Status: Casual

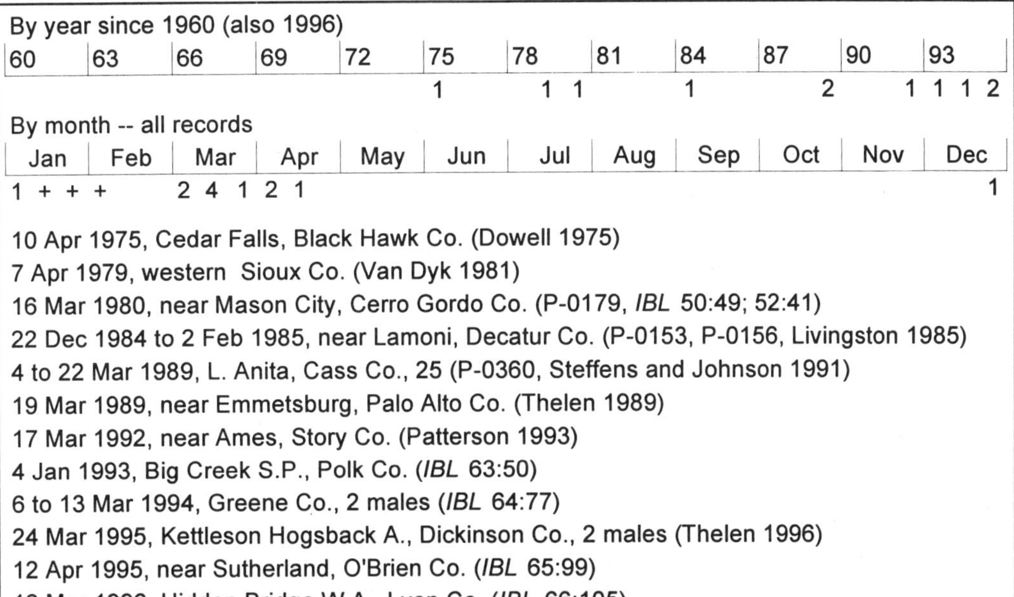

By year since 1960 (also 1996)

60	63	66	69	72	75	78	81	84	87	90	93
					1	1 1		1		2	1 1 1 2

By month -- all records

Jan	Feb	Mar	Apr	May	Jun	Jul	Aug	Sep	Oct	Nov	Dec
1 + + +		2 4 1 2 1									1

10 Apr 1975, Cedar Falls, Black Hawk Co. (Dowell 1975)
7 Apr 1979, western Sioux Co. (Van Dyk 1981)
16 Mar 1980, near Mason City, Cerro Gordo Co. (P-0179, *IBL* 50:49; 52:41)
22 Dec 1984 to 2 Feb 1985, near Lamoni, Decatur Co. (P-0153, P-0156, Livingston 1985)
4 to 22 Mar 1989, L. Anita, Cass Co., 25 (P-0360, Steffens and Johnson 1991)
19 Mar 1989, near Emmetsburg, Palo Alto Co. (Thelen 1989)
17 Mar 1992, near Ames, Story Co. (Patterson 1993)
4 Jan 1993, Big Creek S.P., Polk Co. (*IBL* 63:50)
6 to 13 Mar 1994, Greene Co., 2 males (*IBL* 64:77)
24 Mar 1995, Kettleson Hogsback A., Dickinson Co., 2 males (Thelen 1996)
12 Apr 1995, near Sutherland, O'Brien Co. (*IBL* 65:99)
12 Mar 1996, Hidden Bridge W.A., Lyon Co. (*IBL* 66:105)

Occurrence: Of the 12 records, 2 are from winter and 10 from March to April. The flock of 25 at Lake Anita in early March may have wintered.

Comment: This western species breeds north to east-central Alaska, the southern Yukon, and western Manitoba, east to the western edge of the Prairie States, and south to southern New Mexico. It winters from southern British Columbia, Nevada, southern Colorado, southwestern Kansas, western Oklahoma, and the Texas panhandle, south to northern Mexico. It is considered a regular migrant in western Minnesota, and a male paired with an Eastern Bluebird in east-central Minnesota in 1986 (Janssen 1987). There are more than 10 records each from Wisconsin and Ontario, with fewer from Missouri and Illinois. Farther east, there are records from Quebec, New York, Pennsylvania, New Jersey, Michigan, Kentucky, and Mississippi. The vagrant records are about equally divided between winter and spring.

In spring, this species may migrate with Eastern Bluebirds, and in winter it prefers areas with juniper trees and adjacent water. Unlike Eastern Bluebirds, Mountain Bluebirds often hover. Female bluebirds (Eastern, Western, and Mountain) present an identification challenge (Dunn 1981); however, in Iowa, occurrence of the Western Bluebird should be considered exceedingly unlikely.

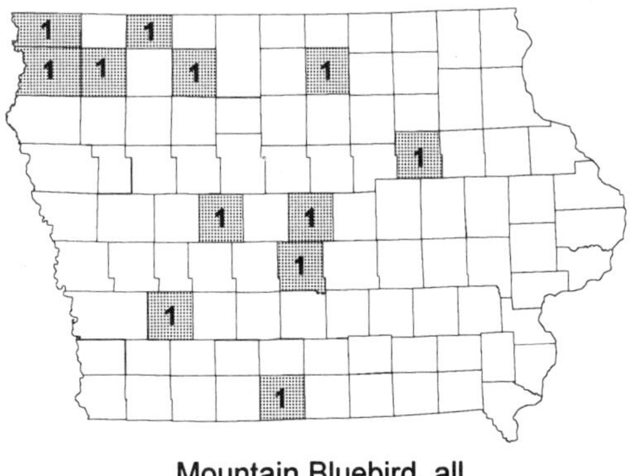

Mountain Bluebird, all

References:

Dowell, V. E. 1975. Mountain Bluebird at Cedar Falls. *Iowa Bird Life* 45:96.

Dunn, J. 1981. The identification of female bluebirds. *Birding* 13:4-11.

Livingston, J. R. 1985. Mountain Bluebird in Decatur County. *Iowa Bird Life* 55:19-20.

Patterson, M. 1993. Mountain Bluebird in Story County. *Iowa Bird Life* 63:102.

Steffens, S., and R. Johnson. 1991. Mountain Bluebirds at Lake Anita State Park. *Iowa Bird Life* 61:119-120.

Thelen, E. 1989. Mountain Bluebird in Palo Alto County. *Iowa Bird Life* 59:124.

Thelen, E. 1996. Mountain Bluebirds in Dickinson County. *Iowa Bird Life* 66:67-68.

Van Dyk, J. 1981. Mountain Bluebird in northwest Iowa. *Iowa Bird Life* 51:132.

Townsend's Solitaire (*Myadestes townsendi*)

Status: Regular

By year since 1960 (also 1954, 1956, 6 in 1958, 2 in 1996)

60	63	66	69	72	75	78	81	84	87	90	93
3		1	1 1	1	1 2 3	1 2	1	3 3	1 2	1 3 5	+ 2

Jan	Feb	Mar	Apr	May	Jun	Jul	Aug	Sep	Oct	Nov	Dec
			x x x	x xx					x xx x	x x	

6 May 1986 | 6 Oct 1968
16 May 1972 | 13 Oct 1989
17 May 1992 | 17 Oct 1970

Occurrence: Of the 47 records, 38 are from December through March; however, this species may arrive in October and remain until mid-May. There are 25 records from western Iowa, 13 from central Iowa, and 9 from eastern Iowa. This rare winter visitor from the West is found in Iowa almost every year, and presumably other undiscovered birds are present.

Townsend's Solitaire is usually found in clumps of junipers (Bock 1982) or other coniferous trees. Many of the Iowa birds have remained in the same area for weeks or months, where they respond readily to tape-recorded calls.

The first Iowa record was on 25 November 1954 at Eagle Point Park in Clinton County (Youngworth 1961). Subsequently, several were found in cemeteries in the Loess Hills in western Iowa (Youngworth 1957, 1959). The first photograph was of 1 that was netted at Shenandoah in Page County on 6 October 1968 (DeLong 1969).

Comment: The winter range is from southern British Columbia and Alberta south into Mexico and east to the Great Plains. The breeding range is from southern Alaska south through western Canada and western United States into northern Mexico.

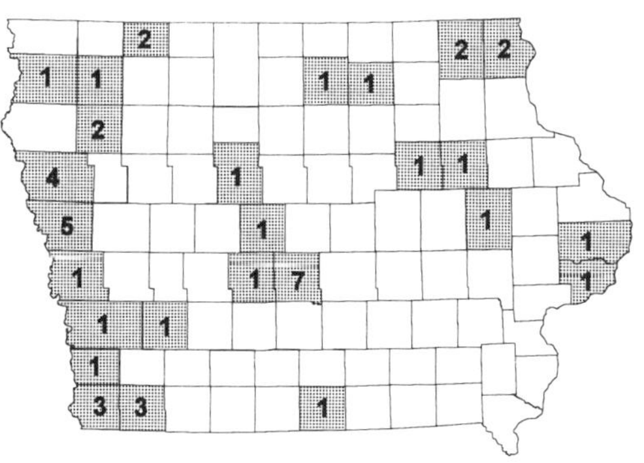

Townsend's Solitaire, all

Wintering birds occur across Canada and in the northeastern United States, but not to the southeast of Iowa. Missouri records are from the northwestern corner of that state. Minnesota has more records than Iowa, and Illinois and Wisconsin have fewer. In Minnesota, many records are in the southern half of the state near juniper groves, and many others are on the north shore of Lake Superior (Svingen 1993).

References:
Bock, C. E. 1982. Factors influencing winter distribution and abundance of Townsend's Solitaire. *Wilson Bull.* 94:297-302.
DeLong, Mrs. W. C. 1969. When you set your trap! *Iowa Bird Life* 39:41-43.
Svingen, P. 1993. The Townsend's Solitaire in Minnesota. *Loon* 65:110-115.
Youngworth, W. 1957. Townsend's Solitaire in Monona County. *Iowa Bird Life* 27:24-25.
Youngworth, W. 1959. Townsend's Solitaire in western Iowa. *Iowa Bird Life* 29:23-24.
Youngworth, W. 1961. A challenge to Iowa bird-spotters. *Iowa Bird Life* 31:74-76.

Veery (*Catharus fuscescens*)

Status: Regular; nests

Jan	Feb	Mar	Apr	May	Jun	Jul	Aug	Sep	Oct	Nov	Dec
			x					x	x		

30 Apr 1976	23 Sep 1966
1 May 1966	30 Sep 1970
3 May 1969	1 Oct 1976

Occurrence: This rare migrant and rarer summer resident arrives in mid-May and departs by mid-September. Although Veerys probably nest in woodlands, especially in eastern Iowa, there are only 2 confirmed nesting records (Faaborg 1969, Koenig 1979). There were no confirmed reports of nesting during the Breeding Bird Atlas project (Jackson et al. 1996). Veery is a secretive species, and, at least during the nesting season, it is heard more often than seen.

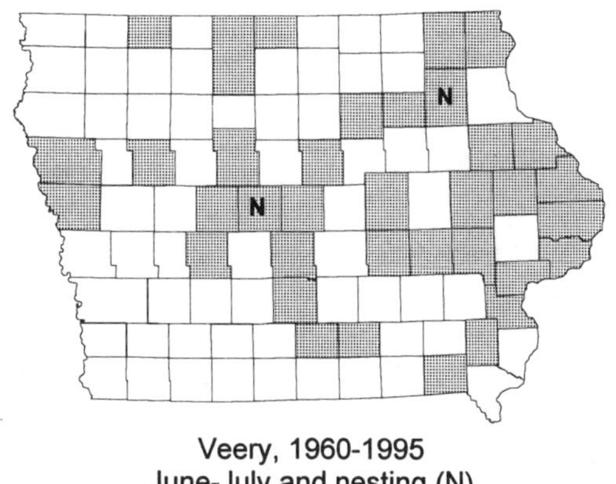

Veery, 1960-1995
June-July and nesting (N)

Comment: The winter range is in northern South America. The breeding range is from southern Canada south to the northern United States. Iowa is at the southern edge of the breeding range.

References:
Faaborg, J. 1969. Notes on the summer birds of Boone County. *Iowa Bird Life* 39:45.
Koenig, D. 1979. Acadian Flycatcher and Veery nests. *Iowa Bird Life* 49:27-28.

Gray-cheeked Thrush (*Catharus minimus*)

Status: Regular

Jan	Feb	Mar	Apr	May	Jun	Jul	Aug	Sep	Oct	Nov	Dec
							xx	x	xx		

22 Apr 1970	1 Jun 1968	14 Aug 1977	22 Sep 1994
25 Apr 1995	2 Jun 1984	17 Aug 1975	13 Oct 1989
26 Apr 1985	2 Jun 1967	22 Aug 1991	14 Oct 1969

Occurrence: This uncommon spring and rare fall migrant is usually found from early May to late May and from late August to mid-September. It is most often seen near the ground in wooded areas such as along paths in parks or in urban yards. In migration it is more common than Veery and less common than Swainson's Thrush.

Thrushes are much less frequently detected by birders in fall as compared to spring, but, compared to other species such as warblers, they make up an expected proportion of the specimens taken at fall tower kills (Mosman 1975, J. Dinsmore et al. 1983, S. Dinsmore et al. 1987).

Comment: The winter range is from Costa Rica south to northern South America. The breeding range is from eastern Siberia and Alaska across northern Canada to Newfoundland and south into the Great Lakes states. This is the most northerly of the migrant thrushes, with some breeding in the Arctic beyond the tree line.

Swainson's Thrush (*Catharus ustulatus*)

Status: Regular

Jan	Feb	Mar	Apr	May	Jun	Jul	Aug	Sep	Oct	Nov	Dec
									x	x x	

20 Apr 1967	3 Jun 1967	16 Aug 1986	30 Oct 1976
22 Apr 1966	3 Jun 1966	18 Aug 1986	6 Nov 1977
22 Apr 1970	4 Jun 1986	19 Aug 1975	14 Nov 1985

Occurrence: This common spring and uncommon fall migrant is usually found from early to late May and from late August to early October. There are undocumented reports from late December (*IBL* 44:5, 21) and mid-July (*IBL* 54:84).

Comment: The winter range is from southern Mexico south through much of South America. The breeding range is from southern Alaska east to Newfoundland and south to the central Rocky Mountains, the Great Lakes, and New England. There are single winter records from Minnesota (Janssen 1987) and Wisconsin (Robbins 1991), and 5, some poorly documented, from Illinois (Bohlen 1989). In summer, this species is not found south of its breeding grounds in northern Minnesota and Wisconsin.

Hermit Thrush (*Catharus guttatus*)

Status: Regular

Jan	Feb	Mar	Apr	May	Jun	Jul	Aug	Sep	Oct	Nov	Dec
								x x			
				11 May 1995		10 Sep 1985					
				12 May 1996		15 Sep 1964					
				13 May 1996		21 Sep 1986					

Occurrence: This uncommon migrant and rare winter resident is usually found during October and April. On Christmas Bird Counts, 41 birds on 41 different counts have been found in 22 of 36 years from 1960 to 1995, with 1 or 2 per year, except for 3 years with 3 birds and 1 year with 4. During the same period, there were only 12 additional winter reports from January and February.

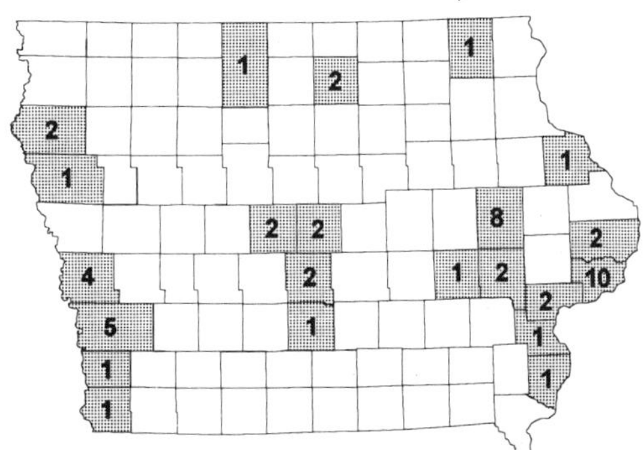

Hermit Thrush, 1960-1995
Christmas Bird Counts and January-February

Comment: The winter range is the southern half of the United States south to the Gulf Coast and Guatemala. Iowa is at the northern edge of its winter range. The breeding range is from southern Alaska east to Newfoundland and south to southern New Mexico, the Great Lakes, and western Virginia.

Wood Thrush (*Hylocichla mustelina*)

Status: Regular; nests

Jan	Feb	Mar	Apr	May	Jun	Jul	Aug	Sep	Oct	Nov	Dec
			x						x x		
19 Apr 1973									13 Oct 1962		
23 Apr 1989									14 Oct 1975		
24 Apr 1982									24 Oct 1977		

Occurrence: This uncommon summer resident arrives in early or mid-May and departs in late September. In summer, it is most common in southern and eastern Iowa, and its distribution is much more localized in northwestern Iowa. There are few specific records of Wood Thrush nests. From 1960 to 1995, there are summer records from all parts of the state, including all counties except for 12 in the western third of the state.

Historically, the Wood Thrush was considered a common to abundant summer resident (Anderson 1907, DuMont 1933). Numbers appear to have declined somewhat since then.

Comment: The winter range is from southern Texas south to northern Colombia. The breeding range is from central Minnesota east to Nova Scotia and south almost to the Gulf Coast. Iowa is near the western edge of its breeding range. Based on Breeding Bird Survey data, Wood Thrush populations have declined in recent years. Both habitat fragmentation and high nest parasitism from Brown-headed Cowbirds have been suggested as causes for those apparent declines. In Iowa, high cowbird nest parasitism was noted even in the late 1800s (Keyes and Williams 1888).

American Robin (*Turdus migratorius*)

Status: Regular; nests

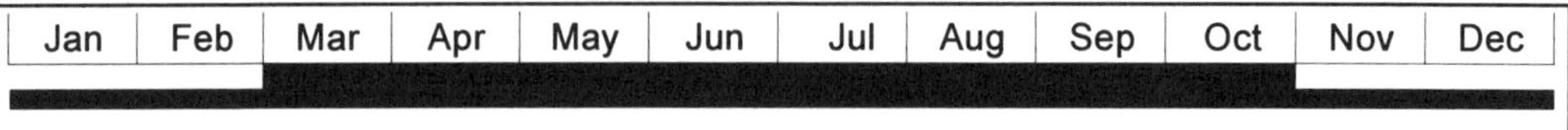

Occurrence: The American Robin is an abundant migrant and summer resident and uncommon winter resident throughout Iowa. Spring migrants arrive in early March and fall migrants generally depart in late October. One of Iowa's most familiar species, robins nest in woodlands, urban areas, farmsteads, and parks throughout the state. Nesting starts in mid- or late April and extends into July with many pairs commonly producing 2 or even 3 broods (Klimstra and Stieglitz 1957, Willson 1978).

Robins are found on about two-thirds of Christmas Bird Counts. By far, the most are found on counts near the Missouri River, especially those in southwestern Iowa. Many robins eventually move south but at least a few winter in Iowa every year, and numbers vary greatly from year to year. Presumably the amount of fruit available to wintering birds accounts for these yearly variations.

Historically, the American Robin was considered an abundant summer resident and an uncommon winter resident (Anderson 1907, DuMont 1933), similar to its present status. Anderson (1907) noted that its numbers had appeared to have increased greatly since the start of settlement of Iowa.

In the 1960s, some American Robin populations apparently were decimated by chemical spraying that was intended to control Dutch elm disease (Weller 1971). Those populations have recovered, and the species is doing well now.

Comment: The winter range is from the United States, except the most northern parts, south to northern Central America. The breeding range is from northern Alaska and Canada south almost to the Gulf of Mexico and to southern Mexico.

References:

Klimstra, W. D., and W. O. Stieglitz. 1957. Notes on reproductive activities of robins in Iowa and Illinois. *Wilson Bull.* 69:333-337.

Weller, M. W. 1971. Robin mortality in relation to Dutch elm disease control programs on the Iowa State University campus. *Iowa State J. Sci.* 45:471-475.

Willson, G. D. 1978. Reproductive biology of American Robins following a Dutch elm disease control program. *Proc. Iowa Acad. Sci.* 85:91-96.

Varied Thrush (*Ixoreus naevius*)

Status: Regular

By year since 1960 (also 1996)

60	63	66	69	72	75	78	81	84	87	90	93
	2	1	1 1		1 2 2	1 1 2	1 2 3	3 4 1	2 1 5	2 5	1 2 4

Jan	Feb	Mar	Apr	May	Jun	Jul	Aug	Sep	Oct	Nov	Dec
			XX X	X					X XX		

19 Apr 1984 — 15 Oct 1991
21 Apr 1989 — 22 Oct 1985
16 May 1976 — 30 Oct 1983

Occurrence: This rare winter visitor is most often found from November through February, with extreme records from mid-October to mid-May. Most of the 50 records are from the northeastern half of the state.

The first record is from 4 Dec 1964 at Grinnell in Poweshiek County (*IBL* 35:26). There have been from 1 to 5 reports every year from 1975 to 1995, except for 1992. Many have been photographed. Most are found at feeders in urban areas, but a few have been found in rural areas near conifer groves.

Comment: The winter range is along the Pacific Coast from British Columbia to northern Mexico. The breeding range is from central Alaska south in western Canada to Washington and Oregon. The winter vagrancy pattern of this species has been known for many years. Birds stray eastward to the eastern Rocky Mountains, to the Midwest, and to the East Coast, apparently by different routes (Keith 1968).

Reference:

Keith, A. R. 1968. A summary of the extralimital records of the Varied Thrush, 1848 to 1966. *Bird-Banding* 39:245-276.

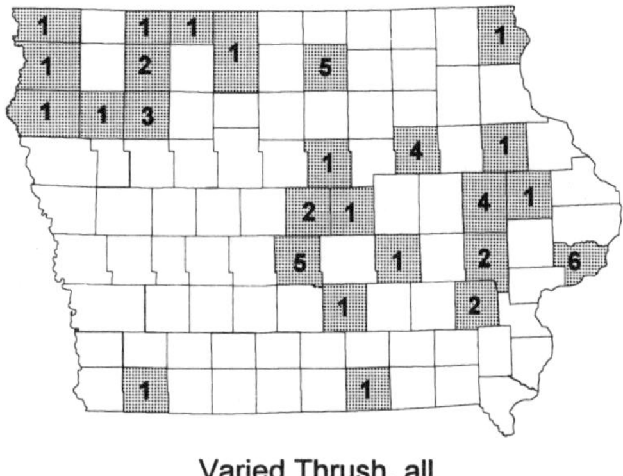

Varied Thrush, all

Mockingbirds, Thrashers, and Allies (Family Mimidae)

Mockingbirds, thrashers, and allies comprise 33 species, with 12 from North America and 5 from Iowa. These species of the New World tropical and temperate zones have long, often decurved, bills; long tails; and short, rounded wings. They are noted singers and mimics. There are no sexual or seasonal plumage differences.

Of the Iowa species, 3 are predominantly summer residents and 2 are Accidental.

Gray Catbird (*Dumetella carolinensis*)

Status: Regular; nests

Jan	Feb	Mar	Apr	May	Jun	Jul	Aug	Sep	Oct	Nov	Dec
X											

20 Apr 1980	2 Jan 1987
22 Apr 1985	9 Jan 1955
22 Apr 1985	24 Jan 1993

Occurrence: This common summer resident arrives in early May and departs by late September or early October. Catbirds are reported on 80 percent of the Breeding Bird Surveys and are most common in northeastern and southern Iowa. They start nesting in mid- or late May and typically attempt 2 broods (Johnson and Best 1980).

On Christmas Bird Counts from 1960 to 1995, Gray Catbirds were found on 21 counts in 13 years. There are 4 reports from early and 1 from mid-January and none from February or March.

Comment: The winter range is from the southern United States south to the West Indies and Panama. The breeding range is from British Columbia east to Nova Scotia and south to northern Arizona and the Gulf Coast. The pattern of late fall birds lingering into December and a few of these remaining into January is typical for nearby states, but a few birds have over-wintered in Minnesota (Janssen 1987) and Wisconsin (Robbins 1991).

Reference:

Johnson, E. J., and L. B. Best. 1980. Breeding biology of the Gray Catbird in Iowa. *Iowa State J. Research* 55:171-183.

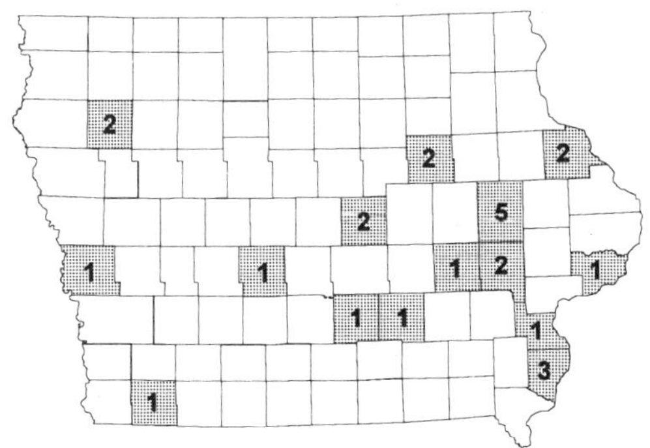

Gray Catbird, 1960-1995
Christmas Bird Counts and January

Northern Mockingbird (*Mimus polyglottos*)

Status: Regular; nests

Jan	Feb	Mar	Apr	May	Jun	Jul	Aug	Sep	Oct	Nov	Dec

Occurrence: This rare summer resident and rarer winter resident is most often found in shrubby fields in the southern half of the state. Most reports from the northern part of the state occur in spring.

Summer and nesting records are mainly from the southern half of the state, although there are a few nesting records from northern Iowa (map). On Breeding Bird Surveys, with 1 exception, mockingbirds were found only in the southern third and in east-central Iowa.

Mockingbirds were found on Christmas Bird Counts in 32 of 36 years from 1960 to 1995, averaging 2.4 counts per year. They are most consistently found along the Mississippi River in southeastern Iowa and in south-central Iowa. The severe winters of 1978-1979 and 1984-1985 may have reduced the wintering population—mockingbirds were found on Christmas Bird Counts in only 7 of 10 years from 1979 to 1988 averaging 1.2 counts per year. In December 1995, 2 found near Whittemore in Kossuth County were the most northerly winter and first county records (*IBL* 66:58).

It is likely that mockingbirds over-winter every year, although they are only reported in January or February in about half of the years, and some are reported as over-wintering without mention of the months in which the birds were seen. The number of mockingbirds seen at any given time of year likely reflects the number of observers present to see them.

Historically, there were only 34 reports of Northern Mockingbird prior to 1930 (Dinsmore et al. 1984). Those reports and others through 1965 are listed in several articles (Keck 1946, Brown 1961, Youngworth 1963, Summy 1967). The 53 reported in the 1930s was clearly an increase. It is difficult to judge how much the population has fluctuated since then.

Comment: The permanent range is in the southern United States south to the West Indies and southern Mexico. Mockingbirds are partially migratory in the northern parts of their range, which includes southern Iowa. Some birds are found north of the usual range to southern Canada. Iowa is clearly on that northern fringe, with the bulk of the population moving south for the winter.

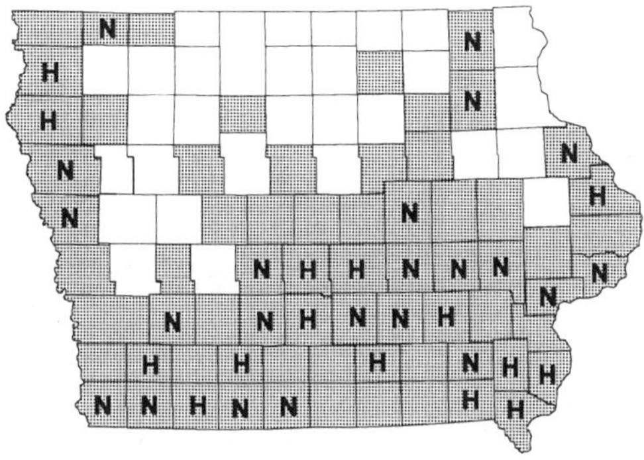

Northern Mockingbird, 1960-1995
June-July and nesting (recent N, historical H)

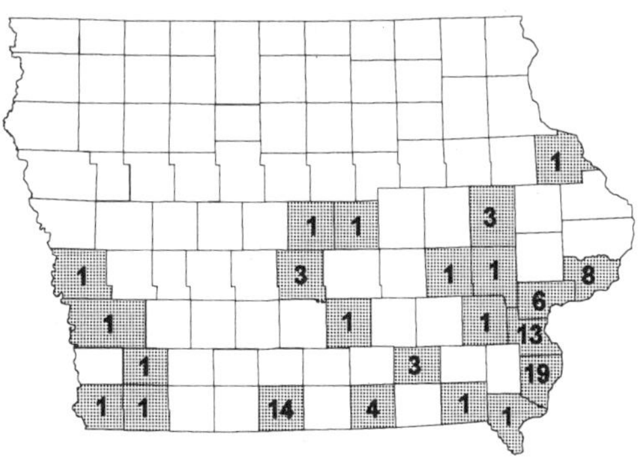

Northern Mockingbird, 1960-1995
Christmas Bird Counts

References:

Brown, W. H. 1961. Mockingbirds in Iowa. *Iowa Bird Life* 31:32-33.

Keck, W. N. 1946. The Mockingbird in Iowa. *Iowa Bird Life* 16:23-27.

Summy, R. 1967. The northward advance in range of the Mockingbird (*Mimus polyglottos*) in Iowa, 1961-1965. *Iowa Bird Life* 37:14-20.

Youngworth, W. 1963. The Mockingbird in northwest Iowa. *Iowa Bird Life* 33:33-35.

Sage Thrasher (*Oreoscoptes montanus*)

Status: Accidental

20 Dec 1952 to 10 Jan 1953, West Des Moines, Polk Co. (Stiles 1953)
26 Dec 1964 to 2 Jan 1965, Des Moines, Polk Co. (*IBL* 35:6, Dinsmore et al. 1984)
23 Sep to 12 Oct 1985, Waterloo, Black Hawk Co. (P-0187, *IBL* 56(1) cover, Moore 1986)

Occurrence: Of the 3 records, 1 is from fall and 2 are from winter.

Comment: This species breeds in arid sagebrush habitat from southern British Columbia east to eastern Montana, eastern Wyoming, central Colorado, northern New Mexico and west to extreme western California and central Oregon. East of the Great Plains states, there are 1 to 5 records in states and provinces east to Ontario, Wisconsin, Illinois, Arkansas, and Louisiana. There are also records from the East Coast and Gulf Coast including Massachusetts, New York, New Jersey, Maryland, Virginia, North Carolina, Florida, and Alabama. Most of the vagrant records are from October, December to January, and May, with a few scattered in other months.

References:

Moore, F. L. 1986. Sage Thrasher in Waterloo. *Iowa Bird Life* 56:28-29.

Stiles, B. F. 1953. Sage Thrasher in Iowa: A sight record. *Iowa Bird Life* 23:22-23.

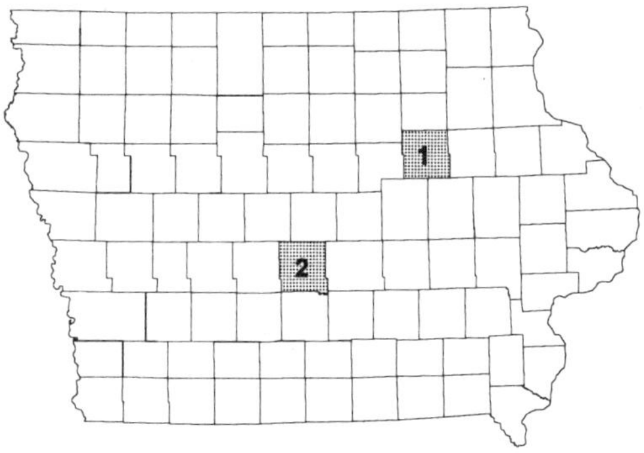

1
2

Sage Thrasher, all

Brown Thrasher (*Toxostoma rufum*)

Status: Regular; nests

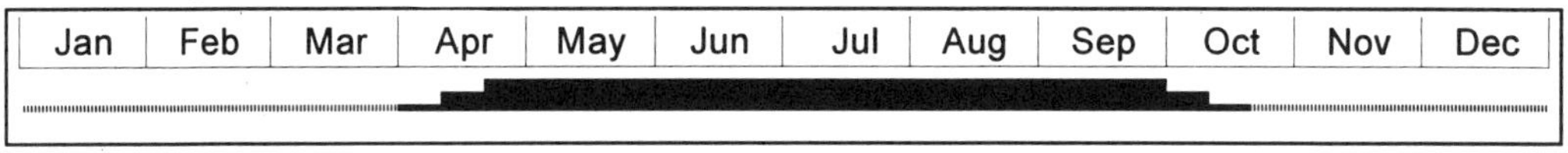

Jan	Feb	Mar	Apr	May	Jun	Jul	Aug	Sep	Oct	Nov	Dec

Occurrence: This common summer resident and rare winter resident arrives in early to mid-April and departs by early or mid-October.

Thrashers were found on Christmas Bird Counts in 35 of 36 years from 1960 to 1995, averaging 3.2 counts per year. Most were singles, but there were 2 on 11 counts, 3 on 4 counts, and 4 and 5 on 1 count each. On Christmas Bird Counts, thrashers are found in all areas of the state, but 59 percent were in central and east-central Iowa and only 9 percent were in the northern third of the state. From 1960 to 1995, there were 9 additional reports from January and February, as well as a few others reported as "over-wintering."

Brown Thrashers are found on all Breeding Bird Survey routes, with the greatest numbers in northeastern and southern Iowa. Thrashers outnumbered catbirds by 2.7 to 1 on these routes, which tend to sample open countryside. On the wooded bluffs of the Coralville Reservoir in Johnson County, catbirds outnumbered thrashers by 9.2 to 1 (Kent et al. 1994).

Comment: The winter range is from southern Missouri and Maryland south to the Gulf Coast and west to central Texas. The breeding range includes all of the eastern United States and southern Canada west through the Great Plains. A few winter north to Minnesota and southern Ontario.

Although the Brown Thrasher and the Gray Catbird occupy somewhat similar habitats, the thrasher seems to be more adaptable to agricultural land and the catbird to heavily wooded areas.

Curve-billed Thrasher (*Toxostoma curvirostre*)

Status: Accidental

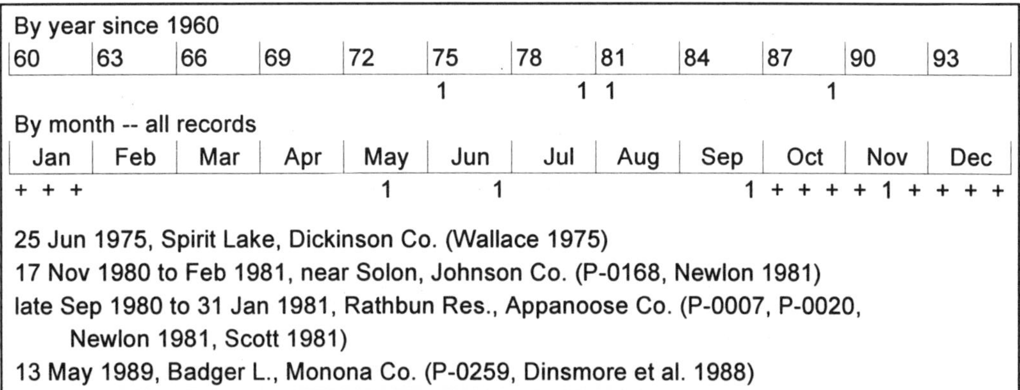

By year since 1960

60 | 63 | 66 | 69 | 72 | 75 | 78 | 81 | 84 | 87 | 90 | 93

1 (1975) 1 1 (1980, 1981) 1 (1989)

By month -- all records

Jan	Feb	Mar	Apr	May	Jun	Jul	Aug	Sep	Oct	Nov	Dec
+ + +				1	1			1	+ + + +	1 + +	+ +

25 Jun 1975, Spirit Lake, Dickinson Co. (Wallace 1975)

17 Nov 1980 to Feb 1981, near Solon, Johnson Co. (P-0168, Newlon 1981)

late Sep 1980 to 31 Jan 1981, Rathbun Res., Appanoose Co. (P-0007, P-0020, Newlon 1981, Scott 1981)

13 May 1989, Badger L., Monona Co. (P-0259, Dinsmore et al. 1988)

Occurrence: There are 2 records from fall-winter and 1 each from May and June. The fall-winter birds occurred in the same year and remained for several months, frequenting feeders. The June bird was found on a gravel road after a dust and hail storm and was caked with mud. After washing and cleaning, it was released. The May bird was found in a parking lot and was quite tame, but did not stay.

Comment: This nonmigratory species of the Southwest ranges from Arizona northeast to the corners of Colorado, Kansas, and Oklahoma, east to west-central and southern Texas, and south to southern Mexico. The relatively few vagrants have occurred west to southeastern California and Nevada, east on the Gulf Coast to Louisiana and Florida, and northeast to Nebraska, South Dakota, Iowa, Minnesota, Wisconsin, and Illinois. Iowa has more records than any other midwestern state. The Minnesota record was in the southwestern corner near Iowa. A Wisconsin bird stayed for 4 years and laid infertile eggs each summer.

References:

Dinsmore, S., T. Sorensen, and D. Gifford. 1988. Curve-billed Thrasher in Monona County. *Iowa Bird Life* 58:116.

Newlon, M. C. 1981. Curve-billed Thrashers in Iowa. *Iowa Bird Life* 51:21-24.

Scott, C. 1981. The Curve-billed Thrasher at Rathbun. *Iowa Bird Life* 51:35.

Wallace, L. 1975. Curve-billed Thrasher at Spirit Lake. *Iowa Bird Life* 45:96-97.

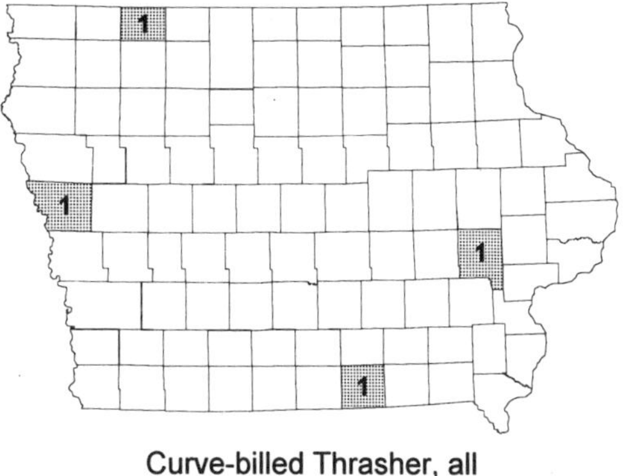

Curve-billed Thrasher, all

Wagtails and Pipits (Family Motacillidae)

Wagtails and pipits comprise 62 species, with 11 from North America and 1 from Iowa. These ground-loving species have thin bills, long legs, long toes, and long tails. They walk or run rather than hop. Some have a spur-like hind claw. Wagtails are Old World birds; pipits occur worldwide.

American Pipit (*Anthus rubescens*)

Status: Regular

Jan	Feb	Mar	Apr	May	Jun	Jul	Aug	Sep	Oct	Nov	Dec
							X X X				X XX

2 Mar 1990	14 May 1950	10 Aug 1991	20 Dec 1969
3 Mar 1956	15 May 1983	20 Aug ??	26 Dec 1964
9 Mar 1986	19 May 1983	28 Aug 1972	29 Dec 1970

Occurrence: This rare to uncommon migrant is usually seen from late March to early May and from late September to late October. Pipits are often found on mudflats, but may be found in open fields. They have a very wide migration interval.

Comment: In North America, the winter range of this Holarctic species is in the southern United States south to northern Central America and north on the East and West coasts. The breeding range is on Arctic tundra and south on alpine tundra in the Rocky Mountains to northern New Mexico.

There are single January records from Minnesota, Wisconsin, and Illinois and 2 from Missouri. This species winters regularly in Arkansas and southern Tennessee.

Waxwings (Family Bombycillidae)

Waxwings comprise 3 species, with 2 from North America and 2 from Iowa. These fruit eaters of temperate and northern climates range widely in search of food. They have a soft plumage with a crest and short, broad-based bills.

Bohemian Waxwing (*Bombycilla garrulus*)

Status: Regular

By year since 1960

60	61	62	63	64	65	66	67	68	69	70	71	72	73	74	75	76	77
1	5	1	1	3		3	3	1	1			1	3			4	1

78	79	80	81	82	83	84	85	86	87	88	89	90	91	92	93	94	95
4	6	3	1	2		5	1	5		2	1	3	1		1	2	2

Jan	Feb	Mar	Apr	May	Jun	Jul	Aug	Sep	Oct	Nov	Dec
				x						x xx	

28 Mar 1964 — 2 Nov 1984
29 Mar 1995 — 11 Nov 1984
4 May 1920 — 15 Nov 1986

Occurrence: This rare winter visitor is found almost every year, usually with 1 to 5 reports. Over a period of 36 years, there were 2 winters in which there were many reports: 18 in 1961-1962 and 14 in 1984-1985. An even larger invasion occurred in northwestern Iowa in 1919-1920, when there were many flocks, some with as many as 100 birds and a record late date of 4 May (Stephens 1920). The largest number on record is 5,000 at Des Moines in Polk County on 18 March 1923 (*IBL* 1:8). A flock of thousands was noted in Clayton County in 1908-1909 (Sherman 1921).

Bohemian Waxwings tend to arrive late in winter, perhaps after exhausting food supplies farther north. Most occur as singles or small groups, sometimes associating with Cedar Waxwings. Flocks of 75 to 150 were noted in Decatur, Linn, Polk, Scott, and Woodbury counties in 1962 (*IBL* 32:19), and 200-500 were in Monona County on 18 January 1964 (Youngworth 1964).

There are records for all areas of the state, with the fewest in southern Iowa. Many are found in cities where there are plantings of fruit trees and people to observe the birds.

Comment: The winter range is from southern Alaska and the northwestern Canadian provinces south through most of the western United States and, in eruptions, east to the northeastern United States and southern Canada. The breeding range is from northern Montana and Manitoba to northern Alaska. Very few are found south of Iowa in winter.

Eruptions are noted more frequently in Wisconsin (Robbins 1991). Only 2 of 5 Iowa eruptions noted above correspond with the years of eruptions in Wisconsin, indicating the erratic nature of this species' movements.

References:

Sherman, A. R. 1921. The Bohemian Waxwing in Iowa in vast numbers. *Auk* 38:278-279.

Youngworth, W. January 18, 1964, in the field. *Iowa Bird Life* 34:53.

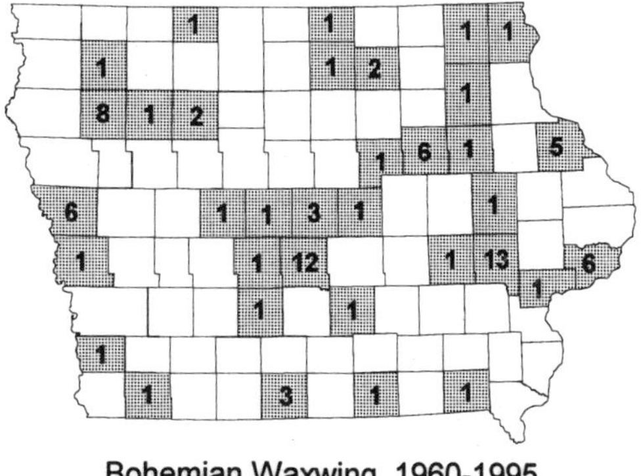

Bohemian Waxwing, 1960-1995

Cedar Waxwing (*Bombycilla cedrorum*)

Status: Regular; nests

Occurrence: This abundant migrant, common summer resident, and rare winter resident is usually most common from late February to early May and from late September to late November when large flocks of migrants appear. Cedar Waxwings are found on about 25 percent of the Breeding Bird Surveys, most commonly in eastern Iowa. They are found on about 70 percent of the Christmas Bird Counts.

Numbers vary greatly from year to year, but Cedar Waxwings are about equally common in all sections of the state. In some years, large flocks appear in January and February to feed on crab apples and other fruits, and, in other years, few are present.

Comment: The winter range is from southern Canada south through the United States to Panama and the West Indies. The breeding range is from southern Alaska to Newfoundland and south to the northern half of the United States.

Shrikes (Family Laniidae)

Shrikes comprise 30 species, with 3 from North America and 2 from Iowa. They are carnivorous and predatory with strong hooked bills, strong legs, and feet with hooked claws. They have a harsh "shriek," hence the name.

Northern Shrike (*Lanius excubitor*)

Status: Regular

Jan	Feb	Mar	Apr	May	Jun	Jul	Aug	Sep	Oct	Nov	Dec
									XX X		
			1 Apr 1979			1 Oct 1989					
			5 Apr 1992			2 Oct 1970					
			6 Apr 1985			18 Oct 1980					

Occurrence: The Northern Shrike is an uncommon winter resident in northern and central Iowa and rare in southern Iowa. It is usually found in open habitats containing scattered trees or shrubs. Northern Shrikes arrive in early November and usually depart in late February.

Northern Shrikes are reported on about 20 percent of the Christmas Bird Counts, most commonly in northern Iowa.

Comment: The winter range is from southern Alaska east to Newfoundland and south to the central United States. The breeding range is across Alaska and northern Canada (north of James Bay). This species is also found in northern Eurasia.

Iowa is on the southern edge of the winter range. This species rarely reaches northwestern Missouri (Robbins and Easterla 1992). Owing to the difficulty in distinguishing Northern and Loggerhead shrikes, it is probably not reasonable to compare numbers in northern and southern Iowa based on undocumented reports. In winter, as a general rule, Northern Shrikes are expected in the north and Loggerheads in the south, but both clearly occur in the central part of the state.

Loggerhead Shrike (*Lanius ludovicianus*)

Status: Regular; nests

Jan	Feb	Mar	Apr	May	Jun	Jul	Aug	Sep	Oct	Nov	Dec

Occurrence: In summer, the Loggerhead Shrike is a rare resident in northern Iowa and an uncommon resident in southern Iowa. It is a rare winter resident in southern Iowa.

Loggerhead Shrikes are found on about 20 percent of the Breeding Bird Surveys, most often in southern Iowa. Along Adair County roadsides, there were 74 pairs and 93 nests in 1988 and 89 pairs and 119 nests in 1989 (DeGeus 1990).

Loggerhead Shrikes are found on about 20 percent of the Christmas Bird Counts, most often in southern Iowa. The number found varies greatly from year to year.

Historically, the Loggerhead Shrike was considered a fairly common summer resident (Anderson 1907, DuMont 1933). The removal of hedgerows and shrubby cover may partially account for the decline in the number of Loggerhead Shrikes since then.

Comment: The winter range is approximately the southern half of the United States south to southern Mexico. Iowa is at the northern edge of its usual winter range. The breeding range is from southern Canada south to the Gulf of Mexico and southern Mexico.

Reference:

DeGeus, D. W. 1990. Productivity and habitat preferences of Loggerhead Shrikes inhabiting roadsides in a Midwestern agroenvironment. Master's thesis, Iowa State Univ., Ames.

Starlings and Allies (Family Sturnidae)

Starlings and allies comprise 110 species, with 2 from North America and 1 from Iowa. These stocky Old World species have strong legs and bill, rounded or pointed wings, and square tail. They are omnivorous and nest in cavities.

European Starling (*Sturnus vulgaris*)

Status: Regular; nests

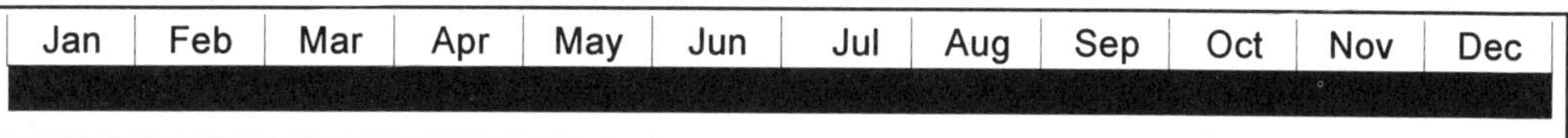

Occurrence: This abundant permanent resident is most common on farmsteads, feedlots, and urban areas but occupies a wide range of habitats. The European Starling is among the most abundant species in Iowa. It is reported on virtually every Christmas Bird Count, with increasing numbers from north to south. Starlings are found on all of the Breeding Bird Surveys and are one of the most common species reported. They are most abundant on counts in eastern and north-central Iowa.

After the nesting season, starlings often join several species of blackbirds in large communal roosts that may contain thousands of birds. In urban areas the droppings below the roosts can be very messy and perhaps a health hazard.

Comment: The permanent range of this introduced Palearctic species is from southern Alaska and the northern portions of the Canadian provinces south to northern Mexico. European Starlings were introduced into New York City in 1890 and were first found in Iowa in December 1922, when 1 was seen at Lamoni in Decatur County. By April 1936, this species had been found in every county in the state (DuMont 1945).

Reference:

DuMont, P. A. 1945. The invasion of the Starling into Iowa. *Iowa Bird Life* 15:30-33.

Vireos (Family Vireonidae)

Vireos comprise 48 species, with 14 from North America and 7 from Iowa. The Iowa species are all regular—5 nest and 2 are migrants. Vireos are insectivorous, arriving in late April or early May and most leaving by October.

Vireos are relatively small, plain, large-headed song birds. Their bills are thicker than those of warblers with a slight hook to the upper mandible. Vireos are more sluggish and less gregarious than warblers. White-eyed, Bell's, and Warbling vireos have distinctive songs and are most commonly located and identified by song. The other four species that occur in Iowa have songs that are similar to each other and require a practiced ear to distinguish. They are easier to identify by their visual differences.

White-eyed Vireo (*Vireo griseus*)

Status: Regular; nests

Jan	Feb	Mar	Apr	May	Jun	Jul	Aug	Sep	Oct	Nov	Dec
			X						X		

Early dates	Late dates
5 Apr 1981	25 Sep 1976
18 Apr 1900	26 Sep 1982
18 Apr 1977	1 Oct 1983

Occurrence: White-eyed Vireo is a rare breeding species in Iowa, where it is near the northern and western edge of its range. From 3 to 14 per year were reported from 1980 to 1995. The first often arrive in southeastern Iowa by late April, and the last are noted in late September. Few are reported during the summer, although they are undoubtedly present. Most are reported from eastern, central, and south-central Iowa, but occasional migrants are reported from all areas of the state. Typical habitat is woodland edge with tangles, where birds remain out of sight, but are easily detected by their loud, distinctive song. Most are reported from previously known locations.

Historically, Anderson (1907) described White-eyed Vireo as tolerably common in southern Iowa and irregular in central Iowa, a pattern that fits current observations. DuMont (1933), however, noted an utter lack of recent records. Reports were irregular until 1960. A nest with 2 eggs was found in Van Buren County on 18 July 1894 (Anderson 1907). Other evidence of nesting includes an adult with young at Cone Marsh in Louisa County on 12 June 1977 (*IBL* 47:102), an adult feeding a cowbird at Yellow River Forest in Allamakee County on 22 June 1985 (*IBL* 55:94), and "nesting" at Wheatland in Clinton County in the summer of 1964 (*IBL* 34:66).

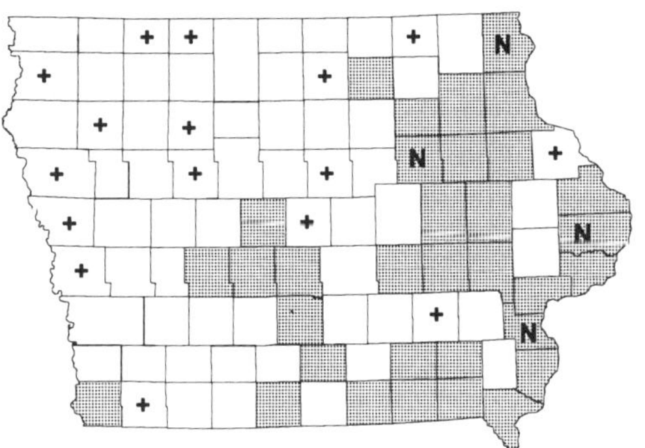

White-eyed Vireo, 1960-1995
June-July, nesting (N), and spring (+)

Comment: The winter range is from South Carolina across the Gulf Coast to southern Texas south to the West Indies and Central America. The breeding range is from northeastern Mexico and the southern United States north to central Iowa, southern Wisconsin, and southern Massachusetts. The western edge of the range extends to eastern Nebraska and Kansas. Migrants are found casually north of the normal breeding range to southern Canada, mainly in spring, and west to California, mainly in fall.

Bell's Vireo (*Vireo bellii*)

Status: Regular; nests

Jan	Feb	Mar	Apr	May	Jun	Jul	Aug	Sep	Oct	Nov	Dec
								XX	X	X	
27 Apr 1996									24 Sep 1969		
29 Apr 1988									16 Oct 1901		
30 Apr 1992									19 Nov 1984		

Occurrence: This rare to locally uncommon summer resident arrives in May, and most leave by mid-September. Birds are most frequently reported from southern, central, and east-central Iowa and are quite rare in northwestern and north-central Iowa. They frequent hedgerows and thickets. They are usually heard rather than seen. The easiest way to find them is to listen in locations where they have been found in previous years. When the vegetation matures, they move to new locations.

Bell's Vireo was found on 8 percent of Breeding Bird Surveys from 1983 to 1992. In Fremont County, 29 singing males were found along 7 miles of a drainage ditch (Roosa 1977). Occasional nests have been found or nesting confirmed.

Historically, Anderson (1907) reported this species from all sections of the state and considered it common to abundant. DuMont (1933) considered it fairly common in southern and western Iowa and somewhat rare in northeastern Iowa. In Sioux City, 13 nests were found from 1908 to 1915 (Bennett 1917). In Boone County, 5 nests were found in 1940 (Rosene 1941).

Comment: The winter range is from Mexico south to Honduras and casually in the southern United States. The breeding range has a southwestern portion that includes northern Mexico and the southern parts of bordering states and a middlewestern portion that extends from central Texas north barely to south-central North Dakota, northwestern Iowa, southeastern Minnesota, and southwestern Wisconsin and east to Indiana and Arkansas.

This species declined sharply in the central United States (Mississippi River to Rocky Mountains) from 1965 to 1979 (Robbins et al. 1986). Early reports from the Sioux City area (Bennett 1917, Youngworth 1964) suggest that it was previously more common in northwestern Iowa, although current reports may underestimate the number of birds present in that area. More data are needed to monitor population changes in future years.

References:

Bennett, W. W. 1917. Bell's Vireo studies (*Vireo belli* Aud.). *Proc. Iowa Acad. Sci.* 24:285-293.

Roosa, D. 1977. Bell's Vireo singing male county. *Iowa Bird Life* 47:137-138.

Rosene, W. M. 1941. Filming the elusive Bell's Vireo. *Iowa Bird Life* 11:2-5.

Youngworth, W. 1964. Bell's Vireo in late summer. *Iowa Bird Life* 34:27.

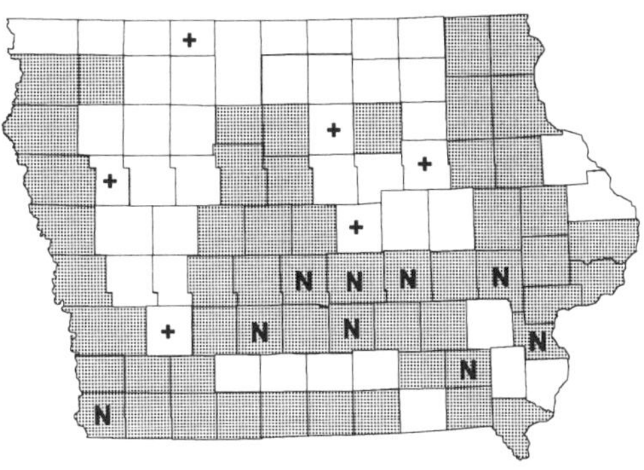

Bell's Vireo, 1960-1995
June-July, nesting (N), and spring/fall (+)

Solitary Vireo (*Vireo solitarius*)

Status: Regular

Jan	Feb	Mar	Apr	May	Jun	Jul	Aug	Sep	Oct	Nov	Dec
					X	X X	X			XX XX	X

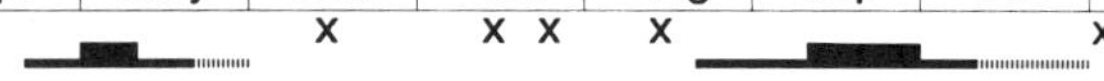

21 Apr 1985	30 May 1995	20 Aug 1994	7 Nov 1984
22 Apr 1989	30 May 1995	22 Aug 1985	11 Nov 1984
24 Apr 1982	14 Jun 1966	24 Aug 1977	14 Nov 1991
summer: 13 Jul 1985, 22 Jul 1989		winter: 20 Dec 1984	

Occurrence: Of the vireos, Solitary is the earliest spring and latest fall migrant, when it is rare to uncommon, usually solitary, and often silent. There are 2 records for summer and 1 for winter.

Comment: The winter range is in the southern coastal United States and Middle America. The breeding range in the East is across southern Canada, the extreme northern United States, and, in the Appalachians, south to Georgia, and in the West from Mexico to Northwest Territories. Late fall/early winter stragglers have also been recorded in nearby states.

Yellow-throated Vireo (*Vireo flavifrons*)

Status: Regular; nests

Jan	Feb	Mar	Apr	May	Jun	Jul	Aug	Sep	Oct	Nov	Dec
									X X		

22 Apr 1989	30 Sep 1986
23 Apr 1989	3 Oct 1982
24 Apr 1974	13 Oct 1951

Occurrence: This uncommon to common summer resident may arrive as early as late April, and most are gone by mid-September. Birds occur across the state, but are more common in the wooded areas of eastern, southern, and central Iowa. They may be found in large wooded tracts with Red-eyed Vireo or sometimes in smaller wooded areas and towns. At the Coralville Reservoir in Johnson County, the ratio of Red-eyed to Yellow-throated vireos was about 3 to 1 (Kent et al. 1994).

Comment: The winter range is from southern Mexico and southern Florida south to northern South America and casually along the Gulf Coast of Texas and Mexico. The breeding range is in the eastern United States from the Gulf Coast north barely into Canada and west to eastern Nebraska.

Warbling Vireo (*Vireo gilvus*)

Status: Regular; nests

Jan	Feb	Mar	Apr	May	Jun	Jul	Aug	Sep	Oct	Nov	Dec

23 Apr 1964	25 Sep 1990
23 Apr 1989	26 Sep 1989
23 Apr 1994	27 Sep 1995

Occurrence: This common summer resident usually arrives in early May, and most are gone by early September. Fewer are detected in fall, when most are not singing their distinctive song. Owing to a preference for riparian habitat, especially cottonwoods, Warbling Vireo is the most widespread of the vireos in Iowa. In the woodland habitat of the Coralville Reservoir, the ratio of Red-eyed to Warbling vireos was about 3 to 1 (Kent et al. 1994). This ratio is reversed on Breeding Bird Surveys, which do not provide a good sample of the more restricted habitat of Red-eyed Vireo.

Comment: The winter range is from Mexico south to El Salvador and casually north to California and Arizona. The breeding range is more extensive than the winter range, extending from the East Coast to the West Coast, and from central Mexico to the Northwest Territories in the West and from Louisiana (but not southern Texas or the Southeast) north to southern Canada in the East.

Philadelphia Vireo (*Vireo philadelphicus*)

Status: Regular

Jan	Feb	Mar	Apr	May	Jun	Jul	Aug	Sep	Oct	Nov	Dec
					x		x		x		

3 May 1986	31 May 1973	4 Aug 1988	8 Oct 1967
3 May 1986	31 May 1968	13 Aug 1992	9 Oct 1975
6 May 1983	5 Jun 1992	14 Aug 1994	18 Oct 1994

Occurrence: This rare migrant is somewhat easier to find in fall when it flocks with Red-eyed Vireos. Most are identified by sight, because this species seldom sings in migration and the song is difficult to distinguish from that of Red-eyed Vireo. Sight identification is not always easy either, because this small, plain vireo can look like Tennessee or Orange-crowned warblers or the larger Red-eyed Vireo. In spring, this species is usually found in trees and usually not singing. In fall, it forages lower in more open areas and may be present in the same area for several weeks.

Comment: The winter range is in Central America. The breeding range is across the forested areas of Canada from eastern British Columbia to western Newfoundland, barely reaching south to Minnesota and Maine.

Red-eyed Vireo (*Vireo olivaceus*)

Status: Regular; nests

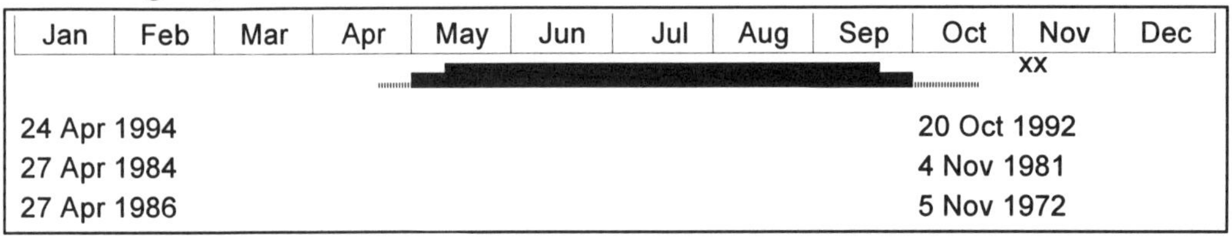

Jan	Feb	Mar	Apr	May	Jun	Jul	Aug	Sep	Oct	Nov	Dec
										XX	

24 Apr 1994	20 Oct 1992
27 Apr 1984	4 Nov 1981
27 Apr 1986	5 Nov 1972

Occurrence: This common to abundant summer resident in large wooded tracts is a fairly late migrant, with most arriving in mid-May. Most are gone by late September. This species breeds throughout the state, but is much more common in the more abundant woodland habitat of eastern Iowa. In spring and summer, this species is often concealed due to its sluggish movements and tendency to be high in the forest canopy, but its presence is easily detected owing to its persistent singing.

In fall, when birds are not singing much, Red-eyed Vireos form small flocks with other vireos and warblers in lower woodland edge habitat. The Red-eyed Vireo was among the most abundant species at tower kills at Alleman in Polk County in the fall of 1973-1974 (Mosman 1975), on 14 September 1982 (Dinsmore et al. 1983), and on 21, 22 September 1985 (Dinsmore et al. 1987).

Comment: The winter range is in the Amazon Basin of South America. The breeding range includes all of the eastern United States, across northern states to northern Oregon, most of the Canadian provinces, and the Northwest Territories. Red-eyed Vireo is by far the most common woodland bird in the eastern deciduous forest (Robbins et al. 1986); however, several other species are more common in the deciduous forest of eastern Iowa (Kent et al. 1994).

Emberizids (Family Emberizidae)

Emberizids or New World nine-primaried oscines comprises the warblers, tanagers, cardinals, grosbeaks, buntings, towhees, sparrows, longspurs, meadowlarks, blackbirds, and orioles. All have 9 primaries, complex syrinx muscles, and similar genetic markers.

Wood Warblers (Subfamily Parulinae)

Wood warblers comprise 116 species, with 58 from North America and 38 from Iowa. Of the Iowa species, 36 are Regular and 2 Accidental. Eighteen species have nested in Iowa.

Warblers are thought to have evolved in northern Central America at a time when North and South America were separated by water (Curson et al. 1994). From their "home base," species evolved, with some remaining sedentary and others moving into South America and the West Indies. With changes in climate, many migrated north to more favorable nesting grounds, and speciation occurred in association with habitat niches. Similar appearing species, such as Black-throated Green, Townsend's, Hermit, and Golden-cheeked warblers, probably separated as recently as the Wisconsinan glacial period.

The frequency and timing of warbler migration in Iowa is related to location of wintering grounds, which broadly can be characterized as Middle America (with many confined to the "home base" in Central America and others extending into Mexico), northern South America, the West Indies, and the southern United States/northern Mexico. For example, birds wintering in northern South America, such as Mourning, Connecticut, and Canada warblers are late spring migrants in Iowa. Birds wintering predominantly in the West Indies, such as Cape May, Black-throated Blue, and Prairie warblers, are more common in the eastern United States than they are in Iowa. The striking difference in spring and fall frequency in Iowa for 2 closely related species, Bay-breasted and Blackpoll warblers, is explained by differences in migration routes (Martsching 1986, 1987). Both species winter in northern South America and breed across Canada (Bay-breasted more to the east and Blackpoll more to the north and west); however, Bay-breasted Warblers migrate predominantly over the Gulf of Mexico and Central America, while most Blackpolls pass through the West Indies and even over the Atlantic Ocean in fall. Thus Bay-breasted Warblers are moving east in the spring, when they are less common in Iowa, and west in the fall, when they are more common in Iowa. The reverse is true for Blackpolls. Other examples can be found in the species accounts. A detailed 5-year study of warbler migration in central Iowa provides data on migration patterns for many of Iowa's warblers (Martsching 1986, 1987).

Most of the warbler migration occurs at night in mixed flocks. Warblers are concentrated by weather patterns. In spring, a stalled low-pressure front may cause warblers to "fall out" in the early morning when they encounter rain or high winds. In the fall, night migrants are brought in by strong cold fronts. In migration, species that nest in Iowa are often found in loose flocks with other warblers, but some are rarely found away from their appropriate habitat. The first species to arrive in spring is Louisiana Waterthrush, which can be found in southeastern Iowa as early as late March. Yellow-rumped Warbler could arrive earlier, but it is not possible to tell an early migrant from an occasional wintering bird. Other early warblers include species that winter in the southern United States: Orange-crowned, Yellow-throated, Pine, Palm, Black-and-white, and Common Yellowthroat.

Of the nesting warblers, Yellow Warbler, American Redstart, Ovenbird, and Common Yellowthroat are widespread. The Iowa breeding ranges of warblers that nest in the southeastern United States (Blue-winged,

Northern Parula, Yellow-throated, Prairie, Cerulean, Prothonotary, Worm-eating, Louisiana Waterthrush, Kentucky, Hooded, and Yellow-breasted Chat) are quite similar—the wooded valleys of the Mississippi, Des Moines, and Missouri rivers and their tributaries. Each of these species, however, has its own habitat niche. The distributional data on these species are biased in favor of certain areas that are heavily birded. Although new sites for these species are likely to be discovered, the pattern of distribution will not change much. The remaining nesting warblers are irregular nesters, with most of their population nesting to the north of Iowa: Golden-winged (historical), Chestnut-sided, Black-and-white, and possibly Canada.

In fall, the nesting species that reach the northwestern edge of their range in Iowa leave early and are rarely encountered in August and September. Northern Parula is an exception, because it also has a northern breeding population. In general, the late fall warblers are the non-nesting species that are early in spring: Orange-crowned, Yellow-rumped, and Palm. Species that have been found in winter include Orange-crowned, Nashville, Yellow-rumped, Pine, Ovenbird, Common Yellowthroat, and Yellow-breasted Chat.

Blue-winged Warbler (*Vermivora pinus*)

Status: Regular; nests

Jan	Feb	Mar	Apr	May	Jun	Jul	Aug	Sep	Oct	Nov	Dec

20 Apr 1987 — 16 Sep 1979
20 Apr 1992 — 18 Sep 1978
22 Apr 1985 — 26 Sep 1981

Occurrence: This uncommon summer resident usually arrives in southeastern Iowa in late April. The breeding range is in eastern, central, and south-central Iowa, with only a few spring and summer records from other areas. It is likely that most leave the state before the fall season, when only 0 to 3 are reported per year. It is a rare migrant in western Iowa (Youngworth 1959).

Blue-winged Warblers nest in areas of new brushy growth adjacent to deep woods. Owing to its low density and selective habitat, it is likely that there are many undiscovered nesting locations. Birders tend to know where to find them and not to look for new locations.

When Blue-winged and Golden-winged warblers mate, the resulting hybrid is a Brewster's Warbler, which shows the dominant features of both species (see Curson et al. 1994 for details). Mating of Brewster's Warblers or their secondary offspring may produce the much rarer Lawrence's Warbler, which shows recessive characteristics. In Iowa, 15 Brewster's and 4 Lawrence's warblers have been reported in the last 50 years.

Historically, the information on distribution of this species (Anderson 1907, DuMont 1933) is similar to the current range.

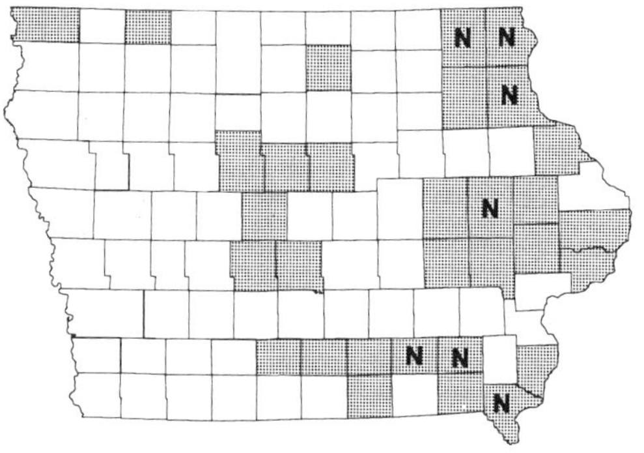

Blue-winged Warbler, 1960-1995
June-July and nesting (N)

Comment: The winter range is in Central America. The breeding range is in the United States (also extreme southern Ontario) from Arkansas and northern Alabama northeast to southern New England. Iowa is on the western edge of its range and near the northern edge, which is in southeastern Minnesota and southern Wisconsin.

Reference:

Youngworth, W. 1959. Blue-winged Warbler at Sioux City. *Iowa Bird Life* 29:103.

Golden-winged Warbler (*Vermivora chrysoptera*)

Status: Regular; formerly nested

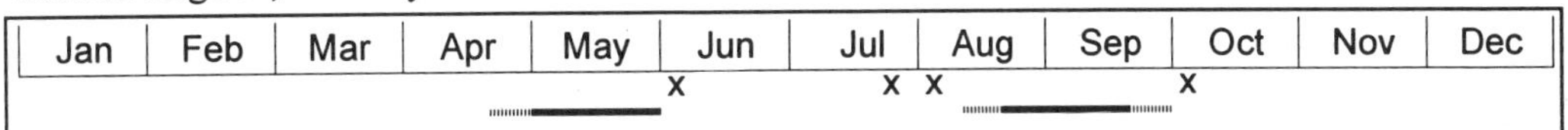

Jan	Feb	Mar	Apr	May	Jun	Jul	Aug	Sep	Oct	Nov	Dec
					X	X	X		X		

28 Apr 1989	27 May 1989	29 Jul 1977	26 Sep 1984
28 Apr 1989	28 May 1996	9 Aug 1988	27 Sep 1986
29 Apr 1986	2 Jun 1979	11 Aug 1985	2 Oct 1983

Occurrence: This rare migrant is usually seen in mixed flocks of warblers during May and from late August to mid-September. The Golden-winged Warbler is rarely reported from west-central, southwestern, and south-central Iowa, and in central Iowa it was among the rarest of migrants with an average of 4 per season in spring and fall (Martsching 1986, 1987). It is somewhat more common in eastern Iowa.

Historically, Anderson (1907) and DuMont (1933) both considered this species a rare migrant. The only evidence for nesting is a nest found near Keokuk in Lee County on 28 May 1888 (DuMont 1936) and a secondhand report of 2 nests in Grundy County in June 1898 (Anderson 1907).

Comment: The winter range is in Central America and the northern tip of South America. The breeding range overlaps with the northern breeding range of Blue-winged Warbler and extends farther north in the United States and into southern Canada and south along the Appalachians. In nearby states, the breeding range includes north-central to east-central Minnesota, all of Wisconsin except the southern 2 to 3 rows of counties, and occasionally in northern Illinois. Blue-winged Warblers appear to compete with Golden-wings and slowly replace them on the interface of their ranges. The amount of hybridization appears to be stable, which argues against combining these 2 closely related species into 1 species.

Tennessee Warbler (*Vermivora peregrina*)

Status: Regular

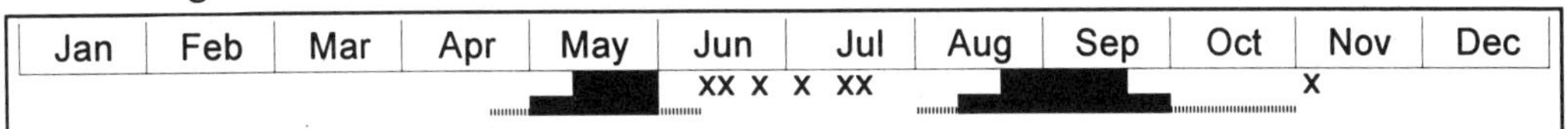

Jan	Feb	Mar	Apr	May	Jun	Jul	Aug	Sep	Oct	Nov	Dec
					XX X	X XX				X	

20 Apr 1986	23 Oct 1979
21 Apr 1982	23 Oct 1982
23 Apr 1989	3 Nov 1985

Occurrence: This relatively late spring and mid-fall migrant may be Iowa's most abundant migrant warbler (Martsching 1986, 1987). It is difficult to compare numbers with Yellow-rumped Warbler, which occurs at a different time and often in different habitat. When Tennessees are heard from every woods, the spring warbler migration is at its peak, and when they are no longer heard, it is over. There are 6 records from mid-June to mid-July, but no evidence of nesting. In fall, they occupy a lower and more open habitat, where they are usually identified by sight rather than song.

Comment: The winter range is in Central America and northern South America. The breeding range extends from southern Alaska and the Yukon across all of Canada and extreme northern parts of the United States.

Orange-crowned Warbler (*Vermivora celata*)

Status: Regular

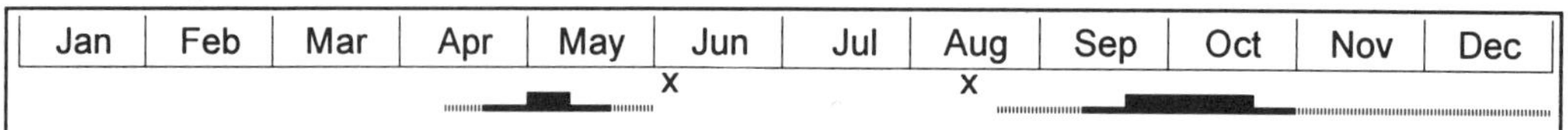

Jan	Feb	Mar	Apr	May	Jun	Jul	Aug	Sep	Oct	Nov	Dec
					x		x				

15 Apr 1977	24 May 1953	18 Aug 1991	23 Dec 1971
15 Apr 1995	28 May 1892	22 Aug 1986	23 Dec 1970
16 Apr 1992	6 Jun 1929	25 Aug 1985	27 Dec 1970

Occurrence: This species is an uncommon early spring and late fall migrant with occasional hardy birds remaining into December. The drab coloration and Chipping Sparrow-like song are not very distinctive.

Comment: The winter range extends from coastal and southern California and South Carolina south to northern Central America. The breeding range includes most of the western United States from New Mexico to northwestern Alaska and most of the Canadian provinces. This common warbler of the West is less common in the East. It has been found in December and occasionally later in nearby states.

Nashville Warbler (*Vermivora ruficapilla*)

Status: Regular

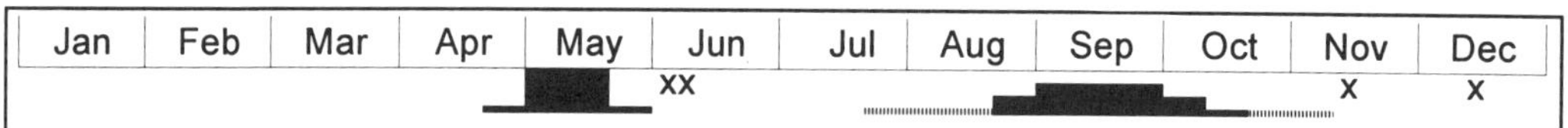

Jan	Feb	Mar	Apr	May	Jun	Jul	Aug	Sep	Oct	Nov	Dec
					xx					x	x

20 Apr 1987	31 May 1992	22 Jul 1979	4 Nov 1984
21 Apr 1994	2 Jun 1992	26 Jul 1993	6 Nov 1987
22 Apr 1985	5 Jun 1979	29 Jul 1988	13 Nov 1995
winter: 19 Dec 1993			

Occurrence: This common to abundant migrant has a wide migration interval in both spring and fall, with more fall stragglers than most warblers. In central Iowa, Nashville was the third most common migrant warbler in spring and second in fall, although more total birds were seen in spring than fall (Martsching 1986, 1987). Nashville Warbler was the most numerous species (228 of 469 birds) at a tower kill near Hinton in Plymouth County on 21, 22 September 1985 (Dinsmore et al. 1987).

There is 1 winter record from a Christmas Bird Count. Although the breeding range is only about 1 county in Wisconsin away from the northeastern corner of Iowa, there are no nesting or mid-summer records for Iowa.

Comment: The winter range is in Mexico and northern Central America, but some birds remain in the southern parts of California and Texas. The breeding range is split. The western part includes the northwestern United States and southern British Columbia. The eastern part extends from Manitoba east to the Maritime Provinces and south to northwestern Minnesota, northern and central Wisconsin, and, in the East, to West Virginia.

Northern Parula (*Parula americana*)

Status: Regular; nests

Jan	Feb	Mar	Apr	May	Jun	Jul	Aug	Sep	Oct	Nov	Dec
			x						x		
9 Apr 1981									10 Oct 1992		
13 Apr 1985									10 Oct 1982		
13 Apr 1985									16 Oct 1982		

Occurrence: This uncommon migrant and rare, local nesting species arrives in southern Iowa by late April. Only a few have been reported between mid-July and mid-August. The fall migration is slightly later than average for warblers. Like other warblers, migrants are more common in eastern Iowa, but may be found anywhere in the state.

Northern Parulas show a preference for sycamore trees, and their breeding range in Iowa is similar to Yellow-throated Warbler, which also is associated with sycamores. The range follows the lower half of the Mississippi River and some of its tributaries, the Des Moines River to central Iowa, and the lower half of the Missouri River. The most consistent locations with the highest density of birds are Shimek Forest in Lee County and Lacey-Keosauqua State Park in Van Buren County, followed by Wildcat Den State Park in Muscatine County, Ledges State Park in Boone County, and Waubonsie State Park in Fremont County. As with other rare nesting species with restricted habitat requirements, it is likely that more regular nesting locations will be discovered in the future. The only nests that have been found were at Lacey-Keosauqua State Park in 1979 and 1993 (Koenig 1979, Pinkston 1994).

Comment: The winter range includes northern Central America to the Gulf Coast of Mexico and the West Indies to southern Florida. The breeding range is from eastern Texas and northern Florida north to southeastern Manitoba and the Maritime Provinces with an odd gap that includes most of Iowa, the southern parts of Minnesota, Wisconsin, and Michigan, and eastern Ohio, northern Kentucky, Indiana, and northern Illinois.

References:

Koenig, D. 1979. Probable nesting of the Northern Parula Warbler in Iowa. *Iowa Bird Life* 49:116-117.

Pinkston, D. R. 1994. Northern Parula nest in Van Buren County. *Iowa Bird Life* 64:19-20.

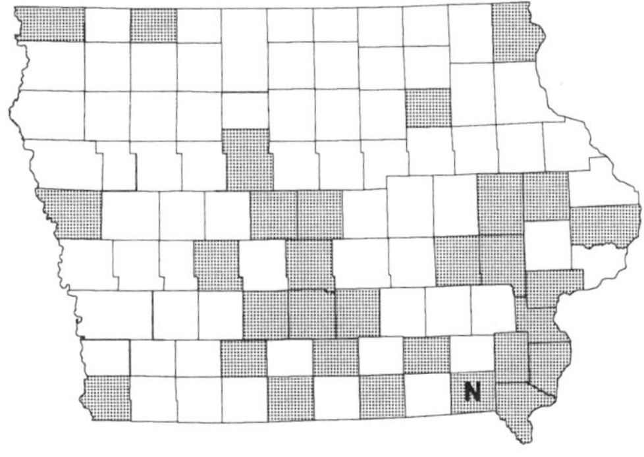

Northern Parula, 1960-1995
June-July and nesting (N)

Yellow Warbler (*Dendroica petechia*)

Status: Regular; nests

Jan	Feb	Mar	Apr	May	Jun	Jul	Aug	Sep	Oct	Nov	Dec
									XX		

Earliest	Latest
24 Apr 1982	26 Sep 1946
24 Apr 1990	2 Oct 1982
26 Apr 1989	5 Oct 1967

Occurrence: This uncommon to locally common migrant and nesting species occurs in all areas of the state. It arrives by early May. Yellow Warblers leave soon after nesting, beginning in mid-July, so few are seen in fall. Breeding birds are found in willows and shrubs near open water. Migrants may be found anywhere. On Breeding Bird Surveys from 1967 to 1991, Yellow Warblers were found on 27 percent of routes. They are most common in the lakes region of northwestern Iowa and along the Mississippi River in northeastern Iowa.

Comment: Yellow Warbler with its several subspecies is the most widespread of the wood warblers. The northern migratory "Yellow Warbler" is referred to as the *aestiva* group. Its winter range extends from the southern portions of California, Arizona, and Florida through Middle America and the West Indies to the Amazon Basin. Its breeding range in the West extends from northern Mexico to well beyond the Arctic Circle in Alaska and Canada, and in the East from the northern parts of states along the Gulf Coast to the Arctic.

Chestnut-sided Warbler (*Dendroica pensylvanica*)

Status: Regular; occasionally nests

Jan	Feb	Mar	Apr	May	Jun	Jul	Aug	Sep	Oct	Nov	Dec
									X X	X	

Earliest	Latest
3 May 1986	5 Oct 1986
3 May 1993	17 Oct 1993
4 May 1987	21 Nov 1992

Occurrence: This common migrant does not arrive until early May and peaks in mid-May. In fall it is among the more common warblers from late August to late September. There are 3 modern confirmed nesting records: 6 July 1978 at Volga Lake in Fayette County (Schaufenbuel 1979), 21 July 1983 in Poweshiek County (Koenig 1983), and near Amana in Iowa County (Jackson et al. 1996). Other summer records since 1978 (map) suggest nesting, especially the successive yearly records in Boone, Fayette, and Allamakee counties.

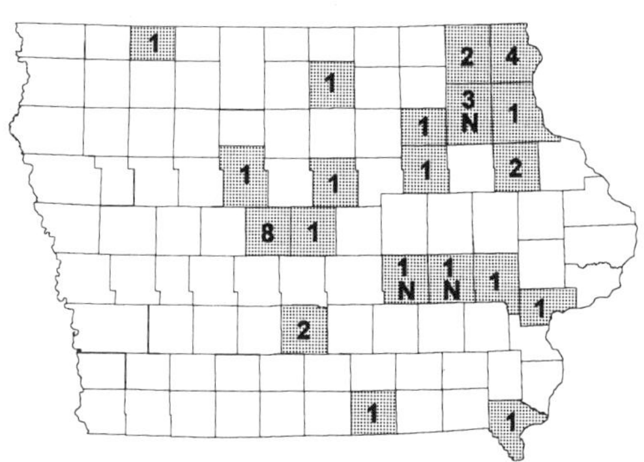

Chestnut-sided Warbler, 1960-1995
June-July and nesting (N)

Historically, Chestnut-sided Warbler was noted as breeding in 12 counties (10 in the eastern half of the state), and it was considered a common summer resident (Anderson 1907). Nests were confirmed in Lee and Van Buren counties in southeastern Iowa, Jackson County in east-central Iowa, Pottawattamie County in southwestern Iowa, and Kossuth County in north-central Iowa (Anderson 1907, DuMont 1936). By 1900 this species had disappeared as a summer resident (DuMont 1933). The next 2 summer records were 19 June 1952 at Des Moines in Polk County and 1 July 1963 at Decorah in Winneshiek County (Brown 1971).

Comment: The winter range is in Central America. The breeding range is in the eastern United States and Canada from Saskatchewan, Minnesota, Wisconsin, and northeastern Illinois east to the Maritime Provinces and south along the Appalachians, with an isolated population in Colorado. The current range in Minnesota is north of Minneapolis (Janssen 1987) and in northern and central Wisconsin (Robbins 1991). The range extended south in these states and into Iowa and Missouri prior to 1900.

Reference:

Koenig, D. 1983. Chestnut-sided Warbler nest. *Iowa Bird Life* 53:77.

Magnolia Warbler (*Dendroica magnolia*)

Status: Regular

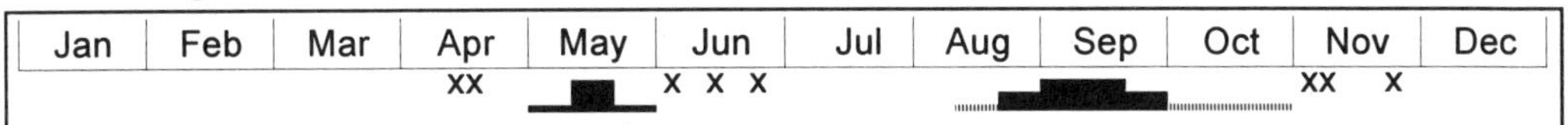

Jan	Feb	Mar	Apr	May	Jun	Jul	Aug	Sep	Oct	Nov	Dec
			XX		X X X					XX X	

18 Apr 1886	6 Jun 1972	12 Aug 1986	2 Nov 1974
18 Apr 1982	16 Jun 1989	14 Aug 1982	2 Nov 1974
2 May 1964	22 Jun 1976	14 Aug 1986	26 Nov 1954

Occurrence: This fairly common migrant has an average spring and fall migration interval with scattered early and late dates.

Comment: The winter range is in southern Mexico, Central America, and the West Indies with casual occurrence in the southern United States. The breeding range includes most of Canada, the northern part of border states from Minnesota east, and the northern Appalachians.

Cape May Warbler (*Dendroica tigrina*)

Status: Regular

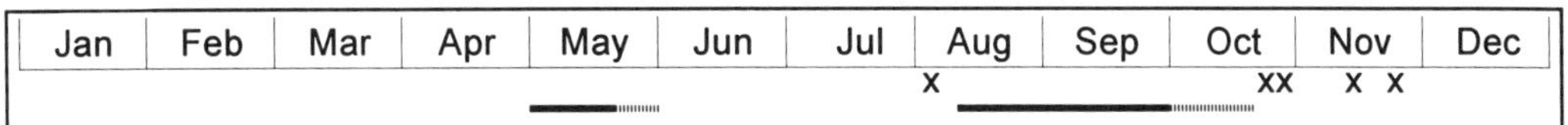

Jan	Feb	Mar	Apr	May	Jun	Jul	Aug	Sep	Oct	Nov	Dec
							X		XX	X X	

1 May 1985	23 May 1983	2 Aug 1988	24 Oct 1987
1 May 1985	24 May 1996	11 Aug 1977	17 Nov 1964
4 May 1991	26 May 1996	11 Aug 1991	27 Nov 1886

Occurrence: The spring migration interval of this rare migrant is compact with two-thirds of records from mid-May. Females arrive later than males and are rarely reported. There are about the same number of fall records as spring records, but they are more widely distributed, from mid-August to late September with a few stragglers into October and November. The number of reports fluctuates from year to year, varying from 3 to 37 locations per year. Records are from all areas of the state, but most are in eastern and central Iowa, with few in the southwest. Birds may be found in almost any habitat; however, this species has a preference for conifers and is often found in cemeteries and windbreaks.

Comment: The winter range is in the West Indies with a few birds remaining in southern Florida. The breeding range stretches from Alberta to the Maritime Provinces dipping into northern states from North Dakota to New England. The relatively late spring arrival in Iowa is consistent with the long distance from wintering grounds. Iowa lies on the southern edge of the diagonal southeast-to-northwest migration route. The population of Cape May Warblers varies from year to year in association with outbreaks of spruce budworms on the nesting grounds. Clutch size averages large in years with plentiful food supply (Harrison 1984), which may partially account for yearly variation in numbers.

Black-throated Blue Warbler (*Dendoica caerulescens*)

Status: Regular

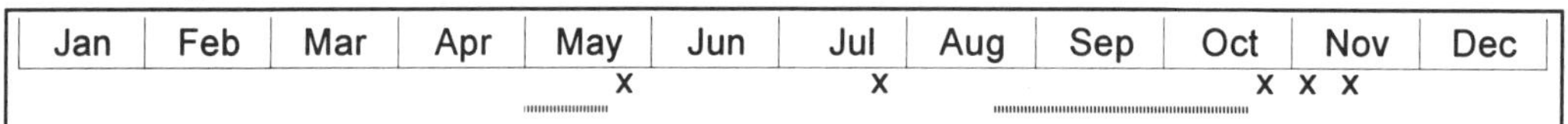

Jan	Feb	Mar	Apr	May	Jun	Jul	Aug	Sep	Oct	Nov	Dec

6 May 1978	19 May 1980	23 Aug 1986	31 Oct 1987
6 May 1983	20 May 1983	24 Aug 1985	3 Nov 1962
6 May 1991	21 May 1983	27 Aug 1989	20 Nov 1943

summer: 26 Jul 1990

Occurrence: Fall records of this very rare migrant outnumber spring records by about 5 to 1. The number of reports varies from 2 to 11 per year. The spring migration interval is short, with three-fourths of the records from mid-May, and the fall migration interval is long, ranging from late August to mid-October, with most of the records in September. There are records from all areas of the state, but very few from the west and south. There is 1 summer record, likely a stray or possibly a very early migrant, in southwestern Iowa at Waubonsie State Park in Fremont County (*IBL* 60:105).

Comment: The winter range is in the West Indies. The breeding range extends from northern Minnesota and Wisconsin and south ern Ontario east to the Maritime Provinces and south in the Appalachians. The relatively late spring arrival in Iowa is consistent with the long distance from wintering grounds. The migration pattern of Black-throated Blue Warbler in Iowa is similar to Cape May Warbler in that both migrate diagonally from the West Indies to areas north of Iowa, but the range of Black-throated Blue Warbler does not go west of Iowa, which may account for it being the rarer of the 2 species here. Very few Black-throated Blues overshoot to Iowa in the spring, but in fall more birds must take a southerly or southwesterly route to reach Iowa. Nearby states also have recorded a few late fall migrants.

Yellow-rumped Warbler (*Dendroica coronata*)

Status: Regular

Jan	Feb	Mar	Apr	May	Jun	Jul	Aug	Sep	Oct	Nov	Dec
					x x		x x				

29 May 1996
2 Jun 1966
17 Jun 1978

6 Aug 1988
13 Aug 1991
23 Aug 1987

Occurrence: This abundant early spring and late fall migrant may be found in large loose flocks, especially from late April to early May and early to mid-October. A few birds have lingered into June and a few have returned in August. Yellow-rumped and Tennessee warblers are the most abundant migrant warblers in Iowa, but their numbers peak at different times.

On Christmas Bird Counts, Yellow-rumped Warblers were reported in 1953 and at 3 locations in 1962. None were reported again until 1972, but since then there have been reports in 17 of 22 years (usually 1 to 4 locations). On the 1992-1993 Christmas Bird Counts, 44 individuals were seen on 12 counts, and individuals lingered through the winter in Cerro Gordo, Polk, and Appanoose counties. The only other January and February records (excluding Christmas Bird Counts) are 7 February 1954 in Linn County (Brown 1971), 22 February 1982 in Polk County (*IBL* 52:28), 28 January 1983 in Cherokee County (*IBL* 53:27), 5 January 1985 in Decatur County (*IBL* 55:29), 19 to 20 January 1985 in Marshall County (*IBL* 55:29), 23 January to 20 February 1988 in Warren County (*IBL* 58:57), and 27 January 1991 in Van Buren County (*IBL* 61:59).

Historically, Yellow-rumped Warbler was not mentioned as occurring in Iowa in winter (Anderson 1907, DuMont 1933), and prior to 1972 only the records listed above are mentioned (Brown 1971). Wisconsin had its first Christmas Bird Count record in 1957 (Robbins 1991).

The western subspecies, Audubon's Warbler (*D. c. auduboni*), has been recorded 3 times: 30 April 1934 in Winneshiek County (DuMont 1944), 27 October 1981 in Johnson County (*IBL* 51:121), and 28 April 1988 in Pocahontas County (*IBL* 58:83).

Comment: The winter range includes all of Middle America, the West Indies, and much of the southern and coastal United States, and occasionally to northern states. The breeding range in the West extends from northern Mexico to northern Alaska and east to western South Dakota, and in the East across Canada and northern parts of northern states and the northern part of the Appalachians. Almost all of the Iowa winter records are from the Christmas Bird Count period, suggesting that the apparent increase in records in recent years could be related to intensity of coverage on these counts; however, the paucity of birds prior to 1972 does suggest a real increase in wintering birds since that time. We do not know how many of the late December birds migrate south, stay through the winter, or perish.

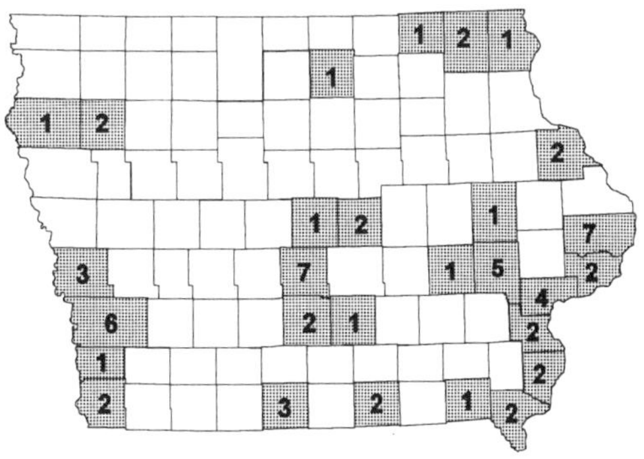

Yellow-rumped Warbler 1960-1995
December-February

Black-throated Gray Warbler (*Dendroica nigrescens*)

Status: Accidental

19 May 1961, Sioux City, Woodbury Co. (Youngworth 1961)

Occurrence: There is 1 sight record from spring.

Comment: This western warbler breeds from southern British Columbia east to Colorado and New Mexico and south to northern Mexico and winters from southern Arizona to southern Mexico. Eastward vagrancy is well established with a few records from most states and provinces northeast to Nova Scotia and southeast to Georgia. There are more records from the East than from the Midwest. About two-thirds of the vagrant records are from September to December and the rest from late April to May.

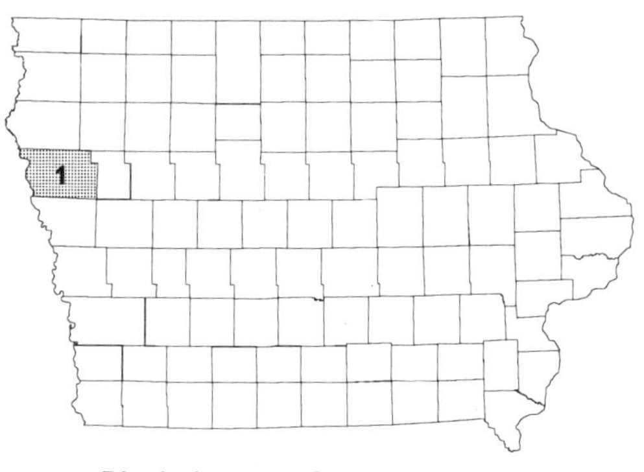

Black-throated Gray Warbler, all

Reference:

Youngworth, W. 1961. Black-throated Gray Warbler at Sioux City. *Iowa Bird Life* 31:69.

Townsend's Warbler (*Dendroica townsendi*)

Status: Accidental

7 May 1950, Davenport, Scott Co. (Feeney 1950) 12 May 1988, Wildcat Den S.P., Muscatine Co. (White 1989) 11 May 1991, Stone S.P., Woodbury Co. (*IBL* 61:95; 62:71)

Occurrence: The 3 sight records are from spring.

Comment: Townsend's Warbler is a more northerly species than Black-throated Gray Warbler, breeding from southern Alaska to Washington and east to Montana and wintering in western California and south to Central America. Vagrant records are from the Great Plains states, centrally from Iowa to New Jersey, and sporadically along the East Coast from Newfoundland to Florida. There are slightly more vagrant records for Townsend's than for Black-throated Gray Warbler, and they are about equally divided between late April to early May and September to December.

References:

Feeney, T. J. 1950. Townsend's Warbler at Davenport. *Iowa Bird Life* 20:61.

White, G. 1989. Townsend's Warbler in Muscatine County. *Iowa Bird Life* 59:62-63.

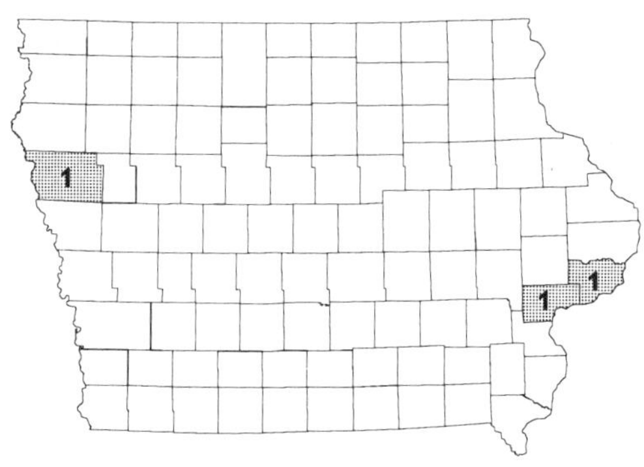

Townsend's Warbler, all

Black-throated Green Warbler (*Dendroica virens*)

Status: Regular

Jan	Feb	Mar	Apr	May	Jun	Jul	Aug	Sep	Oct	Nov	Dec

8 Apr 1986	31 May 1993	13 Aug 1989	28 Oct 1981
14 Apr 1984	1 Jun 1994	13 Aug 1991	3 Nov 1984
22 Apr 1987	1 Jun 1983	16 Aug 1986	10 Nov 1975

summer: 16 Jun 1992, 3 Jul 1994, 12, 14 Jun 1995

Occurrence: This uncommon to common migrant has an average migration peak with a more-than-average number of early and late stragglers. There are 3 records from mid-June to early July.

Comment: The winter range includes southern Texas, eastern Mexico, Central America, southern Florida, and the West Indies. The breeding range extends from Alberta to Labrador, south to northern Minnesota and Wisconsin, and south in the Appalachians to Alabama.

Blackburnian Warbler (*Dendroica fusca*)

Status: Regular

Jan	Feb	Mar	Apr	May	Jun	Jul	Aug	Sep	Oct	Nov	Dec

29 Apr 1981	5 Jun 1985	2 Aug 1988	17 Oct 1981
30 Apr 1944	6 Jun 1993	9 Aug 1988	18 Oct 1984
1 May 1993	8 Jun 1986	10 Aug 1991	16 Nov 1974

summer: 6 Jul 1985

Occurrence: This uncommon warbler has an average migration interval, which includes May and late August to September. The average spring arrival dates are unusual for such a long-distance migrant. There is 1 summer record.

Comment: The wintering grounds are in southern Central America and South America south to Peru. The breeding range is from Saskatchewan and northeastern Minnesota east to the Maritime Provinces and south in the Appalachians to Georgia.

Yellow-throated Warbler (*Dendroica dominica*)

Status: Regular; nests

Jan	Feb	Mar	Apr	May	Jun	Jul	Aug	Sep	Oct	Nov	Dec
			XX					X X XX		X	

5 Apr 1991	22 Sep 1985
6 Apr 1991	27 Sep 1986
11 Apr 1981	4 Nov 1981

Occurrence: This rare summer resident arrives early, often by mid-April, and leaves by September. It is reported most regularly from Lacey-Keosauqua State Park in Van Buren County and Ledges State Park in Boone County. Other counties with records in 3 or more years include Lee, Warren, and Polk along the Des Moines River and Des Moines and Muscatine along the Mississippi River. Sightings at Pine Lake in Hardin County in 1988, 1990, and 1993 were unusually far north. Individual birds seen in other counties (map) could be migrants, strays, or nesting birds. It is likely that undiscovered breeding sites exist, such as in Johnson County where birds were found in June from 1993 to 1995 during an intensive breeding bird survey (Kent et al. 1994).

This species has a strong preference for sycamore trees, where it is usually detected because of its persistent singing. Only 2 nests have been discovered, both at Lacey-Keosauqua State Park (Koenig 1981, *IBL* 56:118). There is no existing specimen and the only photograph is of a bird that was stunned by hitting a window at Seymour in Wayne County on 11 September 1982 (P-0090, *IBL* 52:124). A very late bird was at Cedar Rapids in Linn County on 4 November 1981 (*IBL* 51:121).

Historically, the first report of this species was a specimen taken by George Berry at Keokuk on 4 May 1888 and later examined by Anderson (1907). Other early reports were from Wall Lake in Sac County on 13 May 1913 (Spurrell 1921), Rock Bluff in Wapello County on 28 August 1913 (Spiker 1924), Sigourney in Keokuk County in 1917, 1920-1922, 1924, and 1927 (DuMont 1933), at Des Moines in Polk County on 29 August 1926 and 29 May 1927, at Iowa City in Johnson County on 17 May 1931 (Roberts 1931), and near Cedar Rapids on 16 May 1935 (Serbousek 1936). No more were seen until 17 June 1969, when 1 was discovered at Ledges State Park in Boone County (Brooke 1969). Birds have been found at that location in most years since. In the 1970s other populations were discovered near Burlington in Des Moines County (Fuller 1974), at Wildcat Den State Park in Muscatine County (*IBL* 49:62), at Lacey-Keosauqua State Park in Van Buren County (*IBL* 49:62), and at Shimek Forest in Lee County (*IBL* 49:84).

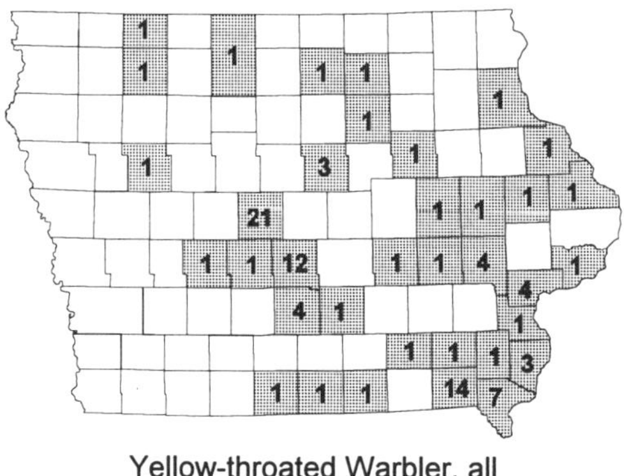

Yellow-throated Warbler, all

Comment: The winter range is from the southern United States to the West Indies and northern Central America. The breeding range is from the Gulf Coast west to eastern Texas and north to southern Iowa and New Jersey. The subspecies *D. d. albilora*, also known as the Sycamore Warbler, breeds west of the Appalachians and winters in Middle America, and can be identified by lack of any yellow in the supercilliary stripe (other subspecies have yellow anteriorly).

In Ohio, there was a decline in Yellow-throated Warblers in the 1800s with few remaining in the 1920s (Peterjohn 1989). The population began to expand in the 1940s but was not widespread in central Ohio until the 1960s. There was a range expansion in Pennsylvania in 1983 (Harrison 1984). The Iowa data are also consistent with a species that is experiencing a range expansion.

References:

Brooke, M. 1969. Yellow-throated Warbler in Ledges State Park. *Iowa Bird Life* 39:64.

Fuller, J. C. 1974. Birding areas in Des Moines County and adjacent Illinois with some Lee County areas. *Iowa Bird Life* 44:95-100.

Koenig, D. 1981. A Yellow-throated Warbler nest in Iowa. *Iowa Bird Life* 51:104-105.

Roberts, F. L. R. 1931. Notes from Iowa City. *Iowa Bird Life* 1:24.

Serbousek, L. 1936. Spring birds in eastern Iowa. *Iowa Bird Life* 6:42.

Pine Warbler (*Dendroica pinus*)

Status: Regular

Jan	Feb	Mar	Apr	May	Jun	Jul	Aug	Sep	Oct	Nov	Dec
+ + + +			x	x			x				xx +

17 Apr 1948	19 May 1951	6 Aug 1989	4 Oct 1986
23 Apr 1992	20 May 1945	24 Aug 1985	4 Oct 1981
24 Apr 1994	24 May 1984	24 Aug 1987	8 Oct 1994

winter: 19 Dec 1991-10 Feb 1992, 20 Dec 1992-6 Jan 1993

Occurrence: This very rare migrant (2 to 9 reports per year) is found from late April to mid-May and late August to early October. There are 2 recent winter records (Schantz and Black 1993, Fuller 1993). Most records are from eastern and central Iowa and are reported by the most active birders, suggesting that this species could be found in more locations if looked for. Several were found in Sioux City in northwestern Iowa by an active observer (Youngworth 1963).

Pine Warblers prefer conifers but may be found in deciduous trees in migration. They are relatively easy to identify in spring when they are in breeding plumage and singing. In fall, some, especially immatures, are quite similar to many Blackpoll and Bay-breasted warblers. Yet, 60 percent of Pine Warblers are reported from fall, some of which may have been misidentified.

Historically, the scattered reports (Anderson 1907, DuMont 1933) suggest a pattern of occurrence similar to the current pattern.

Comment: The winter range is in the southeastern United States and parts of the West Indies. The breeding range includes most of the winter range and north to southern Canada with a gap across the Midwest in areas with few pine trees. It breeds south of Iowa up to the Ozarks in Missouri, north of Iowa in northern Minnesota and Wisconsin, and, historically, east of Iowa in northern Illinois and Indiana. There are scattered late fall and winter records from adjacent states.

References:

Fuller, J. 1993. Pine Warblers in winter at Iowa City. *Iowa Bird Life* 63:106,108.

Schantz, T., and G. Black. 1993. A wintering Pine Warbler in Marion County. *Iowa Bird Life* 63:81-82.

Youngworth, W. 1963. The Pine Warbler as a migrant in the Sioux City area. *Iowa Bird Life* 33:84-85.

Prairie Warbler (*Dendroica discolor*)

Status: Regular; occasionally nests

Jan	Feb	Mar	Apr	May	Jun	Jul	Aug	Sep	Oct	Nov	Dec

30 Apr 1995 — 5 Sep 1977
5 May 1994 — 7 Sep 1991
7 May 1992 — 15 Sep 1984
nesting: 8 Jul 1995, L. Macbride, Johnson Co. (Edwards 1995)

Occurrence: Prairie Warbler barely reaches Iowa as a very rare over-migrant and nesting species, occurring at 1 or 2 locations in all except 2 of the last 15 years. Definite evidence of nesting was not found, however, until 8 July 1995, when a pair were found feeding 4 fledglings at Lake Macbride (Edwards 1995). Most of the reports (15 of 20) have been from 3 widely separated counties in eastern Iowa (Lee, Johnson, and Allamakee), where most are found in old-field scrub habitat. Most have been males that were singing persistently as if on territory; some have remained for a few days and others for weeks or months. Male(s) were present at the same location in the Croton Unit of Shimek Forest in Lee County for at least 6 years beginning in 1984 (Cecil 1985). An immature and an adult female were there on 12 and 15 August 1986, respectively (*IBL* 57:21), and a pair was there on 24 June 1993 (*IBL* 63:98).

Historically, of the 13 reports prior to 1977, none were accepted by the Records Committee, but 4 were considered probably correct and the others lacked sufficient information to make a judgment. The most interesting of these old records was a nest found on 5 June 1886 north of Keokuk in Lee County (DuMont 1935b, 1936). Also, throughout June 1962 a singing male was noted at Yellow River Forest in Allamakee County (Koenig 1974, 1979), a location where birds have been found several times since. Other probably correct records include early migrants on 23 April 1960 at George Wyth State Park in Black Hawk County (Hays 1960) and on 26 April 1954 at Grundy Center in Grundy County (King 1954).

Comment: The winter range is from central Florida south to the West Indies. The breeding range is in the eastern United States and southern Ontario. The western edge of the range extends to eastern Texas and Oklahoma. It is found in the Ozarks and adjacent areas in Missouri and in southern Illinois and Indiana. The edge of the range is irregular with scattered birds north of the usual range in Iowa, Wisconsin, and Illinois, but only accidentally in Minnesota.

References:

Cecil, R. I. 1985. Prairie Warbler in Lee County. *Iowa Bird Life* 55:98.

Edwards, C. 1995. Prairie Warblers nesting in Johnson County. *Iowa Bird Life* 65:105.

Hays, R. 1960. Bird notes from Waterloo. *Iowa Bird Life* 30:68.

King, Mrs. J. R. 1954. Bird notes from central Iowa. *Iowa Bird Life* 24:59.

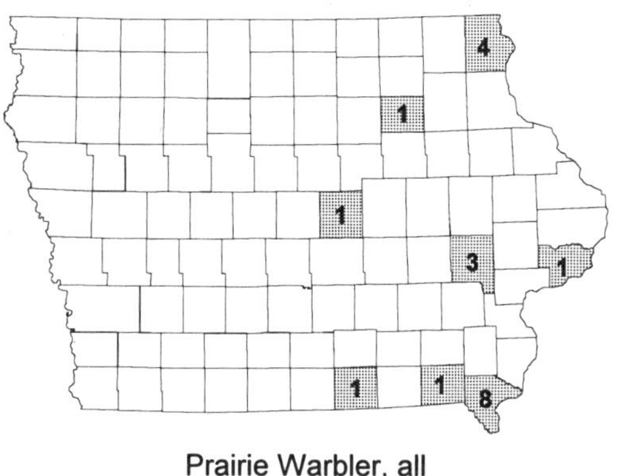

Prairie Warbler, all

Palm Warbler (*Dendroica palmarum*)

Status: Regular

Jan	Feb	Mar	Apr	May	Jun	Jul	Aug	Sep	Oct	Nov	Dec
							x x		x	x	

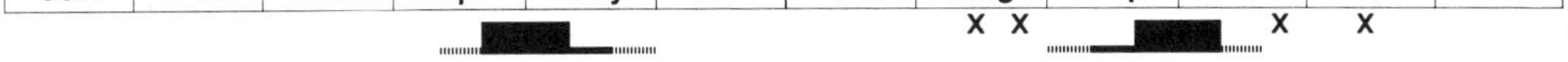

19 Apr 1991	20 May 1992	17 Aug 1991	17 Oct 1992
20 Apr 1986	22 May 1967	28 Aug 1993	21 Oct 1984
20 Apr 1993	29 May 1968	2 Sep 1991	17 Nov 1974

Occurrence: Palm Warbler is a common early spring and late fall migrant. It is often found in open areas.
Comment: The winter range extends from South Carolina to Florida and along the Gulf Coast to northern Central America and to the West Indies. The breeding range is mostly in Canada from Mackenzie and Alberta to Labrador and dipping into the northern parts of Minnesota, Wisconsin, and Michigan. There are at least 5 winter records for Illinois, some as far north as Chicago (Bohlen 1989), and 4 from Missouri (Robbins and Easterla 1992).

Bay-breasted Warbler (*Dendroica castanea*)

Status: Regular

Jan	Feb	Mar	Apr	May	Jun	Jul	Aug	Sep	Oct	Nov	Dec
			x xx		x						

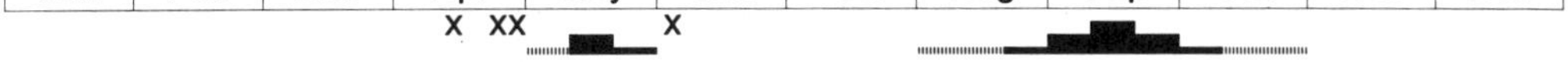

18 Apr 1982	29 May 1968	4 Aug 1989	20 Oct 1979
28 Apr 1989	31 May 1983	5 Aug 1988	23 Oct 1989
28 Apr 1989	7 Jun 1992	10 Aug 1991	30 Oct 1976

Occurrence: This uncommon late spring migrant is much more common in fall, when it is also somewhat late. At Ames, the number per season from 1982 to 1986 averaged 3 in spring and 29 in fall (Martsching 1986, 1987). At Alleman Towers in Polk County, Bay-breasted made up 10 percent of the warblers killed in the fall of 1973 and 4 percent in the fall of 1974, compared to only 1 bird (less than 1 percent) in the spring of 1974 (Mosman 1975). Identification is easy in spring, but in fall immatures must be distinguished from the similar Pine and Blackpoll warblers.
Comment: The winter range is in Panama and northern South America, mainly Colombia. The breeding range is from Mackenzie and northeastern British Columbia to the Maritime Provinces dipping south into northern Minnesota and Wisconsin. The numbers of Bay-breasted Warblers may be influenced by outbreaks on the nesting grounds of spruce budworms, a favored food item (Harrison 1984).

Blackpoll Warbler (*Dendroica striata*)

Status: Regular

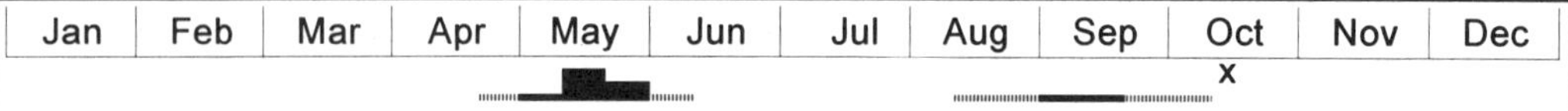

Jan	Feb	Mar	Apr	May	Jun	Jul	Aug	Sep	Oct	Nov	Dec
									X		

26 Apr 1994	1 Jun 1983	16 Aug 1986	5 Oct 1967
27 Apr 1985	7 Jun 1982	18 Aug 1991	5 Oct 1977
28 Apr 1951	9 Jun 1967	20 Aug 1989	12 Oct 1981

Occurrence: This common and relatively late spring migrant is rare in fall. At Ames, the average number per season from 1982 to 1986 averaged 56 in spring and 4 in fall (Martsching 1986, 1987). At Alleman Towers in Polk County, Blackpolls made up 14 percent of the warblers killed in the spring of 1974, compared to only 2 birds (less than 0.3 percent) in the fall of 1974 and none in the fall of 1973 (Mosman 1975). The spring birds heading west hit Iowa, while the fall migration is to the northern Atlantic Coast and south with some birds taking an oceanic route to South America. Fall birds, both adults and immatures, must be distinguished from similar appearing Pine and Bay-breasted warblers.

Comment: The winter range is in South America from Colombia south and east of the Andes to northern Argentina. This long-distance migrant breeds in the northern part of the Canadian Provinces north and west to the Arctic Circle in Alaska and to the Yukon, Mackenzie, and Labrador. The eastern edge of the range extends south to northern New York and New England.

Cerulean Warbler (*Dendroica cerulea*)

Status: Regular; nests

Jan	Feb	Mar	Apr	May	Jun	Jul	Aug	Sep	Oct	Nov	Dec
			XX					X X	X		

18 Apr 1992	2 Sep 1991
19 Apr 1992	26 Sep 1986
22 Apr 1985	3 Oct 1964

Occurrence: This rare summer resident is found in eastern Iowa along the Mississippi River and its tributaries and in central Iowa in counties along the Des Moines River. There are summer records for only 2 counties in western Iowa. The distribution of spring records is similar to that of summer records, suggesting that most birds seen in spring have arrived on their nesting grounds. Ceruleans are rarely seen away from deep-woods habitat, which may be in river bottoms or on bluffs. Most are not found until May, but some arrive in southeastern Iowa in April.

There are fewer than 10 records after July. Ceruleans inhabit treetops where they may not move a lot and are most easily detected by their song. Thus, it is not surprising that few are detected after 1 July or in fall migration. A thorough search of appropriate habitat is needed to find breeding sites. For example, only 5 sites were found in the extensive woodlands of the Coralville Reservoir in 4 years of surveying (Kent et al. 1994). The few recent and old (see below) records along the Missouri River suggest that the range may extend that far west.

Reports of nesting are as follows: May 1957 nest under construction at Yellow River Forest in Allamakee County (Brown 1971); 16 June 1975 nest with young at Yellow River Forest (Koenig 1976); 26 May 1976 carrying nest material at Palisades-Kepler State Park in Linn County (*IBL* 47:61); 21 June 1985 female feeding young cowbird at Shimek Forest in Lee County (*IBL* 55:94); and 17 June 1986 nest with 4 young at Lacey-Keosauqua State Park in Van Buren County (*IBL* 56:118).

Historically, Cerulean Warblers were first noted in early July 1868 at Boonesboro in Boone County by J. A. Allen (Allen 1868) and were still present there in 1931 (DuMont 1933). Old records from western Iowa include August [no year] in Emmet County (DuMont 1933), a specimen taken on 20 May 1899 at Sioux City in Woodbury County (DuMont 1933), and 9 June 1946 at Waubonsie State Park in Fremont County (Youngworth 1946).

Comment: The winter range is in South America from Colombia and Venezuela south and east of the Andes to northern Bolivia. The breeding range is from northern parts of Gulf Coast states north to southern Minnesota and southern Ontario, and from eastern Oklahoma and southeastern Nebraska east to New Jersey and central North Carolina. The population of this species, which is centered in Ohio, is thought to be declining due to loss of habitat on breeding and wintering grounds (Robbins et al. 1992).

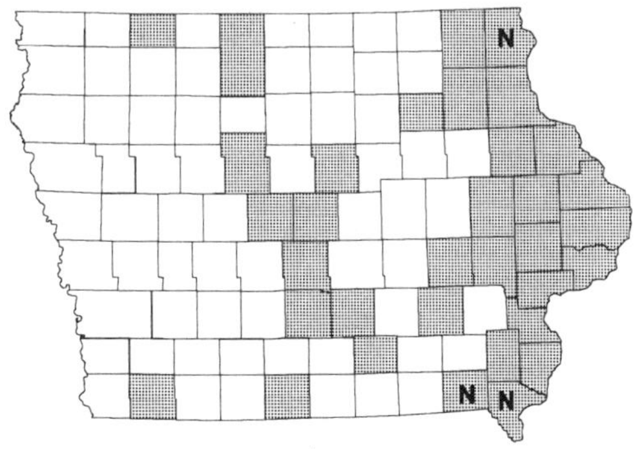

Cerulean Warbler, 1960-1995
June-July and nesting (N)

References:

Robbins, C. S., J. W. Fitzpatrick, and P. B. Hamel. 1992. A warbler in trouble: *Dendroica cerulea.* In: Hagen, J. W., and D. W. Johnston, eds. *Ecology and Conserva-*

tion of Neotropical Migrant Landbirds. Smithsonian Institution Press, Washington, D.C.

Youngworth, W. 1946. Blue Grosbeaks and other birds. *Iowa Bird Life* 16:65.

Black-and-white Warbler (*Mniotilta varia*)

Status: Regular; occasionally nests

Jan	Feb	Mar	Apr	May	Jun	Jul	Aug	Sep	Oct	Nov	Dec
		X	XX						X	X	

Early dates	Late dates
31 Mar 1979	16 Oct 1992
5 Apr 1981	30 Oct 1982
10 Apr 1988	4 Nov 1995

Occurrence: This common migrant is slightly on the early side in spring and average in fall, with scattered early and late dates. From 1 to 4 have been reported in June/July in 12 of the last 15 years. Most of these have been found in the wooded southwestern, southeastern, and northeastern corners of the state.

Although this species should nest in Iowa, the confirmed nesting records are few and mostly old: adults and young taken in 1895 in Allamakee and Winneshiek counties (Bartsch 1897); nest with 6 eggs (2 cowbird) in 1889 near Missouri Valley in Harrison County (Toppan 1889); nest in late May 1896 in Van Buren or Henry County (Anderson 1907); nest with 3 eggs on 4 June 1901 near Keokuk in Lee County (DuMont 1936); young birds on 11 August 1929 at Sioux City in Woodbury County (DuMont 1933); and adult feeding young in June 1968 at Waubonsie State Park in Fremont County (Silcock 1977). More recently, a netted female had a brood patch on 4 July 1988 at West Okoboji in Dickinson County (*IBL* 58:112).

Comment: The extensive winter range includes Florida and the Gulf Coast to Mexico, southern Mexico to northwestern South America, and the West Indies. The breeding range includes the eastern United States north of the narrow Gulf Coast wintering range and Canada northwest to Mackenzie. It extends west to central Texas and the central Great Plains, curiously skipping Iowa. The major breeding areas in adjacent states, however, are not very close to Iowa (the Ozarks in Missouri, southern Illinois, and northern Minnesota and Wisconsin). There are single December records from southern Wisconsin (Robbins 1991) and southern Illinois (Bohlen 1989), and a February record from Duluth, Minnesota (Janssen 1987).

Reference:

Toppan, G. L. 1889. A pleasant hour. *Ornithologist and Oologist* 14:166.

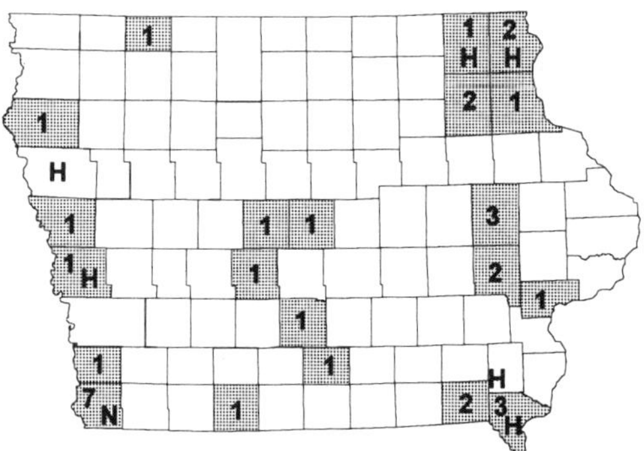

Black-and-white Warbler, 1960-1995
June-July and nesting (recent N, historic H)

American Redstart (*Setophaga ruticilla*)

Status: Regular; nests

Jan	Feb	Mar	Apr	May	Jun	Jul	Aug	Sep	Oct	Nov	Dec
			XX						X XX	X	

27 Apr 1954	23 Oct 1983
29 Apr 1994	23 Oct 1979
30 Apr 1951	18 Nov 1994

Occurrence: This common migrant and summer resident is found throughout the state. It breeds in woodland habitat along major streams and rivers in Iowa. An example of its abundance in summer is the 75 counted along 20 miles of the Des Moines River in Boone County in 1987 (*IBL* 57:122). At the Coralville Reservoir in wooded areas, American Redstarts were about as common as Indigo Bunting and Red-eyed Vireo (Kent et al. 1994).

Comment: The winter range is from southern Florida and central Mexico south to northern South America and the West Indies. The breeding range in the East extends from near the Gulf Coast to Labrador and in the West from northern Colorado to Mackenzie.

Prothonotary Warbler (*Protonotaria citrea*)

Status: Regular; nests

Jan	Feb	Mar	Apr	May	Jun	Jul	Aug	Sep	Oct	Nov	Dec
								XX			

26 Apr 1982	31 Aug 1963
26 Apr 1994	3 Sep 1967
27 Apr 1985	9 Sep 1989

Occurrence: This rare summer resident is found along river bottoms, backwaters, and lakes, where it nests in holes in dead snags. It is usually, but not always, found in the same habitat in migration. It is not surprising that its distribution follows the major rivers in Iowa. Although this species is easy to hear and see, and nests are easy to find because they are usually in stumps over water, there is much river bottom habitat that is difficult to survey. With some effort, more regular nesting sites could be located. Along the Mississippi River, House Wrens competed with Prothonotary Warblers for nest boxes (Brush 1994).

There is old and recent evidence of nesting in northwestern Iowa. A pair nested in a tin can nailed to a tree at West Okoboji in Dickinson County in 1914 (Stephens 1914). Another nest was found at Marble Lake in Dickinson County on 23 June 1991 (*IBL* 61:117). In O'Brien County, a nest was found along the Little Sioux River on 28 May 1989 (*IBL* 59:85).

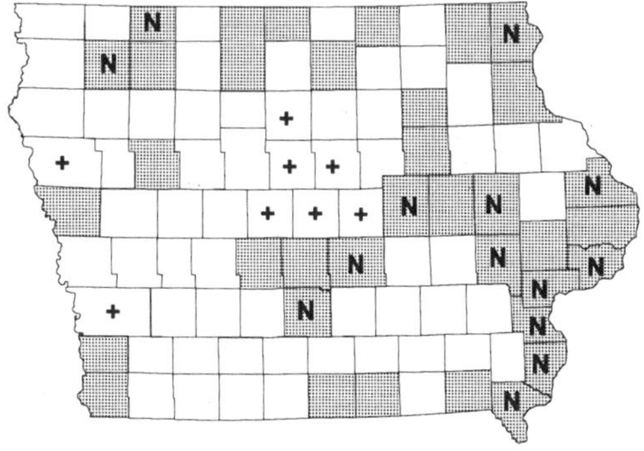

Prothonotary Warbler, 1960-1995
June-July, nesting (N), and spring (+)

There are only 9 reports in the last 10 years for August and September.

Comment: The winter range is from southern Mexico and the West Indies south to extreme northern South America. The breeding range is in the eastern United States and southern Ontario west to central Texas and southwest Iowa. The range extends up along the Mississippi River in Minnesota and Wisconsin to north of the Twin Cities.

References:

Brush, T. 1994. Effects of competition and predation on Prothonotary Warblers and House Wrens nesting in eastern Iowa. *J. Iowa Acad. Sci.* 101:28-30.

Stephens, T. C. 1914. The Prothonotary Warbler at Lake Okoboji, Iowa. *Wilson Bull.* 26:109-116.

Worm-eating Warbler (*Helmitheros vermivorus*)

Status: Regular; nests

Jan	Feb	Mar	Apr	May	Jun	Jul	Aug	Sep	Oct	Nov	Dec
								x x			
23 Apr 1976									31 Aug 1986		
24 Apr 1992									10 Sep 1985		
24 Apr 1994									15 Sep 1984		

Occurrence: This rare nesting species arrives in late April. Few are recorded after mid-July, but 2 have lingered to September. Most summer records are from southeastern Iowa and bordering east-central counties (map). Spring records extend to central and northeastern Iowa, where there are single summer records and nesting is possible. Nesting was confirmed at Croton Unit of Shimek Forest in Lee County from 1984 to 1990 (*IBL* 57:122, 59:114, 60:106; Cecil 1985, 1988).

Historically, Worm-eating Warbler was "a rare summer resident in southern Iowa, very seldom reaching the central part of the state" (Anderson 1907), which suggests that there has been little or no change in the range. A nest with 5 eggs was found in Henry County on 25 May 1893 (Savage 1893, 1899; the year and another record apparently misquoted by Anderson 1907). In Kossuth County, which is far from the usual range, a nest with eggs was found on 4 June 1904 (Anderson 1907).

Comment: The winter range is in the West Indies and from eastern Mexico south to Panama. The breeding range is in the eastern United States north to southeastern Nebraska and southern New York south to North Carolina and Arkansas. Worm-eating Warblers are found on heavily wooded hillsides with deep ravines. They are hard to find and their habitat difficult to survey, so the breeding range may be more extensive than currently known.

References:

Cecil, R. 1985. Possible Iowa nesting of Worm-eating Warbler. *Iowa Bird Life* 55:96-98.

Cecil, R. 1988. Double brooding by Worm-eating Warbler in Lee County. *Iowa Bird Life* 58:60.

Savage, D. L. 1893. Notes on the birds of Henry Co., Iowa. *Oologist* 10:325-326.

Savage, D. L. 1899. The Worm-eating Warbler. *Oologist.* 16:35.

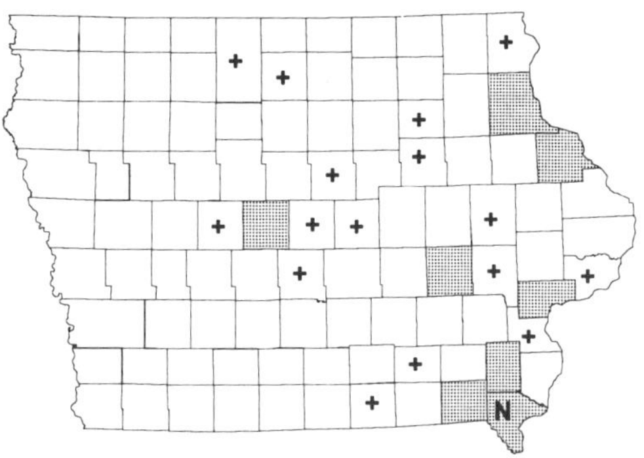

Worm-eating Warbler, 1960-1995
June-July, nesting (N), and spring (+)

Ovenbird (*Seiurus aurocapillus*)

Status: Regular; nests

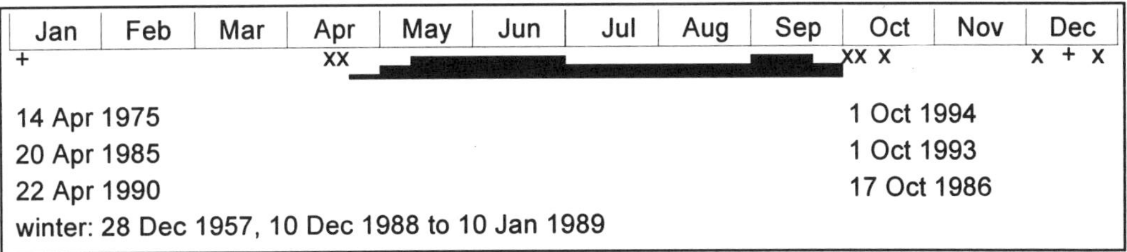

Occurrence: This common migrant and summer resident arrives in late April or early May and leaves by late September. At Alleman Towers in Polk County, Ovenbird was the most common warbler killed in the combined fall seasons of 1973 and 1974 (Mosman 1975), on 14 September 1982 (Dinsmore et al. 1983), and on 21-22 September 1985 (Dinsmore et al. 1987). There are two winter records: 9 and 28 December 1957 at Farley in Dubuque County (*IBL* 28:18), and 10 December 1988 to 10 January 1989 at Coralville in Johnson County (Butler 1989).

In migration, Ovenbird can be found anywhere in the state. Summer residents are also found in all areas of the state, but are most common in eastern and central Iowa and along the Missouri River where there are large wooded tracts. At the Coralville Reservoir in wooded areas, Ovenbirds were slightly less common during breeding season than American Redstart (0.9 vs. 1.4 birds per party-hour) (Kent et al. 1994).

Comment: The winter range is from the Gulf Coast through Middle America and the West Indies. The breeding range extends from northern Arkansas and northern Alabama north through the Canadian provinces and west to the eastern edge of the Rocky Mountains.

Reference:

Butler, J. E. 1989. Winter Ovenbird at Coralville. *Iowa Bird Life* 59:92.

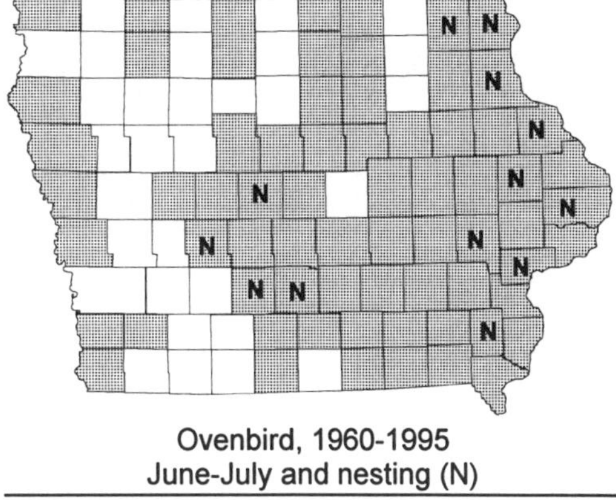

Ovenbird, 1960-1995
June-July and nesting (N)

Northern Waterthrush (*Seiurus noveboracensis*)

Status: Regular

Jan	Feb	Mar	Apr	May	Jun	Jul	Aug	Sep	Oct	Nov	Dec
					x				x	x x	

18 Apr 1985	1 Jun 1990	5 Aug 1987	7 Oct 1984
19 Apr 1980	1 Jun 1968	5 Aug 1988	18 Nov 1962
20 Apr 1985	1 Jun 1967	6 Aug 1976	21 Nov 1969
summer: 15 Jun 1980			

Occurrence: This uncommon migrant arrives slightly earlier than the average warbler in both spring and fall. Early spring birds must be carefully distinguished from Louisiana Waterthrush, which arrives even earlier. There is 1 summer record from 15 June 1980 in Iowa's only tract of sphagnum bog at Dead Man's Lake in Pilot Knob State Park in Hancock County (Schaufenbuel 1981). This habitat is appropriate for breeding, but a long way from the normal range in northern Minnesota. In migration, this species is often found near streams and pools.

Comment: The winter range is from southern Florida south through the West Indies and Middle America to northern South America. The breeding range is across Canada to timberline in northern Alaska and Northwest Territories, and south dipping into the northern United States.

Louisiana Waterthrush (*Seiurus motacilla*)

Status: Regular; nests

Jan	Feb	Mar	Apr	May	Jun	Jul	Aug	Sep	Oct	Nov	Dec
							x	xx			

29 Mar 1994	21 Aug 1985
30 Mar 1991	2 Sep 1968
30 Mar 1993	9 Sep 1958

Occurrence: This rare summer resident breeds in eastern, southern, and central Iowa. Favorite locations are Shimek Forest in Lee County, Lacey-Keosauqua State Park in Van Buren County, Waubonsie State Park in Fremont County, Ledges State Park in Boone County, and Yellow River Forest in Allamakee County; however, it has been found at many other locations. Searches of heavily wooded ravines with small streams would likely reveal more nesting birds. There are 3 summer records from west-central and northwestern Iowa. Nesting was confirmed at 35 percent of summer locations in the breeding bird atlas study, a high level compared to other warblers (Jackson et al. 1996).

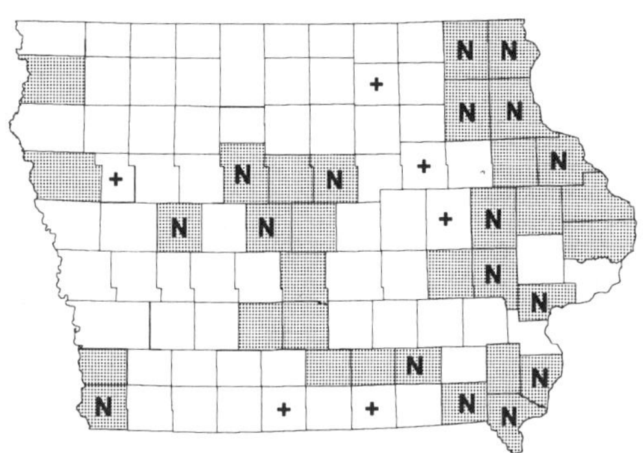

Louisiana Waterthrush, 1960-1995
June-July, nesting (N), and spring (+)

Comment: The winter range is in the West Indies, Middle America, and extreme northern

South America. The breeding range is in the eastern United States north of the Gulf Coast, north to the Twin Cities and southern Ontario, and west to northeastern Texas and eastern Nebraska.

Kentucky Warbler (*Oporornis formosus*)

Status: Regular; nests

Jan	Feb	Mar	Apr	May	Jun	Jul	Aug	Sep	Oct	Nov	Dec
								X			

Early dates	Late dates
24 Apr 1985	15 Sep 1971
26 Apr 1986	19 Sep 1943
27 Apr 1985	23 Sep 1971

Occurrence: This rare summer resident arrives in early to mid-May. Only a few have been seen from July to mid-September. Iowa is on the northern edge of the breeding range, which extends approximately from southwestern Iowa to northeastern Iowa and southeastern Wisconsin. This species is found in heavily wooded tracts along major rivers (map), a habitat preference similar to several other warblers of the southeastern United States. There are only 2 records of a nest being found: June 1884 in Van Buren County (Anderson 1907) and 13 June 1975 at Effigy Mounds National Monument in Allamakee County (Koenig 1976). Other confirmed nesting records are from the breeding bird atlas study (Jackson et al. 1996).

Comment: The winter range is in eastern Mexico and Central America. The breeding range is in the eastern United States from southern Georgia and eastern Texas north to southeastern Nebraska, southern Wisconsin, and southern Pennsylvania.

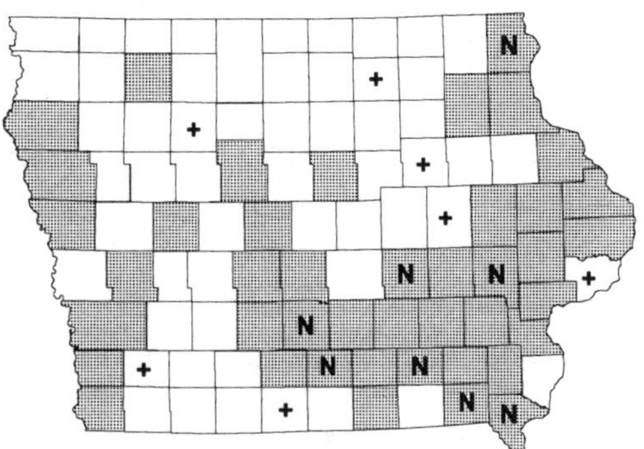

Kentucky Warbler, 1960-1995
June-July, nesting (N), and spring/fall (+)

Connecticut Warbler (*Oporornis agilis*)

Status: Regular

Jan	Feb	Mar	Apr	May	Jun	Jul	Aug	Sep	Oct	Nov	Dec
									X		

7 May 1979	1 Jun 1986	20 Aug 1973	26 Sep 1965
8 May 1993	3 Jun1956	20 Aug 1992	27 Sep 1986
9 May 1991	6 Jun 1982	21 Aug 1984	8 Oct 1970

Occurrence: This rare migrant is recorded about twice as often in spring as in fall. Spring migration is late, with the vast majority found from 15 to 31 May. The fall migration tends to be early. In spring this secretive, ground-loving warbler is usually found when it sings. It is surprising that so many, presumably non-singing birds are seen in fall, when most are said to migrate to the East Coast. The distribution of records follows the distribution of active birders. The most have been found in Hickory Hill Park in Iowa City, a location where many birders routinely look for this species. It is not unexpected, however, to encounter a Connecticut Warbler in any heavily wooded area in late May. Fall birds are said to like jewelweed.

Comment: The winter range is in north-central South America. The breeding range extends from the northern parts of Minnesota, Wisconsin, and Michigan across the central parts of the Canadian provinces from western British Columbia to eastern Quebec. Most birds migrate through the West Indies and Florida. Some move across the Gulf of Mexico in spring, but in fall most birds migrate eastward to New England and then south along the Atlantic coast.

Mourning Warbler (*Oporornis philadelphia*)

Status: Regular

Jan	Feb	Mar	Apr	May	Jun	Jul	Aug	Sep	Oct	Nov	Dec
			X			X			XX		

30 Apr 1994	17 Jun 1956	9 Aug 1983	30 Sep 1986
2 May 1992	19 Jun 1979	11 Aug 1985	1 Oct 1965
2 May 1992	20 Jun 1988	14 Aug 1968	4 Oct 1980

Occurrence: This uncommon to rare migrant tends to be late in spring with some birds lingering into June. Fewer are found in fall.

Comment: The winter range is in Central America and northern South America. The breeding range is across Canada from Alberta to Newfoundland south to central Minnesota and Wisconsin and to the northern Appalachians. The migration route, in contrast with Connecticut Warbler, is through the Midwest, the Gulf of Mexico, and eastern Mexico.

MacGillivray's Warbler (*Oporornis tolmiei*)

Status: Accidental

2 Jun 1995, Eagle City County P., Hardin Co. (*IBL* 66:96)

Occurrence: There is 1 sight record of a male seen briefly in late spring.

Comment: This western warbler winters in western and southern Mexico and in Central America. The breeding range is in the mountains of the western United States and Canada. *Oporornis* warblers are notoriously difficult to identify, especially females and immatures. The definitive wing minus tail measurements can only be applied to netted or dead birds. The pattern of white around the eye, the color of the lores, and the pattern of black on the upper breast are considered by some but not all to be diagnostic in spring males.

MacGillivray's Warbler, all

Common Yellowthroat (*Geothlypis trichas*)

Status: Regular; nests

Jan	Feb	Mar	Apr	May	Jun	Jul	Aug	Sep	Oct	Nov	Dec
X										X	X X X

21 Apr 1976
22 Apr 1985
23 Apr 1973

20 Dec 1984
26 Dec 1993
2 Jan 1994

Occurrence: This abundant summer resident arrives in early May and most are gone by late September, but a few linger into winter. On Breeding Bird Surveys, Yellowthroats are widely distributed, averaging 18.7 birds per route from 1983 to 1992. They are found in a variety of habitats in every county.

Comment: The winter range extends from the southern United States through the West Indies and Middle America to northern Colombia. The breeding range extends from Mexico to the northern edge of Canadian provinces. Winter records from nearby states follow a similar pattern to Iowa's—occasional birds are seen on Christmas Bird Counts or in early January, usually in cattail marshes, but are not reported later in the winter.

Hooded Warbler (*Wilsonia citrina*)

Status: Regular; nests

Jan	Feb	Mar	Apr	May	Jun	Jul	Aug	Sep	Oct	Nov	Dec
			x				x x	x			

8 Apr 1950	29 Aug 1987
13 Apr 1940	30 Aug 1968
19 Apr 1992	6 Sep 1993

Occurrence: This very rare summer resident and over-migrant may arrive as early as April. Only 7 have been recorded in August and September. Two-thirds of the records are from May. Spring records are from all areas of the state, but most are from eastern and central Iowa, and only 10 from the western third of Iowa. This species has been reported every year since 1970 with 1 to 14 reports per year (usually 5 to 7).

The most consistent locations of summer birds have been in Lee and Allamakee counties. Birds were present in the woods near Amana in Iowa County for several years beginning in 1982 (Bendorf 1982) with confirmed nesting (Jackson et al. 1996). Hooded Warblers nest in deeply wooded areas with a preference for bottomland woods.

Historically, Currier reported this species as common in the river bottoms near Keokuk in Lee County and discovered 2 nests in 1894 (Currier 1895, DuMont 1936). It was not common elsewhere, however, with reports from Black Hawk, Des Moines, Jackson, Mahaska, and Poweshiek counties (Anderson 1907). There were only 4 records from 1900 to 1967, all from eastern Iowa: 13 April 1940 in Louisa County (Musgrove and Roberts 1940); 8 April 1950 in Des Moines County (Crossley 1952); 4 May 1950 in Scott County (Feeney 1950); and 3 May 1952 in Dubuque County (Crossley 1952). Suddenly, in 1968, there were 4 reports.

Comment: The winter range is in the West Indies and Middle America. The breeding range is in the eastern United States and southern Ontario, from eastern Texas and northern Florida north to Iowa and New York. Because Iowa is on the northern and western edge of this species range, it is not surprising to see some population shifts. There appears to have been a decline in Missouri since 1900 (Robbins and Easterla 1992). All except 2 of Minnesota's records have been since 1970 (Janssen 1987), but the status in Wisconsin apparently did not change from early days (Robbins 1991). Nearby states also report early April migrants, and there are a few from March. It is not known what happens to all of the birds that are seen in May but not later in summer. The pattern of apparent "over migration" is more pronounced than it is for other southeastern warblers that occur in Iowa.

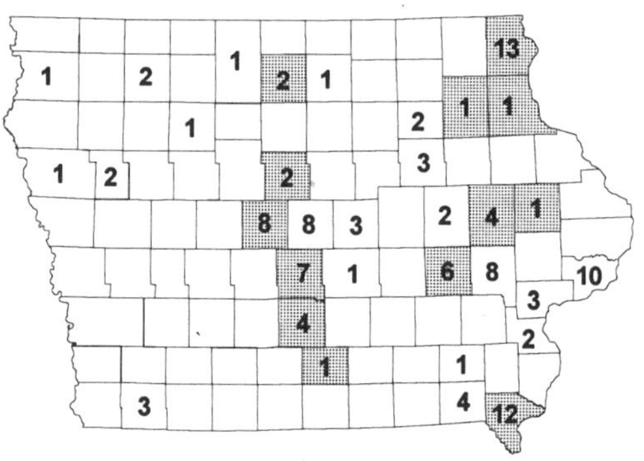

Hooded Warbler, 1990-1995
Records, June-July (shaded)

References:

Bendorf, C. 1982. Summer records of Hooded Warbler. *Iowa Bird Life* 52:115-117.

Crossley, G. E. 1952. Two records of the Hooded Warbler in Iowa. *Iowa Bird Life* 22:30.

Currier, E. S. 1895. The Hooded Warbler. *Iowa Ornithologist* 1:67-70.

Feeney, T. J. 1950. Townsend's Warbler at Davenport. *Iowa Bird Life* 20:61.

Musgrove, J. W., and M. E. Roberts. 1940. Bird records in the Conesville region. *Iowa Bird Life* 10:31.

Wilson's Warbler (*Wilsonia pusilla*)

Status: Regular

Jan	Feb	Mar	Apr	May	Jun	Jul	Aug	Sep	Oct	Nov	Dec
										X	

25 Apr 1993	29 May 1989	8 Aug 1977	18 Oct 1987
28 Apr 1990	30 May 1995	8 Aug 1981	18 Oct 1966
29 Apr 1977	31 May 1995	9 Aug 1988	2 Nov 1980

Occurrence: This fairly common migrant is mostly seen in May (slightly on the late side for spring warblers) and late August through September (average timing for fall). The number seen per year in spring and fall at Ames was about average for warblers (Martsching 1986, 1987). In the fall of 1955 at Webster City, Wilson's was the most common warbler with 18 percent of the total number (Carter 1955).

Comment: The winter range is in Middle America north to southern California and Texas. The breeding range includes the mountains of the western United States and across northern Canada and Alaska. One might expect that Wilson's Warbler would be relatively more common in western Iowa than other warblers, but no data are available to validate this impression.

Canada Warbler (*Wilsonia canadensis*)

Status: Regular

Jan	Feb	Mar	Apr	May	Jun	Jul	Aug	Sep	Oct	Nov	Dec
						X	XX		XX		

9 May 1985	30 Sep 1967
9 May 1993	3 Oct 1979
10 May 1986	8 Oct 1995

Occurrence: This uncommon migrant and very rare summer resident is a late spring and early fall migrant. More were detected at Ames in fall than spring—24 versus 6 per year (Martsching 1986, 1987), and more were banded at Davenport in fall than spring—302 versus 120 (Dinsmore et al. 1984). In the fall of 1955 at Webster City, Canada Warbler was the third most common warbler with 13 percent of the total number (Carter 1955); however, the data from Ames place it as twelfth most common in fall.

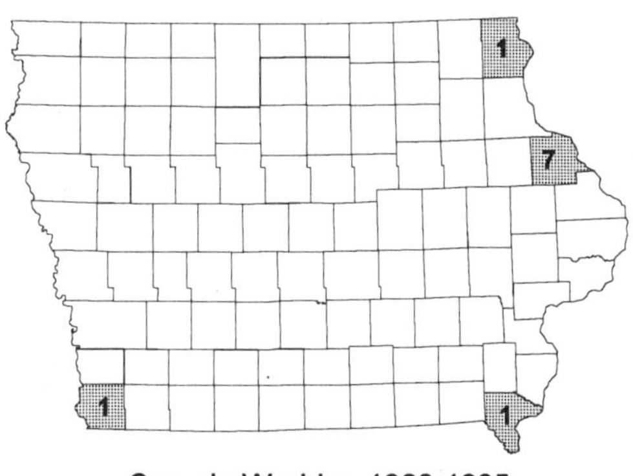

Canada Warbler, 1960-1995
Mid-June-July

Although early authors considered it rare in western Iowa (Anderson 1907, DuMont 1933), current data indicate that this species can be found anywhere in the state. Published records are from sites with the most active warbler watchers.

There are 7 early June records that could be late migrants; however, summer records from White Pine Hollow in Dubuque County in 1979, 1981-1985, and 1994-1995 (*IBL* 49:84, 51:102, 52:93, 53:76, 54:85, 55:95, 64:111, 65:100) suggest nesting. Other late June records are a female on 21 June 1980 at Waubonsie State Park in Fremont County (*IBL* 50:77), 1 on 22 June 1984 at Yellow River Forest in Allamakee County (*IBL* 54:85), and a male on 28 June 1987 at the Croton Unit of Shimek Forest in Lee County (*IBL* 57:123).

Comment: The winter range is in northwestern South America. The breeding range extends across Canada from Alberta to Newfoundland south to northern Minnesota and Wisconsin and south in the Appalachians to northern Georgia. In spring, more birds seem to migrate toward the Atlantic Coast than in fall (Curson et al. 1994), which may explain the greater numbers found in Iowa in fall. In Illinois, there is 1 nesting record from Joliet and other summer records without proof of nesting (Bohlen 1989).

Yellow-breasted Chat (*Icteria virens*)

Status: Regular; nests

Jan	Feb	Mar	Apr	May	Jun	Jul	Aug	Sep	Oct	Nov	Dec
x			x								

19 Apr 1995 — 20 Sep 1985
26 Apr 1972 — 24 Sep 1994
28 Apr 1989 — 28 Sep 1964
winter: 16 Jan 1972

Occurrence: This rare summer resident arrives in early May. Few are found from July to September. Almost all summer records are from southern, central, and eastern Iowa in a pattern similar to other warblers that nest in the southern United States. Although chats may be found in or near oak-hickory forest, they also like areas with scrubby cover. They are easily detected by their loud voice, but they are often silent during the breeding season and difficult to locate. For example, in a 4-year breeding survey at the Coralville Reservoir, 3 birds were found on 1 occasion each at different sites (Kent et al. 1994).

A nest with 2 eggs was found in southern Clinton County on 4 July 1954 (Petersen 1954), and another nest was observed and photographed at Camp Dodge in Polk County from 8 to 29 July 1956 (Peasley and Peasley 1957). Nesting was confirmed without finding a nest in Mahaska (2 sites) and Lee counties (Jackson et al. 1996).

A wintering bird came to a feeder in Davenport in Scott County from mid-November 1971 to 16 January 1972, when it was taken into the home and released on 11 March 1972 (Petersen 1972).

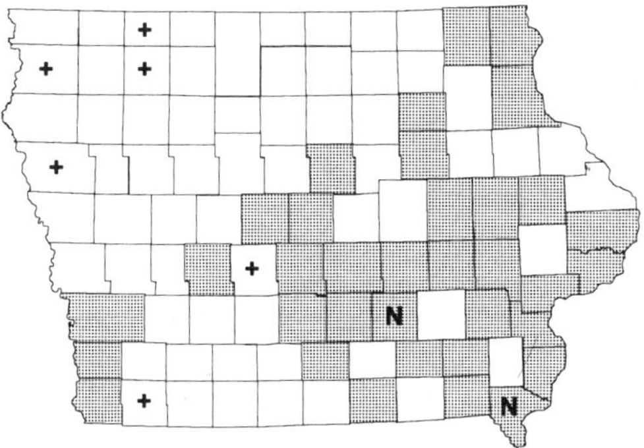

Yellow-breasted Chat, 1960-1995
June-July, nesting (N), and spring/fall (+)

Historically, chats were considered common as far north as central Iowa and abundant in southeastern Iowa (Anderson 1907). They were reported to Anderson as common and nesting in Kossuth County, but in other north-central counties Anderson did not find them in Winnebago or Hancock counties but did have a specimen from Cerro Gordo County taken on 30 May 1891. Chats were reported as uncommon in Woodbury and decreasing in Black Hawk and Des Moines counties (Anderson 1907). DuMont (1933) considered chats as rare except along the Missouri River to Sioux City. He also cited a bird found dead in Dickinson County on 27 May 1933.

Comment: The winter range is in Middle America, southern Florida, and southern Texas with records north to California, the Great Lakes, New York, and New England (American Ornithologists' Union 1983). There are 3 winter records from Illinois (Bohlen 1989). The breeding range includes northern Mexico and almost all of the United States (except southern Florida and around the western Great Lakes), edging into Canada in the West and East. The northern edge of the breeding range dips southward in Minnesota so that it includes only southwestern and southeastern Minnesota; therefore, it is not surprising that this species does not breed in north-central Iowa. Thus, Iowa is on the northern edge of the range only in the center of the state, although modern records from northwestern Iowa have all been from spring (2) and fall (2).

References:

Peasley, H. R., and Mrs. H. R. Peasley. 1956. Nesting record of Yellow-breasted Chat in Polk County. *Iowa Bird Life* 27:2-5.

Petersen, P. C. 1954. Bird notes from southeast Iowa. *Iowa Bird Life* 24:56-57.

Petersen, P. C. 1972. Wintering Yellow-breasted Chat at Davenport. *Iowa Bird Life* 42:26.

Tanagers (Subfamily Traupinae)

Tanagers comprise 414 species, with 6 from North America and 3 from Iowa. Most of the species in this subfamily are found in the Neotropics. Of the Iowa species, 2 are regular nesting species, and 1 is a casual visitor from the West. Iowa tanagers have brightly colored males and plain females. They inhabit woods and brushy areas and eat insects and fruit.

Summer Tanager (*Piranga rubra*)

Status: Regular; nests

Jan	Feb	Mar	Apr	May	Jun	Jul	Aug	Sep	Oct	Nov	Dec
									X		X

20 Apr 1899	7 Oct 1982
27 Apr 1942	8 Oct 1966
28 Apr 1985	27 Oct 1991
winter: 2 Dec 1990	

Occurrence: The vast majority of records of this rare summer resident have been from along the Mississippi River north to Scott County, along the Des Moines River north to Polk County, and in the Loess Hills of Fremont County. The most consistent locations in recent years have been at Waubonsie and Lacey-Keosauqua state parks. All confirmed nesting records are from the southern half of the state, although there are summer records from 6 counties farther north. Scattered spring and fall migrants have been noted throughout the state, and 1 bird was photographed at a feeder in Scott County on 2 December 1990 (*IBL* 62:22).

Historically, there are only about a dozen reports prior to 1906 (Anderson 1907, DuMont 1933) and no more until 21 May 1940 (Serbousek 1959). Summer residents were found at Waubonsie State Park in Fremont County in 1942 (Jones 1942) and have been found there ever since. A nest was found at Des Moines in Polk County in 1956 and summering pairs were there at least through 1971 (Brown 1971). A nest was found at Wildcat Den State Park in Muscatine County in 1961 (Lange 1961), and birds were observed at this location in subsequent years.

Comment: The winter range is from Mexico south along the Andes to Bolivia. The breeding range is in the southern United States and northern Mexico. Iowa is on the northern edge of the breeding range, but a few stragglers are regularly found north to South Dakota, Minnesota, Wisconsin, and southern Canada. In Ohio, a northward extension of the breeding range occurred in the 1950s (Peterjohn 1989). This species appears to be very gradually extending its range northward.

References:

Jones, M. L. 1942. Bird observations at Waubonsie. *Iowa Bird Life* 12:39-40.

Lange, J. W. 1961. The Summer Tanager. *Iowa Bird Life* 31:50-53.

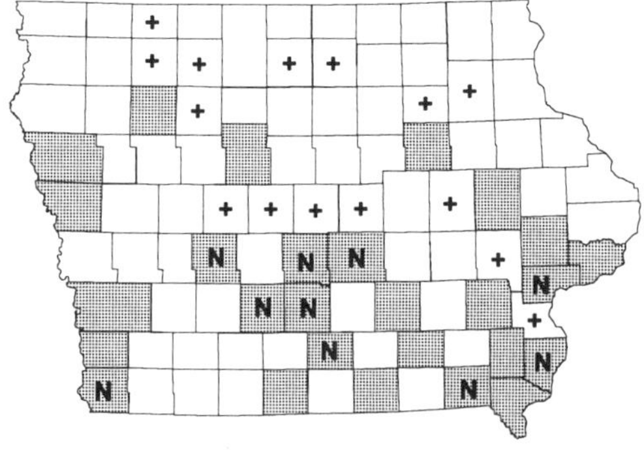

Summer Tanager, 1960-1995
June-July, nesting (N), spring/fall (+)

Scarlet Tanager (*Piranga olivacea*)

Status: Regular; nests

Jan	Feb	Mar	Apr	May	Jun	Jul	Aug	Sep	Oct	Nov	Dec
			X							XX	

Early dates	Late dates
19 Apr 1964	28 Oct 1979
22 Apr 1970	11 Nov 1990
23 Apr 1994	14 Nov 1991

Occurrence: This uncommon to common summer resident nests throughout the state, but is more common in the wooded areas of eastern and southern Iowa. Scarlet Tanager is seldom found on Breeding Bird Surveys, but in a more intensive study of woodland habitat at the Coralville Reservoir, it was as common as Wood Thrush and Yellow-throated Vireo (Kent et al. 1994). In spite of the male's bright color, this species is more often heard than seen and rarely strays from its deep-woods habitat during the nesting season.

Comment: The winter range is from Panama south to Bolivia on the east side of the Andes. The breeding range is in the eastern United States and southern Canada, west to eastern Nebraska and south to central Missouri.

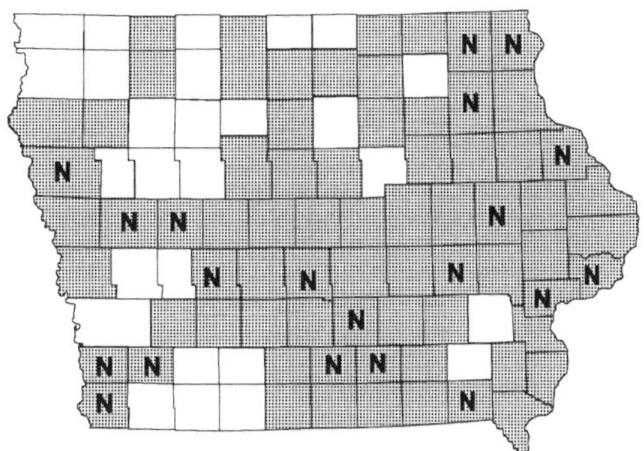

Scarlet Tanager, 1960-1995
June-July, nesting (N)

Western Tanager (*Piranga ludoviciana*)

Status: Casual

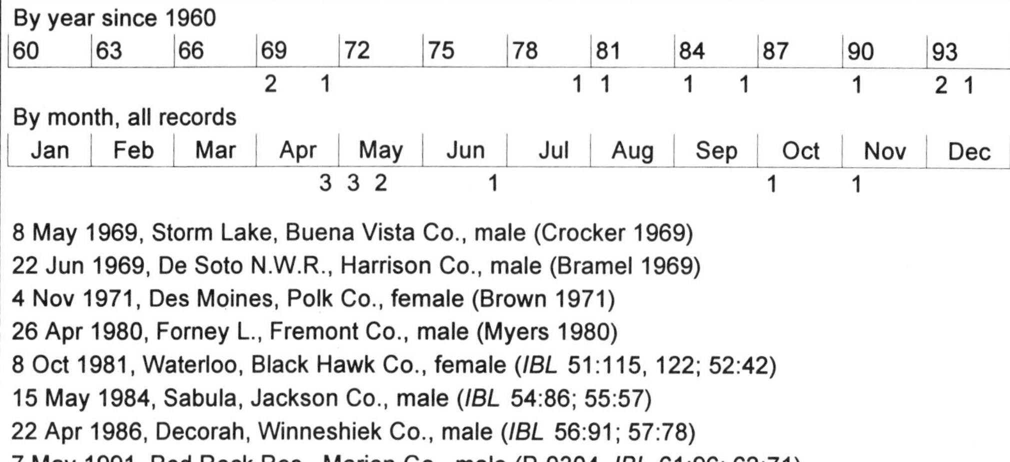

By year since 1960

60 63 66 69 72 75 78 81 84 87 90 93

2 1 1 1 1 1 1 2 1

By month, all records

Jan Feb Mar Apr May Jun Jul Aug Sep Oct Nov Dec

3 3 2 1 1 1

8 May 1969, Storm Lake, Buena Vista Co., male (Crocker 1969)
22 Jun 1969, De Soto N.W.R., Harrison Co., male (Bramel 1969)
4 Nov 1971, Des Moines, Polk Co., female (Brown 1971)
26 Apr 1980, Forney L., Fremont Co., male (Myers 1980)
8 Oct 1981, Waterloo, Black Hawk Co., female (*IBL* 51:115, 122; 52:42)
15 May 1984, Sabula, Jackson Co., male (*IBL* 54:86; 55:57)
22 Apr 1986, Decorah, Winneshiek Co., male (*IBL* 56:91; 57:78)
7 May 1991, Red Rock Res., Marion Co., male (P-0304, *IBL* 61:96; 62:71)
10 May 1993, Lime Creek Nature Center, Cerro Gordo Co., male (*IBL* 63:79)
11 May 1993, L. Manawa, Pottawattamie Co., male (P-0397, *IBL* 63:79)
25 to 26 Apr 1994, Swan L., Johnson Co., male (Dankert 1995)

Occurrence: Of the 11 records, 8 are from spring, 1 from summer, and 2 from fall.

Comment: The winter range of this western species is from Mexico to Panama, with a few also in California and along the Gulf Coast to Florida. The breeding range is from southeastern Alaska and southern Mackenzie, east to the Black Hills, and south to western Texas.

There are records from almost all states and provinces. In the Midwest, two-thirds of the vagrant records are from May with a few from April, June, and July. Most fall records are from August with 1 in September and only the Iowa records in October and November. The pattern in the East, however, is different with most records from August to January and a few in April.

References:

Bramel, G. C. 1969. Another Iowa Western Tanager. *Iowa Bird Life* 39:64-65.

Brown, W. H. 1971. Western Tanager in Des Moines. *Iowa Bird Life* 41:113.

Crocker, Mrs. E. G. 1969. Iowa's first Western Tanager. *Iowa Bird Life* 39:44-45.

Dankert, D. L. 1995. Western Tanager in Eastern Iowa. *Iowa Bird Life* 65:21-22.

Myers, B. 1980. Western Tanager in southwest Iowa. *Iowa Bird Life* 50:53.

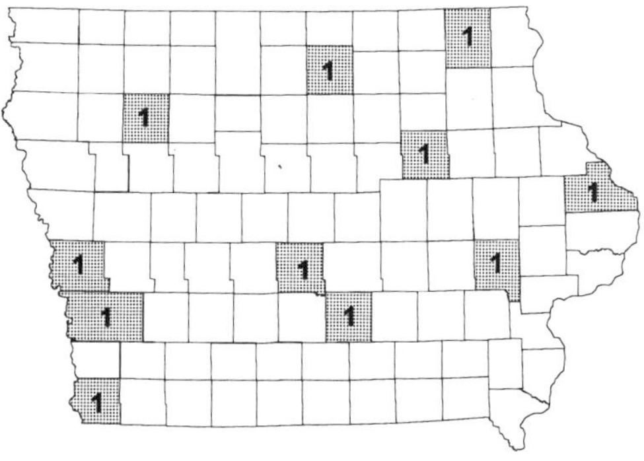

Western Tanager, all

Cardinals and Grosbeaks (Subfamily Cardinalinae)

Cardinals and grosbeaks comprise 42 New World species, with 13 from North America and 7 from Iowa. Of the Iowa species, 5 are Regular and 2 are Accidental. Most of these species are seed eaters with heavy conical bills, but they also eat insects.

Northern Cardinal (*Cardinalis cardinalis*)

Status: Regular; nests

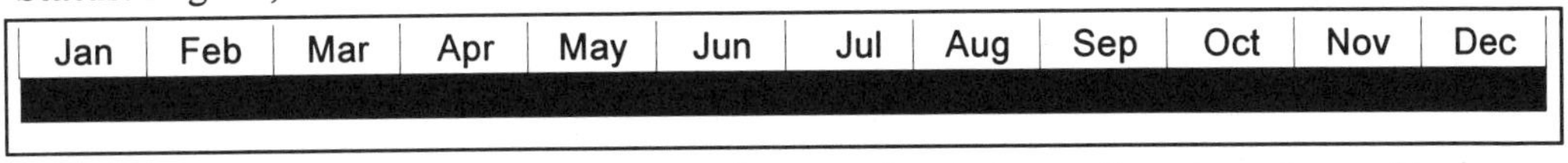

Jan	Feb	Mar	Apr	May	Jun	Jul	Aug	Sep	Oct	Nov	Dec

Occurrence: This abundant permanent resident is found throughout Iowa, but is more common in eastern and southern areas of the state. In northwestern Iowa, cardinals are found in riparian habitat and are rare in agricultural areas. On Christmas Bird Counts, yearly counts ranged from 2.9 to 4.7 per party-hour. Greatest numbers are along the Mississippi River, averaging 5.5 per party-hour, and the fewest numbers are in north-central and northwestern Iowa, with an average fewer than 1 per party-hour at most sites. Similar geographic differences were noted on mid-winter feeder surveys in 1984 (Hollis 1984).

Historically, cardinals were rare in Iowa before 1885, but rapidly expanded from southeast to northwestern Iowa (Anderson 1907, Brown 1920, DuMont 1933).

Comment: The range of this nonmigratory species includes the eastern United States, southern Canada, and the southwestern United States south to northern Central America. It extends north to central Minnesota and west to eastern Colorado. The northward expansion in Minnesota appears to be progressing slowly (Janssen 1987).

Reference:

Brown, H. C. 1920. The Cardinal in north-central Iowa. *Wilson Bull.* 32:123-132.

Rose-breasted Grosbeak (*Pheucticus ludovicianus*)

Status: Regular; nests

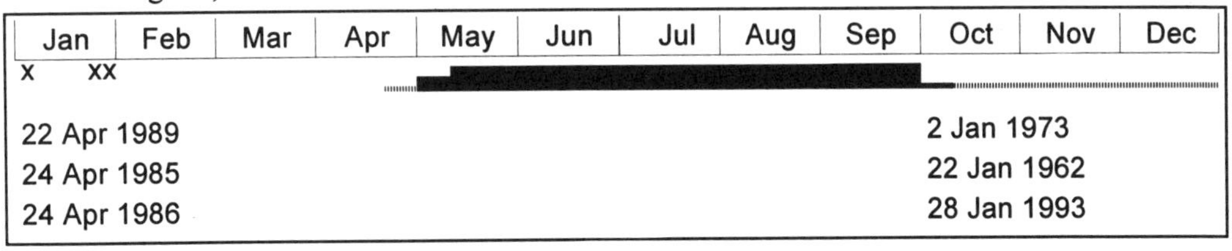

Jan	Feb	Mar	Apr	May	Jun	Jul	Aug	Sep	Oct	Nov	Dec
x xx											

22 Apr 1989
24 Apr 1985
24 Apr 1986

2 Jan 1973
22 Jan 1962
28 Jan 1993

Occurrence: This common summer resident usually arrives in early May, but a few may arrive by late April. Most are gone by late September, but a few stragglers remain into winter. This species of the woodland and woodland edge breeds throughout the state, but is more abundant in eastern and southern Iowa. In the woodland habitat of the Coralville Reservoir, its abundance was similar to Downy Woodpecker (Kent et al. 1994). During migration and early in the nesting period, Rose-breasted Grosbeaks sing repeatedly and appear to be abundant; later they sing less and are less conspicuous.

Comment: The winter range is from central Mexico south to northwestern South America, but a few attempt to over-winter in the Midwest and the East. The breeding range includes the northeastern United States and Canada, south to northern Oklahoma, west to the central Great Plains and Prairie Provinces, and north to southern Mackenzie.

Black-headed Grosbeak (*Pheucticus melanocephalus*)

Status: Accidental

By year since 1960

60	63	66	69	72	75	78	81	84	87	90	93
		1				1	1	1		1	2

By month -- all records

Jan	Feb	Mar	Apr	May	Jun	Jul	Aug	Sep	Oct	Nov	Dec
				2 1					1 1		1 1

30 Oct 1968, Manti Woods, Fremont Co., male (DeLong 1969)
1 to 11 Dec 1978, Cedar Rapids, Linn Co., imm. male (P-0002, Millikin 1979)
13 to 14 Dec 1981, Le Claire, Scott Co., imm. male (P-0037, *IBL* 52:25, 28, 42-43)
13 May 1985, Coralville Res., Johnson Co., imm. male (*IBL* 55:69; 56:44)
30 May 1990, near Booneville, Madison Co., male (*IBL* 62:22)
15 May 1994, Big Creek S.P., Polk Co., male (*IBL* 64:79)
1 Oct 1994, Clayton Co., imm. female (*IBL* 65:18)

Occurrence: Of the 7 records, 3 are from spring and 4 are from fall/early winter.

Comment: The winter range of this western species is central to southern Mexico and occasionally north to California. The breeding range is from southern British Columbia to northwestern Saskatchewan, east to central Nebraska, and south in mountains to southern Mexico. This species may be the most common eastern vagrant passerine, occurring in almost all states and provinces. In the Midwest, it has been recorded in all months with the greatest number from September to January, but the largest peak in May. In the East and South, the pattern is one of fall migrants over-wintering, with most records from September to February.

The ranges of Black-headed and Rose-breasted grosbeaks meet in the middle of the Great Plains states, where there is some hybridization (West 1962, Anderson and Daugherty 1974). Identification of hybrids, females, and immature males is a significant challenge and requires more information than is presented in field guides (West 1962, Anderson and Daugherty 1974, Zimmer 1985, Oberholser 1974).

References:

Anderson, B. W., and R. J. Daugherty. 1974. Characteristics and reproductive biology of grosbeaks (*Pheucticus*) in the hybrid zone in South Dakota. *Wilson Bull.* 86:1-11.

DeLong, Mrs. W. C. 1969. The Black-headed Grosbeak in western Iowa. *Iowa Bird Life* 39:43.

Millikin, S. 1979. Black-headed Grosbeak at Cedar Rapids. *Iowa Bird Life* 49:64-65.

West, D. A. 1962. Hybridization in grosbeaks (*Pheucticus*) of the Great Plains. *Auk* 79:399-424.

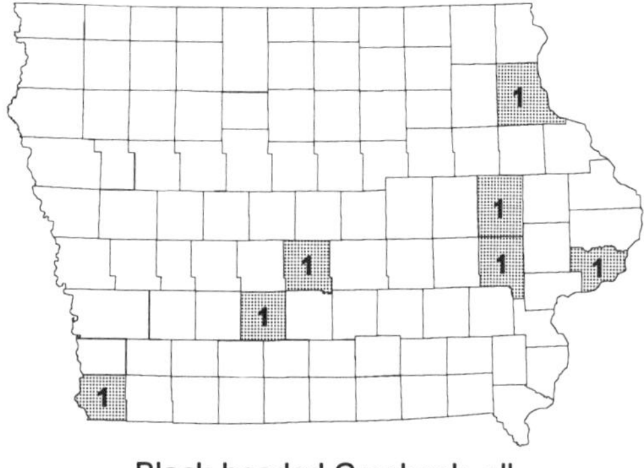

Black-headed Grosbeak, all

Blue Grosbeak (*Guiraca caerulea*)

Status: Regular; nests

Jan	Feb	Mar	Apr	May	Jun	Jul	Aug	Sep	Oct	Nov	Dec
			x						x		

23 Apr 1975	16 Sep 1989
3 May 1992	20 Sep 1969
7 May 1986	4 Oct 1965

Occurrence: This rare to locally uncommon summer resident is found on the western edge and southeastern corner of the state, rarely elsewhere. Most arrive in mid-May and are gone by late August. They are most easily found in the Missouri River floodplain in shrubby habitat along roads and ditches. They can also be found in the northwestern and southeastern corners of the state. There are scattered records in other areas of the state in May and June and 3 later records: 4 July 1988 in Muscatine County (*IBL* 58:112), a dead female presumably at Fort Dodge in Webster County on 4 October 1965 (*IBL* 36:21), and at Cedar Rapids in Linn County on 8 October 1975 (*IBL* 46:24).

Historically, the first birds were recorded at Cedar Falls in Black Hawk County in June 1923 and at Spirit Lake in Dickinson County on 18 May 1924 (DuMont 1933). Next came a series of May records from Dubuque in Dubuque County in 1929, 1931, 1933, and 1935 (Johnson 1937). This pattern was not sustained, however, with the only other records from the upper Mississippi Valley being from Dubuque in May 1947 (*IBL* 17:73) and 1 June 1955 (Heuser 1955), and from Allamakee County in May 1949 (*IBL* 19:33). Increasing numbers were found in western Iowa beginning in 1932 (Youngworth 1958). Birds have been seen in Lee County in southeastern Iowa since they were first discovered there on 1 June 1979 (*IBL* 49:84) and nested there in 1986 and 1987 (*IBL* 56:119; 57:123). An extralimital nesting record was from Des Moines in 1955 (Berkowitz 1956).

Comment: The winter range is in Middle America and rarely in the southern United States. There is a winter record from Illinois (Bohlen 1989). The breeding range is from Central America to the southern United States, with the most northerly extension in the Dakotas and southwestern Minnesota. There are occasional records north to southern Canada.

References:

Berkowitz, A. C. 1956. Blue Grosbeak in Polk County. *Iowa Bird Life* 26:22.

Heuser, E. 1955. Hills over the Mississippi: A place for bird study. *Iowa Bird Life* 25:54-56.

Johnson, Mrs. R. W. 1937. Observations in the Dubuque region. *Iowa Bird Life* 7:53-54.

Youngworth, W. 1958. The Blue Grosbeak in western Iowa, a summary. *Iowa Bird Life* 28:57-59.

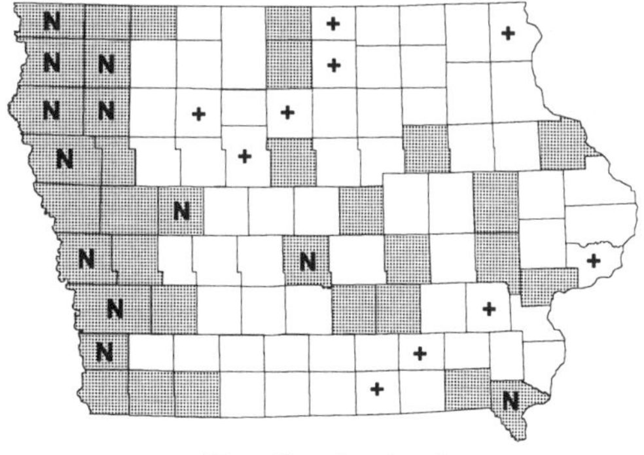

Blue Grosbeak, all
June-July, nesting (N), spring/fall(+)

Lazuli Bunting (*Passerina amoena*)

Status: Accidental

By year since 1960 (also 1929, 2 in 1958, 2 in 1996)

60	63	66	69	72	75	78	81	84	87	90	93
								1			1 1

By month, all records

Jan	Feb	Mar	Apr	May	Jun	Jul	Aug	Sep	Oct	Nov	Dec
				3 2	1 1	1					

20 May 1929, Sioux City, Woodbury Co., male (Youngworth 1929)
14 May 1958, Big Sioux R., Plymouth Co. (?), male (Youngworth 1959)
18 Jun 1958, Plymouth Co., hybrid male (Youngworth 1959)
16 May 1986, Martin-Little Sioux R.A., Cherokee Co., male (Brewer 1986)
7 Jul 1994, Calhoun Co., male (P-0415, *IBL* 64:50)
28, 29 May 1995, Clay Co., male (*IBL* 65:77)
16 May 1996, Shenandoah, Page Co. (*IBL* 66:107)
1 to 2 Jun 1996, Little Sioux W.A., Clay Co. (in press)

Occurrence: There are 8 records from northwestern and 1 from southwestern Iowa. All were males, but 1 was a hybrid nesting with a female Indigo Bunting (Youngworth 1959). There are 8 other reports (Dinsmore et al. 1984); most lack descriptions, but are likely correct.

Comment: The winter range is from southern Arizona to southern Mexico. The breeding range is from southern Canada, east in the Great Plains states to northeastern South Dakota and east-central Nebraska, and south to central Texas and northern Baja California.

The ranges of Lazuli and Indigo buntings overlap in the Great Plains states, where hybrids may occur (Emlen et al. 1975). There are only a few vagrant records of Lazuli Bunting to the east of Illinois and Wisconsin; these are from Ontario, Maine, Pennsylvania, Maryland, Virginia, South Carolina, and Florida. In contrast to the Iowa records, which are near the breeding range, Minnesota and Wisconsin records are widely scattered. Almost all of the Midwest records are from May to June, and the few eastern records are from fall-winter.

References:

Brewer, M. M. 1986. Lazuli Bunting in Cherokee County. *Iowa Bird Life* 56:96.

Emlen, S. T., J. D. Rising, and W. L. Thompson. 1975. A behavioral and morphological study of sympatry in the Indigo and Lazuli buntings of the Great Plains. *Wilson Bull.* 87:145-179.

Youngworth, W. G. 1929. The Lazuli Bunting in Iowa. *Wilson Bull.* 41:190.

Youngworth, W. 1959. The Lazuli Bunting along the western border of Iowa: A summary. *Iowa Bird Life* 29:3-5.

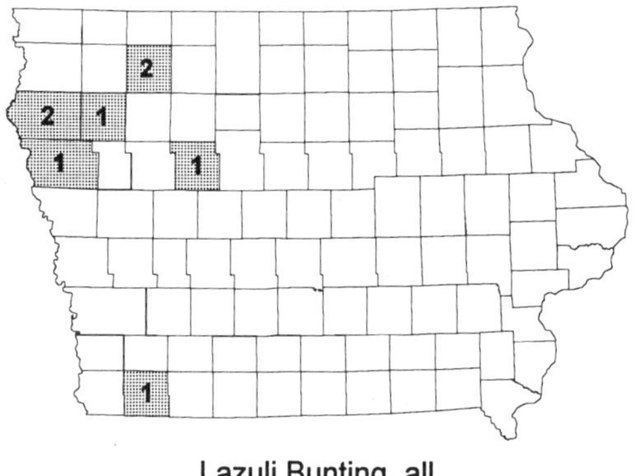

Lazuli Bunting, all

Indigo Bunting (*Passerina cyanea*)

Status: Regular; nests

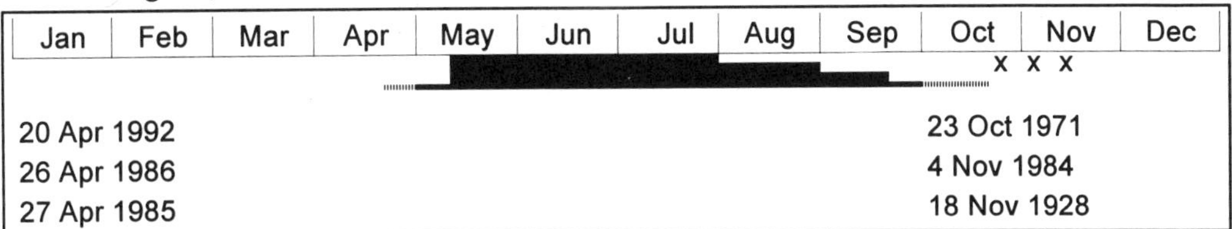

Occurrence: This abundant summer resident nests throughout the state. It is somewhat more abundant in eastern and southern Iowa where there is more edge habitat. Most Indigo Buntings arrive in mid-May and leave by mid-September.

Comment: The winter range includes the West Indies, Middle America, northern Colombia, and the southern extremes of Texas and Florida. The breeding range is in the eastern United States and southern Canada, and in southwestern states. There are a few winter records from Missouri, Illinois, Wisconsin, and states to the east.

Dickcissel (*Spiza americana*)

Status: Regular; nests

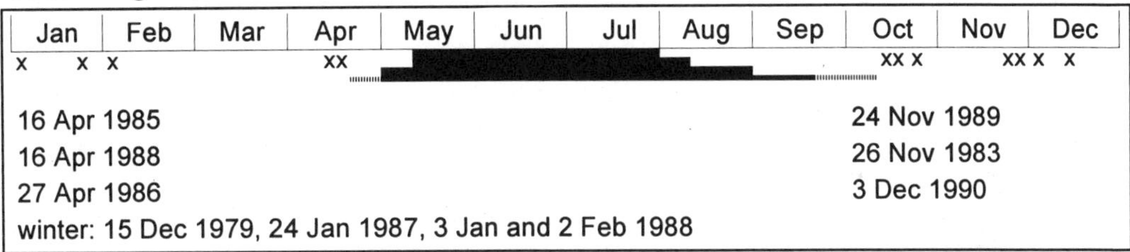

Occurrence: This abundant summer resident occurs in grasslands and roadsides throughout the state. Birds arrive abruptly in early to mid-May and gradually disappear by mid-September. Based on Breeding Bird Surveys, they are most abundant in western Iowa and least abundant in northeastern Iowa. Populations have shown dramatic fluctuation, with a sharp decline from 1970 to 1983, followed by a sharp increase to a peak in 1989, and then another decline.

Comment: The winter range is from central Mexico to northern South America, but a few birds also winter coastally from New England to Texas. The breeding range is from Texas to southern Saskatchewan, east to western Ohio and locally from South Carolina to Maryland. Scattered late fall and winter records, mostly at feeders, have been recorded in nearby states in a pattern similar to that for Iowa.

Emberizines (Subfamily Emberizinae)

Emberizines, which include towhees, sparrows, and longspurs, comprise 259 species, with 59 from North America and 29 from Iowa. This large subfamily, which is often lumped with other subfamilies includes about 43 Old World buntings, 150 South American emberizines, and 69 North American sparrows. Of the Iowa species, 24 are Regular and 5 Accidental.

Most of the Iowa species are confined to North America and are migrants. Two are Holarctic migrants (Lapland Longspur, Snow Bunting). Most sparrows winter south of Iowa. Species that breed to the north and winter in Iowa in large numbers include American Tree Sparrow, Dark-eyed Junco, Lapland Longspur, and Snow Bunting. Song Sparrow breeds and winters in Iowa. Species that regularly winter in Iowa in small numbers (Iowa is on the northern edge of their winter range) include Swamp, White-throated, White-crowned, and Harris's sparrows. Several other species winter irregularly or in very small numbers; many of these are mainly reported in December. Christmas Bird Counts, which are biased by extensive field observation and automatic reporting, supply most of the information on wintering sparrows. More information, with substantiating details, is needed on the presence or absence of the following species between mid-November and mid-March: Chipping, Field, Vesper, Savannah, Fox, and Lincoln's sparrows. A few towhees also winter in Iowa. The relative distribution of Eastern and Spotted towhees needs further delineation. Species that are not expected at all in winter include Clay-colored, Lark, Grasshopper, Henslow's, Le Conte's, and Nelson's Sharp-tailed sparrows and Smith's Longspur.

Species in this family that regularly nest in Iowa include Eastern Towhee and Chipping, Field, Vesper, Lark, Savannah, Grasshopper, Henslow's, Song, and Swamp sparrows. Clay-colored Sparrow has been found irregularly in summer in northern Iowa. Species that are predominantly migrants and are not expected in summer include Le Conte's, Nelson's Sharp-tailed, Fox, Lincoln's, White-throated, White-crowned, and Harris's sparrows, as well as the abundant winter species.

Sparrows are easily identified by their distinctive songs, and most adults in appropriate habitat with good views are not identification problems. Out-of-season birds, especially juveniles, require experience and good views for accurate identification and should be thoroughly documented.

The 5 accidental species reach Iowa from the Great Plains (Lark Bunting, Chestnut-collared Longspur), Southwest (Black-throated Sparrow), West (Green-tailed Towhee), or Northwest (Golden-crowned Sparrow). The first 2 could be more common migrants in western Iowa than the number of records indicates. The other 3 have been found near feeders. Spotted Towhee is also a vagrant from the West, but it winters in small numbers every year.

Green-tailed Towhee (*Pipilo chlorurus*)

Status: Accidental

5 May 1975, Storm Lake, Buena Vista Co. (Crocker 1975)
22 May to early Jun 1990, West Des Moines, Polk Co. (P-0366, *IBL* 60(3) cover, Quinn 1990)

Occurrence: The 2 records are both from spring.

Comment: This species breeds in western mountainous states from Montana to New Mexico and winters from southern California to southern Texas south to central Mexico. This uncommon but widespread vagrant has been recorded in almost all states and provinces north and east to Nova Scotia. States with the most records include Missouri, Illinois, Wisconsin, and Massachusetts. Most of the records in the Midwest and East are from September to March, but the Midwest also has a cluster of records from April to June, and there are a few from the East at this time.

References:

Crocker, V. R. 1975. Green-tailed Towhee at Storm Lake. *Iowa Bird Life* 45:61.

Quinn, C. A. 1990. Green-tailed Towhee in West Des Moines. *Iowa Bird Life* 60:77-78.

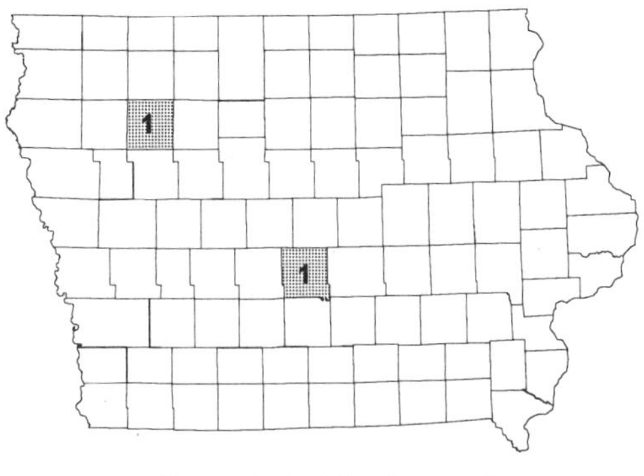

Green-tailed Towhee, all

Eastern Towhee (*Pipilo erythrophthalmus*)

Status: Regular; nests

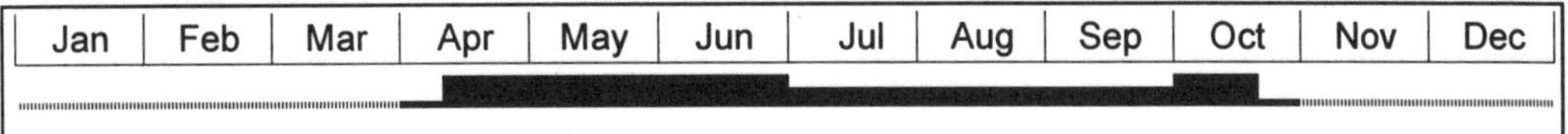

Occurrence: This fairly common summer resident and rare winter resident occurs throughout the state, but is more common in the wooded areas of eastern and southern Iowa and wooded river valleys elsewhere in the state. Many arrive by mid-April and most are gone by late October.

Most winter reports in the past have not distinguished between Eastern and Spotted towhees. Those that have suggest that the 2 species are about equally common and both may occur anywhere in the state. Most reports of winter towhees are from the Christmas Bird Count period, with an average of 10 towhees per year from 1985 to 1994. Only 10 percent of the Christmas Bird Count records are from the northern third of the state. It is not known how many of the birds that are seen in early winter survive. Wintering birds are often associated with feeders. Mid-winter reports of Eastern Towhees include the following: 6 January 1963 near Marion in Linn County (*IBL* 33:19); 22 January 1977 in Fremont County (*IBL* 48:51); 11 February 1989 in Dallas County (*IBL* 59:53); winter 1989 at Princeton in Scott County (*IBL* 59:53); January 1990 at Ledges State Park in Boone County (*IBL* 60:53); and winter 1992-1993 at Johnston in Polk County (*IBL* 63:51).

Comment: The winter range is in the eastern United States from Nebraska, Iowa, and Massachusetts south to the Gulf Coast. Towhees are found irregularly in winter north to central Minnesota (Janssen 1987) and central Wisconsin (Robbins 1991). The breeding range includes most of the winter range except for the southwestern portions, and it extends north to southern Canada and west to Manitoba, western Iowa, and southeastern Nebraska.

The splitting of Rufous-sided Towhee into Eastern and Spotted towhees, which occurred in 1995, should provide the stimulus for more complete reporting of winter towhees and better delineation of their winter distribution in Iowa.

Spotted Towhee (*Pipilo maculatus*)

Status: Regular

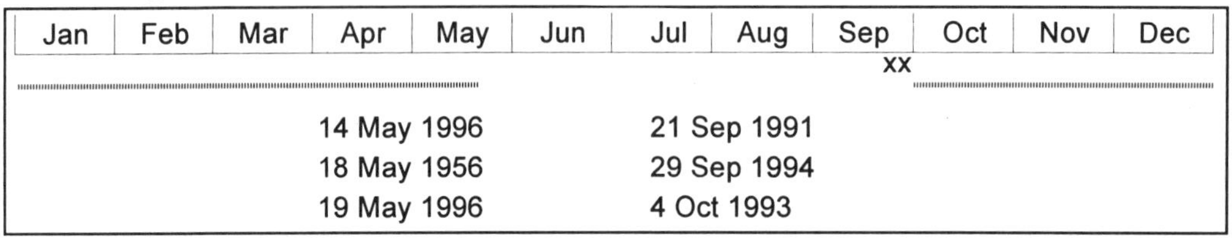

Jan	Feb	Mar	Apr	May	Jun	Jul	Aug	Sep	Oct	Nov	Dec
								XX			

Spring	Fall
14 May 1996	21 Sep 1991
18 May 1956	29 Sep 1994
19 May 1996	4 Oct 1993

Occurrence: This rare winter resident is found every year in small numbers from late September to early May. Most records are from Christmas Bird Counts or birds wintering near feeders. Prior to the recent splitting of Rufous-sided Towhee into Eastern and Spotted towhees, published reports have inconsistently made the distinction between the 2 species. Spotted Towhees have been reported from all areas of the state, but there are clusters of records from southwestern Iowa and central Iowa. An average of 3 per year have been reported from 1985 to 1994, but this number is likely to increase with more specific reporting in future years. In western Iowa, Spotted Towhees were thought to be migrants with a few wintering (Youngworth 1960). The first record of this species was from Sioux City in Woodbury County on 18 October 1928 (Youngworth 1932).

Comment: The winter range is from southern British Columbia and Colorado south to Guatemala and casually in the eastern United States. The breeding range overlaps the winter range and extends northeastward to the central Great Plains and southern Saskatchewan. The closest nesting populations are in western Nebraska and South Dakota.

Reference:

Youngworth, W. G. 1960. The Arctic Towhee along the western border of Iowa: A discussion and summary. *Iowa Bird Life* 30:51-53.

American Tree Sparrow (*Spizella arborea*)

Status: Regular

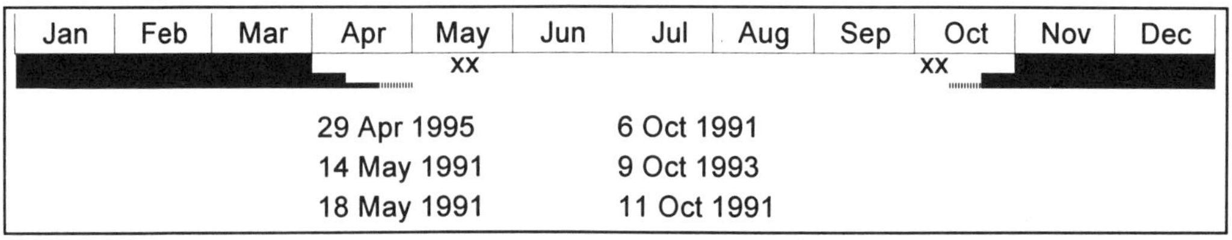

Jan	Feb	Mar	Apr	May	Jun	Jul	Aug	Sep	Oct	Nov	Dec
				XX					XX		

Spring	Fall
29 Apr 1995	6 Oct 1991
14 May 1991	9 Oct 1993
18 May 1991	11 Oct 1991

Occurrence: This abundant winter resident is found in flocks along roadsides and in open areas throughout the state. Birds may be found at feeders, especially in rural areas. Based on Christmas Bird Count data, the number of birds per party hour in the north is about half of that in the central and southern portions of the state. Numbers reported on Christmas Bird Counts also vary from year to year.

American Tree Sparrow is most easily confused with Chipping Sparrow, a species that leaves just as American Tree Sparrows arrive in late October and arrives in mid-April just as American Tree Sparrows leave. American Tree Sparrows frequently occur in mixed flocks with Dark-eyed Junco, a species that typically arrives 2 weeks earlier and leaves 2 weeks later. Unusually early or late American Tree Sparrows should be carefully documented. There are 3 reports from 14 September (*IBL* 45:80, 54:120; Brown 1971), which are undocumented and would be very unusual for any midwestern state. Details are available for the late spring dates.

Comment: The winter range is in the United States east of the Cascade Mountains south to northern Texas and northern North Carolina, and north to the extreme southern portions of Canada. The breeding range includes Alaska and northern parts of the Canadian provinces to the Arctic Coast.

Chipping Sparrow (*Spizella passerina*)

Status: Regular; nests

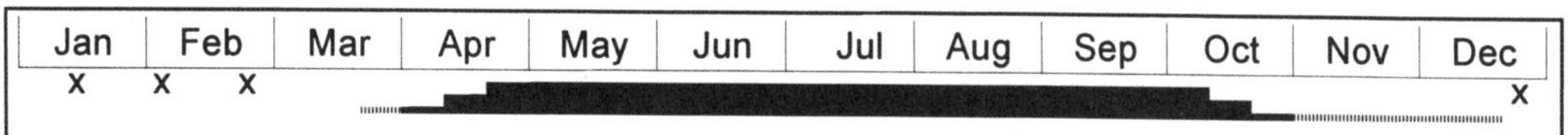

Jan	Feb	Mar	Apr	May	Jun	Jul	Aug	Sep	Oct	Nov	Dec
x	x x										x

26 Mar 1992
27 Mar 1988
27 Mar 1994

18 Dec 1994
19 Dec 1993
27 Dec 1992

winter: 9 Feb 1988, 1991-1992, 12 Jan, 28 Feb 1995

Occurrence: This common summer resident arrives in April and leaves in October. Chipping Sparrows are often found near farmsteads and in towns where there are conifers. Based on Breeding Bird Surveys, this species is most common in eastern Iowa and least common in southern Iowa. The number per count steadily increased from 2 to 10 from 1970 to 1993.

There are 20 reports from December to February, all from the southern two-thirds of Iowa and all except 3 from Christmas Bird Counts. Most are undocumented. Mid-winter birds include individuals caught and banded on 9 February 1988 in Linn County (*IBL* 58:57), at a feeder at Red Rock Reservoir in Marion County all winter in 1991-1992 (*IBL* 62:57), and at a feeder in Indianola in Warren County on 12 January and 28 February 1995 (*IBL* 65:50).

Comment: The winter range is from central California, Arkansas, and Maryland (and casually farther north) south to northern Central America. The pattern of winter records in Minnesota, Wisconsin, and northern Illinois is similar to that in Iowa. Missouri has fewer winter records than Iowa with only 1 in the north (Robbins and Easterla 1992). The breeding range is from mountainous areas in northern Central America to the Yukon, James Bay, and southern Newfoundland.

Chipping Sparrows can be confused with American Tree Sparrows. All winter and March records of Chipping Sparrow should be reported and carefully documented.

Clay-colored Sparrow (*Spizella pallida*)

Status: Regular; occasionally nests

Jan	Feb	Mar	Apr	May	Jun	Jul	Aug	Sep	Oct	Nov	Dec
			x x							x x	

8 Apr 1944
19 Apr 1985
23 Apr 1990

31 Oct 1984
13 Nov 1961
23 Nov 1992

Occurrence: This rare migrant and occasional summer resident is most easily found in western Iowa in early May. Although it occurs regularly in eastern Iowa, it is easy to miss. Fall migrants are less frequently reported and are difficult to identify amongst the many immature Chipping Sparrow that are likely to be present. Fall birds leave the Midwest by mid-October. The late fall dates for Iowa are unusually late when compared to those for nearby states.

Clay-colored Sparrows have been found with increasing frequency at a few locations in northern Iowa in summer, including the following counties and years: Winneshiek (1974), Fayette (1981, 1984, 1985), Emmet (1984), Lyon (1986, 1988, 1989), Dickinson (1986), Kossuth (1989, 1990), Story (1991), Cerro Gordo (1992, 1994), and Allamakee (1994). They were also found in Woodbury and Franklin counties on the breeding bird atlas project (Jackson et al. 1996).

Historically, nesting was described in Kossuth, Winnebago, and Jackson counties (Anderson 1907) and in Emmet County (DuMont 1933). Nesting birds disappeared from extreme southern Minnesota in the 1920s, but a few have been noted in recent years (Janssen 1987).

Comment: The winter range includes southern Texas and most of Mexico. Winter records in the upper Midwest are quite unusual, with 1 January record for Minnesota (Janssen 1987) and 2 December records for Missouri (Robbins and Easterla 1991). The breeding range is in the central United States and Canada from Nebraska, northern Iowa, and southern Ontario northwest to western British Columbia and southern Mackenzie.

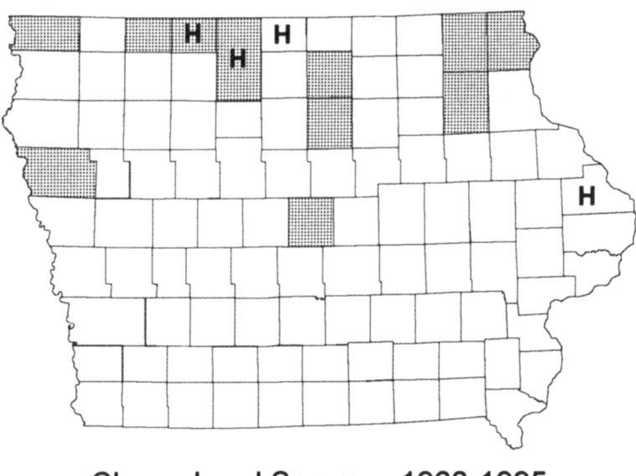

Clay-colored Sparrow, 1960-1995
June-July and historical nesting (H)

Field Sparrow (*Spizella pusilla*)

Status: Regular; nests

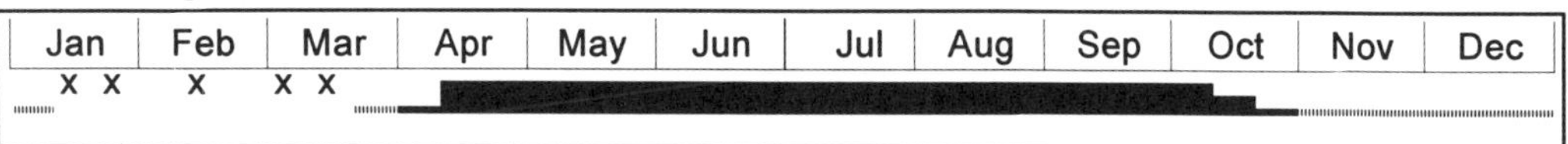

Occurrence: This common summer resident arrives in mid-April and leaves in October, with a few remaining into winter. The preferred habitat of scattered shrubs and low conifers explains the Breeding Bird Survey data, which show the highest counts in southern Iowa and the lowest counts in north-central Iowa.

From 1 to 38 per year (mean 11) have been reported on Christmas Bird Counts from 1960 to 1995, with half of the birds being reported along the Mississippi River from Clinton to Louisa counties. In the northern third of Iowa, Field Sparrow was recorded on 6 of 36 counts from Decorah and once each from 3 other counts. Excluding counts along the Mississippi River, Field Sparrows were found on 5 percent of counts in central Iowa and 10 percent of counts in southern Iowa. There are very few winter records from after the Christmas Bird Count period to late March, including the following: January 1982 at Burlington in Des Moines County (*IBL* 52:29); 19 January 1995 in Monona County (*IBL* 65:50); 30 January 1955 at Webster City in Hamilton County (Carter 1955); 12 February 1980 at Yellow River Forest in Allamakee County (*IBL* 50:28); 8 March 1970 at Waterloo in Black Hawk County (*IBL* 40:50); and 13 March 1955 at Iowa City in Johnson County (Serbousek 1959).

Comment: The winter range is in the eastern United States from Kansas and northern Pennsylvania south to the Gulf Coast and northeastern Mexico. The winter range is just south of Iowa in southern Illinois and southern Missouri. On Christmas Bird Counts, Field Sparrows are regular (a few counts) in Wisconsin, but rare in Minnesota. There are only a few mid-winter records from Minnesota, Wisconsin, and northern Illinois. The breeding range is from northeastern Texas and northern Florida north to New Brunswick, southern Ontario, central Minnesota, and North Dakota.

In Missouri, Field Sparrows are most commonly found in early winter along the Mississippi River in southeastern Missouri (Robbins and Easterla 1992). The paucity of Iowa records in November, early December, and early January may be due to the limited amount of birding activity and reporting at these times. Winter records of this species should be documented.

Reference:

Carter, D. L. 1955. Winter records from the Webster City region. *Iowa Bird Life* 25:41-42.

Vesper Sparrow (*Pooecetes gramineus*)

Status: Regular; nests

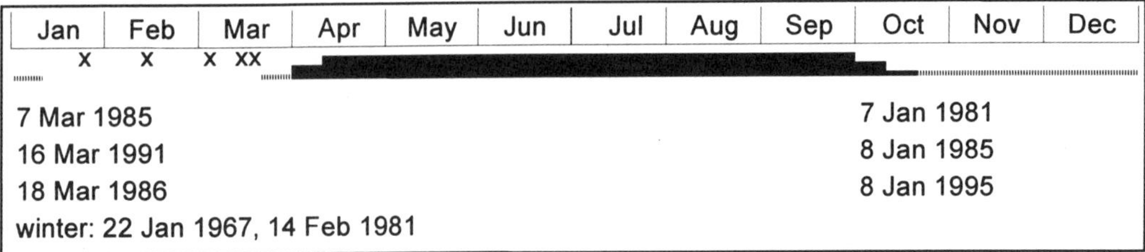

Occurrence: This common summer resident arrives in early April and leaves in October. This species of the roadsides and farmlands is quite noticeable when it first arrives, but by mid-summer birds are scattered across agricultural land and less often seen. Breeding Bird Surveys show high counts in north-central Iowa and very low counts in southern Iowa. Nests are commonly placed in row-crop fields, where they are often destroyed (Rodenhouse and Best 1983). On Breeding Bird Surveys, average numbers have varied from 7 to 28 per count and have been at the higher end of the range in the 1980s and 1990s.

There are 2 records from Christmas Bird Counts prior to 1960 and 34 from 1960 to 1994. About half of these records are along the Mississippi River from Clinton to Burlington; the others are widely scattered. Winter records after early January include the following: 22 January 1967 at Jefferson in Greene County (*IBL* 37:22) and 14 February 1981 at Cedar Falls in Black Hawk County (*IBL* 51:34).

Comment: The winter range is in Mexico and the southern United States north to Arkansas and North Carolina and casually farther north. There are only a few January and February records from Minnesota, Wisconsin, Illinois, and Missouri. The breeding range spans the continent from Missouri north to southern Mackenzie.

Reference:

Rodenhouse, N. L, and L. B. Best. 1983. Breeding ecology of Vesper Sparrows in corn and soybean fields. *Amer. Midland Naturalist* 110:265-275.

Lark Sparrow (*Chondestes grammacus*)

Status: Regular; nests

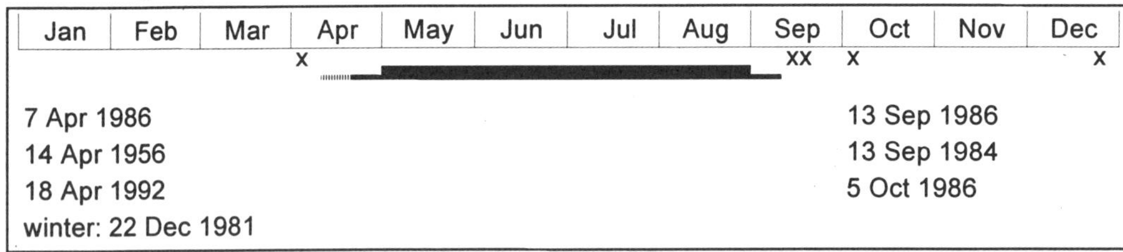

Occurrence: This rather local and uncommon summer resident arrives in late April and leaves by early September. It prefers sandy fields in open bottomlands and is most common in western and southern Iowa. This species is rare in the northern parts of the Des Moines Lobe in the flat glaciated areas, and nesting records are distributed along major rivers in other areas of the state (Jackson et al. 1996).

There is 1 documented winter record: 22 December 1981 at Rathbun Reservoir in Appanoose County (*IBL* 52:6).

Comment: The winter range is from Mexico north to central California, central Texas, and along the Gulf and East coasts. There are single December records from Wisconsin and Missouri. The breeding range is in northern Mexico and the western United States and southern Canada. The range is irregular east of the Mississippi River to western North Carolina and southern Ontario.

Black-throated Sparrow (*Amphispiza bilineata*)

Status: Accidental

16 Mar to 9 Apr 1993, Waterloo, Black Hawk Co. (P-0385, *IBL* 63:79)

Occurrence: The 1 record is of a bird found in March that likely arrived the previous fall with the many others that occurred in the Midwest that winter.

Comment: This bird of the southwestern deserts breeds north in the Great Basin to Oregon, west to eastern California, east to western and southern Texas, and south to central Mexico. In winter, northern birds move south to the southern edge of the United States.

There are up to 6 records in states north to Minnesota and Wisconsin and east to Illinois and Ohio. In addition, there are records from Ontario, Quebec, Maine, New Jersey, Virginia, Florida, and Louisiana. Vagrants to the Midwest and East are evenly scattered from September to early May.

The eruption in the winter of 1992-1993 produced about half as many records as in all previous years, with birds in New Jersey, Quebec, Ontario, Michigan, Wisconsin, Minnesota, Iowa, Missouri, Nebraska, Kansas, and at unusual locations in Texas (*Amer. Birds* 47:90, 98, 230).

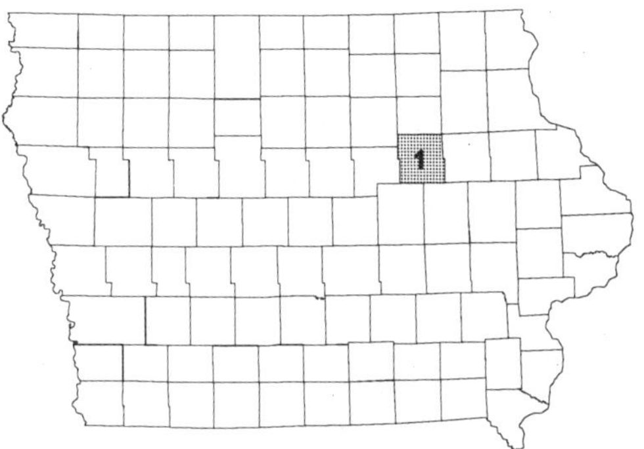

Black-throated Sparrow, all

Lark Bunting (*Calamospiza melanocorys*)

Status: Accidental

By year since 1960 (also 15 reports prior to 1960)

60	63	66	69	72	75	78	81	84	87	90	93
	2 2	1 1	1 3 2	1		1	1 2	2 1			1

By month -- all records

Jan	Feb	Mar	Apr	May	Jun	Jul	Aug	Sep	Oct	Nov	Dec
			1	4 7 8	9 2 1	2 + +					

30 Apr 1994	1 Jul 1970
4 May 1982	1 Jul 1894
9 May 1914	29 Jul 1980

Occurrence: This spring over-migrant and possible summer resident has varied from casual to accidental in its occurrence. It was reported in all but 1 year from the periods 1925 to 1928, 1964 to 1972, and 1980 to 1985. Of the 36 records (excluding a few that are questionable or lack details), 60 percent are from Lyon, Sioux, Plymouth, and Woodbury counties in northwestern Iowa, 86 percent are from western Iowa, and 75 percent are from May and early June.

Reports from 2 early dates do not include descriptions: 28 March 1970 in Adams County (Bliese 1970) and 15 April 1965 in Lucas County (*IBL* 35:52). They are mentioned, however, because there are scattered records on early dates from nearby states for this generally late spring migrant.

It is not known whether the cyclic pattern of records is due to sampling or variation in extent of over-migration. One observer who searched for this species only recorded it once between 1928 and 1957 (Youngworth 1942, 1958), while another who farmed in Plymouth County observed it each spring (Bryant 1971). Attempts to find this species along roadsides and in fields in northwestern Iowa from mid-May to mid-June have occasionally been successful.

There is no proof of nesting. Up to 12 pairs were observed in 4 fields on a farm in Plymouth County from 14 May to 1 July 1970 (Bryant 1971). In 1927, large numbers were present during the breeding season at Gitchie Manitou State Preserve in Lyon County (Roberts and Roberts 1928), and a few were there in the summer of 1928 (DuMont 1933).

One was photographed in Bremer County on 13 May 1981 (P-0013, Moore and Myers 1981). Other records from central and eastern Iowa include the following: 15 May 1958 in Boone County (Keenan 1958), 24 May 1964 in Wright County (Roosa 1964), 28 May 1965 in Decatur County (*IBL* 35:89), and 30 April 1994 in Des Moines County (Fuller 1995).

Historically, the first report of Lark Bunting comes from John James Audubon in Harrison County where 2 were shot on 13 May 1843 (Audubon and Coues 1897). Others were collected on 1 July 1894 and 6 June 1897 in Woodbury County (Stephens 1942), but the specimens are not known to exist.

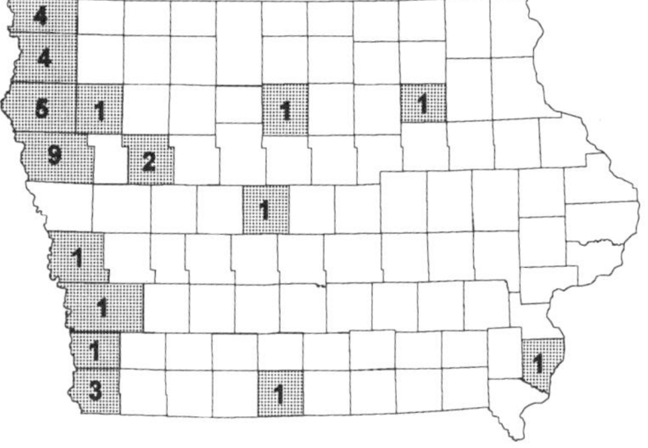

Lark Bunting, all

Comment: The winter range is from north-central Texas and southeastern California south to central Mexico. The breeding range is in the Great Plains from northern Texas and southern Canada east to eastern Nebraska and casually to western Minnesota, and west to northeastern Utah. There were 2 nesting colonies in northwestern Missouri in 1969 (Robbins and Easterla 1992). Vagrant records are widely scattered throughout the eastern United States and Canada. Based on these occurrences, fall and even winter records are potentially possible for Iowa.

References:

Bliese, J. C. W. 1970. Lark Bunting observations. *Iowa Bird Life* 40:52-53.

Bryant, E. 1971. Lark Bunting in Plymouth County. *Iowa Bird Life* 41:55.

Fuller, C. 1995. Lark Bunting in Des Moines County. *Iowa Bird Life* 65:22.

Keenan, J. 1958. Lark Bunting near Ogden. *Iowa Bird Life* 38:43.

Moore, F. L., and R. K. Myers. 1981. Eastern Iowa Lark Bunting. *Iowa Bird Life* 51:105.

Roberts, F. L. R., and M. Roberts. 1928. Notes on some Iowa and South Dakota birds. *Wilson Bull.* 40:50.

Roosa, D. M. 1964. Lark Bunting in Wright County. *Iowa Bird Life* 34:52.

Stephens, T. C. 1942. Another record of the Lark Bunting in Woodbury County. *Iowa Bird Life* 12:30.

Youngworth, W. 1942. Summer bird notes from western Iowa. *Iowa Bird Life* 12:45.

Youngworth, W. 1958. The Lark Bunting in northwest Iowa. *Iowa Bird Life* 38:44.

Savannah Sparrow (*Passerculus sandwichensis*)

Status: Regular; nests

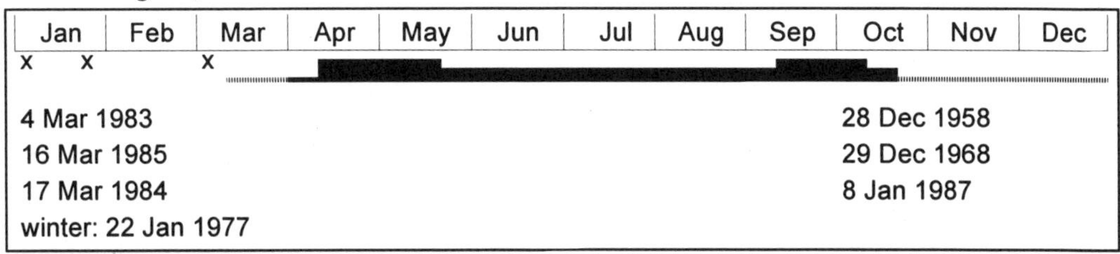

Occurrence: This common migrant and uncommon summer resident arrives in April and leaves in October. Few are reported in November and early December. In fact, December records are almost all from Christmas Bird Counts, with 2 in the 1950s, 9 in the 1960s, 4 in the 1970s, 3 in the 1980s, and 3 in the 1990s. Some, but not all, of these December records are well substantiated. All are from the southern half of the state except for 1 on 20 December 1962 at Estherville in Emmet County (*IBL* 33:4, 7). There are 2 well-described January records: 8 January 1987 at Bays Branch W.A. (*IBL* 57:58) and 22 January 1977 in Fremont County (*IBL* 47:21).

Savannah Sparrows nest throughout Iowa, but are rare in southern and west-central Iowa. Breeding Bird Surveys show by far the highest counts in northeastern Iowa. This species may be easily overlooked in summer unless the observer can detect its high-pitched song.

Comment: The winter range is from northern Central America north to the southern and coastal United States. The winter range extends north to Oklahoma and southern Missouri, and casually farther north. There are occasional winter records from Wisconsin and northern Illinois. The breeding range extends across North America from the northern edge of the winter range to the Arctic Coast, and overlaps the winter range in the highlands of Middle America and California.

Grasshopper Sparrow (*Ammodramus savannarum*)

Status: Regular; nests

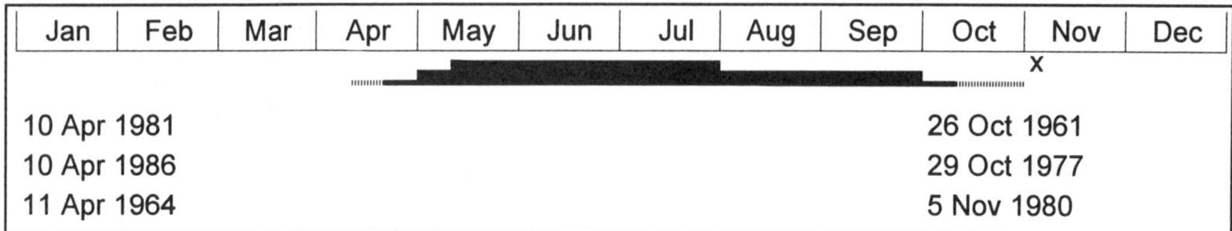

Occurrence: This common summer resident arrives in late April to early May and departs by early October. Based on Breeding Bird Surveys, this species is most common in grasslands and hayfields of southern Iowa and least common in the corn and soybean fields of north-central Iowa. Numbers on Breeding Bird Surveys dropped sharply from 1980 to 1985, but recovered by 1990.

Comment: The winter range is from northern Central America north to southern Arizona, Arkansas, and North Carolina. There are single January records from central Missouri and central and southern Illinois. The breeding range is in the United States, southern Canada, and extreme northwestern Mexico, but does not include southern Florida and some parts of the southwestern and northwestern United States. Local resident populations occur in Middle America, northern South America, and the West Indies.

Henslow's Sparrow (*Ammodramus henslowii*)

Status: Regular; nests

By year since 1960 -- also 27 reports prior to 1960

60 63 66 69 72 75 78 81 84 87 90 93

2 1 4 7 3 5 1 2 2 3 2 3 2 1 4 4 3 2 2 7 9 4 1 3 2 5 2

Jan Feb Mar Apr May Jun Jul Aug Sep Oct Nov Dec

x x x x x xx

29 Mar 1963
3 Apr 1979
16 Apr 1954

19 Oct 1963
24 Oct 1974
29 Oct 1966

Occurrence: This rare summer resident is usually found at only a few locations each year. Birds are found in thick grasslands with much residual cover. They may be found at suitable sites for a number of years and then disappear. For example, there were reports from Cedar Falls in Black Hawk County from 1943 to 1948, from Hayden Prairie in Howard County from 1954 to 1984 (Youngworth 1955, Ennis 1959), and Volga Lake in Fayette County from 1978 to 1983. Since 1987, up to 14 have been found in the grasslands southwest of Lacey-Keosauqua State Park in Van Buren County. Although this species may be found in any part of the state, recent records have been concentrated in the southern row of counties.

Although rarely detected, most migrants probably arrive in April, and few have been seen after July. The 2 latest October dates represent birds netted at Davenport (*IBL* 36:105, 44:103). Specimens include a juvenile at the Museum of Zoology, Ann Arbor, Michigan, taken at Ruthven in Clay County on 29 August 1907 (DuMont 1933), a mounted specimen at the University of Iowa taken in Johnson County prior to 1907 (Anderson 1907, DuMont 1933), a male at Iowa State University (#2178) taken at Brenton Slough in Polk County on 31 May 1934, and a mounted specimen at the University of Iowa (#32425) taken in Johnson County on 16 April 1954.

Historically, the first record was recorded by John James Audubon on 9 May 1843 in Pottawattamie County (Audubon and Coues 1897). Early ornithologists found Henslow's Sparrow to be uncommon to common (Anderson 1907). There are only 3 specific records from 1907 to 1942, after which there were reports from 1 to 3 locations on the Spring Bird Censuses that were carried out from 1943 to 1948. These data suggest that Henslow's Sparrow was common on Iowa's prairies, but became scarce once they were plowed.

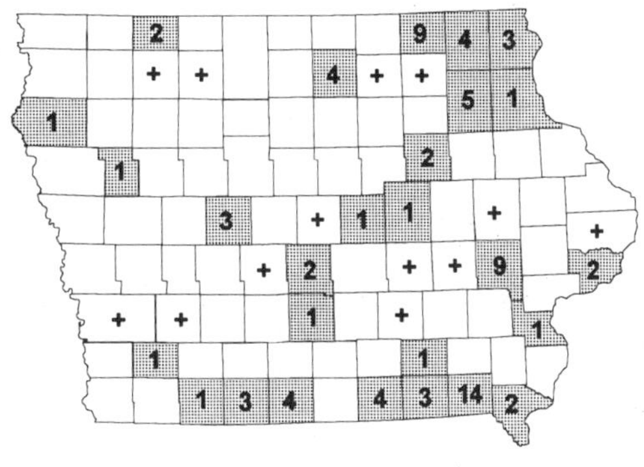

Henslow's Sparrow, all
1960-1995 and prior to 1960 (+)

Comment: The winter range is in the United States from southern South Carolina to eastern Texas. The breeding range is in the northeastern United States and Ontario from eastern Nebraska to New Hampshire and from southern Missouri to central Minnesota. There is a record from 20 December 1942 in Dodge County, Wisconsin (Robbins 1991).

It is likely that Henslow's Sparrow is more common than the records indicate. Extensive search of grassland habitat would be required to determine how many are present.

References:
Ennis, J. H. 1959. Some notes on the Hayden Prairie, with special reference to Henslow's Sparrow. *Iowa Bird Life* 29:82-85.

Youngworth, W. 1955. Birding on the Hayden Prairie area. *Iowa Bird Life* 25:13-14.

Le Conte's Sparrow (*Ammodramus leconteii*)

Status: Regular

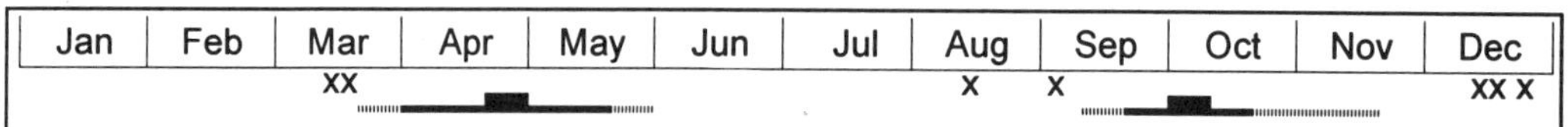

Jan	Feb	Mar	Apr	May	Jun	Jul	Aug	Sep	Oct	Nov	Dec
		XX					X	X			XX X

12 Mar 1955	21 May 1994	10 Sep 1896	12 Nov 1976
19 Mar 1977	21 May 1983	14 Sep 1974	15 Nov 1986
27 Mar 1954	23 May 1995	14 Sep 1986	15 Nov 1970

summer: 19 Aug 1933

winter: 13 Dec 1952, 20 Dec 1954, 26 Dec 1969

Occurrence: This uncommon migrant can be found if looked for in grassy fields in spring and dry marsh edge in fall. In spring, individual birds tend to sit tight until flushed, and then fly straight away and disappear into the grass again. Fall birds are more cooperative and easier to identify. Late April and early October are good times to look for this species.

The earliest spring date represents 7 birds shot in Johnson County on 12 and 13 March 1955 (University of Iowa #32631 to #32637). The only summer record involved 4 birds, 1 shot, at Brenton Slough in Polk County on 19 August 1933 (DuMont 1933). The December records, which are quite unusual, are as follows: 13 December 1952 presumably at Des Moines (Brown 1971); 20 December 1954 in Hamilton County (*IBL* 25:11-12); and 26 December 1969 at Goose Lake in Greene County (*IBL* 40:12).

Comment: The winter range is in the southeastern United States from southern South Carolina and northern Florida to central Texas and southeastern Kansas. Wintering birds in variable numbers are found north to central Missouri (Robbins and Easterla 1992) and southern Illinois (Bohlen 1989). The breeding range extends from Quebec to western British Columbia and from central Wisconsin and central Minnesota to southern Mackenzie.

Reference:
DuMont, P. A. 1933. Bird notes during August 1933 from Polk County, Iowa. *Iowa Bird Life* 3:56-57.

Nelson's Sharp-tailed Sparrow (*Ammodramus nelsoni*)

Status: Regular

Jan	Feb	Mar	Apr	May	Jun	Jul	Aug	Sep	Oct	Nov	Dec
			XX	X	X		X		X		

24 Apr 1976	29 May 1978	30 Aug 1931	19 Oct 1986
26 Apr 1952	29 May 1963	13 Sep 1971	19 Oct 1975
2 May 1963	4 Jun 1964	14 Sep 1986	25 Oct 1972

Occurrence: There are 1 to 10 reports per year since 1971 (except for 1980) for this rare migrant. It is almost always found in wetlands, typically at the edge of tall marshy vegetation, where it may walk on the ground and elude good views. Records are scattered in all areas of the state, but most are from known stopover areas such as Snake Creek Marsh in Greene County. Numbers are undoubtedly underestimated because of the difficulty in walking through its specific habitat and getting good looks at this elusive bird. In fall, it is often found in the same locations as Le Conte's Sparrow, but it is less common and more restricted to the marsh's edge.

Nelson's Sharp-tailed Sparrow tends to be a late spring migrant, with almost all records from mid- to late May. The early spring records (prior to 15 May) are not well substantiated. Minnesota, Wisconsin, and Missouri also have a few April and early May records, but in Illinois, Bohlen (1989) considers April records suspect without a specimen or photograph. Fall birds are easier to find and may remain in the same area for several weeks from mid-September to mid-October.

Historically, there were only 3 records prior to 1928: a specimen at the University of Iowa from 12 October 1894 at Iowa City in Johnson County (Bartsch 1899); a specimen at Iowa State Teachers College from 21 May 1900 at Cedar Falls in Black Hawk County (DuMont 1933); and a specimen at the University of Iowa from 27 May 1904 at Coralville in Johnson County (Anderson 1907). There were 14 reports from central Iowa from 1928 to 1934 and then only 1 report until 1950. There were 3 reports in the 1950s and 5 in the 1960s.

Comment: The winter range is coastal from South Carolina to Texas. The breeding range extends from northeastern South Dakota and northwestern Minnesota across the Prairie Provinces to western British Columbia and southern Mackenzie.

Sharp-tailed Sparrow was split into Nelson's Sharp-tailed and Saltmarsh Sharp-tailed sparrows in 1995. Their identification and ranges are described by Sibley (1996).

References:

Bartsch, P. 1899. *Ammodramus nelsoni* in Iowa. *Auk* 16:276-277.

Sibley, D. 1996. Field identification of the Sharp-tailed Sparrow complex. *Birding* 28:197-208.

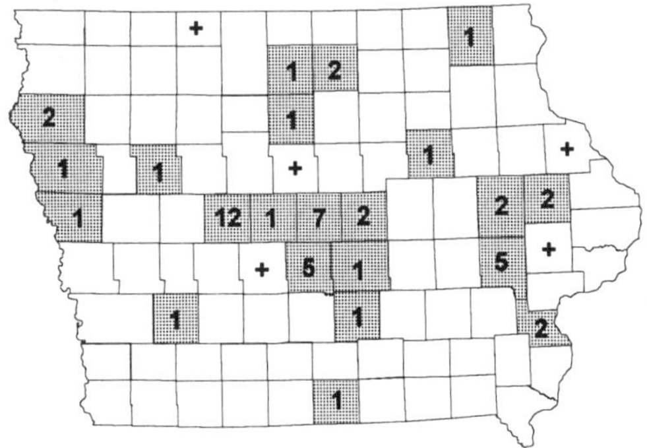

Nelson's Sharp-tailed Sparrow, all 1960-1995 and prior to 1960 (+)

Fox Sparrow (*Passerella iliaca*)

Status: Regular

Jan	Feb	Mar	Apr	May	Jun	Jul	Aug	Sep	Oct	Nov	Dec
				x				x			
			23 Apr 1988			18 Sep 1995					
			23 Apr 1993			21 Sep 1974					
			6 May 1984			22 Sep 1975					

Occurrence: This uncommon migrant and rare winter resident is most easily found from late March to mid-April and in October. It was reported on 35 of 36 Christmas Bird Counts from 1960 to 1995, with a mean of 12 birds per year. December birds are recorded in all areas of the state, with greatest numbers along the lower Mississippi River valley and lowest numbers in the north. Over the same time period, there were 15 reports from January and February. It is likely that others go undiscovered or unreported.

Comment: The winter range is across the southern United States (except southern portions of Florida and Texas) and along the Pacific Coast to British Columbia. The winter range extends north to central Missouri, but some are found as far north as southern Canada. The breeding range is across northern Canada and in the mountains of the western United States.

Song Sparrow (*Melospiza melodia*)

Status: Regular; nests

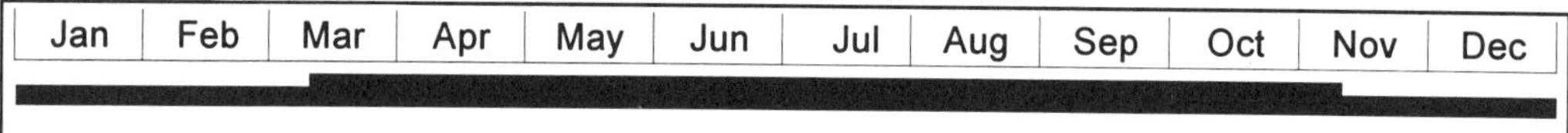

Occurrence: This common summer resident and uncommon winter resident is even more common during migration. It breeds throughout the state in a variety of habitats. On Breeding Bird Surveys, the lowest numbers are found in southern and northwestern Iowa.

In winter, Song Sparrows can usually be found along streams and ditches where there is open water. The best data on winter distribution comes from Christmas Bird Counts, where the highest counts are found along the lower portions of the Mississippi and Missouri rivers. There is also a gradation from north to south, with only one-fourth as many per party hour in the north as compared to the south.

Comment: The winter range includes northern Mexico and most of the United States except for the southern tips of Florida and Texas and north to central Minnesota. The breeding range includes much of the winter range with birds leaving the southeastern United States and southern Great Plains and moving north throughout the Canadian Provinces and into southern Mackenzie.

Lincoln's Sparrow (*Melospiza lincolnii*)

Status: Regular

Jan	Feb	Mar	Apr	May	Jun	Jul	Aug	Sep	Oct	Nov	Dec
x	x +	x					x				

26 Mar 1989	27 May 1990	28 Aug 1988	2 Jan 1971
7 Apr 1996	27 May 1982	2 Sep 1995	3 Jan 1981
8 Apr 1983	30 May 1995	4 Sep 1989	5 Jan 1983

winter: 27 Jan 1979, 3 to 18 Feb 1983

Occurrence: This uncommon migrant is most common in early to mid-May and late September to mid-October.

There are 61 winter (December to February) reports from 1960 to 1995, with all except 4 from the Christmas Bird Count period. Most are undocumented. Of these records, 60 percent are from Clinton, Scott, Muscatine, and Louisa counties, 22 percent from southwestern counties, and 14 percent from Polk, Story, and Marshall counties. The 2 mid-winter records are 1 banded at a feeder on 27 January 1979 at Shenandoah in Page County (*IBL* 49:26) and 1 at a feeder from 3 to 18 February 1983 at Fairfield in Jefferson County (*IBL* 53:54).

Comment: The winter range is from northern Central America north to California, Arkansas, and Georgia. A few are found in winter in southern Missouri in most winters, with more in mild winters (Robbins and Easterla 1992). There are only a few winter records from Minnesota, Wisconsin, and northern Illinois. Bohlen (1987) points out that Lincoln's Sparrow can be confused with immature Swamp Sparrow. The breeding range is across the Canadian provinces, northern Wisconsin, and northern Minnesota northwest to southern Alaska and south in the mountains of the western United States.

Swamp Sparrow (*Melospiza georgiana*)

Status: Regular; nests

Jan	Feb	Mar	Apr	May	Jun	Jul	Aug	Sep	Oct	Nov	Dec

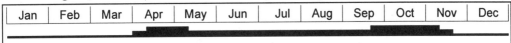

Occurrence: This common migrant is uncommon in summer and rare in winter. Migrants are widespread; in fall, they may be found in dry upland areas with Song Sparrows, as well as in the more traditional wetland habitat. Swamp Sparrow is a regular summer resident in the marshes of north-central and northwestern Iowa, and more localized in other areas of the state. Nests with 4 eggs were located at Dewey's Pasture in Clay County on 10 May 1982 (Johnson 1982) and at Sweet Marsh in Bremer County on 26 May 1983 (Schaufenbuel 1983).

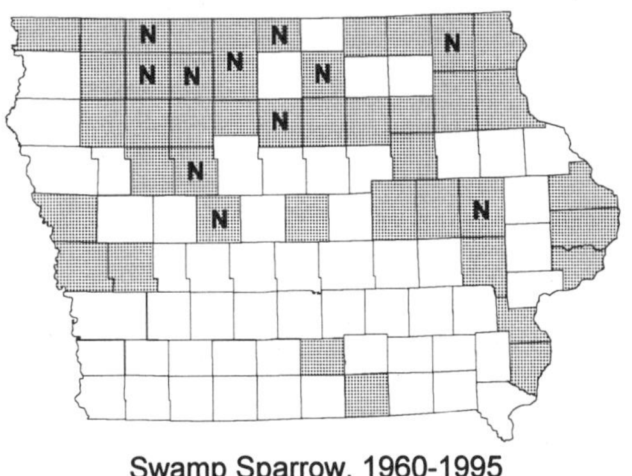

Swamp Sparrow, 1960-1995
June-July and nesting (N)

Wintering birds are found in grassy areas with open water. On Christmas Bird Counts, the mean number for the state is 50 per year, with the highest density along the Mississippi River from Clinton south and very few in the northern third of the state, where there are records for only 6 of 36 years. Swamp Sparrows may over-winter in appropriate habitat, but the extent to which they do so is poorly documented because observers do not search for them and are less likely to report them than on Christmas Bird Counts. The only mid-winter record from the northern third of the state was at Big Marsh in Butler County on 30 January 1993 (*IBL* 63:51).

Comment: The winter range extends from northeastern Mexico, southern New Mexico, and Arkansas north to Iowa and Ohio, and east to Massachusetts and Florida. Occasional winter birds are found in Minnesota and Wisconsin. The breeding range extends from eastern Nebraska, central Iowa, and Delaware north across the Canadian Provinces to Alberta and southern Mackenzie.

References:

Johnson, R. R. 1982. Swamp Sparrow nesting in Iowa. *Iowa Bird Life* 52:128-129.

Schaufenbuel, J. P. 1983. Swamp Sparrow nest at Sweet Marsh. *Iowa Bird Life* 53:59.

White-throated Sparrow (*Zonotrichia albicollis*)

Status: Regular

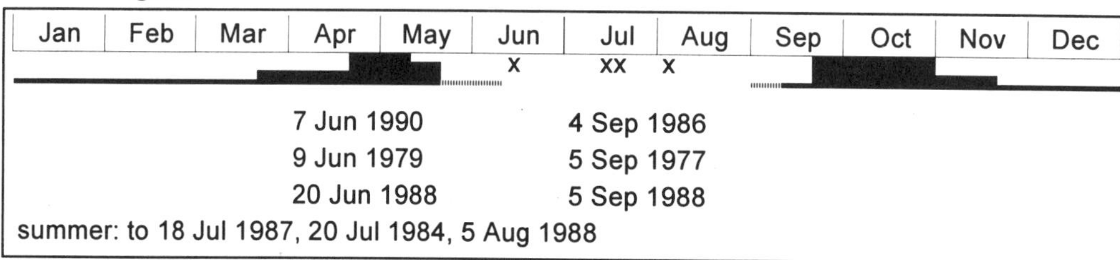

Occurrence: This abundant migrant and rare winter resident has occasionally remained into summer. Migration peaks are from late April to mid-May and from late September through October. Late summer records include 7 June to 18 July 1987 at Davenport in Scott County (*IBL* 57:123), 20 July 1984 in Emmet County (*IBL* 54:86), and 5 August 1988 at Union Slough National Wildlife Refuge in Kossuth County (*IBL* 59:17).

Over-wintering birds are found at feeders or with flocks of sparrows and juncos. Based on Christmas Bird Count data, winter birds are most common along the Mississippi River and least common in northern Iowa. The number per year averaged 55 from 1960 to 1995, with some fluctuation from year to year and over 100 per year from 1991 to 1994. In the northern third of the state, this species is recorded almost every year on Christmas Bird Counts, but with an average of only 2 birds per year. On 29-30 January 1984, White-throated Sparrows were found at 7.3 percent of 1,754 feeders in Iowa (Hollis 1984). The greatest numbers were in central and eastern Iowa, and there was little difference between north and south.

Comment: The winter range is from eastern Arizona, southern Colorado, Iowa, and New England south to the Gulf Coast and northeastern Mexico. Some also winter in western California. Over-wintering birds are also regular in southern Minnesota and southern Wisconsin. The breeding range is in eastern Canada and the northeastern United States west to north-central Minnesota and northwest across Canada to northeastern British Columbia and the southern Yukon.

Golden-crowned Sparrow (*Zonotrichia atricapilla*)

Status: Accidental

3 to 7 May 1977, Jamaica, Guthrie Co. (Burns 1977)
early May 1995, Hamilton Co. (P-0459, *IBL* 65:77)

Occurrence: Both records are from early May in the central part of the state.

Comment: This far-western species breeds from the Bering Straits south and east to the Yukon, British Columbia, southwestern Alberta, and barely to Washington. It winters on the West Coast from southern Alaska to northern Baja California. In winter, this species is casual east to Colorado and Texas, and there are vagrant records from about half of the states and provinces east of the Rocky Mountains. Although birds in the Midwest and East must be wintering birds, records are clustered in October to November, in January, and in April to May.

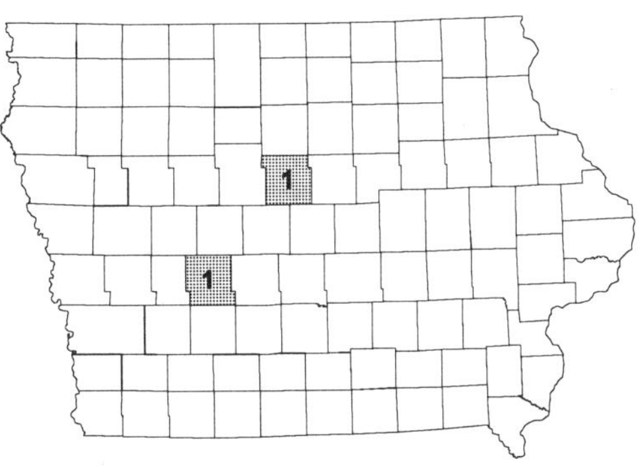

Golden-crowned Sparrow, all

Reference:

Burns, G. 1977. Golden-crowned Sparrow (first Iowa sighting). *Iowa Bird Life* 47:63.

White-crowned Sparrow (*Zonotrichia leucophrys*)

Status: Regular

Jan	Feb	Mar	Apr	May	Jun	Jul	Aug	Sep	Oct	Nov	Dec
								x			
			24 May 1968			17 Sep 1988					
			25 May 1983			25 Sep 1989					
			27 May 1996			26 Sep 1987					

Occurrence: This uncommon migrant and rare winter resident reaches peak numbers from late April to mid-May and during October. Based on Christmas Bird Counts, winter distribution varies strikingly from north to south with 0.002, 0.043, and 0.062 per party hour for northern, central, and southern counts, respectively. Otherwise, the distribution appears to be patchy, with some counts consistently finding this species and others not. This species is found in rural edge habitat in winter as well as in migration. It was found at 5.5 percent of 1,754 feeders in 1984 (Hollis 1984). The differences from north to south were far less striking than for Christmas Bird Count data.

Comment: The winter range extends from the east-central United States to northern Mexico and southwestern British Columbia. It misses the extreme southeastern United States and extends north to Massachusetts, Ohio, southern Wisconsin, Iowa, and occasionally Minnesota. The breeding range is from Newfoundland across the northern parts of Canadian provinces to the Arctic Ocean, west to Alaska and south in the western United States to northern Arizona.

Harris's Sparrow (*Zonotrichia querula*)

Status: Regular

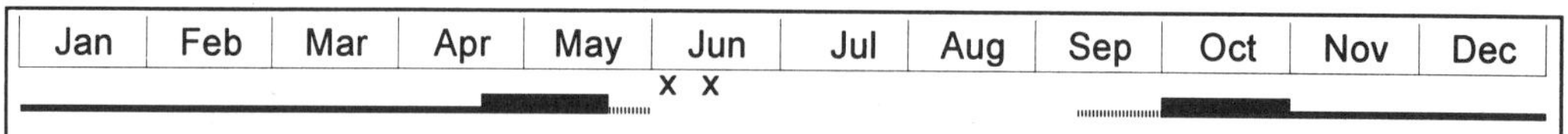

Jan	Feb	Mar	Apr	May	Jun	Jul	Aug	Sep	Oct	Nov	Dec

25 May 1983 — 17 Sep 1994
26 May 1983 — 18 Sep 1994
30 May 1993 — 19 Sep 1993
summer: 9 to 15 Jun 1977, 13 to 14 Jun 1989

Occurrence: In migration, Harris's Sparrow is common in western and rare in eastern Iowa, and, in winter, it is rare but regular in western and irregular in eastern Iowa. There are 2 summer records: 9 to 15 June 1977 at Trumbull Lake in Clay County (*IBL* 47:104) and 13, 14 June 1989 at West Okoboji in Dickinson County (banded, *IBL* 59:115).

On Christmas Bird Counts from 1960 to 1995, there were 0.913 Harris's Sparrows per party-hour on counts from the Missouri River valley compared to 0.002 per party-hour for counts from the Mississippi River valley. The highest winter counts are from southwestern Iowa based on Christmas Bird Counts and winter feeder surveys (Hollis 1984), but this species is regular along the entire western edge of the state. Winter counts are fairly stable, except for 1989, when numbers were twice the average on Christmas Bird Counts. There are scattered mid-winter records for eastern Iowa.

Comment: The winter range is in the southern Great Plains from central Texas north to southern South Dakota and from central Colorado to western Iowa. The breeding range is in northern Manitoba and Mackenzie.

Dark-eyed Junco (*Junco hyemalis*)

Status: Regular

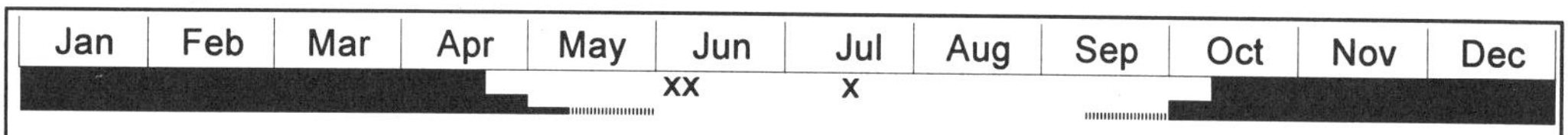

Jan	Feb	Mar	Apr	May	Jun	Jul	Aug	Sep	Oct	Nov	Dec

26 May 1996 — 11 Sep 1976
7 Jun 1980 — 14 Sep 1994
9 Jun 1950 — 16 Sep 1988
summer: 19 Jul 1987

Occurrence: This abundant winter resident arrives abruptly in October and most are gone by the end of April. There is 1 summer record: 19 July 1987 at Des Moines (*IBL* 57:123).

Based on Christmas Bird Count data, juncos are about twice as abundant in central and southern Iowa as they are in northern Iowa, and numbers fluctuate up and down each year. Based on mid-winter feeder surveys, juncos were the most consistently present species (89 and 87 percent of feeders in 1984 and 1985) and were only outnumbered by American Goldfinch and House Sparrow (Hollis 1984, 1986).

Dark-eyed Juncos vary considerably in appearance in different geographic locations. The western subspecies, Oregon Junco, is found at scattered locations across Iowa on a regular basis. Two were collected in Polk County on 16 January 1947 (Musgrove 1948). The various subspecies of Dark-eyed Junco are not regularly reported, and intergrades make accurate identification difficult.

Comment: The winter range includes southern Canada, northern Mexico, and all of the United States except for the southern tips of Florida and Texas. The breeding range extends across Canada and Alaska except for the extreme northern portions south in the mountainous areas of the eastern and western United States and south centrally to southern Manitoba, northeastern Minnesota, and northern Wisconsin.

Reference:

Musgrove, J. W. 1948. Records of the Montana Junco and the Cassiar Slate-colored Junco for Iowa. *Iowa Bird Life* 18:36-37.

Lapland Longspur (*Calcarius lapponicus*)

Status: Regular

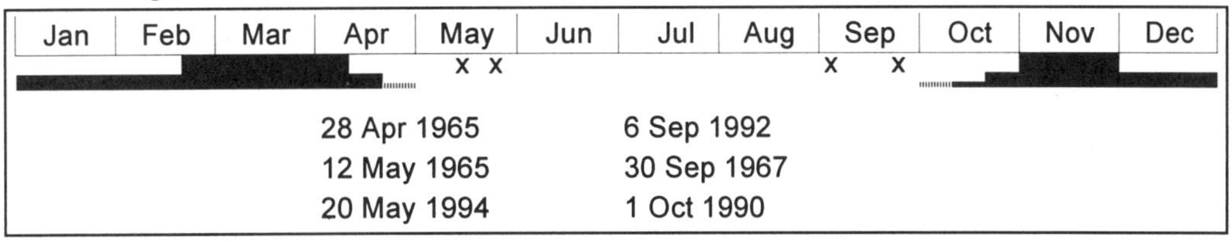

Jan	Feb	Mar	Apr	May	Jun	Jul	Aug	Sep	Oct	Nov	Dec
				x x				x x			

28 Apr 1965
12 May 1965
20 May 1994

6 Sep 1992
30 Sep 1967
1 Oct 1990

Occurrence: This abundant migrant and common winter resident may be difficult to find because it occurs in large flocks that, depending on snow cover and other conditions, may be present in some areas of the state and absent in others. It is most easily found in spring and fall after snowstorms, when birds typically flock to roadsides. It may occur in mixed flocks with Horned Lark, Snow Bunting, and Smith's Longspur. Swirling flocks move rapidly and seemingly disappear into the ground as birds land in stubble fields or short grass.

Based on Christmas Bird Count data, birds are found on about one-third of counts, with considerable year-to-year variation and with only slightly more in the north than in the south. It is difficult to estimate numbers of this species, but it must be one of the most abundant in Iowa. It is certainly the most common passerine on the Arctic tundra. In March 1904 and January 1938, huge numbers were killed in snowstorms in northwestern Iowa (Roberts 1907, Stephens 1939). About 50,000 were seen between Cherokee and Sac City on 27 February 1984 (*IBL* 54:19).

Comment: The winter range is from southern Canada south to Maryland, Tennessee, Arkansas, Colorado, Utah, and southern California in the Nearctic and in north-central Europe and Asia in the Palearctic. The breeding range follows the Arctic Coast and extends south to the Aleutians and James Bay.

References:

Roberts, T. S. 1907. A Lapland Longspur tragedy. *Auk* 24:369-377.

Stephens, T. S. 1939. The 1938 longspur tragedy in northwest Iowa. *Proc. Iowa Acad. Sci.* 46:383-395.

Smith's Longspur (*Calcarius pictus*)

Status: Regular

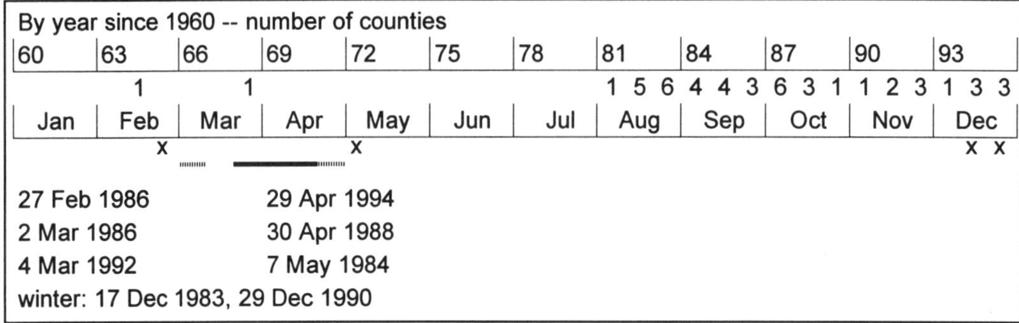

Occurrence: This rare spring migrant has been found in Iowa each year since 1981, when it was discovered in Johnson County (Kent 1981). Smith's Longspurs are usually found in flocks, which are often large, and may stay in one area for several weeks from late March to mid-April or later. They may be in mixed flocks with Lapland Longspurs. They have been most consistently found in grassy fields and old stubble in the flat lands of southeastern Johnson and northwestern Louisa counties, but these locations are extensively searched each year.

There are 2 modern winter records: 17 December 1983 in Pocahontas County (P-0136, *IBL* 64:70) and 29 December 1990 near Almont in Clinton County (*IBL* 61:59).

Historically, large numbers were located in Decatur County in late October 1872 (Trippe 1973). Early and late fall dates for Poweshiek County were 18 October 1888 and 4 November 1889 and for Lee County were 7 November 1899 and 28 November 1889 (Cooke 1911). It was found commonly in Poweshiek County from February to April from 1887 to 1890 (Jones 1892, 1895). Other records prior to 1900 were from spring in Black Hawk, Lee, Mills, Polk, Pottawattamie, Poweshiek, and Scott counties (Kent 1981). There were 9 reports from 1900 to 1930 and then only 2 from 1931 to 1980, which were in 1964 and 1968 (Kent 1981).

There is a female specimen for 18 April 1885 from Des Moines in Polk County at Iowa State University and a female or immature male from 22 April 1928 and 4 males from 13 April 1929 in Iowa County at Coe College. A road-killed specimen from Cherokee County on 29 April 1994 is at Iowa State University (#2608, *IBL* 64:79-80).

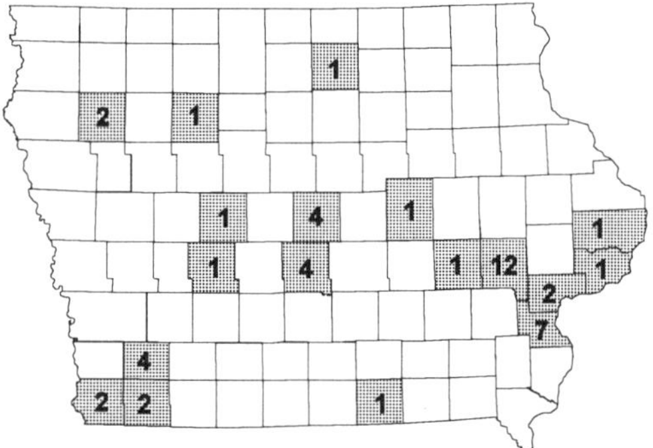

Smith's Longspur, 1960-1995
Number of years seen

Comment: The winter range is centered in the southern Great Plains from northeastern Texas to Kansas. The breeding range extends in a narrow band along the western edge of Hudson Bay to northeastern Alaska and discontinuously to an area southeast of Mt. McKinley.

It is unclear why so few were discovered from 1930 to 1980 and why there are no modern fall records. Minnesota does not experience large flocks in spring (Janssen 1987); perhaps, after lingering in Iowa, these birds head more or less directly for the Arctic. Fall records occur in western Minnesota and western Missouri from mid-October in Minnesota to late November in Missouri. Perhaps fall birds take a more westerly route and should be looked for in western Iowa. The winter range appears to be well away from Iowa—Missouri has only 5 winter records (Robbins and Easterla 1992).

References:

Cooke, W. W. 1911. The migration of North American sparrows. *Bird-Lore* 13:15-16.

Kent, T. H. 1981. Smith's Longspur in Iowa. *Iowa Bird Life* 51:53-55.

Trippe, T. M. 1873. The Painted Bunting. *Amer. Naturalist* 7:500.

Chestnut-collared Longspur (*Calcarius ornatus*)

Status: Accidental

By year since 1960

60	63	66	69	72	75	78	81	84	87	90	93
							1 1	1 1		1	2

By month -- all records

Jan	Feb	Mar	Apr	May	Jun	Jul	Aug	Sep	Oct	Nov	Dec
		2	1 3 1								

4 Apr 1982, northwestern Muscatine Co., male (*IBL* 52:63; 53:35)
12 Mar 1983, near Hills, Johnson Co., male (*IBL* 53:55; 54:39)
20 Mar 1985, Hendrickson M., Story Co., 2 males (*IBL* 55:70; 56:44)
15 Apr 1986, Woodbury Co. (Iowa State Univ. #2509, P-0239, Bierman 1986)
23 Apr 1992, southwestern Fremont Co., flocks of 5, 25 (Iowa State Univ. #2568, P-0335, *Amer. Birds* 46:432, *IBL* 62:81; 63:70)
12 Apr 1995, Sioux Co. (P-0447, Kent 1996, *Field Notes* 49:260)
12 Apr 1995, Lyon Co. (*IBL* 65:77, Kent 1996)

Occurrence: The 7 records are all from spring, 2 with specimens. The 4 records from the western edge of the state are of birds found after April snowstorms. The birds in central and eastern Iowa were found while searching flocks of other longspurs. There are 16 reports prior to 1940, but none with satisfactory evidence (Dinsmore et al. 1984).

Comment: This species breeds in the northern part of the Great Plains south to northeastern Colorado and northwestern Nebraska and east to the western edge of Minnesota. The winter range includes Arizona, New Mexico, Oklahoma, northwestern Louisiana, northern Texas, and northern Mexico. Although the western edges of Iowa and Missouri are on a direct line between the eastern edges of the winter and summer ranges for this species, both states have experienced only a few spring records in the west and a few other records to the east. There are a few records from Wisconsin, Illinois, and Florida and scattered records from Michigan, Ontario, Nova Scotia, Maine, Massachusetts, Connecticut, New York, New Jersey, Maryland, and Virginia. Midwest vagrant records are from March to May, except for 2 December records from Illinois. More easterly records are scattered from March to August and October to January.

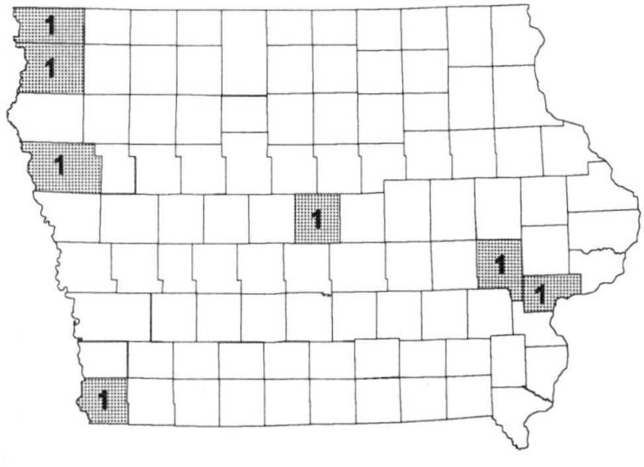

Chestnut-collared Longspur, all

References:

Bierman, D. 1986. Chestnut-collared Longspur in Woodbury County. *Iowa Bird Life* 56:95.

Kent, T. H. 1996. Chestnut-collared Longspurs in Sioux and Lyon counties. *Iowa Bird Life* 66:61-63.

Snow Bunting (*Plectrophenax nivalis*)

Status: Regular

Jan	Feb	Mar	Apr	May	Jun	Jul	Aug	Sep	Oct	Nov	Dec
			1 Apr 1993			20 Oct 1962					
			5 Apr 1975			20 Oct 1989					
			9 Apr 1982			20 Oct 1990					

Occurrence: The number and location of Snow Buntings varies from year to year. Small numbers may be found near sandy or rocky areas at reservoirs and lakes or small or large numbers may be found along roads in open country, where they often associate with Lapland Longspur and Horned Lark. Snowstorms in February and March often concentrate birds along roadsides.

Comment: The winter range includes southern Canada and the northern United States, as well as the Pacific Coast from British Columbia to the Aleutians. The winter range extends south to southern Illinois and central Missouri. This species also winters in northern Europe and Asia. The breeding range is circumpolar near the Arctic Coast, reaching the Aleutians but only the northern parts of Hudson Bay.

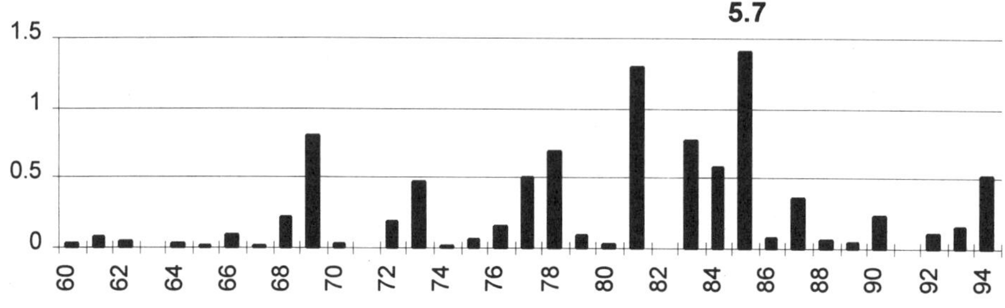

Snow Bunting, 1960-1994
Christmas Bird Counts, number per party-hour

Blackbirds and Allies (Subfamily Icterinae)

Blackbirds and their allies comprise 96 New World species, with 25 from North America and 13 from Iowa. All of the Iowa species are Regular except for Bullock's Oriole, which is Accidental and was split from Baltimore Oriole in 1995. Great-tailed Grackle was first found in Iowa in 1983, but since then it has become a regular nesting species and continues to expand its range. This family contains some of Iowa's most common species: Red-winged Blackbird, Eastern and Western meadowlarks, Common Grackle, Brown-headed Cowbird, and Baltimore Oriole. Bobolink, Yellow-headed Blackbird, and Orchard Oriole also nest in Iowa and are locally common. The only transients in the group are Rusty and Brewer's blackbirds.

Bobolink (*Dolichonyx oryzivorus*)

Status: Regular; nests

Jan	Feb	Mar	Apr	May	Jun	Jul	Aug	Sep	Oct	Nov	Dec
									x	x	
23 Apr 1992									10 Oct ??		
26 Apr 1969									15 Oct 1954		
28 Apr 1962									25 Nov 1975		

Occurrence: This common summer resident nests throughout Iowa. Based on Breeding Bird Surveys, it is much more common in northern and eastern Iowa than it is in southern and western Iowa. Numbers have declined steadily from 13 to 2 per survey route from 1970 to 1992.

Most Bobolinks arrive suddenly in early May and disappear gradually in late summer. When found, late summer birds are often in flocks, with males having molted to a female-like basic plumage.

Comment: The winter range is in South America east of the Andes from central Brazil to northern Argentina. There are 3 winter records from Illinois (Bohlen 1989), but none from other nearby states. The breeding range is across the northern United States and southern Canada. The range extends south to northern Missouri.

Red-winged Blackbird (*Agelaius phoeniceus*)

Status: Regular; nests

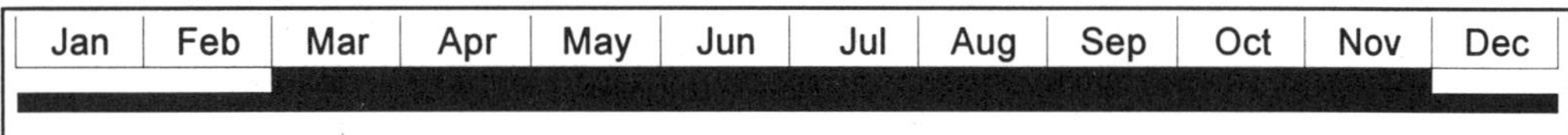

Occurrence: This abundant breeding species occupies marshes and open upland areas including roadsides. Based on Breeding Bird Surveys, counts are highest in eastern and southern Iowa and lowest in north-central and western Iowa.

The winter distribution is quite variable. On Christmas Bird Counts, this species is found on half of the counts in the northern third and on two-thirds of the counts in the southern third of the state, but numbers are much greater in the south, often due to large flocks. There is little quantitative data on birds wintering beyond the Christmas Bird Count period, but scattered individuals or small flocks, most of which are males, are not unusual. The highest winter count was 255,000 at a roost in Glenwood in Mills County on 22

December 1984 (*IBL* 55:12, 17). In midwinter, Red-winged Blackbirds were found at 2.5 percent of bird feeders, making them slightly less common at feeders than Brown-headed Cowbirds and Common Grackles (Hollis 1986).

Comment: The winter range is from central Central America north throughout the United States except for the northern edge. The breeding range encompasses the same areas and extends north to southern Alaska, Mackenzie, and Newfoundland.

Eastern Meadowlark (*Sturnella magna*)

Status: Regular; nests

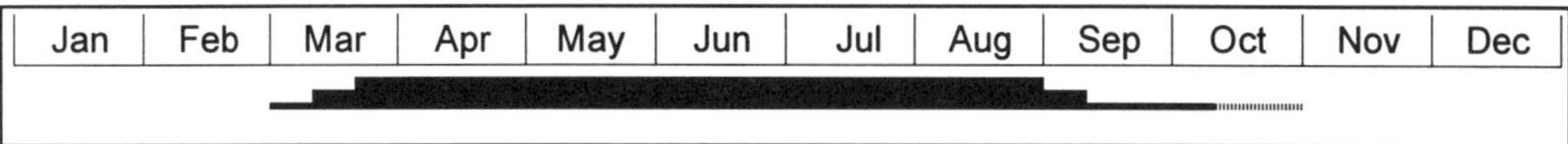

Occurrence: Eastern Meadowlarks are a common breeding bird in eastern and southern Iowa and gradually become uncommon to rare or absent from some counties in northwestern Iowa. Eastern Meadowlark, a bird of grassy fields along river valleys, is the predominant meadowlark in southeastern and parts of south-central Iowa. In Winneshiek County in northeastern Iowa, 42 percent of the meadowlarks were Eastern and 58 percent Western, and both species were often found in the same fields (Hochstetler et al. 1991).

Singing meadowlarks in March identify spring arrivals. Fall birds are mostly silent, with no reliable data on fall departure dates for this species. The vast majority of wintering meadowlarks appear to be Westerns, although adequate documentation of this impression is lacking. Up until 1982, Eastern Meadowlarks were listed on Christmas Bird Counts, but this practice was discontinued after a discussion of identification problems (*IBL* 53:4, Wilson 1983). At that time, all winter specimens located were Westerns (Wilson 1983). Road-killed birds from Tama and Johnson counties, initially identified as Eastern Meadowlarks, on closer examination proved to be Westerns. There are a few other winter sight and song records that may be of Eastern Meadowlarks (*IBL* 58:49, 76; 61:60).

Historically, the relative east-west distribution of meadowlarks was noted by early ornithologists (Anderson 1907). Since then there has been some range expansion of both species with more overlap in distribution (Lanyon 1956, Hochstetler et al. 1991).

Comment: The winter range extends from Arizona diagonally to New York and southern New England south to the Amazon. In Missouri, Easterns are said to be the predominant meadowlark in winter, except in the northwestern part of the state (Robbins and Easterla 1992). In Illinois, Easterns are most common in the southern part of the state in winter, and only a few winter records of Western Meadowlark are cited (Bohlen 1989). The breeding range includes the winter range and extends north to south-central South Dakota, eastern Minnesota, southern Ontario, and the Maritime Provinces.

References:

Hochstetler, K. J., E. L. Garza, W. Lohmann, and T. A. Sordahl. 1991. Distribution of Eastern and Western meadowlarks in Winneshiek County. *Iowa Bird Life* 61:8-13.

Lanyon, W. E. 1956. Ecological aspects of the sympatric distribution of meadowlarks in the north-central states. *Ecology* 37:98-108.

Wilson, B. L. 1983. Identifying meadowlarks in Iowa. *Iowa Bird Life* 53:83-87.

Western Meadowlark (*Sturnella neglecta*)

Status: Regular; nests

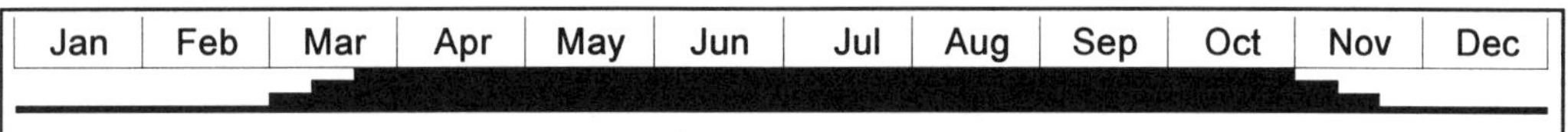

Occurrence: This abundant summer resident and rare winter resident is found throughout the state, but is rare in southeastern and parts of south-central Iowa. Western Meadowlarks prefer more open and drier habitat than Easterns, but both may be found in the same fields. Most wintering meadowlarks are thought to be Westerns, but adequate documentation is lacking.

Comment: The winter range extends diagonally from southern British Columbia to the panhandle of Florida south to southern Mexico. The breeding range includes the highlands of northern Mexico, the western United States and southern Canada east to northern Louisiana and southeastern Ontario.

Yellow-headed Blackbird (*Xanthocephalus xanthocephalus*)

Status: Regular; nests

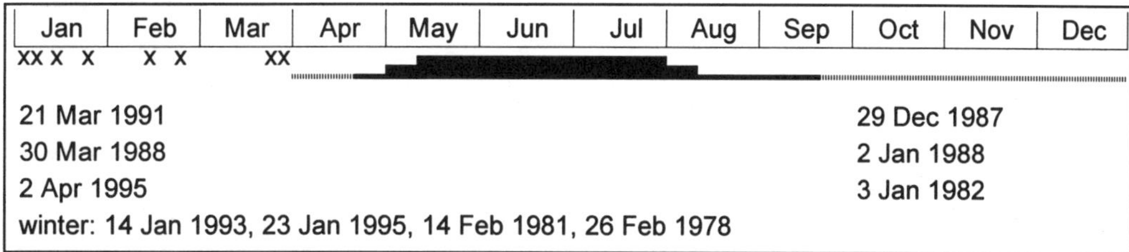

Occurrence: This species is a common summer resident in the marshes of the Wisconsinan glacial areas of north-central Iowa and is also found in marshes along the Missouri River and in scattered other locations. For a blackbird, it arrives rather late and departs early in the fall. Yellow-headed Blackbirds are typically found in the same deep-water marshes from year to year. Of 27 marshes occupied in the years 1960 to 1962, 24 were still occupied in 1983 to 1984 (Weller 1969, Brown 1988). Additional areas may be occupied in high-water years such as the 11 areas mentioned in 1990 (*IBL* 60:106).

There are about 22 winter records from 1960 to 1995, with all but 4 from December to early January, and most from Christmas Bird Counts. Winter records are scattered across the state, but half have been from the western edge.

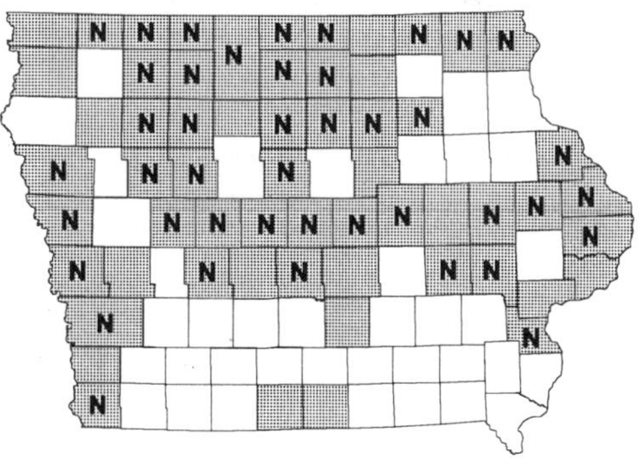

Yellow-headed Blackbird, 1960-1995
June-July and nesting (N)

The mid-winter records are a young male at a feeder in Council Bluffs in Pottawattamie County on 26 February 1978 (*IBL* 48:70), 1 at a feeder in Waterloo in Black Hawk County on 14 February 1981 (*IBL* 51:33), a male in a cattle lot in Kossuth County on 14 January

1993 (*IBL* 63:52), and 3 at Ingham Lake in Emmet County on 23 January 1995 (*IBL* 65:51).

Comment: The winter range is from central California and western Texas south to southern Mexico. Winter records from nearby states parallel the pattern in Iowa, except for regular occurrence in northwestern Missouri (Robbins and Easterla 1992). The breeding range is in the western United States and western Canadian provinces east to northwestern Missouri, Ohio, and extreme southern Ontario.

References:

Brown, M. 1988. Yellow-headed Blackbird nesting in Iowa: A twenty-year follow-up. *Iowa Bird Life* 58:38-39.

Weller, M. W. 1969. Distribution of the Yellow-headed Blackbird in Iowa. *Iowa Bird Life* 39:3-5.

Rusty Blackbird (*Euphagus carolinus*)

Status: Regular

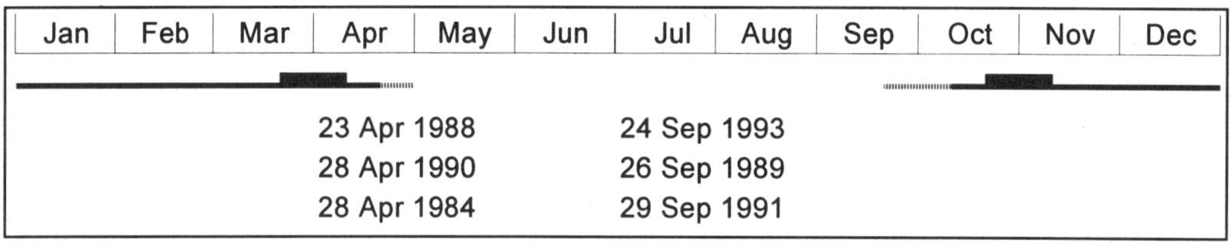

Jan	Feb	Mar	Apr	May	Jun	Jul	Aug	Sep	Oct	Nov	Dec
			23 Apr 1988			24 Sep 1993					
			28 Apr 1990			26 Sep 1989					
			28 Apr 1984			29 Sep 1991					

Occurrence: This uncommon migrant and rare winter resident is most common from late March to early April and from late October to early November. It is most common near marshes, streams, and lakes and can be found anywhere in the state.

On Christmas Bird Counts, Rusty Blackbirds are found in all areas of the state in variable numbers from year to year. They are found most consistently (about 50 percent of counts) and in the largest numbers (may be over 100 birds) along the western edge of the state. The number per party-hour is greater in northern Iowa and along the Mississippi River than it is in central and southern Iowa. Birds are reported in January and February almost annually from all areas of the state. Birds have been found near marshes, in feedlots, and occasionally at feeders. Many of the birds seen on Christmas Bird Counts may move south, but the number that over-winter is also likely to be much greater than reported.

Comment: The winter range is mostly in the United States east of the Rocky Mountains (excluding southern Florida), but some are found north to southern Canada and along the Pacific Coast to Alaska. The breeding range extends across Canada and Alaska, barely dipping into northeastern Minnesota.

Brewer's Blackbird (*Euphagus cyanocephalus*)

Status: Regular

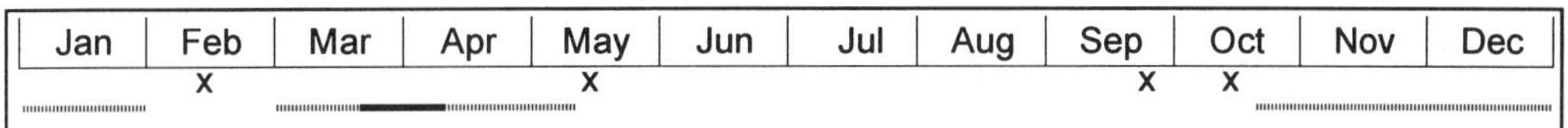

Jan	Feb	Mar	Apr	May	Jun	Jul	Aug	Sep	Oct	Nov	Dec
	x			x				x	x		

6 May 1983	30 Sep 1989
10 May 1981	14 Oct 1932
11 May 1996	24 Oct 1984

Occurrence: Although this species nests just north of Iowa in southern Minnesota, it is a surprisingly rare migrant and winter visitant. It is much less common than Rusty Blackbird. The best time to look for this species is in late March and early April in grassy areas near water and in plowed fields or feedlots. It is somewhat less likely than Rusty Blackbird to associate with other icterids. There are fewer fall than spring records, most in late October and November.

Rusty Blackbird, and even other species such as immature male Red-winged Blackbirds, immature Common Grackles, and Brown-headed Cowbirds, can be misidentified as Brewer's. It is impossible to determine the validity of the 94 reports of Brewer's Blackbirds for December through February from 1960 to 1995. Of these winter records, 77 percent have been from Christmas Bird Counts and 88 percent from the southern two-thirds of the state. There are 8 reports from January and 1 from February, most without details of identification. There are a number of reports from early March, which indicate the beginning of migration.

Comment: The winter range is from southern British Columbia, southern Wyoming, Arkansas, and western South Carolina south to southern Mexico. Winter birds are noted in Minnesota, Wisconsin, Illinois, and Missouri with comments on identification problems. The breeding range is in the western United States north to central Alberta and east along the northern part of the range to southern Michigan. In Minnesota, the breeding range extends to within 1 county of Iowa, but in Wisconsin it is in the northeastern half of the state. During the twentieth century, Brewer's Blackbird has undergone a gradual range expansion from west-central Minnesota to eastern Ontario (Stepney and Power 1973).

The validity of winter records might be increased if detailed descriptions of such birds were required for reporting. Confirmation of early fall dates is also needed.

Reference:

Stepney, P. H. R., and D. M. Power. 1973. Analysis of the eastward breeding expansion of Brewer's Blackbird plus general aspects of avian expansions. *Wilson Bull.* 85:452-464.

Great-tailed Grackle (*Quiscalus mexicanus*)

Status: Regular; nests

Jan	Feb	Mar	Apr	May	Jun	Jul	Aug	Sep	Oct	Nov	Dec
	x xx										x xx

26 Feb 1995	19 Dec 1987
5 Mar 1994	22 Dec 1984
5 Mar 1996	27 Dec 1992

Occurrence: The first Great-tailed Grackles identified in Iowa were a pair in a flooded field in the Missouri River bottoms in northwestern Mills County on 19 May 1983 (*IBL* 54:39). The first evidence of nesting occurred later that summer when a female was observed feeding young at Riverton Area in Fremont County on 15 July 1983 (Silcock 1983). By 1992, there were 58 reports of Great-tailed Grackles with nesting in six counties (S. Dinsmore and J. Dinsmore 1993). The spread has been along the Missouri River and to the marshes of central and north-central Iowa. The arrival and departure dates are similar to those for other blackbirds. Over-wintering birds occur in northwestern Missouri (Robbins and Easterla 1992) and are likely to occur in Iowa in the future.

Comment: This resident species is migratory in the northern parts of its range, which extends from Iowa and Louisiana west to southeastern California and south to northwestern South America. The range has been expanding northward from Texas since 1900, reaching Oklahoma in the 1950s, northwestern Missouri in 1976, and eastern Nebraska in 1977 (J. Dinsmore and S. Dinsmore 1993).

References:

Dinsmore, J. J., and S. J. Dinsmore. 1993. Range expansion of the Great-tailed Grackle in the 1900s. *J. Iowa Acad. Sci.* 100:54-59.

Dinsmore, S. J., and J. J. Dinsmore. 1993. Range expansion of Great-tailed Grackles in Iowa, 1983-92. *Iowa Bird Life* 63:85-89.

Silcock, W. R. 1983. Great-tailed Grackle in southwest Iowa: Continuation of an explosive range expansion. *Iowa Bird Life* 53:106-107.

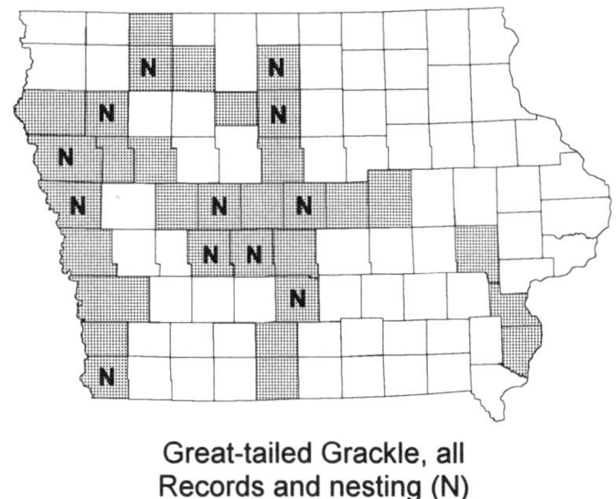

Great-tailed Grackle, all Records and nesting (N)

Common Grackle (*Quiscalus quiscula*)

Status: Regular; nests

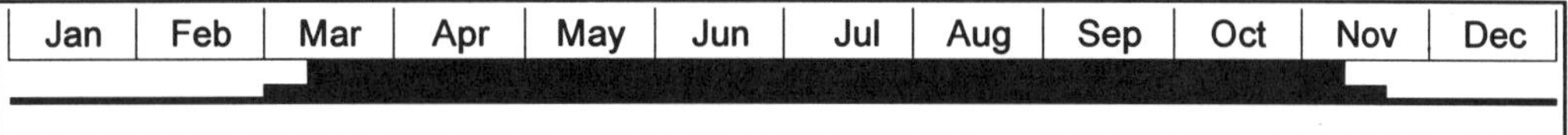

Occurrence: This abundant summer resident is even more conspicuous in migration, and variable numbers remain into early winter and over-winter. It nests throughout Iowa in conifers, hedgerows, and other dense cover, often in loose colonies. Based on Breeding Bird Surveys, numbers are highest in north-central and lowest in eastern Iowa.

Common Grackles are found on about two-thirds of Christmas Bird Counts, with the greatest numbers in southern Iowa. Over-wintering birds may be found in any part of the state, but are most common in southern Iowa. Grackles were found at 4 and 13 percent of feeders in mid-winter in 1984 and 1985, the most of any icterid (Hollis 1986).

Comment: The winter range is in the eastern United States west to western Kansas and north to southern Minnesota. The breeding range includes the winter range and extends west to the Rocky Mountains and north to southern Mackenzie.

Brown-headed Cowbird (*Molothrus ater*)

Status: Regular; nests

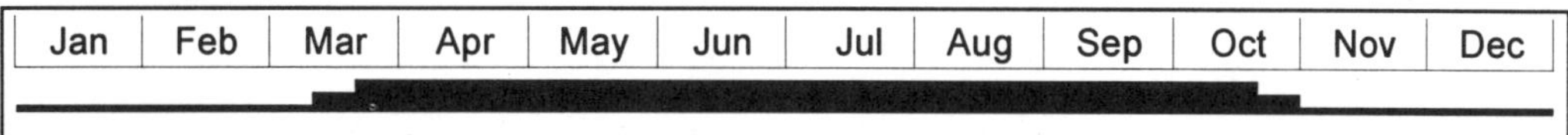

Occurrence: This common summer resident and rare winter resident occurs in all areas of the state. On Breeding Bird Surveys, numbers are evenly distributed and have steadily increased from 18 to 36 per survey route from 1970 to 1992. In a survey of breeding birds at Coralville Reservoir, cowbirds were more common in lowland open areas than on wooded bluffs (Kent et al. 1994).

Cowbirds are dependent on other species to incubate their eggs and raise their young. Of 64 host species recorded in Iowa, Red-winged Blackbird, Northern Cardinal, and Indigo Bunting are most frequently parasitized (Lowther 1985, 1991).

On Christmas Bird Counts, cowbirds are found on one-third of counts with highest numbers in the south. They were found at 3.6 percent of feeders in mid-winter in 1984 and 1985 (Hollis 1986). Over-wintering birds are more common in the south, but may be found anywhere in the state, often in feedlots or with flocks of starlings.

Comment: The winter range extends from the Maritime Provinces, the southern Great Lakes, Iowa, southern Arizona, and California south to southern Mexico. The breeding range extends across North America from northern Mexico to southern Mackenzie, excluding southern Florida.

References:

Lowther, P. E. 1985. Catalog of Brown-headed Cowbird hosts from Iowa. *Proc. Iowa Acad. Sci.* 92:95-99.

Lowther, P. E. 1991. Catalog of Brown-headed Cowbird hosts from Iowa—an update. *Iowa Bird Life* 61:33-38.

Orchard Oriole (*Icterus spurius*)

Status: Regular; nests

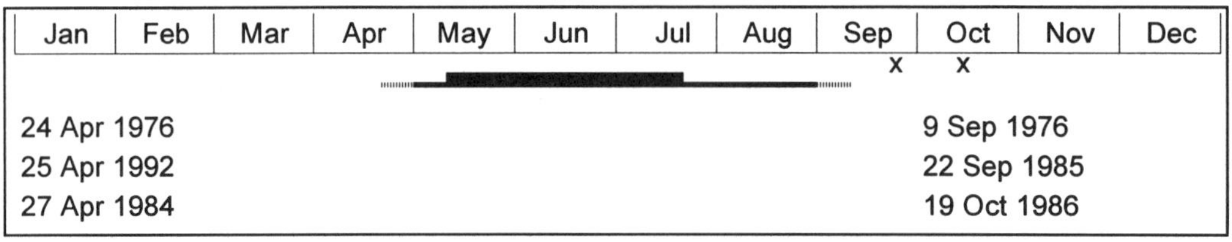

Jan	Feb	Mar	Apr	May	Jun	Jul	Aug	Sep	Oct	Nov	Dec
								x	x		

24 Apr 1976	9 Sep 1976
25 Apr 1992	22 Sep 1985
27 Apr 1984	19 Oct 1986

Occurrence: This summer resident may be considered common in western Iowa, especially along the Missouri River, and rare and widely scattered elsewhere in the state. On Breeding Bird Surveys, it is found on about 20 percent of surveys in central and southern Iowa, but on less than 10 percent in northern Iowa. There are summer records for most of the counties in the state (Jackson et al. 1996). Orchard Orioles occupy edge habitat and are easy to overlook. They leave early, with only a few records beyond August.

Comment: The winter range is from central Mexico to northwestern South America. Overwintering birds are not found in the Midwest, although Illinois has 2 December records (Bohlen 1989). The breeding range includes northern Mexico and most of the United States east of the Rocky Mountains.

Baltimore Oriole (*Icterus galbula*)

Status: Regular; nests

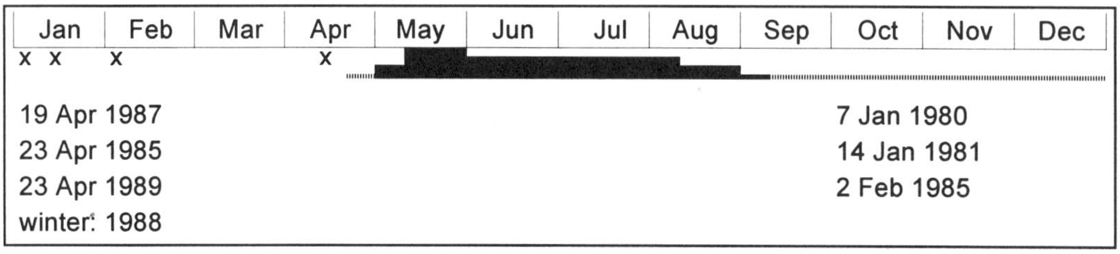

Jan	Feb	Mar	Apr	May	Jun	Jul	Aug	Sep	Oct	Nov	Dec
x x	x		x								

19 Apr 1987	7 Jan 1980
23 Apr 1985	14 Jan 1981
23 Apr 1989	2 Feb 1985
winter: 1988	

Occurrence: This common summer resident may be considered abundant during spring migration and early in the nesting season when males are singing loudly. Based on Breeding Bird Surveys, Baltimore Orioles are evenly distributed across the state. With such a conspicuous and unique nest, it is not surprising that nesting has been verified in almost every county (Jackson et al. 1996).

Most Baltimore Orioles arrive in early May and are gone by early September, but a few linger into winter, mostly at feeders where suet and fruit are available. There are 9 winter records from 1960 to 1995, all initially found in December except for 1 at Fairport in Muscatine County on 14 January 1981 (*IBL* 51:33). One was at a feeder in Atlantic in Cass County from 26 November 1984 to 2 February 1985 (*IBL* 55:30). Another was said to overwinter at Iowa City in Johnson County 1988 (*IBL* 58:58).

Comment: The winter range is from the West Indies and central Mexico south to northern South America, and casually farther north in the United States. The pattern of winter birds at feeders with few surviving into January is found in Minnesota, Wisconsin, Illinois, and Missouri and bears a remarkable resemblance to the pattern in Iowa. The breeding range is the eastern United States (excluding the extreme southeast) and southern Canada west to the western edge of the Great Plains.

Bullock's Oriole (*Icterus bullockii*)

Status: Accidental

12 May 1993, Clemens, Marshall Co., male (*IBL* 63:80)
3 Sep 1995, Red Rock Res., Marion Co., male (*IBL* 66:25)

Occurrence: There are 2 Accepted records of this recently split species, both males.

Baltimore and Bullock's orioles were lumped into Northern Oriole by the American Ornithologists' Union in 1973 and split in 1995. There are no historic records for this species in Iowa (Anderson 1907, DuMont 1933, Brown 1971). Identification of females is difficult and will be a topic of further discussion as more Bullock's Orioles are reported in Iowa. There are 2 reports of females that are Not Accepted, but may be worthy of further consideration: 20 December 1981 at Cedar Falls in Black Hawk County (P-0038, *IBL* 52:28) and 21 November 1987 at Maysville in Scott County (*IBL* 58:23).

Comment: The winter range is from central Mexico to northern Central America and, in smaller numbers, in coastal California and along the Gulf Coast. The breeding range is in northern Mexico, the western United States, and southern Canada west of the central Great Plains.

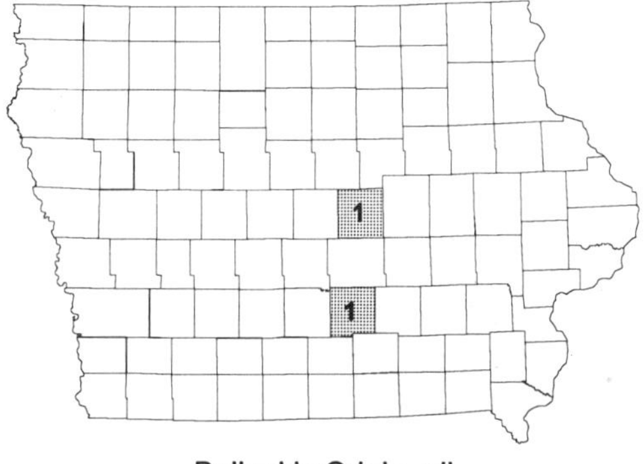

Bullock's Oriole, all

Fringilline and Cardueline Finches and Allies
(Family Fringillidae)

Fringilline and cardueline finches and allies comprise 133 species, with 23 from North America and 11 from Iowa. Of the Iowa species, 8 are Regular, 1 Casual, and 2 Accidental. In addition to the New and Old World finches, which have short, conical, seed-eating bills, this family also includes the Hawaiian honeycreepers, which have a variety of bill shapes.

Two species are resident in Iowa (House Finch, American Goldfinch); the others visit Iowa in the winter or during migration. Most of the winter finches are cyclical, with invasion years separated by years with few or no records (see chart on next page). Winter incursions of several of the finches sometimes coincide, such as in 1969 and 1975, while in other years they may be confined to 1 or 2 species.

Finches

Purple Finch

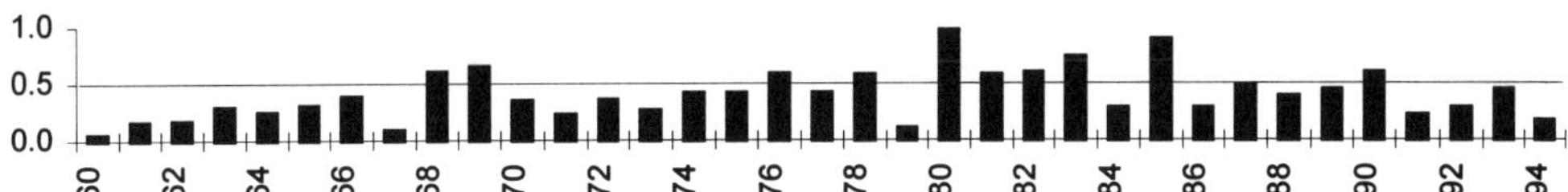

Red Crossbill

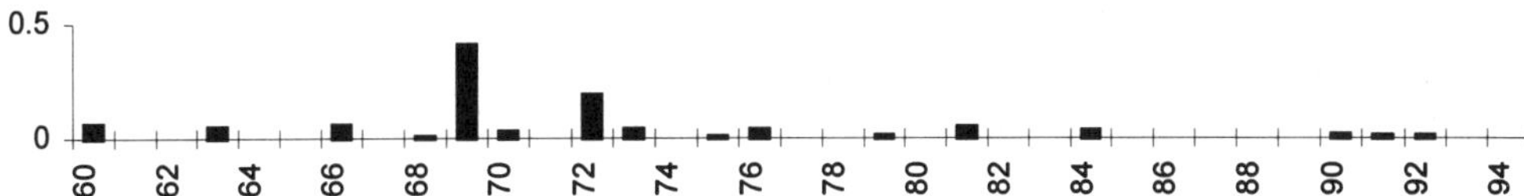

White-winged Crossbill

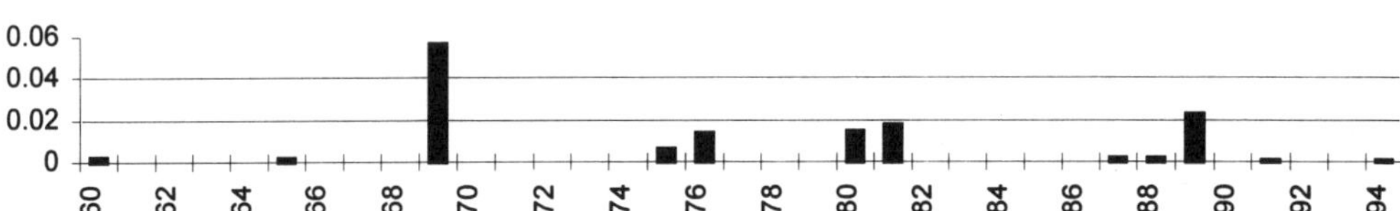

Common Redpoll

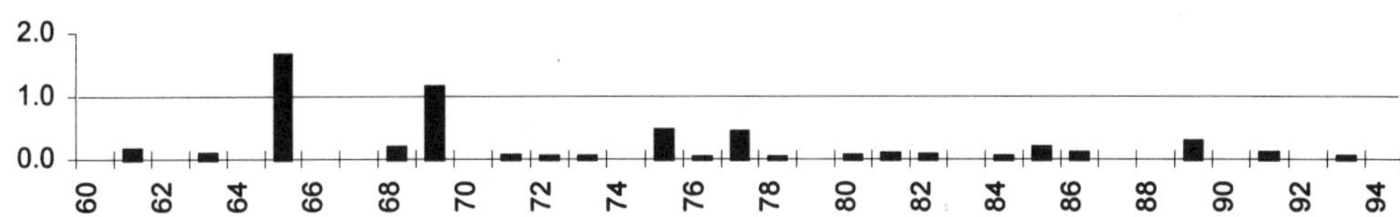

Pine Siskin

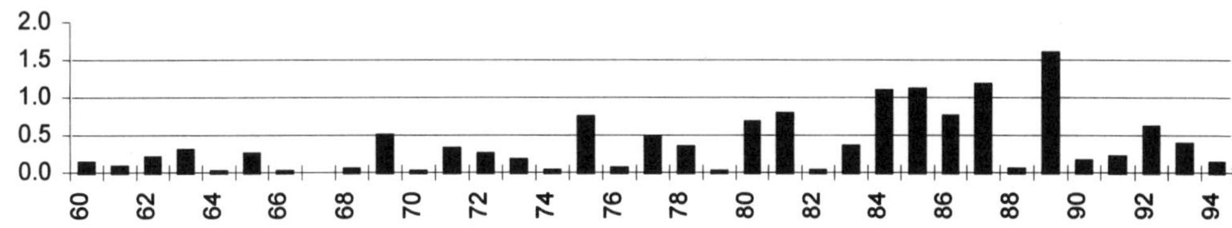

Evening Grosbeak

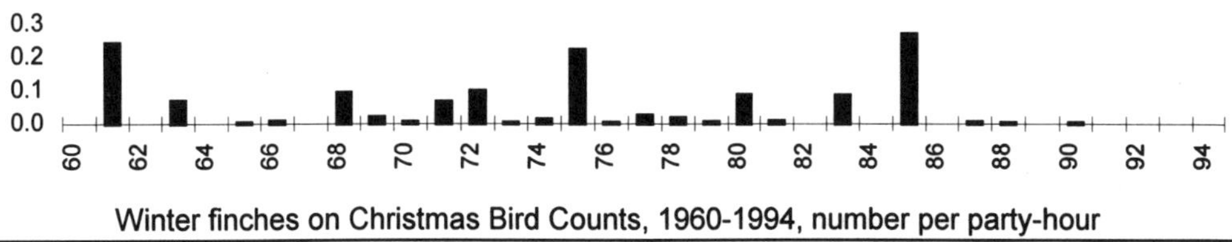

Winter finches on Christmas Bird Counts, 1960-1994, number per party-hour

Gray-crowned Rosy-Finch (*Leucosticte tephrocotis*)

Status: Accidental

Feb 1883, Sioux City, Woodbury Co. (Talbot 1883)
Jan to 19 Mar 1978, Oelwein, Fayette Co. (P-0017, Wilkinson 1978)

Occurrence: The 2 winter records of Gray-crowned Rosy-Finch include 1 that was captured and described in detail as it molted and 1 that was photographed at a feeder. Talbot kept the Sioux City bird until at least August 1883.

Comment: Gray-crowned Rosy-Finches breed in the western mountains and Low Arctic from northern New Mexico and central California north to the Yukon and all except extreme northern Alaska and to Kamchatka and central Siberia. In winter, birds move to lower elevations and, in Asia, south to Korea and Japan. Vagrants have been found in the northern Great Plains and the northern Midwest including Minnesota, Iowa, Wisconsin, Ontario, Michigan, and Ohio. There are outlying records from Maine and Oklahoma. Records are scattered from late October to early April.

In 1982, Gray-crowned, Brown-capped, and Black rosy-finches were lumped into one species, Rosy Finch, but in 1993 they were split again. Most of the eastern vagrants are Gray-crowned, but 1 of 2 Ohio records is of Black Rosy-Finch.

References:

Talbot, D. H. 1883. The Gray-crowned Finch in confinement. *Bull. Nuttall Ornithological Club* 8:240-242.

Wilkinson, R. 1978. 'Rosy the Finch' creates stir in birdwatching. *Iowa Bird Life* 48:79-80.

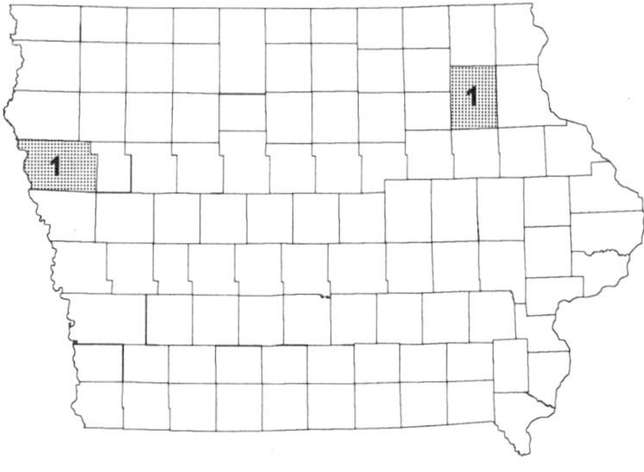

Gray-crowned Rosy-Finch, all

Pine Grosbeak (*Pinicola enucleator*)

Status: Casual

By year since 1960 (also 18 records prior to 1960)

60 63 66 69 72 75 78 81 84 87 90 93

1 1 1 1 1 1 3 1 5 5 2 2 4 2 1 4 1 1 1

Jan	Feb	Mar	Apr	May	Jun	Jul	Aug	Sep	Oct	Nov	Dec

X XX X XX

8 Mar 1995 24 Oct 1922
8 Mar 1981 30 Oct 1938
28 Mar 1989 2 Nov 1924

Occurrence: This eruptive species from the north has occurred in 19 of 36 years from 1960 to 1995, with 1 to 6 records per year. There are 18 older records dating back to 1878. It tends to be found 2 to 4 years in a row and then be absent for 2 to 4 years. The period of winter residence is from late October to early March. Only 3 of 56 records are from the southern third of Iowa, and there are more from eastern (25) and central (20) than from western (11) Iowa.

Pine Grosbeaks may be found in conifers, feeding on ash trees, or at feeders. A specimen at the State Historical Museum in Des Moines is dated 31 January 1973.

Comment: The breeding range includes the boreal forest of Canada and the western United States, with movement southward from the northern parts of the range in winter. This species is regular in winter in northeastern Minnesota and northern Wisconsin and irregular as far south as northern Texas. Only 11 records are listed for Missouri (Robbins and Easterla 1992) and only 2 for southern Illinois (Bohlen 1989). There are 2 August records from northern Minnesota and 1 September record from southern Minnesota (Janssen 1987). The range also extends across the Palearctic.

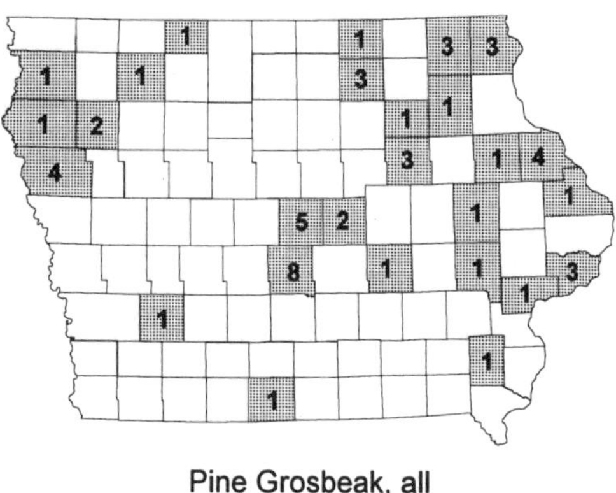

Pine Grosbeak, all

Purple Finch (*Carpodacus purpureus*)

Status: Regular

Jan	Feb	Mar	Apr	May	Jun	Jul	Aug	Sep	Oct	Nov	Dec
			15 May 1966 15 May 1978 17 May 1966			26 Aug 1986 28 Aug 1985 29 Aug 1976					

Occurrence: This common migrant and uncommon winter resident is most common in October and from late April to early May. On Christmas Bird Counts, numbers vary considerably from year to year, with slightly higher than average counts in southern Iowa and lowest counts in western Iowa. In 1984 and 1985, Purple Finches were found at 35 and 19 percent of feeders in mid-winter (Hollis 1986).

Historically, a nest was said to have been found in Henry County, which is in southeastern Iowa, on 2 June 1892 (Anderson 1907). Although such a record seems unlikely based on current distribution, Illinois has 3 reports of nesting from the 1800s (Bohlen 1989).

Comment: The winter range is in the far west from southern British Columbia to Baja California and from the Great Plains east in the United States and southern Canada. The breeding range is from California to the Yukon and across the Canadian provinces and the northern part of the eastern United States, south to central Minnesota and central Wisconsin.

House Finch (*Carpodacus mexicanus*)

Status: Regular; nests

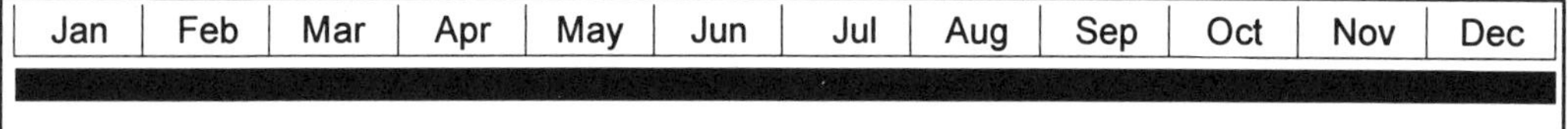

Occurrence: The first House Finch in Iowa, a male, was found in Pocahontas County on 3 June 1982, and it was followed by males at Ottumwa in Wapello County on 26 June 1982 and at Perry in Dallas County on 27 July 1982 (*IBL* 52:94). A female appeared in Mason City in Cerro Gordo County in September 1982 (*IBL* 52:125). In 1986, the first nests were found in Wayne and Scott counties (Dinsmore and Petersen 1986). After that, House Finches rapidly occupied most of Iowa (Cecil and Dinsmore 1995).

House Finches now are resident in most towns in Iowa and are spreading to rural areas. They are found on most Christmas Bird Counts, with numbers up to 10 times that of Purple Finch and 0.1 times that of House Sparrow (Cecil and Dinsmore 1995).

Comment: Once a resident of Mexico, the western United States, and southern British Columbia, this species now occupies all of the United States and southern Canada and the Hawaiian Islands. Most probably reached Iowa from the East, where introduced or escaped birds became established about 1940. A more gradual range expansion also occurred from the West.

References:

Cecil, B., and J. J. Dinsmore. 1995. Range expansion of the House Finch in Iowa. *Iowa Bird Life* 65:61-68.

Dinsmore, S. J., and P. C. Petersen, 1986. First House Finches nesting in Iowa. *Iowa Bird Life* 56:122.

Red Crossbill (*Loxia curvirostra*)

Status: Regular; occasionally nests

Jan	Feb	Mar	Apr	May	Jun	Jul	Aug	Sep	Oct	Nov	Dec

XX X X X X X X

Nesting records:

22 to 25 Apr 1982, Des Moines, Polk Co., nest building (*IBL* 52:62)

9, 10 Jul 1986, Des Moines, Polk Co., pair feeding 4 yg. (*IBL* 56:119)

Occurrence: This rare and erratic winter visitant may arrive as early as August, and some have lingered late into spring and summer. Nest building was observed in Des Moines in Polk County from 22 to 25 April 1982, but the nest was destroyed (*IBL* 52:62). A pair were feeding 4 young in Des Moines in Polk County on 9, 10 July 1986 (*IBL* 56:119).

Other summer reports include birds at Ames in Story County on 7 June 1970 (*IBL* 40:74), a bird found dead near Newton in Jasper County in late June or early July 1986 (*IBL* 56:119, Iowa State University specimen), 3 at Algona in Kossuth County from 7 to 9 July 1990 (*IBL* 60:106), 1 at Rippey in Greene County on 16 July 1990 (*IBL* 60:106), 1 from 29 to 31 July 1990 at Carroll in Carroll County (*IBL* 60:106), 2 at Boone in Boone County on 5 June 1992 (*IBL* 61:118), and a female near Luther in Boone County on 22 June 1992 (*IBL* 61:118). In late July and early August 1996, Red Crossbills were reported from numerous counties throughout Iowa (in press).

Red Crossbills may be found anywhere in the state, but most records have been from metropolitan areas where there are the most conifers, feeders, and observers. On Christmas Bird Counts, they were found in 20 of 36 years from 1960 to 1995. Most of the records are from mid-October through March, but there are scattered early records beginning in August and more in May, especially in invasion years. Red Crossbills tend to be found for 2 to 5 years in a row followed by 1 or 2 years with few or no reports. The maximum number of reports was 20 in 1984.

Comment: This resident of Palearctic and Nearctic coniferous forests is erratic in its movements and may nest at any time of year. It is a rare summer resident in northern Minnesota and northern Wisconsin. In winter it has been found as far south as Florida.

There are at least 8 Nearctic and 3 Palearctic types of Red Crossbill based on song, bill type, body size, and type of cones eaten, and these types are potentially separate species (DeBenedictis 1995).

Reference:

DeBenedictis, P. A. 1995. Red Crossbills, one through eight. *Birding* 27:494-501.

White-winged Crossbill (*Loxia leucoptera*)

Status: Regular

Jan	Feb	Mar	Apr	May	Jun	Jul	Aug	Sep	Oct	Nov	Dec
				X		X	X		XX		

27 Apr 1994	late Aug 1969
28 Apr 1981	26 Oct 1965
4 May 1974	28 Oct 1980

summer: 24 Jul 1979

Occurrence: This rare winter resident is slightly less common and more confined to winter than Red Crossbill. Almost all records fall in the period from late October to late April. White-winged Crossbills were found on Christmas Bird Counts in 12 of 36 years from 1960 to 1995. They tend to be found for 2 or 3 years in a row followed by 1 to 3 years with few or no reports. The only summer record involved a bird found dead near Anita in Cass County on 24 July 1979 (*IBL* 49:85).

White-winged Crossbills may be found anywhere in the state, but most records have been from metropolitan areas where there are the most conifers, feeders, and observers. This species shows a definite preference for hemlocks, which have small cones.

Comment: This species occurs in coniferous forests across Canada and patchy areas of the northern United States. The range extends farther north than that of Red Crossbill and does not extend as far south into the mountains of the western United States. In winter, this species moves erratically as far south as Missouri and northern Texas.

Common Redpoll (*Carduelis flammea*)

Status: Regular

Jan	Feb	Mar	Apr	May	Jun	Jul	Aug	Sep	Oct	Nov	Dec
			X	XX					XX X		

8 Apr 1982	15 Oct 1981
1 May 1978	18 Oct 1989
2 May 1988	23 Oct 1965

Occurrence: This rare winter resident has major eruptions about every 10 years, with minor eruptions in intervening years. Birds first arrive in late October, and the last leave in early April, although most are found in midwinter.

On Christmas Bird Counts, Common Redpolls have been found in 31 of 36 years from 1960 to 1995, on 0 to 16 counts per year. They are reported least frequently from southern Iowa. The highest average counts are from northern Iowa, but these high counts are greatly influenced by large flocks in invasion years.

Comment: The main winter range extends from southern Greenland across the northern edge of the Canadian provinces to southern Alaska. A few, and periodically large numbers, winter south as far as Missouri. The breeding range is from the northern parts of the Canadian provinces to the Arctic Ocean. This species also occupies the northern Palearctic.

Hoary Redpoll (*Carduelis hornemanni*)

Status: Accidental

By year since 1960 (also 3 in 1996)

60	63	66	69	72	75	78	81	84	87	90	93
						3	1 + 1				1

By month -- all records

Jan	Feb	Mar	Apr	May	Jun	Jul	Aug	Sep	Oct	Nov	Dec
+ 2	2 1 1	1									2

22 Jan to 5 Feb 1978, Marion, Linn Co. (P-0016, Halmi 1978, Anon. 1978)
12 Feb 1978, Davenport, Scott Co. (Anon. 1978)
10 Mar 1978, Coralville Res., Johnson Co. (*IBL* 48:76)
27 Dec 1980-3 Jan 1981, Waterloo, Black Hawk Co. (*IBL* 51:3-4, 19, 33; 52:41)
23 to 30 Jan 1982, Pine L., Hardin Co. (P-0036, *IBL* 52:28)
23 Dec 1995, Spirit L., Dickinson Co. (*IBL* 66:60)
3 to 12 Feb 1996, near Norwalk, Warren Co. (P-0496, *IBL* 66:60)
4 Feb 1996, near Iowa City, Johnson Co. (*IBL* 66:60)
28 Feb 1996, Ames, Story Co. (*IBL* 66:60)

Occurrence: Of the 9 Accepted records, 5 occurred in the winters from 1978 to 1982. The first and last years of this period were massive invasion years for Common Redpoll. There are other reports from these years that may have been correct. The other 4 records occurred in the winter of 1995-1996. Three old specimens were determined to be Common Redpolls (Dinsmore et al. 1984).

Comment: This Holarctic species lives in the Arctic tundra, with some birds moving south sporadically in winter. The southern extent of records includes Washington, Nevada, Wyoming, Nebraska, Iowa, Illinois, Indiana, Ohio, Pennsylvania, Maryland, and New Jersey. Records span the period from late October to early April.

The differences between Hoary and Common redpolls are subtle. It is difficult to substantiate that they are different species. At least 3 of the Iowa records are substantiated by photographs, 1 after being mist netted. Only the most obvious examples of Hoary Redpoll will be identifiable, and then only with good views or photographs. The most reliable field mark is said to be the lack of bold streaks on the undertail coverts (Czaplak 1995). This species is most likely during Common Redpoll invasion years.

References:

Anon. 1978. Editor's note. *Iowa Bird Life* 48:54.

Czaplak, D. 1995. Indentifying Common and Hoary redpolls in winter. *Birding* 27:447-457.

Halmi, N. S. 1978. Hoary Redpoll (*Carduelis hornemanni*) in Iowa. *Iowa Bird Life* 48:53-54.

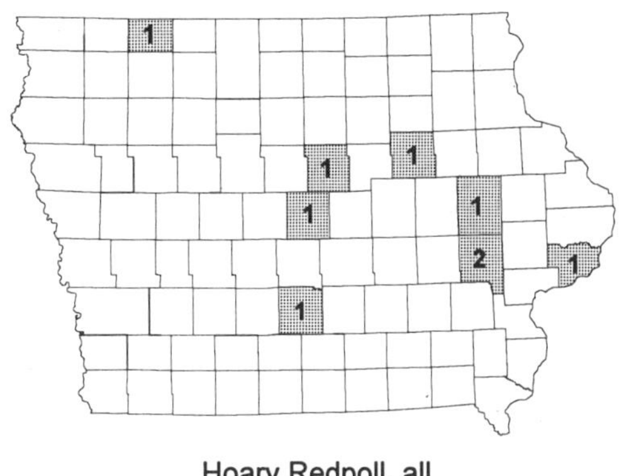

Hoary Redpoll, all

Pine Siskin (*Carduelis pinus*)

Status: Regular; occasionally nests

Jan	Feb	Mar	Apr	May	Jun	Jul	Aug	Sep	Oct	Nov	Dec
							X X	XX			

Occurrence: This uncommon to common winter resident and irregular nesting species varies in numbers from year to year. First arrivals vary from late September to mid-October. On Christmas Bird Counts, siskins are found every year. The percentage of counts with siskins and the number per party-hour have increased about three-fold from the 1960s to the 1990s. Siskins were found at 15 and 20 percent of feeders in mid-winter in 1984 and 1985 (Hollis 1986). They are found in conifers and at feeders. A few linger into summer, most often in peak invasion years.

The first evidence of nesting was from 13 April to 5 May 1914 with 1 young fledged at Sioux City (Hayward and Stephens 1914). From 1973 to 1982, there were 12 more reports of nesting (Dinsmore et al. 1984), and from 1983 to 1995 there were 9 more reports. The earliest date is 8 April 1978 at Des Moines with an adult incubating (Brooke 1978), and the latest date for fledging is 23 June 1982 at Davenport (*IBL* 52:94). Most of the nesting records are from the central part of the state, including 6 from Story County. There are 2 records each from Scott, Polk, and Woodbury counties. Most of the nesting birds disappear in summer, with only a few records from July and only 2 from August. The earliest fall records are 16 September 1990 in Fremont County (*IBL* 61:25) and 19 September 1992 in Pottawattamie County (*IBL* 63:22).

Comment: The winter range is from southeastern Alaska and southern Canada south throughout the United States to northern Mexico. The breeding range extends throughout the mountainous west from Mexico to the Yukon and in the east across the southern parts of the Canadian provinces and the northern parts of the United States. Breeding occurs regularly in the northern parts of Minnesota and Wisconsin and irregularly farther south.

References:

Brooke, M. 1978. Pine Siskin nest in Des Moines. *Iowa Bird Life* 48:102.

Hayward, W. J., and T. C. Stephens. 1914. The Pine Siskin breeding in Iowa. *Wilson Bull.* 26:140-146.

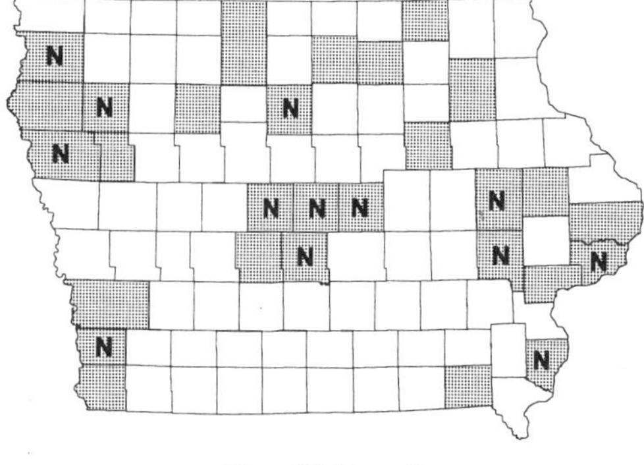

Pine Siskin, all
June-August and Nesting (N)

American Goldfinch (*Carduelis tristis*)

Status: Regular; nests

Jan	Feb	Mar	Apr	May	Jun	Jul	Aug	Sep	Oct	Nov	Dec

Occurrence: This common permanent resident is the state bird of Iowa (Zaletel 1992). It is found throughout the state and is fairly evenly distributed on Breeding Bird Surveys and Christmas Bird Counts. It was found at 73 and 72 percent of feeders in mid-winter in 1984 and 1985 (Hollis 1986). The late nesting season, from early July to late September, corresponds with the occurrence of thistle blossoms, which are used for nest lining and food (Lynch 1970).

Comment: The winter range includes patchy locations in southern Canada, the United States, and northern Mexico. In Minnesota and Wisconsin, migration is noted—most leave the northern parts of these states in winter. During summer, this species leaves Mexico and the southern row of states, and the range extends north to the central parts of the Canadian provinces. Little is known on the movements of goldfinches in Iowa.

References:

Lynch, C. B. 1970. The reproductive strategy of the American Goldfinch, *Spinus tristis tristis*, in Iowa. *Proc. Iowa Acad. Sci.* 77:164-168.

Zaletel, H. 1992. How the goldfinch became Iowa's state bird. *Iowa Bird Life* 62:68-69.

Evening Grosbeak (*Coccothraustes vespertinus*)

Status: Regular

Jan	Feb	Mar	Apr	May	Jun	Jul	Aug	Sep	Oct	Nov	Dec
							x	x x			
				12 May 1984		25 Aug 1947					
				14 May 1976		8 Sep 1961					
				14 May 1976		18 Sep 1972					

Occurrence: This rare and eruptive winter visitant has been seen every year from 1961 to 1995 except for 1991. Birds may arrive as early as mid-September and remain until mid-May. Most are found at feeders. Records are quite evenly distributed across the state. Evening Grosbeaks were found on Christmas Bird Counts in 25 of 36 years from 1960 to 1995 and were reported on 0 to 27 counts per year.

Comment: The breeding range is across southern Canada and the extreme northern United States and in the Rocky Mountains to northwestern Mexico. The winter range includes the breeding range and extends south in the eastern United States except for the southern edge.

Old World Sparrows (Family Passeridae)

Old World Sparrows comprise 2 species, both of which were introduced into North America and spread to Iowa.

House Sparrow (*Passer domesticus*)

Status: Regular; nests

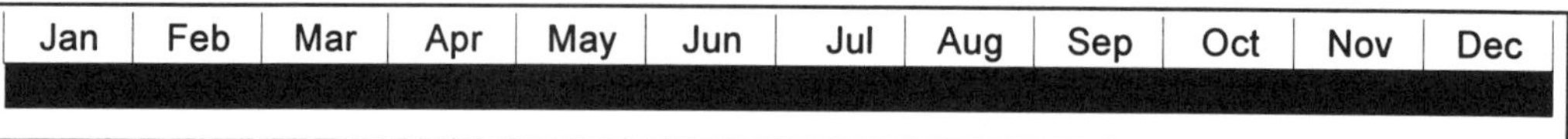

Occurrence: This abundant permanent resident has an affinity for towns and farmsteads, but also is found in other areas, especially where there are dead trees to provide nest sites. Based on Christmas Bird Counts, it is evenly distributed across the state, but on Breeding Bird Surveys, numbers are somewhat higher in the east.

Historically, House Sparrows were introduced in Brooklyn, New York, in 1851 and 1852 and reached Iowa by 1869 (Barrows 1889). They were also introduced at Davenport in 1870, Cedar Rapids in 1874, Dubuque in 1876, and Iowa City in 1881, and by 1907 they were said to be the most abundant bird in Iowa (Anderson 1907).

Comment: This resident species is found throughout northern and southern hemispheres, except in the coldest portions, and on many islands such as the Hawaiian Islands.

Reference:

Barrows, W. B. 1889. The Engish Sparrow (*Passer domesticus*) in North America. *U.S. Department of Agriculture Division of Economic Ornithology and Mammalogy Bull.* No. 1.

Eurasian Tree Sparrow (*Passer montanus*)

Status: Regular; nests

Jan	Feb	Mar	Apr	May	Jun	Jul	Aug	Sep	Oct	Nov	Dec

Occurrence: The first Iowa record was of 2 birds at West Branch in Cedar County from 14 March to early April 1987 (Veal 1987). On 16 December 1989, 10 to 15 were reported north of Burlington in Des Moines County (*IBL* 60:46, 54), and many have been found regularly at that location ever since. The first confirmed evidence of nesting was on 17 June 1993 (*IBL* 63:99).

Records from other counties include northern Lee County in the winter of 1993-1994 (*IBL* 64:52), western Johnson County from late December 1993 to 15 May 1994 (*IBL* 64:52, 80), southeastern Louisa County on 13 May 1995 (*IBL* 65:78), and Muscatine County on 16 January 1966 (*IBL* 66:60). Christmas Bird Count records were across the river from Iowa in Illinois opposite Scott County on 21 December 1980, opposite Lee County on 28 December 1985 and 3 January 1987, and in Missouri opposite Lee County 23 December 1990. More recent Christmas Bird Count reports from Keokuk, Muscatine, and Oakville have not indicated the state in which the birds were seen.

Comment: This species is widespread across Europe and Asia and also occurs in Australia. It was introduced at St. Louis in 1870 in an area where there were not yet any House Sparrows (Lang 1992). The range gradually spread to include the St. Louis area and west-central Illinois as far north as Lee County in Iowa. Since 1970, spread has been noted along the Mississippi River to Iowa and along the Illinois River in Illinois, with extralimital records in Kentucky, Wisconsin, Minnesota, and Manitoba (Lang 1992).

This species appears to be well-established in Des Moines County and probably at other locations along the Mississippi River. If the trend continues, more will be found in southeastern Iowa and occasionally at other locations.

References:

Lang, A. 1992. The Eurasian Tree Sparrow population in North America: Evolving and expanding. *Birders Journal* 1:298-307.

Veal, S. 1987. Eurasian Tree Sparrow at West Branch. *Iowa Bird Life* 57:95.

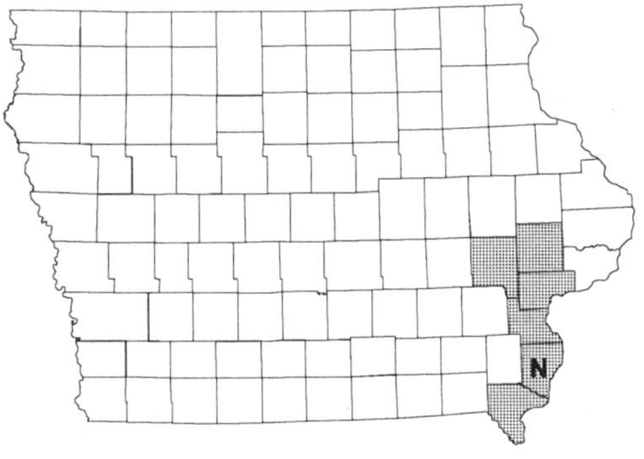

Eurasian Tree Sparrow, all Locations and nesting (N)

Appendix A. SELECTED OTHER SPECIES REPORTED IN IOWA

Included in this appendix are selected species for which there are no Accepted records, but for which there are probable records or for which significant literature exists. The purpose of this appendix is to provide the interested reader access to information on reports of birds that have not been judged by the Records Committee to be Accepted. Also included are several species for which the origin of birds is uncertain and several that have been introduced but not established.

In addition to the species discussed below, the following species are mentioned by Dinsmore et al. (1984) with little or no evidence for their occurrence in Iowa: Emperor Goose, Masked Duck, Gray Hawk, Scaled Quail, Gull-billed Tern, Greater Roadrunner, Boreal Owl, Common Poorwill, Brown-headed Nuthatch, Western Bluebird, Kirtland's Warbler, Swainson's Warbler, Bachman's Sparrow, and Baird's Sparrow.

The Records Committee has reviewed and not accepted reports of 12 other species that are not on the Iowa list, only two of which have significant literature citations: A possible Red-naped Sapsucker at Sioux City in Woodbury County on 14 April 1966 (Youngworth 1966) and 2 Lesser Goldfinches at Sioux City in Woodbury County on 16 January 1964 (Hanna and Hanna. 1964).

References:

Hanna, D. H., and Mrs. D. H. Hanna. 1964. Lesser Goldfinch at Sioux City, Iowa. *South Dakota Bird Notes* 16:102-103

Youngworth, W. 1966. The Red-naped Sapsucker ? at Sioux City. *Iowa Bird Life* 36:52

Fulvous Whistling-Duck (*Dendrocygna bicolor*)

Occurrence: A bird at Goose Lake in Clinton County from 17 July to 8 September 1994 was accepted in the category "Accepted—Origin Uncertain" (P-0420, *IBL* 64:107, 65:11, 81). A report from Dewey's Pasture in Palo Alto County on 11 June 1963 (Horak and Kaufmann 1965) lacks descriptive details but is likely correct. There is an incomplete, second-hand description of a bird shot in the Estherville–Spirit Lake area in Emmet or Dickinson county in the fall of 1931 (Roberts 1932).

Comment: This species is found in tropical and warm temperate areas of Asia, Africa, South America, Middle America, and the southern United States. There are a few Fulvous Whistling-Duck reports from most northern states and Canadian provinces that are scattered throughout all months of the year. This species is commonly held by waterfowl breeders and collectors and some may escape captivity.

References:

Horak, G. J., and G. W. Kaufmann. 1965. Fulvous Tree Duck in Iowa. *Iowa Bird Life* 35:29.

Roberts, F. L. R. 1932. Two Iowa duck records. *Wilson Bull.* 44:180.

Harris's Hawk (*Parabuteo unicinctus*)

Occurrence: An adult was south of Blairstown in Benton County from 10 to 14 September 1989 (P-0292, *IBL* 60:13, 61:85). The identification was Accepted but the origin was considered uncertain. A painting was made of a bird caught in a trap in Van Buren County about 1895 (Anderson 1907), but the painting is now lost, and there is no way to verify the record.

Comment: The permanent range is from central Texas, southern New Mexico, and southern Arizona to southern South America. There are a few records from Oklahoma, Kansas, and Nebraska. The few reports from other locations are difficult to evaluate because this relatively tame hawk is easy to maintain and is often kept by falconers (Palmer 1988).

Chukar (*Alectoris chukar*)

Occurrence: This introduced game bird was noted in Marion County from 1966 to 1968, in Plymouth County in 1967, and in Scott County from 1974 to 1981 (Dinsmore et al. 1984). Birds have been reported periodically from Scott County to 1995, where 100 were released in 1970, 1 was photographed on a nest on 14 June 1974 (P-0010), and another photographed in January 1995 (P-0441). A manager of a game farm in Clinton County imports birds for fall hunting. He indicated that birds not killed by hunters sometimes nest, but the young do not survive (personal communication with T. H. Kent).

Comment: Introductions of this Eurasian species have not produced sustained and expanding populations except in arid areas of the West. It is not known whether the recent Scott County birds are offspring from the 100 released in 1970 or whether new birds have been added.

Mountain Plover (*Charadrius montanus*)

Occurrence: Two records were Accepted and later retracted. The description of a bird at Credit Island in Scott County on 25-26 March 1964 (Petersen 1964, *IBL* 59:76) did not exclude the much more likely American Golden-Plover. A plover in basic plumage on 9 to 10 July 1987 was seen by many and thought to be a Mountain Plover, but reconsideration and help from an outside reviewer made it clear that this bird was an American Golden-Plover at an odd time in an odd plumage (*IBL* 56:115, 57:77, 59:76, Zaletel 1987)

Comment: The winter range is from southern Texas across northern Mexico, and north in central California. The breeding range is in the western Great Plains from northern Texas and New Mexico to northern Montana. This species does not show an eastward vagrancy pattern, except for a few records along the Gulf Coast to Florida.

References:

Petersen, P. 1964. Mountain Plover at Davenport. *Iowa Bird Life* 34:49.

Zaletel, H. 1987. Mountain Plover in Story County. *Iowa Bird Life* 57:25.

Purple Sandpiper (*Calidris maritima*)

Occurrence: A partial description of a bird on a rocky waterfall at the mouth of the Upper Iowa River in Allamakee County on 12 May 1946 (Stewart 1946) could have been this species. Another report was considered doubtful by the Records Committee (Dinsmore et al. 1984).

Comment: The winter range is on the East Coast and in Europe. The breeding range is in the Arctic from eastern Siberia to northeastern Canada. Vagrants are expected on the Great Lakes and have occurred as far south as Texas. This species is not expected west of Iowa, but could occur here. Most vagrants occur in late fall and early winter (October to January), but there are mid- to late May records in Wisconsin (Robbins 1991) and June records in Illinois (Bohlen 1989).

Reference:

Stewart, C. A. 1946. A sight record of the Purple Sandpiper in Iowa. *Iowa Bird Life* 16:70

Band-tailed Pigeon (*Columba fasciata*)

Occurrence: A partial description of a bird on a farm with Rock Doves on 5 September 1970 in Webster County seen by a biologist familiar with this species was suggestive of this species. It was present from summer to late September (Crawford 1971).

Comment: The winter range is from Oregon and California to Central America. The breeding range includes the winter range and extends north to southern Alaska and in the eastern Rocky Mountains north to northern Colorado. Band-tailed Pigeons are also resident in South America. They are very rare vagrants to more than half of the states and provinces of eastern North America at any time of year, but with most records from September to December.

Reference:

Crawford, J. A. 1971. First Iowa Band-tailed Pigeon. *Iowa Bird Life* 41:30.

Ringed Turtle-Dove (*Streptopelia risoria*)

Occurrence: There are a number of records of this species (Dinsmore et al. 1984).

Comment: This human-associated species with no known natural occurrence was never considered established in Iowa and was removed from the American Birding Association's checklist in 1992 (DeBenedictus 1994).

Monk Parakeet (*Myiopsitta monachus*)

Occurrence: The only record is of a bird at Davenport in Scott County from 22 December 1973 to 15 January 1974 that was photographed (Petersen 1974).

Comment: This native species of South America was brought to North America beginning in the 1960s and was widely reported by the 1970s. It was added to the American Birding Association's checklist in 1992 based on established populations in Florida and Texas (DeBenedictus 1994). It is also found on the East Coast from New England south and in Chicago.

Reference:

Petersen, P. C. 1974. First Monk Parakeet record for Iowa. *Iowa Bird Life* 44:22-23.

Three-toed Woodpecker (*Picoides tridactylus*)

Occurrence: A weakened bird seen on 28, 29 May 1975 at Bettendorf in Scott County was taken into captivity and died 2 days later (Fredericksen 1976). The bird was kept in freezers for some time. It was later destroyed by a taxidermist after his freezer was disconnected. There is no description or photograph.

Comment: This northern resident species of coniferous forests occurs south into the mountains of the western United States but barely reaches the northern United States in the East. The nearest records to Iowa are from the Twin Cities in Minnesota and northwestern Nebraska. Immature Hairy Woodpeckers may exhibit a yellow crown and have been mistaken for Three-toed Woodpecker even on the Gulf Coast (Kaufman 1993). This rare winter visitor in northern Minnesota is found from October to mid-April.

References:

Fredericksen, M. 1976. Northern Three-toed Woodpecker in Iowa. *Iowa Bird Life* 46:27-28.

Kaufman, K. 1993. Identifying the Hairy Woodpecker. *Amer. Birds* 47:311-314.

Carolina Chickadee (*Parus carolinensis*)

Occurrence: There is a correctly identified specimen of this species at Coe College labeled "Keokuk, Ia. 1896 5/4/88" which was examined by H. C. Oberholser (P-0071, Anderson 1907, DuMont 1933). The specimen was contributed by George Berry. The origin of some of Berry's specimens has been questioned (Meyer 1959). There are 2 other unsubstantiated reports (Dinsmore et al. 1984).

Comment: This common resident species of the southeastern United States does not move north of the boundary zone with Black-capped Chickadee, which is in central Missouri and central Illinois. Although this species can be distinguished from the very similar Black-capped Chickadee, it is likely that a convincing record would require photographs, measurements, a tape recording, or a specimen.

American Dipper (*Cinclus mexicanus*)

Occurrence: An unlabeled specimen in a collection at Macedonia in Pottawattamie County was said to have been taken in Fremont County in the spring of 1885 or 1886 (Hendrickson 1957). The information on the origin of the specimen was secondhand.

Comment: This species of the western mountain streams occurs in the Black Hills of South Dakota, and there are 3 extralimital records from the north shore of Lake Superior in Minnesota.

Reference:

Hendrickson, G. O. 1957. A Dipper specimen at Macedonia, Iowa. *Iowa Bird Life* 27:72.

Sprague's Pipit (*Anthus spragueii*)

Occurrence: None of the 15 reports of this species, including 1 that was initially accepted by the Records Committee, is complete or without discrepancies (Dinsmore et al. 1984, *IBL* 64:70).

Comment: Sprague's Pipits winter in the south-central United States and breed in the northern Great Plains, and there are records from all states bordering Iowa and many other eastern states. It is likely that some of the Iowa reports of this species are correct, but the documentation is less than convincing.

Yellow Grosbeak (*Pheucticus chrysopeplus*)

Occurrence: An immature male visited a rural feeder near Elkhart in Polk County from 24 November 1990 to 7 January 1991 (P-0398, *IBL* 61:59, 62:22).
Comment: Three forms of Yellow Grosbeak are resident from northern Mexico through South America. There are about 15 summer records from Arizona and an unaccepted record from California in June. The Iowa bird is unprecedented for location and time of year. There is no way of determining how it got to Iowa.

Painted Bunting (*Passerina ciris*)

Occurrence: "An adult in all its glorious plumage" was seen as close as 6 feet in a yard at Fort Defiance State Park in Emmet County on 30 May 1956 by an experienced birder and bander and by 5 other people but eluded being photographed (Jones 1956). A male was present near a feeder for a few hours on 6 January 1987 at Bettendorf in Scott County and was photographed (P-0218, *IBL* 57:57).
Comment: The winter range is in Middle America and southern Florida. The breeding range is in the south-central United States and northern Mexico and in the southeastern United States. Over-migrants occur in the upper Midwest from late April to early June, but there are only a few fall records. Although now illegal, this species was frequently kept in captivity. The Iowa spring bird tested the limits of acceptance of sight records by the Records Committee. An expected vagrant at an expected time of year seen by an experienced observer at close range lacked description, and the report did not even indicate the sex of the bird. On 3 separate occasions the Records Committee failed to accept this record by 1 or 2 votes. The winter bird in an urban setting that stayed only briefly below a feeder is much more likely to be an escaped bird even though having such birds is illegal.
Reference:
Jones, M. L. 1956. Storm-driven birds at Fort Defiance State Park. *Iowa Bird Life* 26:69-70.

McCown's Longspur (*Calcarius mccownii*)

Occurrence: A flock of 20 were noted, but not described, at Grinnell in Poweshiek County from 3 to 8 March 1887 (Jones 1892). The only other reference is from I. S. Trostler who found this species to be a common migrant in Pottawattamie County and identified specimens that he shot (Anderson 1907).
Comment: This species winters from Oklahoma and southeastern Arizona south to northern Mexico and breeds in the high western plains from northern Colorado to southern Alberta and Saskatchewan. A few have been found in Missouri, Minnesota, and western Ontario, and there are exceptional records from Michigan and Massachusetts.

Appendix B.
SPECIES NOT REPRESENTED BY A SPECIMEN

Red-throated Loon (photograph)
Pacific Loon (photograph)
Clark's Grebe (photograph)
Brown Pelican (photograph)
Neotropic Cormorant (photograph)
Anhinga (documentation)
Magificent Frigatebird (photograph)
Little Blue Heron (photograph)
Tricolored Heron (documentation)
Reddish Egret (photograph)
White Ibis (photograph)
Glossy Ibis (photograph)
Roseate Spoonbill (photograph)
Wood Stork (documentation)
Mute Swan (photograph)
Bean Goose (photograph)
Garganey (documentation)
Cinnamon Teal (photograph)
Common Eider (photograph)
Barrow's Goldeneye (photograph)
Mississippi Kite (photograph)
Ferruginous Hawk (documentation)
Gyrfalcon (photograph)
Black Rail (documentation)
Snowy Plover (photograph)
Black-necked Stilt (photograph)
Whimbrel (photograph)
Sharp-tailed Sandpiper (documentation)
Curlew Sandpiper (photograph)
Red Phalarope (photograph)
Pomarine Jaeger (photograph)
Laughing Gull (photograph)
Little Gull (photograph)
Black-headed Gull (photograph)
Mew Gull (photograph)
California Gull (photograph)
Thayer's Gull (photograph)
Iceland Gull (photograph)
Lesser Black-backed Gull (photograph)
Slaty-backed Gull (photograph)
Glaucous Gull (photograph)
Great Black-backed Gull (photograph)
Black-legged Kittiwake (photograph)
Ross's Gull (photograph)
Ivory Gull (photograph)
Thick-billed Murre (documentation)
Marbled Murrelet (documentation)
Ancient Murrelet (documentation)
Common Ground-Dove (photograph)
Carolina Parakeet (documentation)
Groove-billed Ani (photograph)
Northern Hawk Owl (photograph)
Chuck-will's-widow (photograph)
Lewis's Woodpecker (photograph)
Black-backed Woodpecker (photograph)
Western Wood-Pewee (documentation)
Alder Flycatcher (recording)
Western Flycatcher species (photograph)
Say's Phoebe (photograph)
Vermilion Flycatcher (photograph)
Gray Jay (photograph)
Pinyon Jay (documentation)
Fish Crow (documentation)
Boreal Chickadee (photograph)
Pygmy Nuthatch (photograph)
Rock Wren (photograph)
Mountain Bluebird (photograph)
Townsend's Solitaire (photograph)
Varied Thrush (photograph)
Sage Thrasher (photograph)
Curve-billed Thrasher (photograph)
White-eyed Vireo (photograph)
Black-throated Gray Warbler (documentation)
Townsend's Warbler (documentation)
Yellow-throated Warbler (photograph)
Prairie Warbler (photograph)
Worm-eating Warbler (photograph)
MacGillivray's Warbler (documentation)
Western Tanager (photograph)
Black-headed Grosbeak (photograph)
Lazuli Bunting (photograph)
Green-tailed Towhee (photograph)
Spotted Towhee (photograph)
Black-throated Sparrow (photograph)
Lark Bunting (photograph)
Golden-crowned Sparrow (photograph)
Great-tailed Grackle (photograph)
Bullock's Oriole (documentation)
Gray-crowned Rosy-Finch (photograph)
Hoary Redpoll (photograph)
Eurasian Tree Sparrow (photograph)

Appendix C. **First Accepted Records By Year**

In this appendix, species are listed by the year of their first definite sighting in Iowa. Excluded are most of the common species based on the list of Keyes and Williams (1889). They listed a few species for which they did not have specimens. Of these, Western Bluebird and Bachman's Sparrow are not currently accepted, and Carolina Parakeet, Western Kingbird, and Rock Wren are accepted but not on the basis of the citations by Keyes and Williams. Species listed by Keyes and Williams that were regular then but not now are Swallow-tailed Kite, Greater Prairie-Chicken, Sharp-tailed Grouse, Whooping Crane, Long-billed Curlew, and Passenger Pigeon. All other species on the Keyes and Williams list are now regular except for Pine Grosbeak, which is Casual.

References are to an account of the first definite record. Citations preceded by an asterisk can be found in the Species Accounts in Chapter 4; the others are in Literature Cited. References to *IBL* are in the Field Reports of *Iowa Bird Life*.

1804 Least Tern (Moulton 1986)
1819-20 Long-billed Dowitcher (James 1823)
Black-billed Magpie (James 1823)
1843 Yellow-crowned Night-Heron (Audubon and Coues 1897)
Carolina Parakeet (Audubon and Coues 1897)
Lark Bunting (Audubon and Coues 1897)
1864 Brewer's Blackbird (DuMont 1933)
1866 Eskimo Curlew (*Hough 1901)
1867 Swallow-tailed Kite (Allen 1868)
1868 Peregrine Falcon (Anderson 1907)
1869 House Sparrow (*Barrows 1889)
1872 Smith's Longspur (*Trippe 1873)
1883 Sharp-tailed Grouse (Kent and Schrimper 1996)
Gray-crowned Rosy-Finch (*Talbot 1883)
1884 Mississippi Kite (DuMont 1933)
Hudsonian Godwit (Anderson 1907)
Buff-breasted Sandpiper (Anderson 1907)
Kentucky Warbler (Anderson 1907)
1886 Carolina Wren (DuMont 1933)
1888 Yellow-throated Warbler (Anderson 1907)
1889 Caspian Tern (Anderson 1907)
1890 White-winged Scoter (Nutting 1895)
Burrowing Owl (Anderson 1907)
1891 White-faced Ibis (Anderson 1907)
Baird's Sandpiper (Nutting 1893)
Sabine's Gull (*Bartsch 1899)
1892 Oldsquaw (Nutting 1895)
Prairie Falcon (Anderson 1907)
Ruddy Turnstone (*Bartsch 1898)
Bewick's Wren (Bartsch 1897)
Pine Warbler (Nutting 1893)
1893 Surf Scoter (Anderson 1907)
Semipalmated Plover (Anderson 1907)
Piping Plover (DuMont 1933)
Short-billed Dowitcher (DuMont 1933)
Common Tern (Nutting 1893)
1894 Cinnamon Teal (Anderson 1907)
Red-necked Phalarope (Anderson 1907)
Clark's Nutcracker (Nutting 1895)
Nelson's Sharp-tailed Sparrow (*Bartsch 1899)
1895 Pacific Loon (*Giddings 1896)
Whimbrel (Anderson 1907)
Western Sandpiper (Anderson 1907)
Western Kingbird (Anderson 1907)
1896 Parasitic Jaeger (Praeger 1925)
Thick-billed Murre (*Brown 1897)
1897 Connecticut Warbler (Anderson 1907)
1899 Black Rail (Anderson 1907)
1900 Brown Pelican (*Henning 1905)
Ring-necked Pheasant (Farris et al. 1977)
1901 Common Eider (*DuMont 1934)
1902 American Avocet (Anderson 1907)
Bonaparte's Gull (Anderson 1907)
1903 Magnificent Frigatebird (*Bartsch 1922, *Briggs 1969)
1905 Gray Partridge (DuMont 1933)
1907 Long-tailed Jaeger (*Anderson 1908)
1910 Rock Wren (*Bennett 1925)
1913 Dunlin (Gabrielson 1918)
1922 European Starling (DuMont 1933)
1923 Blue Grosbeak (DuMont 1933)
1926 Red-necked Grebe (Pierce 1930)
Western Grebe (DuMont 1933)

1928 Lewis's Woodpecker (*Bailey 1929, *Youngworth 1929)
Spotted Towhee (*IBL* 2:52)
1929 Lazuli Bunting (*Youngworth 1929)
1931 Black-legged Kittiwake (*DuMont 1933)
1932 Harlequin Duck (*DuMont 1934)
1933 Eurasian Wigeon (*DuMont 1935)
Black Vulture (*Dill 1933)
Chuck-will's-widow (*DuMont 1935)
1934 Red Knot (Bennett 1935)
1937 Purple Gallinule (*Dix 1937)
1940 Ruff (*Dill 1941)
1941 Glaucous Gull (*Stiles 1941)
1945 Ross's Goose (Brown 1971)
1946 Scissor-tailed Flycatcher (*Brown 1946)
1950 Townsend's Warbler (*Feeney 1950)
1952 Black Scoter (*Morrissey 1954)
Sage Thrasher (*Stiles 1953)
1953 Anhinga (*Collins 1953)
1954 Townsend's Solitaire (*Youngworth 1961)
1956 Common Raven (*Sieh 1957)
1960 Roseate Spoonbill (*Burgess 1960)
Say's Phoebe (*Bryant and Youngworth 1962)
1961 Cattle Egret (*Weller 1961)
Black-throated Gray Warbler (*Youngworth 1961)
1962 Mute Swan (Musgrove and Musgrove 1977)
1964 Varied Thrush (*IBL* 35:26)
1966 Groove-billed Ani (*IBL* 64:70)
1968 Black-headed Grosbeak (*DeLong 1969)
1969 Western Tanager (*Crocker 1969)
1970 King Eider (*Newlon and Kent 1981)
1972 Red-throated Loon (*Burns and Burns 1972)
Pinyon Jay (*Zollars 1973)
1973 Ferruginous Hawk (*Wilson 1988)
1974 Sharp-tailed Sandpiper (*Halmi 1974)
Great Gray Owl (*Berg 1974)
Alder Flycatcher (P. Petersen, note to Records Committee)
1975 Ivory Gull (Ayres 1976)
Mountain Bluebird (*Dowell 1975)
Curve-billed Thrasher (*Wallace 1975)
Green-tailed Towhee (*Crocker 1975)
1976 Gray Jay (*Koenig 1977)
Boreal Chickadee (*Brown 1976)
1977 Wood Stork (Dinsmore et al. 1984)
Black-bellied Whistling-Duck (*Barratt 1977)
Pygmy Nuthatch (*Brooke 1977)
Prairie Warbler (*IBL* 47:61)
Golden-crowned Sparrow (*Burns 1977)
1978 Great Black-backed Gull (*IBL* 49:56)
Black-backed Woodpecker (*IBL* 49:26, 56)
Hoary Redpoll (*Halmi 1978)
1979 Western Wood-Pewee (*Schaufenbuel 1979)
1980 Brant (*Dinsmore et al. 1981)
1981 Northern Hawk Owl (*Myers 1982)
1982 Mew Gull (*Kent 1983)
Chestnut-collared Longspur (*IBL* 52:63)
House Finch (*IBL* 52:94)
1983 Clark's Grebe (*IBL* 53:48)
Vermilion Flycatcher (Van Dyk 1983)
Great-tailed Grackle (Silcock 1983)
1984 Bean Goose (*Wilson 1985, *Wright and Grenon 1985)
Barrow's Goldeneye (*Silcock 1984)
Black-necked Stilt (*IBL* 54:82; 55:57)
Lesser Black-backed Gull (*Kent and Bowles 1985)
1985 Curlew Sandpiper (*Moore 1985)
Thayer's Gull (*Bendorf 1986)
1986 Rufous Hummingbird (*Stone 1986)
1987 Ancient Murrelet (*Hansen 1988)
Eurasian Tree Sparrow (*Veal 1987)
1988 Snowy Plover (*Dinsmore and Fix 1988)
Red Phalarope (*Dinsmore and Engebretsen 1989)
Pomarine Jaeger (*Dinsmore 1989)
Little Gull (*IBL* 59:14; 65:83)
1989 Tricolored Heron (*Kent 1991)
Laughing Gull (*Kent 1991)
Black-headed Gull (*Dinsmore 1993)
California Gull (*Petersen 1991)
Slaty-backed Gull (*Fuller 1989)
1991 Garganey (*IBL* 61:90)
Iceland Gull (*Kent 1992)
Marbled Murrelet (*Dinsmore 1993)
Common Ground-Dove (*Fuller 1992)
Fish Crow (*IBL* 61:94)
1992 Glossy Ibis (*Kenne 1994)
Gyrfalcon (*Bolduan 1994)
Western Flycatcher sp. (*Johnson 1994)
1993 Reddish Egret (*Schantz 1996)
Ross's Gull (*Fuller 1994)
Black-throated Sparrow (*IBL* 63:79)
Bullock's Oriole (*IBL* 63:80)
1995 White Ibis (*IBL* 66:18)
MacGillivray's Warbler (*IBL* 66:96-97)
1996 Neotropic Cormorant (*IBL* 66:100)

Literature Cited

Allen, J. A. 1868. Notes on birds observed in western Iowa, in the months July, August, and September. *Memoirs Boston Society Natural History* 1:488-502.

——. 1870. Catalogue of the birds of Iowa. In: White, C. A., ed. *Report on the Geological Survey of the State of Iowa*, Vol. 2. Mills and Co., Des Moines.

American Ornithologists' Union. 1982. Thirty-fourth supplement to the American Ornithologists' Union Check-list of North American Birds. *Auk* 99(3) [Supplement]:1-16CC.

——. 1983. *Check-list of North American Birds*, 6th edition.

——. 1989. Thirty-seventh supplement to the American Ornithologists' Union Check-list of North American Birds. *Auk* 106:532-538.

Anderson, R. M. 1897. *An Annotated List of the Birds of Winnebago and Hancock Counties, Iowa.* Published by author, Forest City.

——. 1907. The birds of Iowa. *Proc. Davenport Acad. Sci.* 11:125-417.

Andrews, R., D. Garner, S. Berg, T. Bogenschutz, W. Suchy, and G. Zenner. 1995. *Trends in Iowa Wildlife Populations and Harvest 1994.* Iowa Department of Natural Resources, Des Moines.

Andrews, R., and R. Righter. 1992. *Colorado Birds.* Denver Museum of Natural History, Denver.

Anonymous. 1881. *History of Fremont County, Iowa.* Iowa Historical Company, Des Moines.

——. 1883. *History of Johnson County, Iowa.* Iowa City.

Audubon, M. R., and E. Coues. 1897. *Audubon and His Journals.* Charles Scribner's Sons, New York.

Bailey, B. H. 1906. *200 Wild Birds of Iowa.* Audubon Nature Publications, Cedar Rapids.

——. 1910. *Two Hundred Wild Birds of Iowa.* The Superior Press, Cedar Rapids.

——. 1918. The raptorial birds of Iowa. *Iowa Geological Survey Bull.,* No. 6.

Bartsch, P. 1897. Summer birds of the Oneota Valley (June, July 1895). *Iowa Ornithologist* 3:51-61.

——. 1899. The literature of Iowa birds, 3 vols. Master's thesis, Univ. of Iowa.

Baumgartner, F. M., and A. M. Baumgartner. 1992. *Oklahoma Bird Life.* Univ. of Oklahoma Press, Norman.

Behle, W. F., E. D. Sorensen, and C. M. White. 1985. Utah birds: A revised checklist. *Utah Museum of Natural History Occasional Publication,* No. 4.

Bennett, L. J. 1934. Notes on nesting waterfowl and other marsh nesting birds in northwest Iowa. *Oologist* 51:101-104.

——. 1935. The 1934 spring migration of shore birds through Clay and Palo Alto Counties, Iowa. *Iowa State College J. Sci.* 9:609-616.

——. 1938a. *The Blue-winged Teal: Its Ecology and Management.* Collegiate Press, Ames.

——. 1938b. The 1934 spring migration of some birds through Clay and Palo Alto counties, Iowa. *Iowa Bird Life* 8:2-6.

Bennett, W. W. 1931. *Birds of Sioux City Iowa.* Sioux City Bird Club, Sioux City.

Black, G. 1979. *Birds of Iowa.* Iowa Chapter of The Nature Conservancy.

——. 1992. *Iowa Birdlife.* Univ. of Iowa Press, Iowa City.

Bohlen, H. D. 1978. *An Annotated Check-list of the Birds of Illinois.* Illinois State Museum, Springfield.

——. 1989. *The Birds of Illinois.* Indiana Univ. Press, Bloomington.

Bray, T. E., B. K. Padelford, and W. R. Silcock. 1985. *The Birds of Nebraska: A Critically Evaluated List.* Published by the authors, Bellevue.

Brown, W. H. 1957. Twenty years of Christmas Bird Censuses in Iowa—analysis and criticism. *Iowa Bird Life* 27:85-91.

——. 1971. An annotated list of the birds of Iowa. *Iowa State J. Sci.* 45:387-469.

——. 1973. Shorebirds at Des Moines. *Iowa Bird Life* 43:77.

——. 1975. Population changes in the Tufted Titmouse and Black-capped Chickadee. *Iowa Bird Life* 45:97.

Brown, W. H., N. S. Halmi, and R. F. Vane. 1977. I.O.U. checklist of Iowa birds. *Iowa Bird Life* 47:31-40.

Burns, F. L. 1915. A bibliography of scarce or out of print North American amateur and trade periodicals devoted more or less to ornithology. *Oologist* 32 [Supplement]:1-32.

Carter, D. L. 1955. A study of fall warbler migration. *Iowa Bird Life* 25:17-18.

Checklist Committee of the American Birding Association. 1975. *A.B.A. Checklist: Birds of the Continental United States and Canada.* American Birding Association, Austin, TX.

——. 1996. *A.B.A. Checklist: Birds of the Continental United States and Canada, Fifth Edition.* American Birding Association, Colorado Springs.

Clements, J. F. 1991. *Birds of the World: A Checklist.* Ibis Publishing Co., Vista, CA.

Cole, J. 1920. Story County, Iowa birds. *Oologist* 37:11-13.

Cooke, W. W. 1888. Report on bird migration in the Mississippi valley in the years 1884 and 1885. *U.S. Department of Agriculture Division of Economic Ornithology Bull.*, No. 2.

Cooper, T. C., and N. S. Hart, eds. 1982. *Iowa's Natural Heritage.* Iowa Natural Heritage Foundation and Iowa Academy of Science, Des Moines.

Crim, G. B. 1976. Kinglets in Iowa. *Iowa Bird Life* 46:45-47.

Crone, J. V. 1890. Summer residents of Buena Vista Co., Iowa. *Oologist* 7:45-47.

Curson, J., D. Quinn, and D. Beadle. 1994. *Warblers of North America.* Houghton Mifflin, Boston.

DeBenedictus, P. A. 1994. ABA Checklist report, 1992. *Birding* 26:93-102.

DeSante, D., and P. Pyle. 1986. *Distributional Checklist of North American Birds.* Artemisia Press, Lee Vining, CA.

Dinsmore, J. J. 1981. Iowa's avifauna: Changes in the past and prospects for the future. *Proc. Iowa Acad. Sci.* 88:28-37.

——. 1992. Recent additions to the Iowa State University bird collection. *Iowa Bird Life* 62:1-8.

——. 1993. Early Christmas Bird Counts in Iowa. *Iowa Bird Life* 63:3-9.

——. 1994. *A Country So Full of Game: The Story of Wildlife in Iowa.* Univ. of Iowa Press, Iowa City.

Dinsmore, J. J., T. H. Kent, D. Koenig, P. C. Petersen, and D. M. Roosa. 1984. *Iowa Birds.* Iowa State Univ. Press, Ames.

Dinsmore, J. J., R. B. Renken, and J. P. Schaufenbuel. 1983. TV tower kill in central Iowa. *Iowa Bird Life* 53:91-93.

Dinsmore, S., E. Munson, J. J. Dinsmore, and G. M. Nelson. 1987. Two television tower kills in Iowa. *Iowa Bird Life* 57:5-8.

Dinsmore, S. J. 1995. *The Birds of Polk County.* Published by the author, Ames.

Dinsmore, S. J., and H. Zaletel. 1996. *The Birds of Story County.* Published by the authors, Ames.

Dorn, J. L., and R. D. Dorn. 1990. *Wyoming Birds.* Mountain West Publishing, Cheyenne.

Ducey, J. 1983. A partial list of the birds of Franklin County, Iowa: A view from the 1890s. *Iowa Bird Life* 53:63-68.

DuMont, P. A. 1931. *Birds of Polk County Iowa.* Des Moines Audubon Society, Des Moines.

——. 1932. Some Iowa birds in a Des Moines collection. *Wilson Bull.* 44:236-237.

——. 1933. A revised list of the birds of Iowa. *University of Iowa Studies in Natural History*, Vol. 15, No. 5.

——. 1933a. Extinct birds in Iowa collections. *Iowa Bird Life* 3:28-29.

——. 1935a. The role of the accidental or straggling species of birds in Iowa. *Iowa Bird Life* 5:8-9.

——. 1935b. Additional Iowa species of birds substantiated by specimens. *Wilson Bull.* 47:205-208.

——. 1936. Old nesting records of rare birds in Iowa. *Oologist* 53:8-10.

——. 1944. A review of ornithology in Iowa. *Iowa Bird Life* 14:64-68.

Ennis, J. H., T. J. Feeney, T. Morrissey, J. W. Musgrove, W. Youngworth, and W. H. Brown. 1954. Iowa distributional check-list. *Iowa Bird Life* 24:72-79.

Fagan, L. P. 1909. The summer-resident birds of Polk County, Iowa—A guide to local study. *Proc. Iowa Acad. Sci.* 16:197-215.

Farris, A. L., E. D. Klonglan, and R. C. Nomsen. 1977. *The Ring-necked Pheasant in Iowa.* Iowa Conservation Commission, Des Moines.

Fenton, C. L. 1916. Preliminary list of the birds of Floyd County, Iowa. *Wilson Bull.* 28:130-138.

——. 1923-1924. The birds of Floyd County, Iowa. *Amer. Midland Naturalist* 8:189-208, 230-256; 9:63-79.

Fleskes, J. P., and E. E. Klaas. 1991. Dabbling duck recruitment in relation to habitat and predators at Union Slough National Wildlife Refuge, Iowa. *U.S. Fish and Wildlife Service, Fish and Wildlife Technical Report*, No. 32.

Gabrielson, I. N. 1914. Breeding birds of a Clay County, Iowa, farm. *Wilson Bull.* 26:69-81.

——. 1917. A list of the birds observed in Clay and O'Brien counties, Iowa. *Proc. Iowa Acad. Sci.* 24:259-272.

——. 1918. A list of the birds found in Marshall County, Iowa. *Proc. Iowa Acad. Sci.* 25:123-153.

——. 1919. The birds of Marshall County, Iowa, II. *Proc. Iowa Acad. Sci.* 26:47-75.

Garrett, K., and J. Dunn. 1981. *Birds of Southern California.* Los Angeles Audubon Society, Los Angeles.

Gilligan, J., M. Smith, D. Rogers, and A. Contreras. 1994. *Birds of Oregon.* Cinclus Publications, McMinnville, OR.

Godfrey, W. E. 1986. *The Birds of Canada, Revised Edition.* National Museum of Natural Sciences, Ottawa.

Grant, M. L. 1963. A checklist of Iowa birds, coded with status symbols. *Iowa Bird Life* 33:50-62.

Haney, J. C., P. Brisse, D. R. Jacobson, M. W. Oberle, and J. M. Paget. 1986. Annotated checklist of Georgia birds. *Georgia Ornithological Society Occasional Publication*, No. 10.

Harrison, H. H. 1984. *Wood Warblers' World.* Simon and Schuster, New York.

Hemesath, L. 1994. 1994 rookery survey results. *Wildlife Diversity News* 10(4):9-10.

Hendrickson, G. O. 1944. The Allert bird collection passes to Iowa State College. *Iowa Bird Life* 14:68-69.

Henning, C. F. 1900. Notes on the birds of Boone County, Iowa. *Western Ornithologist* 5:15-19, 36-39, 54-57.

Hodges, J. 1959. Birds of Scott County, Iowa: 1900-1925. *Iowa Bird Life* 29:33-36.

Hollis, R. J. 1984. The 1984 Iowa feeder survey. *Iowa Bird Life* 54:91-101.

——. 1986. The 1985 Iowa feeder survey. *Iowa Bird Life* 56:11-16.

Hoopes, B. A. 1873. Description of a new variety of buteo. *Proc. Acad. Natural Sci.* 25:238-239.

Howell, S. N. G., and S. Webb. 1995. *The Birds of Mexico and Northern Central America.* Oxford Univ. Press, Oxford.

I.O.U. Records Committee. 1986. Official Checklist of Iowa Birds 1986 Edition. *Iowa Bird Life* 56:46-55.

Jackson, L. S., C. A. Thompson, J. J. Dinsmore, B. Ehresman, J. Fleckenstein, R. Cecil, L. M. Hemesath, and S. J. Dinsmore. 1996. *The Iowa Breeding Bird Atlas.* Univ. of Iowa Press, Iowa City.

James, D. A., and J. C. Neal. 1986. *Arkansas Birds, Their Distribution and Abundance.* Univ. of Arkansas Press, Fayetteville.

James, E. 1823. *Account of an Expedition from Pittsburgh to the Rocky Mountains Performed in the Years 1819, 1820.* Longman, Hurst, Rees, Orme and Brown, London.

James, R. D. 1991. *Annotated Checklist of the Birds of Ontario, Second Edition.* Royal Ontario Museum, Toronto.

Janssen, R. B. 1987. *Birds in Minnesota.* Univ. of Minnesota Press, Minneapolis.

Jones, L. 1889. A list of birds found in eastern Jasper and western Poweshiek Counties, Iowa. *Curlew* 1:50-53, 57-60.

——. 1892. Report of the committee on migration and distribution. *Wilson Quarterly* 4:27.

——. 1895. Bird migration at Grinnell, Iowa. *Auk* 12:117-134.

Kaufman, K. 1990. *A Field Guide to Advanced Birding.* Houghton Mifflin, Boston.

Keller, C. E., S. A. Keller, and T. C. Keller. 1986. *Indiana Birds and Their Haunts, Second Edition.* Indiana University Press, Bloomington.

Kelsey, C. 1891. Birds of Poweshiek County, Iowa. *Ornithologist and Oologist* 16:131-134.

Kent, F. W., and T. H. Kent. 1975. *Birding in Eastern Iowa.* Published by the authors, Iowa City.

Kent, T. H. 1995. Report of the Records Committee for 1994. *Iowa Bird Life* 65:80-84.

——. 1996. Official checklist of Iowa birds 1996 edition. *Iowa Bird Life* 66:76-85.

Kent, T. H., and C. J. Bendorf. 1991. Official checklist of Iowa birds 1991 edition. *Iowa Bird Life* 61:101-109.

Kent, T. H., J. J. Dinsmore, D. Koenig, M. C. Newlon, P. C. Petersen, J. Schaufenbuel, and W. R. Silcock. 1982. Official checklist of Iowa birds: 1982 edition. *Iowa Bird Life* 52:67-76.

Kent, T. H., and G. D. Schrimper. 1996. The University of Iowa bird collection. *Iowa Bird Life* 66:86-94.

Kent, T. H., G. Walsh, and C. Edwards. 1994. Breeding birds of the Coralville Reservoir area. *Iowa Bird Life* 64:89-105.

Keyes, C. R., and H. S. Williams. 1889. Preliminary annotated catalogue of the birds of Iowa. *Proc. Davenport Acad. Natural Sci.* 5:113-161.

Koenig, D. 1974. Birding areas of Iowa: Northeast Iowa. *Iowa Bird Life* 44:45-49.

——. 1975. Winter hawk population trends in Iowa. *Iowa Bird Life* 45:42-48, 67-78.

——. 1976. Some unusual nest discoveries. *Iowa Bird Life* 46:19-20.

——. 1977. Winter population trends of woodpeckers in Iowa. *Iowa Bird Life* 47:75-92.

——. 1979. Annotated list of Allamakee County foray birds. *Iowa Bird Life* 49:71-77.

Krider, J. 1879. *Forty Years Notes of a Field Ornithologist.* J. H. Weston Press, Philadelphia.

Laffoon, J. 1941. Late fall and winter bird records, 1938 to 1941, in the Sioux City area. *Proc. Iowa Acad. Sci.* 48:425-436.

Lange, D. 1906. *How to Know the Wild Birds of Iowa and Nebraska.* North-Western School Supply Co., Minneapolis.

Legg, R. G., and P. J. Frye. 1981. Effect of effort and environmental variables on Christmas Bird Count outcomes in Iowa. *Iowa Bird Life* 51:43-49.

Madge, S., and H. Burn. 1988. *Waterfowl.* Houghton Mifflin, Boston.

Martsching, P. 1986. Spring warbler migration at Brookside Park in Ames. *Iowa Bird Life* 56:107-111.

——. 1987. Fall warbler migration at Brookside Park in Ames. *Iowa Bird Life* 57:112-117.

McNair, D. B., and W. Post. 1993. Supplement to Status and Distribution of South Carolina Birds. *Charleston Museum Ornithological Contribution,* No. 8.

McPeek, G. A., and R. J. Adams, eds. 1994. *The Birds of Michigan.* Indiana Univ. Press, Bloomington.

Meyer, A. W. 1959. George Berry, Iowa naturalist. *Iowa Bird Life* 29:74-78.

Monroe, B. L., Jr. 1994. *The Birds of Kentucky.* Indiana Univ. Press, Bloomington.

Monroe, B. L., Jr., and C. G. Sibley. 1993. *A World Checklist of Birds.* Yale Univ. Press, New Haven.

Mosman, D. 1975. Bird casualties at Alleman, Ia. TV tower. *Iowa Bird Life* 45:88-90.

Moulton, G. E., ed. 1986. *The Journals of the Lewis and Clark Expedition, Vol. 2.* Univ. of Nebraska Press, Lincoln.

——. 1993. *The Journals of the Lewis and Clark Expedition, Vol. 8*. Univ. of Nebraska Press, Lincoln.

Musgrove, J. 1949. Check list of Iowa birds. *Iowa Conservationist*, April 1949 [supplement].

——. 1952. Check list of Iowa birds. *Iowa Conservationist*, May 1952 [supplement].

Musgrove, J. W., and M. R. Musgrove. 1943. *Waterfowl in Iowa*. State Conservation Commission, Des Moines.

——. 1977. *Waterfowl in Iowa* [5th edition]. State Conservation Commission, Des Moines.

National Geographic Society. 1987. *Field Guide to the Birds of North America, Second Edition*. National Geographic Society, Washington, D.C.

Nauman, E. D. 1926. An Iowa bird census. *Wilson Bull.* 38:83-91.

Newhouse, D. 1982. *Iowa's Nest Record Card Program*. Iowa Conservation Commission, Des Moines.

Nutting, C. C. 1893. Report of Committee on State Fauna. *Proc. Iowa Acad. Sci.* 1:39-42.

——. 1895. Report of the Committee on State Fauna. *Proc. Iowa Acad. Sci.* 2:43-51.

Oberholser, H. C. 1974. *The Bird Life of Texas*. Univ. of Texas Press, Austin.

Osborn, H. 1891. *A Partial Catalogue of the Animals of Iowa, Represented in the collections of the Department of Zoology and Entomology, Iowa Agricultural College*. Published by Authority of the Board of Trustees, Ames.

Palmer, R. S., ed. 1988. *Handbook of North American Birds Volumes 4 and 5*. Yale Univ. Press, New Haven.

Parker, H. W. 1871. Iowa birds. *Amer. Naturalist* 5:168-170.

Paulson, M. C. 1922. List of breeding birds in Story County, Iowa. *Oologist* 39:20.

Payne, R. B. 1983. A distributional checklist of the birds of Michigan. *Miscellaneous Publications Museum of Zoology Univ. of Michigan*, No. 164.

Peck, G. D. 1913. List of eggs collected in Black Hawk Co., Iowa, 1875. *Oologist* 30:133-135.

Pellett, F. C. 1913. Birds that nest at Tamakoche. *Bird-Lore* 15:305-307.

Peterjohn, B. G. 1989. *The Birds of Ohio*. Indiana Univ. Press, Bloomington.

Petersen, P. C., ed. 1979a. *Birding Areas of Iowa*. Iowa Ornithologists' Union.

——. 1979b. Birds seen on the Lee County foray. *Iowa Bird Life* 49:99-107.

Petersen, W. J. 1971a. Birds along the Missouri. *Palimpsest* 52:550-570.

——. 1971b. Barging down from Fort Union. *Palimpsest* 52:571-583.

Peterson, R. T. 1980. *A Field Guide to the Birds*. Houghton Mifflin, Boston.

——. 1990. *A Field Guide to Western Birds*. Houghton Mifflin, Boston.

Pierce, F. J. 1921. Buchanan County, Iowa, birds. *Oologist* 38:4-7.

——. 1930. Birds of Buchanan County, Iowa. *Wilson Bull.* 42:253-285.

——. 1933a. County lists of Iowa birds. *Iowa Bird Life* 3:7-10.

——. 1933b. The early Iowa bird magazines. *Iowa Bird Life* 3:48-51.

——. 1936. Bird notes in the mimeographed letters of the Iowa Ornithologists' Union. *Iowa Bird Life* 6:48-53.

Post, W., and S. A. Gauthreaux, Jr. 1989. *Status and Distribution of South Carolina Birds*. The Charleston Museum, Charleston.

Praeger, W. E. 1925. The birds of the Des Moines Rapids. *Auk* 42:563-577.

Prior, J. C. 1991. *Landforms of Iowa*. Univ. of Iowa Press, Iowa City.

Robbins, C. S, and W. T. Van Velzen. 1969. The Breeding Bird Survey 1967 and 1968. *Bureau of Sports Fisheries and Wildlife Special Scientific Report—Wildlife*, No. 124.

Robbins, C. S., D. Bystrak, and P. H. Geissler. 1986. The Breeding Bird Survey: Its first fifteen years, 1965-1979. *U.S. Fish and Wildlife Service Resource Publication*, No. 157.

Robbins, M. B., and D. A. Easterla. 1992. *Birds of Missouri*. Univ. of Missouri Press, Columbia.

Robbins, S. D., Jr. 1991. *Wisconsin Birdlife*. Univ. of Wisconsin Press, Madison.

Robinson, J. C. 1990. *An Annotated Checklist of the Birds of Tennessee*. Univ. of Tennessee Press, Knoxville.

Roosa, D. M. 1978. *Winter Raptor Survey*. State Preserves Board, Des Moines.

Roosa, D. M., and P. Bartelt. 1977. *Winter Raptor Survey—1977*. State Preserves Board, Des Moines.

Roosa, D. M., P. Bartelt, and D. Koenig. 1979. *Winter Raptor Survey—1979*. State Preserves Board, Des Moines.

Roosa, D. M., and J. Stravers. 1989. Nesting of raptors uncommon in Iowa: Summary and new records. *J. Iowa Acad. Sci.* 96:41-49.

Rosene, W. M. 1932. A bit of history. *Iowa Bird Life* 2:3-5.

Ross, W. G. 1938. *Bird Notes from the Journal of a Nature Lover*. W. B. Conkey.

Savage, D. L., M. E. Peck, J. V. Crone, C. R. Keyes, P. Bartsch, and H. J. Giddings. 1897. A complete and annotated list of Iowa birds. *Iowa Ornithologist* 3:25-28.

Schaufenbuel, J. 1979. Recent breeding records of uncommon or rare birds of Iowa. *Iowa Bird Life* 49:104-107.

——. 1981. Breeding marsh-bird survey. *Iowa Bird Life* 51:111-114.

Schlicht, D. 1973. Historical notes on the birds of Black Hawk County, Iowa. *Iowa Bird Life* 43:87-96.

Schrimper, G. D. 1982. A brief history of the University of Iowa Museum of Natural History and its ornithological collections. *Iowa Bird Life* 52:103-111.

Scott, O. K. 1993. *A Birder's Guide to Wyoming*. American Birding Association, Colorado Springs.

Serbousek, L. 1959. Bird records of the Cedar Rapids Bird Club. *Iowa Bird Life* 29:63-69.

Sherman, A. R. 1952. *Birds of an Iowa Dooryard*. Christopher Publishing House, Boston.

Shoemaker, F. H. 1896. *A Partial List of the Birds of Franklin County, Iowa*. Published by the author.

Silcock, W. R. 1977. Annotated list of foray birds. *Iowa Bird Life* 47:123-132.

Skaar, D., D. Flath, and L. S. Thompson. 1985. P. D. Skaar's Montana bird distribution, third edition. *Proc. Montana Acad. Sci.* 44 [supplement]: Monograph No. 3.

Small, A. 1994. *California Birds: Their Status and Distribution*. Ibis Publishing, Vista, CA.

South Dakota Ornithologists' Union. 1991. *The Birds of South Dakota Revised Edition*. Aberdeen.

Spiker, C. J. 1924. Birds of Wapello County, Iowa. *Proc. Iowa Acad. Sci.* 31:419-426.

——. 1926. Winter bird records, 1922 to 1926, in northwestern Iowa. *Proc. Iowa Acad. Sci.* 33:307-313.

Spurrell, J. A. 1917. Annotated list of the water birds, game birds and birds of prey of Sac County, Iowa. *Wilson Bull.* 29:141-160.

——. 1919. An annotated list of the land birds of Sac County, Iowa. *Wilson Bull.* 31:117-126.

——. 1921. An annotated list of the land birds of Sac County, Iowa. *Wilson Bull.* 33:123-132.

Stephens, T. C. 1917. Bird records during the past winter, 1916-1917, in northwestern Iowa. *Proc. Iowa Acad. Sci.* 24:245-258.

——. 1918. Bird records of the past winter, 1917-1918, in the upper Missouri valley. *Proc. Iowa Acad. Sci.* 25:71-83.

——. 1920. Bird records of the past two winters, 1918-1920, in the upper Missouri valley. *Proc. Iowa Acad. Sci.* 27:395-407.

——. 1930. Bird records of two winters, 1920-1922, in the upper Missouri valley. *Proc. Iowa Acad. Sci.* 37:357-366.

——. 1957. An annotated bibliography of Iowa ornithology. *Nebraska Ornithologists' Union, Occasional Paper*, No. 4.

Stevenson, H. M., and B. H. Anderson. 1994. *The Birdlife of Florida*. Univ. Press of Florida, Gainesville.

Texas Bird Records Committee. 1995. *Checklist of the Birds of Texas, Third Edition*. Texas Ornithological Society, Austin.

Thompson, M. C., and C. Ely.1989. *Birds in Kansas, Volume One*. Univ. of Kansas Museum of Natural History, Lawrence.

——.1992. *Birds in Kansas, Volume Two*. Univ. of Kansas Museum of Natural History, Lawrence.

Thornburg, D. D. 1973. Diving duck movements on Keokuk Pool, Mississippi River. *J. Wildlife Management* 37:382-389.

Thwaites, R. G. 1905. *Early Western Travels, 1748-1846, vol. 14. Part I of James's Account of S. H. Long's Expedition, 1819-1820*. Arthur H. Clark Co., Cleveland.

——. 1906a. *Early Western Travels, 1748-1846, vol. 22. Part I of Maximilian, Prince of Wied's Travels in the Interior of North America, 1832-1834*. Arthur H. Clark Co., Cleveland.

——. 1906b. *Early Western Travels, 1748-1846, vol. 24. Part III of Maximilian, Prince of Wied's Travels in the Interior of North America*. Arthur H. Clark Co., Cleveland.

Tinker, A. D. 1914. Notes on the ornithology of Clay and Palo Alto counties, Iowa. *Auk* 31:70-81.

Toups, J. A., and J. A. Jackson.1987. *Birds and Birding on the Mississippi Coast*. Univ. Press of Mississippi, Jackson.

Trippe, T. M. 1873. Notes on the birds of southern Iowa. *Proc. Boston Society Natural History* 15:229-242.

Tufts, R. W. 1986. *Birds of Nova Scotia. Third Edition*. Nova Scotia Museum, Halifax.

Veit, R. R., and W. R. Petersen.1993. *Birds of Massachusetts*. Massachusetts Audubon Society.

Weller, M. W. 1961. Cattle Egret and other uncommon Iowa water-birds. *Iowa Bird Life* 31:44-45.

——. 1962. Recommendations for collecting data on nesting birds. *Iowa Bird Life* 32:2-6.

——. 1979. Birds of some Iowa wetlands in relation to concepts of faunal preservation. *Proc. Iowa Acad. Sci.* 86:81-88.

Weller, M. W., L. H. Fredrickson, and F. W. Kent. 1963. Small mammal prey of some owls wintering in Iowa. *Iowa State J. Sci.* 38:151-160.

White, M. 1995. *A Birder's Guide to Arkansas*. American Birding Association, Colorado Springs.

Wilson, B. H. 1906. The birds of Scott County, Iowa. *Wilson Bull.* 18:1-11.

Wood, D. S., and G. D. Schnell. 1984. *Distributions of Oklahoma Birds*. Univ. of Oklahoma Press, Norman.

Youngworth, W. 1931. Late fall and winter bird records, 1926 to 1930, in the upper Missouri valley. *Proc. Iowa Acad. Sci.* 38:277-285.

——. 1932. Fall migration dates from Sioux City, Iowa. *Iowa Bird Life* 2:52.

Zeranski, J. D., and T. R. Baptist. 1990. *Connecticut Birds*. University Press of New England, Hanover, NH.

Zimmer, K. J. 1985. *The Western Bird Watcher*. Prentice Hall, Endlewood Cliffs, NJ.

Index To Species Accounts

Page numbers refer to location of account in Species Accounts or Appendix A.

Accipiter
cooperii, 109
gentilis, 110
striatus, 108
Actitis macularia, 150
Aechmophorus
clarkii, 37
occidentalis, 36
Aegolius acadicus, 214
Agelaius phoeniceus, 349
Aix sponsa, 73
Ajaia ajaja, 60
Alectoris chukar, 371
Ammodramus
henslowii, 337
leconteii, 338
nelsoni, 339
savannarum, 336
Amphispiza bilineata, 333
Anas
acuta, 76
americana, 83
clypeata, 80
crecca, 74
cyanoptera, 79
discors, 78
penelope, 82
platyrhynchos, 75
querquedula, 77
rubripes, 75
strepera, 81
Anhinga, 43
Anhinga anhinga, 43
Ani, Groove-billed, 204
Anser
albifrons, 68
fabalis, 67
Anthus
rubescens, 278
spragueii, 373
Aquila chrysaetos, 117
Archilochus colubris, 219
Ardea
alba, 48
herodias, 47
Arenaria interpres, 156
Asio
flammeus, 213
otus, 212
Avocet, American, 147
Aythya
affinis, 88
americana, 85
collaris, 86
marila, 87
valisineria, 84
Bartramia longicauda, 151
Bittern
American, 45
Least, 46
Blackbird
Brewer's, 353
Red-winged, 349
Rusty, 352
Yellow-headed, 351
Bluebird
Eastern, 266
Mountain, 267
Bobolink, 349
Bobwhite, Northern, 127
Bombycilla
cedrorum, 280
garrulus, 278
Bonasa umbellus, 124
Botaurus lentiginosus, 45
Brachyramphus marmoratus, 197
Brant, 71
Branta
bernicla, 71
canadensis, 72
Bubo virginianus, 207
Bubulcus ibis, 53
Bucephala
albeola, 97
clangula, 95
islandica, 96
Bufflehead, 97
Bunting
Indigo, 325
Lark, 334
Lazuli,
Painted, 374
Snow, 348
Buteo
jamaicensis, 114
lagopus, 116
lineatus, 111
platypterus, 112
regalis, 115
swainsoni, 113
Butorides virescens, 54
Calamospiza melanocorys, 334
Calcarius
lapponicus, 345
mccownii, 374
ornatus, 347
pictus, 346
Calidris
acuminata, 167
alba, 158
alpina, 163
bairdii, 161
canutus, 157
ferruginea, 163
fuscicollis, 160
himantopus, 164
maritima, 372
mauri, 159
melanotos, 161
minutilla, 160
pusilla, 158
Canvasback, 84
Caprimulgus
carolinensis, 216
vociferus, 217
Cardinal, Northern, 321
Cardinalis cardinalis, 321
Carduelis
flammea, 364
hornemanni, 365
pinus, 366
tristis, 367
Carpodacus
mexicanus, 362

purpureus, 362
Catbird, Gray, 274
Cathartes aura, 102
Catharus
fuscescens, 269
guttatus, 271
minimus, 270
ustulatus, 270
Catoptrophorus semipalmatus, 150
Certhia americana, 255
Ceryle alcyon, 221
Chaetura pelagica, 218
Charadrius
alexandrinus, 143
melodus, 144
montanus, 371
semipalmatus, 144
vociferus, 145
Chat, Yellow-breasted, 316
Chen
caerulescens, 69
rossii, 70
Chickadee
Black-capped, 251
Boreal, 251
Carolina, 373
Chlidonias niger, 195
Chondestes grammacus, 332
Chordeiles minor, 215
Chuck-will's-widow, 216
Chukar, 371
Cinclus mexicanus, 373
Circus cyaneus, 107
Cistothorus
palustris, 262
platensis, 261
Clangula hyemalis, 92
Coccothraustes vespertinus, 367
Coccyzus
americanus, 203
erythropthalmus, 202
Colaptes auratus, 227
Colinus virginianus, 127
Columba
fasciata, 372
livia, 198
Columbina passerina, 200
Contopus
borealis, 228
sordidulus, 229
virens, 229
Conuropsis carolinensis, 201
Coot, American, 137
Coragyps atratus, 101
Cormorant
Double-crested, 41
Neotropic, 42
Corvus
brachyrhynchos, 248
corax, 250
ossifragus, 249
Coturnicops noveboracensis, 129
Cowbird, Brown-headed, 355
Crane
Sandhill, 138
Whooping, 140
Creeper, Brown, 255
Crossbill
Red, 363
White-winged, 364
Crotophaga sulcirostris, 204
Crow
American, 248
Fish, 249
Cuckoo
Black-billed, 202
Yellow-billed, 203
Curlew
Eskimo, 152
Long-billed, 154
Cyanocitta cristata, 245
Cygnus
buccinator, 65
columbianus, 64
olor, 66
Dendrocygna
autumnalis, 63
bicolor, 370
Dendroica
caerulescens, 296
castanea, 303
cerulea, 305
coronata, 297
discolor, 302
dominica, 300
fusca, 299
magnolia, 295
nigrescens, 298
palmarum, 303
pensylvanica, 294
petechia, 294
pinus, 301
striata, 304
tigrina, 295
townsendi, 298
virens, 299
Dickcissel, 325
Dipper, American, 373
Dolichonyx oryzivorus, 349
Dove
Mourning, 199
Rock, 198
Dowitcher
Long-billed, 166
Short-billed, 166
Dryocopus pileatus, 227
Duck
American Black, 75
Harlequin, 91
Ring-necked, 86
Ruddy, 100
Wood, 73
Dumetella carolinensis, 274
Dunlin, 163
Eagle
Bald, 106
Golden, 117
Ectopistes migratorius, 199
Egret
Cattle, 53
Great, 48
Reddish, 52
Snowy, 49
Egretta
caerulea, 50
rufescens, 52
thula, 49
tricolor, 51
Eider
Common, 89
King, 90
Elanoides forficatus, 104
Empidonax
alnorum, 231
flaviventris, 230
minimus, 232

traillii, 231
virescens, 230
Eremophila alpestris, 239
Eudocimus albus, 57
Euphagus
carolinus, 352
cyanocephalus, 353
Falco
columbarius, 119
mexicanus, 122
peregrinus, 120
rusticolus, 121
sparverius, 118
Falcon
Peregrine, 120
Prairie, 122
Finch
House, 362
Purple, 362
Flicker, Northern, 227
Flycatcher
Acadian, 230
Alder, 231
Great Crested, 236
Least, 232
Olive-sided, 228
Scissor-tailed, 238
Vermilion, 235
Western, species, 233
Willow, 231
Yellow-bellied, 230
Fregata magnificens, 44
Frigatebird, Magnificent, 44
Fulica americana, 137
Gadwall, 81
Gallinago gallinago, 167
Gallinula chloropus, 136
Gallinule, Purple, 135
Garganey, 77
Gavia
pacifica, 29
immer, 31
stellata, 28
Geothlypis trichas, 313
Gnatcatcher, Blue-gray, 265
Godwit
Hudsonian, 155
Marbled, 155
Golden-Plover, American, 142
Goldeneye
Barrow's, 95
Common, 95
Goldfinch, American, 367
Goose
Bean, 67
Canada, 72
Greater White-fronted, 68
Ross's, 70
Snow, 69
Goshawk, Northern, 110
Grackle
Common, 355
Great-tailed, 354
Grebe
Clark's, 37
Eared, 35
Horned, 33
Pied-billed, 32
Red-necked, 34
Western, 36
Grosbeak
Black-headed, 322
Blue, 323
Evening, 367
Pine, 361
Rose-breasted, 321
Yellow, 374
Ground-Dove, Common, 200
Grouse
Ruffed, 124
Sharp-tailed, 126
Grus
americana, 140
canadensis, 138
Guiraca caerulea, 323
Gull
Black-headed, 178
Bonaparte's, 179
California, 182
Franklin's, 176
Glaucous, 187
Great Black-backed, 188
Herring, 183
Iceland, 185
Ivory, 192
Laughing, 175
Lesser Black-backed, 186
Little, 177
Mew, 180
Ring-billed, 181
Ross's, 190
Sabine's, 191
Slaty-backed, 87
Thayer's, 184
Gymnorhinus cyanocephalus, 245
Gyrfalcon, 121
Haliaeetus leucocephalus, 106
Harrier, Northern, 107
Hawk
Broad-winged, 112
Cooper's, 109
Ferruginous, 115
Harris's, 371
Red-shouldered, 111
Red-tailed, 114
Rough-legged, 116
Sharp-shinned, 108
Swainson's, 113
Helmitheros vermivorus, 308
Heron
Great Blue, 47
Green, 54
Little Blue, 50
Tricolored, 51
Himantopus mexicanus, 146
Hirundo
pyrrhonota, 242
rustica, 243
Histrionicus histrionicus, 91
Hummingbird
Ruby-throated, 219
Rufous, 220
Hylocichla mustelina, 271
Ibis
Glossy, 58
White, 57
White-faced, 59
Icteria virens, 316
Icterus
bullockii, 357
galbula, 356
spurius, 356
Ictinia mississippiensis, 105
Ixobrychus exilis, 46
Ixoreus naevius, 273
Jaeger
Long-tailed, 174
Parasitic, 173

Pomarine, 172
Jay
Blue, 245
Gray, 244
Pinyon, 245
Junco hyemalis, 344
Junco, Dark-eyed, 344
Kestrel, American, 118
Killdeer, 145
Kingbird
Eastern, 237
Western, 236
Kingfisher, Belted, 221
Kinglet
Golden-crowned, 263
Ruby-crowned, 264
Kite
Mississippi, 105
Swallow-tailed, 104
Kittiwake, Black-legged, 189
Knot, Red, 157
Lanius
excubitor, 281
ludovicianus, 282
Lark, Horned, 239
Larus
argentatus, 183
atricilla, 175
californicus, 182
canus, 180
delawarensis, 181
fuscus, 186
glaucoides, 185
hyperboreus, 187
marinus, 188
minutus, 177
philadelphia, 179
pipixcan, 176
ridibundus, 178
schistisagus, 187
thayeri, 184
Laterallus jamaicensis, 131
Leucosticte tephrocotis, 360
Limnodromus
griseus, 166
scolopaceus, 166
Limosa
fedoa, 155
haemastica, 155
Longspur
Chestnut-collared, 347
Lapland, 345
McCown's, 374
Smith's, 346
Loon
Common, 31
Pacific, 29
Red-throated, 28
Lophodytes cucullatus, 98
Loxia
curvirostra, 363
leucoptera, 364
Magpie, Black-billed, 247
Mallard, 75
Martin, Purple, 240
Meadowlark
Eastern, 350
Western, 351
Melanerpes
carolinus, 223
erythrocephalus, 223
lewis, 222
Melanitta
fusca, 94
nigra, 93
perspicillata, 94
Meleagris gallopavo, 127
Melospiza
georgiana, 341
lincolnii, 341
melodia, 340
Merganser
Common, 98
Hooded, 98
Red-breasted, 99
Mergus
merganser, 98
serrator, 99
Merlin, 119
Mimus polyglottos, 275
Mniotilta varia, 306
Mockingbird, Northern, 275
Molothrus ater, 355
Moorhen, Common, 136
Murre, Thick-billed, 196
Murrelet
Ancient, 197
Marbled, 197
Myadestes townsendi, 268
Mycteria americana, 61
Myiarchus crinitus, 236
Myiopsitta monachus, 372
Nighthawk, Common, 215
Night-Heron
Black-crowned, 55
Yellow-crowned, 56
Nucifraga columbiana, 246
Numenius
americanus, 154
borealis, 152
phaeopus, 153
Nutcracker, Clark's, 246
Nuthatch
Pygmy, 254
Red-breasted, 253
White-breasted, 254
Nyctanassa violacea, 56
Nyctea scandiaca, 208
Nycticorax nycticorax, 55
Oldsquaw, 92
Oporornis
agilis, 312
formosus, 311
philadelphia, 312
tolmiei, 313
Oreoscoptes montanus, 276
Oriole
Baltimore, 356
Bullock's, 357
Orchard, 356
Osprey, 103
Otus asio, 207
Ovenbird, 309
Owl
Barn, 205
Barred, 211
Burrowing, 210
Great Gray, 211
Great Horned, 207
Long-eared, 212
Northern Hawk, 209
Northern Saw-whet, 214
Short-eared, 213
Snowy, 208
Oxyura jamaicensis, 100
Pagophila eburnea, 192
Pandion haliaetus, 103
Parabuteo unicinctus, 371

Parakeet
    Carolina, 201
    Monk, 372
Partridge, Gray, 123
Parula americana, 293
Parula, Northern, 293
Parus
    atricapillus, 251
    bicolor, 252
    carolinensis, 373
    hudsonicus, 251
Passer
    domesticus, 368
    montanus, 369
Passerculus sandwichensis, 335
Passerella iliaca, 340
Passerina
    amoena, 324
    ciris, 374
    cyanea, 325
Pelecanus
    erythrorhynchos, 38
    occidentalis, 40
Pelican
    American White, 38
    Brown, 40
Perdix perdix, 123
Perisoreus canadensis, 244
Phalacrocorax
    auritus, 41
    brasilianus, 42
Phalarope
    Red, 171
    Red-necked, 170
    Wilson's, 169
Phalaropus
    fulicaria, 171
    lobatus, 170
    tricolor, 169
Phasianus colchicus, 124
Pheasant, Ring-necked, 124
Pheucticus
    chrysopeplus, 374
    ludovicianus, 321
    melanocephalus, 322
Philomachus pugnax, 165
Phoebe
    Eastern, 233
    Say's, 234
Pica pica, 247
Picoides
    arcticus, 226
    pubescens, 225
    tridactylus, 373
    villosus, 225
Pigeon
    Band-tailed, 372
    Passenger, 199
Pinicola enucleator, 361
Pintail, Northern, 76
Pipilo
    chlorurus, 327
    erythrophthalmus, 327
    maculatus, 328
Pipit
    American, 278
    Sprague's, 373
Piranga
    ludoviciana, 320
    olivacea, 319
    rubra, 318
Plectrophenax nivalis, 348
Plegadis
    chihi, 59
    falcinellus, 58
Plover
    Black-bellied, 141
    Mountain, 371
    Piping, 144
    Semipalmated, 144
    Snowy, 143
Pluvialis
    dominicus, 142
    squatarola, 141
Podiceps
    auritus, 33
    grisegena,34
    nigricollis, 35
Podilymbus podiceps, 32
Polioptila caerulea, 265
Pooecetes gramineus, 332
Porphyrula martinica, 135
Porzana carolina, 134
Prairie-Chicken, Greater, 125
Progne subis, 240
Protonotaria citrea, 307
Pyrocephalus rubinus, 235
Quiscalus
    mexicanus, 354
    quiscula, 355
Rail
    Black, 131
    King, 132
    Virginia, 133
    Yellow, 129
Rallus
    elegans, 132
    limicola, 133
Raven, Common, 250
Recurvirostra americana, 147
Redhead, 85
Redpoll
    Common, 364
    Hoary, 365
Redstart, American, 307
Regulus
    calendula, 264
    satrapa, 263
Rhodostethia rosea, 190
Riparia riparia, 242
Rissa tridactyla, 189
Robin, American, 272
Rosy-Finch, Gray-crowned, 360
Ruff, 165
Salpinctes obsoletus, 256
Sanderling, 158
Sandpiper
    Baird's, 161
    Buff-breasted, 164
    Curlew, 163
    Least, 160
    Pectoral, 161
    Purple, 372
    Semipalmated, 158
    Sharp-tailed, 162
    Solitary, 149
    Spotted, 150
    Stilt, 164
    Upland, 151
    Western, 159
    White-rumped, 160
Sapsucker, Yellow-bellied, 224
Sayornis
    phoebe, 233
    saya, 234
Scaup
    Greater, 87
    Lesser, 88
Scolopax minor, 168

Scoter
  Black, 93
  Surf, 94
  White-winged, 94
Screech-Owl, Eastern, 207
Seiurus
  aurocapillus, 309
  motacilla, 310
  noveboracensis, 310
Selasphorus rufus, 220
Setophaga ruticilla, 307
Shoveler, Northern, 80
Shrike
  Loggerhead, 282
  Northern, 281
Sialia
  currucoides, 267
  sialis, 266
Siskin, Pine, 366
Sitta
  canadensis, 253
  carolinensis, 254
  pygmaea, 254
Snipe, Common, 167
Solitaire, Townsend's, 268
Somateria
  mollissima, 89
  spectabilis, 90
Sora, 134
Sparrow
  American Tree, 328
  Black-throated, 333
  Chipping, 329
  Clay-colored, 330
  Eurasian Tree, 369
  Field, 331
  Fox, 340
  Golden-crowned, 343
  Grasshopper, 336
  Harris's, 344
  Henslow's, 337
  House, 368
  Lark, 332
  Le Conte's, 338
  Lincoln's, 341
  Nelson's Sharp-tailed, 339
  Savannah, 335
  Song, 340
  Swamp, 341
  Vesper, 332
  White-crowned, 343
  White-throated, 342
Speotyto cunicularia, 210
Sphyrapicus varius, 224
Spiza americana, 325
Spizella
  arborea, 328
  pallida, 330
  passerina, 329
  pusilla, 331
Spoonbill, Roseate, 60
Starling, European, 283
Stelgidopteryx serripennis, 241
Stercorarius
  longicaudus, 174
  parasiticus, 173
  pomarinus, 172
Sterna
  antillarum, 194
  caspia, 192
  forsteri, 193
  hirundo, 193
Stilt, Black-necked, 146
Stork, Wood, 61
Streptopelia risoria, 372
Strix
  nebulosa, 211
  varia, 211
Sturnella
  magna, 350
  neglecta, 351
Sturnus vulgaris, 283
Surnia ulula, 209
Swallow
  Bank, 242
  Barn, 243
  Cliff, 242
  N. Rough-winged, 241
  Tree, 241
Swan
  Mute, 66
  Trumpeter, 65
  Tundra, 64
Swift, Chimney, 218
Synthliboramphus antiquus, 197
Tachycineta bicolor, 241
Tanager
  Scarlet, 319
  Summer, 318
  Western, 320
Teal
  Blue-winged, 78
  Cinnamon, 79
  Green-winged, 74
Tern
  Black, 195
  Caspian, 192
  Common, 193
  Forster's, 193
  Least, 194
Thrasher
  Brown, 276
  Curve-billed, 277
  Sage, 276
Thrush
  Gray-cheeked, 270
  Hermit, 271
  Swainson's, 270
  Varied, 273
  Wood, 271
Thryomanes bewickii, 259
Thryothorus ludovicianus, 258
Titmouse, Tufted, 252
Towhee
  Eastern, 327
  Green-tailed, 327
  Spotted, 328
Toxostoma
  curvirostre, 277
  rufum, 276
Tringa
  flavipes, 149
  melanoleuca, 148
  solitaria, 149
Troglodytes
  aedon, 260
  troglodytes, 260
Tryngites subruficollis, 164
Turdus migratorius, 172
Turkey, Wild, 127
Turnstone, Ruddy, 156
Turtle-Dove, Ringed, 372
Tympanuchus
  cupido, 125
  phasianellus, 126
Tyrannus
  forficatus, 238
  tyrannus, 237
  verticalis, 236

Tyto alba, 205
Uria lomvia, 196
Veery, 269
Vermivora
celata, 292
chrysoptera, 291
peregrina, 291
pinus, 289
ruficapilla, 292
Vireo
bellii, 285
flavifrons, 286
gilvus, 287
griseus, 284
olivaceus, 288
philadelphicus, 287
solitarius, 286
Vireo
Bell's, 285
Philadelphia, 287
Red-eyed, 288
Solitary, 286
Warbling, 287
White-eyed, 284
Yellow-throated, 286
Vulture
Black, 101
Turkey, 102
Warbler
Bay-breasted, 303
Black-and-white, 306
Black-throated Blue, 296
Black-throated Gray, 298
Black-throated Green, 299
Blackburnian, 299
Blackpoll, 304
Blue-winged, 290
Canada, 315
Cape May, 295
Cerulean, 305
Chestnut-sided, 294
Connecticut, 312
Golden-winged, 291
Hooded, 314
Kentucky, 311
MacGillivray's, 313
Magnolia, 294
Mourning, 312
Nashville, 292
Orange-crowned, 292
Palm, 303
Pine, 301
Prairie, 302
Prothonotary, 307
Tennessee, 291
Townsend's, 298
Wilson's, 315
Worm-eating, 308
Yellow, 294
Yellow-rumped, 297
Yellow-throated, 300
Waterthrush
Louisiana, 310
Northern, 310
Waxwing
Bohemian, 279
Cedar, 280
Whimbrel, 153
Whip-poor-will, 217
Whistling-Duck
Black-bellied, 63
Fulvous, 370
Wigeon
American, 83
Eurasian, 82
Willet, 150
Wilsonia
canadensis, 315
citrina, 314
pusilla, 315
Wood-Pewee
Eastern, 229
Western, 229
Woodcock, American, 168
Woodpecker
Black-backed, 226
Downy, 225
Hairy, 225
Lewis's, 222
Pileated, 227
Red-bellied, 223
Red-headed, 223
Three-toed, 373
Wren
Bewick's, 259
Carolina, 258
House, 260
Marsh, 262
Rock, 256
Sedge, 261
Winter, 260
Xanthocephalus
xanthocephalus, 351
Xema sabini, 191
Yellowlegs
Greater, 148
Lesser, 149
Yellowthroat, Common, 313
Zenaida macroura, 199
Zonotrichia
albicollis, 342
atricapilla, 343
leucophrys, 343
querula, 344

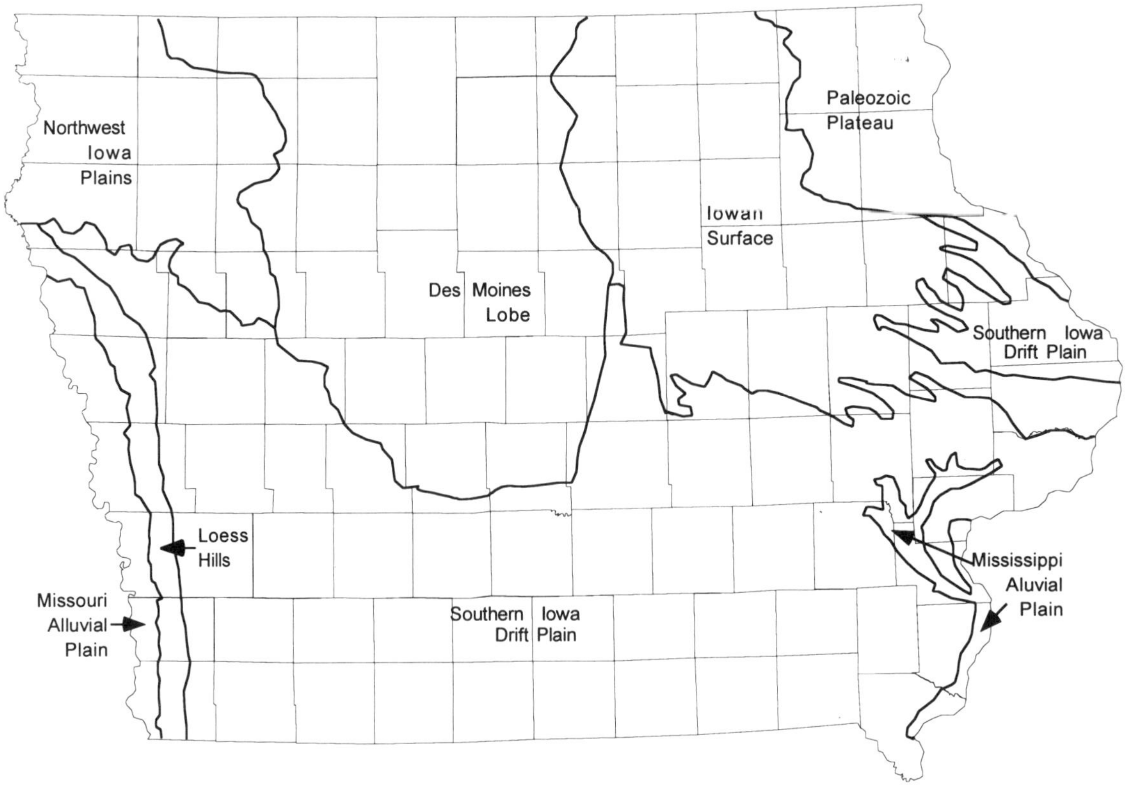

Natural Regions of Iowa

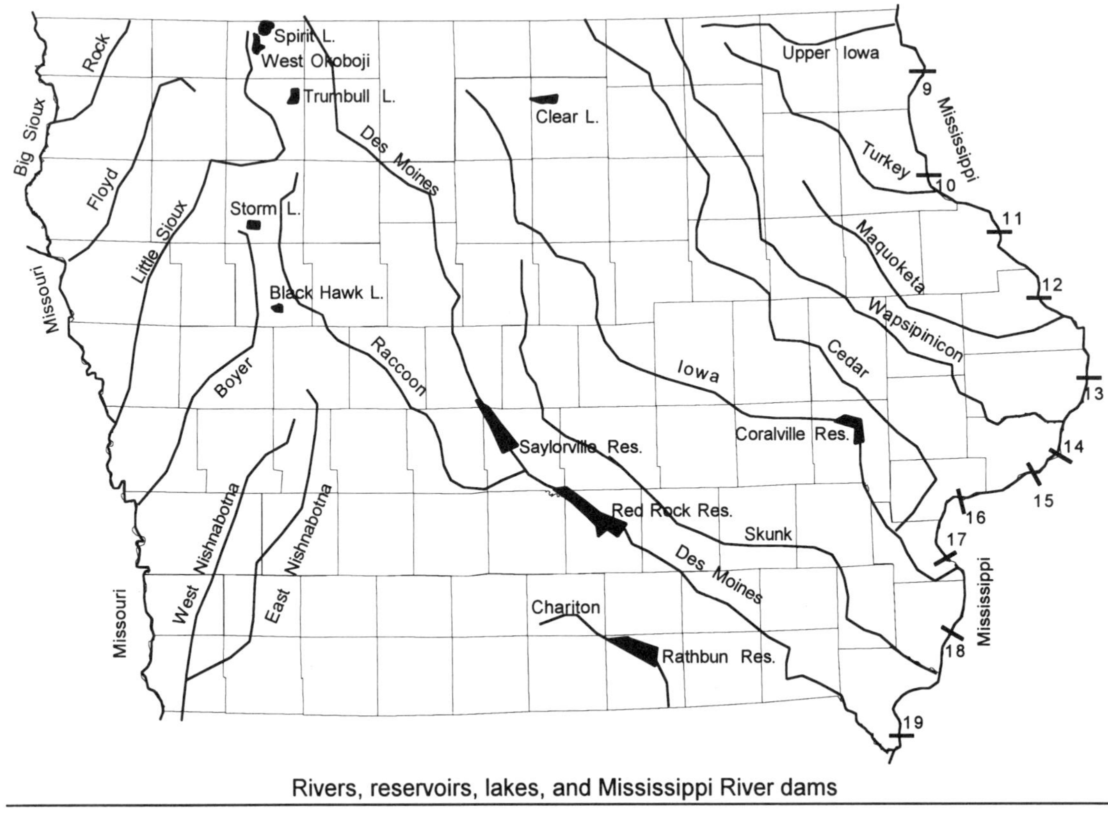

Rivers, reservoirs, lakes, and Mississippi River dams